RESSOURCEMENT

Gabriel Flynn is Lecturer in Systematic Theology, Mater Dei Institute, Dublin City University, Ireland.

Paul D. Murray is Professor of Systematic Theology and Dean and Director of the Centre for Catholic Studies, Department of Theology and Religion, Durham University, UK.

Contributors

Lewis Ayres, Hans Boersma, Michael A. Conway, Brian E. Daley, SJ, Henry Donneaud, OP, Stephen M. Fields, SJ, Gabriel Flynn, Étienne Fouilloux, Janette Gray, RSM, David Grumett, James Hanvey, SJ, Thomas Humphries, Patricia Kelly, Joseph A. Komonchak, Richard Lennan, Gerard Loughlin, Andrew Louth, John McDade, Paul McPartlan, Jürgen Mettepenningen, Francesca Aran Murphy, Paul D. Murray, Edward T. Oakes, SJ, Gerald O'Collins, SJ, Keith F. Pecklers, SJ, Bernard Pottier, SJ, Marcus Pound, Christopher Ruddy, John Saward, Gemma Simmonds, CJ, Benedict T. Viviano, OP, John Webster, A. N. Williams, Jake C. Yap

Ressourcement

A Movement for Renewal in Twentieth-Century Catholic Theology

EDITED BY
GABRIEL FLYNN
AND
PAUL D. MURRAY
WITH THE ASSISTANCE OF PATRICIA KELLY

OXFORD
UNIVERSITY PRESS

Great Clarendon Street, Oxford, OX2 6DP,
United Kingdom

Oxford University Press is a department of the University of Oxford.
It furthers the University's objective of excellence in research, scholarship,
and education by publishing worldwide. Oxford is a registered trade mark of
Oxford University Press in the UK and in certain other countries

Published in the United States of America by Oxford University Press
198 Madison Avenue, New York, NY 10016, United States of America

British Library Cataloguing in Publication Data

Data available

Library of Congress Control Number: 0000000000

ISBN 978–0–19–955287–0 (Hbk)
ISBN 978–0–19–870208–5 (Pbk)

This book is dedicated to
Henri de Lubac (1896–1991)
&
Yves Congar (1904–95)

Acknowledgements

Our thanks are due to the contributors to this volume, for their graciousness in accepting this extra work in the midst of many other responsibilities, and above all for the uniformly high quality of their contributions. We acknowledge the assistance, courtesy, and unfailing generosity of Robert Bonfils, SJ, Archivist, Jesuit Archives, Vanves, Paris; Jérôme Rousse-Lacordaire, OP, Librarian at Le Saulchoir, Paris; and Isabelle Séruzier. Our thanks to our colleagues for their encouragement and advice, to the anonymous reviewers, for their helpful comments and suggestions, and to the translators, for their important work. Particular thanks are due to Henry Donneaud, Stephen M. Fields, David Ford, Étienne Fouilloux, Claude Geffré, Jean-Pierre Jossua, Dermot A. Lane, Richard Lennan, and Fearghus Ó Fearghail for their expertise and assistance. We are grateful to Tom Perridge and Elizabeth Robottom of Oxford University Press for their professionalism and generous support. Special thanks are due to Patricia Kelly for her invaluable contribution. We acknowledge the financial assistance of the Research Committee of Mater Dei Institute and of the Centre for Catholic Studies at Durham University. Lastly, we thank our students, families, and close friends, for their loyalty and unstinting support.

All Scripture references are taken from the New Revised Standard Version, unless within citations of other sources. All English language citations of the documents of the Second Vatican Council are taken from Norman P. Tanner, SJ (ed.), *Decrees of the Ecumenical Coucils*. Two volumes. i. Nicaea I-Lateran V. ii. Trent-Vatican II (London/Washington DC: Sheed & Ward/Georgetown University Press, 1990). An earlier version of Etienne Fouilloux's essay, 'A new "Lyon School" (1919–39)', appeared in Emmanuel Gabellieri and Pierre de Cointet (eds.), *Actes du Colloque Maurice Blondel et la philosophie française* (Paris: Parole and Silence, 2007); an earlier version of Paul D. Murray's essay, 'Expanding catholicity through ecumenicity in the work of Yves Congar: *ressourcement*, receptive ecumenism, and Catholic reform' was published in the *International Journal of Systematic Theology*, 13.3 (2011); an earlier version of Gabriel Flynn's essay 'The twentieth-century renaissance in Catholic theology' was published in the *Irish Theological Quarterly*, 76.4 (2011).

The Editors

Table of Contents

x   *Table of Contents*

List of Contributors

Lewis Ayres holds the Bede Chair of Theology at Durham University. His research focuses on trinitarian theology in Augustine and fourth-century Greek writers, the later development of trintarian theology, the place of Scripture in the early church, and in the modern reception of patristic trinitarian theology. His books include *Nicaea and its Legacy: An Approach to Fourth Century Trinitarian Theology* (Oxford: Oxford University Press, 2004), *Augustine and the Trinity* (Cambridge: Cambridge University Press, 2010), and the forthcoming *The Practice of Christian Doctrine: A Catholic Essay*. He is also co-editor of the forthcoming *Oxford Handbook of Catholic Theology*.

Hans Boersma is J. I. Packer Professor of Theology at Regent College, Vancouver. Educated in Canada and the Netherlands, he is the author of a number of articles, and has written several books, including *Violence, Hospitality, and the Cross: Reappropriating the Atonement Tradition* (Grand Rapids, MI: Baker Academic, 2004); *Nouvelle Théologie and Sacramental Ontology: A Return to Mystery* (Oxford: Oxford University Press, 2009); and *Heavenly Participation: The Weaving of a Sacramental Tapestry* (Grand Rapids, MI: Eerdmans, 2011).

Michael A. Conway is Professor of Faith and Culture at St Patrick's College, Maynooth, Ireland. He is Editor of the *Irish Theological Quarterly* and Director of the Irish Centre for Faith and Culture at Maynooth. He holds a doctorate in theology from the Albert-Ludwigs-University, Freiburg i. Br. He is the author of *The Science of Life: Maurice Blondel's Philosophy of Action and the Scientific Method* (Frankfurt am Main: Peter Lang, 2000 [European University Studies; Series XX - Philosophy, Vol. 616]) and has contributed articles to *Ephemerides Theologicae Lovanienses, Gregorianum*, the *Irish Theological Quarterly*, the *Heythrop Journal*, and the *Cambridge Dictionary of Christianity*.

Brian E. Daley, SJ is Catherine F. Huisking Professor of Theology at the University of Notre Dame, IN. He is a historical theologian, specializing in the study of the early church, particularly the development of Christian doctrine from the fourth to the eighth centuries. He is preparing a critical edition of the works of the sixth-century Greek theologian Leontius of Byzantium for Oxford University Press, and has written a number of articles for scholarly journals on ancient Christology, trinitarian theology and eschatology. His books include *The Hope of the Early Church* (Cambridge: Cambridge University Press, 1991), *On The Dormition of Mary: Early Patristic Homilies*

(New York: St Vladimir's Seminary Press, 1997), and *Gregory of Nazianzus* (New York: Routledge, 2006). A past president of the North American Patristic Society, he is an editor of *Traditio*, and has served as a member of the editorial board of *Traditio* and of the *Journal of Early Christian Studies*. He is executive secretary of the Orthodox-Roman Catholic Consultation in North America.

Henry Donneaud, OP is Professor of Fundamental Theology at the Faculty of Theology of the Institut Catholique de Toulouse where he is Dean of Graduate Studies. His principal research interests include the history of the nature of theology, particularly in the medieval period, as well as the history of contemporary Thomism. He is author of *Théologie et intelligence de la foi au XIIIe siècle* (Paris: Parole et Silence, 2005). He is a member of the editorial board of the *Revue thomiste* and the *Mémoire dominicaine*.

Stephen M. Fields, SJ is Associate Professor of Theology at Georgetown University, Washington, DC, where his research interests include metaphysics and the philosophy of religion, historical and systematic theology, John Henry Newman, Karl Rahner, Hans Urs von Balthasar, and recent papal thought. He is the author of *Being as Symbol: On the Origins and Development of Karl Rahner's Metaphysics* (Washington DC: Georgetown University Press, 2000). He has published scholarly articles in *Theological Studies*, *Philosophy and Theology*, *Louvain Studies*, *Logos*, *American Catholic Philosophical Quarterly*, and elsewhere. He holds a doctorate from Yale University and has served as President of the Jesuit Philosophical Association.

Gabriel Flynn is College Lecturer in Systematic Theology at Mater Dei Institute, Dublin City University. He is a priest of the Diocese of Meath, Ireland. He completed his doctorate at the University of Oxford in 2000. His publications include *Yves Congar's Vision of the Church in a World of Unbelief* (Aldershot/Burlington VT: Ashgate, 2004) and the edited volumes *Yves Congar: Theologian of the Church* (Louvain: Peeters, 2005)/*Yves Congar: théologien de l'Église* (Paris: Éditions du Cerf, 2007), *Leadership and Business Ethics*, Issues in Business Ethics 25 (New York: Springer, 2008). He has been Guest Editor at *Louvain Studies*, and has also contributed to *La vie spirituelle*, *New Blackfriars*, *Theology Digest*, and the *Journal of Business Ethics*.

Étienne Fouilloux is Emeritus Professor of Contemporary History at the Université Lumière-Lyon II and former director of the Centre d'histoire religieuse A. Latreille. He is a world-renowned expert on the social and political situation of the Catholic Church in France during the nineteenth and twentieth centuries; the history of religious orders in France, and French Catholicism during the Second World War. His works include, among others, *Une Eglise en quête de liberté: La pensée catholique française entre* *modernisme et Vatican II*, 2nd edn (Paris: Desclée de Brouwer, 2006); *Eugène cardinal Tisserant (1884-1972): Une biographie* (Paris: Desclée de Brouwer, 2011).

Janette Gray, RSM was educated at Macquarie University, Melbourne College of Divinity, and Cambridge University. She teaches systematic theology at the Jesuit Theological College in Parkville, Victoria, Australia.

David Grumett is Chancellor's Fellow in Christian Ethics and Practical Theology at the University of Edinburgh. He is also Secretary to the Society for the Study of Theology, and Assistant Editor of *Ecclesiology*. His books include *De Lubac: A Guide for the Perplexed* (London: T&T Clark, 2007) and *Teilhard de Chardin: Theology, Humanity and Cosmos* (Leuven: Peeters, 2005). He has produced articles on Maurice Blondel and Yves de Montcheuil in *Modern Theology, Political Theology* and *Theological Studies*, and on other aspects of *nouvelle théologie* in the *International Journal of Systematic Theology* and *New Blackfriars*. His other interests include theology and material practice, and he has written (with Rachel Muers) *Theology on the Menu: Asceticism, Meat and Christian Diet* (London: Routledge, 2010).

James Hanvey, SJ is Master of Campion Hall, Oxford. He received his doctorate from Oxford University with a thesis investigating the thought of Hegel, Barth, and Rahner, and the attempt to construct a contemporary metaphysics of the Trinity. He was a visiting scholar at Weston Jesuit School of Theology, Cambridge MA, and Head of the Department of Systematic Theology at Heythrop and Director of the Heythrop Institute for Public Life, Heythrop College, University of London before taking up his new post as Master of Campion Hall. In addition to being a distinguished lecturer in some American Universities he has also held the Veale Chair in Ignatian Studies at the Milltown Institute, Dublin. He has contributed to *Gregorianum, The Way*, and the *International Journal of Systematic Theology*.

Thomas Humphries' doctoral research at Emory University was on fifth- and sixth-century Latin pneumatology. He is currently Assistant Professor of Philosophy, Theology, and Religion at Saint Leo University, Florida, USA.

Patricia Kelly is Senior Lecturer in Catholic Studies at Leeds Trinity University, UK. Her PhD at Durham University is on twentieth-century Catholic theologies of work.

Joseph A. Komonchak is a priest of the Archdiocese of New York. After teaching systematic theology for 45 years at St. Joseph's Seminary, Dunwoodie, and at The Catholic University of America, he now lives in retirement in New York State. He has published extensively on twentieth-century theology and on the Second Vatican Council. He is the editor of the

English edition of the five-volume *History of Vatican II* (Maryknoll NY: Orbis/ Leuven: Peeters, 1995–).

Richard Lennan is Professor of Systematic Theology at Boston College's School of Theology and Ministry. Originally from New South Wales, Australia, and a priest of the Diocese of Maitland-Newcastle, Australia, he holds a doctorate from the University of Innsbruck, Austria. He taught Systematic Theology in the Catholic Institute of Sydney from 1992 to 2007, before moving to Weston Jesuit School of Theology, and Boston College. He is author of *The Ecclesiology of Karl Rahner* (Oxford: Clarendon Press, 1995) and *Risking the Church: The Challenges of Catholic Faith* (Oxford: Oxford University Press, 2004).

Gerard Loughlin studied Theology and English Literature at Lampeter (University of Wales), followed by doctoral research at Cambridge on the philosophy and theology of John Hick. He taught in and was Head of the Department of Religious Studies at the University of Newcastle from 1990 to 2004, when he moved to the newly named Department of Theology and Religion at Durham University. He is the author of several books, including *Telling God's Story: Bible, Church and Narrative Theology* (Cambridge: Cambridge University Press, 1996), *Alien Sex: The Body and Desire in Cinema and Theology* (Oxford: Blackwell, 2004), and editor of *Queer Theology: Rethinking the Western Body* (Oxford: Blackwell, 2007). He is co-editor of *Theology & Sexuality* (Equinox) and serves on the editorial board of *Literature & Theology* (Oxford University Press).

Andrew Louth is a graduate of Cambridge and Edinburgh Universities. After academic posts at Oxford and Goldsmiths College, University of London, he became Professor of Patristic and Byzantine Studies in Durham, and is now Professor Emeritus. He is author of several books and many articles, mostly on the Greek/Byzantine tradition, including works on Dionysios the Areopagite, Maximos the Confessor, and John Damascene. His most recent work is a history of the Church from 681 to 1071, the period during which Greek East and Latin West came to form their separate identities. He was ordained priest in the Russian Orthodox Diocese of Sourozh (Patriarchate of Moscow) in 2003 to serve the Orthodox community in Durham.

Dr John McDade was Head of Systematic Theology at Heythrop College, University of London, before becoming Principal there until 2011. He is currently Lecturer in Theology at St Mary's University College, Twickenham, London, and Visiting Lecturer at Arcadia University in London.

Paul McPartlan is a priest of the Archdiocese of Westminster (UK) and Carl J. Peter Professor of Systematic Theology and Ecumenism at the Catholic

University of America in Washington DC. He is a member of the Roman
Catholic Church's International Theological Commission, and also a member
of the Joint International Commission for Theological Dialogue between the
Roman Catholic Church and the Orthodox Church. He is the author of *The
Eucharist Makes the Church: Henri de Lubac and John Zizioulas in Dialogue*
(Edinburgh: T & T Clark, 1993; 2nd edn Fairfax VA: Eastern Christian
Publications, 2006), *Sacrament of Salvation: An Introduction to Eucharistic
Ecclesiology* (Edinburgh: T & T Clark, 1995), *A Service of Love: Papal Primacy,
the Eucharist, and Church Unity* (Washington DC: Catholic University of
America Press, 2013), and many articles on ecclesiology, Eucharist and
ecumenism.

Jürgen Mettepenningen is Guest Lecturer at the Faculty of Theology and
Religious Studies, Catholic University of Louvain (KU, Leuven), Belgium. His
most recent publications are *Nouvelle Théologie—New Theology: Inheritor of
Modernism, Precursor of Vatican II* (London/NewYork: T&T Clark, 2010)
and—together with Karim Schelkens and John A. Dick—*Aggironamento?
Catholicism from Gregory XVI to Benedict XVI* (Leiden/Boston: Brill, 2013).

Francesca Aran Murphy took her BA from Manchester University and her
Ph.D. from King's College, London, in 1988. She taught at Aberdeen
University from 1995-2010, and is now Professor of Systematic Theology at
the University of Notre Dame, USA. Her most recent books include a
theological commentary on *I Samuel* (Grand Rapids MI: Brazos Press,
2010), *God is not a Story: Realism Revisited* (Oxford: Oxford University
Press, 2007) and *Art and Intellect in the Philosophy of Etienne Gilson*
(Columbia MO: University of Missouri Press: 2004). She has edited several
works such as *The Providence of God: Deus Habet Consilium* (London:
Continuum, 2009).

Paul D. Murray, a married lay Roman Catholic, is Professor of Systematic
Theology and Dean and Director of the Centre for Catholic Studies,
Department of Theology and Religion, Durham University, UK. He serves on
the British Methodist—Roman Catholic Committee and is a member of
ARCIC III. His first monograph was *Reason, Truth and Theology in
Pragmatist Perspective* (Leuven: Peeters, 2004). He is editor of *Receptive
Ecumenism and the Call to Catholic Learning: Exploring a Way for
Contemporary Ecumenism*, (Oxford: Oxford University Press, 2008) and has
also contributed a number of well-received essays to various leading journals
and scholarly collections. He serves on the editorial boards of *Concilium:
International Review for Theology* and the *Ecclesiological Investigations*
monograph series (Continuum International).

Gerald O'Collins, SJ is professor emeritus of Fundamental and Systematic Theology of the Gregorian University in Rome. He has authored or co-authored fifty-nine books, including *Salvation for All* (Oxford University Press, 2008), *Jesus Our Priest* (Oxford University Press, 2010), and *Rethinking Fundamental Theology* (Oxford University Press, 2011).

Edward T. Oakes, SJ, currently teaches theology at University of St. Mary of the Lake/Mundelein Seminary, the Catholic seminary for the Archdiocese of Chicago. He earned his Ph.D. in Systematic Theology from Union Theological Seminary in New York City in 1987. He is the author of *Pattern of Redemption: The Theology of Hans Urs von Balthasar* (New York: Continuum, 2nd edition 1997), editor of *German Essays on Religion* (Continuum, 1994) and co-editor, with David Moss, of the *Cambridge Companion to Hans Urs von Balthasar*. His translations of Balthasar's works include *Epilogue*, the concluding volume to Balthasar's fifteen-volume theological trilogy, *The Theology of Karl Barth: Exposition and Interpretation*, and *Spirit and Institution*, the fourth volume of Balthasar set of collected essays, collectively called *Explorations in Theology*. His latest book *Infinity Dwindled to Infancy: A Catholic and Evangelical Theology* has just appeared from Eerdmans. He can be contacted through the Mundelein website: www.usml.edu.

Keith F. Pecklers, SJ has been Lecturer in Liturgical History at the Pontifical Liturgical Institute since 1996 and Professor of Liturgy at the Pontifical Gregorian University since 2002. He has published seven books and numerous articles and reviews and is the co-editor of the recently published volume by Archbishop Piero Marini, *A Challenging Reform: Realizing the Vision of the Liturgical Renewal* (Collegeville MN: The Liturgical Press, 2007). His books *The Genius of the Roman Rite* (London and Collegeville, MN: Continuum/ Liturgical Press, 2009, and *Worship* (London and Collegeville MN: Continuum/ Liturgical Press, 2003) both won the Catholic Press Association First Place Award in Liturgy. He is Founding President of the International Jungmann Society. He serves on the Board of the American Friends of the Anglican Centre Rome and was the Roman Catholic representative to the 'Cloud of Witnesses' Project co-sponsored by the World Council of Churches and the Ecumenical Monastery at Bose. He also serves as a Vatican consultant for ABC NEWS.

Bernard Pottier, SJ, is Professor at the Jesuit Faculty of Theology at Brussels (IET), where he teaches dogmatic and fundamental theology, and philosophy. He studied psychology and philosophy, and his thesis in patristics was entitled *Dieu et le Christ selon Grégoire de Nysse* (Namur: Culture et Vérité, 1994). He has also published *Le péché originel selon Hegel* (Namur: Culture et Vérité, 1990) and, with A. Borras, *La grâce du diaconat* (Brussels: Lessius, 1998). He published the *Nouvelle Revue Théologique* for seven years. He published, with Lessius, a new translation of Gregory of Nyssa's

The Soul and Resurrection. A parish priest for twenty years in the Portuguese parish in Brussels, he is also a member of AIEMPR (Association Internationale d'Études Médico-psychologiques et religieuses), and published in 2012, with D. Struyf, *Psychologie et spiritualité. Enjeux pastoraux* (Lessius).

Marcus Pound is Catholic Research Fellow in the Department of Theology and Religion at Durham University. His *Theology, Psychology and Trauma* appeared in 2007 (London: SCM Press), and his *Žižek: A (Very) Critical Introduction* (Grand Rapids MI: Eerdmans, 2008), has been acclaimed by Žižek himself. His research interests are on the boundary between theology and psychoanalysis.

Christopher Ruddy is Associate Professor of Systematic Theology at The Catholic University of America, Washington, DC. A graduate of Yale College and Harvard Divinity School, he received his doctorate in systematic theology from the University of Notre Dame. He is the author of *The Local Church: Tillard and the Future of Catholic Ecclesiology* (New York: Herder & Herder, 2006), and *Tested in Every Way: The Catholic Priesthood in Today's Church* (New York: Herder & Herder, 2007). He writes regularly for America and Commonweal, and his articles and reviews have appeared in the *Catholic Historical Review, Christian Century, Horizons, Josephinum Journal of Theology, Logos, Origins,* and *Worship.*

John Saward is a Senior Research Fellow of Blackfriars Hall, Oxford, and a priest of the Archdiocese of Birmingham, England. He formerly held the St Francis of Assisi Chair in Dogmatic Theology at the International Theological Institute at Gaming, Austria, and taught systematic theology at St Charles Borromeo Seminary, Wynnewood, Pennsylvania. He is the author of numerous books and articles, including *The Beauty of Holiness and the Holiness of Beauty* (San Francisco: Ignatius, 1996) and *Sweet and Blessed Country* (Oxford: Oxford University Press, 2005), and is the translator of works by Hans Urs Von Balthasar, Christoph Schonborn, and Joseph Ratzinger. He is the editor, with John Morrill and Michael Tomko, of *Firmly I Believe and Truly: The Spiritual Tradition of Catholic England* (Oxford: Oxford University Press, 2011).

Gemma Simmonds, CJ, lectures in Pastoral Theology at Heythrop College, University of London. Her research interests include Mary Ward, Jansenism, and ecclesiology. She is the translator of de Lubac's *Corpus Mysticum* (London: SCM Press, 2007).

Benedict T. Viviano, OP, is Professor Emeritus of Biblical Studies at the University of Fribourg (Switzerland). With a Ph.D. in Bible Studies from Duke University, he has worked in the US, Jerusalem, and Switzerland. He has written numerous articles on the Synoptic Gospels and Catholic Letters, and was lead editor of the Synoptic Gospels and Catholic Epistles for the 3rd edition of the *Bible de Jérusalem*.

John Webster is Professor of Divinity at the University of St Andrews. He studied English and Theology at Cambridge, taught in Durham and Toronto, and was Lady Margaret Professor of Divinity at the University of Oxford before moving to Aberdeen. A founding editor of *International Journal of Systematic Theology*, he has written extensively on the work of Karl Barth, and on dogmatic and moral theology.

A.N. Williams lectures in theology at the University of Cambridge. She is the author *of The Ground of Union: Deification in Aquinas and Palamas* (Oxford: Oxford University Press, 1999), *The Divine Sense: The Intellect in Patristic Theology* (Cambridge: Cambridge University Press, 2007), and *The Architecture of Theology: Structure, System and* Ratio (Oxford: Oxford University Press, 2011).

Jake C. Yap is Associate Professor of Dogmatic and Systematic Theology at the Loyola School of Theology, Quezon City, Philippines. He is a lay person living a consecrated life in a missionary brotherhood called The Servants of the Word. He has published in *Communio: Revue Catholique Internationale* and *Quaderni del Centro Studi Asiatico*. His Oxford D.Phil. dissertation is entitled '"Word" and "Wisdom" in the Ecclesiology of Louis Bouyer' (2003).

List of Abbreviations

ASS	*Acta Sanctae Sedis*
AAS	*Acta Apostolici Sedis*
ASSCOVII	*Acta Synodalia Sacrosancti Concilii Œcumenici Vaticani II* (Vatican City: Typis Polyglottis Vaticanis, 1970–1978)

Augustine, Complete Works

Augustine, *The Works of Saint Augustine*, ed. John Rotelle, OSA, 50 volumes (Hyde Park NY: New York City Press, 1990–)

CCSL	*Corpus Christianorum Series Latina* (Turnhout: Brepols, 1953–)
CCSG	*Corpus Christianorum Series Graeca* (Turnhout: Brepols, 1976–)
DS	Heinrich Denzinger & Adolf Schönmetzer, SJ (eds.), *Enchiridion symbolorum, definitionum et declarationum de rebus fidei et morum* 34th rev. edn. (Barcelona/Freiburg im Breisgau/Rome/New York: Herder, 1967)
ST	Thomas Aquinas, *Summa Theologiae*, trans. and ed. Dominicans of the English Province, rev. edn. 61 volumes. (Cambridge: Cambridge University Press, 2006)
Tanner	Norman P. Tanner, SJ (ed.), *Decrees of the Ecumenical Councils.* Two volumes. i. Nicaea I-Lateran V. ii. Trent-Vatican II. (London/Washington DC: Sheed & Ward/Georgetown University Press, 1990)
Le Saulchoir	Marie-Dominique Chenu, *Une école de théologie: le Saulchoir* (Kain-lez-Tournai/Étiolles: Le Saulchoir, 1937).
Une école	Marie-Dominique Chenu, *Une école de théologie: le Saulchoir*, eds G Alberigo, É Fouilloux, J Ladrière, J-P Jossua (Paris: Éditions du Cerf, 1985).

Papal and conciliar documents

Second Vatican Council

Ad GD	*Ad Gentes Divinitus*
	Second Vatican Council, Decree on the Missionary Activity of the Church.
DV	*Dei Verbum*
	Second Vatican Council, Dogmatic Constitution on Divine Revelation.
GS	*Gaudium et Spes*
	Second Vatican Council, Pastoral Constitution on the Church in the World Today.
LG	*Lumen Gentium*
	Second Vatican Council, Dogmatic Constitution on the Church.
SC	*Sacrosanctum Concilium*
	Second Vatican Council, Constitution on the Sacred Liturgy.

Papal Encyclicals

AP   *Aeterni Patris*

                    Leo XIII, Encyclical Letter on the Restoration of Christian Philosophy (4th August 1879), Acta Leonis XIII, 1 (1881), 255–84.

DAS   *Divino Afflante Spiritu*

                    Pius XII, Encyclical Letter on Promoting Biblical Studies (30th September 1943), AAS 35 (1943), 297–325.

DCE   *Deus Caritas Est*

                    Benedict XVI, Encyclical Letter on Christian Love (25th December 2005), AAS 98 (2006), 217–52.

HG   *Humani Generis*

                    Encyclical Letter concerning some False Opinions Threatening to Undermine the Foundations of Catholic Doctrine (12th August 1950), AAS 42 (1950), 561–78.

Lamentabili   *Lamentabili Sane Exitu*

                    Pius X, Syllabus Concerning the Errors of the Modernists, Lamentabili Sane (3rd July 1907), ASS 40 (1907), 470–8.

MCC   *Mystici Corporis Christi*

                    Pius XII, Encyclical Letter on the Mystical Body of Christ (29th June 1943), AAS 35 (1943), 195–248.

Pascendi   *Pascendi Dominici Gregis*

                    Pius X, Encyclical Letter on the Doctrines of the Modernists (8th September 1907), AAS 40 (1907), 593–650

Journals/Series

Ang   *Angelicum*

BETL   *Bibliotheca Ephemeridium Theologicarum Lovaniensem*

EphThL   *Ephemerides Theologicae Lovanienses*

Gr   *Gregorianum*

IJST   *International Journal for Systematic Theology*

LS   *Louvain Studies*

NRT   *Nouvelle revue théologique*

RevTh   *Revue Thomiste*

RSPT   *Revue des Sciences philosophiques et théologiques*

RSR   *Recherches de Science Religieuse*

RThL   *Revue Théologique de Louvain*

TR   *Theologische Revue*

TS   *Theological Studies*

VI   *Vie Intellectuelle*

ZkT   *Zeitschrift für katholische Theologie*

Unless otherwise stated, biblical quotations are taken from the *New Revised Standard Version* (Oxford: Oxford University Press, 1995).

Introduction

The Twentieth-Century Renaissance in Catholic Theology

Gabriel Flynn[1]

The renowned generation of French *ressourcement* theologians whose influence pervaded French theology and society in the period 1930 to 1960, and beyond, inspired a renaissance in twentieth-century Catholic theology and initiated a movement for renewal that made a decisive contribution to the reforms of the Second Vatican Council (1962–5).[2] The foremost exponents of *ressourcement* were principally, though not exclusively, leading French Dominicans and Jesuits of the faculties of Le Saulchoir (Paris) and Lyon-Fourvière, respectively. They included the Dominicans Marie-Dominique Chenu (1895–1990),[3]

---

[1] I wish to thank Professor Norman Tanner, SJ, and other reviewers, for helpful comments on earlier drafts of this chapter.

[2] See Rosino Gibellini, *Panorama de la théologie au XXe siècle*, trans. Jacques Mignon, new edn. (Paris: Cerf, 2004), 173–289; Bernard Sesboüé, *La théologie au XXe siècle et l'avenir de la foi: Entretiens avec Marc Leboucher* (Paris: Desclée de Brouwer, 2007), 11–51; Étienne Fouilloux, '"Nouvelle théologie" et théologie nouvelle (1930–1960)', in Benoît Pellistrandi (ed.), *L'histoire religieuse en France et Espagne*, Collection de la Casa Velázquez, 87 (Madrid: Casa de Velázquez, 2004), 411–25; Fouilloux, *Une Église en quête de liberté: La pensée catholique française entre modernisme et Vatican II (1914–1962)*, Anthropologiques (Paris: Declée de Brouwer, 1998); Étienne Fouilloux and Bernard Hours (eds.), *Les jésuites à Lyon XVIe–XXe siècle* (Lyon: ENS Editions, 2005); Jean-Yves Lacoste *et al.*, *Histoire de la théologie* (Paris: Éditions du Seuil, 2009), 429–35; Aidan Nichols, OP, 'Thomism and the Nouvelle Théologie', *The Thomist*, 64 (2000), 1–19; John Milbank, 'Radical Orthodoxy and twentieth-century theology' in John Milbank and Simon Oliver (eds.), *The Radical Orthodoxy Reader* (London: Routledge, 2009), 368–79; Milbank points to the importance of Félix Ravaisson in the trajectory of the *nouvelle théologie*. See further John R. T. Lamont's comments on *nouvelle théologie* and *ressourcement* in his 'Conscience, Freedom, Rights: Idols of the Enlightenment Religion', *The Thomist*, 73 (2009), 169–239 (169, 235–9).

[3] See Claude Geffré *et al.*, *L'hommage différé au Père Chenu* (Paris: Cerf, 1990); Jacques Duquesne (ed.), *Jacques Duquesne interroge le Père Chenu: 'un théologien en liberté'* (Paris: Centurion, 1975).

Yves Congar (1904–95),[4] Dominique Dubarle (1907–87),[5] and Henri-Marie
Féret (1904–92),[6] and the Jesuits Jean Daniélou (1905–74),[7] Henri de Lubac
(1896–1991),[8] Henri Bouillard (1908–81),[9] and Hans Urs von Balthasar (1905–
88) who, under the influence of Adrienne von Speyr, left the Society of Jesus
in 1950 in order to found a 'secular institute' for lay people.[10] The movement
also encompassed Belgium and Germany.[11] The American historian John
W. O'Malley aptly describes the importance and effectiveness of *ressourcement*
as follows: 'In brief, some form of *ressourcement* lay behind every reform

[4] See Victor Dunne, *Prophecy in the Church: The Vision of Yves Congar*, European
University Studies, 23 (Frankfurt: Lang, 2000); Joseph Famerée, *L'Ecclésiologie d'Yves Congar
avant Vatican II: Histoire et Église*, BETL, 107 (Louvain: Leuven University Press, 1992); Flynn
(Guest ed.), *Louvain Studies*, 29 (Fall–Winter, 2004) 'This Church that I Love: Essays Celebrating the Centenary of the Birth of Yves Cardinal Congar'; Douglas M. Koskela, *Ecclesiality and
Ecumenism: Yves Congar and the Road to Unity*, Marquette Studies in Theology, 61 (Milwaukee WI: Marquette University Press, 2008). See further references in my essay on Congar in
this volume.

[5] Dominique Dubarle, OP, was a *peritus* at Vatican II, professor at Le Saulchoir and Dean of
the Faculty of Philosophy at the Institut Catholique de Paris. An expert in the thought of
Aristotle and St Thomas, he contributed to the understanding of the relationship between
theology and philosophy. See Dominique Dubarle, *L'Ontologie de Thomas Aquinas*, Philosophie
& Théologie (Paris: Cerf, 1996). Also, Jacques Courcier, 'Dominique Dubarle et la Géométrie
Projective', *RSPT*, 92 (2008), 623–36.

[6] See Henri-Marie Féret, 'La théologie concrète et historique et son importance pastorale
présente', in Gérard Philips *et al.*, *Le service théologique dans l'Église: Mélanges offerts au Père
Yves Congar pour ses soixante-dix ans*, Cogitatio Fidei, 76 (Paris: Cerf, 1974), 193–247; further,
Jean Puyo (ed.), *Jean Puyo interroge le Père Congar: 'une vie pour la vérité'*, Les Interviews (Paris:
Centurion, 1975), 45–6.

[7] See Jacques Fontaine (ed.), *Actualité de Jean Daniélou* (Paris: Cerf, 2006); Jean Daniélou,
Carnets spirituels, ed. Marie-Joseph Rondeau (Paris: Cerf, 2007).

[8] See Hans Urs von Balthasar, *The Theology of Henri de Lubac: An Overview*, trans. Joseph
Fessio, SJ, and Michael M. Waldstein (San Francisco: Ignatius Press, 1991); Jean-Pierre
Wagner, *Henri de Lubac*, Initiations aux théologies (Paris: Cerf, 2007); Wagner, *La théologie
fondamentale selon Henri de Lubac*, Cogitatio Fidei, 199 (Paris: Cerf, 1997); Rudolf Voder-
holzer, *Meet Henri de Lubac* (San Francisco: Ignatius Press, 2008); John Milbank, *The
Suspended Middle: Henri de Lubac and the Debate concerning the Supernatural* (London:
SCM, 2005); a collection of essays in *Communio*, 35 (2008) 'Henri de Lubac's *Catholicism* at
70 Years' with an important article by Georges Chantraine, SJ, '*Catholicism*: On "Certain
Ideas"', *Communio*, 35 (2008), 520–34; Paul McPartlan, *The Eucharist Makes the Church:
Henri de Lubac and John Zizioulas in Dialogue* (Edinburgh: T&T Clark, 1993).

[9] See Michel Castro, 'Henri Bouillard (1908–1981): éléments de biographie intellectuelle',
Mélanges de science religieuse, 60 (2003), 43–58; also, *RSR*, 97/2 (2009); this issue of *RSR* is
devoted to the thought of Bouillard, with essays by Étienne Fouilloux, Claude Geffré, and others.

[10] See John O'Donnell, SJ, *Hans Urs Von Balthasar* (London: T&T Clark, 1991); Kevin
Mongrain, *The Systematic Thought of Hans Urs Von Balthasar: An Irenaean Retrieval*
(New York: Crossroad, 2002); Edward T. Oakes, *Pattern of Redemption: The Theology of Hans
Urs von Balthasar* (New York: Continuum, 1994).

[11] See Jürgen Mettepenningen, *Nouvelle Théologie—New Theology: Inheritor of Modernism,
Precursor of Vatican II* (London: Continuum, 2010), especially Ch. 3; also Marcellino
D'Ambrosio, '*Ressourcement* theology, *aggiornamento*, and the hermeneutics of tradition',
Communio, 18 (1991), 530–55.

movement in Western Christianity—and behind every reform movement in Western culture—at least up to the Enlightenment.'[12]

A host of new initiatives emerged in the French church during and after the Second World War. This included the movement for the reform of the liturgy, *Centre de Pastorale Liturgique*, the return to biblical and patristic sources, exemplified especially in the foundation of the *Sources chrétiennes* series, the renewal of ecclesiology, demonstrated by the establishment of the Unam Sanctam series, and the realization of the church's missionary task.[13]

The *ressourcement* passed through various stages of development.[14] The biblical renewal, which began in Germany in the course of the inter-war period, spread progressively to the rest of the Catholic world and even to what may be considered the less progressive countries. The liturgical renewal is older than the biblical renewal. Although known in France from before the First World War, its first intense period of activity was linked with the name of Dom Lambert Beauduin (1873–1960), the Belgian liturgist and founder of Chevetogne, who was condemned by a Roman tribunal in 1930 following the publication of his view that the Anglican Church should be 'united to Rome, not absorbed' ('unie non absorbée'). But it was in Germany during the inter-war period that the liturgical renewal blossomed when the church was forced, especially during the Nazi era, to renounce social action and to focus instead on the lively celebration of the divine mysteries. The liturgical renewal, which was not limited to Germany and France, could count on the active goodwill of the Holy See. The biblical renewal and the liturgical movement were

---

[12] John W. O'Malley, *What Happened at Vatican II* (Cambridge MA/London: Harvard University Press, 2008), 41.

[13] As Congar remarks: 'Anyone who did not live through the years 1946 and 1947 in the history of French Catholicism has missed one of the finest moments in the life of the Church. In the course of a slow emergence from privation and with the wide liberty of a fidelity as profound as life, men sought to regain evangelical contact with a world in which we had become involved to an extent unequalled in centuries.' See Yves M.-J. Congar, *Dialogue between Christians: Catholic Contributions to Ecumenism*, trans. Philip Loretz (London: Geoffrey Chapman, 1966), 32; ET of Congar, *Chrétiens en dialogue: contributions catholiques à l'œcuménisme*, Unam Sanctam, 50 (Paris: Cerf, 1964), p. xliii. De Lubac also refers to the spirit of hope, creativity, and originality that pervaded this period in the history of the French church, with *Chantiers de Jeunesse*, and the *Cahiers du Témoignage chrétien* producing a rich harvest. See de Lubac, *At the Service of the Church: Henri de Lubac Reflects on the Circumstances that occasioned His Writings*, trans. Anne Elizabeth Englund (San Francisco: Ignatius Press, 1993), 45, 48; ET of *Mémoire sur l'occasion de mes écrits*, ed. Georges Chantraine, SJ, *Œuvres complètes*, xxxiii (Paris: Cerf, 2006), 44–5, 47. '[B]oth in 1940–1942 and under the total occupation in 1942–1944, Lyons was quite different. Just as earlier, in the sixteenth century, it had been the "intellectual capital" of France, it became in 1940, the "capital of the Resistance".'

[14] See Congar, 'Tendances actuelles de la pensée religieuse', *Cahiers du monde nouveau*, 4 (1948), 33–50; Daniélou, 'Les orientations présentes de la pensée religieuse', *Études*, 249 (1946), 5–21; Roger Aubert, *La Théologie Catholique au milieu du XXe siècle* (Tournai: Casterman, 1954).

completed by a patristic rejuvenation.[15] The movement towards fuller contact with patristic thought is perhaps the most interesting and challenging of the various currents of renewal in theology in the early part of the twentieth century, as it provides an authentic witness to the faith in a way that is sensitive to the ever changing needs of humanity. There were new missionary strategies in France, including the Young Christian Worker/Young Christian Student movements, which developed during the inter-war period, and, during World War II, Godin and Daniel's *La France: Pays de mission?*,[16] and Cardinal Suhard's pastoral letters.[17]

Like Modernism, *ressourcement* engendered controversy from its inception and attracted considerable attention beyond those directly concerned with it. An inevitable part of that controversy related to the vexed question of terminology. The word *ressourcement* was coined by the poet and social critic Charles Péguy (1873–1914).[18] According to Congar, Péguy was a great influence in favour of *ressourcement*, though in his view Péguy's understanding of the Christocentric dimension of the faith was weak. The liturgical changes inaugurated by Pope Pius X (1835–1914) were also an inspiration for *ressourcement*.[19] Congar adopted *ressourcement* as the standard for church reform understood as an urgent call to move from 'a less profound to a more profound tradition; a discovery of the most profound resources'.[20] Much later, Congar would restate this original emphasis in the context of a glowing tribute to his beloved master and *confrère* Chenu:

> One day the balance will be drawn up, but already the positive quality can be sensed. What would a little later be called 'ressourcement' was then at the heart of our efforts. It was not a matter either of mechanically replacing some theses by other theses or of creating a 'revolution' but of appealing, as Péguy did, from one tradition less profound to another more profound.[21]

---

[15] See Louis Bouyer, 'Le Renouveau des études patristiques', *VI*, 15 (1947), 6–25; Bouyer, *Life and Liturgy*, 3rd edn. (London: Sheed & Ward, 1965).

[16] Henri Godin and Yvan Daniel, *La France: pays de mission?*, 7th edn. (Paris: Cerf, 1950).

[17] Emmanuel Suhard, *Essor ou déclin de l'Église: lettre pastorale Carême de l'an de grâce 1947* (Paris: Lahure, 1947); ET: *Growth or Decline?: The Church Today*, trans. James A. Corbett (Montreal: Fides Publishers, 1948); Suhard, *Le sens de Dieu: lettre pastorale Carême de l'an de grâce 1948* (Paris: Lahure, 1948); Suhard, *Le prêtre dans la cité: lettre pastorale Carême de l'an de grâce 1949* (Paris: Lahure, 1949); ET: *The Pastoral Letters of Emmanuel, Cardinal Suhard: Rise or Decline of the Church (1947), The Meaning of God (1948), The Priest in the Modern World (1949)* (London: New Life Publication Service, 1955).

[18] Congar, 'Le prophète Péguy', *Témoignage Chrétien*, 26 August 1949, 1.

[19] See Congar, 'Autour du renouveau de l'ecclésiologie: la collection "Unam Sanctam"', *VI*, 51 (1939), 9–32 (11).

[20] Congar, *Vraie et fausse réforme dans l'Église*, Unam Sanctam, 20 (Paris: Cerf, 1950), 601–2.

[21] Congar, 'The Brother I have known', trans. Boniface Ramsey, OP, *The Thomist*, 49 (1985), 495–503 (499). See also Congar, 'Le frère que j'ai connu', in Geffré et al., *L'hommage différé au Père Chenu*, 239–45 (242).

The *ressourcement* project was severely criticized by M.-Michel Labourdette,[22] as well as by Réginald Garrigou-Lagrange[23] who seems to have borrowed the phrase '*la nouvelle théologie*' to describe it. The epithet *nouvelle théologie* in fact corresponds to a theology that is concerned to know the tradition, as opposed to a purely scholastic and repetitive theology. The view of tradition proposed by the *nouvelle théologie*, far from being traditionalist, in the sense of a repetition of the recent past, was concerned rather with the unity of the ever-living tradition. As we have seen, this was precisely Congar's position.[24]

In September 1946, Pope Pius XII expressed his concerns regarding the *nouvelle théologie* to representatives of both the Dominicans and the Jesuits, warning against an attack on the fundamental tenets of Roman Catholic doctrine. Then in late November 1946, an unknown group of Jesuits published an anonymous and impassioned defence of *Sources chrétiennes* in the Jesuit periodical *Recherches de Science Religieuse*,[25] thereby making a difficult situation worse. In an atmosphere of suspicion and controversy, *Humani Generis* was published on 12 August 1950.[26] As the clouds began to gather over the church in France in the wake of the controversial encyclical, it is hardly surprising that both Congar and de Lubac, astute political analysts, rejected the term *nouvelle théologie*. In 1950 Congar compared *nouvelle théologie* to the 'tarasque', a legendary monster of Provence.[27] The distinguished French liturgist, Pierre-Marie Gy, OP (1922-2004), a lifelong friend and colleague of Congar, commented that for Congar, as also for Chenu, 'l'appellation de "nouvelle théologie" et l'enumération de ses représentants étaient artificielles,

---

[22] M.-Michel Labourdette, 'La Théologie et ses sources', *RevTh*, 46 (1946), 353–71; see further Labourdette, 'La Théologie, intelligence de la foi', *RevTh*, 46 (1946), 5–44; Aubert, *La Théologie Catholique*, 84–6.

[23] Réginald Garrigou-Lagrange, 'La nouvelle théologie où va-t-elle', *Ang*, 23 (1946), 126–45. The controversial term was first used by Pietro Parente, Secretary to the Holy Office, in an article entitled 'Nuove tendenze teologiche' which appeared in *L'Osservatore Romano*, 9–10 February 1942, 1. Parente saw this '*nouvelle théologie*' as a crude attempt to demolish the by then classical system of the schools ('. . . tenta di demolire rudemente il sistema ormai classico delle nostre scuole').

[24] Congar, *Tradition and the Life of the Church*, trans. A. N. Woodrow, Faith and Fact Books, 3 (London: Burns & Oates, 1964), 146; ET of Congar, *La tradition et la vie de l'Église*, 2nd edn, Traditions chrétiennes, 18 (Paris: Cerf, 1984), 118–19. 'While it is extension and progress, Tradition remains linked to its roots. The Holy Spirit is the divine guarantee of its fidelity.'

[25] 'La Théologie et ses sources: réponse aux Études critiques de la Revue thomiste (mai–août) 1946', *RSR*, 33 (1946), 385–401; see Joseph A. Komonchak's chapter in the present volume.

[26] Pius XII, *Humani Generis*. Encyclical Letter concerning some False Opinions Threatening to Undermine the Foundations of Catholic Doctrine, *AAS* 42 (1950), 561–78. ET, *False Trends In Modern Teaching: Encyclical Letter (Humani Generis)*, trans. Ronald A. Knox, rev. edn. (London: Catholic Truth Society, 1959). See Robert Guelluy, 'Les Antécédents de l'encyclique "Humani Generis" dans les sanctions Romaines de 1942: Chenu, Charlier, Draguet', *Revue d'histoire ecclésiastique*, 81 (1986), 421–97.

[27] Puyo (ed.), *Jean Puyo interroge le Père Congar*, 99.

polémiques, étrangères à la réalité'.[28] De Lubac expressed his view vehemently. 'I do not much like it when people talk of "new theology", referring to me; I have never used the expression, and I detest the thing. I have always sought, on the contrary, to make the Tradition of the Church known . . . "New theology" is a polemical term . . . which most of the time signifies nothing.'[29] De Lubac's confrere Henri Bouillard argued in 1947 along similar lines that 'the creation of a *théologie nouvelle* was not something to which he pretended', a conviction he was to repeat forcefully some three years later.[30]

Although no names had been mentioned in *Humani Generis*, the Jesuit and Dominican superiors felt compelled to act. Congar read *Humani Generis* very attentively, having been advised by Emmanuel Suárez, OP, the then Master of the Dominican Order, that there were things in it which concerned himself. Congar denied, however, that either he or anyone in his ecumenical milieu ever practised a bad 'irenicism'.[31] In February 1954, he was summoned to Paris by the Master of the Dominican Order and together with his *confrères* Chenu, Féret, and Pierre Boisselot, was dismissed from his post at Le Saulchoir. At his own suggestion, Congar went into exile in Jerusalem. Then, in November 1954, he was assigned to Blackfriars, Cambridge. The fate of the leading Jesuits was no different. De Lubac was permanently removed from all lecturing duties at Fourvière. *Humani Generis* had effectively signalled the end of his academic career, while his books were withdrawn from Jesuit libraries. As he writes:

> Around the end of August 1950, the encyclical *Humani generis* appeared in *La Croix*; I read it, toward the end of the afternoon, in a dark, still-empty room, in front of an open trunk . . . I later wrote about it to someone asking me for information: 'It seems to me to be, like many other ecclesiastical documents, unilateral: that is almost the law of the genre; but I have read nothing in it, doctrinally, that affects me [4:28].' [. . .] I should also have said above that, shortly after the publication of the encyclical *Humani generis*, a new measure had been taken. The order was given to withdraw from our libraries and from the trade, among other publications, three of my books: *Surnaturel*, *Corpus mysticum* and *Connaissance de Dieu*.[32]

[28] Letter from Gy to the author (9 July 1998); see further Congar, 'Bulletin de théologie dogmatique', *RSPT*, 35 (1951), 591–603 (596, n. 12).

[29] De Lubac, *At the Service of the Church*, 361; *Mémoire*, 362. See further de Lubac, *Entretiens autour de Vatican II: Souvenirs et Réflexions*, Théologies, 2nd edn. (Paris: France Catholique/Cerf, 2007 (1985)), 12; Chantraine, *Henri de Lubac: De la naissance à la démobilisation (1896–1919)*, vol. i, Études lubaciennes, vi (Paris: Cerf, 2007); Chantraine, *Henri de Lubac: Les années de formation (1919–1929)*, vol. ii, Études lubaciennes, vii (Paris: Cerf, 2009).

[30] Bouillard, *Vérité du christianisme*, Théologie (Paris: Desclée De Brouwer, 1989), 401, 406.

[31] See Puyo (ed.), *Jean Puyo interroge le Père Congar*, 106–13.

[32] De Lubac, *At the Service of the Church*, 71, 74; ET of *Mémoire*, 72, 75.

De Lubac's *confrères*, Henri Bouillard and Gaston Fessard, were temporarily exiled from the lecture theatre and were forbidden to publish, while Daniélou, with characteristic serendipity, remained active at the Institut Catholique de Paris.[33] But neither war nor persecution could deflect Congar or de Lubac from their vocation to service of the church and of truth.

Congar is honoured as a pioneer of church unity and a champion of the laity. At the same time, his role as reformer is ambiguous and his theology remains obfuscated to the present day.[34] Careful study of his contribution to church reform shows him to be an architect of the contemporary church. Congar, in fact, viewed his theology as an integral part of the Second Vatican Council, a point he expressed succinctly as follows: 'If there is a theology of Congar, that is where it is to be found.'[35] While Congar's participation in the proceedings of that Council, notably his close association with the Belgian theologians, indicates his obvious political adroitness, we must ever bear in mind that it is primarily as a servant of truth, and of the bishops, that he perceived his role there. As he explains:

> All the things to which I gave special attention issued in the Council: ecclesiology, ecumenism, reform of the Church, the lay state, mission, ministries, collegiality, return to the sources and Tradition.... I've consecrated my life to the service of truth. I've loved it and still love it in the way one loves a person. I've been like that from my very childhood, as if by some instinct and interior need.[36]

At Vatican II, the path of church reform and renewal by way of a return to the biblical and patristic sources was pursued not only by Congar, but also by de Lubac, Daniélou, Rahner, and Ratzinger, among others.[37] Congar's most significant contribution to *ressourcement* is undoubtedly the Unam Sanctam series launched by *La Vie intellectuelle* in November 1935, which became a

---

[33] See Brian Daley, 'The *Nouvelle Théologie* and the Patristic Revival: Sources, Symbols and the Science of Theology', *IJST*, 7 (2005), 362–82.

[34] See Flynn, 'Yves Congar and Catholic Church Reform: A Renewal of the Spirit', in Flynn (ed.), *Yves Congar: Theologian of the Church* (Louvain/Grand Rapids MI: Peeters/Eerdmans, 2005), 99–133; also Paul J. Philibert, OP, 'Retrieving a Masterpiece: Yves Congar's Vision of True Reform', *Doctrine and Life*, 61 (2011), 10–20.

[35] Congar, 'Letter from Father Yves Congar, O.P.', trans. Ronald John Zawilla, *Theology Digest*, 32 (1985), 213–16 (215).

[36] Congar, 'Reflections on being a Theologian', trans. Marcus Lefébure, *New Blackfriars*, 62 (1981), 405–9 (405–6). That Congar considered himself a servant of the Church is clear from the guiding principle he adopted to govern his work at the Council: 'As a pragmatic rule, I have taken this one: to do nothing except that solicited by the bishops. IT IS THEY who are the Council. If, however, an initiative bore the mark of a call of God, I would be open to it'. See Congar, *Mon journal du Concile*, Éric Mahieu, (ed.), 2 vols (Paris: Cerf, 2002), i.177 (31 October 1962); also Flynn, 'Book Essay: *Mon journal du Concile* Yves Congar and the Battle for a Renewed Ecclesiology at the Second Vatican Council', *LS*, 28 (2003), 48–70.

[37] See George Lindbeck, 'Ecumenical Theology', in David F. Ford (ed.), *The Modern Theologians: An Introduction to Christian Theology in the Twentieth Century*, 2 vols (Oxford: Blackwell, 1989), ii.255–73 (258).

highly influential ecclesiological and ecumenical library of Éditions du Cerf, running to some 77 volumes. Congar acknowledged that Unam Sanctam prepared the way for Vatican II while Chenu saw in this new collection 'one of the most beautiful fruits of our theology at Le Saulchoir'.[38]

De Lubac, like Congar, had a dynamic view of tradition: 'What I have more than once regretted in highly regarded theologians, experienced guardians, was less, as others have made out, their lack of openness to the problems and currents of contemporary thought than their lack of a truly traditional mind (the two things are moreover connected).'[39] His prodigious theological programme impacted directly on the documents of Vatican II.[40] As Paul McPartlan states: 'Joseph Ratzinger pays a remarkable tribute to de Lubac when he affirms that: "in all its comments about the Church [Vatican II] was moving precisely in the direction of de Lubac's thought".'[41] De Lubac was instrumental, with others, in the foundation of the *Théologie* series, a project of the Fourvière Jesuits, dedicated to the 'renewal of the Church'. He launched the series before the end of the Second World War with Fr Henri Bouillard, who became the project's first secretary. Bouillard said that the twofold objective of the project was 'to go to the sources of Christian doctrine, to find in it the truth of our life.'[42] But it was *Sources chrétiennes*, a bilingual collection published by Éditions du Cerf, under the general editorship of de Lubac and Daniélou, which was the crowning glory of the Fourvière Jesuits, as well as their greatest and most enduring contribution to *ressourcement*.[43] De Lubac elucidates the importance of *Sources chrétiennes* for renewal as follows: 'Each time, in our West, that Christian renewal has flourished, in the order of thought as in that of life (and the two are always connected), it has flourished under the sign of the Fathers.'[44] This project was thought up and elaborated between 1932 and 1937 by Victor Fontoynont, SJ († 1958), who was the true founder of the collection, as de Lubac acknowledges in his *Mémoire sur l'occasion de mes écrits*.[45] Perhaps the most eloquent testimony to the relevance and success of this venture, the principal aim of which was to provide

---

[38] See Congar, 'Reflections on being a Theologian' (405); Fouilloux, 'Frère Yves, Cardinal Congar, Dominicain: itinéraire d'un théologien', *RSPT*, 79 (1995), 379–404 (386).

[39] De Lubac, *At the Service of the Church*, 145; ET of *Mémoire*, 148.

[40] See de Lubac, *Carnets du Concile*, Löic Figoureux, (ed.), 2 vols (Paris: Cerf, 2007), i.421–5 (30 November 1962); de Lubac, *Entretiens autour de Vatican II: Souvenirs et Réflexions*, 41–69.

[41] McPartlan, 'The Eucharist, the Church and Evangelization: The Influence of Henri de Lubac', *Communio*, 23 (1996), 776–85 (780).

[42] See de Lubac, *At the Service of the Church*, 31; ET of *Mémoire*, 29.

[43] See Fouilloux, *La Collection 'Sources chrétiennes': éditer les Pères de l'Église au XXᵉ siècle* (Paris: Cerf, 1995), 219. Fouilloux notes that one of the aims of *Sources chrétiennes*, from its beginnings, was a *rapprochement* between separated Christians of East and West. See further Aubert, *La Théologie Catholique*, 84–6.

[44] De Lubac, *At the Service of the Church*, 95–6; ET of *Mémoire*, 96.

[45] De Lubac, *At the Service of the Church*, 94; ET of *Mémoire*, 95.

high quality translations of the Fathers in contemporary French, is the publication to date of over 500 volumes of Greek, Latin, and occasionally Syriac and Aramaic authors. The limitations of *Sources chrétiennes* notwithstanding, the series has certainly contributed to making the Fathers the normal spiritual *milieu* of theologians and the educated laity.[46] The eminent American Jesuit, John Courtney Murray (1904–67), aptly describes the success of *Sources chrétiennes*: 'We are all familiar with that definite, if undefinable reality known . . . as a "climate of opinion". And we know, too, that in the patristic climate of opinion the uniniated rather tends to gasp for breath. It is to this problem and its solution that the recently inaugurated series of patristic texts, *Sources chrétiennes*, directly addresses itself, with altogether remarkable success.'[47]

The achievement of the *ressourcement* theologians lay not so much in their rejection of a long since arid neo-scholasticism as in their dual concern to engage with the contemporary world and to ensure the essential unity of theology.[48] Indeed, the greatest legacy of the entire *ressourcement* enterprise rests in its enduring significance for the Christian Churches in the contemporary world, as A. N. Williams has demonstrated in a masterly essay.[49]

While the *ressourcement* theologians were the harbingers of the new era of openness, ecumenism, and dialogue inaugurated at the Second Vatican Council, it should not be forgotten that the ecclesial reforms and academic freedom for which they laboured were won in the midst of bitter acrimony, public recrimination, and intense personal suffering. In *Chrétiens en dialogue*, Congar portrays his anguish in stark terms: 'I only succeeded in overcoming all this, both spiritually and at the level of ordinary human sanity, by complete resignation to the cross.'[50] Furthermore, *Mon journal du Concile* provides unequivocal evidence of the official and quasi-official suspicion in which he was held for so long, and from which he apparently could not escape. In an entry on 14 March 1964, he wrote: 'Personally, I have never [. . .] emerged

---

[46] See Congar, 'L'Esprit des Pères d'après Moehler', *Supplément à la 'Vie Spirituelle'*, 55 (1938), 1–25 (2).

[47] See John Courtney Murray, '*Sources Chrétiennes*', TS, 9 (1948), 250–5 (251).

[48] Following the Council of Trent, a juridical model of faith with a strong emphasis on orthodoxy and certitude was imposed universally throughout the Catholic Church. In most seminaries and universities, theology and philosophy were taught without reference to the primary sources and gave an impression of rigidity and narrowness through excessive dependence on scholastic philosophy. In order to overcome the intransigence and aridity of the manuals, Congar, together with his colleagues Marie-Dominique Chenu and Henri-Marie Féret, embarked on an enterprise to eliminate 'baroque theology' and initiate 'the return to the sources'. See further Marie-Dominique Chenu, *Une école*, 127.

[49] A. N. Williams, 'The Future of the Past: The Contemporary Significance of the *Nouvelle Théologie*', *IJST*, 7 (2005), 347–61.

[50] Congar, *Dialogue between Christians*, 43; ET of *Chrétiens en dialogue*, p. lv.

from the apprehensions of a man, suspected, sanctioned, judged, [and] discriminated against.'[51]

De Lubac's travails are perhaps best illustrated in his memoirs where it is possible to discern the dark contours of an intense, tumultuous drama, the origins and extent of which were normally hidden from its central protagonist:

> Pius XII declared: 'There has been too much talk for some time about new theology'—which shows besides that his personal information was rather vague, for none of the members of what was called the 'Fourvière school', as far as I know, ever used that expression, and it was precisely Fr Garrigou-Lagrange who, picking up an old cliché, had launched it in a recent article with a threatening tone: 'New Theology: Where is it going?' (Angelicum, 1946). [. . .] [C]ritics abounded everywhere. 'Refutations' of *Surnaturel* increased. [. . .] It was in June 1950 that lightning struck Fourvière. I will not give here the chronicle of events. It would be rich in dramatic and melodramatic incidents. [. . .] The fact is that I then found myself at the center of the cyclone. [. . .] The decisions made in Rome in June 1950 officially emanated solely from the General of the Society. The latter was motivated to make them, however, by the fact of 'pernicious errors on essential points of dogma' maintained by the five professors in question, who had been removed from their duties and changed to a different residence: Fathers Emile Delaye, Henri Bouillard, Alexandre Durand, Pierre Ganne and I. [. . .] [T]he houses of the Society were not open to me.[52]

Whatever the motivation for de Lubac's and Congar's analyses of their relationship with *nouvelle théologie*, it is clear that they found themselves at the epicentre of a most acrimonious and fractious controversy in the period immediately prior to Vatican II. Moreover, some of the bitterest disagreements emanating from the *ressourcement* continue to reverberate today, notably in the domains of tradition and liturgy.

There is one further point which can be alluded to briefly. In the post-conciliar period, some of the leading *ressourcement* thinkers expressed concerns about the *aggiornamento* in unambiguous terms. In 1967, Congar described his own response as follows: 'Where are we to go from here? Where shall we be in twenty years? I, too, feel almost every day a temptation of uneasiness (*inquiétude*) in the face of all that has changed or is being called into question.'[53] Furthermore, de Lubac made no secret of his concerns.[54] In 2005, at the commencement of his papal ministry, Pope Benedict XVI, following Pope John Paul II, confirmed his 'determination to continue to put the Second

---

[51] Congar, *Mon journal du Concile*, ii.56 (14 March 1964).

[52] De Lubac, *At the Service of the Church*, 60, 62, 67–8, 79; ET of *Mémoire*, 62–3, 68–9, 80.

[53] Congar, 'Theology's Tasks after Vatican II', in Laurence K. Shook, (ed.), *Renewal of Religious Thought*, 2 vols (New York: Herder and Herder, 1968), i.47–65 (50); ET of 'Les tâches de la théologie après Vatican II', in L. K. Shook and Guy-M. Bertrand, (eds.), *La Théologie du renouveau*, 2 vols, Cogitatio Fidei, 27 (Montreal: Fides; Paris: Cerf, 1968), ii.17–31 (19).

[54] De Lubac, *At the Service of the Church*, 158–9; ET of *Mémoire*, 162–3.

Vatican Council into practice' as the '"compass" by which to take our bearings in the vast ocean of the third millennium'.[55] Five years later, Benedict alluded to the unresolved tensions concerning the Council's reception, a kind of antinomy, when, in his 2010 Pastoral Letter to the Catholics of Ireland, he called into question both the interpretation and the implementation of that Council's programme of renewal.[56] Such difficulties notwithstanding, the advantages of the Council's reform and renewal are clear at all levels of church life.

RESSOURCEMENT OR NOUVELLE THÉOLOGIE?

De Lubac and Daniélou were the leading practitioners of *ressourcement*. Their books often seem like a rich, intricately woven tapestry of texts from the tradition. Congar and Chenu, without diminution or denial of the return to the sources, represent a strongly historical theology, what their neo-Thomist confreres would doubtless call a 'historicist' approach to theology, including the theology of St Thomas. What distinguishes the *ressourcement* theologians from the *nouveaux théologiens* is that the former were also *nouveaux théologiens* while the latter were not always committed to *ressourcement*. Rahner's approach sets him apart from other *nouveaux théologiens*; his 'supernatural existential' is an attempt to rethink the supernatural—one of the preoccupations of the *nouveaux théologiens*. In his later writings, however, he does not tend to refer explicitly to the Fathers or to cite them. What unites these overlapping elements is a certain *froideur* towards Thomism, or what they insist on calling neo-Thomism.[57] Étienne Fouilloux contends that Congar became, with Chenu, de Lubac and Daniélou 'the incarnation of a "new theology", French-style, less concerned with conformity to Scholasticism as with the return to the sources of Christianity and to a dialogue with the great prevailing currents of thought'.[58]

The twentieth-century renaissance in Catholic theology coincided with the terrible barbarity of totalitarianism.[59] In the face of evil, the *ressourcement*

---

[55] Benedict XVI, 'First Message of His Holiness Benedict XVI at the end of the Eucharistic Concelebration with the Members of the College of Cardinals in the Sistine Chapel', 20 April 2005, available at: <http://www.vatican.va/holy_father/benedict_xvi/messages/pont-messages/2005/documents/hf_ben-xvi_mes_20050420_missa-pro-ecclesia_en.html>.

[56] See, Benedict XVI, 'Pastoral Letter of the Holy Father Pope Benedict XVI to the Catholics of Ireland', 19 March 2010, para. 4, available at: <http://www.vatican.va/holy_father/bene-dict_xvi/letters/2010/documents/hf_ben-xvi_let_20100319_church-ireland_en.html>.

[57] I am grateful to John Saward for our discussions on the complexities of *ressourcement* and *nouvelle théologie*.

[58] Congar, *Journal d'un théologien (1946–1956)*, ed. with notes by Étienne Fouilloux and others, 2nd edn. (Paris: Cerf, 2001), 12.

[59] See Hannah Arendt, *The Origins of Totalitarianism*, 9th edn. (New York: Schocken Books, 2004).

theologians were not afraid to accept responsibility and to summon others in their respective spheres of influence to judgement and action. However, the staunch opposition of many of the Catholic *ressourcement* theologians to Nazism is little known compared with that of some of their leading Protestant counterparts. Failure to document their contribution to the French Resistance would also be a failure to recognize that *ressourcement* is essentially a practical theology engaged in an open, critical, and sometimes militant fashion with the most pressing issues affecting contemporary society.[60] In the next section of this chapter, therefore, I propose to discuss how leading French *ressourcement* theologians contributed to the battle against Nazism while also confronting the complicity of the Vichy regime and the quiescence of the majority of French bishops.

'HISTORICALLY TRAGIC TIMES'—POPE PIUS XI[61]

Catholic and Protestant bishops, priests, and pastors, both German and French, are often accused of being either sympathetic to the Nazi regime or generally tolerant of its anti-Jewish stance during the period of the Third Reich (1933–45). Among the notable exceptions, on the Protestant side, were Dietrich Bonhoeffer (1906–45), head of the German Confessing Church's seminary near Stettin, and Max Metzger (1887–1944); both were influential religious activists, writers, and martyrs. Bonhoeffer's heroic opposition to German National Socialism, a political system which he publicly condemned as corrupt and misleading, is well known because of his execution at the hands of the SS Black Guards on 9 April 1945.[62]

On the Catholic side, the honour roll includes, among others, Romano Guardini (1885–1968) and Engelbert Krebs (1881–1950), both of whom publicly criticized Hitler and were eventually dismissed from their professor-ships by the Minister for Education.[63] The courageous witness of Cardinal Clemens August, Count von Galen (1878–1946), Bishop of Münster, who

---

[60] See further John Milbank, 'Henri de Lubac', in David F. Ford with Rachel Muers (eds.), *The Modern Theologians: An Introduction to Christian Theology since 1918*, 3rd edn. (Oxford: Blackwell, 2005), 76–91 (77–8).
[61] On 24 February 1934, Pius XI stated: 'We are living in historically tragic times.... We are living in times when racial pride has been exalted to the point of being a pride of thoughts, doctrines and practices, which is neither Christian nor human.' Cited in de Lubac, *Christian Resistance to Anti-Semitism: Memories from 1940–1944*, trans. Elizabeth Englund, OCD (San Francisco: Ignatius Press, 1990), 28.
[62] G. Leibholz, 'Memoir', in Dietrich Bonhoeffer, *The Cost of Discipleship*, trans. R.H. Fuller, with some revision by Irmgard Booth, complete edn. (London: SCM, 1959), 9–27 (25).
[63] See Robert A. Krieg, *Catholic Theologians in Nazi Germany* (New York: Continuum, 2004), 118–19, 148–50.

exposed and publicly condemned the attacks of the Nazi regime against persons with intellectual disability, must also be acknowledged. When he died on 22 March 1946, the President of the regional association of the Jewish communities wrote to the Vicar Capitular in Münster: 'Cardinal von Galen was one of the few upright and conscientious men who fought against racialism in a most difficult time. We shall always honour the memory of the deceased Bishop.'[64] The actions of von Galen and his fellow bishops Konrad von Preysing and Johannes Baptist Sproll would have gained greater papal support if Pius XI had lived long enough to issue his planned new encyclical *Humani Generis Unitas*, denouncing anti-Semitism much more vociferously than he had in *Mit Brennender Sorge*.[65]

Congar was an implacable enemy of National Socialism. He considered his period of detention in the prisons of Colditz and Lübeck (1941–5), following a brief time of combat, to be a moment of grace, the occasion of the finest companionship of his entire life. The atmosphere of war and captivity was also a time of profound authenticity when as a prisoner of war Congar demonstrated a defiant and obstinate '[d]evelopment of opposition to the enemy'.[66] As he recounts:

> In captivity, I adopted a militant anti-Nazi attitude which had its own consequences and inconveniences. However, it admitted me to the fellowship of courageous men in an atmosphere of resistance which was a great tonic. I then began to realize that one of the most important things in life, particularly in difficult times—and what times are not?—is to seek out men of courage and enlightenment with whom one can associate and keep faith. In this respect I was overwhelmed for I had some wonderful friends and comrades.[67]

De Lubac's strident opposition to anti-Semitism during the Nazi occupation of France merits consideration, notably, his role as co-editor of the clandestine *Cahiers du Témoignage chrétien*.[68] The spirit of the *Cahiers* was always informed by the fight against anti-Semitism, with de Lubac as one of the principal theologians striving to show the incompatibility between Christianity and Nazism. The *Cahiers'* profound concern for the soul of France is

---

[64] Cited in Reinhard Lettmann, Bishop of Münster, 'Introduction', Bishop von Galen, *Three Sermons in Defiance of the Nazis*, 1–28 (5), available at: <http://www.churchinhistory.org/pages/booklets/vongalen(n).htm>.

[65] See Georges Passelecq and Bernard Suchecky, *The Hidden Encyclical of Pius XI*, trans. Steven Rendall (New York: Harcourt Brace, 1997); Guenter Lewy, *The Catholic Church and Nazi Germany* (London: Weidenfeld & Nicolson, 1964).

[66] Congar, *Dialogue between Christians*, 30; ET of *Chrétiens en dialogue*, p. xli.

[67] Congar, *Dialogue between Christians*, 29–30; ET of *Chrétiens en dialogue*, pp. xl–xli.

[68] See de Lubac, 'La question des évêques sous l'occupation', *Revue des Deux Mondes* (février 1992), 67–82. A note on the file containing this essay, the authenticity of which cannot be proven, reads as follows: 'Jacques Guillet and Bernard Sesboüé are in favour of its authenticity.' De Lubac Papers, Jesuit Archives, Vanves, Paris, Dossier 5, 'Résistance spirituelle au nazisme, 1940–1945'.

manifested in its first edition, entitled *France, prends garde de perdre ton âme*. It provided a ministry to souls and gave a voice to the churches during the painful years of occupation from 1941 to 1944, years of general confusion, military defeat, and breakdown of the institutions of the Third Republic.

In the midst of much profound sorrow, de Lubac enjoyed the 'grace of friends' and none more than that of his *confrère* Yves de Montcheuil (1900–44), sometime Professor of Theology at the Institut Catholique de Paris. De Montcheuil was indisputably a man '*omnium horarum*', to borrow Erasmus' famous description of St Thomas More. He shared de Lubac's theological vision as well as his engagement with the French Resistance for which he was executed by the Gestapo on 12 August 1944. De Lubac praised de Montcheuil's service to the French church. 'Today, Fr de Montcheuil is practically forgotten, the Church is not a party: it's a mother, who accepts that the sacrifice of its children remains buried in obscurity, according to the laws of the gospel.'[69] The editor of *Recherches de Science Religieuse* wrote the following tribute: 'Fr de Montcheuil had a profound influence on the theologians who attended his courses at the Institut Catholique and, beyond the Faculty of Theology, on the student body, in particular on those students who heard his lectures and who received spiritual direction and counsel from him.'[70]

There are two principal sources for de Lubac's role in the Christian resistance to Nazism and anti-Semitism, namely, *Résistance chrétienne à l'antisémitisme*, a memoir which he completed in 1984, and *Théologie dans l'histoire*.[71] He was fully cognizant of the 'formidable spiritual drama', the 'diabolical hurricane' which was blowing violently across France, while Marshal Pétain (1856–1951), 'Head of State' (1940–4), together with his cabinet, remained oblivious to the violence. De Lubac unambiguously aligned himself with Pope Pius XI, and was deeply critical of historians who sought to minimize the significance of the encyclical *Mit brennender Sorge*.[72] He was at pains to illustrate the moral courage, diplomacy, and political acuity of the elderly Pope who from 1930 until his death persisted in his combat against Nazism with his courageous battle cry 'Spiritually we are Semites!'[73]

---

[69] De Lubac, *Trois jésuits nous parlent: Yves de Montcheuil 1899–1944 Charles Nicolet 1897–1961 Jean Zupan 1899–1968* (Paris: Lethielleux, 1980), 71.

[70] Jules Lebreton, '"In Memoriam" Le Père Yves de Montcheuil', *RSR*, 33 (1946), 5–9 (5).

[71] De Lubac, *Theology in History*, trans. Anne Englund Nash (San Francisco: Ignatius Press, 1996); ET of *Théologie dans l'histoire. II Questions disputées et résistance au nazisme*, Théologie (Paris: Desclée de Brouwer, 1990).

[72] Pius XI, 'Mit brennender Sorge: Encyclical of Pope Pius XI on the Church and the German Reich March 14, 1937', *AAS* 29 (1937), 145–67. ET available in *The Papal Encyclicals 1903–1939*, iii, ed. Claudia Carlen, 5 vols (Raleigh: Pierian, 1990), 525–35.

[73] See further, de Lubac, *Christian Resistance to Anti-Semitism*, 27–8.

In the context of a discussion of the 'Theological Foundations of the Missions',[74] de Lubac responded to the 'brutal objection' to the church's mission based on race. He repudiated the principal Nazi theoretician of race, Alfred Rosenberg. In a powerful and compelling defence of truth and humanity, de Lubac rallied French Catholics to church and country in defence of the defenceless against the ruthless forces of tyranny:

> Appeal as constantly as racists may to what they call 'the undeniable results of the science of the races', if we deduct from their theories the part of literary Christianity and that of ideological or political propaganda (not to speak of blasphemies), nothing remains to which the name of science applies. [. . .] Christians of France, in the misfortune that has struck our land, we have undoubtedly not been insensitive to the evils that struck the Church at the same stroke. [. . .] We do not know what God holds in reserve, and we may be permitted to hope that he will not allow the shadow of a new paganism, coming from the old Christian Europe, to extend over the entire world (and even then, we well know that all would not be lost). But this is on condition that, instead of giving way to despair, we stand by our Church and that her conscience might resound through all our consciences.[75]

In a wartime pamphlet challenging theological accommodations to Nazi ideology, de Lubac movingly restated 'the Christian vocation of France': 'For a spiritual and metaphysical crisis, only a remedy of the same nature is appropriate. [. . .] Now, the vocation of France is a Christian vocation. [. . .] France has also received a certain genius that carries its children either to spread this Christianity around them or to propagate in the world the great human values that we owe to Christianity.'[76]

In a letter to his superiors on 25 April 1941, de Lubac described the conquests by Germany as 'an anti-Christian revolution' the aim of which was 'to subjugate the Church' and to impose Nazi methods and ideas. As evidence of this, he pointed to the presence on French soil of concentration camps, the propagation of anti-Semitism and, at the same time, the rise in France of a wave of neo-paganism.[77] In the course of his letter, he raised the spectre of church leaders seemingly unaware of the harshest realities on the ground while at the same time articulating bewildering platitudes based on self-interest:

> Do our spiritual leaders share, even a little, such a state of mind? [. . .] We hear some of them publicly express satisfaction with the present situation from the

---

[74] De Lubac, 'Theological Foundations of the Missions', *Theology in History*, 367–427; ET of 'Le fondement théologique des missions', *Théologie dans l'histoire*, ii.159–219.

[75] De Lubac, 'Theological Foundations of the Missions', *Theology in History*, 410, 421–2; ET of 'Le fondement théologique des missions', *Théologie dans l'histoire* ii.202, 214.

[76] De Lubac, 'Christian explanation of our times', *Theology in History*, 440–56 (446–7); ET of 'Explication chrétienne de notre temps', *Théologie dans l'histoire* ii.232–49 (238, 240).

[77] De Lubac, 'Letter to My Superiors', *Theology in History*, 428–39 (431–5); ET of 'Lettre à mes supérieurs', *Théologie dans l'histoire*, ii.220–31 (221–5).

religious point of view; hyperboles abound on their lips and in their writings; they speak freely of 'providential defeat', of 'miracles', and so forth. But not the most timid reminder of doctrine, the most modest warning, at least in public, has yet reached us. It does not seem that most are concerned with enlightening their clergy on the present situation of Catholicism and on the danger to the faith. Priests and faithful are thus left without any warning, without direction.[78]

De Lubac acknowledges without dissimulation the common responsibility for the present state of affairs: '[E]ach one always bears his little part in great collective responsibilities, and that in times of exceptional crisis.[. . .] [I]t is a more urgent duty for each to become aware and act in consequence.'[79]

Nothing could have prepared de Lubac, Congar, and their erstwhile colleagues for the extraordinarily difficult leadership role they were to play in the renewal of Catholic theology and liturgy, the reform of the churches, and the rejuvenation of European culture in the period after World War II. Their critical voice in a Nazi wasteland bespeaks a deep-seated respect for humanity. Essentially they were religious men of ideas, driven along by the emerging currents of the times which they helped to create and in which they lived. Possessed of an unwavering love of the church and a profound compassion for others, they were fearless in the execution of their mission, an important part of which was the construction of a Christian humanism in response to the challenges of the Enlightenment, European totalitarianism, and secular modernity. The present volume seeks to emulate the style and method of the *ressourcement* by pursuing a historical approach in the analysis of *nouvelle théologie*.[80]

RESSOURCEMENT: A MOVEMENT FOR RENEWAL IN CATHOLIC THEOLOGY

This volume is essentially about theology and history. It attempts to articulate the history of the *ressourcement* movement, its antecedents and leading exponents, and to assess the relevance of their prodigious theological output for the contemporary churches and modern society. The book is divided into four parts.

Part I, 'The *Ressourcement* Movement: History and Context', presents a series of chapters on the background to *ressourcement* and delineates the

---

[78] De Lubac, *Theology in History*, 434–5; ET of *Théologie dans l'histoire*, ii.226–7.
[79] De Lubac, *Theology in History*, 438; ET of *Théologie dans l'histoire*, ii.230.
[80] See Fouilloux, 'Dialogue théologique? (1946–1948)', in Serge-Thomas Bonino (ed.), *Saint Thomas au XXᵉ siècle*, Actes du colloque du Centenaire de la *Revue Thomiste*, (Paris: Centre National de Livre-Saint Paul, 1994), 153–95; also Donneaud's chapter in the present volume.

historical phases of the so-called *nouvelle théologie*. Gemma Simmonds reveals a remarkable similarity between seventeenth-century Jansenism and key aspects of the later *ressourcement*. She argues that if the reforms envisaged by the Jansenists had not been so comprehensively crushed by church and state, the later reforms spearheaded by de Lubac, Congar, Daniélou, and their companions might have come about considerably earlier. Moving to the cusp of the twentieth century, Gerard Loughlin examines the relationship between *nouvelle théologie* and Modernism, paying careful attention to the neo-scholastic critique of Modernism. Interestingly, his response to the question, 'Was Garrigou-Lagrange correct when he said that the new theology was but a return to the old heresy?', is both yes and no. Continuing our examination of the background influences on *ressourcement* theology, Francesca Aran Murphy and Michael A. Conway assess the contribution of two of the most significant philosophers of the twentieth-century Catholic Church, Étienne Gilson and Maurice Blondel, respectively.

Étienne Fouilloux, Henry Donneaud, A. N. Williams, and John Saward assess, in turn, the originality of the new 'Lyon School' (1919–39), amid the French intellectual currents between the wars, the contribution of the Dominican province of Toulouse to *ressourcement*, with particular reference to Marie-Rosaire Gagnebet and what has been called a Thomist *ressourcement*, and the contribution of Pierre Teilhard de Chardin and Charles Journet. None of these chapters makes any claim to be the last word in the history of a complex and controversial movement.

The final four chapters in this section present a more long-term view of *ressourcement* in twentieth-century Catholic theology. Joseph A. Komonchak skilfully demarcates the complex relationship between *Humani Generis* and *nouvelle théologie*. He shows how Vatican II articulated a new language of dialogue, which displaced the near-monopoly in theology enjoyed by scholastic method, language, principles, and concepts. Hans Boersma argues, from a Reform perspective, that the answer to the enigma of *nouvelle théologie* is not to place it on a historical trajectory from Modernism to post-conciliar pluralism but rather to ground it in the traditional doctrine of analogy, thus presenting a sacramental epistemology that offers a theological recovery of mystery to the modern world. Jürgen Mettepenningen assesses the development of the consecutive phases of *nouvelle théologie* and its relationship to the broader *ressourcement* movement. Finally, Christopher Ruddy considers the enduring legacy of post-Tridentine theology. He verbalizes the danger of allowing the 'hermeneutic of reform' in Vatican II to become a 'hermeneutic of discontinuity and rupture'.

Part II, 'Central Figures of the *Ressourcement*' considers the leading exponents of twentieth-century *ressourcement*. Janette Gray and Gabriel Flynn assess the contribution of Chenu and Congar, respectively, while David Grumett, Bernard Pottier, James Hanvey, and Edward T. Oakes examine the role of the leading Jesuit thinkers, de Lubac, Daniélou, Bouillard, and von Balthasar. This consideration of the great thinkers from the faculties of Le Saulchoir (Paris) and Lyon-Fourvière and beyond is complemented by Jake Yap's essay on Louis Bouyer, seen as one of the great *ressourcement* theologians, who viewed the relationship between God and creation as the fundamental question of theology.

Part III, '*Ressourcement* as a threefold programme of renewal', takes its title from Roger Aubert's seminal work *La Théologie Catholique au milieu du XXe siècle*. It has chapters on the renewal in biblical studies, liturgy, and patristics. Benedict T. Viviano's essay, 'The renewal of biblical studies in France 1934–54 as an element in theological *ressourcement*', systematically outlines the history of the biblical renewal. In the face of discontent with modern exegetical methods among younger Jewish and Christian scholars, he makes the case for the continued relevance of French *ressourcement* theologians. Keith F. Pecklers presents a historical/theological assessment of the twentieth-century Catholic recovery of the church's liturgical sources. In this context, he supports the case for the liturgy as 'the primordial source of renewal in the church'.[81] Brian E. Daley's essay 'Knowing God in history and in the church: *Dei Verbum* and *nouvelle théologie*' considers how *Dei Verbum* and *nouvelle théologie* assist in reading scripture and human history as the church Fathers had read them for centuries, and finds in them a new key to understanding the church.

Part IV, '*Ressourcement* and the Church in the Modern World', assesses the continued relevance of the twentieth-century movement for renewal. Stephen M. Fields presents a response to an awkward question that may arise in readers' minds concerning the philosophical underpinnings of *ressourcement*. Following Aidan Nichols, he argues that the polemic between Thomism and *ressourcement* concerns integrating patristic insights about subjectivity and event into a sound metaphysics. He articulates the case for a continuing dialogue between *ressourcement* and Thomism for the benefit of the contemporary world. Gerald O'Collins examines the impact of *ressourcement* theology on Vatican II through a careful examination of the documents, and by reference to the ways in which the theologians worked with the bishops in the revision of the texts. Paul McPartlan draws upon such perennially important issues as Eucharist and ecumenism to demonstrate the importance of the Second Vatican Council and its *ressourcement* theologians in shaping the future agenda of the Catholic Church. Turning to the contribution of Karl Rahner, who, it is widely acknowledged, was one of the dominant theological voices of the Catholic Church in the twentieth century, Richard Lennan

---

[81] Archbishop Piero Marini, Interview with John L. Allen, Jr., Archbishop's House, Westminster, London, 15th December 2007, available at: <http://www.natcath.com/mainpage/specialdocuments/marini_interview.pdf>, 6.

considers possible convergences between his thought and the *ressourcement*. Lewis Ayres, Patricia Kelly, and Thomas Humphries question whether Joseph Ratzinger (Benedict XVI), one of the last surviving theologians of the pre-Vatican II era, views *ressourcement* as a hermeneutic of continuity rather than as a rupture with the church's past. Marcus Pound proposes a case of theological *ressourcement* in Roland Barthes, George Bataille, and Jacques Lacan. He considers the wider influence of *ressourcement* on the historic emergence of French psychoanalytic thought and Catholic psychology.

The final chapters by Paul D. Murray, John Webster, and Andrew Louth discuss in turn the groundbreaking contribution of Congar to ecumenism and church reform, the relationship between *ressourcement* and Protestantism, and the links between French *ressourcement* theology in the second and third quarters of the twentieth century and the Orthodox scholars who came to settle in the West, especially in Paris, during this period. Certain dogmatic differences notwithstanding, Webster suggests that *ressourcement* theology offers an invitation to Protestant theology to renew its vocation as ecclesial science and to see the present situation of theology for what it is, a moment in the history of redemption. It is not insignificant that Louth argues that the relationship is a mutual one, each side learning from the other, and, moreover, that in this engagement one can see something of the dynamics of a genuine, mutually receptive, ecumenism. In the epilogue, John McDade assesses the legacy of the *ressourcement* thinkers. The editors and contributors to this volume present the transformative *ressourcement* vision for renewal and rejuvenation in the hope that future generations will draw strength and life from it.

This introductory chapter can perhaps be fittingly brought to a close with reference to de Lubac's articulation of the human search for meaning:

> To remind man what constitutes the final end is not to tell him something that substantially fails to interest him . . . It is rather to illustrate the total meaning of his being by helping him to find and then to interpret the inscription written into his heart by his Creator.[82]

---

[82] De Lubac, 'The Total Meaning of Man and the World', trans. of the first four sections (of six total) of *Athéisme et sens de l'homme* by D. C. Schindler, *Communio*, 35 (2008), 613–41 (613); ET of 'Sens total de l'homme et du monde', *Athéisme et sens de l'homme: Une double requête de Gaudium et spes* (Paris: Cerf, 1968), 91–130.

Part I

The *Ressourcement* Movement: History and Context

1

Jansenism: An Early *Ressourcement* Movement?

Gemma Simmonds, CJ

JANSENISM AND *RESSOURCEMENT*

The primary purpose of the *ressourcement* movement of twentieth-century France was a theological and spiritual renewal based on a return to the original sources of Christian tradition, namely scripture, the Fathers, and liturgy. Proponents of the so-called 'new' theology (a title they vigorously opposed) included within this renewal a concern for a dialogue between faith and the major issues of their day, and for a renewed ecclesiology which gave due place to the role of the laity and to a conciliar concept of governance. *Ressourcement* is often seen as the harbinger of the Second Vatican Council, which modernized the Catholic Church and swept away much of what was considered 'traditional', so it may appear perverse to link it with another French phenomenon generally blamed for all that is considered rigid and obscurantist in Catholicism. Nevertheless, a closer look at seventeenth-century Jansenism reveals a remarkable similarity to key aspects of the later *ressourcement*. Had the reforms envisaged by the Jansenists not been so comprehensively crushed by church and state, it could be argued that the reforms spearheaded by de Lubac, Congar, Daniélou and their companions might have come about considerably earlier.

Like the word 'Puritan', 'Jansenist' has become detached from its historical moorings to serve as a catch-all phrase for rigidity, sanctimoniousness, and oppressive religious austerity, used, as in Patrick Kavanagh's *Lough Derg*, to describe the 'foul legend' of a certain type of French or Irish Catholicism, brutally pessimistic in its concentration on sin and allegedly responsible for everything from endemic sexual repression to mental illness.[1] It fares little

---

[1] See Michael Sheehy, *Is Ireland Dying? Culture and the Church in Modern Ireland* (London: Hollis and Carter, 1968); Nancy Scheper-Hughes, *Saints, Scholars and Schizophrenics: Mental Illness in Rural Ireland* (Berkeley: University of California Press, 1979).

better in film and literature, Tag Gallagher describing Rossellini's film *Blaise Pascal* as a horror movie, in which 'everything is drenched in suffering, torture, fear, superstitious dread; everyone is writhing in desperate faith, self-mortification and pain [. . .] everything seem[s] drenched in blood and penance'.[2] He sees the film as a portrayal of the 'appalling heroism', with which, through 'endless misery and dogged persistence', the Jansenists struggle with 'absurdity systematised into terror'.[3]

In their own day the Jansenists of seventeenth-century France were similarly demonized by their enemies, and with as little care for truth or accuracy. While undoubtedly there were tragic distortions in Jansenist views on grace and the sacraments, early Jansenism can nevertheless be seen as one of the foremost contributors to the development of modern consciousness in advocating the rights of the individual conscience. In espousing the rights of the lower clergy, the emancipation of slaves, and the restoration of civil status to Jews and Protestants, later Jansenism stands at the forefront of social, political, and philosophical radicalism.[4] In terms of ecclesiology, Jansenism fostered stronger roles for the laity and especially women in the church. The outstanding scriptural scholarship of Port-Royal and its efforts to promote a vernacular missal were aimed at the fuller lay participation in liturgy promoted by the Second Vatican Council.[5] In a close parallel to the *ressourcement* movement, the Jansenist recourse to the past was a radical response to the questions posed by a society in transit and a church in disarray after long periods of conflict and stagnation. Yet the positive dynamic within Jansenism burned itself out in an ideological quarrel that ultimately thwarted the very reform at which it was aimed.[6]

JANSENISM: A MOVEMENT FOR CHURCH REFORM IN SEVENTEENTH-CENTURY FRANCE

In the first half of the seventeenth century the convent of Port-Royal, outside Paris, became the centre of a reform movement which attracted many of the

---

[2] Frank McGuinness, 'Rimbaud', *Irish Times*, 14 October 2000.

[3] Tag Gallagher, *The Adventures of Roberto Rossellini: his Life and Films* (New York: Da Capo Press, 1998), 626-7.

[4] Alexander Sedgwick, *Jansenism in Seventeenth-Century France: Voices from the Wilderness* (Charlottesville: University of Virginia Press, 1977), 201–2.

[5] F. Ellen Weaver, 'Liturgy for the Laity: the Jansenist Case for Popular Participation in Worship in the Seventeenth and Eighteenth centuries', *Studia Liturgica*, 19 (1989), 47–59. The first recorded case of a celebration of the Mass in French was in Jansenist circles at Versailles in 1794. See also Linda Timmermans, *L'accès des femmes à la culture (1598–1715): un débat d'idées, de Saint François de Sales à la marquise de Lambert* (Paris: Champion, 1993), 14–16, 692–4.

[6] Jean-Louis Quantin, *Le catholicisme classique et les Pères de l'église—un retour aux sources (1669–1713)* (Paris: Institut d'Études Augustiniennes, 1999), 979–84.

most brilliant social, political, and intellectual figures of the day. Led by Mère Angélique Arnauld, the community extended to the *solitaires* or *Messieurs*, laymen or priests who were famed as much for their erudition as for their austerity of life. Like the proponents of *la nouvelle théologie*, the Port-Royal circle rejected the name given to them by their critics, preferring 'Friends of the Truth' or 'Disciples of St Augustine' to 'Jansenists'. Foremost in its spiritual leadership were the Abbé de Saint-Cyran and Antoine, brother of Angélique, 'Le Grand Arnauld', and their nephew Louis-Isaac Lemaistre de Sacy, the biblical translator.

The Jansenists drew inspiration from the condemned radical Augustinian-ism of Michel Baius, Professor of Scripture at Louvain. Similarly inspired, the monumental *Augustinus* of Cornelius Otto Jansen (1585–1638), Bishop of Ypres and friend of Saint-Cyran, was published posthumously in 1640. In 1653 Innocent X condemned as heretical five propositions allegedly found in it. The bitter *fait* and *droit* controversy that ensued over whether or not the propositions were in the book set individual conscience over ecclesial author-ity. This controversy led to the eventual condemnation of the Jansenists not only by the church but also by Louis XIV, who saw in Jansenist insistence on conscience an emerging resistance to his increasing absolutism.

In his book on the Reformation, Diarmaid MacCulloch observes: 'The issues of authority which Jansenism raised are still those that threaten to blow apart the modern Roman Catholic Church. That is reflected in the call back to a vision of papal monarchy, away from the conciliarism of the Second Vatican Council, sounded by Pope John Paul II from 1978.'[7] The way that theology relates to history and the understanding and interpretation of Christian sources lay at the heart of the question over the extent to which Augustine's teaching should be considered as doctrinally normative. The relation of theology to history and original context was also to become a crucial issue in the twentieth century with the *nouvelle théologie*.

In the search for a clear understanding of Augustine's doctrine of grace, Port-Royal made a major contribution to the study of patristics and to scholarly research into original texts. In this stress on historical sources, there is a strong parallel with the re-appropriation of Christian sources by twentieth-century French theologians, though there is a major difference of focus between the *ressourcement*s of the seventeenth and twentieth centuries. It was largely the lack of contextualization and the tendency towards a narrow, primitivist interpretation that gave birth to the distortions for which Jansen-ism was condemned. If their radical Augustinian zeal betrayed the Jansenists into error, Owen Chadwick gives a comprehensive and impressive list of their achievements by the nineteenth century: stronger parish life, better education of priests, better work in schools, a more congregational liturgy, a love of early

---

[7] Diarmaid MacCulloch, *Reformation: Europe's House Divided 1490–1700* (London: Penguin, 2004), 483.

Christianity and of the Bible, and 'the renewal of a quest for the authentic and
innermost meaning of Catholicism'.[8] This might well sum up those achievements of the Second Vatican Council spearheaded by the *nouvelle théologie*.

In 1643 Antoine Arnauld's *De la fréquente Communion* argued for a
return to the more rigorous sacramental practice of the patristic era. Arnauld
held that the ecclesial body founded by Christ 'is the same today as it has
been for sixteen hundred years and [. . .] will be the same at the end of the
world'.[9] Notions of necessary changes in legislation, culled from the structure
of secular society, could have no place in the church of God. He and his
opponents took as their champion Vincent of Lérins, whose *Commonitorium*
offers as the criteria for orthodoxy 'what has been believed everywhere, always
and by all'.[10] What was left open was the question as to who might provide an
authoritative interpretation of the Fathers, whose works were even more open
to multiple understandings than scripture itself.[11]

While Port-Royal played a major part in the revival of patristic and biblical
scholarship, the indiscriminate Jansenist passion for Augustine came to be
seen as an indirect threat to Roman authority since it pitted the Fathers and
ancient councils against the Pope. The final years of the seventeenth century
saw a concerted effort between papacy and throne to outlaw Jansenism and
crush Port-Royal. The convent was closed, the nuns and *Messieurs* imprisoned
or evicted and finally the house razed to the ground. This only drove its
supporters and their work underground. Pasquier Quesnel's *Réflexions mor-
ales* on Sacy's 1665 translation of the New Testament precipitated the Bull
Unigenitus in 1713 and with it the appellant crisis, where bishops, religious,
and clergy who appealed against *Unigenitus* and called for a general council of
the church to arbitrate the matter found themselves unwilling heretics over-
night. The definitive break between Rome and the Jansenist remnant came
about in 1871 in the aftermath of the First Vatican Council and its pronounce-
ment of the dogma of papal infallibility.[12] The present-day 'Gallican Catholic
Church of France', founded in 1883, is a far cry from Port-Royal. Arnauld and
Saint-Cyran would certainly be bemused by the monthly Mass for animals
where retired television stars and pretenders to the throne of France are joined
in church by an assortment of llamas, dogs, cats, and guinea pigs.[13]

---

[8] Owen Chadwick, *The Popes and European Revolution* (Oxford: Oxford University Press,
1981), 612.
   [9] Antoine Arnauld, *La tradition de l'Église sur le sujet de la pénitence et de la communion*
(Paris: Antoine Vitré, 1644), 52.
   [10] Vincent of Lérins, *Commonitorium*, ed. Reginald Stewart Moxon (Cambridge: Cambridge
University Press, 1915), 2–3, 6–7.
   [11] Yves Congar, *La tradition et les traditions: essai historique* (Paris: Fayard, 1960), 254–5.
   [12] Quantin, *Catholicisme*, 17, 97–8.
   [13] See article and photograph of the Mass (and animals) in the Église Catholique Gallicane de
Ste Rita, Paris, available at <http://eglisesainterita.free.fr> (accessed 1 February 2010).

The Jansenist reformers have been described as looking to recover the earthly paradise of the past as a means of arriving at the heavenly paradise of the future, while their twentieth-century counterparts are seen as looking to the past in order to learn how to construct the future.[14] For the Jansenists, the translation of the scriptures and the reform of the liturgy were a key part in promoting full participation in church of the laity whose baptism required it of them as a duty.[15] Within their passion for 'the truth' lay also the notion of the theologian's freedom to exercise reason and conscience, submitting not to authority for authority's sake, but to truth, and authority insofar as it proves to be its guardian.[16] Not only theologians but bishops were eager to follow Arnauld and claim their authority and autonomy directly from God rather than Rome.[17]

JANSENIST *RESSOURCEMENT* IN CONFLICT WITH ROME

If Jansenist *ressourcement* brought Port-Royal into conflict with Rome over the authority of Augustine, their reference to the tradition of the church with regard to the Bible and Tridentine liturgical reforms would prove equally contentious. They developed a particularly high theology of the laity. Their enthusiasm for the use of the scriptures and even, with the exception of the prayers of consecration, the celebration of Mass in the vernacular, the promotion of lay participation in the liturgy, including praying the breviary, and the reading of the Canon of the Mass aloud, put clear water between Trent and the Augustinian reformers.[18]

The rules which preceded the Index of forbidden books stressed that those reading the Bible should have the capacity to interpret it according to Catholic tradition, and that this capacity should have been verified by a qualified cleric.[19] Arnauld, echoing Chrysostom, argued that the simple faithful should

---

[14] Nicholas Lash, *Voices of Authority* (London: Sheed & Ward, 1976), 56.

[15] Jacques-M. Grès-Gayer, 'Le gallicanisme d'Antoine Arnauld: éléments d'une enquête', *Chroniques de Port-Royal*, 44 (1995), 31–51 (34–5, 41); Bernard Chédozeau, 'Les grandes étapes de la publication de la Bible catholique française', in Jean-Robert Armogathe (ed.), *Le grand siècle et la Bible*, vi (Paris: Beauchesne, 1989), 341–60 (352).

[16] Letter to M. N., 9 June 1661, quoted in Antoine Arnauld Œuvres, 42 vols (Paris: Sigismond d'Arnay, 1775–1782), iii.250; and Letter to Du Vaucel 5 October 1691, *Œuvres*, iii.388.

[17] Pierre Blet, 'L'idée de l'épiscopat chez les évêques français du XVIIe siècle', in B. Vogler (ed.), *Miscellanea historiae ecclesiasticae: Colloque de Strasbourg, septembre 1983, sur 'L'institution et les pouvoirs dans les églises de l'antiquité à nos jours'* (Brussels: Nauwelaerts, 1987), 315–19.

[18] Pierre Blet, 'La querelle de la moralité du théâtre avant Nicole et Bossuet', *Revue d'histoire littéraire de la France*, 5–6 (1970), 553–76. See also Heinrich Denzinger, *The Sources of Catholic Dogma*, 1954, trans. Roy Defferari, 30th edn. (St Louis MO: Herder, 1957), 291–2 (946, 956), 390 (1566–7), and reference to *Unigenitus* in 398–400 (1602–6).

[19] Bernard Chédozeau, *La Bible et la liturgie en français: l'église tridentine et les traductions bibliques et liturgiques (1600–1789)* (Paris: Cerf, 1990), 25–9; and 'Grandes étapes', 346, 359.

have a voice in the church and have as much access as possible to the sources of Christian doctrine and holiness: 'I am [. . .] struck by the wrong that is done to the church and to faith by those who try to prevent the children of God from reading what the Holy Spirit has caused to be written for them.'[20] He criticized the papal ban on vernacular translations of the breviary, in a critique that was a comprehensive rejection of the Index and the very notion of forbidding books.

The Spanish Index, more rigorous than the Roman one, issued an all-out ban, valid in all Spanish territories, on translations of the scriptures into the vernacular. This set up tensions between those of Ultramontanist tendencies and members of the theology faculties of Louvain (in the Spanish Netherlands) and the Sorbonne, whose close acquaintance with Protestantism and nationalistic pride led them to favour translations into French.[21] The years between 1660 and 1708 marked the golden era of biblical translation at Port-Royal. As Professor of Scripture at Louvain, Jansen himself had published several studies of the New Testament and the Pentateuch, and Saint-Cyran, whose spiritual doctrine was largely based on the New Testament, persuaded Antoine Le Maistre to translate the Gospels. This translation would be continued and edited after his death by his brother, Le Maistre de Sacy, in what would become known as the *Nouveau Testament de Mons*.

Despite his own struggles with the language, Saint-Cyran promoted the learning of Hebrew at Port-Royal and further inspired Le Maistre to translate the Psalms.[22] Saint-Cyran himself never wrote a word of commentary on scripture without first verifying that it was in line with the patristic tradition.[23] In addition the *Messieurs* produced erudite, patristically-inspired biblical commentaries, concordances, and histories.[24] The translations included commentaries and prefaces emphasizing Augustine's pre-eminence as an interpreter of scripture.[25]

In the face of Trent's support for the Latin Vulgate as the sole authentic version of the Bible, these laymen translated directly from the Greek and Hebrew. Such gestures challenged the clerical hegemony of Trent to an extent that unnerved even the Gallicans among French bishops and theologians.[26]

---

[20] Letters to Du Vaucel, 5 and 12 October 1691, quoted in Arnauld, *Œuvres*, iii.388–90.

[21] See Chédozeau, 'Grandes étapes', 343–6; and *La Bible et la liturgie en français*, 186–9, 195.

[22] See Jean Lesaulnier, 'Les hébraïsants de Port-Royal', *Chroniques de Port-Royal*, 53 (2004), 29–45.

[23] Claude Lancelot, *Memoires touchant la vie de M. de Saint-Cyran* (1738), ed. Denis Donetzkoff (Paris: Nolin, 2003), 219.

[24] Chédozeau, 'La publication de l'Écriture par Port-Royal. Première partie: 1653–1669', *Chroniques de Port-Royal*, 33 (1984), 35–42; and 'La publication de l'Écriture par Port-Royal. Deuxième partie: 1672–1693', *Chroniques de Port-Royal*, 35 (1986), 195–203.

[25] Chédozeau, 'Préfaces de la *Bible de Port-Royal*', *Chroniques de Port-Royal*, 53 (2004), 47–66, (50–1).

[26] Chédozeau, 'Grandes étapes', 349–50; and Jean Lesaulnier, 'Les hébraïsants de Port-Royal', 35–41.

Arnauld's insistence on making the Bible available to all was vindicated in 1757 by a brief of Benedict XIV liberalizing the ban on biblical translation. By then Port-Royal's dominance in biblical translation had been firmly established. But if Benedict's brief vindicated Port-Royal's insistence on access to scripture, with the Fathers as its primary interpreters, it did so by insisting on clerical regulation of who had permission to read the Bible. Port-Royal's attempt to make Bible reading obligatory for all Catholics not only failed but would be condemned after the Synod of Pistoia.[27]

JANSENISM AND REFORM OF THE LITURGY

Zeal for the reform of the liturgy predates Port-Royal, French delegates to the Council of Trent urging liturgical and sacramental reforms, experimenting with vernacular liturgies and conducting baptisms in French.[28] But in the following centuries the liturgy became the battleground in a struggle for local autonomy against Roman centralization.[29] Concerns to preserve the Gallican heritage by returning to the practices of the ancient church provoked major liturgical revisions at local and diocesan levels in the eighteenth century.[30] By the mid-nineteenth century, a sustained counter-surge of Romanization took place in order to avoid Jansenist and Gallican 'errors'. The chief culprit in Ultramontanist eyes was the *Heures de Port-Royal*, a translation of the breviary aimed at giving the laity access, like the clergy, to the prayer of the church.[31] Both in its preference for the Hebrew text of the Psalms and its encouragement of laity to participate in a prayer generally reserved to priests and religious, it raised a storm of protest.[32]

The scholars of Port-Royal culled the legendary content of saints' lives within the breviary, replacing them with patristic texts of undisputed provenance.[33] Jansenist polemic against 'indiscreet' Marian devotions in favour of scripture and the Fathers was inspired by a purist preference for historical realities and the

[27] Chédozeau, 'Grandes Étapes', 359–60.

[28] Alain Tallon, *La France et le Concile de Trente (1518–1563)* (Rome: École Française de Rome, 1997), 709–30.

[29] Henri Leclercq, 'Liturgies Néo-Gallicanes', in F. Cabrol (ed.), *Dictionnaire d'archéologie chrétienne et de liturgie* (Paris: Letouzey et Ané, 1907), ix, 2, cols. 1636–129.

[30] By the eighteenth century, 90 out of 139 dioceses in France had distinct local liturgies; c.f. Hans Bernhard Meyer (ed.), *Eucharistie: Geschichte, Theologie, Pastoral*, Gottesdienst der Kirche, 4 vols (Regensburg: Pustet, 1989), iv.270.

[31] Nicolas Le Tourneux, *L'Office de l'Eglise en latin et en françois contenant l'office des dimanches et des fêtes* (Paris: Le Petit, 1650).

[32] Chédozeau, *Bible et liturgie*, 117–23.

[33] Quantin, *Catholicisme*, 249–58.

simplicity of the primitive church.[34] In 1660 Joseph Voisin produced a hugely successful four-volume bilingual missal.[35] Intended to promote greater understanding of and participation in the Mass by the laity, it was perceived in Rome as a challenge to the authority of Trent and condemned by papal decree. The missal remained on the Index until 1897, the pope threatening to excommunicate automatically all those involved in producing or using it. Voisin's translations were included in Le Tourneux's '*L'Année Chrétienne*', a highly popular series of commentaries on the feasts and seasons of the liturgical year, together with a translation of the Canon of the Mass, which the French bishops thought reflected Jansenist tendencies, and had put on the Index in 1691.[36] Arnauld wrote several defences of the translation of scriptures, patristic, and liturgical texts, arguing repeatedly, among other points, that it enabled women to have access to these cornerstones of Christian life.[37]

JANSENISM AND VATICAN II

It has been suggested that the liturgical reforms of the Second Vatican Council did little more than take up where the Jansenists left off.[38] Filled with partisan invective and conspiracy theories about Jansenism, the famed liturgist Dom Prosper Guéranger of Solesmes rejected the austere Gallican passion for scriptural and historical accuracy.[39] He accused Jansenist liturgical translators of promoting anarchic theological autonomy among the faithful, let loose on the scriptures and prayers in French. Others defended the recovery of ancient liturgical rites and texts by the likes of Jubé of Asnières, despite his reputation for consecrating asparagus during Mass.[40]

[34] See Blaise Pascal, *Les Provinciales: Pensées et opuscules divers*, eds. Gérard Ferreyroles and Philippe Sellier (Paris: Librairie Générale Française, 2004), 9; Philippe Sellier, *Pascal et la liturgie* (Paris: Presses Universitaires de France, 1966), 92–7.

[35] Joseph Voisin, *Messel Romain, selon le règlement du Concile de Trente* (Paris: de la Haye et Piget, 1660).

[36] Keith Pecklers, *Dynamic Equivalence* (Collegeville MN: Liturgical Press, 2003), 12–15.

[37] Arnauld, 'Défense des versions de l'Ecriture Sainte, des Offices de l'Eglise et des Ouvrages des Pères, et en particulier de la nouvelle traduction du Bréviaire, contre la Sentence de l'Official de Paris du 10 avril 1688', in *Œuvres*, viii.246–54; 'De la lecture de l'Ecriture Sainte, contre les paradoxes extravagants et impies de M. Mallet [. . .]', in *Œuvres*, viii.684–5, 655: 'It is an intolerable error to think it good to prevent women from reading Holy Scripture on the sole grounds of their being women.'

[38] Pierre Jounel, 'Les Missels diocésains français du 18ᵉ siècle', *La Maison-Dieu*, 141 (1980), 91–6 (91).

[39] See Pecklers, *Dynamic Equivalence*, 28; Gaston Fontaine, 'Présentation des Missels diocésains français du 17ᵉ au 19ᵉ siècle', *La Maison-Dieu*, 141 (1980), 97–166 (98–9).

[40] See Ernest Koenker, *The Liturgical Renaissance in the Roman Catholic Church* (Chicago: University of Chicago Press, 1954), 22–4. The matter of the asparagus is a misinterpretation of Jubé's return to an ancient tradition of the offering of first fruits.

Jansenist emphasis on the Eucharist as prayer of all the faithful, rather than an exclusively priestly sacrifice, prompted moves for greater lay participation in corporate acts of worship, including from women and the uneducated, and an assertion of local rites and customs which implied resistance to monarchical papal governance.[41] In the eighteenth century, similar attempts were made to combine reform of the liturgy and greater local autonomy in ecclesial matters. The 1786 Synod of Pistoia in Italy called for liturgical reforms of distinctly Jansenist flavour: maximum involvement of the laity, introduction of vernacular worship, elimination of unnecessary private Masses, proclamation aloud of the Eucharistic Prayer, consecration and distribution of communion at one and the same Mass, and serious preparation for reception of the sacraments.[42] The people and clergy were ill-prepared for such a reforming synod, and the presiding bishop was deposed in 1790.[43] Not until the Second Vatican Council would these reforms, underpinned by the *ressourcement* movement, become part of the familiar Catholic liturgical landscape.

While the beginnings of the modern notion of a 'hierarchical church' were emerging from the Tridentine reforms, the Jansenists were busy espousing patristic authority in the name of Catholic orthodoxy.[44] Pushing to obtain the condemnation of Jansenism in Rome, its enemies tried to imply that papal pronouncements carried the obligation to obedience of dogmatic truths.[45] Arnauld resisted vigorously: 'The church would be running a risk beyond any daring if popes were permitted to claim to act as prophets, and to sit in judgment on all matters with an infallibility born of religious enthusiasm.'[46]

Implicit in Port-Royal's exaltation of the primitive Christian past and its push towards *ressourcement* was the question of the relationship between tradition and the magisterium.[47] In the *Augustinus*, Jansen effectively subordinates the authority of the church to that of Augustine by claiming that his doctrine is that of the church. As the congregations in Rome met over the Five Propositions one consulter insisted; 'Either all the Holy Fathers, the

[41] Pecklers, *Dynamic Equivalence*, 23; and Quantin, *Catholicisme*, 532–53.

[42] Keith Pecklers, 'The Jansenist critique and the Liturgical Reforms of the Seventeenth and Eighteenth Centuries', *Ecclesia Orans*, 20 (2003), 325–39.

[43] Weaver, 'Erudition, Spirituality and Women: the Jansenist Contribution', in Sherrin Marshall (ed.), *Women in Reformation and Counter-Reformation Europe: Public and Private Worlds* (Bloomington IN: Indiana University Press, 1989), 189–206 (205, n. 23); Pecklers, *Worship* (London: Continuum, 2003), 83–4.

[44] Congar, *Essai historique*, 232. See also Bernard Chédozeau, 'Port-Royal et le jansénisme: la revendication d'une autre forme du tridentinisme?' *XVIIe Siècle*, 43 (1991), 119–25.

[45] Lucien Ceyssens, 'Le Cardinal Jean Bona et le Jansénisme', *Benedictina*, 10 (1956), 79–119, 267–327 (94–5).

[46] Arnauld, Letter to anon., January 1664 in *Œuvres*, i.462.

[47] Bruno Neveu, 'Augustinisme janséniste et magistère romain', *XVIIe siècle*, 135 (1982), 191–209 (194–5).

Councils, the Scholastics and even the Holy Spirit, who is Lord of Scripture, are heretical, or the doctrine of Jansen is.'[48] The Jansenist party held that papal pretensions to divinely-inspired doctrinal authority stood in direct contradiction to the patristic tradition.[49] In Arnauld's judgement, support for the infallibility of the pope that overrode the consent of the universal church or council was a denial of the unbroken tradition of the church: 'To take him as the arbiter of the truth is to put a man in the place of God.'[50]

The Four Gallican Articles of 1682 confronted papal claims to ultimate authority with a 'tradition of the church' firmly established by historical criticism and the example of the African church under Cyprian and Augustine, in which bishops and councils decided on matters of faith, on an equal footing with Rome.[51] The notion of episcopal collegiality and a high regard for councils, so foundational to the concept of church put forward by the Second Vatican Council, was at the heart of Arnauld's ecclesiology.

Congar offers a detailed analysis of what was at stake in the censure of the Five Propositions.[52] For Arnauld, whoever opposes Jansen opposes Augustine and whoever opposes Augustine denies God's revelation of divine truth to the church.[53] Sacy put the matter succinctly into rhyme:

> Whoever follows Augustine follows the church:
> Whoever rejects him despises her:
> Since she alone has brought him to
> This height of authority.[54]

THE JANSENIST CRISIS AND AUTHORITY

What the Jansenist crisis brings into sharp relief is the question of authority, whether that of internal conviction, based on a person or group's interpretation of dogma and history, or that of the formal, external criteria of papal governance that the post-Tridentine church sought to establish and reinforce. Against a papacy modelling itself on the patterns and structures of a civil authority, which itself was becoming increasingly absolutist, stood the

---

[48] Yves Congar, *Vraie et fausse réforme dans l'église*, 2nd edn. (Paris: Cerf, 1968), 856.

[49] Letter to M. d'Angers, January 1664, quoted in Arnauld, *Œuvres*, i.462.

[50] Letter to Singlin 1 September 1663, quoted in *Œuvres*, i.410. See also letter to du Vaucel, 9 October 1686, *Œuvres*, ii.722–30.

[51] See entries on 'Quatre Articles' and 'Libertés de l'Eglise Gallicane' in René and Suzanne Pillorget, *France baroque, France classique 1589–1715 Dictionnaire* (Paris, Laffont, 1995), 964–5, 656–69.

[52] Yves Congar, *Sainte Eglise: études et approches ecclésiologiques* (Paris: Cerf, 1963), 357–73.

[53] Nicolas Piqué, 'Arnauld, Rome et la tradition', *Chroniques de Port-Royal*, 46 (1997), 169–84.

[54] Isaac-Louis Le Maistre de Sacy, *Les enluminures du fameux Almanach des PP. iesuites, intitulé la déroute et la confusion des iansenistes: Ou triomphe de Molina iesuite sur S. Augustin* (n.p: n.pub., 1654), 80.

sacrosanct authority of scripture and its interpretation by Augustine and the early Fathers. The Jansenists saw their doctrine and practice as the touchstone for a faith that simultaneously stood against the transient fashions of 'the world' while providing answers to its challenges.[55]

For Port-Royal, Augustine's work stood as what Gadamer terms a 'classic', something that continues down the generations to occupy a central place in thought and 'conversation' between the historical context of a text and the contemporary context of its interpreter, working out the dialectic between tradition and understanding in a 'fusion of horizons'.[56] Modern theologians like David Tracy have developed and sometimes challenged Gadamer's hermeneutical theory, suggesting that if texts are to claim this 'classical' status, there can be no definitive interpretation that would effectively close their history.[57] No such theory operated in the seventeenth century, so the drama for the 'Disciples of Saint-Augustine' and their allies in the University of Paris lay in being confronted with two apparently incompatible claims to absolute authority, those of tradition and of the papacy.[58] The voice of the French university theologians would not be heard so loudly in the church again until Vatican II.[59]

Outside the specialist world of Jansenist studies, little has been done, except in the field of liturgical studies, to relate the movement to the development of the modern church.[60] The major aspects of the Jansenist theological position received focused consideration from the 'new' theologians of twentieth-century France. Like the Jansenists themselves, they were seen as dangerous innovators and suffered censure by the church, though unlike the Jansenists they were subsequently rehabilitated to play a pivotal role in conciliar reforms.[61] Congar was aware of the futility of 'archaeolatry' and denied that twentieth-century *ressourcement* was a scholarly reconstruction or 'repristination'. Repeating Pius XII's criticism of the Synod of Pistoia's 'exaggerated and senseless

---

[55] Lash, *Voices of Authority*, 11–24.

[56] Hans-Georg Gadamer, *Truth and Method* (New York: Crossroad, 1975), 256, 267–70.

[57] David Tracy, *The Analogical Imagination: Christian Theology and the Culture of Pluralism* (New York: Crossroad, 1981), 73–5, 135–7, n. 8, n. 16, 115–24.

[58] Richard Gaillardetz, 'The Reception of Doctrine: New Perspectives', in Bernard Hoose (ed.), *Authority in the Roman Catholic Church: Theory and Practice* (Aldershot/Burlington VT: Ashgate, 2002), 95–114 (100–2).

[59] See Hugh Lawrence, 'Spiritual Authority and Governance: A Historical Perspective', in Hoose (ed.), *Authority in the Roman Catholic Church*, 37–57 (54–6); Francis Oakley, *The Conciliarist Tradition: Constitutionalism in the Catholic Church 1300–1870* (Oxford: Oxford University Press, 2003), 250–1.

[60] Pecklers, *Dynamic Equivalence*, 12–15.

[61] Giacomo Martina, 'The Historical Context in which the Idea of a New Ecumenical Council Was Born', in René Latourelle (ed.), *Vatican II Assessment and Perspectives: Twenty Five Years After (1962–1987)* 3 vols. (New York: Paulist Press, 1988), i.3–73 (30–40); Wolfhart Pannenberg and Richard J. Neuhaus, 'The Christian West?' *First Things*, 7 (1990), 24–31 (25–6).

antiquarianism', he did less than justice to the Synod's long-term goals and Jansenism's clear development, by the 1660s, into a movement that had reforming aims based on concrete contemporary pastoral needs.[62]

JANSENISM: A PRACTICAL *RESSOURCEMENT* IN SCRIPTURE, THE FATHERS, AND LITURGY

Louis Bouyer saw the failure of Jansenist attempts at liturgical reform as a tragedy that thwarted the legitimate introduction of vernacular translation, lay participation, and practical *ressourcement* into the liturgy.[63] The *Sources chrétiennes* series sought to 'trace Christian doctrine to its sources, in order to find there the truth on which our lives are based'.[64] In this, the twentieth-century *ressourcement* owes a major debt to the renewal of biblical, patristic, and liturgical scholarship, and of ecclesiology, in the Port-Royal circle. What united the 'new' theologians was the conviction that theology must present itself as relevant to the present and that the source of this relevance lay in the recovery of the past.[65] The intentions of Antoine Arnauld of Port-Royal and of de Lubac sound remarkably similar: 'The great effort lies in rediscovering Christianity in all its fullness and purity. It is an effort that lies ceaselessly before us, as does the task of reform within the heart of the church itself.'[66] The similarities lie not only in their methodology but also in their anxiety to provide answers from the past to the dilemmas of the present.

It was in the result that they differed so radically, since the *ressourcement* of the seventeenth century led to an overall rejection of modern life, whereas it led the twentieth-century theologians to embrace it as a potential source of divine revelation. The contribution of *nouvelle théologie* must be acknowledged in recovering a tradition of thought, grounded in appeal to historical sources and oriented towards a conciliar construct of church authority that was particularly strong in France and stretched from the patristic era into the middle ages and the doctrines of Gerson via the Jansenists to the Second

---

[62] Congar, *Sainte Église*, 305, 309; and *Mediator Dei*, 64. The crucial charitable role played by Port-Royal during the *Fronde* and the contribution of Jansenist spiritual directors to Catholic renewal points to their engagement with contemporary anxieties and contradicts suggestions that Jansenism had little pastoral perspective.

[63] Louis Bouyer, *Life and Liturgy* (London: Sheed & Ward, 1956), 41, 50–6, 67.

[64] Henri de Lubac, *Mémoire sur l'occasion de mes écrits* (Namur: Culture et Vérité, 1992), 29.

[65] Marcellino d' Ambrosio, '*Ressourcement* theology, *aggiornamento* and the hermeneutics of tradition', *Communio*, 18 (1991), 530–55 (531–2).

[66] De Lubac, *Paradoxes, suivis de Nouveaux Paradoxes* (Paris: Seuil, 1959), 38.

Vatican Council.[67] In this, there is a clear link between both *ressourcement* movements; as de Lubac says, 'every time that a Christian renewal has flourished here in the West [...] it has flourished under the sign of the Fathers'.[68]

[67] Congar, *Divided Christendom: a Catholic Study of the Problem of Reunion*, trans. M. A. Bousfield (London: Bles, 1939), 64–90.

[68] De Lubac, *Mémoire*, 96.

2

Nouvelle Théologie: A Return to Modernism?

Gerard Loughlin

Réginald Marie Garrigou-Lagrange, writing in 1946, famously asked where *nouvelle théologie* was heading—'La nouvelle théologie, où va-t-elle?'—and replied that it was returning to modernism—'Elle revient au modernisme.'[1] At the time of asking, Garrigou-Lagrange (1877–1964) was already a pre-eminent, much published teacher of neo-scholastic theology at the Angelicum, the Dominican House of Studies in Rome. He was also a staunch defender of the faith against the encroachments of Modernism, obsessed with the threat it posed to the certainties he had found in the Catholic magisterium.[2] His answer to his own question was not a compliment but a damning judgement, intended to close rather than engage discussion.

It is more than tempting to follow Garrigou-Lagrange and read the story of *nouvelle théologie* as repeating that of Modernism. For both stories concern groups of theologians—a more coherent group in the case of *nouvelle théologie*—who wished to retrieve traditions of thought earlier than the neo-scholastic, in order to correct the rationalism of the latter and confront the growing challenges of modernity. Both groups—Modernists and *nouveaux théologiens*—looked to the tradition of Christian mysticism that found the transcendent in the material and the immanent; the quotidian transformed. But in challenging the reigning theology of their day, they attracted the hostility of others, whose careers were invested in the certainties now being questioned. Both groups were named—and so formed—by the instruments of their destruction. In 1907, Pope Pius X subscribed his name to the Encyclical

---

[1] Réginald Garrigou-Lagrange, 'La Nouvelle Théologie, où va-t-elle?' *Ang*, 23 (1946) 126–45 (143).

[2] See further Michael J. Kerlin, 'Anti-Modernism and the Elective Affinity Between Politics and Philosophy', in Darrell Jodock (ed.), *Catholicism Contending with Modernity: Roman Catholic Modernism and Anti-Modernism in Historical Context* (Cambridge: Cambridge University Press, 2000), 308–36 (314). Kerlin offers a fascinating discussion of the elective affinities between Garrigou-Lagrange and Jacques Maritain, and their mutual abhorrence of Modernism and fascination with the proto-fascist *Action française*.

Pascendi Dominici Gregis, which declared 'modernism' the 'synthesis of all heresies', though the synthesis was entirely the work of the pope's letter, itself almost certainly the work of Fr Joseph Lemius (1860–1923).[3] And in 1947, Garrigou-Lagrange named *nouvelle théologie* as such, the new theology that was in fact nothing but the old, returned to life through his naming of it, and by that designation destroyed.[4] The *nouvelle théologie* had been noted already by Pietro Parente in 1942,[5] but Garrigou-Lagrange's attention was the more defining, and followed closely on the heels of addresses by Pope Pius XII to the Jesuits and Dominicans, in which he had condemned the 'nova theologia'.[6] And then, in August 1950, came the 'lightning bolt' that was Pius' *Humani Generis*,[7] aimed against 'some false opinions threatening to undermine the foundations of Catholic doctrine'.

As with *Pascendi, Humani Generis* does not name its opponents, whose discussions it nevertheless aimed to close. Also as with *Pascendi*, the final concern of *Humani Generis* was that people should attend to what the church taught and, when all other justification was lacking, simply submit to its authority and assent to its teaching. The encyclical asserts its own status as that of the ordinary teaching authority of the church, which is to say of Christ himself.[8] Thus the encyclical permits the discussion of evolution 'provided that all are prepared to submit to the judgment of the Church',[9] which insists that whatever the case with bodies, souls are the immediate creation of God[10] and there is no question of polygenism.[11] But the real interest of the encyclical

---

[3] See Alec R. Vidler, *A Variety of Catholic Modernists* (Cambridge: Cambridge University Press, 1970), 17–18; and Gabriel Daly, *Transcendence and Immanence: A Study in Catholic Modernism and Integralism* (Oxford: Clarendon Press, 1980), Appendix 1 (232–4).

[4] The article is dated 1946, but appeared in February 1947; Jürgen Mettepenningen, *Nouvelle Théologie – New Theology: Inheritor of Modernism, Precursor of Vatican II* (London: Continuum, 2010), 4.

[5] Pietro Parente, 'Nouve tendenze teologiche', *L'Osservatore Romano* (9–10 February 1942), 1.

[6] Mettepenningen, *Nouvelle Théologie – New Theology*, 4.

[7] De Lubac described *Humani Generis* as the 'lightning bolt' which 'killed the project' that he and others were developing, of a 'theology less systematic than the manuals, but more saturated with tradition, integrating the valid elements in the results of modern exegesis, of patristics, liturgy, history, philosophical reflection'. Cited in Hans Urs von Balthasar, *The Theology of Henri de Lubac*, trans. Joseph Fessio, SJ and Michael M. Waldstein (San Francisco: Ignatius Press, 1991 [1976]), 10–11.

[8] Pius XII, *Humani Generis*. Encyclical Letter concerning some False Opinions Threatening to Undermine the Foundations of Catholic Doctrine (12th August 1950), *AAS* 42 (1950), 561–78, § 20. ET available at http://www.vatican.va/holy_father/pius_xii/encyclicals/documents/hf_p-xii_enc_12081950_humani-generis_en.html.

[9] Pius XII, *HG* § 36.

[10] Pius XII, *HG* § 36.

[11] Pius XII, *HG* § 37. The encyclical insists on monogenism (from Adam) in order to preserve the transmission of original sin from one to all, even though such sin is nowhere mentioned in Genesis, which clearly assumes polygenism (Gen. 4.16); and this even though *HG* applauds the literal reading of the Bible over and against its symbolic interpretation (§ 23), which is needed to find the doctrine of monogenetic sin in the text.

is with those ideas already identified by Garrigou-Lagrange in his attack on the new theology.[12]

Garrigou-Lagrange took aim at Henri Bouillard and his argument that the truths of faith need to be expressed in current terms, in the language of the day. Maintaining Thomas Aquinas' Aristotelian vocabulary might prove more of a hindrance than a help. For Garrigou-Lagrange, unchangeable truths take unchangeable forms, and truth is always the relation of mind to reality, rather than of mind to life. The latter substitution was proposed by Maurice Blondel, another target of Garrigou-Lagrange's critique, which identifies Blondel's misconception as characteristically Modernist. De Lubac is also rebuked, and the danger presented by all three authors is the aping in thought of the world's supposed fluidity, a changeableness that threatens the unchangeable dogmas of the faith and the church which proclaims them. Thus the requirement in *Humani Generis*, to limit the allowed discussion of evolution, to maintain what is necessary for the unchanging doctrine of original sin, is also a concern of Garrigou-Lagrange's article, where he refers to Teilhard de Chardin.

The final example that shows where the new theology is heading is the proposal to change the language of transubstantiation so as to better render the mystery of Christ's presence at the Eucharist. To abandon Thomas' rendition of Aristotelian ontology is to abandon the doctrine of the real presence and embrace the 'position moderniste', which views Christ's arrival as a change in the subject rather than in the object of adoration: 'comporte toi à l'égard de l'Éucharistie comme à l'égard de l'humanité du Christ'.[13] Garrigou-Lagrange called for a return to Thomas, and Thomas as interpreted in the neo-scholastic tradition stemming from the nineteenth century.

The immediate effects of *Humani Generis* were as devastating as those of *Pascendi*, though the latter was part of a tripartite offensive. It had been preceded by *Lamentabili Sane Exitu* (17 July 1907), a compilation of condemned teachings, and was followed, a few years later, by the institution, on 1 September 1910, of an anti-Modernist oath that was to be taken by all priests and teachers of priests, and which remained in force until 1967.[14] It was this last which really achieved the work of the Encyclical, and helped to create a culture of paranoia and conformity, enabling any perceived theological deviancy to be denounced as Modernist—heresy *à la mode*. Mark Schoof likens the situation in the church to that of the Netherlands under Nazi occupation. 'People thought that enemies and traitors were lurking everywhere'; that

[12] It is not known who wrote the encyclical, but it is quite likely that Garrigou-Lagrange was one of the contributors. See further Joseph A. Komonchak's essay in this volume.

[13] Garrigou-Lagrange, *La nouvelle théologie*, 141.

[14] The oath was prescribed in the *motu proprio, Sacrorum Antistitum*, and is reprinted in Fergus Kerr, *Twentieth-Century Catholic Theologians: From Neoscholasticism to Nuptial Mystery* (Oxford: Blackwell, 2007), 223–5.

everywhere the fifth columnists of Modernism were hiding, needing to be rooted out before they destroyed the citadel.[15] It was in such a climate that the work of the new theology developed, attempting a rapprochement with modernity under the radar of the thought police.

Catholic theologians would rarely admit to continuity with the Modernists, lest the contagion of heresy be thought to infect their own work. Marie-Dominique Chenu was foolhardy enough to quote the Irish Modernist George Tyrrell (1861–1909) with approval in his book on the theology of Le Saulchoir, when he embraced a historicism that could only be read as Modernism by such as Garrigou-Lagrange.[16] The book was withdrawn from circulation in 1938, and placed on the Index of Prohibited Books in 1942,[17] where other works of *nouvelle théologie* were to join it.[18] At the same time, Chenu, Louis Charlier, and Réne Draguet were removed from their teaching posts. They were suspected of Modernism, of introducing change and contingency into the fixed certainties of Christian faith. Also suspect was Henri de Lubac and others working at or associated with the Jesuit faculty at Fourvière: Henri Bouillard and Jean Daniélou. Several of these, including de Lubac, lost their posts in the lead-up to *Humani Generis*, and the circulation of de Lubac's books—*De la connaissance de Dieu* (1941, 1948), *Corpus mysticum* (1944, 1949), and *Surnaturel* (1946)—was restricted. As in so much else, these erasures repeated those suffered by the Modernists, and were but the continuing effects of the purge begun in 1910.

Persecution always started, not with the burning, but with the banning of books. The French Modernist, Alfred Loisy (1857–1940), had five of his books prohibited in 1903, a sign of the distaste that would lead to his excommunication in 1908. He might have averted this fate through recanting, but chose not to. More tragic was Tyrrell's loss to the church. A convert to Catholicism (1879), he had become a Jesuit priest in 1891, and thereafter one of the Jesuit's most able and well-known teachers and writers. But he was effectively forced to leave the Order in 1905. He was excommunicated two years later, having published articles against *Pascendi*, and two years after that he was dead, most likely from Bright's disease.[19] Though he had devoted his life to the church and its faith, he could not abjure his writings, and so was refused a Catholic burial. Nevertheless, his old friend, Henri Brémond, said a few prayers at the

[15] Mark Schoof, OP, *Breakthrough: Beginnings of the New Catholic Theology*, introduced by E. Schillebeeckx OP, trans. N. D. Smith (Dublin: Gill and Macmillan, 1970 [1968]), 45.
[16] Marie-Dominique Chenu, *Le Saulchoir*.
[17] See further Fergus Kerr, 'Chenu's Little Book', *New Blackfriars*, 66/777 (1985), 108–112.
[18] For example, Louis Charlier's *Essai sur le problème théologique*, Bibliothèque Orientations: Section scientifique, 1 (Thuillies: Ramgal, 1938).
[19] For an account of Tyrrell's death see Nicholas Sagovsky, *'On God's Side': A Life of George Tyrrell* (Oxford: Clarendon Press), ch. 15.

graveside. Bremond was duly censured and made to take the anti-Modernist oath.[20]

Other Modernists fared better. The Austro-Scottish Baron Friedrich von Hügel (1852–1925) was a layman, and so of no real interest to the ecclesial authorities, and had always been more circumspect in his own writings than he had often urged in those of his friends, like Tyrrell.[21] Edouard Le Roy and Lucien Laberthonnière (a priest) found their books prohibited. Tyrrell's close friend and indefatigable biographer, Maude Petre (1863–1942), was for a time forced to go outside of her diocese in order to receive the sacraments, but was otherwise left alone. The church's treatment of the Modernists was thus variable, ranging from the petty to the vindictive. But it was chilling, with no qualms about destroying those it deemed insubordinate; and it was effective.

In light of the repetitions between the stories of Modernism and of the *nouvelle théologie*, one might take a hint from those from whom one would otherwise hesitate to learn lessons, and suppose a continuity of ambition and thought between the early and the mid-twentieth-century Modernists or neo-Modernists. But such is the taint of the term 'Modernism', that even today exponents of *nouvelle théologie*, including Protestant ones (who are presumably immune to the anxieties of Catholic culture), will seek to distance the *nouveaux théologiens* from their predecessors. Thus Hans Boersma, while he does not deny certain similarities between the two groups, argues for a fundamental difference between their agendas.[22]

Boersma allows for an 'overlap' between Modernism and *nouvelle théologie*, but denies that the former was a significant harbinger of the latter. Both shared a distaste for the aridities of neo-Thomism, and honoured the importance of experience for theology, but the Modernists did not espouse anything like the sacramental ontology that Boersma finds in *nouvelle théologie*. Indeed, Boersma asserts that the Modernists maintained the same 'gap between the natural and the supernatural' as otherwise held by their opponents.[23] With reference to Loisy and Tyrrell, Boersma insists that both 'scholars evinced the modern incapacity to reach beyond the natural horizons'. They focused on 'historical critical exegesis' and collapsed 'revelation into mystical experience'

---

[20] Maisie Ward, *The Wilfred Wards and the Transition*, 2 vols (London: Sheed & Ward, 1934–37), vol. 2: Insurrection versus Resurrection, 492–3.
[21] On von Hügel see further Michael de la Bedoyere, *The Life of Baron von Hügel* (London: Dent, 1951); and John J. Heaney, *The Modernist Crisis: Von Hügel* (London: Geoffrey Chapman, 1968).
[22] Hans Boersma, *Nouvelle Théologie and Sacramental Ontology: A Return to Mystery* (Oxford: Oxford University Press, 2009), 18. Though much of this essay takes issue with Boersma's reading of Modernism in relation to *nouvelle théologie*, it is nevertheless indebted—at almost every point—to his exhilarating study. I would also like to thank my colleague, Paul D. Murray, for his encouragement and assistance in the writing of this essay.
[23] Boersma, *Nouvelle Théologie*, 20.

rather than finding 'divine truth' in 'doctrinal statements', when the latter are treated sacramentally or analogically.[24]

Boersma notes the wide range of people, from throughout Europe, who were named or self-named as Modernist, but he deals with but two: Loisy and Tyrrell. This enables him to evoke a much more coherent movement than actually existed, and indeed he largely follows *Pascendi* in not challenging its claim that Modernism was a matter of 'agnosticism, immanentism, and relativism'.[25] As perhaps befits his argument that *nouvelle théologie* worked to overcome divisions, most particularly that between nature and grace, Boersma charges Loisy and Tyrrell with failing to do so. Loisy, he says, divided history from theology, while Tyrrell divided theology from revelation, making the latter an interior enlightenment divorced from external expression, which never guides and forms but only articulates a preceding experience.

The charge against Loisy is more nearly correct than that against Tyrrell, for Loisy did separate history from theology, arguing that the scriptures needed to be considered apart from their later theological interpretations.[26] Loisy made his argument in the context of *Providentissimus Deus* (1893), which had asserted the inspired and error-free status of scripture.[27] The encyclical lambasted the 'higher criticism',[28] yet called upon it to defend scripture's innocence.[29] The book that brought Loisy to prominence was *L'Évangile et l'Église* (1902), described by Tyrrell as the 'classical exposition of Catholic Modernism'.[30] And yet in this book, Loisy argued for the necessity of tradition, as alone delivering the full truth of the Christian faith, which is to be found in the interpretation of the scriptures as in the scriptures themselves. Thus, even as Loisy separated history from theology, he conjoined them, and thus led many—including the future Pope Pius X—to welcome his book.[31] But others noticed that Loisy's position handed the faith over to the contingencies of ceaseless interpretation, for it denied the possibility of finding a definitive

---

[24] Boersma, *Nouvelle Théologie*, 21.

[25] Pius X, *Pascendi Dominici Gregis*. Encyclical Letter on the Doctrines of the Modernists (8th September 1907), *AAS* 40 (1907), 593–650. ET, *Encyclical Letter* ('Pascendi Gregis') *of our most Holy Lord Pius X by Divine Providence Pope on the Doctrines of the Modernists* (London: Burns & Oates, 1907) § 39; cited in Boersma, *Nouvelle Théologie*, 18.

[26] Alfred Loisy, *Études bibliques*, 3rd edn. (Paris: Picard, 1903). The first edition of *Études bibliques* had been published in 1894, the second in 1901.

[27] Leo XIII, *Providentissimus Deus*. Encyclical Letter on the Study of Holy Scripture (18th November 1893), § 20. *Acta Leonis XIII* 13 (1893), 326–64 (342). ET available at <http://www.vatican.va/holy_father/leo_xiii/encyclicals/documents/hf_l-xiii_enc_18111893_providentissimus-deus_en.html>.

[28] *Providentissimus Deus*, § 21.

[29] *Providentissimus Deus*, § 22.

[30] George Tyrrell, *Christianity at the Cross-Roads* (London: Longmans, Green & Co., 1909), 92. Alfred Loisy, *L'Évangile et l'Église* (Paris: Picard, 1902).

[31] Bernard Reardon (ed.), *Roman Catholic Modernism* (London: Adam & Charles Black, 1970), 32.

core that once stated was stated for all time. The book was condemned in 1903, and Loisy's defence, *Autour d'un petit livre* (1903) only made matters worse, for it found revelation, and not only faith, in the one who sees rather than in what is seen. 'La révélation se réalise dans l'homme, mais elle est l'œuvre de Dieu en lui, avec lui et par lui.'[32] Loisy's mistake was to make the faith dependent on faith.

But if there is some substance in the charge against Loisy, there is very little in that against Tyrrell. Boersma follows the Jesuit's contemporary critics in being too quickly dismissive, too uninterested in Tyrrell's concern to avoid some of the very things with which he was and is charged. If we take George Tyrrell and Friedrich von Hügel as our representative Modernists we will find a movement much more closely aligned with its successor than some defenders of the latter want to allow.

Modernism is too readily excised from Boersma's account of *nouvelle théologie*. He introduces the movement's nineteenth-century predecessors— Johann Adam Möhler, Maurice Blondel, Joseph Maréchal, Pierre Rousselot— but then jumps from them to the mid-twentieth century, mentioning Modernism only in passing, and then in order to deny its relationship to what came before or after. But even if the *nouveaux théologiens* were more directly influenced by Möhler and Blondel than by Tyrrell or von Hügel, the latter were not so dissimilar to their predecessors as to constitute a significant divergence from the tradition of thought that Boersma wants to trace from the nineteenth to the twentieth century. Indeed, at each point where he marks a difference between the predecessors of the *nouveaux théologiens* and the Modernists, one can discern an overlooked continuity. One can come to these points by considering the charge that the Modernists were agnostic, immanentist, and relativist; for the same was said of the new theologians, but said by those who misunderstood.

AGNOSTICISM AND ANALOGY

Hans Boersma cites the judgement of Alessandro Maggiolini, that George Tyrrell 'could not admit that our statements about God have an authentically analogical character. In this way, *Pascendi*'s charge of agnosticism does indeed apply to Tyrrell.'[33] But this judgement betrays a defective knowledge of either Tyrrell or Thomas, or of both, for not only did Tyrrell intend to uphold

[32] Alfred Loisy, *Autour d'un petit livre* (Paris: Picard, 1903), 197.
[33] Alessandro Maggiolini, 'Magisterial Teaching on Experience in the Twentieth Century: From the Modernist Crisis to the Second Vatican Council', trans. Andrew Matt and Adrian Walker, *Communio* 23/2 (1996) 225–43 (235–6); cited in Boersma, *Nouvelle Théologie*, 21, n. 79.

analogy, as Maggiolini allows,[34] he did so by insisting that statements about God are true insofar as they are analogical, with their truth attested by the spiritual fruits of their deployment. For such truths are always practical and representative, inciting desire for the God they describe.

Tyrrell so favoured analogy that he held all knowledge to be in some sense analogical. Even when speaking of the world we have to use terms that are never fully adequate to what they signify.[35] He does admit that the analogical relationship between the terms drawn from the 'natural world' to describe the 'spirit-world' can never be precisely known, but must remain hidden, 'just because we cannot compare its terms as we can those of thought and extension'.[36] But in this he was not saying other than that taught by Thomas Aquinas, who was his guide here as elsewhere. Indeed, as Fergus Kerr has argued, the dispute between, on the one hand, Modernists and neo-Modernists (Tyrrell or de Lubac), and, on the other hand, the neo-scholastics (Lemius or Garrigou-Lagrange), was a dispute about the interpretation of Thomas and the Thomist tradition.[37]

Tyrrell's understanding of analogy was properly Thomistic, and presented as such. Having set out an account of how the truths of God's mystery cannot be 'conceived save under the forms of analogy', he appended a more detailed exposition of Thomas' teaching, for precisely the reason that some had mistaken his Thomistic apophaticism for agnosticism.[38] There is of course an argument as to the extent that Thomas' brief remarks on analogy are open to an agnostic interpretation, an argument that is still alive in the twenty-first century.[39] But to the extent that one favours the readings of Victor White and Herbert McCabe rather than those of John Milbank and Catherine Pickstock, one can say that Tyrrell was being faithful to the Angelic Doctor, and, moreover, to that proper reticence demanded by the distinction between creator and creature.[40] Far from being agnostic, as Maggiolini avers, Tyrrell was being appropriately apophatic.

Tyrrell distinguishes between religious truth and its expression, as between a body and its clothing. But such clothing is said to be sacramental. The words

---

[34] Maggiolini, 'Magisterial Teaching', 235.

[35] Boersma finds this teaching in Pierre Rousselot (*Nouvelle Théologie*, 71). See further, Pierre Rousselot, *The Eyes of Faith*, trans. Joseph Donceel, SJ (New York: Fordham University Press, 1990 [1910]).

[36] George Tyrrell, *Lex Orandi or Prayer and Creed* (London: Longmans, Green, 1903), 58.

[37] Cf. Kerr, *Twentieth Century Catholic Theologians, passim.*

[38] Tyrrell, *Lex Orandi*, 80–2.

[39] For a discussion of this debate see Paul DeHart, 'On Being Heard but Not Seen: Milbank and Lash on Aquinas, Analogy and Agnosticism', *Modern Theology*, 26/2 (2010), 243–77.

[40] See further Victor White, OP, *God the Unknown: And Other Essays* (London: Harvill Press, 1956); Herbert McCabe, OP, 'Appendix 4: Analogy' in Thomas Aquinas, *Summa Theologiae* (London: Eyre & Spottiswoode, 1964), vol. 3, Knowing and Naming God, *Ia. 12–13*, 106–107; and John Milbank and Catherine Pickstock, *Truth in Aquinas* (London: Routledge, 2001).

that express truth 'belong to the world of sense and also to the world of spirit; to the apparent, the relative, the transitory; and also to the real, the absolute, the eternal'.[41] The sacramentality of religious truths is said to consist in their having a 'literal and a spiritual value', with the latter being more real than the former.[42] The words of the Creed are said to be like this, indicating both historical facts and spiritual realities.[43] This is not very far from what Boersma claims to be a distinguishing mark of *nouvelle théologie*, namely a concern with retrieving a 'pre-modern spiritual interpretation' of scripture, whereby 'historical appearances' conceal and disclose 'eternal realities'.[44]

Moreover, it is not the case that Modernists like Tyrrell or von Hügel downplayed doctrinal statements in favour of inner experience. They well understood how scripture, creeds, and liturgies foster and elicit the very experience they are said to express. There is for them an intimate, integral relationship between word and spirit. Tyrrell understood the creed as forming a spiritual sensibility, even as it expresses spiritual realities that might be otherwise expressed. 'It is by living in the light of these beliefs, by regulating our conduct according to them that we can reproduce and foster the spirit of Christ within ourselves. They furnish us with an effectual guide to eternal life.'[45] And they do this because they show that life; 'their practical value results from, and is founded in, their representative value'.[46]

IMMANENTISM AND THE SACRAMENTAL PRINCIPLE

George Tyrrell came to hold a modern, ecological understanding of human life, viewing our bodies as 'woven' into the woof and weft of the physical universe, 'the very tissue of the world of appearances of which each particle exerts a ceaseless influence on every other'.[47] But such a view, however attractive to modern sensibilities, might be thought to betray that immanentism which so frightened the neo-scholastic: an immersion in nature so deep that the super-natural is reduced to the same level, and so rendered a *faux* transcendence.

The distinction and proper relationship between the natural and the super-natural—the world in itself and the world graced by God—was arguably at the heart of the *nouvelle théologie* project, and its achievement, as Boersma argues, was to have secured a happily sacramental understanding of the world. *Nouvelle théologie*, it is claimed, steers between the Scylla of neo-scholasticism, which overly separated nature and grace, and the Charybdis of Modernism, which collapsed one into the other—Tyrrell's very failing.

---

[41] Tyrrell, *Lex Orandi*, 3.   [42] Tyrrell, *Lex Orandi*, 4.   [43] Tyrrell, *Lex Orandi*, 5.
[44] Boersma, *Nouvelle Théologie*, 21.   [45] Tyrrell, *Lex Orandi*, 57.
[46] Tyrrell, *Lex Orandi*, 57–8.   [47] Tyrrell, *Lex Orandi*, 68.

For the neo-Thomists it seemed necessary to maintain a sharp distinction between the natural and the supernatural, between the gift and the place of its reception. For if the natural could itself attain to that by which it was exceeded, then its perfecting was already its own possibility, and so in a sense already achieved. What need then of Christ's arrival and, more to the point, of the church through whom Christ arrives again in the sacraments that the church so jealously guards?

In some sense, *nouvelle théologie* wanted to return to a medieval world view, when the natural and the supernatural were conjoined, with everything—from worms to angels—having its place in a continuous hierarchy of being. This conception dissolved with modernity, when the natural became ever more autonomous, ever more a realm ruled by its own laws, that once known to a reason that has no need to evoke the supernatural, becomes ever more susceptible to manipulation and compliant to human devising. This is not to say that *nouvelle théologie* simply adopted a neo-Platonism in which all flowed from an absolute source. De Lubac, for one, warned against this, while also insisting on the gratuity of God's grace.[48]

Neo-Thomism had imagined a pure nature (*pura natura*) that was entirely autonomous with regard to the divine, and that had, in itself, no desire (*desiderium naturale*) for the divine, since it had no means to its attainment. This was a world in which no one had a sense of the world's mystery, of its inexplicable existence. Needless to say, this is not really our world, even if most of us most of the time take existence for granted. But having imagined such a world, neo-scholasticism contended that desire for the beatific vision, not to mention its attaining, must be understood as a gift of the divine charity, an entirely extrinsic bestowal.[49] Such a stress on the gratuity of grace is somewhat strange, since the nature to which it comes, is itself, as de Lubac noted, 'freely given'.[50]

De Lubac argued that the idea of a pure nature graced by a celestial desire was the gift of sixteenth- and seventeenth-century theologians, spread abroad by de Lubac's fellow Jesuit, Francisco Suárez (1548–1617), but first really invented by the Dominican, Cajetan (1469–1534).[51] The idea of two orders, the natural and the supernatural, each with their own ends, made it possible to think a wholly human realm, to which the divine was alien, rather than its given fulfilment, and this in turn enabled the possibility of a pure secularity.[52] It was this that de Lubac feared and strove against.

---

[48] Henri de Lubac, SJ, *The Mystery of the Supernatural*, trans. Rosemary Sheed, introduced by David L. Schindler (New York: Crossroad, 1998 [1965]), 236; cited in Boersma, *Nouvelle Théologie*, 90. Boersma suggests that de Lubac was arming himself against possible attack from the neo-Thomists.

[49] Boersma, *Nouvelle Théologie*, 91–2.

[50] De Lubac, *The Mystery of the Supernatural*, 30.

[51] Boersma, *Nouvelle Théologie*, 94.

[52] Boersma, *Nouvelle Théologie*, 96–7. This, of course, is the great theme of John Milbank's study, *Theology and Social Theory* (Oxford: Blackwell, 1990): that theology invented the secular

For de Lubac, Thomas was to be read as positing a human nature that desires that which it cannot attain save for the graciousness of God, who gives to humanity the vision for which it yearns, and yearns for because made so by God.[53] This is 'the paradox of the spiritual creature that is ordained beyond itself by the innermost reality of its nature to a goal that is unreachable for it and that can only be given as a gift of grace'.[54] Thus our desire for God is suspended between the natural and the supernatural, in the middle.[55] If this idea of a desire for the unobtainable that is yet given, as faith hopes, seems unduly paradoxical, then this was all to the good, since it pointed to the mystery of God, which de Lubac worked to maintain against the rationalisms of positive theology.[56]

These issues are not to be found in Tyrrell, or at least not in the terms of the mid-twentieth-century debate. But it is entirely wrong to charge him with maintaining a strict dualism between nature and grace, or of collapsing the latter into the former. On the contrary, Tyrell sought the mediation of one through the other, in a fashion not dissimilar to that which Boersma applauds. This can be seen most clearly in Tyrrell's book, *Lex Orandi* (1903), the first chapter of which is entitled 'The Sacramental Principle'. Here we learn that the 'religion of Incarnation' is 'sacramental in principle'.[57]

In *Lex Orandi*, Tyrrell distinguishes between the natural and the supernatural as between two worlds—'one the shadow and the sacrament; the other, the substance and the signified reality'.[58] But just insofar as there is a gap between these two domains, he conceives it as crossed, for we are said to live in both of them simultaneously. Tyrrell sees the world as indwelt by God, and

---

by withdrawing the supernatural from the natural, by imagining an ungraced world, with no knowledge of its own gratuity. Of course the possibility might be said to lie in the making of the natural/supernatural distinction itself, which in these terms is largely a thirteenth-century scholastic development, and which Thomas Aquinas did much to advance. The distinction's growing deployment had much to do with the need to distinguish miracles from marvels in the process of the interrogatory, which from 1233 onwards was the means by which saints, starting with St Dominic, were canonized. The need to evidence the supernatural furthered its ever-greater distinction from the natural, which had once seemed miraculous in itself (Augustine, *City of God*, 21.7). See Robert Bartlett, *The Natural and the Supernatural in the Middle Ages* (Cambridge: Cambridge University Press, 2008), 9–14. For an insistent defence of *natura pura*, and one opposed to de Lubac and Milbank, see Steven A. Long, *Natura Pura: On the Recovery of Nature in the Doctrine of Grace* (New York: Fordham University Press, 2010). For Long, humanity has an 'end proportionate to nature', as distinct from a 'supernatural *finis ultimus*' (29). The first is God as first cause of being, while the second is God as eternal beatitude. But both divinities must be the same God.

[53] Boersma, *Nouvelle Théologie*, 97–8.

[54] Balthasar, *The Theology of Henri de Lubac*, 13.

[55] See John Milbank, *The Suspended Middle: Henri de Lubac and the Debate Concerning the Supernatural* (Grand Rapids MI: Eerdmans, 2005).

[56] Boersma, *Nouvelle Théologie*, 98–9.

[57] Tyrrell, *Lex Orandi*, 2.

[58] Tyrrell, *Lex Orandi*, 10.

this indwelling he understands as God's grace, when God's love and will indwells ours, and ours lives in God's. It is a matter of mutual ensphering and embrace. 'Under whatever metaphor, spatial or otherwise, we may represent will-union and indwelling, it is neither more nor less than mutual love.'[59]

If Maurice Blondel was careful to distinguish between immanence and immanentism, between a method and a dogma, Modernists are said to have not been careful enough.[60] Alfred Loisy was the chief offender. Yet for someone like Tyrrell, the immanent order is shot through with the transcendent, penetrated by the mystery that shows in its materiality. Similarly, von Hügel found revelation to be the mark of all experience insofar as attending to the world reveals its givenness.[61] But such revelation is only partial, a prelude to the '[s]elf-manifestation of Perfect Spirit', which not only comes to us, but in that arrival is the cause of our 'very capacity for apprehending It'. The movement of Spirit is always prior to our own, so there is never a moment in which human subjectivity has priority over divine disclosure, since any such priority is itself the Spirit's disclosing movement.

> Because Spirit, God, works in our midst and in our depths, we can and we do know Him; because God has been the first to condescend to us and to love us, can we arise and love Him in return.[62]

RELATIVISM AND *RESSOURCEMENT*

When comparing the Modernists and the neo-Modernists, the *nouveaux théologiens*, it is important to remember that the latter, as a group, were more integrated and more professionalized. It should also be borne in mind that much that the Modernists wrote was intended for a general, educated readership. There were some, such as Loisy, who held academic posts and wrote academic treatises. But others, such as Tyrrell and von Hügel, were chiefly writing to be understood by educated Catholics, and not just professional readers of theology. This contrasts with the *nouveaux théologiens*, who wrote in university and seminary settings, for students of theology in the first instance. Tyrrell's theology was less technical, less consciously scientific than that of his successors, but it was no less robust or incisive; no less committed to the church and its faith.

However, it is less plausible to describe the Modernists as engaged in that process of *ressourcement* that was so integral to the project of *nouvelle*

---

[59] Tyrrell, *Lex Orandi*, 32.
[60] 'Unlike . . . George Tyrrell and Lucien Laberthonnière, Blondel remained convinced of the need for divine revelation coming from the outside.' Boersma, *Nouvelle Théologie*, 59.
[61] Baron Friedrich von Hügel, *Essays and Addresses on the Philosophy of Religion First Series* (London: Dent, 1928 [1921]), 56.
[62] Hügel, *Essays and Addresses*, 57.

théologie that the latter often goes by that name. Jean Daniélou penned the programmatic essay of *ressourcement*, which appeared in the year before Garrigou-Lagrange's critique of the new theology.[63] For Daniélou, *ressourcement* meant a return to the scriptures, to the Fathers, and to the liturgy, in order to retrieve a fuller, more contemplative understanding of the faith, one more securely focused on the mystery that gives life to faith and in which faith lives. Today most attention is given to the retrieval of the Fathers, figures such as Irenaeus, Origen, and Gregory of Nyssa. *Nouvelle théologie* is rich with patristic insight. The same can hardly be said of Modernism. And yet, in its own way, it too was attempting a return and a retrieval. Though Modernism is thought to have too readily embraced the certain results of the 'higher criticism', with little regard for, if not actively denigrating, the rich tradition of allegorical interpretation, this is more of a caricature than an accurate reading. Even Loisy, the steeliest of biblical critics, argued for tradition as the site of theological reflection, while Daniélou recognized the need to integrate symbolic interpretation with scientific exegesis.[64]

But Modernism was most clearly engaged in *ressourcement* in its retrieval of medieval sources. As already indicated, much of Tyrrell's theology is based on his reading of Thomas against the Thomists, a reading that might almost be said to find its fulfilment in the work of people such as the Dominicans, Victor White and Herbert McCabe. Tyrrell fully accepted Thomas's distinction between first and secondary causation, the presence of the 'First Mover in every movement',[65] and so could never have held anything other than a sacramental view of the world. Moreover, he understood that such a view was fostered through the liturgies of the church, and did not doubt to find in them resources for theology. The same is true of von Hügel, whose crowning achievement was his study of St Catherine of Genoa, *The Mystical Element of Religion*.[66] Like Tyrrell, he looked to find transcendence in immanence, in the lives of Christian people, and so turned to the study of one to find what he believed true of all.

But it was the Modernists' interest in history, their appreciation of how context determines concept, and of how time alters both, that led to the charge of relativism: the recurring charge of the neo-scholastics against both the Modernists and the neo-Modernists. Here one has to understand that Rome was an embattled institution. It had increasingly lost political and social power throughout the nineteenth century and would continue to do so throughout

[63] Jean Daniélou, 'Les orientations présentes de la pensée religieuse', *Études*, 249 (1946), 5–21.
[64] Exponents of *nouvelle théologie* can sometimes too easily forget about 'scientific exegesis', even developing arguments that turn on just such forgetfulness.
[65] Tyrrell, *Lex Orandi*, 90.
[66] Friedrich von Hügel, *The Mystical Element of Religion as Studied in Saint Catherine of Genoa and Her Friends*, 2 vols, 2nd edn. (London: Dent, 1961 [1923]). The first edition appeared in 1908.

the twentieth and twenty-first. It is instructive to note that Garrigou-Lagrange was inspired to pursue a religious rather than a medical career through reading Ernest Hello's *L'Homme* (1872). This work presented the fantasy of an adamantine church, fixed for all time against the world's flux.

> [T]he Catholic Church not only has not changed, but is not able to change and will not change. In proclaiming the Catholic Church immutable, the human word repeats for it the promise made to it by the word of God. This word immutable engages the future.[67]

It was this promise of certainty that attracted Garrigou-Lagrange, a promise he was to fulfil through the tireless pursuit and rooting out of any and all deviations and relativisms. If he relaxed, the promise would fail.

Thus both Modernists and the *nouveaux théologiens* were suspect as soon as they distinguished, as both did, between the truths of faith and the expressions of those truths. When Henri Bouillard distinguished between 'affirmations' and 'representations' of those affirmations, he was likened to Loisy and Tyrrell, the arch-relativists. Bouillard insisted that there were 'invariants'—'defined dogma, that is to say, propositions canonized by the Church, but also everything that is contained explicitly or implicitly in Scripture and the Tradition'— but also held that these invariants are expressed in 'contingent concepts'.[68] History teaches no less, but Garrigou-Lagrange was not wrong to then wonder how the invariants could ever be known in themselves. He solved the problem by turning the variants into invariants, but Modernism realized that something more subtle was needed. Boersma argues that Bouillard's distinction between invariants (affirmations) and contingencies (representations) shows that he was 'no Modernist'.[69] But in fact it shows just the opposite.

Boersma claims that 'Modernism regarded historical or contingent statements as merely the relative expressions of one's ultimately ineffable subjective experience. This implied that for Modernism there were no eternal or absolute truths in which our statements might participate in some fashion.'[70] But Modernists such as Tyrrell or von Hügel never doubted that there were 'eternal and absolute' truths. They devoted their lives to living into and out of such truths, and helping others to do so. They merely recognized, with the mystical tradition, that there was more failure than success in our representations of the truth. To put it another way, they recognized the distinction between propositions and statements, and that propositions are only shown in the *judgement* that different statements express the same proposition.

---

[67] Ernest Hello, *L'Homme* (Paris: Librairie Academique, 1897 [1872]), 269: cited in Kerlin, 'Anti-Modernism', 310.

[68] Henri Bouillard, *Conversion et grace chez S. Thomas d'Aquin: Étude historique*, Théologie 1 (Paris: Aubier, 1944), 221; cited in Boersma, *Nouvelle Théologie*, 102 n. 67.

[69] Boersma, *Nouvelle Théologie*, 102 n. 67.

[70] Boersma, *Nouvelle Théologie*, 108.

Eternal and absolute truths are known in the *recognition* of a community, and this is not to look inward, to some supposed psychological resource, to 'one's ultimately ineffable subjective experience', nor upward, to some plane of reality just out of sight. It is to look *between*, to the relationships that constitute the *communitas* of the community, the commonality of shared agreement and disagreement, of dispute in conversation, and of reconciliation in worship. Thus the invariant affirmation is always finally elusive, and in this a lure to further exploration, to continued conversation and contemplation. All such would have ceased long ago if matters were as imagined by neo-scholasticism.

OÙ VA LE MODERNISME? IL REVIENT AU MYSTÈRE

Was Garrigou-Lagrange correct when he said that the new theology was but a return to the old heresy? The answer has to be yes and no. No, insofar as *nouvelle théologie* existed in a different modernity to that of the beginning of the twentieth century, a modernity that had, by 1946, suffered two 'world' wars; and no insofar as *nouvelle théologie* had learned to read further back and more deeply into the tradition than had been possible for the Modernists. And, above all, no, because the Modernism to which *nouvelle théologie* might have returned was but a chimera of the neo-Thomists. But yes, insofar as, reluctantly accepting the name of Modernist, Tyrrell declared for a Modernism whose 'dominant interest' is tradition.[71] And yes, insofar as Modernism, too, looked to find a theology that was not that of neo-scholastic rationalism, but one that answered, as Tyrrell and others saw it, to the yearning of the human heart, to a desire for God, that for him was elicited, nurtured, and fulfilled through the sacraments and sacrament of the church. And this notwithstanding 'the "beggarly elements" through which the Spirit is communicated'.[72] For despite everything, the 'Church is not merely a society or school, but a mystery and sacrament; like the humanity of Christ of which it is an extension'.[73]

If *nouvelle théologie* was a return to mystery, then it was also a return to Modernism.[74]

---

[71] Tyrrell, *Christianity at the Cross-Roads*, 2.

[72] Tyrrell, *Christianity at the Cross-Roads*, 276.

[73] Tyrrell, *Christianity at the Cross-Roads*, 275. Compare de Lubac: 'The Church is a mystery: that is to say that she is also a sacrament. She is "the total locus of the Christian sacraments", and she is herself the great sacrament that contains and vitalizes all the others. In this world she is the sacrament of Christ, as Christ himself, in his humanity, is for us the sacrament of God.' Henri de Lubac, *The Splendor of the Church*, trans. Michael Mason (San Francisco: Ignatius Press, 1999 [1956]), 202; cited in Boersma, *Nouvelle Théologie*, 255.

[74] For more on Modernism see Gerard Loughlin, 'Catholic Modernism', in David Fergusson (ed.), *The Blackwell Companion to Nineteenth-Century Theology* (Oxford: Wiley-Blackwell, 2010), 486–508.

3

Gilson and the *Ressourcement*

Francesca Aran Murphy

INTRODUCTION: DID GILSON BELONG TO THE *RESSOURCEMENT*?

Clio, the muse of historians, would remind us that the dates tell against it. Étienne Gilson (1884–1978) fought in the Great War: of the *ressourcement* figures, only Henri de Lubac (1896–1991) shares this distinction. Gilson was closer to the generation of Réginald Garrigou-Lagrange, OP (1877–1964). When de Lubac entered the Jesuit scholasticate on Jersey, Gilson was an 'old master', the 2nd edition of *Le Thomisme* (1922) locked in a 'bookcase . . . under the category marked "Modern Philosophy"'.[1] The political turmoils culminating in the Second World War and the problems of post-war Catholicism shaped the appreciation of the need for *ressourcement* in Yves Marie-Joseph Congar (1904–95), Jean Daniélou (1905–74), Henri Bouillard (1908–81), and Hans Urs von Balthasar (1905–88). Steering close to the post-war French winds in his 1956 *Habilitationsschrift* on Bonaventure, late arrivals like Joseph Ratzinger (1927–) could take Gilson's pioneering expansion of the range of medieval thought for granted.[2] But not even Gilson's friend Marie-Dominique Chenu, OP (1895–1990) had witnessed the Modernist drama at first hand as Gilson had; only Garrigou-Lagrange shares this distinction. A 'medievalist of the first rank' by 1913,[3] Gilson wrote *Le Thomisme* (1914/1919) during the 'Loisy crisis'.

The recovery of the Greek Fathers informed the change which the Jesuit theologians desired. For Gilson, patristics meant Augustine. In the 1930s he refused 'to engage in a new crusade for the *Défence de l'Occident*' 'because I am

---

[1] Henri de Lubac (ed.), *Letters of Étienne Gilson to Henri de Lubac*, trans. Mary Emily Hamilton (San Francisco: Ignatius Press, 1988), 7–8.

[2] See Ratzinger, *Milestones: Memoirs 1927–1977*, trans. Erasmo Leiva-Merikakis (San Francisco: Ignatius Press, 1998), 108.

[3] Gerald A. McCool, *From Unity To Pluralism: The Internal Evolution of Thomism* (New York: Fordham University Press, 1989), 164.

a Thomist' and in the 1960s he denied that there is anything '"Western" about Saint Thomas's writings. Not only are they packed with the Eastern Fathers, but their spiritual home is Jesus Christ, born in "Bethlehem".'[4]

Though Gilson recognized that the church was in trouble after World War II, and though his writings have a *theological* stamp, no book of his carries an *imprimatur*. Though he argued from 1914 until 1978 that Thomas Aquinas was a theologian, Gilson did so as a historian and philosopher. Though he told a dying soldier in 1916 that Albert the Great argued that laymen can hear confession *in extremis*,[5] Gilson had a modest conception of the role of lay people in theology. He compared the act of transfiguring 'philosophy into theology' to 'chang[ing] water into wine'.[6] It sounds like a gift an office-holder would exercise. Contrary to the *ressourcement* clerics, Gilson was not driven by a need to alter the practice of *theology*.

Most sharply, the divergence between the Jesuit and Dominican *ressourcement* leaders and Gilson lay in their respective evaluations of *action*. Daniélou claimed in 1946 that the time for 'theoretical speculation separated from action and disengaged from life' is over.[7] Having objected to the separation between theology and 'pastoral practice' since the 1930s, having been prevented from exercising medieval scholarship by Garrigou-Lagrange and helping the worker-priests instead in the 1950s, Chenu observed in 1965 that, 'to be a theologian really means not to be cut off from the daily, concrete life of the Church'.[8] Two years later, Gilson stated that the 'disorder' which 'invades Christianity . . . today . . . will not cease until Dogmatics retrieves its natural primacy over the practical'.[9]

For his part, Garrigou-Lagrange had reacted to Daniélou's 1946 shot across the Thomist bows by describing the 'substitution' of action for theory as a redefinition 'of truth, no longer *adaequatio rei et intellectus* but *conformitatis mentis et vitae*'. He traced the source of the idea that truth is 'the conformity of the judgement with the exigencies of action' to Maurice Blondel's writings of 1906.[10] Similarly, Gilson's objection went back to the turn of the century too, when Charles Maurras put the 'action' into *Action française*. Unlike Garrigou-Lagrange, Gilson extended his objections to '*Action*' even to politics, noting how peculiar it was that 'a master in theology belonging to the order of Saint

---

   [4] Étienne Gilson, *Les tribulations de Sophie* (Paris: Vrin, 1967), 47–8.
   [5] Laurence K. Shook, *Étienne Gilson* (Toronto: Pontifical Institute of Mediaeval Studies, Toronto, 1984) 382–3, 66–7, 76: Gilson heard the dying man's confession.
   [6] Gilson, *Le philosophe et la théologie* (Paris: Fayard, 1960), 112.
   [7] Daniélou, 'Les orientations présentes de la pensée religieuse', *Études*, 251 (1946), 5–21 (7).
   [8] 'A conversation with Père Chenu', *Dominicana*, 50 (1965), 141; cited in Marcellino D'Ambrosio, 'Ressourcement theology, *aggiornamento* and the hermeneutics of tradition', *Communio*, 18 (1991), 530–55 (535).
   [9] Gilson, *Tribulations*, 13.
   [10] Garrigou-Lagrange, 'La nouvelle théologie où va-t-elle?' *Ang*, 23 (1946), 126–46 (130, 127), referring to Blondel, *L'Action*.

Dominic . . . was able in conscience to sustain the notion that the "best political regime" defended by Charles Maurras was the same as that taught by saint Thomas'.[11] Encouraged by observation of the prioritizing of action over theory in European fascism, Gilson's commitment to theory marked his preference for Thomas over Augustine. He begins his book on Augustine by defining him as a thinker who 'regarded philosophy as something . . . different from the speculative pursuit of a knowledge of nature': Augustine's 'metaphysics', he says, 'rests on an ethics'.[12] So far as the *ressourcement* foregrounded doing over being, Gilson thought they were mistaken.

At the same time, this difference precisely marks where Gilson made his contribution to the *ressourcement*, the point where their confluence enabled the *ressourcement* to be a theology which endures. For Gilson, it is not the abstract logic of the method for demonstrating and accumulating truths which counts, it is the seizure, in judgement, of the *res*, the *thing*. For Garrigou-Lagrange, what matters in Thomas's definition of truth as the adequation of thing and intellect is the *formal* principle: the *logic* of the method is precisely what is at stake in his defence of truth. He used Thomas's definition of truth as a formal methodological principle, developing a metaphysics of essences, which left him ill-placed to influence the Blondelians other than by the traditional methods of the Index, barring from teaching, and so on. In contrast, Gilson used Thomist theology as a way of knowing and speaking about existent realities. He reacted fiercely to those scholastics who imposed a formalist bias on Thomas's thought, noting, for instance, that Thomas never used the term 'principle of non-contradiction', central to the Thomism of Sanseverino and Garrigou-Lagrange.[13] Gilson's aversion to the Thomism of the commentators expressed well the sentiment of many *ressourcement* theologians:[14] but he was more than one of a chorus proclaiming that the commentators have served 'to emasculate' Thomas's 'doctrine and to make of his theology a brew of watered-down *philosophia aristotelico-thomistica*'.[15] Distinguishing Gilson's approach was an *aesthetic* decision to present Thomism as an *artistic* theology, anchored in *sensory* appreciation of existence.

When he first banged his head on Descartes's *Meditations*, in 1903, the most 'obstinate' of efforts left Gilson without 'illumination': 'Without my knowing it, I already suffered that incurable metaphysical malady which is "chosisme".' The disease of 'chosisme' or *thingism* renders the victim 'incapable of comprehending that anyone could speak of an object which is neither an object nor

---

[11] Gilson, *Le philosophe*, 67.

[12] Gilson, *The Christian Philosophy of Saint Augustine*, trans. L. E. M. Lynch (London: Golancz, 1961), 3, 24.

[13] Gilson, 'Les principes et les causes', *RTh* 52 (1952), 39–63.

[14] D'Ambrosio, '*Ressourcement* theology', 537.

[15] Gilson to de Lubac, July 8, 1956, in *Letters*, 24.

conceived in relation to an object'.[16] Because he could not write about Thomas Aquinas without knowing him to be an 'object' in space and time, a historical personality, Gilson endeavoured to present Thomism as true without presenting it as a timeless perennial wisdom with only a contingent connection to the revelation of Christ and historical ecclesial tradition. By disassociating Thomas from scholastic formalism, Gilson enabled a generation with different intellectual appetites to his own to harbour a certain Thomism within their Augustinianism or Blondelianism. Gilson led the *ressourcement* leaders back to the factual, historical Thomas. He thereby enabled men like Chenu and de Lubac to incline their interest in a philosophy of 'action' towards Thomas's 'theorism' and so ensured that they would not suffer the fate of being required to subscribe to a Thomism committed to a formalist conception of 'truth', resistant to being and reality.

THOMISM AND THE MODERNIST DRAMA

On his own testimony, Alfred Loisy learned in his seminary to understand truth in a logical rather than realistic manner, that is, in a way which excluded contingency and temporality.[17] This was a drawback when, as a scholar of historical-biblical criticism, he had to account for temporally indexed changes within the Old Testament, and when he surveyed the developments which seemed to him to separate Jesus' preaching from the doctrines of the church. How are Jesus' Gospel and church doctrine related if each is timelessly complete in its truth, but non-identical? Landed with the problem of the temporal 'relativity' of Christian doctrine, Loisy solved it by equating tradition with an *evolution*, by claiming that doctrines *evolve*, from germ to seed to perpetually growing tree. In 1895, when 'important exegetical work' had 'already . . . brought him problems', his reading of Newman led him to articulate the 'idea [of doctrinal development] which . . . enabled him to reconcile this relativism with his faith'.

Though Loisy imagined that his adaptation of Newman's theory 'preserved history from theological control and theology from the danger of history',[18] Pius X thought otherwise, and rightly, since Loisy inadmissibly made dogma a product of historical change. However inadvertently, Loisy promoted the historicism which remained Garrigou-Lagrange's bugbear for the next sixty years. Loisy had a real dilemma: if, as the scholasticism he had assimilated indicated, truth is only a *principle* of judgement, there is no way doctrine can

---

[16] Gilson, *Le philosophe*, 23–4.

[17] Alfred Loisy, *My Duel with the Vatican: The Autobiography of a Catholic Modernist*, trans. Richard Wilson Boynton (New York: Greenwood Press, 1968 [French original 1913]), 78.

[18] Henri Gouhier, *Études sur l'histoire des idées en France depuis le XVIIᵉ siècle* (Paris: Vrin, 1980), 141–2.

'evolve' without its truth evolving too. If truth is not conceived as creative or active in the judging event, and if the discovery of doctrinal change tarnishes doctrines' 'timelessness', truth will be taken to be *created* by the flow of time. Historicism is an inevitable outcome of combining a passive, essentialist idea of truth with the actual historicity of doctrine.

Prior to the First World War, the young Gilson inhabited 'peri-modernist' circles.[19] He felt a sympathy for Loisy right down until reading an essay by Henri Gouhier in 1963 contrasting Bergson and Loisy.[20] Gouhier observes that for Loisy, Christ's message is *mobile*, moving in time, whereas, if Bergson had written *L'Évangile et l'église*, he would have described Christ's teaching as *mobilizing*,[21] that is, driving time creatively before it, absorbing and changing it, bringing the times into 'adequation' with its truth. Just as for Gouhier a Bergsonian rather than 'scholastic' Loisy would have enabled revealed truth to *mobilize* the development of doctrines, so, in Gilson's conception of the relation of philosophy to theology, philosophy is the (relatively) relative and temporally indexed partner, and theology creatively regenerating it, into timeless truth. In the first edition of *Le Thomisme*, Gilson maintained that 'One can isolate the philosophy from the theology in Saint Thomas' system dogmatically, but one cannot isolate them historically. This system of the world is born in and of theology; its plan and its content never allows us completely to forget its origin.' Thomas's 'philosophical demonstrations' are given their aim by 'a theological plan and . . . theological ends'.[22]

'CHRISTIAN PHILOSOPHY'

These early formulations of Gilson's are moving towards claiming that a Christian's philosophy is mobilized by theology, but they have yet to arrive there. The 'theological ends' are not yet given a very productive role. In his early books on Thomas and Bonaventure, Gilson describes their systems as the philosophies of Christians, not as Christian philosophies. When he states that no one had thought about *Christian Philosophy* during the Modernist crisis, Gilson includes himself in this oversight. He had started his career intending to undermine the prevalent conception in French universities that no philosophical advances occurred between the ancient Greeks and Descartes. He thought he had

---

[19] Henry Bars, 'Gilson et Maritain', *RTh*, 7 (1979), 237–71 (260).

[20] Gilson to Gouhier, 19 July 1963, in Géry Prouvost, 'Lettres d'Étienne Gilson à Henri Gouhier', *RTh*, 94 (1994), 460–78 (473–4).

[21] Gouhier, *Études sur l'histoire des idées*, 155.

[22] Gilson, *Introduction au système de S. Thomas d'Aquin* (Strasbourg: Vix, 1919), 15 and 24–5, citing *ST* 1a.1. ad2: 'the theology of holy teaching differs in kind from that theology which is ranked as a part of philosophy'. Blackfriars, i.8–9.

shown in his doctoral dissertation ('La liberté chez Descartes et la théologie', 1913) that Descartes did not invent his conception of God as a free, all-powerful Creator, or take it from Aristotle. Descartes drew his idea of God from philosophers who were *Christians*, and hence, Gilson believed he could prove, a philosophy lived amongst the medieval schoolmen. He proceeded to write books detailing the philosophies of Aquinas and Bonaventure. He was taken aback when a Dominican reviewer, Gabriel Théry, pointed out that Aquinas' work was as much a *theology* as Bonaventure's: Gilson realized that, as a 'young professor', he had been one of those 'historians, philosophers and theologians' who are 'deterred' from 'calling theology what they prefer to name philosophy' by imagining that 'the notion of theology excludes that of philosophy'.[23]

It was in the controversy over Christian philosophy, in 1929–33, conducted on public platforms in Paris and Aberdeen, that his professional personae, and his faith and spirituality first evidently chanted in unison. Marie-Dominique Chenu called *The Spirit of Mediaeval Philosophy* Gilson's 'most beautiful book'.[24] In depicting the *Spirit*, or life-giving force, of all medieval philosophy, from Athenagoras to Duns Scotus, Gilson aims to show that, in each of the Christian thinkers, 'revelation generates reason'.[25] Faith mobilizes reason, not extrinsically, but from within. As a historian, against those who denied that faith can influence reason, Gilson argued that the 'reality' of medieval Christian philosophies, substantially different from their non-Christian precursors and contemporaries, disproves their theory.[26] His own account gives the credit to the historian's Muse: 'We owe the rediscovery of the notion' of Christian philosophy to 'Clio', he claimed, that is, to his having been inspired to use the Gifford Lectures of 1931–2 to show that what Anselm, Aquinas, and Bonaventure have *in common* is the Christian spirit of their thinking.[27]

The scholars stimulated by *Aeterni Patris* had tended to present 'Medieval Men' as participating in a single, undifferentiated 'Medieval Thought'. It was Gilson's great contribution to show that that the idea of a 'common Scholastic doctrinal synthesis' was an ahistorical myth.[28] With this, the genius of *The Spirit of Mediaeval Philosophy* is its inclusiveness.

Maritain defended a more limited notion of Christian philosophy in these debates, backing up behind only a moral impact of faith upon reason. For

[23] Gilson, *Le philosophe*, 192–3, 97–102, 105–7.
[24] Chenu, 'L'interprète de Saint Thomas d'Aquin', in Monique Couratier (ed.), *Étienne Gilson et nous: la philosophie et son histoire*, Bibliothèque d'histoire de la philosophie (Paris: Vrin, 1980), 43–8 (44–5).
[25] Gilson, in Maurice Blondel *et al.*, 'La notion de philosophie chrétienne', *Bulletin de la société française de la philosophie*, 31 (1931), 37–93 (39).
[26] Gilson, *The Spirit of Mediaeval Philosophy*, The Gifford Lectures 1931–1932, trans. A. H. C. Downes (London: Sheed & Ward, 1936), 41.
[27] Gilson, *Le philosophe*, 194.
[28] McCool, *From Unity to Pluralism*, 170–5.

Maritain, as de Lubac put it, 'it is in the men who philosophize that something has changed, not in the philosophy'.[29] For Gilson, the change is ontological. Faith, as he saw it, stimulated all of the Christian philosophers to philosophical *realism*, including simple *empiricism*. For Maritain, Bergson's weakness lay in remaining at the level of 'integral empiricism', whereas Gilson 'found empiricism in Saint Thomas' and 'recognized in authentic Augustinism "a consistent psychological empiricism".'[30] For Gilson, Augustine uses revelation, not only as a theological premise, but also '*as a source of light for his reason*', as a '*Christian philosopher*'.[31]

For his contemporary Thomists, proud of their epistemological realism, the drawback to Augustine's epistemology was its apparent 'Platonism'. Gilson endeavoured both to exempt Augustine from the aura of non-realist illuminationism which Descartes and the nineteenth-century Ontologists had attached to him, and to show that Augustine deployed metaphysical realism in exploring his congenial territory of the soul, individual persons, and history. The presentation of Augustine, Anselm, and Bonaventure in *The Spirit of Mediaeval Philosophy* is not just a debater's ploy. It is based in a carefully prepared interpretation of realism as the bond uniting the Christian philosophers as a whole, sufficiently elastic to include a realism of the historical individual (the Augustinians) and a realism of the universal (the Thomists). This rehabilitation of the 'Augustinian family' as realists enabled the *ressourcement* leaders of the 1950s to exercise their preference for Augustine, whilst excising any tendency they may have had to interpret Augustine in an unduly 'spiritualising' way. More generally, Gilson's work, pre-eminently so in his masterpiece, *The Spirit of Christian Philosophy*, set the stage for how Chenu, de Lubac, and Daniélou conceived of the unity of faith and philosophy.[32]

GILSON AND THE *NOUVELLE THÉOLOGIE* CRISIS (1950)

Daniélou spoke of the 'masterpiece' in an article simultaneously congratulating Gilson upon his 1947 reception into the Académie française and canvassing him for the *ressourcement* cause: in addition to influencing historians of

[29] De Lubac, 'Sur la philosophie chrétienne: Réflexions à la suite d'un débat', *NRT*, 42 (1936), 225–53 (227); also Maritain, 'La notion de philosophie chrétienne', 63.

[30] Bars, 'Gilson et Maritain', 257, citing Maritain, *De Bergson à Thomas d'Aquin: essais de métaphysique et de morale* (Paris: Hartmann, 1947), 16; Gilson, 'L'avenir de la métaphysique augustinienne', *Revue de Philosophie*, 1 (1930), 690–714. The latter appeared in English as 'The Future of Augustinian Metaphysics', trans. Edward Bullough, in *A Monument to St. Augustine* (New York: Meridian Books, 1957 (1930)), 289–315.

[31] Gilson, *Christian Philosophy of Augustine*, 242.

[32] Daniélou, 'Étienne Gilson à l'Académie', *Études*, 251 (1946), 263–4 (264).

philosophy, 'Gilson has also exercised a seminal influence on theological thought' by showing 'that mediaeval philosophy comprehends diverse systems which are equally orthodox'. The editor of *Sources chrétiennes* was using the inclusivism of *The Spirit* to argue that, far from being restricted to a narrow Thomist orthodoxy, Christian philosophy 'consists in a collection of specific positions which taken together as a whole system can call itself Christian'.[33] Gilson did not, however, welcome being publically press-ganged into serving Daniélou's ends.

In 1950, *Humani Generis* brought the conflict between Thomists and the *nouvelle théologie* to a head. The idea is abroad, the encyclical notes, 'that the history of dogmas consists in the reporting of the various forms in which revealed truth has been clothed, forms that have succeeded one another in accordance with the different teachings and opinions that have arisen over the course of the centuries' (*HG* § 15). People surmised that Garrigou-Lagrange was behind this. The encyclical's analysis of current theological trends reflects his assertion of 1946 that the *nouvelle théologie* was speeding 'toward modernism'. Taking issue with Henri Bouillard's efforts to extract Thomas's theology of grace from the ancient 'Aristotelian notions', such as form and formal causality, in which is cast, Garrigou-Lagrange argued that, though Trent 'did not canonise the Aristotelian notion of form . . . it approved it as a *stable, human idea*'.[34]

In the summer of 1950, Gilson discussed the problem in letters to M.-Michel Labourdette, OP, editor of the *Revue thomiste*. Labourdette had also been suborned into the conflict (in this case, by Garrigou-Lagrange), and like Gilson had refused to play ball. For Gilson, the problem was that using philosophy does indeed invite historical 'contingency' into theology; the solution was a 'sort of symbiosis' between the two, enabling their mutual illumination. The way in which we explain a doctrine makes it believable to us, and, simultaneously, we are enabled to give it some cogency *by dint of* our belief in it. It is neither an unchangeable 'foundation' (Garrigou-Lagrange) for doctrine nor its changeable 'husk' (Bouillard).

Garrigou-Lagrange did not attempt to dragoon Gilson as an ally. Instead, at the close of the first Scotist Congress, he accused Gilson of reducing metaphysics to an 'adventure, a story told for fun' and threatened to criticize his heresies from the podium at the Thomist Congress.[35] Gilson responded so resiliently that the bully backed off.[36]

---

[33] Daniélou, 'Gilson à l'Académie', 264.

[34] Garrigou-Lagrange, 'La nouvelle théologie', 143, 127–8.

[35] Gilson to Labourdette, 26 September 1950, in Henry Donneaud (ed.), 'Correspondance Étienne Gilson–Michel Labourdette', *RTh*, 94 (1994), 479–529 (512).

[36] Fernand van Steenberghen, 'Un incident révélateur au congrès thomiste de 1950', *Revue philosophique de Louvain*, 86 (1988), 379–90, 381–2.

Gilson and Garrigou-Lagrange had one thing in common: both interpreted the current 'crisis' in relation to the Modernist drama. Gilson's thinking had continued to live and grow since 1905. His paper for the Thomist Congress is about the relation between what is time-bound in Christian thinking, and what is eternal. He accepts that all scholastic thought is defined by philosophical 'master theses', like '[a]ct and potency, form and matter', the four Aristotelian 'causes': 'But if this were the whole truth', Gilson claimed, 'the Christian Middle Ages remained philosophically sterile and . . . did no more than repeat *ad nauseam* a more or less deformed Aristotle.' In fact though, the 'master theses' of scholastic reasoning, its philosophical ideas, become consubstantial with the light that illuminates them.

Viewing the positions of Garrigou-Lagrange and Bouillard as two sides of the same coin, Gilson rejects their shared anxiety that someone must *act* to shore up theology in either an ancient or an updated foundation. 'To those who request a new Scholastic theology, founded on modern philosophy', like Bouillard, 'there are others', Gilson affirmed, 'who reply that there is only one true philosophy, which is that of Aristotle, and that it is because Scholastic theology is founded on this true philosophy that it is itself true.' But theology is not founded on *any* philosophical practice. *Philosophically* an unswerving Thomist, Gilson follows out the logic of his anti-foundationalism to the extent of claiming that a plurality of philosophies can be engendered by faith: 'neither Duns Scotus nor St. Thomas Aquinas *founded* their theologies on any philosophy . . . As theologians, they have made use of philosophy within the light of faith; and it is from this usage that philosophy has come forth transformed.[37] The *formulas* are Aristotle's; the philosophical *notions* are new, created by the truth of doctrine.

GILSON AND NEWMAN

Gilson terrified the philosophers with his commanding finale: 'Scholastic philosophy must return to theology!'[38] The injunction is impossibly restrictive, if one imagines that Gilson was speaking as a *philosopher*, as he was best known for doing.[39]

A different interpretation appears in the light of Gilson's 1954 introduction to Newman's 'epoch-making contribution to the history of Christian thought',

[37] Gilson, 'Historical Research and the Future of Scholasticism', *Modern Schoolman*, 29 (1951), 1–10 (7–8).
[38] Gilson, 'Future', 8–9.
[39] Serge-Thomas Bonino, OP, 'Historiographie de l'école thomiste: le cas Gilson', in Serge-Thomas Bonino (ed.), *Saint Thomas aux XXᵉ siècle*, Actes du colloque du Centenaire de la *Revue Thomiste* (Paris: Centre National de Livre-Saint Paul, 1994), 299–313 (310).

Grammar of Assent.[40] Gilson first wrote about Newman as the debate about
the *ressourcement* played itself out. Though he notes the objections generated
by Newman's distinction between 'the notional assent given by the mind to
theology', that is, to the science of faith, 'and the real assent which the same
mind gives to the truth of religion', that is to its dogmatic articles, Gilson does
not dissent from it.[41] The articles of faith and the science of faith are distinct:
the 'symbiosis' which exists between them in the mind of the Christian
philosopher and theologian can generate a plurality of philosophies and
theologies, indeed, must do so, for Gilson, since as *Being and Some Philosophers* argues, every existent entity is individual, including those entities we call
Christian philosophers.[42] Whereas the genius of the *Spirit* is to harmonize the
Christian philosophers, the lonelier genius of *L'être et l'essence* is to point out
their individuality and variegation. From opposite angles, both are necessary
to a genuine *ressourcement* of Christian thought.

This clarifies the meaning of Gilson's imperative. He does not mean that
scholastic philosophy should be *theology*, a science of faith, but that it should
take its life from theology, from the articles of faith. As 'Newman conceives
it . . . theology exercises a necessary . . . function, but this function is different
from that of religion'.[43] In Gilson's understanding, the *Grammar* is not about
theology—the 'notional' explication of the articles of faith—but about the
articles themselves, the ever 'real' and 'particular' dogmas of Christian *religion*.

Gilson describes Newman, born an Anglican, as bringing to the Catholic
Church 'a more purely patristic intellectual formation than would have
been the case' if he had received a scholastic training like Loisy's: 'owing to
him, the great theological style of the Fathers has been worthily revived in the
nineteenth century'.[44] So, on the one hand, Gilson's injunction to scholastic
philosophers to 'return to theology!' meant to return to the sources, the
biblical dogmas. But on the other hand, he saw it as advantageous that Newman's philosophical theology had a 'theological formation' which 'owed little
to the scholastics'.[45]

For Newman and Gilson alike, dogma and its truth is not an abstract
principle by which theology regulates itself but a concrete and active event.
It acts as the sacraments of the church act. As Schmitz points out, Gilson's
'early and continuing experience of sacramental realities helped him to shape
his sense of the concrete . . . Through the sacraments [he] entered into the
presence of a spiritual reality in which the drama of the very life of the divine

---

[40] Étienne Gilson, 'Introduction', in John Henry Newman, *An Essay in Aid of a Grammar of
Assent* (Image Books/Doubleday: New York, 1955), 9–21 (20).
[41] Gilson, 'Introduction', 13.
[42] Gilson, *Being and Some Philosophers* (Toronto: Pontifical Institute of Mediaeval Studies,
1952 [1949]), 50.
[43] Gilson, 'Introduction', 19.   [44] Gilson, 'Introduction', 18.
[45] Gilson, 'Introduction', 17.

persons is made manifest by the bodies which signify their grace.'[46] At his first
communion, the child knows nothing of the theological theory of 'transubstantiation . . . but his piety toward the eucharist does not mistake its object':
the real ontological event precedes our intellectual appropriations of it.[47] Just
as the Parisian cradle-Catholic illustrates the electrifying force of dogma from
the child's religious initiation, so the English adult convert puts before us the
rituals of Christmas, Epiphany, and, especially, Corpus Christi to show how
Dogma acts: 'Are' these festivals, each of them a living commentary on the
words, 'The Son is God' 'addressed to the pure intellect, or to the imagination?'
Newman asks, '[Do] they interest our logical faculty, or excite our devotion?
Why is it that personally we find ourselves so ill-fitted to take part in them,
except that . . . in our case the dogma is far too much a theological notion, far
too little an image living within us?'[48]

A sacramental perception of created reality as radiating electricity from
an uncreated source runs through Gilson's existential Thomism. Whatever its
theoretical truth, any philosophical notion created to explicate the articles of
faith is only a human reflection of their energy. The basic example of a
sacrament is baptism: 'held in the baptismal font, the baby passively receives
a sacrament which decides his future for him in time and in eternity' and is
none the less '*engagé*'.[49] Anti-Pelagianism lies behind Gilson's conviction that
dogma *acts* before we think about it.

As Gilson notes, the 'assent' of which Newman speaks 'is the one which faith
gives to religious truth, that is, such an assent whose nature is so absolute that
its own certitude . . . is far stronger than that of all the motives of credibility by
which it may have been prepared'.[50] Whether as a child, an adult, or a
'professional', anyone who adheres to the articles of faith performs the primary
act from which theology flows by being enabled, by God, to participate in him.
The 'articles of faith', as believed by us, do not exhibit the truth of *our*
judgements, but of the 'Judge', whose Truth measures ours: 'I know through
my reason that there is a God, but this certitude is not for me that of my own
knowledge. In telling me himself that he exists and in inviting me to believe his
word, God offers me to partake in the knowledge which he himself has of his
own existence. This is not just information, it is an invitation.'

Thus, the 1885 Catechism of Meaux, which begins, '*The first truth we must
believe is that there is a God* and that He is one', goes on, '*I believe that there is
a God because he has revealed his existence to us*'; and only then states that
reason tells us there is a God, for otherwise, heaven and earth would not exist.
By contrast, the 1923 Paris Catechism begins by asking whether we can 'know

---

[46] Kenneth L. Schmitz, *What has Clio to do with Athena?: Étienne Gilson, historian and
philosopher* (Toronto: Pontifical Institute of Mediaeval Studies, 1987), 2.
[47] Gilson, *Le philosophe*, 14–15.   [48] Newman, *Grammar*, 122.
[49] Gilson, *Le philosophe*, 13.   [50] Gilson, 'Introduction', 12.

God in a certain manner'. By the time the 1949 Catechism of Tours was circulated, the first article has been reduced to, '*I believe in God because nothing can create itself by itself.*' Pastorally disastrous, since the child will eventually realize its faith is *based* on a 'pseudo-philosophy', the development is equally inauspicious theologically. 'The God of rational certitude . . . comes before that of revelation.'[51] In a pointed study of the first article of the first question of the *Summa Theologiæ*, in 1953, Gilson observed that Thomas maintains that God revealed even the truths about himself which reason can, in principle, attain, and he revealed those truths because 'it was *necessary to human salvation*'. Since God 'wanted to save' the 'human species', not just a tiny elite of intellectuals, God *acted*, in history 'to make human salvation possible'.[52]

Gilson insists that Newman was no 'fideist', despite his *Essay*'s concentrating 'exclusively' on truths 'accepted on the strength of the word of God alone'.[53] Gilson complains of being labelled a 'fideist' and barricaded with Vatican I and *Sacrorum Anistitum* on occasions when he stated that 'I believe in the existence of God.'[54] Gilson emphasizes that the assent of faith draws its 'unconditionality' from its *object*, from the Truth which activates it.[55] Those rationalists 'who reproach him with a leaning to fideism or with an ingrained mistrust in the validity of theological demonstrations' are 'irrelevant' because, for Newman, real assent 'is an assent to realities', 'that is, assent to *res*'.[56] Gilson notes Newman's debt to 'British empiricism': 'apprehension', the empirically-minded Augustinian said, 'is real in the experimentalist', because his 'language expresses things external to us', not, as with the 'grammarian', 'our own thoughts', or what is 'notional'.[57]

For Gilson, the 'Patristic and mediaeval thinkers differ from the ancient Greek philosophers' because they were different as *persons*, and they differed as persons because they had been made so by the *acts* of a personal God: 'the transforming agency in the history of thought is not' the evolution of its notions about God, 'but a divine event'. All of the Thomists of his generation were formally or notionally realists, but Gilson's 'defence of the sensible' was 'in the service . . . of a philosophy of the *concrete*, i.e., of the concrete make up of individual beings, some of which include spiritual reality in their make-up'.[58] The metaphysical image governing this existential philosophy is the individuality of the *personal* act. It calls for a 'phenomenology' like that of Newman.[59] Our notional acts, our abstract thinking, that apparent exercise of our *own* minds, Newman says, are what we have in common with

---

[51] Gilson, *Le philosophe*, 15, 13, 76–8.
[52] Gilson, 'Note sur le *revelabile* selon Cajetan', *Medieval Studies*, 15 (1953), 199–206 (200).
[53] Gilson, 'Introduction', 15.   [54] Gilson, *Le philosophe*, 93–4.
[55] Gilson, 'Introduction', 12, citing Newman's *Grammar*, 51–2.
[56] Gilson, 'Introduction', 14.   [57] Newman, *Grammar*, 37.
[58] Schmitz, *Clio*, 9, 11.   [59] Gilson, 'Introduction', 20.

others, whereas our 'real' thinking, which submits us to forcible external impressions, 'by bringing facts home' to us 'as their motive causes', 'are of a personal character, each individual having his own'.[60] Moreover, 'the images in which . . . [r]eal assent . . . [or] [b]elief . . . lives . . . have the power of the concrete upon the affections and passions, and by means of these indirectly become operative' and thus 'lead to action'.[61]

'Theology', Newman affirmed, 'deals with notional apprehension, religion with imagination.' The 'theology of a religious imagination' holds the 'key' to 'that maze of complicated disorder' it meets in our world: 'and thus it gains a more and more consistent and luminous vision of God from the most unpromising materials'. Gliding from *a priori* truth to truth, the Anglican scholasticism of Samuel Clarke found it easy to deduce that God's being implies his perfect knowledge, which implies his Eternity, which entails his Justice, and so on. 'Ordinarily speaking', though, Newman suggested, 'such deductions do not flow forth, except according as the Image, presented to us through conscience, on which they depend, is cherished within us.' The chain of entailments will not hold together unless harnessed to the 'living hold on truths'[62] which real assent delivers. 'Instead of leading us simply to God as to a terminus', an authentic Christian philosopher like Augustine 'makes use of digression in order to refer us constantly to him as to a center to which we must return'.[63]

Gilson thus recalled Thomas's proposal that theology is to the 'philosophical disciplines' as the *sensus communis* is to the five senses: 'The common sense knows . . . . Here is thus a sense which . . . can consider a mass of information . . . which it does not produce itself, but which it can apprehend, distinguish, and judge.'[64] It is the Image, the total *Gestalt* supplied by theology, which gives life and coherence to the philosophies of Christians. Though both Newman and Gilson distinguished between notional and real assent, both asserted that the distinction is not a 'demarcation'. Both recognized that, in their time, the splitting asunder of notional and real assent had been to the detriment of the real. Newman set out to combat the abstract, Bible 'religion' of English Protestantism he knew, and, Gilson says, the 'lack of real assent . . . does not seem to have grown less common in our own days. . . . countless baptized men and women not wholly ignorant of their religion seem to live, to behave, and to think as though they were wholly foreign to the truth of Christian dogma. This is the precise evil which Newman has attempted to define and for which he has sought a cure in the notion of assent.'[65] Gilson not only enabled Augustinians to acknowledge their kinship with Thomists, he also enabled Thomists

[60] Newman, *Grammar*, 31, 82.   [61] Newman, *Grammar*, 86–7.
[62] Newman, *Grammar*, 108, 106, 249.   [63] Gilson, *Christian Philosophy of Augustine*, 236.
[64] Gilson, *Le philosophe*, 113–14.   [65] Gilson, 'Introduction', 20.

to be Augustinians, and hence for the *ressourcement* to live on in Thomism until the present day.

CONCLUSION

Drawing on a submerged baptismal analogy, Gilson compared scholastic philosophers to submarine creatures: 'There are certain fish that live only in warm water. To say that they will die in cold water is not to deny that they are fish. As for the fish that, as some insist . . . , must be made to live in cold water in order to maintain the purity of their essences, they do not become true fish, but dead fish.'[66] Two generations on from Gilson, a Bonaventurian theologian, the last living partisan of the pre-Vatican II *ressourcement*, observed that, 'just as we cannot learn to swim without water, so we cannot learn theology without the spiritual praxis in which it lives'.[67] What was at stake in the crises of 1905 and 1950, and of many spiritual dramas, even in our own time, was not the truth of deduction, but the truth of real assent.

[66] Gilson, 'Future', 10.
[67] Ratzinger, *Principles of Catholic Theology: Building Stones for a Fundamental Theology*, trans. Mary Frances McCarthy (San Francisco: Ignatius Press, 1987), 322.

4

Maurice Blondel and *Ressourcement*

Michael A. Conway

Born in Dijon in 1861, Maurice Blondel is renowned (somewhat inaccurately) as the 'philosopher of action' who hailed from Aix-en-Provence, where he taught and lived until his death in 1949. A brilliant philosopher and a devout Roman Catholic, he sought in his philosophy to reflect a personal synthesis of life so as to coherently combine these realities without, on the one hand, denying the autonomy of philosophical reflection or, on the other, the very gratuity of the gift of faith. Although born into a family that was traditionally connected to the legal profession, he chose early in life to follow a career in philosophy, presenting his famous doctoral thesis in 1893 with the robust title *L'Action: Essai d'une critique de la vie et d'une science de la pratique*, which was to remain his masterpiece.[1] Embarrassingly, on being awarded his doctorate, he was refused a teaching post (which would have been his due) because his philosophical conclusions were deemed to be too 'Christian' and, therefore, compromising of philosophical reason. In 1895, however, thanks to the intervention of his former teacher, Emile Boutroux, he was appointed to Lille, and shortly afterwards to Aix-en-Provence, where he remained until his early retirement due to failing eyesight.

A number of years after presenting his thesis, Blondel published two further significant works, which were more directly connected to the philosophical problem of religion, namely, the *Letter on Apologetics* (1896) and *History and*

---

[1] Maurice Blondel, *L'Action: Essai d'une critique de la vie et d'une science de la pratique* (Paris: Alcan, 1893, 2nd ed., Paris: PUF 1950). For the English translation, see Maurice Blondel, *Action: Essay on a Critique of Life and a Science of Practice*, trans. Olivia Blanchette (Notre Dame IN: Notre Dame University Press, 1984). Blondel's doctoral thesis is also available in the first volume of a planned nine-volume edition of his complete works, two of which have already been published. See Maurice Blondel, *Œuvres complètes*, i, ed. Claude Troisfontaines (Paris: PUF, 1995), 15–526. This French thesis was accompanied, as was the tradition, by a minor Latin thesis on Leibniz. See Maurice Blondel, *De vinculo substantiali et de substantia composita apud Leibnitium*, in Blondel, *Oeuvres complètes*, i.531–687.

Dogma (1904).[2] These specific publications, together with his thesis, unleashed an enormous controversy at the time of publication and would *de facto* have a considerable influence on twentieth-century Catholic thought, particularly through their impact on the so-called *ressourcement* theologians. Bishop Peter Henrici, a specialist in Blondelian studies, surmises, for example, that 'no other author had co-determined so decisively and extensively Catholic thought in the twentieth century as Blondel'.[3]

Blondel's entire philosophical endeavour could be labelled as establishing the correct relationship between autonomous philosophical reasoning and Christianity. Importantly, Blondel insisted that he was not a theologian and, even from his earliest years, protested whenever his work was presented as being an apologetic for religion (against Brunschvicg in 1896 and Bréhier in 1931, for example). Having said that, however, his philosophy of action, thought, and being, from its earliest formulation, included an examination not only of religion in its general contours, but also in its most strict form, in a consideration of the notion of the supernatural. This is the concern that pervades all of Blondel's work and explains why his 'philosophy' would emerge, in time, to be foundational to the entire edifice of *ressourcement* theology.

From an early age, Blondel was sensitive not just to responding to what we would now call the secularizing influences in society, but also to do so from *within* the frameworks of contemporary reflection. It is this that made his endeavour so different (and effective), in comparison with the reigning neo-scholasticism of Catholic theology, sorely ill-equipped to meet the challenge. If France is to be granted the honour of being the undisputed centre of theological reflection in the period associated with *ressourcement* (1930–50), then it is to Blondel's philosophy that one must turn to find the substantial philosophical under-girding of this 'new' endeavour.

L'ACTION (1893)

Blondel submitted his doctoral thesis to the Sorbonne after several years' work and numerous drafts with the final title: 'L'Action: Essai d'une critique de la vie et d'une science de la pratique'. It is a multi-levelled, complex philosophical

[2] Maurice Blondel, *The Letter on Apologetics* and *History and Dogma*, texts presented and trans. by Alexander Dru and Illtyd Trethowan (London: Harvill Press, 1964).

[3] 'So hat wohl kein anderer Autor das Katholische Denken des 20. Jahrhunderts so entscheidend und weitreichend mitbestimmt wie Blondel' (Peter Henrici, 'Blondel und Loisy in der modernistischen Krise', *Internationale katholishe Zeitschrift "Communio"*, 16 (1987), 513–530 (530.) See also Albert Raffelt, 'Maurice Blondel und die katholische Theologie in Deutschland', in Albert Raffelt, Peter Reifenberg, and Gotthard Fuchs (eds.), *Das Tun, der Glaube, die Vernunft: Studien zur Philosophie Maurice Blondels 'L'Action' 1893–1993* (Würzburg: Echter, 1995), 180–205.

work structured around five main sections with an Introduction and a Conclusion, whereby the central section (the Third Part) takes up more than half of the main text. This Third Part is itself subdivided into five stages. The work opens with the famous question: 'Yes or no, does human life have a meaning, and does man have a destiny?' The first lines of the thesis clearly pose the question of meaning and of human destiny as *the* philosophical question, and the one that embraces all other concerns. It is universal in scope, personal in character, and demands a (tacit or explicit) response from everyone. To study this question is to investigate concrete human action in its integrity and determine its precise import in so much as it is a synthesis of the voluntary and the obligatory. It is this complex reality that the thesis aspires to unravel and the very last lines of the Conclusion suggest, in the light of the *démarche* of the text, where the answer might ultimately be found and ends simply: *c'est* (it is).

Very briefly, Blondel begins his discussion by asking if action is a legitimate philosophical problem (which included, importantly, the moral component) and, having established that it is indeed so, he proceeds to show, through an analysis of the position taken by the dilettante and the pessimist, that the solution to the problem of action cannot be a negative one. This leaves us with the first important determination of the thesis, namely, that *there is something* (*il y a quelque chose*). This something is then investigated in the major Third Part in a phenomenological-type inquiry that is effected from within the positivist tradition and post-metaphysical in not assuming any of the presuppositions associated with an *a priori* metaphysics.[4] At this point Blondel examines a whole series of connected phenomena that include the natural sciences, the emergence of consciousness, freedom, duty, the physiological bearing of action, the family, and social order, culminating in an investigation of superstitious action. He does this, importantly, through the technical apparatus of the will in the action of willing by examining the gap that pertains between what is explicitly willed (*la volonté voulue*) and the willing will (*la volonté voulante*).[5] This spectrum of interconnected phenomena is examined meticulously in order to determine the degree to which that which is willed as phenomenon meets the originating aspiration of the very willing (the act) that willed it. There is in us a voluntary, spontaneous, and foundational movement of our willing that is expressed through the particular choices that we make and on which we reflect in order to redirect this very movement:

> Everything is in equating the reflected movement to the spontaneous movement
> of my willing (vouloir). Now it is in action that this relation of either harmony or

---

[4] See Michael A. Conway, 'A Positive Phenomenology: The structure of Maurice Blondel's early philosophy', *Heythrop Journal*, 47 (2006), 579–600.

[5] See René Virgoulay, *L'Action de Maurice Blondel (1893): Relecture pour un centenaire* (Paris: Beauchesne, 1992), 53–76.

discordance is determined. Hence the supreme importance of studying action; for it manifests at the same time the double will of man; it constructs in him all his destiny, like a world that is his original work and which ought to contain the complete explanation of his history.[6]

At the end of this Third Part we are left, *de facto*, facing a dilemma in human action where, on the one hand, we have established a fullness in action and, on the other, we are unable to give an adequate account of this situation:

> It is impossible not to raise the problem of action; impossible to give it a negative solution; impossible to find oneself as one wills to be, either in ourselves or in others; in short, impossible to stop, to go back, or to go forward by oneself. In my action there is something I have not yet been able to understand and equal; something which keeps it from falling back into nothingness, and which is only something in being nothing of what I have willed up to now. What I have voluntarily posited, therefore, can neither surpass nor maintain itself: it is this conflict that explains the forced presence of a new affirmation in consciousness; and it is the reality of this necessary presence that makes possible in us the consciousness of this very conflict.[7]

The Fourth Part deals with this conflict and, in doing so, raises the question of the relationship that subsists between the natural and the supernatural order. The dilemma places us before the alternative for or against what Blondel designates as *l'unique nécessaire* (*the one thing necessary*)—in allusion, perhaps, to Lk. 11.41–2 and Pascal's *Pensées*.[8] This is the genesis point of the supernatural order in the natural. He writes (the much quoted):

> Absolutely impossible and absolutely necessary to man, that is properly the notion of the supernatural: man's action goes beyond man; and all the effort of his reason is to see that he cannot, that he must not restrict himself to it. A sincere expectation of an unknown messiah; a baptism of desire, which human science lacks the power to evoke, because this need itself is a gift. It can show its necessity, it cannot give birth to it.[9]

This (philosophical) determination of the relationship of the natural to the supernatural order led in the period after the publication of *L'Action* and, more particularly, with the publication of the *Letter on Apologetics*, to wide-spread misunderstanding, criticism, and controversy.

Now, depending on the *option* we take at this point, Blondel proceeds in the Fifth Part to discuss the achievement of action which includes a discussion of positive religion (i.e., religion with its rites, structures, dogmas, etc.) as a means of bringing human destiny to its term and integrating knowledge and action in

---

[6] *L'Action*, p. xxiv.   [7] *L'Action*, 339.
[8] See Blaise Pascal, *Pensées*, ed. Louis Lafuma (Paris: Du Seuil, 1962), no. 270.
[9] Blondel, *L'Action*, 388. This celebrated formulation may have been influenced by Pascal's equally celebrated fragment on the 'disproportion of man' (see Pascal, *Pensées*, no. 199).

being. The option itself is a free choice for or against the transcendent that is immanent to our action. It, in turn, leads to either a privative (in its negation) or complete (in its acceptance) appropriation of reality. Blondel, however, in the Conclusion, makes it clear that this final term is reached only through an action (of belief) that goes beyond the parameters of any philosophical examination and as such beyond the text of *L'Action*. It is only at this point that the phenomenological inquiry reaches the fullness of ontological deter-mination and the circle of thought, action, and being might be ultimately closed.

The complexity of Blondel's work, which draws on a vast matrix of material—most of which is unacknowledged, since all of it has been thoroughly reworked so as to serve, independently of its origin, in the Blondelian register—meant that the work was destined to be the source of massive controversy on several fronts: the secular philosophical world of the French university saw it as an affront on the autonomy of independent reason; many in ecclesiastical circles (particularly of the neo-Thomist persuasion) would eventually charge it with violating the gratuity, and denying the absolute transcendence, of the supernat-ural order. His conclusion that human action is discovered to be intrinsically open to the supernatural order was seriously misunderstood on both sides of this divide.

Blondel was never completely satisfied with his early thesis: he saw it as an initial sketch (required to attain a university qualification) of a much bigger project that would need to include a greater spectrum of concerns and discussions. Indeed, this is the task he would set himself for much of his later career. Nothing that he would write later, however, could live up to the juvenile energy, to the intensity of argument, and to the structural elegance of this seminal work. And for all its deficiencies, it still remains *the* text in which to access Blondel's philosophy, and nothing that he subsequently writes can be adequately approached without having understood first its connection to the seminal argument of *L'Action*.

Written at the end of the nineteenth century, *L'Action* was read by a whole generation of young philosophers and theologians (often secretly), who would not only be highly influenced by it, but would also take up many of its concerns anew in the next generation.[10] Many of these emerged to be the

---

[10] It is rather difficult to track directly Blondel's influence on theologians. In the wake of the papal encyclical, *Pascendi Dominici Gregis* (Pius X, *Pascendi Dominici Gregis*. Encyclical Letter on the Doctrine of the Modernists (8 September 1907), *AAS* xl (1907), 593–650; ET available at <http://www.vaticholy_/holy_father/pius_x/encyclicals/documents/hf_p-x_enc_19070908_pascendi-dominici-gregis_en.html>, in which, to some degree, he was targeted, his thought remained compromised through his rather tenuous 'link' with the so-called Modernists. He was thus considered suspect in some Roman Catholic circles and especially in Rome. This means that theologians whom he inspired were not free to declare this in public, even after the end of the Modernist crisis. It is for this reason that, rightly, René Virgoulay speaks of a 'subterranean

major figures of the *ressourcement* movement. Blondel's thesis attempted to reflect life and human action in its fullness and to follow the intimate contours of every consciousness as it seeks its own equilibrium. In making action, and not reason, its subject, it at once projected a concrete philosophy of universal import and avoided proffering an abstract rationalism that was limited to the squirrel-cage of a theoretical reasoning. Through his treatment of action, Blondel recovered—even for philosophy in the positive tradition—the subjective, the personal, and the historical, not merely as categories of reflexive thought but as living realities that always go beyond the determinations of explicit formulations. His concern with attending to the concrete in its dialectical relationship with the abstract would mirror later concerns of the *ressourcement* theologians.

BLONDEL AND APOLOGETICS

The older apologetics had attempted to prove the fact of divine revelation without considering its meaning in relation to human existence and any intrinsic relationship to those who welcomed it. Faith was considered to be an essentially complete and closed system of established truths to which one had to give full assent, because of the authority of God. The church guaranteed their validity, and this authority, in turn, was attested to in the Bible through miracles and anticipatory prophecy. Working in the register of an ahistorical consciousness that had emerged to a large extent through a deficient reading of Thomas Aquinas, the proponents of this apologetics saw no reason to consider as part of their work showing that there was an intrinsic relationship between the order of creation and that of redemption. Revelation was treated in an excessively supernaturalistic and alien way that portrayed it as a series of mysteries that were to be believed ultimately on the strength of miracles. This led not only to a totally extrinsic notion of revelation, but also to a fideistic reduction of the real contribution of human reason to Christian faith.

Blondel was the first of his generation to see clearly the radical insufficiency of this position and to understand that faith can be understood (and lived) in a salutary way only from within the movement of faith itself as a living and lived reality. In *L'Action*, he showed, over the widest possible spectrum of experiences and analyses, the fundamental human openness to faith and revelation that could be established in an apodictic fashion by means of a thoroughgoing, critical study of human action in all its variant forms. If the older apologetics might be deemed to be extrinsic with very little appreciation of the existential

influence' on theologians; see Virgoulay, *Philosophie et Théologie chez Maurice Blondel* (Paris: Cerf, 2002), 183–8.

character of faith, Blondel's method (which cannot be said to be apologetics in any traditional sense) might be said to be intrinsic, in that it calls each person to follow the contours of their own world and action so as to establish what is in deepest accord with their most intimate needs. His philosophy could be described as a discernment of the mystery of divine presence, which penetrates concrete human existence and bestows upon the drama of human action a transcendent bearing and meaning.

After the publication of *L'Action*, Blondel published a number of articles that were aimed at making more explicit the argument of his doctoral thesis, and clarifying misunderstandings that had emerged in the literature. One such article (or, rather, a series of six articles) reacted to a serious misreading of the 'apologetic character' of the thesis. As his response, the young philosopher published his (in)famous *Lettre sur les exigences de la pensée contemporaine en matière d'aplogétique et sur la méthode de la philosophie dans l'étude du problème religieux*, commonly called simply *La Lettre* in French, and the *Letter on Apologetics* in English. This letter brought a major whirlwind of controversy in its wake, particularly when read by scholastic theologians who did not have Blondel's secular philosophical background and were ill-equipped to understand its *démarche*.

Published in 1896, three years after the thesis, the *Letter on Apologetics* is not so much an apologetic essay as a philosophical study that is concerned with the issue of method in treating religion in a philosophical enquiry. Blondel re-presents the salient methodological structure of *L'Action*, albeit now in the light of the early controversies with the rationalist philosophy of the university. He was almost completely unaware that this work was going to be read by theologians, who were little prepared to accept some of his claims and conclusions. Responding to the critique from the university, Blondel accepted (and equally adopted) the notion of immanence, recognizing that it was perfectly appropriate to the methodology of the philosopher, even in the study of religion. What he wished to show, however, is that, employed as a 'method', far from leading to a 'doctrine' of immanence or to a closed framework, so to speak, it allows one, on the contrary, to examine philosophically even that which is most opposed to it, viz., the idea of the supernatural taken in its most rigorous Catholic understanding. Thus extending the domain of philosophy to even a consideration of the depths of religion, and enlarging the ambit of reason without denaturing faith, however, was the ambition of the young philosopher. The *Letter on Apologetics* further clarifies how the method of immanence—implied and utilized in principle in the earlier *L'Action*—allows one to achieve this. When the *Letter* expresses specifically how one ought to do this it, in effect, summarizes the procedure of the thesis: 'put into equation, in consciousness itself, that which we appear to think and to will and to do, with that which we do, we will and we think in reality: in such a manner that in the artificial negations or in the ends artificially willed are to be found

still the deep affirmations and the incoercible needs that they imply'.[11] As part
of this process, in the first section of the *Letter*, the *pars destruens*, Blondel
critiques traditional forms of apologetics and hits a particular nerve when
he critiques those forms of apologetics that ratify an extrinsic relationship
between the natural and supernatural orders.

Already in 1893, in a letter to the director of the *École Normale*, Blondel had
noted that scholasticism had subordinated nature to grace, and reason to faith,
in a form that resulted in the juxtaposition of two orders that were completely
exterior to one another. This juxtaposition was untenable, he maintained at
the time, since in the final analysis one had to choose one to the detriment of
the other.[12]

Now, in the *Letter on Apologetics*, he underlined that in the traditional tract
on revelation theologians limited themselves, on the one hand, to showing the
non-impossibility of a supernatural revelation from the side of God and then,
on the other, outlining the historical factual proof that this revelation had
taken place in Jesus Christ (and this was confirmed by miracles).

> It is not enough that there should be no recognised impossibilities on the one side
> and certain real facts on the other for the connection between this possibility and
> this reality (ce réel) to impose itself on my conscience, to oblige my reason and to
> govern my whole life. Why must I take account of this fact when I can legitimately
> disregard so many other facts that are equally real? How far am I responsible for
> a voluntary abstention in this regard? So many questions remain unanswered,
> because it is not sufficient to establish separately the *possibility* and the *reality*, but
> one must show further the *necessity for us* (nécessité pour nous) of adhering to this
> reality of the supernatural.[13]

Thus Blondel explicitly criticized the apologetics of the (neo-) scholastic schools,
unaware of the torrent of negative reactions that this would unleash against
him from a spectrum of Thomist theologians, which would include the priests,
Marie-Benoît Schwalm, OP, Hippolyte Gayraud, and Xavier-Marie Le Bachelet.
Given the particular period, however, in which scholastic philosophy was
considered the sacrosanct philosophical presentation of Roman Catholicism,
these pages from Blondel were profoundly refreshing and, indeed, courageous.
He affirms that Thomism had turned the matter of faith into a static account
and argued from principles that had become obsolete. Above all it had
completely neglected the question of the *subjective disposition* in the reception
of the matter of faith:

---

[11] Blondel, 'Lettre sur les exigences de la pensée contemporaine en matière d'apologétique et
sur la méthode de la philosophie dans l'étude du problème religieux', in Blondel, *Œuvres
complètes*, ii, *1888–1913: La philosophie de l'action et la crise moderniste*, ed. Claude Troisfontaines (Paris: PUF, 1997), 97–173 (128).

[12] See Blondel, *Lettres philosophiques* (Paris: Aubier, 1961), 32–7 (35).

[13] Blondel, 'Lettre sur les exigences de la pensée', 107.

And since [the Thomist] starts from principles which, for the most part, are disputed today; since he does not offer the possibility of restoring them by his method; since he presupposes a host of assertions which are just those which are called in question; since he cannot provide, in his systematic form, for the new requirements of minds which must be approached on their own ground, one must not tend towards contentment with this triumphant exposition. We are still in the life of struggle and suffering; and to understand this is itself a good and a gain. We must not exhaust ourselves refurbishing known arguments and presenting an *object* for acceptance while the *subject* is not disposed to listen. It is not ever the side of divine truth which is at fault but human preparation, and it is here that our effort should be concentrated.[14]

We have here in a nutshell a critique of the (neo-)scholastic system that would be enlarged and further investigated by *ressourcement* theologians, particularly in de Lubac's monumental work.[15] Blondel, however, was the one who introduced this serious concern into Roman Catholic theology.

HISTORY AND DOGMA

The so-called Modernist crisis is the *Sitz-im-Leben* for one of Blondel's most important contributions in view of twentieth-century theology.[16] A primary scene of conflict was the reception of the historical sciences and with this, severe disagreement around exegesis, church history, apologetics (as understood at the time), and the relationship between faith and politics. A central issue was the appropriate adoption of the historical critical method. It was his reading of *L'Évangile et l'église* (1902) that would give rise to an exchange of letters between Blondel and Alfred Loisy, its author, in early 1903, which constitutes one of the significant contributions of the whole 'Modernist' movement on the questions of historical and theological method. Whereas he expressed the highest regard and deepest approval for Loisy's undertaking, Blondel did articulate an early reservation in regard to Loisy's assertion that Jesus had a limited consciousness, a position, Blondel feared, that concealed an implicit and deficient Christology. Indeed, he spoke of Loisy's 'occult Christology', which, for Blondel, was effectively one that did not have a solid foundation. In the face of such criticism, Loisy, influenced by the *Leben-Jesu-Forschung*, maintained that he was writing as an historian and that his conclusions were the inevitable results of a critical

---

[14] Blondel, 'Lettre sur les exigences de la pensée', 119.

[15] For confirmation of Blondel's influence on de Lubac, see, for example, Henri de Lubac, *Mémoire sur l'occasion de mes écrits* (Namur: Culture et Verité, 1992), 15–16, 33 *et passim*.

[16] In the older secondary literature, Blondel is more often than not aligned with the so-called 'Modernists'. In latter years, however, it has been well established (ironically) that he was one of the very first to see through the essence of 'Modernism' and to chart the way to overcoming its shortcomings (see Henrici, 'Blondel und Loisy', 514).

examination of New Testament texts. Despite not being an exegete, Blondel immediately challenged a historical method that would lead to such a conclusion. Acting on pressure from a number of friends, he finally agreed to go public with his reservations and began the painfully difficult composition of an extraordinary series of articles, entitled *Histoire et Dogme. Les lacunes philosophiques de l'exégèse moderne*, which appeared in early 1904.[17] There he critiqued two 'Catholic mentalities' that were absolutely incompatible. One was a historical relativism (à la Loisy), termed 'historicism' by Blondel, and the other, a position that he designated as *extrinsicism* (à la Gayraud, for example), which was reflective of the dogmatism of theologians who would claim to impose on facts an interpretation drawn from faith. Historicism, in Blondel's understanding, is concerned wholly with the investigation and determination of facts which it subsequently treats as if they were in themselves substantial units of reality. The antagonistic and deficient positions of both historicism and extrinsicism called for a resolution of the conflicting positions through a principle of mediation.[18] Blondel proceeds to present his own solution through a re-discovery of the dynamic, vital character of *tradition* as this very principle. He argued that Christian tradition is not something closed and complete in the past, but rather a vital and dynamic reality that is both a retrograde view in terms of the past and equally a progressive one in terms of the present and the future. In short, his position renewed the place of *tradition* in Christian self-understanding.

With exceptional clarity, Blondel saw that it was only in turning to *tradition* as a primary category that one could solve the problem of the relationship between history and dogma. He suggests valuing *tradition* as a living reality and according to its own principle as a 'power of conservation and preservation that also instructs and initiates'.[19] Far, however, from being an occult 'knowledge' placed side-by-side with the knowledge accessible to the historian, or, for that matter, an oral tradition that might compliment the written one, tradition is the condition of possibility of even its own understanding as articulated at the level of real, effective history. In this sense, as a principle, it anticipates absolutely every explicit formulation. As a dynamic, living reality it cannot be purely and simply assimilated to the explicit, be that expressed in either spoken or written form, in the exact measure that tradition itself makes tradition possible:

[17] See Blondel, *Histoire et Dogme: Les lacunes philosophique d'exégèse moderne*, in Blondel, *Œuvres complètes*, 2., 387–453; also Yves Krumenacker, 'La science historique à l'époque d'"Histoire et Dogme"', *Théophilyon*, 9 (2004), 99–110. It should be noted that Blondel's series of articles was not intended as an exclusive, one-sided critique of Loisy, who is not even mentioned in the text.

[18] Blondel's French thesis can be read as a philosophy that is rooted in the reality of mediation. See, for example, Paul Favraux, *Une philosophie du médiateur: Maurice Blondel* (Paris: Lethielleux, 1986); and Jacques Flamard, *L'idée de médiation chez Maurice Blondel* (Paris: Béatrice-Nauwelaerts, 1969).

[19] Blondel, *Histoire et dogme*, 434.

Turned lovingly towards the past where its treasure lies, it moves towards the future, where lies its conquest and its light. It has a humble sense of faithfully *recovering* even what it thus *discovers*. It does not have to innovate because it possesses its God and its all; but it has always to teach us something new because it transforms something of the lived implicit to the known explicit.[20]

This understanding of tradition opened not merely the possibility, but indeed, the necessity of returning to the fullness and the richness of this very tradition so as to be constantly nourished and taught anew by it. This was the very challenge of *ressourcement avant la lettre*. There is little doubt that Balthasar, Daniélou, Congar, Chenu, de Lubac, and many others were deeply inspired by Blondel's contribution on the importance of tradition as sketched in this remarkable essay.[21]

Blondel's position, at its core, is founded on his so-called *panchristism*, i.e., his earliest synthesis of the intellectual and the spiritual that found its first public expression in the (much debated) last chapter of *L'Action*, entitled 'The connection of knowledge and of action in being.'[22] This was effectively a Christocentric view of reality, itself, a transposition into philosophy of the *primogenitus omnis creaturae*.[23] For the thesis, in an obvious, though camouflaged, manner, the mediation of Christ is what establishes and guarantees the reality and the objectivity of the sensible world. It is Christ who is the cornerstone of the created order and who assures its solidity (even philosophically).[24] This means that, for Blondel, any historical enquiry into the person of Christ must not lose sight of the reality that this cannot, with impunity, be cut off from the living Christ who is met in the intimacy of living faith. This living reality of Christ is not to be confused with the dissected and reductive moments of either historical research or, for that matter, dogmatic statement.

For the *ressourcement* theologians a central concern was history; not in an historicist register that would search out the solutions for the present in the closed responses of the past, but rather in history as a creative hermeneutical exercise in which the 'sources' of Christian faith were revisited with a set of new questions. This appreciation of history understood as a living tradition stands in marked contrast to neo-scholasticism which, as Daniélou chided in his famous article from 1946, has no historical sense.[25] In being resolutely

---

[20] Blondel, *Histoire et dogme*, 434.

[21] For Congar's case (as an example) and the subsequent link to the Second Vatican Council, see Gabriel Flynn, *Yves Congar's Vision of the Church in a World of Unbelief* (Aldershot/Burlington VT, Ashgate, 2004), 198–211. See also David Grumett's and James Hanvey's chapters in this volume.

[22] Blondel, *L'Action*, 424–99.

[23] See, for example, Virgoulay, *Philosophie et Théologie*, 88–94.

[24] In its more personal and spiritual contours and inspiration this constellation is more explicitly evident in Blondel's private *Carnets intimes*.

[25] Jean Daniélou, 'Les orientations présentes de la pensée religieuse', *Études*, 249 (1946), 1–21.

essentialist and objectivist in its approach, it was oblivious to human subjectivity, to contemporary thought, and to the daily life of the people of God. Blondel was first to recognize the weakness of this position.

It is of particular note that in reading philosophers (and theologians, to the degree that this distinction makes any sense) of the past, Blondel had underlined, on several occasions, that it was insufficient to reproduce the mere theoretical system that corresponded to the work of isolated reflective reason, without penetrating to the personal core of a philosopher's world and understanding the entire edifice from this perspective, which gave it its unique quality. In this regard he himself would present highly original contributions on, say, Augustine, Thomas Aquinas, Descartes, Malebranche, and Pascal to name but a few.[26] Similarly, the *ressourcement* thinkers' return to the Fathers was not ultimately a concern with bare scholarship but rather with a work of revitalization. It was a matter of connecting with a deeper dynamic of the spiritual life which continues to be active. All the elements of the church's tradition—scripture, creeds, rites, etc.—are channels of the one, incomparable source which is the mystery of Christ. Referring, for example, to his studies of the Greek Fathers, Balthasar remarks: 'To be faithful to the Tradition is not, therefore, to repeat and transmit literally theses of philosophy or of theology that one imagines abstracted from time and the contingencies of history. It is much more to imitate our Fathers in the faith in regard to the attitude of intimate reflection and their effort of audacious creation, which are the necessary preludes to true spiritual fidelity.'[27] And he goes on to add: 'We would...hope to penetrate to the vital source of their spirit, to the fundamental and secret intuition which directs the entire expression of their thought and which reveals to us one of these possible great attitudes that theology has adopted in a concrete and unique situation.'[28]

BLONDEL AND THOMISM

With Pope Leo XIII's promulgation of *Aeterni Patris* in 1879,[29] the philosophy of St. Thomas Aquinas—as interpreted by neo-scholasticism—became the

---

[26] See, for example, Blondel, *Dialogues avec les philosophes: Descartes; Spinoza; Malebranche; Pascal; Saint Augustin*, Preface, Henri Gouhier (Paris: Aubier, 1966).

[27] Hans Urs von Balthasar, *Présence et pensée: essai sur la philosophie religieuse de Grégoire de Nysse* (Paris: Beauchesne, 1942), p. x.

[28] Von Balthasar, *Présence et pensée*, p. xi. We note, in passing, that Balthasar had translated Blondel into German.

[29] Leo XIII, *Aeterni Patris*: Encyclical Letter on the Restoration of Christian Philosophy (4th August 1879), *Acta Leonis XIII*, i (1881), 255–84. ET available at <http://www.vatican.va/holy_father/leo_xiii/encyclicals/documents/hf_l-xiii_enc_04081879_aeterni-patris_en.html>.

standard philosophy and theology of Roman Catholic thought and seminary formation. Not unconnected to this, Blondel maintained, from an early age, a substantial interest in the thought of St Thomas. However, in the period after publishing his doctoral thesis he moved into his most critical period vis-à-vis Thomism, which culminates with the (rather over-enthusiastic) critique that appeared in the *Letter on Apologetics*. Until this point, however, his contact with the thought of Thomas was limited to the lens of scholastic manuals.[30] In the aftermath of the publication of the controversial letter, and partly in order to respond to various objections that had been raised against it, Blondel turned to a path that would lead him eventually to a direct engagement with Thomas's thought. In this transition he significantly corrects the major error he had made in his earlier work in identifying too closely the codifications of the neo-Thomist manuals with the thought of Thomas himself.[31] In subsequent debates he would study with particular intensity, Thomas's understanding of the role of tradition, of the act of faith, and of the role of finality in his philosophy. A range of publications during the first decade of the twentieth century help Blondel clarify, through Thomas's writings, his own 'method of immanence' and show the essential role of the will in the matter of belief. Blondel would also teach a number of courses at university, in which Thomas's works featured as major sources and in which he treated his philosophy as the counterpoint to Descartes's achievement and, derivatively, contemporary philosophy.[32] The crucial point—in terms of the later *ressourcement* thinkers—is that, in being forced to read Thomas at first hand, Blondel discovered not only serious lacunae in many of the manual accounts of his thought on key issues, but also that he had an essential role to play in contemporary thought in correcting some of the deviations induced through an overzealous appropriation of the Cartesian heritage. All of this means that Blondel began to read Thomas directly without the 'benefit' of tutelage from the classical commentators. This allowed him to read the medieval texts with fresh eyes, so to speak, and so discover a philosopher-theologian who stood apart from his commentators, and who, at times, was (surprisingly) more in harmony with the concerns of contemporary philosophy than many had been led to believe.[33]

---

[30] Later Blondel clearly recognizes this. See, for example, Blondel, *Le problème de la philosophie catholique* (Paris: Bloud et Gay, 1932), 47.

[31] For a more complete discussion, see Michael A. Conway, 'From Neo-Thomism to St. Thomas: Maurice Blondel's Early Encounter with Scholastic Thought', *EphThL*, 83 (2007), 1–22.

[32] For more detail, see Michael A. Conway, 'A Thomistic Turn? Maurice Blondel's Reading of St Thomas', *EphThL*, 84 (2008), 87–122.

[33] There were, certainly, a number of exceptions to the dominant neo-scholastic take on theology. One might mention the Tübingen School that, before its time, was conscious of the importance of not only the historical, but also even of the ecumenical dimension to Christian theology. The leading figures here included Johann Sebastian Drey and Johann Adam Möhler. One might also, in this regard, mention John Henry Newman and Matthias Scheeben.

Half a century later, Daniélou and many others would accuse the neo-Thomism of school theology, for example, of being an abstract rationalism that was incapable of offering any intellectual or spiritual nourishment. The rupture between theology and life which Daniélou laments goes against one of the major insights of the century, viz., that thought is not meant merely to contemplate the world, but, through action, to transform it. This insight was Blondel's earliest motivation for undertaking a study specifically of action in his thesis and remained the vital stimulus of all his philosophy.

It is no surprise that later the Fourvière theologians, in particular, many of whom were dedicated Thomists, had a deep sense that the Thomism of the manuals was not the Thomism of Thomas himself. This realization was also Blondel's, who began to have a suspicion that this might, indeed, be the case. He was not, it must be said, uncritical of St Thomas, and his critique too filters through—via, for example, Henri Bouillard—to the *ressourcement* thinkers. But it did, in part, initiate a return to a direct reading of Thomas that was independent of the commentators—such as John of St Thomas, Francisco Suarez, Domingo Bañez, and Thomas Cajetan—to reveal a thinker who was far less rigidly ahistorical and rationalistic than had been projected, and thus much more in tune with the concerns of modern philosophical method.

BLONDEL AND SOCIAL ACTION

Unquestionably Blondel was of the mindset of social Catholicism and—even though he never presented a formal treatise of social philosophy as such—had a keen interest in social issues, both practically and theoretically.[34] Through family connections and past pupils, he was closely attached to the group of democratically oriented 'Social Catholics' who were centred around the *Semaines sociales de France* and, on three occasions, contributed to the issues at hand: *La Semaine Sociale de Bordeaux et le Monophorisme* (1909–10); *Patrie et humanité* (1928); and *La conception l'ordre sociale* (1947).[35]

It is no surprise that Blondel reads concrete social engagement in line with the treatment of social action in *L'Action*, viz., within the integral framework of moral, even religious, action. Social action is a sort of bridge or union between the self as the centre of personal action and the universal, moral, and religious dimension of this action. As Peter Henrici points out, the forms of social life that Blondel examines, for example, in *L'Action*—i.e., the family,

[34] On the personal level, he was a member of a Conference of St Vincent de Paul, where he regularly visited 'ses pauvres'. He also commented regularly on social issues in *La Croix de Provence*.
[35] One could add to this list his short work from 1939, *Lutte pour la civilisation et philosophie de la paix* (Paris: Flammarion, 1939).

country, and humanity—while being fully natural, are moral realities, since the free will that grounds them is necessarily moral, i.e., universalizing, altruist, and humanitarian.[36] Blondel designates this will 'love' and in retrospect, in the light of the supernatural vinculum to which it tends in its realization, ought to be called, simply, 'charity'.[37]

Thus, Blondel critiques, in the circumstantial writings mentioned above, those social theories and practices that do not reflect this balancing of components that characterizes his own integral vision of social reality. The most important of these writings, for the purposes of this present study, is the series of articles drafted in view of the *Semaine sociale de Bordeaux* and published first as seven articles, under the relatively transparent pseudonym *Testis*, in the *Annales de Philosophie Chrétienne* and later as a separate monograph with the title: *La Semaine Sociale de Bordeaux et le monophorisme*.[38]

When Henri Lorin publicly called on Blondel to come to the defence of the *Semaines sociales* against Maurras' monarchical and rabidly anti-Modernist *Action française*, he had the additional incentive of responding to those critics, who from scholastic and integrist (intégrist) circles had persistently attacked him since the *Letter on Apologetics*.[39] The *Testis* series first outlined the position of the *Semaines sociales* and then undertook a critical analysis of the opponents' position so as to highlight a number of fundamental errors in terms of the doctrine of knowledge, on the relationship between diverse orders of reality, on the connection of the social order to the moral and religious one, and, foundationally, of the relationship between the natural and supernatural orders. It is with this fundamental issue that the *Testis* articles are principally concerned, and this so, especially, in its ecclesiological implications.

Blondel summarizes this collection of deficient positions into a system of connected ideas that he terms, rather, enigmatically, *monophorism*, which could be best rendered as a 'one-way system'. In the face of Modernism, which might now be designated as an immanentist monophorism (since everything comes from inside), there exists its mirror image, so to speak, namely, an extrinsicist monophorism (everything comes from outside), that he critiques

---

[36] See Peter Henrici, 'Simples remarques sur la philosophie sociale de Blondel', in *Blondel entre l'Action et la Trilogie*, ed. Marc Leclerc, *Actes du Colloque international sur les 'écrits intermédiaires' de Maurice Blondel, tenu à l'université Grégorienne à Rome du 16 au 18 novembre 2000* (Bruxelles: Lessius, 2003), 361–4.

[37] Henrici, 'Simples remarques', 363.

[38] See Blondel, *Une alliance contre nature: catholicisme et intégrisme, La Semaine sociale de Bourdeaux 1910*, reprint (Brussels: Editions Lessius, 2000).

[39] I use the translation 'integrist' rather than the more usual 'integralist' to translate the French 'intégriste', not only because as its homologue it is closer to the original French (itself a neologism adapted from the Spanish), but, more particularly in the case of Blondel, I wish—in order to avoid confusion—to reserve the word 'integral' (and its variants) for a separate setting, since one of Blondel's explicit concerns is to formulate what he terms an 'integral realism'. See Yvette Périco, *Maurice Blondel: Genèse du sens* (Paris: Editions Universitaires, 1991), 23–5.

as the position of the opponents to the *Semaines sociales*. Here he denounces the dangers incurred, for example, by those Catholics who accepted support- ing *Action française*, in whom he sees a representative selection of this mono- phorism in politics. The theoretical position corresponds to a conceptual realism that ultimately makes the human ability to understand the measure of all intelligibility. This, in turn, permits a radically nationalistic image of reality in which the fragmentary aspects appear as self-sufficiently subsistent and, crucially, delimited from consideration of others.[40] In this same mindset, the supernatural is understood as an external, additional story that is added on to a nature that is already complete in itself. The greater part of Blondel's discussion is concerned with a trenchant analysis of this anti-Modernist position since if reality is divided, in such a manner, into hermetically sealed compartments, an unscrupulous politics, for example, will permit and (illegit- imately) justify any means to achieve its desired end. Over against this, the Social Catholics understand reality to be an interconnected totality in which the economic order, for example, cannot be separated absolutely from social, ethical, and even religious concerns.

In this way, Blondel was the one to have exposed the dangers and aberra- tions of the integrist mentality within Catholicism with its deficient philo- sophical and indeed, theological, foundations. Balthasar would later point to 'the interest and importance of these "controversies" with a view to a philo- sophical and theological analysis of Catholic integrism'.[41] And one of the leading *periti* at the Second Vatican Council, Yves Congar, has remarked that 'if it were necessary for us to characterize in one word the theological approach of the Council, we would evoke the ideal of knowledge proposed by Maurice Blondel, which protested against what he rather enigmatically called "monophorism", that is to say a reified (*chosiste*) conception of knowledge'.[42]

LATER YEARS

Because of deterioration in his eyesight, Blondel took early retirement from teaching at the university of Aix-en-Provence and dedicated the remainder of his life to drafting the definitive form of his integral philosophy. From 1934–7 he dictated (to his secretary, Mlle Panis) and published five volumes of a 'trilogy': two volumes on *Thought*, two volumes on *Action*, and a fifth volume

---

[40] See Henrici, 'Blondel und Loisy', 529.

[41] See Peter Henrici, 'De *l'Action* à la critique du *Monophorisme*', *Bulletin des Amis de Maurice Blondel*, nouvelle série 3 (1991), 9–28 (9).

[42] Yves Congar, 'L'inspiration: Un catholicisme rajeuni et ouvert bilan et perspectives', *Informations catholiques internationales*, 255 (1966), 5–15 (13). See also Yves Congar, *Mon Journal du Concile*, ed. Éric Mahieu (Paris: Cerf, 2002), i.49.

on *Being and beings*. Two further volumes appeared between 1944 and 1946 on *Philosophy and the Christian Spirit*; the third, planned volume remained outstanding at his death in 1949.

It is really only of late that this spectrum of later works is beginning to enjoy the sustained attention of the European philosophical and theological community.[43] Much of the research is carried out in conjunction with important centres of Blondel study that regularly hold conferences and research days on aspects of his philosophy (together with its influence on theology). Apart from the Blondel Archives at Louvain-la-Neuve, for the study of Blondel and his intellectual heritage, important centres include Paris, Lyon/Aix-en-Provence, Rome, Mainz, and Freiburg im Breisgau. Areas of particular interest that are presently emerging in the literature include Blondel's relationship to the philosophical and theological tradition and his re-appraisal of the same, his relationship to a number of leading figures of the period (John Henry Newman, Henri Bergson, Teilhard de Chardin, Louis Lavelle, and Jacques Paliard), his understanding of metaphysics and mediation (which is of enormous importance in understanding philosophically a sacramental world view), his treatment of mysticism (and its relation to the French School), the integral and spiritual realism of his later philosophy, his appropriation of Leibniz's philosophy, his treatment of the relationship between science and metaphysics, and his social philosophy.

Strictly speaking, Blondel is not part of the *ressourcement* movement per se. The acknowledgement of his contribution, which is indirect, is, nonetheless, vital if one is to understand the seismic shift that took place in the early part of the twentieth century in Roman Catholic thought and which culminated in the Second Vatican Council. What he offered, though indirectly, is foundational, and, it is this that one must understand in order to appreciate his importance for the movement. He discovers and clarifies the very principles that will become, in time, so central to *ressourcement*, and these he grounds in a philosophy that, at the same time, is original and deeply rooted in the Christian tradition. This philosophy and these principles could not but inspire a generation of young philosophers and theologians who were increasingly unhappy with the more classical scholastic system in which they were being formed. I have outlined in this paper how and in what context these various principles emerged for Blondel, and it is now a monumental task to track the detail of this influence. Later discussions, for example, on grace and nature, on the role of tradition, on reading Thomas, on integrating history and dogma, on

---

[43] See, for example, Emmanuel Gabellieri and Pierre de Cointet (eds.), *Maurice Blondel et la philosophie française*, Colloque tenu à Lyon (Paris: Parole et Silence, 2007); Emmanuel Tourpe (ed.), *Penser l'être de l'Action: La métaphysique du 'dernier' Blondel* (Louvain: Peeters, 2000); Marc Leclerc (ed.), *Blondel entre l'Action et la Trilogie*, Actes du Colloque international sur les 'écrits intermédiaires' de Maurice Blondel, tenu à l'Université Grégorienne à Rome du 16 au 18 novembre 2000 (Brussels: Lessius, 2003).

the role of the natural sciences in regard to religious faith, on obedience and autonomy, and on a Christocentric view of reality were all explored by Blondel and given a new, dynamic formulation. None of these issues were discussed later by the *ressourcement* theologians without giving a nod, directly or indirectly, to Blondel's earlier achievement.

5

A New 'Lyon School' (1919–1939)?[1]

Étienne Fouilloux

'THE NEW INTELLECTUAL AND CATHOLIC SCHOOL OF LYON'

What better witness could there be than Fr François Varillon, who barely set foot outside Lyon between his birth in 1905 and his death in 1978? When his Jesuit brethren left Fourvière at the beginning of the 1970s he wrote:

> These are the people I knew. Some of them have died, some are alive and still active among us: Marius Gonin, Pierre Lachièze-Rey, Emmanuel Gounot, Fr Joseph Chaine, René Biot, Gabriel Madinier, Victor Fontoynont, Albert and Auguste Valensin, Louis Richard, Albert Gelin, Joseph Vialatoux, Paul Couturier, Jules Monchanin, Victor Carlhian, Joseph Hours, André Roullet, Henri de Lubac, Jean Lacroix, André Latreille, Joseph Folliet, Pierre Jouguelet, Pierre Chaillet, Victor-Henri Debidour, Henri Rambaud, Louis Aguettant.[2]

Several other names could easily be added to this list of laypeople and priests, which I propose calling the new intellectual and Catholic school of Lyon. Why 'new'? In the spiritual history of the city since the beginning of the nineteenth century, historians have discovered several earlier 'Lyon Schools': one is a 'mystical school', rich in artists, writers, and scholars, but above all in founders of works and congregations, which Joseph Folliet, one of its faithful heirs, defined as representing 'the refusal to separate contemplation, speculative thought and action'.[3] Another is esoteric or occult in type, going from Jean-Baptiste

---

[1] Translated from the French by Gemma Simmonds, CJ. This is an extended and corrected version of the text which appeared in Emmanuel Gabellieri and Pierre de Cointet (eds.), *Actes du Colloque Maurice Blondel et la philosophie française* (Paris: Parole et Silence, 2007), 263–73.

[2] Quotation from François Varillon, 'Feuilles de route', *Chronique sociale*, reproduced in *Beauté du monde et souffrance des hommes, entretiens avec Charles Ehlinger* (Paris: Centurion, 1980), 75.

[3] Joseph Folliet, 'L'École mystique de Lyon et la Chronique sociale', in M. Pacaut, J. Gadille, J.-M. Mayeur, and H. Beuve-Méry (eds.), *Religion et politique; les deux guerres mondiales; histoire*

Willermoz to Nizier Philippe, via Allan Kardec; this was less concerned with action than with speculative thought.[4] At the other extreme, there is a social school, which closely linked contemplation and action from the end of the nineteenth century, whose crowning glory is none other than the *Chronique sociale*, the origin and underpinning of many initiatives mentioned here.[5]

At the beginning of the twentieth century, when anticlericalism reigned triumphant and the Modernist crisis was brewing, its enemies from both the left and the right thought they had identified another 'Lyon School', a small, informal group of Catholic figures who had been brought together, according to Bernard Comte, by a threefold concern. First, the rejection of a brutal confrontation with the lay republic; second, 'the demand for free enquiry and a critical spirit' within the ecclesial domain; and third, 'the desire for a purified religion which went beyond narrow confessionalism'.[6] This project did not survive the storms of anti-Modernism, being subject to severe attack by an intransigent Catholicism. The quiet voice of this 'Lyon School' and the weekly *Demain*, which was associated with it, fell silent of its own accord in 1907, in the aftermath of the Holy Office's decree *Lamentabili*, without leaving any real heirs. After World War I, only one of its members, the 'broad-minded' Joseph Serre could be found within the *Chronique sociale* and in the Lyon Society of Philosophy, until his death in 1937.

The principal aim of this chapter is to prove the existence of a new 'Lyon School' in the inter-war period. This school was in no way the offspring of the one that preceded it, but driven by the anti-Modernist reaction, it echoed in minor ways at least part of the earlier spirit without being its direct heir. Apart from this partial affinity, at least two other characteristics make it possible to develop the analogy. On the one hand, it was formed as a network with neither fixed borders nor a single point of origin, incorporating instead the cross-over

de Lyon et du Sud-Est: mélanges offerts à M. le doyen André Latreille (Lyon: Marius Audin, 1972), 581–602 (588); and, earlier, Joseph Buche, *L'École mystique de Lyon (1776–1847): Le grand Ampère, Ballanche, Cl.-Julien Bredin, Victor de Laprade, Blanc Saint-Bonnet, Paul Chenavard, etc.* (Lyon: A. Rey, 1935).

[4] Christine Bergé, *L'au-delà des Lyonnais: Mages, Médiums et Francs-Maçons du XVIIIᵉ au XXᵉ siècle* (Lyon: Lugd, 1995).

[5] Bruno-Marie Duffé, 'Gabriel Matagrin et l'École lyonnaise: Dialogue social et transcendance', in Denis Maugenest (ed.), *Le mouvement social catholique en France au XXᵉ siècle* (Paris: Cerf, 1990), 89–115 ('Une école lyonnaise de la pensée chrétienne', 91); see also Jean-Dominique Durand and Bernard Comte (eds.), *Cent ans de catholicisme social à Lyon et en Rhône-Alpes* (Paris: Éditions Ouvrières, 1992); and 'Catholicisme social: l'École lyonnaise', *Théophilyon*, X/1, (2005) 7–143.

[6] Quotations taken from Bernard Comte, 'Un rassemblement de catholiques libéraux: la naissance à Lyon de la revue *Demain* (1905)', in *Les catholiques libéraux au XIXᵉ siècle* (Grenoble: Presses universitaires de Grenoble, 1974), 239–80 (268); see also Louis-Pierre Sardella, 'Autour de l'École de Lyon et de la revue *Demain*: L'émergence d'une nouvelle forme d'anticléricalisme croyant?', in *L'anticléricalisme croyant (1860–1914): Jalons pour une histoire* (Annecy-le-Vieux: Université de Savoie, 2004), 161–81.

of multiple intellectual initiatives applied in varying ways by institutions like the *Chronique sociale*, the Catholic faculties or the university seminary. On the other hand, it also held a minority position, although it had a bright future at the heart of Lyon Catholicism, which was then largely dominated by the intransigence of the Congrégation des Messieurs, the daily *Le Nouvelliste*, and the archbishop's office, at least until the death of Cardinal Maurin. The three last names in Fr Varillon's list are worth noting: Victor-Henri Debidour, Henri Rambaud, and Louis Aguettant. It was they and a few others[7] who between 1918 and 1928 gathered around the *Revue fédéraliste*, whom Antoine Lestra did not hesitate to name 'The Lyon School' in *La Croix* on 23 April 1921. This school, close to Charles Maurras in literature as in politics, and anxious to establish intellectual and ecclesial order, was in fact more representative of the Catholicism of 1920s Lyon than the one whose emergence is being traced here.[8] In many respects it was not the new Lyon schools, however, which became famous, but rather their rival, the 'new' Catholic school of Lyon.

AN EARLY ORGANIZATION

It is striking how the new Lyon school spread in the aftermath of the Great War, as if it was necessary to work twice as hard to fill a double void: the one left by the victims of the conflict, of course; but also the one left by the victims of the increasing anti-Modernist rigidity of the years 1907–14. We will have to be satisfied with establishing the chronology of the birth of this new 'Lyon School', without being able to investigate every one of the branches within its own history, before attempting to describe its originality in comparison with its precursors.

Although they challenged a number of Modernist innovations, Albert Valensin, a Jesuit professor in the faculty of theology from 1910, the master gilder Victor Carlhian, and the philosopher Joseph Vialatoux, suffered the full rigours of the end of Pius X's pontificate. Albert Valensin, a close disciple of Maurice Blondel, was affected by the suspicion that surrounded Blondel on account of his article on the 'Method of Immanence' in the *Dictionnaire apologétique de la foi catholique*, jointly edited by the Valensin brothers, Albert, and the philosopher Auguste.[9] The principal coordinator within the

---

[7] Charles Forot and Louis Pize from the Ardèche or Louis Émile Mercier from Forèze.

[8] Louis Aguettant, *La vie comme une œuvre d'art: Biographie*, (ed.), Jacques Longchampt (Paris: L'Harmattan, 2006), 342–3; see further, Alexis Mercier, 'La Revue fédéraliste: Une tentative décentralisatrice lyonnaise, 1918–1928', unpublished Master's dissertation (Université Lumière-Lyon II, 1997).

[9] A pamphlet published in 1912 in which the younger brother undertook the task of explaining the method in question, while the elder analysed it; article republished in vol. ii,

Lyon branch of the Sillon,[10] Victor Carlhian, submitted without hesitation, but not without regret, to its pontifical condemnation in 1910, and with still greater difficulty to the silencing of his teacher, the Oratorian Lucien Laberthonnière, in 1913.[11] Joseph Vialatoux, a member of staff at the *Chronique sociale*, long retained an unhappy memory of the polemic raised within fundamentalist circles against it.[12] It was men such as these, in mourning for what they loved and believed in, who, along with certain others, played the key roles in the new 'Lyon School', which came together surprisingly quickly after the dual massacre, military and religious, from which they had just escaped.

In 1917 the Bourbonnais Jacques Chevalier, a disciple of the disapproved-of Guillaume Pouget, himself forbidden to teach in 1905 on account of his non-conformism, arrived to teach philosophy to the boys of the Lycée Ampère and the Lycée Parc in Lyon, gathering a group of second-year students around him who stayed in touch with him when he was appointed Professor at the University of Grenoble in 1919–20 (André Fugier, Léon Husson, André Latreille, and others).[13] In October 1919, at the time when Pierre Lachièze-Rey succeeded Chevalier at the Lycée du Parc, Victor Fontoynont, a recently demobilized Jesuit, was assigned to teach humanities at the day school in rue Sainte-Hélène, before distinguishing himself as Chair of Philosophy of the *grand collège* of Notre-Dame de Mongré, near Villefranche-sur-Saône. His superiors argued that his proximity to Auguste Valensin, and thus to the thought of Maurice Blondel, rendered him questionable as a member of the teaching body of the Scholasticate in philosophy in Jersey, where he was destined. The blessing of the temporary chapel and the foundation stone of the church of Notre-Dame Saint-Alban took place on 14 October and 23 November 1919. This project had been nurtured before and during the war by Frs Jean and Laurent Remillieux with Victor Carlhian, who owned a

---

(Paris: Beauchesne, 1915, cols. 579–612). Maurice Blondel was delighted with this publication (letter to Auguste Valensin of 22 September 1912, *Correspondance* ii (Paris: Aubier, 1957), n° 285).

[10] Editorial note: The journal *Le Sillon*, and its associated movement, developed in 1894 out of meetings led by Marc Sangnier, whose 'Cercles d'Études', encompassing students and young workers, sought to form an elite of young Catholics to evangelize France.

[11] 'Since the *Annales de Philosophie Chrétienne* disappeared in 1913, I do not think I have felt so scandalized as I did on Friday when I learned that you have been relieved of your duties', he wrote to de Lubac on 19 June 1950, having also declared in 1929 that 'Laberthonnière's *Essais de philosophie religieuse* [had been for him] what Descartes was for Malebranche' (Maurice Villain, *Portrait d'un précurseur: Victor Carlhian, 1875–1959* (Paris: Desclée de Brouwer, 1965), 126).

[12] 'Being no longer young, I have painful memories of the years before 1914 in which we suffered under the unbridled curse of this distortion [fundamentalism]. Those who remember it can have no difficulty in recognizing its revival in our own day'; letter to Régis Jolivet, still on the de Lubac affair, 13 July 1950.

[13] For a definitive reference, see the Lyon volume of *Le Lyonnais—Le Beaujolais* du *Dictionnaire du monde religieux dans la France contemporaine*, in which most of the names quoted here appear, (ed.) Xavier de Montclos (Paris: Beauchesne, 1994).

property on the edge of the deprived zone of the Monplaisir *quartier*. The new 'Lyon School' would often meet in this modest building, which became the centre of a fully-fledged parish from October 1924.[14]

In May 1920, Victor Carlhian bought a summer residence in the northern Vercors, opposite the Charterhouse. Immediately he brought Fr Paul Couturier there, his sons' science teacher in the Institution des Chartreux and one of his part-time chaplains, who was one of the first to participate in one of Albert Valensin's earliest retreats for priests on the Ignatian *Spiritual Exercises*. In October 1920, Auguste Valensin was removed from the Scholasticate in Jersey, for the same reasons as Victor Fontoynont a year before him, and assigned to Lyon, as his brother's substitute in theology, then as Professor of Philosophy in the Catholic faculty of Literature at the start of the academic year in 1921. Also in October 1920, Jacques Chevalier sent a 'Note on the organization of intellectual collaboration and of work in common' to his young disciples in Lyon and Grenoble (Paul Belmont, Louis Bourgey, Louis Garrone, Jean Lacroix, and others). This was followed a year later by the constitution of the 'Work in Common Group', led by Chevalier with the support of Victor Carlhian, whom he had met in 1919. The Group, which rarely met in plenary session, functioned as an exchange of ideas by means of carbon-copied notes which circulated among its members from June 1921 onwards.[15] Finally, it was probably in the autumn of 1920 that another, more discreet, group, the *Elegi Principem Iesum* or EPI[16] was born, at the instigation of Colonel André Rouillet with Albert Valensin as chaplain. What was its aim? The formation and religious education of influential members of society, priests and laity, from Lyon or elsewhere, by means of two sets of carbon-copied notes per month, one of spiritual content, the other on a current topic. With certain reservations, on account of the deliberate confidentiality within the EPI, whose members only gathered once a year during the summer in the Jesuit retreat house in Châtelard, Francheville, we find something like the new 'Lyon School' at prayer.

In January 1921, Victor Carlhian, at his own expense, published a small bibliographical review, *Le Van*, which was set the task of sifting through everything being published, above all in the religious, philosophical, scientific and social fields. Besides Carlhian's editorials, which deserve to be studied for their own sake, since they constitute the distilled thought of this intellectual who was turned aside from his philosophical and scientific vocation by business, *Le Van* paid honour to his friends' work, beginning with that of Chevalier, who

---

[14] Natalie Malabre, 'Le religieux dans la ville du premier vingtième siècle: La paroisse Notre-Dame Saint-Alban d'une guerre à l'autre', unpublished Ph.D. thesis (Université Lumière-Lyon II, 2006).

[15] Étienne Fouilloux, 'Le Groupe de travail en commun de Jacques Chevalier (1920–1940)', in *Bulletin de la Société Historique, Archéologique et Littéraire de Lyon* 2002, xxxii (Lyon, 2004), 361–77.

[16] 'J'ai choisi Jésus pour roi'; see Henri Hours, 'L'E.P.I.', *Église à Lyon*, 3 February, 1997, 63–4.

envisaged using the bulletin as the cornerstone of his Group's major philosophical journal . . . which would never see the light of day.[17]

After a break in 1922, the movement resumed in February 1923, with the
establishment of the Lyon Philosophical Society by Charles Chabot, Dean of
the Faculty of Letters in the State University. Far be it from me to give the
credit for this lay initiative to the Catholics of Lyon! It is striking, however, to
note the extent of the place occupied within it by Catholic thinkers. Carlhian,
Chevalier, Vialatoux, and Auguste Valensin figure among its founder members, soon to be reinforced by Pierre Lachièze-Rey, Jean Lacroix or Gabriel
Madinier; Carlhian and Valensin would hold the presidency; and the new
'Lyon School' participated actively in its work. Although admittedly an exception, six out of eight communications during 1925–6 session came from
within it, among whose authors were Dr René Biot, Jacques Chevalier, and
Joseph Vialatoux. Lacking a proper editorial outlet the Society published a
typed report of its speeches and discussions, edited by Victor Carlhian.[18]

Along with the Notes of the EPI and those of the Work in Common Group,
these are three archives of unofficial literature, which a group of some of
the most noteworthy intellectuals of Lyon received every month. *Le Van*, the
'Revue critique des Idées et des Livres', according to its own definition,[19]
having little in common with the weekly *Demain*, we can say that the new
'Lyon School' was a carbon-copied school, even a *samizdat* school before its
time, less than twenty years after the Modernist crisis.

In 1924, for example, not without opposition from the bishops of Grenoble
and Lyon, Chevalier and Carlhian edited and circulated *ad usum privatum*,
thus without an *imprimatur*, Guillaume Pouget's major work, *L'origine surna-
turelle ou divine de l'Église catholique d'après les données de l'histoire*. Supplemented by a series of related publications,[20] in a spirit of openness, while
wishing to remain compatible with orthodoxy, this book resumed some of the
key questions which were being asked at the time of the Modernist crisis. At
the beginning of the 1930s the Carlhian organization also reproduced unpublished texts by Teilhard de Chardin, beginning with *Le Milieu divin*.[21]

[17] He listed several hundred examplars. The total of 3,000, suggested by Jean Guitton and
Maurice Villain subsequently, seems a considerable exaggeration; see Françoise Buclet, '"Le
Van", Revue lyonnaise de bibliographie, 1921–1939', unpublished Master's dissertation (Université Lumière-Lyon II, 1995).
[18] Victor Carlhian, 'Rappel d'histoire', communication of 2 June 1935, 8 carbon-copied pages.
[19] 'Avertissement au lecteur', January 1921, 2.
[20] *L'origine du mal moral et de la chute primitive*, 1927; *Le Christ et le monde moral*, 1929;
Inspiration de la Bible, 1930; *La rédemption du monde moral par le Christ*, 1931 (list taken from a
letter sent by Carlhian to the director of the Bibliothèque Nationale, 22 March 1950, copy).
[21] Note by de Lubac on the letter of 17 October 1932 to Fr Auguste Valensin, in *Lettres
intimes de Teilhard de Chardin* (Paris, Aubier Montaigne, 1974), 234.

On 22 November 1924, under the protective shadow of the *Chronique sociale*, there gathered for the first time the medical, philosophical, and biological study group from Lyon on the initiative of Dr René Biot, the local promoter of a form of a holistic medicine. After Auguste Valensin turned down the invitation, the theological accompaniment of this group fell to the young Fr Jules Monchanin, a neighbour of Notre-Dame Saint-Alban. Supported financially by Carlhian, Dr Biot was a member of the Work in Common Group and of the Lyon Philosophical Society, as was Monchanin.[22]

When the university year resumed in 1926, the Jesuit Theologate of the provinces of Lyon and Paris returned to Fourvière for almost half a century. There, an 'academy', which gave itself the ironic name of 'La Pensée', persisted around Joseph Huby. He had been diverted from theology towards exegesis because he was a disciple of Fr Pierre Rousselot, whose ideas about the 'eyes of faith' were banned from being taught within the Society of Jesus from 1920 onwards. Its keenest members were some scholastics at the end of their studies, Gaston Fessard, Henri de Lubac, and Yves de Montcheuil. Although he was supported by Victor Fontoynont, who had known him during his regency at Mongré, this fact drew early attention to Fr de Lubac, preventing him from being able to pursue doctoral studies in Rome, and 'promoting' him in 1929 to a chair in the faculty of Theology, replacing Albert Valensin, who was increasingly taken up with his retreat and preaching ministry.[23]

At the end of the 1920s the key members of the new 'Lyon School' were therefore in place. The beginning of the 1930s brought few additions. Mention should nevertheless be made of the appointment in 1932 of Victor Fontoynont as prefect of studies in the Fourvière Theologate, at the end of a crisis which he seemed best able to resolve. Around him there gathered a group of professors and scholastics, familiarly christened 'the Fontoynont Group', from which would eventually emerge not only Éditions du Cerf's *Sources chrétiennes* series in 1942 and Éditions Aubier's *Théologie* two years later, but also the clandestine *Cahiers* and *Courriers du Témoignage Chrétien* from 1941 onwards.[24] In January 1933, after Albert Valensin had freed him from some of his inhibitions, Paul Couturier launched the Week of Prayer for Christian Unity in Lyon, which was to have a bright future. Who was his first preacher? Albert

[22] Régis Ladous (ed.), *Médecine humaine, médecine sociale: Le Docteur René Biot (1889–1966) et ses amis* (Paris: Cerf, 1986); Rachel Laulagnier, 'Le Groupe lyonnais d'études médicales, philosophiques et biologiques, 1924–1969', unpublished Master's dissertation (Université Lumière-Lyon II, 1997).

[23] Fouilloux, *La collection 'Sources chrétiennes': Éditer les Pères de l'Église au XXᵉ siècle* (Paris: Cerf, 1995), 54–64.

[24] To the well-known work of François and Renée Bédarida, we should add Bernard Comte's contribution 'Les jésuites', in *L'intelligence d'une ville: Vie intellectuelle et culturelle à Lyon entre 1945 et 1975* (Lyon: Bibliothèque municipale, 2006), 55–66.

Valensin, naturally, who had awoken him to the problem by immersing him in work helping Russian refugees in 1922 and 1923.[25]

At the heart of the network, as will be realized simply by the recurrence of the same names, the same men engaged in a proliferation of collaborations, whether it was Victor Carlhian, ubiquitous in managing and organizing, the Valensin brothers, in particular the elder, Albert, whose role as a spiritual director as much as a thinker is deserving of separate study, or the laymen René Biot and Joseph Vialatoux. The example of the French *Semaines sociales* clearly shows the pivotal role played by the new 'Lyon School', well beyond the confluence of the Saône and the Rhône: five times over the Albert Valensin–Joseph Vialatoux duo furnished them with an important part of their intellectual armour, in 1922, 1923, 1924, 1927 and 1933; at Clermont-Ferrand in 1937, on the theme of human rights, 'four or five lessons [were] given by one of the members of the EPI', rejoiced Colonel Roullet.[26]

WAS IT A REAL SCHOOL?

If we take it in the strict sense, the term hardly applies: in fact no permanent organization employed all these characters of such divergent status and interests. Nevertheless, their contributions and their work bear a distinct family resemblance which allows us to think of them, despite their particularities, as a true school of thought.

But what drew together men who can be found at the dawn of several daring innovations within French Catholicism, beyond the bonds of friendship to which their correspondence bears ample witness? It was certainly not the desire to play a role on the political, local, or national scene. From this point of view, the condemnation of the Sillon movement had had an impact: the Édouard Aynard of the new 'Lyon School' would be sought in vain.[27] Such a rejection of explicit commitment, even in view of the great ideological conflicts of the end of the 1930s, is nevertheless not evidence of a lack of interest. Whether intellectuals by profession or by desire, the members of the new 'Lyon School' only intervened in the sphere of politics, in its broad sense, within their own territory, that of ideas, when it seemed to them that the integrity of Christian faith was under threat. This was how they were all,

---

[25] Fouilloux, 'La vocation tardive de l'abbé Couturier', in *L'œcuménisme spirituel de Paul Couturier aux défis actuels* (Lyon: Profac, 2003), 15–43.

[26] Roullet himself, René Biot, Jean Lacroix, Joseph Vialatoux, and no doubt the lawyer Emmanuel Gounot (Note for the month of August); see Jean-Dominique Durand (ed.), *Les Semaines sociales de France, 1904–2004* (Paris: Parole et Silence, 2006).

[27] Sylvie Geneste, 'Édouard Aynard, banquier, député, mécène et homme d'œuvres (1837–1913)', unpublished Ph.D. thesis (Université Jean-Moulin–Lyon III, 1998).

including Jacques Chevalier, immunized by their teachers Pouget, Blondel, and Laberthonnière against the attraction of *Action française*.[28] And in the person of Joseph Vialatoux, Lyon supplied one of the most vigorous critics of Maurras's positivism at the time of the Roman sanctions at the end of the 1920s.[29] After the riots of February 1934[30] and, even more so after the Spanish Civil War, an irreparable breach nevertheless opened up between Chevalier and his companions (Fugier, Garronne, Guitton, and Husson), driven by a growing fear of Communist subversion, and most of the Lyon School, who for their part refused to choose between the two totalitarian threats of Communism and Fascism. There is nothing surprising, therefore, in the fact that different choices disrupted their public relationship after the calamity of 1940: whereas Jacques Chevalier was briefly in charge of national education in Vichy, from September 1940 to February 1941, most of his former friends from Lyon leaned towards the side of the Resistance. These political differences nevertheless did not prevent their philosophical or theological convergences, which would re-emerge after the War.

On the intellectual and spiritual planes which were most familiar to them, the members of the new 'Lyon School' found themselves first of all sharing the same concern for fidelity to the heritage they had received. Their teachers, whether it was Pouget and Bergson in the case of Chevalier, Blondel in the case of the Valensin brothers, or Laberthonnière for Carlhian, had fallen victim, to varying degrees, to the anti-Modernist repression. At the beginning of the 1920s, teachers and disciples were still suffering the consequences of this trial, which in their eyes was unjustified.[31] Far from denying the positive legacy of the questions and some of the responses from before 1914, on the contrary, they sought to make them bear fruit by demonstrating their perfect compatibility with the Catholic faith. If they rejected any relationship with the Modernism condemned by the church, they nevertheless did not belong in the camp of the zealots who tended to stigmatize as Modernist the least divergence from the fundamentalist authorized version.

What is significant in this respect is their attitude to Thomism, whose hardening orthodoxy, according to Marie-Dominique Chenu's much deplored expression, served as a doctrinal instrument of repression. Some among them,

---

[28] There were nevertheless two exceptions: Paul Couturier, whom Victor Carlhian and Albert Valensin separated from Maurras; and the young Joseph Hours.

[29] Bernard Comte, "'*Morale et politique*'" (1927–1934): collaboration and exchanges between Vialatoux, J. Maritain and H. de Lubac', *Théophilyon*, X/1 (2005), 45–65.

[30] Editorial note: Anti-parliamentary demonstrations by far-right groups in Paris on 6 February 1934 ended in riots, but were perceived, especially on the left, as a failed fascist coup attempt.

[31] In 1926, without asking his opinion, Fr Adhémar d'Alès, editor of the *Dictionnaire apologétique de la foi chrétienne*, substituted Albert Valensin's comprehensive opinion with a lively critique of the method of immanence by his *confrère* Joseph de Tonquédec, who had also attacked Maurice Blondel.

such as Victor Carlhian, were frankly allergic to it. Others, like Joseph Vialatoux and the Jesuits carried solid Thomist baggage; some a reformulated
Thomism in the spirit of Rousselot and Maréchal, found in the likes of Joseph
Huby or Henri de Lubac; and yet others, a Thomism severely obliterated by
familiarity with Pascal or Newman, and even more with Blondel's philosophy
of action in the Valensin brothers, or Bergson's philosophy of movement and
duration in Jacques Chevalier. The men of the new 'Lyon School' were less in
search of a metaphysics of being than of a philosophy of the person committed
to the common work of constructing a world worth living in. They did not
conceive of this philosophy as separate from the theology to which it aspired
and which potentially generated a theology of a collective history of salvation
nourished in its essentials by a return to biblical sources and the rediscovery
of the patristic sources of the Christian faith. This is the origin of their
role as organic intellectuals of social Catholicism, in the footsteps of Maurice
Blondel,[32] and their privileged, courteous but firm debate with the semi-
official philosophy of the state university, that critical idealism with Kantian
roots incarnated by Léon Brunschvicg, which they considered to be individualistic and disembodied.

CONCLUSION

Of necessity less bold than its predecessor, the new 'Lyon School' knew how
to hold the balance between two sets of symmetrical pitfalls: a full-blooded
nationalism and an aggressive rationalism, on the one hand, and modernist
hypercriticism and Roman intransigence on the other. At the level of Lyon and
its radius, its intellectual and spiritual research participated fully in this third
way, whose fruitfulness I have tried to demonstrate elsewhere, as born of the
desire to escape the reductionist Modernism-conservatism polarization of
the preceding period.[33] It assumed this function with varying fortunes during
the 1930s. Certain of its initiatives would be increasingly successful. Without
claiming to reform the church, a task that remained forbidden, the Notre-
Dame Saint-Alban parish project carved out a considerable reputation with
its concrete results in this area.[34] The spiritual ecumenism of Fr Couturier
successfully resumed, though of course on other foundations, the desire for

[32] Emmanuel Gabellieri, 'Catholicisme social et "métaphysique en action": La pensée de
Joseph Vialatoux', *Théophilyon*, X/1, (2005) 9–43; 'L'esprit de *L'Action*: Lyon et le *Vinculum*
blondélien', in *Maurice Blondel et la philosophie française*, 277–90.
[33] Étienne Fouilloux, *Une Église en quête de liberté: La pensée catholique française entre
modernisme et Vatican II, 1914–1962*, 2nd edn. (Paris: Desclée de Brouwer, 2006).
[34] Natalie Malabre, 'Le religieux dans la ville du premier vingtième siècle'.

reconciliation of the 'Belle Époque'.[35] The annual publications of the Biot Group, published by Lavandier, courageously approached delicate questions at the frontiers of medicine and psychology. As for the Lyon Philosophical Society, it welcomed the second congress of similar societies in April 1939.[36]

However, other endeavours perished. Such is the case of the Work in Common Group, which fell victim to the growing differences between Chevalier and his associates from Lyon; or to the attraction for several of its members of the journal *Esprit*, founded in October 1932 by Emmanuel Mounier, a former student of Chevalier in Grenoble. It can nevertheless pride itself on two late successes: the historic encounter in Paris on 12 February 1933, between Chevalier's two great reference points, Guillaume Pouget and Henri Bergson; and the re-edition by Gallimard in 1941 of Jean Guitton's *Portrait de Monsieur Pouget*, published in the preceding years in instalments in the *Cahiers du Van*, which thus became a publishing success.

The new 'Lyon School' was impoverished by Auguste Valensin's assignment to Nice in 1935, after the severe Jesuit censure of his book on Maurice Blondel, published in collaboration with Yves de Montcheuil the previous year, and when his brother Albert left to preach the *Spiritual Exercises* of Saint Ignatius to his missionary confrères in Asia at the end of 1936. Like Fr Jules Monchanin, who left for India three years after him, he would not return. The School benefited from Jean Guitton's visit from St Étienne to the Lycée du Parc, and above all from the historian Joseph Hours' stay in its preparatory classes in 1936,[37] and the visit in 1937 of the philosopher Jean Lacroix, who became the beacon of the local *Esprit* Group and its link with the *Chronique sociale*.[38] It enjoyed brilliant success with the publication in 1938 of de Lubac's *Catholicisme*, which had been patiently mulled over for years previously by several sections of the network. His definition of Catholicism as an eminently social phenomenon, drawn from the best sources of the church's ancient tradition, but also from his teachers and friends Blondel or Teilhard de Chardin, is undoubtedly one of the best illustrations of the new 'Lyon School', and is recognized as such at the heart of the nebula whose unity this paper has tried to restore.[39] One of its last collective manifestations was nevertheless an indignant protest against the sanction which banished de Lubac from Lyon in June 1950, a

---

[35] Editorial Note: The 'Belle Époque' refers to the period leading up to the First World War, subsequently perceived as a 'Golden Age'.

[36] Jean-Marc Gabaude, *Un demi-siècle de philosophie en langue française (1937–1990): Historique de l'Association des Sociétés de philosophie de langue française* (Montréal: Éditions Montmorency, 1990).

[37] He returned to teach in Lyon in 1928.

[38] Bernard Comte, 'Jean Lacroix dans les années 30: militant et pédagogue', in *Cahiers Emmanuel Mounier*, n° 96, December 2006, 19–44.

[39] See, among others, Dominique Bertrand, 'Patristique et apologétique, *Catholicisme*', in *Bulletin de l'Institut Catholique de Lyon*, n°116, January–March 1997, 17–29; and Pierre Vallin, '*Catholicisme*: le Père de Lubac au seuil d'une œuvre', *Théophilyon*, X/1 (2005), 67–108.

protest launched by Victor Carlhian and relayed to the Roman authorities by Cardinal Gerlier, Maurin's successor who, in contrast to his predecessors, rapidly forged personal bonds with a number of its members.

Without going as far as to ratify Varillon's opinion that 'Lyon was at that time the religious capital of France',[40] I have tried to show the originality of the new 'Lyon School' amid the French intellectual currents between the wars. In a national context largely dominated by the different variants of Thomism in Catholic circles and by the secular rationalism of Kantian origin in university circles, despite the late breakthrough of phenomenology emanating from beyond the Rhine, the new 'Lyon School' maintained a line of interpretation of Christianity that was at the same time personalist and social, a tributary of its return to biblical and patristic sources and considerable borrowings from philosophies of conscience or from action cruelly shaken by the Modernist crisis.

---

[40] François Varillon, *Beauté du monde et souffrance des hommes*, 74.

6

Gagnebet's Hidden *Ressourcement*: A Dominican Speculative Theology from Toulouse

Henry Donneaud, OP[1]

INTRODUCTION

Marie-Rosaire Gagnebet[2] entered the Dominican province of Toulouse in 1927,[3] studying at the *studium* in Saint-Maximin and doing his doctorate in Rome under the supervision of Réginald Garrigou-Lagrange from 1935 to 1937. Garrigou-Lagrange immediately recruited him onto the teaching faculty at the Angelicum, where he spent his entire career. From 1939 onwards, he became noted for his relentless critique of the controversial *Essai sur le problème théologique* by his Belgian *confrère* Louis Charlier, which was placed on the Index three years later.[4] He was a member of the preparatory

---

[1] Translated from the French by Gemma Simmonds, CJ.

[2] The only study available today on Gagnebet is Étienne Fouilloux's serious, precise, and balanced account, 'Du rôle des théologiens au début de Vatican II: un point de vue romain', in A. Melloni, D. Menozzi, G. Ruggieri, and M. Toschi (eds.), *Cristianesimo nella storia, Saggi in onore di Giuseppe Alberigo* (Bologna: Il Mulino, 1996), 279–311; see also his 'Dialogue théologi-que? (1946–1948)', in Serge-Thomas Bonino (ed.), *Saint Thomas au XXe siècle*, Actes du colloque du Centenaire de la *Revue Thomiste* (Paris: Centre National de Livre-Saint Paul, 1994), 153–95.

[3] Editorial Note: The French Dominicans, restored in 1840 as one Province, were divided in 1865 into three Provinces, France, Paris, Lyon (1862), and Toulouse (1865). The Saint-Maximin *studium* would henceforth only serve the Toulouse Province, with a new foundation educating the French friars, first in Flavigny, then in Belgium (Le Saulchoir) in 1903. Ambroise Gardeil and Marie-Dominique Chenu both served as Regent of Studies at Le Saulchoir. The journals *Revue des sciences philosophiques et théologiques* and *Bulletin thomiste* were founded at Le Saulchoir, while *Revue thomiste* was founded by Thomas Coconnier, of Toulouse, in Fribourg. Fouilloux points out that, 'the new editors of the *Revue thomiste* from 1939 had little sympathy for the "historicism" at Le Saulchoir'. Fouilloux, 'Le Saulchoir en process (1937–1942), in *Une école*, 39–59 (53).

[4] Cf. R. Guelluy, 'Les antécédents de l'encyclique *Humani generis* dans les sanctions romaines de 1942: Chenu, Charlier, Draguet', in *Revue d'histoire ecclésiastique*, 81 (1986), 421–97 (469–70).

theological commission for the Second Vatican Council from 1960, participating actively in the drawing up of several preparatory schemas, particularly *De Ecclesia*, before suffering the full force of the 'trauma' of the 'little revolution' during the first months of the Council.[5]

In view of Garrigou-Lagrange's relentless opposition to *ressourcement*, it is somewhat surprising to find Gagnebet listed among the movement's instigators. Nevertheless, a careful reading of his two articles, in 1938 and 1939, devoted to the nature of theology, leads to the adoption of this view. The second article would generally stand as *a priori* evidence to the contrary, since on behalf of scholasticism itself it constitutes a resounding refutation of Charlier's book, which was the origin of *nouvelle théologie*.[6] This long review, however, only serves to set out clearly, as a response to Charlier, the positions developed in Gagnebet's first article, based on a section from his doctoral thesis.[7] Now, beneath the appearance of a pure 'defence and illustration' of scholastic Thomism, these positions in fact introduce important shifts within Thomism by means of a return to a more authentic Aquinas. It would appear, therefore, that we are dealing with what Mettepenningen judiciously suggested calling 'Thomist *ressourcement*'.[8]

Theological *ressourcement* means a theological renewal based on the revitalization of the authentic sources of Christian tradition (scripture, the Fathers, liturgy), supposedly obscured, rendered sterile, even distorted by more recent, less pure traditions. By analogy, it seems appropriate to apply this concept to the Thomist tradition, itself part of the Christian tradition and living largely by the same spiritual and intellectual laws. *Ressourcement* therefore means a return to the authentic Aquinas, with a view to extricating certain of his insights and key positions, which later scholastic tradition may have neglected, ossified, changed, or even contradicted. The appeal to history and its methods, as well as an openness to contemporary concerns, appear to be the primary indicators of such a process. In this sense, according to Mettepenningen, the names Chenu, Congar, Gilson, and Maritain spring immediately to mind.

This chapter will focus on three essential criteria of *ressourcement*, in order to establish the extent to which Gagnebet's theory concerning the nature and method of theology belongs to it. First, a reformist aim which, beginning with a critique of the dominant understanding of theology as too rigid to adapt to

---

[5] Fouilloux, 'Du rôle des théologiens', 309, 311.

[6] M.-R. Gagnebet, 'Un essai sur le problème théologique', *RevTh*, 45 (1939), 108–45.

[7] Gagnebet, 'La nature de la théologie spéculative', *RevTh*, 44 (1938), 1–39, 213–55 and 645–74. The two first editions were later collected into one volume, *La nature de la théologie spéculative* (Paris: Desclée De Brouwer, 1938). For the sake of convenience I refer to the series of articles.

[8] J. Mettepenningen, 'L'*Essai* de Louis Charlier (1938): Une contribution à la *nouvelle théologie*', *RThL*, 39 (2008), 211–32 (231–2).

contemporary needs, argues for a renewed way of conceiving of and practising theology which is more in harmony with current concerns. Second, a historic judgement which moves 'from a more superficial tradition to a deeper one',[9] in order to return to more authentic sources of Christian doctrine. Third, an implementation of the historical method, with a view to a concrete and precise rediscovery of the traditional understanding of theology.

We will therefore discover in Gagnebet the paradoxical case of a *ressourcement* which does not identify itself as such.

A PROFOUND THOUGH HIDDEN REFORM

Gagnebet formulated his theological project as a 'defence and illustration' of Thomist scholasticism in its continuing tradition: on the one hand, defending the truth in the face of attacks which threaten to mutilate it, and on the other exploring and clarifying the truth for its own sake in order to reach a deeper understanding of its inner intelligibility. In seeking to disentangle the essence of speculative theology, his first article, made up of extracts from his doctoral thesis, corresponds to this search for a speculative understanding of truth, according to a specifically speculative aim which Gagnebet seeks to demonstrate precisely characterizes Thomism.[10] His second article, which refutes Charlier's theories, exemplifies his defensive and apologetic intention, namely to re-establish Aquinas' genuine thought deformed (as he saw it) by Charlier, and to avenge the scholastic tradition which he unjustly disparaged. There was already faint but firm evidence of his defensive intention in the notes of his first article, responding to the claims of the Franciscan Jean-François Bonnefoy, whose articles on theology as a science according to Aquinas foretold several of Charlier's conclusions, although from a perspective foreign to the *nouvelle théologie*.[11]

We now turn to what Gagnebet thought he was defending against Charlier. Charlier had mounted an open attack on the 'scholastic doctrine', which he accused of having betrayed Aquinas by increasingly rigidly applying the Aristotelian notion of science to theology, whereas Aquinas, he said, had

---

[9] C. Péguy, 'Avertissement', *Cahiers de la quinzaine*, V, 11 (1 March 1904), in R. Burac (ed.), *Œuvres en prose complètes*, La Pléiade (Paris: Gallimard, 1987–1992), 3 vols., ch. 1, 1305. Quoted with regard to the theological 'revolution' undertaken by the *ressourcement* in the 1930s at Le Saulchoir in Y. Congar, 'Le frère que j'ai connu', in *L'hommage différé au père Chenu* (Paris: Cerf, 1990), 239–45 (242).

[10] Gagnebet, 'La nature de la théologie spéculative', 2–3.

[11] J.-F. Bonnefoy, 'La théologie comme science et l'explication de la foi selon S. Thomas d'Aquin', *EphTh*, 14 (1937), 421–46, 600–31; and 15 (1938), 491–516; reprinted in one volume, *La nature de la théologie selon S. Thomas d'Aquin* (Paris/ Bruges: Vrin/Beyaerts, 1939).

carefully side-stepped such a pitfall by retaining a 'broad' and 'vague' notion of science and by understanding theology as a simple 'explanation of what has been revealed'. The scholastics, he said, had turned theology into a machine for drawing 'new conclusions' and, producing a 'virtual revelation', added to the 'formal revelation' via syllogistic reasoning, thus distancing it from the heart of the faith which Aquinas himself had designated as its proper end.[12] Charlier therefore appealed for a return to Aquinas' position, which did not see theology as a true science and did not conceive its purpose to be drawing new conclusions. In this respect, Aquinas was said to be on the side of 'the current tendencies of theology', in opposition to scholastic ossification.

Gagnebet is not seeking to defend what Charlier is attacking. He wants to demonstrate that what Charlier is attacking, particularly his fixation with 'theological conclusions', is not the true scholastic position; Charlier's critique, therefore, is unfounded. Beneath his apparently conservative purpose lies an authentic return to Thomist sources, with a profound modification of the way in which Thomist theology understands itself, difficult to grasp because it is carefully hidden beneath the apparently unanimous Thomist tradition on this matter. Gagnebet's dominant theory, which supports the value of the speculative and contemplative ends both of faith and of doctrine in Aquinas, consists in separating doctrine from any strictly theological conclusion in favour of the connection of the truths contained in revelation, whereby theological reasoning does not so much allow us to 'deduce' them as to make clear the causal links which unite them.

Without saying as much, Gagnebet does nothing less than overturn the way in which Thomists understand the Aristotelian conception of science. Giving a scientific demonstration does not consist in deducing new, hitherto unknown truths, starting from previously known principles, but in discovering the causal links by which certain already materially known truths find themselves reconnected, like properties, to a greater truth in which they find their *raison d'être* as they do in their own subject.[13] As Gagnebet comments: 'The purpose of scientific demonstration is not essentially the establishment of the existence of facts: its aim is to explain them, to make clear their cause and purpose.'[14]

For Gagnebet, according to the very purpose of theology, adding science to faith therefore consists not in adding new truths deduced from the terms of faith, but in explaining the truths of faith from within, by adding to them a knowledge and intensification of the intelligible links which unite and explain them. Theology's conclusions, like its principles, may well already belong to

---

[12] Louis Charlier, *Essai sur le problème théologique*, Bibliothèque Orientations: Section scientifique, 1 (Thuillies: Ramgal, 1938), 115.

[13] Gagnebet, 'La nature', 229–30.

[14] Gagnebet, 'Le problème actuel de la théologie et la science aristotélicienne d'après un ouvrage récent', *Divus Thomas*, 46 (1943), 237–70 (249).

the formal deposit of revelation; they become conclusions when reasoning makes it possible to 'manifest' them as so many attributes connecting themselves like effects to the essence of their subject, that is, to God, insofar as he has made himself known.[15]

In thus discovering a new interpretation of Aristotelian science, and therefore of the way in which Aquinas understood theology as a science, Gagnebet rejected both Charlier, and his opponents, who held a strictly theological conclusion. Charlier was correct to say that the deduction of new theological conclusions does not correspond to Aquinas' essential intention but, because he did not truly understand what Aquinas meant by science, he wrongly took issue with the scientific quality of theology and the validity of the work of reason thus applied to revelation.

AN INTIMIDATED HISTORICAL JUDGEMENT

In Gagnebet's writing historical judgement is no less discreet, almost to the point of being invisible, as if it dared not declare itself. It is nevertheless clearly present as an underlying, if embryonic, theme.

In his first article, according to the purely speculative purpose which consists in the contemplation of speculative theology's essence for its own sake, we hardly see any historical consideration intervening, unless it be the comparison between Aquinas' speculative concept of theology and the affective and practical concept of St Augustine and his thirteenth-century disciples such as Alexander of Hales, Bonaventure, or Albert the Great. Gagnebet presents his own understanding of the scientific nature of theology as being not new, but in complete conformity with that of the 'great disciples of Aquinas', without thinking it worthwhile to demonstrate this assertion, except by some sketchy references which even careful analysis reveals to be highly inconclusive.[16]

Only three times, in a very discreet and allusive fashion, does Gagnebet offer a glimpse of the way in which he is drawing back from an erroneous interpretation which he hesitates to admit had become current among Thomists: once in the body of the text, without naming any names or periods,[17] twice in notes, of which one refers to Melchior Cano, with no further explanation,[18] and the other cites the names of Vacant and Gardeil, merely quoting the former:

---

[15] Gagnebet, 'La nature', 234.

[16] Gagnebet, 'La nature', 235.

[17] Gagnebet, 'La nature', 234.

[18] Gagnebet, 'La nature', 236, n. 2: 'Nevertheless, if the custom of finding within these texts the understanding of theology deriving from M. Cano and normally attributed to Saint Thomas, were to raise difficulties . . .'.

Fr. Bonnefoy seems above all to wish to demonstrate that Aquinas' theology does not consist in an effort to develop 'the virtualities contained in a proposition of faith', as some say. It seems to be a reaction against a concept of theology attributed to Aquinas which is expressed accurately enough in a text by Vacant quoted by Fr. A. Gardeil (*Le donné révélé et la théologie*, 2nd edn., Juvisy, p. 196): 'Theology understood in its strict sense has as its object theological conclusions, that is to say, not revealed truths, but the consequences which are contained in these truths and which can be drawn by deduction.'

This is what a theologian of the last century expressed in another way when he wrote: 'Deducing truths revealed to people and for people *ex revelatione divina publica* and the greatest number of consequences which they contain, that is the aim and the essential task of the theologian.' If it is to this interpretation that Fr. B. objects, I have to confess that I am in agreement with him that it cannot be found in Aquinas. I believe that it stems from a very materialist interpretation of Aquinas and his principal commentators.[19]

Even knowing from elsewhere the general outline of the position which Gagnebet contradicts without saying so, it would be difficult to guess at the breadth of what is at stake in a quarrel of interpretation introduced within Thomism. Gagenebet clearly does not want to risk compromising the unity, and therefore the authority, of the Thomist school. The same reserve no doubt explains why he refuses to name the author of the second quotation, Thomas Coconnier, none other than the founder of the *Revue thomiste* and principal architect of the Thomist renewal in the Dominican province of Toulouse under the pontificate of Leo XIII.[20]

Clearly, Gagnebet refused to admit that the erroneous position which he criticized in certain people is quite simply that which up until then was held by nearly everyone on the subject, even the most forward-looking Thomists. It can be found in Garrigou-Lagrange[21] and Chenu.[22] Gagnebet seems therefore to have been overwhelmed by his own results, partially similar to those of Charlier.

In Gagnebet's second article, his comparative and historical judgement is barely more explicit. It is a little more insistent on the strict exactitude between Aquinas and his commentators, since this is one of the major points of

[19] Gagnebet, 'La nature', 240, n. 2. The anonymous quotation comes from Thomas Coconnier, 'Spéculative ou positive?', *RevTh*, 10 (1902), 629–53 (643).

[20] On Thomas Coconnier, cf. Henri Donneaud, 'Les cinquante premières années de la *Revue thomiste*', *RevTh*, 93 (1993), 5–25 (5–10); and 'Les origines fribourgeoises de la *Revue thomiste*', in *Mémoire dominicaine* V, Autumn 1994, 43–60.

[21] Cf. R. Garrigou-Lagrange, *De Deo uno, Commentarium in primam partem S. Thomae*, Bibliothèque de la *Revue thomiste* (Paris: Desclée De Brouwer, 1938), 43–4.

[22] M.-D. Chenu, 'La théologie comme science au XIIIᵉ siècle: Genèse de la doctrine de Saint Thomas', *Archives d'histoire doctrinale et littéraire du moyen âge*, 2 (1927), 31–71 (66–7).

Charlier's offensive against the scholastic position.[23] Further, he says little more with regard to the reinterpretation of Thomist exegesis in which he is engaging. In order to limit the spread of the deviation from which the authentic Thomist position was said to have suffered, Gagnebet evokes 'some contemporary authors', and this time goes so far as to name Gardeil himself as the principal culprit, if not the one responsible for its current diffusion:

> In order for Aquinas to have made a science out of theology, it is not necessary for him to have assigned as the purpose of theology, *as several contemporary theologians hold*, non-revealed proposals, it is enough that he should have found room within given revelation for demonstrative reasoning [. . .] Now for [Fr. Charlier], demonstration within theology identifies itself with the reasoning by which a non-revealed proposition is demonstrated, with the help of a proposition of faith, and a proposition of reason. He also wishes to prove, above all else, the impossibility of *the theological conclusion in the strict sense in which Fr. Gardeil has spoken of it*.[24]

Gagnebet did not stop at Gardeil any more than at 'those few contemporary authors'. Presumably he had no intention of publicly refuting his honoured Dominican *confrères*, even when he dared, this time, refer to the one whom he held to be the source of the error: Melchior Cano, the inventor of the 'theological places' and the great master of Dominican Thomism in sixteenth-century Salamanca.

Gagnebet had launched his denunciation from the outset of his article, indicating immediately to Charlier that the 'scholastic position' which he opposed in Gardeil was not that of the 'great Thomist' Cano, whom Gardeil held to be his 'great master in Thomist methodology'. Now, it was Cano who was said to have fundamentally displaced the function and therefore the purpose of theological reasoning. For him, reasoning meant using 'truths held to be certain by the interlocutor in order to make him admit other positions with which he is arguing'. Cano was thus said to have displaced the sense of the words 'principles' and 'conclusions' in theology. From that time on, the principles of theology were assimilated into the truths of faith as a whole, held as certain by the mass of the faithful, whereas conclusions, which were the object of theology, 'were all the truths which the faithful were persuaded to hold by means of these revealed truths'.[25] From here stemmed the fatal deviation according to which the purpose of the work of theology is no longer knowing God in himself by understanding God's revelation, but guaranteeing the truth of deduced conclusions by means of this revelation.

---

[23] Cf. Gagnebet, 'Un essai', 112, Cf. 127, 130, n. 2.
[24] Gagnebet, 'Un essai', 128 (my emphasis); also 113.
[25] Gagnebet, 'Un essai', 108–9.

Gagnebet nevertheless remained discreet to the point of evasion, not attempting the slightest demonstration or even quoting texts. Nor did he say anything of what was at stake at the time, limiting his historical judgement to Cano, who remained for him an exception within the School, so there was no criticism of the other great commentators' fidelity to Aquinas. No historical continuity seemed to link them to 'those contemporary authors' who, like Coconnier, Vacant, Gardeil, or Marin-Sola, were said to have recently witnessed to his regrettable influence.

Gagnebet analysed Cano's work at length in his doctoral thesis, insisting in particular on the extent of the epistemological displacement for which he was responsible, under the direct influence of Renaissance humanism and in response to the attacks of the Reformers. Under the pressure of controversy, Cano was said to have concentrated the purpose of theology on the determination of what is revealed—was such and such a proposition attached to revelation or not (*an sit*)—thus marginalizing, *de facto*, the internal search for an understanding of revelation (*quid sit*). The analytical description of formulas according to how close they were to the sources of revelation would have ended up mattering more than the contemplative meaning of the truths of faith, the real science of the God of revelation.

> As for theological science itself, Cano also places it in this theological perspective of *an est*. Its goal is to know what is taught by God. In the explicit formulations contained in Scripture and Tradition, there are others which can only be seen with the help of human argument. The essential goal of theology, as of science, is to lay them bare.[26]

It is strange that in these articles Gagnebet remains so elliptical about Cano, whereas he was more precise and incisive in the unpublished part of his thesis. Behind the eirenicism of a purely speculative intention, or his anxiety to focus his Thomist defence on an incorrect contemporary interpretation of Aquinas and of scholasticism, it is possible to detect the anxiety of a Thomist viscerally attached to the tradition of the commentators, hesitating in the face of a reproach he would have to address to one of the great names within that tradition.

Furthermore, one wonders if Gagnebet entered easily into this process of shedding light on a contemporary deviation, given that epistemological displacements stemming from certain historical conditionings risked affecting not only a particular author but an entire period within Catholic thought. Was it possible that the intellectual struggle against the Protestant reformers, so legitimate and necessary in his eyes, could have led to such damaging consequences at the very heart of the Thomist tradition? And how was it possible

---

[26] Gagnebet, 'La nature de la théologie spéculative', thesis (Rome: Angelicum, 1937), 321, 333–4. A copy is available in the library of the Dominican friary in Toulouse.

not to suspect that the deviation confirmed in Cano had not in some way contaminated the other 'great commentators' of the modern era? While Chenu, Congar, and Charlier were working valiantly, all flags flying, towards the 'liquidation of baroque theology',[27] with Gagnebet one suspects that, although he had arrived at similar conclusions on precisely this point of the nature of theology, an inner anxiety forbade him to join the militant ranks of the return to sources.

It would not be until the publication of his course on *De natura theologiae* in 1952 that Gagnebet would make explicit certain conclusions drawn from his previous analyses. At that time he recognized that it was not only Cano but 'the writers of the period' who, faced with the Reformation, elaborated 'a new notion of theology which was manifestly different from that of Aquinas and the other medieval Schoolmen'. He then clearly contrasted the theological position of Aquinas and the great Schoolmen of the thirteenth century, including the 'Augustinians' whose goal was the knowledge of God and God's word, with that of modern theologians who were above all concerned with the validity of the propositions of Catholic teaching. But on the precise point of the nature of theology he still said nothing about any of the great Thomist commentators except Cano.[28]

AN EFFECTIVE HISTORICAL DEMONSTRATION

Although formed at the Toulouse *studium*, far from Le Saulchoir, Gagnebet was a rigorous and detailed pioneer of the historical method. It is difficult to avoid thinking that, resentful of the demonstrative power of Chenu's work on the same subject, he did everything possible to show that he was no less scientific in the value he set on genuine Thomism. In a discreet but direct allusion to Chenu, the Regent of Le Saulchoir, he certainly makes clear that his 'aim is not to retrace the historical origins' of Aquinas' conception of sacred science.[29] But he conscientiously defers to the demands of historical method, as much in his speculative research on the essence of this science as in his refutation of Charlier. It is particularly notable that in determining Aquinas' thought, he rarely quotes the great commentators, only referring to them when he tries, *contra* Charlier, to prove their commonality of view with Aquinas.

---

[27] Cf. Y. Congar, *Journal d'un théologien*, ed. with an introduction by Étienne Fouilloux (Paris: Cerf, 2000), 58–9 (extract from 'Mon témoignage', written between 1946 and 1949).

[28] Gagnebet, *De natura theologiae ejusque methodo secundum sanctum Thomam* (Rome: Pontificium Athenaeum Angelicum, 1952), ii.3–4, 57–8.

[29] Gagnebet, 'La nature', 2.

Elsewhere, and doubtless still under the same implicit influence of Le Saulchoir, particularly Chenu's pioneering article on 'Theology as science in the thirteenth century', he developed a long comparative and contextual approach to the Thomist position. Whereas Charlier restricted himself to Aquinas alone without saying anything about his predecessors and contemporaries, Gagnebet was careful, before approaching Aquinas' position, to analyse at length that of Aquinas' Franciscan and Dominican contemporaries. Certainly, in contrast to Chenu, his purpose was more comparative than historical, but Aquinas was effectively resituated in the context of his time, at least doctrinally speaking. Moreover, the idea of theological pluralism, unexpected in the writing of a 'Roman' theologian, is clearly apparent here. Far from being concordist, Gagnebet presented these divergences between an affective theology of Augustinian inspiration (Bonaventure and Albert) and Aquinas' truly speculative theology as completely legitimate, each of them coming under the patronage of Doctors of the Church whose authority was beyond question.

In his exegesis, Gagnebet did not proceed like Charlier, who would juxtapose long and copious passages from Aquinas, with only the occasional brief overall remark, and no further explanation. Gagnebet generally put the numerous quotations from Aquinas into footnotes, often giving only the references for them. But he used detailed explanations, setting one text with another or several notions among themselves, and gave a critical evaluation of the appropriateness of such juxtapositions.[30] Still under the influence of Le Saulchoir, he signalled developments in Aquinas' thought, as for example between the *Sentences* and the *Summa* with regard to theology's procedural methods.[31]

And so we reach the content of the demonstration. The significance of Gagnebet's position rests on the manner in which he manages to prove, by relying on texts, how Aquinas clearly distinguished between two complementary methods within theology, the demonstration 'by authorities' on the one hand, and the demonstration 'by reason' on the other.[32] The first allows us to establish the fact that certain truths belong to revelation and thus to faith (*an ita sit*). The second, by a scientific method, serves to separate a certain explanatory understanding from these truths (*propter quid*). For this Gagnebet used and developed an article from the fourth *Quodlibet*,[33] which became

---

[30] For example, regarding the use made by Aquinas of 1 Cor. 15.12 in order to prove the presence of scientific reasoning within *sacra doctrina*, cf. Gagnebet, 'La nature', 229, n. 1 and 'Un essai', 126–7.

[31] Cf. Gagnebet, 'La nature', 228, n. 2.

[32] Aquinas, *Super Boetium de Trinitate*, prologus et expositio prohemii (Léonine l.76–7). Commentary in Gagnebet, 'La nature', 221–2.

[33] Aquinas, *Quaestiones quodlibetales*, IV, q. 9, a. 3 [18] (Marietti, 83). Commentary in Gagnebet, 'La nature', 223–5; and 'Un essai', 111, 120, 142; and 'Le problème actuel', 253.

emblematic of his exegetical crypto-revolution, since he used it in a pivotal way in all his work on the nature of theology. It is striking that Chenu makes no mention of it in his 1927 article, and Charlier only refers to it once, and then briefly.[34] It is, however, the only article in the whole of his work in which Aquinas treats of theological method, *strictu sensu*, for its own sake, that is, the one used by the university teachers for 'magisterial discussion in their classes'. Here the distinction between the method of authority and the method of reason is made clear. A theological discussion can have two goals: either to do away with a doubt about the existence of a truth of faith, in the face of someone who disputes it (*an ita est*). It is then that authority intervenes, starting from beliefs already held as true by the opponent. But when it is a case of 'making known how a thing is true' which is taught by faith, only reason can intervene, since it alone can help us to penetrate to 'the root of truth'. A teacher of theology should not only 'do away with error but instruct those who hear by leading them to an understanding of the truth with which he is dealing', without which the student 'would leave with an empty head', contenting himself with 'believing' a truth without really 'knowing' it.

On the basis of such a topical text, Gagnebet sets out the heart of his own thesis, before explaining it: 'theology has not for its only goal the demonstration of the existence of revealed truth, but it is seeking to be understood'.[35] Thanks to the *Quodlibet* text, he can both oppose the theory of a new theological conclusion with Charlier against the dominant position illustrated by Gardeil and Chenu, by showing that it does not constitute the proper object of theology according to Aquinas; and, *contra* Charlier, Draguet, and Bonnefoy, he can show how Aquinas applies to theology what is for him most specific within the Aristotelian notion of science, in the proper sense of the word: enquiry into the cause. The *Quodlibet* furnishes all the elements of his exegetical demonstration.

The Aristotelian notion of science finds itself explicitly evoked here by Aquinas, as much in his own way of proceeding as in his goal. When Aquinas speaks of 'reasons which allow us to know', he directly evokes the scientific syllogism whose *raison d'être* is precisely to 'make known'.[36] By saying that the proper purpose of a teacher of theology is the search for the 'root of truth', which is not knowledge of the facts alone, but of its why and wherefore, Aquinas evokes the very purpose of Aristotelian science which is 'an understanding of the truth of the conclusion by means of the demonstration'.[37] The conclusion is not reached simply as a true proposition; it is grasped in its

---

[34] Cf. Charlier, *Essai*, 112.   [35] Gagnebet, 'La nature', 224.
[36] Aquinas, *Expositio libri posteriorum*, I, 4 (Léonine i.ii, 20, ln. 146–7): 'Demonstratio est syllogismus scientialis, id est faciens scire.' The expression comes directly from Aristotle, *Posterior Analytics* i.iv (71b18).
[37] Aquinas, *Expositio libri posteriorum*, i.iv (Léonine i.ii, 20, ln. 142–144). Cf. Aristotle, *Posterior Analytics* i.iv (71b17).

internal truth which is its cause.[38] Now, Aquinas applies this notion of science directly to scholastic theology, insofar as reason seeks within it not faith, which is a matter of authority, but an understanding of faith, 'an understanding of' the already raw truth.

The scientific quality of theology being thus proven, in the Aristotelian sense, Gagnebet can make clear the concrete way in which his way of proceeding is used. Theological reasoning aims to unite revealed truths whose immediate principles play the role of precepts whereas others, being secondary and mediated, become conclusions by their causal attachment to the first. A teacher of theology therefore has the role of leading his hearers to an understanding of faith by drawing out, through scientific reasoning, the connections which structure revelation from within like a prior divine science. Gagnebet refers to the thousands of articles edited by Thomas: according to the explanations given in the article from the *Quodlibet*, nearly all his articles aim to establish such an internal explanation for faith. Gagnebet takes as an example the demonstration of the priesthood of Christ.[39] Here it is certainly not a matter of a new truth obtained through a process of reasoning, since the fact of the priesthood belongs already to faith, through explicit revelation. But theological reasoning allows us to reveal its *raison d'être* by uniting it to its explanatory principles, that is to say the sanctification of humanity and its reconciliation to God. It is therefore clearly the discernible connection between truths of faith which defines the goal of the theologian.[40]

Gagnebet, strengthened by his interpretation of Thomas, used the historical method to criticize Charlier for not having known how to discover the authentic concept of Aristotelian science, in particular as it was understood by Aquinas, and thus of thinking wrongly that the latter did not wish to apply it to theology. Charlier said that he was struck by the 'tide of expressions' Aquinas used to make clear the scientific nature of theology. Gagnebet responded by blaming Charlier for having dispensed himself from needing to prove this claim 'in a scientific manner', for want of having really 'studied in depth' the Aristotelian notion of science in the way Aquinas explained it.[41] It is a fact that Charlier attributed too easily to Aristotle, and to Aquinas' commentary, an understanding of science as the drawing of new conclusions, whereas this is a distorted interpretation which post-dates them both. He did not return to the sources but remained stuck in the same watered-down notion of Aristotelian science as Gardeil, only to draw from it the opposite conclusion: Aquinas did not want to make theology a science in the strict sense.

---

[38] Aquinas, *Expositio libri posteriorum* i.iv (Léonine i.ii, 19, ln. 82–7).
[39] Aquinas, *ST*, 3a.22.1, Blackfriars, l.136–57. Cf. Gagnebet, 'La nature', 235.
[40] Gagnebet, 'La nature', 235.
[41] Charlier, *Essai*, 121; Gagnebet, 'Un essai', 123.

In order to prove that, *de facto*, Aquinas had only presented theology as a science 'in a broad sense', Charlier relied on an objection imported from Aquinas, according to which science cannot be applied to God on account of the simplicity of the divine essence. Gagnebet had no difficulty in retorting that in raising this objection, Aquinas precisely intends to demonstrate, by virtue of another Aristotelian principle, that negations and divine actions *ad extra* take the place of passion that could demonstrably be attributed to the divine essence, and thus 'that theology is indeed a science despite the simplicity of its subject, who is God'.[42] Aquinas finds within Aristotle himself the wherewithal to raise an objection against the application to theology of the Aristotelian notion of science. It is difficult to extract from it, as Charlier does, the opposite conclusion, except by contradicting Aquinas himself.

According to Gagnebet, Charlier had been justified in remarking that Aquinas does not assign as principles of theology every revealed truth, as Gardeil and his companions believed, but only the articles, that is to say the principal truths of faith, but drew the false conclusion that the attachment of conclusions to principles is purely artificial, not scientific, based on the fact that there is no logical necessity uniting the truths of faith to one another. As proof he offered Paul's verse linking the resurrection of believers to Christ's resurrection (1 Cor. 15.12), used by Aquinas as an example of theological argument.[43]

Gagnebet has no difficulty in responding both from reason and from authority. The truths of faith, far from lacking connection, are all united 'by the proper necessity of the science of God and the blessed, in which the divine decrees bestow a hypothetical necessity on the free dispositions of divine wisdom'. It is God himself who desired that, within divine revelation, such means should be ordained to such ends, so that theologians could find within the latter the explanation of the former and thus treat it scientifically. Aquinas' own commentary on this verse of Paul's, which Charlier clearly misses, brings to it an authoritative proof, which explicitly affirms that Paul was here proceeding to an authentic explanation 'by cause' (*locus a causa*), God having willed that the resurrection of humanity should be accomplished through that of Christ. Aquinas, whatever Charlier might say, sees a genuine example of scientific argument in Paul's writing.[44]

The critique of the use of philosophical premises shows that Charlier thinks of the speculative theology he is criticizing in terms of a pure 'metaphysic of what is revealed', applying to the matter of faith a rigid philosophical system and ready-made rational notions, in themselves foreign to revelation. Gagnebet quotes Maritain here in the latter's critique of the Cartesian position in

---

[42] Charlier, *Essai*, 121–3; Gagnebet, 'Un essai', 124–5.   [43] Charlier, *Essai*, 136.
[44] Aquinas, *Super primam epistolam ad Corinthios*, cap. 15, lect. 2 (Marietti, 409–10, n° 913). Quoted with commentary, Gagnebet, 'Un essai', 126–7.

theology, in saying that this would, in fact, amount to 'the actual destruction of speculative theology'.[45] This is not real theology: in real theology, not only does faith control reason, but it subordinates it to itself, in order to rectify it, to orient and perfect it. Theologians, enlightened by faith, continually transform philosophical and revealed concepts in order to render them ever more adequate for their supernatural object, in such a way that it is not reason which appropriates faith to itself, but faith which raises and perfects reason by using it in its service.

Finally, one phrase sums up Gagnebet's judgement on the Thomist exegesis attempted by Charlier with regard to theology as a science: 'He has ended up with an astonishingly primitive notion of that science which is entirely encapsulated within the following expression: "a habitus of conclusions".'[46]

RESSOURCEMENT AND NOUVELLE THÉOLOGIE

At the end of this chapter it seems reasonable to enrol Gagnebet's project within the *ressourcement* movement. A rigorous application of the historical method restored to Aquinas one of his authentic positions obscured in the work of most contemporary Thomists. Strengthened by this, Gagnebet fought for a renewed understanding of the essence of speculative theology that was less materially deductive, more contemplative, and altogether centred on revelation and its understanding. He went as far as promoting a certain theological pluralism. First, by recognizing its true historical place in the affective theology of the Augustinian school, and second, by approving the diversity current within types of Christian thought. It was not only the essential complementarity of positive and speculative theologies, but also the peaceful co-existence of a properly scientific theology, aimed at a speculative understanding of truth, with other types of theological reflection desirous of paying greater attention to the variety of pastoral, spiritual, or cultural expectations of the time. Why should the laudable rediscovery of a symbolic theology like that of the Fathers necessarily imply the disqualification of scientific and speculative theology such as that conceived by Aquinas, each one applied to its proper end and contributing to the expression of an aspect of the Christian mystery and the mission of the church?[47]

---

[45] Gagnebet, 'Un essai', 134, quoting J. Maritain, *Le Songe de Descartes* (Paris: Buchet et Chastel, 1932); J. and R. Maritain, *Œuvres complètes* v.67–8.

[46] Gagnebet, 'Un essai', 143.

[47] Gagnebet, 'Le problème actuel', 265–70. A. Nichols, 'Thomism and the Nouvelle Théologie', *The Thomist*, 64 (2000), 1–19, has successfully depicted this timid but nevertheless genuine openness among the Saint-Maximin Dominicans to the pluralism of methods and goals inherent

Gagnebet's historical demonstration undoubtedly hid a blind spot: the dubious fidelity to Aquinas of the 'great commentators' concerning theological conclusions and the true notion of science. His anxiety, fed by scholastic convictions, about what he might discover seems to have prevented him from venturing too far in his exegesis of the Thomist tradition, and from understanding the origin of the distortion he recorded in Coconnier and Gardeil.

Gagnebet's Thomist exegesis, on the other hand, rapidly gained strength as the most accurate. Congar endorsed it against that of Bonnefoy and Charlier, adopting it with all its underlying implications for the nature of theology.[48] Chenu followed close on his heels with a generous retraction of his earlier claims.[49] Little by little, Gagnebet's discreet exegetical revolution spread slowly but surely, so that nowadays it is part of the common interpretation of theology as a science according to Aquinas.[50] In this regard, insofar as it aims at a return to authentic sources, Thomist *ressourcement* finds itself better expressed in Gagnebet than in Charlier.

Even if not from the outset, Gagnebet's work also laid the foundations of the theological programme of the Dominican school of Saint-Maximin and the *Revue thomiste* between 1935 and 1950. M.-M. Labourdette made full use of it in his manifesto on the nature of theology in 1946, at the very moment when the impossible *Dialogue théologique* was beginning with the Jesuits of Paris and Lyon.[51] Once again we find the *nouvelle théologie*, even though the Dominicans of the Toulouse province, strengthened by their understanding of the sources of the nature of theology, defended its rationality and speculative ambition in the face of those who argued against its relevance and even its validity, in the name of the demands of contemporary culture.

Might we not find here an invitation not to assimilate *nouvelle théologie* and *ressourcement* too hastily? Does not *ressourcement* designate a broader movement than the former which is not co-extensive and not always even consonant with it? *Ressourcement* does not imply, of itself, opposition, marginalization, and finally abandonment of metaphysical reasoning in its

---

in Christian thought, although this would not prevent speculative theology, perfectly constituted in its scientific state, from continuing to be its pinnacle.

[48] Cf. Congar, listed works of Draguet, Bonnefoy, Charlier, and Gagnebet, in *Bulletin thomiste*, 5 (1938), 490–505 (505); and 'Théologie', in *Dictionnaire de théologie catholique* xv, 1946, col. 383–5, 453–6, 459–62; and *La foi et la théologie*, Le mystère chrétien (Paris: Desclée, 1962), 131–2, 171–2.

[49] Chenu, *La théologie comme science au XIIIe siècle*, Pro manuscripto, 2nd edn. 1943, 8–9, 84–5; 3rd edn. (Paris: Vrin, 1957), 10–11, 78, 83–4; and *La théologie est-elle une science?*, Je sais—Je crois 2 (Paris: Fayard, 1957), 63–5.

[50] Cf. J.-P. Torrell, *La théologie catholique*, 2nd edn. (Paris: Cerf, 2008), 60–4.

[51] M.-M. Labourdette, 'La théologie, intelligence de la foi', *RevTh*, 46 (1946), 5–44.

theological assumptions—above all when it is a matter of a Thomist *ressourcement*, and this theological rationality, authentically retrieved and traced to its sources in its speculative aim through the advantages of the historical method, is confirmed as being more in keeping with the teachings of Aquinas, *doctor communis Ecclesiae.*

7

The Traditionalist *malgré lui*: Teilhard de Chardin and *Ressourcement*

A. N. Williams

INTRODUCTION

Pierre Teilhard de Chardin is not an obvious entry in the lists of champions of tradition. Known chiefly for his mystical mix of evolutionary natural science and theology, he seems very much a creature of the twentieth century. Unlike the leading names associated with the *ressourcement* movement, he neither wrote studies of patristic or medieval theology, nor does he even allude frequently to the classic texts and authors of the theological tradition. Although Teilhard is sometimes mentioned in passing in connection with the 'new theologians', he is more usually taken as *sui generis*. One suspects his scientific interests in themselves mitigated against his being viewed as engaged with the Christian past. Sometimes faulted for his lack of knowledge of the tradition, his most obvious commonality with *ressourcement* theologians is that he, too, was censured by the Vatican. This last fact is significant, however: if his interests in the natural sciences and apparent lack of interest in the Fathers and the scholastics makes him seem remote from *ressourcement* theologians, it must equally be said that official censure in itself indicates little of his relation to tradition, given that some of those most obviously engaged in retrieval of the tradition were similarly subject to censure.

Nevertheless, there is no case to be made for Teilhard as a theological archaeologist: his excavations were purely geological. He cannot be taken as engaged in *ressourcement* in the sense that Daniélou or Chenu were, revealing older authors in fresh perspective and with new relevance. Such deliberate and loving unearthing of old treasures is not, however, the only way in which a tradition may be honoured, illuminated, or regenerated from within. Teilhard's theology in fact bears some striking resemblances to patristic and medieval theology and arguably stands in a relation of continuity and development with it. My concern here is not to posit any direct causal link between Teilhard's own engagement with the tradition and the fresh voice he gave to it, but simply to highlight some significant commonalities between his theology and that of the tradition. These commonalities extend well beyond those areas of earlier theology that have entered into general circulation; it is not simply a matter of reiterating the standard doctrines of the Trinity and Christ's person, for example, but in some cases, of a re-presentation of theology now scarcely found outside histories of doctrine.

Before turning to the continuities, though, it is as well to acknowledge the chief difference between the theology of Teilhard and that of either the Fathers or the schoolmen. It is a point, not of doctrinal departure from the theological past, but simply of weight and emphasis. One characteristic which links patristic and medieval theology is their theocentricism. As one progresses beyond the patristic period through the Middle Ages, an increasing turn towards humanity becomes evident. An increased emphasis in piety on the humanity, and especially the sufferings, of Christ, is paralleled by an increased focus on the human person. In piety, this anthropological focus expresses itself in themes such as sin, penitence, and judgement, and in theology, on the development of fuller anthropologies. The theology of the continental Reformers is in this sense the logical extension of—not a reaction against—medieval theology, taking one of its trajectories to a point beyond what the high medieval theologians asserted. Teilhard's theology resembles most post-medieval Western theology in its Christocentricism and anthropocentricism: the Incarnate Christ and the human person lie at the heart of his theology. This focus on the human shifts the weight of his theology away from the purely divine, which was always at the centre of the earlier tradition's theological reflection. This difference is, however, very much a matter of focus rather than substance and, as we shall see, even given this difference of focus, Christology remains an important link between Teilhard's theology and that of the Fathers.

TEILHARD AND THE TRANSFIGURATION OF MATTER

Other differences of emphasis may be more apparent than real. One of these is the theme of matter. Teilhard's interest in—indeed, passion for—matter is one of the leading themes of his theology. Here the contrast with patristic theology seems obvious: on the conventional reading, its pervasive Platonism accounts for both its supposedly negative estimation of the body and its high Christology, the latter not simply oriented towards the cosmic Word rather than the man Jesus, but shy of expatiating on such elements of his humanity as his ignorance or anger, and reluctant to say much of the cross. If one takes this picture to be an accurate portrayal of patristic theology, then Teilhard's emphasis on matter would seem discontinuous.

The notion that patristic theology adopts the Platonic preference for soul over body is arguably a misreading, however: the emphasis on ascetical themes clearly indicates the Fathers did not see matter in general, or the human body in particular, as something to be somehow bypassed in the quest for union with God, but rather as something so integral to human nature that it, too, must be disciplined and sanctified.[1] Teilhard's interest lies admittedly not so much in the body and its need for discipline if the person is to be sanctified, but on matter and the fact that it can be, has been, and is being sanctified. The weight of his analysis lies on divine engagement with matter. In this respect, Teilhard's treatment of matter might be said to exhibit the theocentrism of patristic theology in an area where the Fathers themselves tend towards anthropocentrism.

Nevertheless Teilhard was aware his approach to matter would sound startling to some, even though not necessarily new: 'like the pagan', he wrote, 'I worship a God who can be touched ... I shall only touch God in the world of matter, when, like Jacob, I have been vanquished by him'.[2] Here Teilhard engages in rhetorical artifice (the latter being also a feature of the Fathers' prose), by mischievously suggesting his devotion to the Incarnate Christ in some way resembles pagan idolatry. In one sense, the Christian doctrine of the Incarnation (and its consequents, the doctrines of the resurrection and the sacraments) does bear a resemblance to pagan adoration of material images, though Teilhard could not have been unaware of the significant differences between worshipping God in the flesh and worshipping, say, a bronze statue. We can conjecture the reason for stressing the similarity, rather than the difference: we are accustomed to thinking of idolatry as remote from Christianity, and in shocking his readers into perceiving an element of commonality, Teilhard confronts us with the blunt fact of materiality. Thus far, his assertion seems far from the spirit of the Fathers, for whom idolatry looms large as a theological reference point and constant warning: idolatry is what is strenuously to be avoided. Teilhard's qualification, however, returns him to the spirit of the tradition: although the Incarnate Christ is there to be touched—in the first century in the flesh, and after the Ascension through the sacraments— one can only draw close to this Incarnate One when the whole person is prepared for the encounter. Here, in a provocative affront to the reader's expectations, the insights of the Christian past combine: we worship the Word made flesh, whose way requires surrender to the Holy One, the stripping away of the habits and desires of the world, the flesh, and the devil.

---

[1] I have argued this point more fully in Williams, *The Divine Sense: The Intellect in Patristic Theology* (Cambridge: Cambridge University Press, 2007).
[2] Teilhard, *Hymn of the Universe*, trans. Simon Bartholomew (London: Collins, 1965), 26.

Matter is for Teilhard not merely the crucible in which the embodied human creature meets God, but the means by which the creature is paradoxically drawn closer to the immaterial God. Part of the way he envisages this encounter is sacramental, but for Teilhard, what are properly called sacraments are part of a wider phenomenon. So, in the absence of an altar on which to celebrate, he proposes to make the whole cosmos his altar, offering on it 'the labours and sufferings of the world'.[3] The transformation he sees and seeks is not only that which God works in Christians through the sacraments, but through a fundamental change in orientation, a new way of perceiving and making sense of all creation. 'By means of all created things,' he writes, 'without exception, the divine assails us, penetrates us, and moulds us.'[4] In such bold claims, some saw incipient, or even flagrant, pantheism, but Teilhard is not far from Aquinas' notion that God is in all things by power, presence, and essence,[5] or, as we shall see, from the Eastern Fathers with their sense of the cosmos as the theatre of divine energy.

THE UNION OF ALL THINGS IN GOD

The cosmic dimension of Teilhard's thought is its overarching principle, and one might view it as the product of a scientist's training and habits of looking at the world. Whether prompted in Teilhard by his scientific or his theological training, his constant reference to a universe transfigured by divine energy links him strongly to the thought-world of the Greek Fathers. 'See!', he writes, 'the universe is ablaze!'[6] Matter, which seems to instantiate the particular, the individual, in fact attests to the unity of all creation: 'The farther and more deeply we penetrate into matter . . . the more we are confounded by the interdependence of its parts'.[7] Because of this interdependence, the only way of considering the universe is to take it as a whole 'in one piece'.[8] This conception of interdependence is in turn tied to Teilhard's notion of unity, a unity whose source is the Divine One:

> [T]aken in its main lines, [Christianity] contains an extremely simple and astonishingly bold solution of the world. In the centre, so glaring as to be disconcerting, is the uncompromising affirmation of a personal God: God as

---

[3] Teilhard, *Hymn*, 19.
[4] Teilhard, *Le Milieu Divin: An Essay on the Interior Life*, trans. Siôn Cowell (London: Collins, 1964), 112.
[5] *ST* 1a.8 ad.3, Blackfriars ii.116–17.
[6] Teilhard, *The Prayer of the Universe*, trans. René Hague (London: Collins, 1968), 120.
[7] Teilhard, *The Phenomenon of Man*, rev. ed., trans. Bernard Wall (London: Collins, 1970), 48.
[8] *Phenomenon*, 48.

providence, directing the universe with loving, watchful care; and God the revealer, communicating himself to man on the level of and through the ways of intelligence.[9]

The emphasis on the unity of all things in God as their source and telos is, as it were, the synchronic axis of Teilhard's thought, balanced by the diachronic axis of his notions of development and evolution. The theme of union links the two: he sees both a unity that already exists, in the fact of the created order's origin in God, and a unity that is constantly evolving. That universe is clearly distinct from God (*contra* the accusations of pantheism sometimes laid against Teilhard), though 'invaded' by God, producing union 'without mixture, without confusion'.[10] Its beauty may be 'pagan',[11] but its unity with God is a unity-in-distinction, and it is significant that Teilhard expresses this idea using the language of the Chalcedonian Definition's condemnation of Eutyches.[12] As, per Chalcedon, the divine and human natures in Christ are perfectly united without blending into each other and becoming a *tertium quid*, so are God and the universe.[13] In keeping with the synergistic tenor of his thought, Teilhard regards union as both accomplished by God, and advanced through our perception of what has been and is being done with the universe. Union increases through an increase in consciousness.[14] Humankind does not finally accomplish this union, however: 'Man is not at the centre of the universe as we once thought in our simplicity, but something much more wonderful—the arrow pointing the way to the final unification of the world.'[15] From one perspective, our increased awareness increases union; from another, the rise of our consciousness is the effect of union worked by God.[16]

The fact that we need to grasp the union that already exists in order to further it indicates it has not yet been perfectly accomplished. We see about us both fragmentation and unity, hence we cry 'Lord make us *one*'.[17] Disunity and fragmentation stand in tension with the activity of God: 'the pure heart is the heart which, surmounting the multiple and disruptive pull of created things, fortifies its unity in the fire of simplicity'.[18] The union that stands in contrast to this fragmentation nevertheless represents, not the return to an

---

[9] *Phenomenon*, 320–1.

[10] *Milieu*, 47.

[11] *Milieu*, 47.

[12] Cf. Theodore of Mopsuestia, *On the Incarnation*, V fragment 1; and Maximus the Confessor, *Mystagogy*, 1.

[13] *Hymn*, 109.

[14] *Phenomenon*, 35.

[15] *Phenomenon*, 247.

[16] *Phenomenon*, 268; cf. Maximus the Confessor, *Commentary on the Our Father*, 2.

[17] *Prayer*, 20; cf. Ignatius of Antioch, *Philadelphians*, 2.4; *Didache*, 9; Hippolytus, *Apostolic Tradition*, 4.

[18] *Hymn*, 114; cf. Pseudo-Denys, *Ecclesiastical Hierarchy*, III.1.

original, now lost, state, but a consummation towards which the cosmos was always evolving: 'What is to be brought about is more than a simple union: it is a *transformation*.'[19] Evolution for Teilhard is both the natural process described by scientists and the spiritual progression towards God known to the church, a progression wrought by God but aided by human accord with the divine plan.

There is therefore a deeply synergistic element to Teilhard's thought, and here, too, his consonance with the Greek Fathers is striking.[20] At times, it almost seems as if he believes we can do work that would appear to be quintessentially divine: 'Through practising that charity towards man which alone can gather up the multitude into a single soul.'[21] Whatever Teilhard meant exactly by the problematic notion of a 'single soul', what is clear is that he regards the work of effecting unity as one in which human beings take their part. It is not just that the one who practises charity effects unity among others, but that this alliance with charity brings about the union of the one who loves with the divine Lover. 'My dearest wish, Master,' he wrote, 'is that I might offer so little resistance to you that you could no longer distinguish me from yourself—so perfectly would we be united, in a communion of will.'[22] Correlatively, the human will can, by failing to align itself with the greater, impede the work in which it is meant to assist: the life-giving power even of the sacraments can be blocked because of our misuse of the divine gift of freedom.[23] Not blocking this purpose means aligning oneself with it, rather than choosing a purpose for oneself: 'I know that the divine will, will only be revealed to me at each moment if I exert myself to the utmost.'[24]

The balance between divine and human endeavour is often very delicate. 'For me, my God, all joy and all achievement, the very purpose of my being and all my love of life, all depend on this one basic vision of the union between yourself and the universe.'[25] Human effort is based on the divine work of union, but also on humanity's capacity to see that union and work with it:

> [T]hrough the necessary operation of the Incarnation, the divine so thoroughly permeates all the creaturely energies that, in order to meet it and lay hold of it, we could not find a more fitting setting than that of our action.[26]

Human effort even joins in making the fullness of this mystery known on earth: 'we labour . . . to build the Pleroma; that is to say, we bring to Christ a little fulfilment'[27] so that there is a sense in which 'the Incarnation will be complete only when the part of chosen substance contained in every object . . . shall

---

[19] *Hymn*, 140.
[20] cf. Pseudo-Denys, *Celestial Hierarchy*, III.2.   [21] *Prayer*, 167.
[22] *Prayer*, 167.   [23] *Hymn*, 123.   [24] *Hymn*, 26.
[25] *Hymn*, 35.   [26] *Milieu*, 62.
[27] Cf. Maximus the Confessor, *Ambigua*, 41.

have rejoined the final centre of its completion'.[28] Teilhard distinguishes between the Christ of the earthly years and the Incarnate, but risen and ascended Lord of the church: the mystical and cosmic Christ have not yet attained to the fullness that is divine intention.[29] The Incarnation of Christ is both a restoration, the crown of all perfection, and a making new.[30] The transfiguration of matter is inaugurated by Christ's advent in human nature, but will be fully complete only when the whole cosmos is transformed.[31] There is therefore a strong analogy between Teilhard's Christocentric conception of the renewal of the cosmos in history and the Irenaean notion of recapitulation.[32]

The Incarnation is the fulcrum of Teilhard's theology, linking the themes of matter and evolution and expressing how deeply theological was his understanding of these, how at once original and traditional. Hence he could claim that through Christ's incarnation, all matter is incarnate.[33] This strange statement seems to make little sense if taken at face value: the Incarnation meant divine nature joined matter, but matter is of its nature material and cannot become more so. However the use of 'incarnate' here implies more, that matter has become the bearer of the divine, has been transformed and is a sign of the transformation God is working in the universe. The cosmos is centred on Christ,[34] but Christ stands also at the telos of a linear development, both the centre and the end of the animated and material creation, which is through him created, sanctified, and vivified.[35]

DEIFICATION AND SACRAMENTALITY

The extension and fulfilment of Teilhard's cosmic theology is found in his theology of deification. This ancient conception of redemption and sanctification, drawn notably from the notion of participation in divine life in 2 Pet. 1.4, characterizes the theology of the Eastern Fathers, but is also found in major Western theologians such as Augustine, Aquinas, Luther, and Calvin. At some point after the Reformation, however, Western theology ceased to formulate its understanding of redemption and sanctification using the traditional language of deification. It was not so much that anyone denied deification, as that the language conveying it fell into desuetude. All the more striking, then, that it should surface so frequently in the theology of Teilhard.

---

[28] *Milieu*, 62.   [29] *Prayer*, 92; *Hymn*, 121.
[30] Teilhard, *L'Avenir de l'homme* (Paris: Seuil, 1959), 396–7; *Prayer*, 162, 91.
[31] Cf. Pseudo-Denys, *Divine Names*, VIII.9.
[32] Irenaeus, *Against Heresies*, V.i.2 and V.xx.2; and Maximus, *Ambigua*, 41.
[33] *Hymn*, 23.   [34] *Prayer*, 95.   [35] *Avenir*, 396–7.

Teilhard takes it up in ways that are both traditional and yet extend organically beyond what was said in the past. For Teilhard, deification is not only a matter of the human person's being drawn more deeply into participation in divine life, but the whole created order's being drawn towards God:

> Not only the bread of the altar but (to some degree) everything in the universe that nourishes the soul for the life of spirit and grace, has become yours and has become divine—it is divinized divinizing [sic.] and divinizable.[36]

The 'all' consists not only in existing things, but the operations of those things, 'the divinization of endeavour'.[37] In extending the doctrine in this way, Teilhard could be said to be operating on a principle both patristic and medieval: things are known through their natures, through their characteristic operations.[38] Deification is both accomplished by God and in God and is in the process of being brought about through humankind's response to God. It is the particular task of the Christian to deify the world in Jesus Christ.[39] At one level, it would seem impossible for a human being to do this: if deification means participation in divine life, then to say a human being could effect it would seriously compromise the sovereignty of God. The link between Teilhard's sacramental theology and his theology of deification clarifies this point: 'Transubstantiation', he writes, 'is encircled by a halo of divinization ... that extends to the whole universe.'[40] Teilhard's conception of deification extends the patristic doctrine outwards from humanity to encompass all creation, but is also more explicitly sacramental than the traditional doctrine.

The stress on sacramental life is not in itself novel, however. The Fathers did not have a sacramental theology in the sense of sustained reflection on the sacraments treated separately from other theological topics; they reason from baptism to the divinity of the Spirit, from the reality of Christ's presence in the Eucharist to his divinity. The closest they come to any dedicated and sustained examination of the sacraments are the sequences of catechetical orations delivered to candidates for baptism either just before or just after the rite, which most often took place during the Great Vigil of Easter. While these discourses certainly exhibit focused reflection on the sacraments, they are embedded in an account of theology that is much broader: the baptizands are being instructed in the great rites of baptism and Eucharist in the context of the seamless fabric that is the Christian faith. To say the sacraments are part of this fabric is both to say they cannot be treated in isolation from the rest of it, but also to say that the faith cannot be understood apart from the sacraments. That sensibility runs throughout patristic theology, from its very

---

[36] *Prayer*, 137.   [37] *Milieu*, 55.
[38] Maximus, *Trial*, 8; Aquinas, *ST* III.19.1; Blackfriars l.87–95.   [39] *Milieu*, 72.
[40] *Prayer*, 159; cf. *Milieu*, 125; cf. Gregory of Nyssa's notion that the deity extends to every part of nature, in his *Catechetical Oration*, 79.

beginning with a writer such as Ignatius of Antioch, who makes sense of his own martyrdom in light of his theology of the Eucharist.[41] Teilhard continues and extends this integration by insisting on the relation of the sacraments and deification.

Teilhard signals he is aware of the ancient rooting of theology in sacramental life, for he speaks of 'the most traditional Christianity, expressed in Baptism, the Cross, and the Eucharist'[42] and, in a rare explicit reference to patristic theology, cites Gregory of Nyssa, who speaks of the water running off the body of Christ after his baptism, which elevates the whole world.[43] Linked to Teilhard's strong sense of the cosmic dimension of sanctification, this sacramental theology becomes a theology of the transfiguration of matter:

> If I firmly believe that everything around me is the body and blood of the Word, then for me . . . is brought about that marvellous 'diaphany' which causes luminous warmth of a single life to be objectively discernible.[44]

The theme of the Incarnation becoming real in all creation here reaches its pinnacle, as Teilhard envisages the world not only as altar, but in the very sacrament of the altar itself:

> Mysteriously and in very truth, at the touch of the substantial Word, the universe, an immense Host, becomes flesh. From now on, my God, all matter is by your incarnation incarnate.[45]

This theology is a logical extension of the patristic theology of the Eucharist as the agent of deification.[46]

INFINITE QUALITATIVE DIFFERENCE

At the heart of this ecstatic proclamation of the transfiguration of the material, however, remains a firm conviction of the distinction of creature from creator. Like the Fathers, Teilhard has a strong sense of the kenosis that must precede union with God: 'If God is definitively to enter into us, he must in some way hollow us out, empty us, so as to make room for himself',[47] a notion which strikingly echoes that of Bernard of Clairvaux, who speaks of the divine and deifying experience of losing oneself in God, as a drop of water in a quantity of wine.[48] For Teilhard, all initiative comes from God alone,[49] and every element

---

[41] Ignatius of Antioch, *Romans*, 4.1.   [42] *Milieu*, 43.
[43] *Milieu*, 110.   [44] *Hymn*, 27.
[45] Teilhard, *La Messe sur le monde* (Seuil, 1965), 26, my translation; cf. *Hymn*, 23.
[46] Cf. Gregory of Nyssa, *Catechetical Oration*, 37.
[47] *Hymn*, 118.   [48] *On Loving God*, X.27, 28.   [49] *Hymn*, 22.

of which we are made up is an overflow of God;[50] hence our emptiness is the precondition of sanctification. Teilhard has the deep awareness of the transience of created things[51] which is also characteristic of patristic theology, combined with a sense of the immensity of God's intentions for his ephemeral creation. The Baby of Bethlehem and the Man of the Cross is 'principle of all movement and the unifying centre of the world'.[52] The restlessness of creation has its purpose, then, for its term can only be God, as Augustine saw.[53]

Like Gregory of Nyssa, Teilhard combines a sense of our movement towards God with the strong awareness of divine infinity, not just a metaphysical assertion, but as a principle of sanctification: 'I can never set a boundary to the perfection of my fidelity nor to the fervour of my intention.'[54] In Gregory's spiritual theology, divine infinity stipulates that there can be no term to human spiritual striving, nor limit to human attainment: we can progress ever farther along the path to holiness and knowledge of God and yet never 'catch up' with the infinite God.[55] Teilhard takes this theme and extends it epistemologically: in the cosmos, there is always something more to be seen.[56] By this, he does not mean simply that there is more for natural science to learn about the structure and operations of nature. He means we are oriented towards an ever deeper understanding of the true nature of creation as God's and therefore a truer understanding of divine nature itself. For the Fathers, the mind, as that in us which is properly in the *imago Dei*, is the prime point of connection between us and God.[57] Knowledge of God is therefore not solely a matter of increasing one's intellectual acumen, but of spiritually drawing closer to God. Exactly this sensibility animates Teilhard's theology: knowledge is a privilege, 'it is so vital and blessed to know'.[58] Equating vision and knowledge, he also ascribes a general growth to this greater knowledge, so that to see is to become more and vision means 'fuller being'.[59]

ORIGINAL SIN: REVISION OR *RESSOURCEMENT*

One might well ask, however, where sin fits into this beautiful picture, whether Teilhard had forgotten the ugly and the mean. The point at which Teilhard seems farthest from the classical tradition, the point on which he criticized it most openly and at which he claimed to have parted company with it, is on the

[50] *Prayer*, 93.   [51] *Prayer*, 114–15.   [52] *Hymn*, 126.
[53] Augustine, *Confessions*, I, 1 in Augustine, *Complete Works*, Part I i.39.   [54] *Milieu*, 63.
[55] Cf. *The Life of Moses*, II.226, 239, 236–8; cf. Gregory Nazianzen *Oration*, 28.21.
[56] *Phenomenon*, 35.
[57] Cf. Gregory Nazianzen, *Oration*, 28.17.
[58] *Phenomenon*, 37, 35; cf. Maximus the Confessor, *The Church's Mystagogy*, V.
[59] *Phenomenon*, 37.

doctrine of original sin. He states bluntly 'Christian thought is being gradually obliged to abandon its former ways of conceiving original sin'.[60] In his view, the standard doctrine is 'a static solution to the problem of evil', an 'intellectual and emotional straitjacket'.[61] In his view, the doctrine was not merely misguided, but itself misleading: 'how could man *fail to be robbed of his zest for action* by this alleged revelation of his radical uselessness?'[62] In particular, he disapproved of the scholastic notion of participation:

> I have allowed myself so sharply to criticize the Scholastic notion of 'participation' . . . because it humiliates the man in me, but also, and equally, because it offends the Christian in me.[63]

Prima facie, then, it would seem that Teilhard rejects the traditional doctrine. What is striking about his own declarations that he did so, however, is their vagueness. Teilhard's writings do not in general abound with references to patristic or medieval theology—or to any later theology, for that matter. Here and there one finds references to the schoolmen or scholastic theology, but these are striking in their lack of specificity.[64] Equally hazy, for the most part, is the delineation of the doctrine Teilhard rejects. At times, it seems his objection is to a literal interpretation of Genesis, taking Adam and Eve as specific individuals from whom all the rest of humankind is generated, with original sin passed down like a hereditary physical disease. Given his assumption that the traditional account requires an Adam who is 'born adult', Teilhard outlines two options: either an account requiring a fundamental change in the natural laws of speciation, or a radical revision of the doctrine, such as his own.[65]

Teilhard is however insistent—on this point as at others—that his own view of the cosmic dimension of Christianity is Pauline.[66] He does not therefore quite portray himself as the innovator he was reproached with being, but rather, as the true interpreter of the biblical text. Indeed, he acknowledges—albeit in passing and somewhat grudgingly—that his approach accords with 'recent advances in exegesis'.[67] This last remark is telling: arguably, part of the reason Teilhard saw his own version of the doctrine of original sin as so far removed from that of the tradition was precisely because he did not know the tradition well enough to realize it did not interpret Genesis quite as he believed it did. It can be difficult at times to know exactly what the Fathers made of texts such as the creation accounts in Genesis. In general, however, they are much more aware of the specifically literary qualities of texts than post-Enlightenment interpreters are, much more sensitive to narrative, symbolism,

---

[60] Teilhard, *Christianity and Evolution* trans. René Hague (London: Collins, 1971), 45.
[61] *Evolution*, 80.   [62] *Evolution*, 225.   [63] *Evolution*, 226.
[64] *Evolution*, 21, 38, 43, 224, 226.   [65] *Evolution*, 210–11.
[66] *Evolution*, 129.   [67] *Evolution*, 210–11.

and the figurative nature of language, and these considerations caution against an overly-hasty determination that they all assumed Adam and Eve were historical individuals. They were, in any case, not so much interested in the Bible as a chronicle of historical events, but as the saga of God's dealings with humanity—in theology, in other words.[68]

Teilhard's critique of the traditional doctrine of original sin is bound up with the assumption that it rests on the interpretation of scripture as history.[69] Against this reading of Genesis, he juxtaposes the Pauline picture of the two Adams.[70] It does not seem to occur to him that Paul's successors in the tradition might have been just as capable of reading Genesis as something other than purported history.[71] When one considers what Teilhard wants to affirm, however, it is entirely consistent with the articulation of the doctrine found in patristic writings: 'the *whole* world has been corrupted by the Fall and the *whole* of everything has been redeemed'.[72] At times he hints at an awareness that his version of the doctrine is not, after all, so novel.[73] What appears to be its most novel element may in fact be one of its most traditional traits. 'Original sin', he writes, 'expresses, translates, personifies, in an instantaneous and localized act, the perennial and universal law of imperfection which operates *in virtue* of its being *"in fieri"*.'[74] Although part of Teilhard's objection to what he believes the standard doctrine is rests on its reading of Genesis as history, part relates to its supposedly static quality. Against this static picture he juxtaposes an evolutionary one, this evolution being novel and spiritual, but analogous to natural evolution, which was so central to his scientific thought. However the notion that humankind is *'in fieri'* (in the process of becoming) finds a strong counterpart in early Christian theology.[75] The notion of a solidarity among human beings, which is the basis for most doctrines of original sin, is also both traditional and Teilhardian.

Similarly, it is not clear that what Teilhard proposes as an alternative to the scholastic doctrine of participation he so dislikes is all that remote from the tradition itself. What he dislikes in the doctrine he understands to be

---

[68] Take, for example, Michael Fiedorowicz's reading of Augustine, claiming that even where Augustine seeks to render the Biblical text literally, he explicitly rejects the idea that the Bible is a natural scientific treatise: 'Augustine's position is nonetheless clear: there can be no opposition between two certainties; true science cannot be in conflict with a true interpretation of the scriptures' (157). See also Origen's comments on the absurdity of interpreting certain aspects of Genesis literally in *De principiis*, V.iii.1.

[69] *Evolution*, 36.

[70] *Evolution*, 36.

[71] Cf. Gregory Nazianzen, *Orations*, 30.1; and Athanasius, *Orations against the Arians*, III.33.

[72] *Evolution*, 39.

[73] *Evolution*, 53.

[74] *Evolution*, 51.

[75] Cf. Irenaeus, *Against Heresies*, IV.38.2–3, V.1.2, V.20.2; and Gregory of Nyssa, *Catechetical Oration*, 29.

scholastic is the distinction between *Ens a se* (being in itself) and *Ens ab alio* (being from another/dependent being).[76] He wants to replace this 'metaphysics of *Esse*' with a 'metaphysics of *Unire*'.[77] At one level, his proposal really is on a collision course with the tradition, though not only with its doctrine of the Fall, but the entire doctrine of creation, for he wants to hold that each element—God and creature—has 'an equal need both to exist in themselves and to be combined with each other'.[78] This approach not only seems to compromise divine aseity, by making God dependent on creation, but also by asserting the creature's independence of God. Creation *ex nihilo* and divine sovereignty would appear to be severely compromised, if not abandoned outright, by this critique. Nevertheless, what Teilhard proposes as an alternative is actually very close to the position of the tradition. The language and conceptualities of participation derived as much from expansive reflection on 2 Pet. 1.4 as from any philosophical doctrine. In that framework—a biblical and patristic legacy which continued into medieval theology—participation in divine life meant being united to God. While the tradition was careful to preserve the distinction of creature from creator, even as it asserted their union, and equally careful to preserve divine aseity (as Teilhard is not), the end of both is a theology centred on the union of God and humanity.

CONCLUSION

Considering Teilhard's theology in relation to the tradition raises the question of what *ressourcement* is, precisely. The cry with which other twentieth-century French theologians were associated was '*Ad fontes*'. In the rush to affirm the goodness of inquiring of the tradition, we might pause to ask why exactly we would go back to the sources. One answer might be that the sources voice a theology which is eternally valid and which must be preserved intact and followed, in precisely the form in which it was first articulated. Few, I suspect, would admit to holding such a view, but it is in fact the operative attitude to the tradition in some quarters. The luminaries of what came to be called *la nouvelle théologie* did not, either in principle or practice, hold to such a position. The purpose of returning to the sources was for theology to refresh itself, not merely to repeat what had been said centuries before. If we view *ressourcement* in this light, then Teilhard can be considered party to its deepest concerns.

True, he shows little interest in understanding patristic and medieval theology for its own sake (at times, culpably so, given his willingness to

---

[76] *Evolution*, 226.   [77] *Evolution*, 227.   [78] *Evolution*, 227.

criticize it). The fact remains that the theology he articulates lies in many respects very close to the spirit and substance of the tradition. Teilhard apparently arrived at this theology via reflection on the Bible and the experience of sacramental and contemplative life, which was also how the patristic and medieval theologians arrived at their theology. In Teilhard's case, observation of the natural world and deep love of it provided an additional context in which his thought matured. Yet, by a different route, he reached a view of human life and the natural world *coram Deo* in which, as Hopkins put it, 'the world is charged with the grandeur of God'. Nature, indeed material nature, is being transfigured by its relation to the cosmic Christ, and Teilhard's theology shows us how at once ancient and utterly modern is this understanding of the world and human existence as ablaze with the living God.

8

L'Église a ravi son cœur: Charles Journet and the Theologians of *Ressourcement* on the Personality of the Church

John Saward

INTRODUCTION

Charles Journet was not a *ressourcement* theologian. He was sceptical of the movement's methods and critical of many of the opinions of its protagonists. However, he was willing to commend these *nouveaux théologiens* whenever he perceived the truth of their insights, and in 1953 told his closest friend, Jacques Maritain, that he thought 'people like Father de Lubac' were 'more with us than against us'.[1] On one question, in particular, there was a meeting of minds: both Journet and the *ressourcement* school looked upon the church as by analogy a *person*, not only something to be analysed and assessed, but *someone* to be recognized and loved. The 'fervent profession of faith', as Journet described de Lubac's evocation of the true 'man of the Church' in an article of 1953, can fittingly serve as the watchword of Journet's own life's work: *L'Église a ravi son cœur*.[2] What follows is a sketch of Journet's portrait of this captivating personality, the Bride who has stolen his heart.

---

[1] *Journet—Maritain Correspondance* (JMC), iv, 1950–1957 (Paris: Éditions Saint-Augustin, 2005), 315.

[2] Charles Journet, *Primauté de Pierre dans la perspective protestante et dans la perspective catholique* (Paris: Alsatia, 1953), 39. Journet is quoting de Lubac's article, 'L'Église notre Mère', *Études* (1953) 3–19 (5). '[The true man of the Church] loves the beauty of the House of God. The Church has ravished his heart. She is his spiritual homeland. She is his "mother and brethren".'

NOT STARTING FROM ZANZIBAR: CHARLES JOURNET AND *RESSOURCEMENT*

Two Approaches to Theology: Historical and Speculative

In 1963 Journet reviewed Yves Congar's newly published *Sainte Église*.[3] He was warm in his praise, and expressed his gratitude for the 'privileged' place the Dominican had accorded his work.[4] However, he also confessed reservations about Congar's *ressourcement* methodology. He approaches the church from the angle of history, seeking 'to unravel from the *historical* complexities of the Middle Ages, on the one hand, what the Church truly is, and, on the other, what is either a secular value or a deviation and perversion'. Journet borrows an analogy from another Dominican to illustrate the path that he himself prefers to tread.

> I recalled what Father A[mbroise] Gardeil . . . liked to say about Catholic theology: *Its method is regressive.* To illustrate what he meant, he told the story, which he claimed was historical, of two explorers looking for the sources of the Congo. One, straightforwardly, decides to follow the river's course, starting from its mouth; the other, more subtly, starts from Zanzibar and comes upon the source . . . of the Nile. This 'regressive method' can without doubt be a useful corrective to the present-day method of *ressourcement*. My plan has not been, on each theme, to list the multitude of solutions presented by different theologians, to create a kind of thicket. Still less has it been to create new paths. No, my aim has been to enter, as far as I could, into the depth of thought of the one whom the Church, when I was a seminarian, distinguished with the title, the 'Common Doctor', and of his most attentive commentators. I was convinced that [the thought of St Thomas Aquinas] would contain the light that, in continuity with the Tradition and in coherence with the whole message of Scripture, would enable me to respond to the gravest questions of our times without expecting facile solutions, without diminishing the mystery, but seeking instead to lose oneself within it in order to come back from it less blind.[5]

Divergent Lives

For all its richness of thought, Journet's theological writing has a blessed simplicity of style. His life, too, was modest and inconspicuous.[6] Here was a Swiss diocesan priest content to spend nearly five decades lecturing in the

---

[3] Yves Congar, OP, *Sainte Église: Études et approches ecclésiologiques* (Paris: Cerf, 1963).

[4] Charles Journet, 'Regard rétrospectif. À propos du dernier livre du R. P. Congar sur l'Église', *Nova et vetera*, 38 (1963), 294–312 (294).

[5] Journet, 'Regard rétrospectif', 306–7.

[6] For biographical information, see Guy Boissard, *Charles Journet, 1891–1975* (Boissard) (Paris: Salvator, 2008).

seminary, delivering conferences to enclosed religious, and exercising a weekend ministry of spiritual direction and preaching. True, there were activities of wider influence. He founded, edited, and wrote for the journal *Nova et vetera*; interested himself in modern poetry and painting; collaborated with Jacques Maritain in efforts to apply the light of the Gospel to the political questions of the day; and during the war actively supported spiritual resistance to National Socialism. Having been appointed a Cardinal by his old friend, Pope Paul VI, he took part in the closing stages of the Second Vatican Council and undertook 'delicate missions' on behalf of the Pope, including the defence of *Humanae Vitae*.[7] Still, as Cardinal Newman said of himself, Journet's life's journey was that of an 'indoors' man, day by day moving between altar and blackboard, tabernacle, and desk. As a disciple of St Thomas, he never wavered in his conviction that *sacra doctrina* was principally a speculative rather than practical science, ordered to a more perfect understanding of revealed truth,[8] and that his duty as a theologian was the humble one of leading others to such an understanding according to the mind of the church. He never tried to be a subtle explorer. By contrast, the *ressourcement* theologians were 'outdoors men', peripatetic religious, Jesuits and Dominicans speaking to a diversity of audiences in the wider Catholic world. These were priests with a strong sense of being an *avant-garde*, of taking theology off in new directions, convinced they could get to the Congo by way of Zanzibar.[9]

Divergent Opinions

Journet was a Thomist, and never sought to be anything else, whether in philosophy or theology. In 1927 he defended the metaphysics of St Thomas and proclaimed himself a Thomist pure and simple: 'We change nothing in the metaphysical and theological principles of St. Thomas. Thomism is a metaphysics to which we *raise* ourselves by the intellect; we do not seek to *adapt* it.'[10] In the same period, he also took to task what he regarded as perverse interpretations of the Angelic Doctor being encouraged by Maurice Blondel.[11] Journet remained ever grateful to St Thomas for setting him free

[7] Cf. Boissard, 537–8.   [8] Cf. *ST* 1a.1 ad 4, Blackfriars i.14–17.
[9] Fr Labourdette, OP suspected the founders of the flagship of *ressourcement, Sources chrétiennes,* of glorifying patristic theology to the detriment of scholasticism (M.-M. Labourdette, OP, *et al., Dialogue théologique: Pièces du débat* (Var: Les Arcades, 1947), 65). By contrast, Journet was generous in the welcome he gave the series: he thought it was heroic, an expression of Christian hope, for such a project to be inaugurated 'in the heat of war' (*Nova et vetera,* 19 (1944), 26–37 (26)).
[10] See 'Chronique de philosophie', *Nova et vetera,* 2 (1927), 406–21 (408n).
[11] Letter of 20 January 1926 to the editor of *Les Lettres*; JMC i.360.

from the temptation in his youth to subjectivism,[12] and could therefore not look with equanimity on, as he saw it, Blondel's determination to cut loose from Thomist realism.[13]

De Lubac was always linked in Journet's mind with the anti-Thomistic Blondel. In 1936, at the height of the controversy about 'Christian philosophy',[14] writing to Raïssa Maritain, he says that de Lubac 'sees the only true solution in Blondel'.[15] In 1950, commenting on Pope Pius XII's *Humani Generis*, whose censures were generally thought to be directed against positions held by de Lubac and the other *nouveaux théologiens*, he says that the encyclical censures 'a mass of propositions circulating within the whole *Blondelian movement*'.[16]

Convergent Concerns

The relations between Journet and the *nouveaux théologiens* were never entirely comfortable. In 1938 Journet wrote a positive review of Congar's *Chrétiens désunis*,[17] of which the author had sent him a copy with a personal dedication.[18] By 1964, in the preface to *Chrétiens en dialogue*, Congar seems to regret his earlier alignment with Journet: 'At that time I was still too close to scholastic Thomism . . . I was also too much under the influence of the Abbé Charles Journet's book, *L'union des Églises* (1926), which was already "dated" in 1937.'[19]

In the 1950s, Journet and his friends followed the fortunes of de Lubac with interest and anxiety. In July 1951, writing to Journet from Princeton, Maritain says how much he admires American Catholics, and states his belief that their faith has been safeguarded by the Pope's recent teaching: '[H]ad it not been for the encyclical [*Humani Generis*], they would have started getting interested in de Lubac, Daniélou, "theological pluralism"; they would have got lost in that pseudo-intellectual *mess*.'[20] When Maritain tells Journet that de Lubac agrees with what Maritain says in *Approches de Dieu*, Journet suggests that de Lubac reads only the introductions of his own and Maritain's books, and that his agreement is only 'with regard to general intention'. However, he does not

---

[12] See Boissard, *Charles Journet*, 43–4.   [13] On Blondel, see Boissard, 316.

[14] For an account of the course of this controversy, see the appendix in JMC, i. 1930–1939 (Fribourg/Paris: Éditions universitaires/Éditions Saint-Paul, 1996), 924.

[15] JMC, ii.553.

[16] JMC, iv.81

[17] Yves Congar, OP, *Divided Christendom: A Catholic Study of the Problem of Reunion*, trans. M. A. Bousfield (London: Bles, 1939); *Chrétiens désunis: Principes d'un 'oecuménisme' catholique* (Paris: Cerf, 1937).

[18] JMC, ii.737.

[19] Yves Congar, OP, *Dialogue between Christians: Catholic Contributions to Ecumenism*, trans. Philip Loretz, SJ (London: Chapman, 1966), 24; *Chrétiens en dialogue: Contributions catholiques à l'oecuménisme* (Paris: Cerf, 1964), p. xxxv.

[20] JMC, iv.76.

underestimate the significance of these displays of solidarity across the divisions of theological schools: 'You can't talk any longer of the "Fourvière school", or of *nouvelle théologie*'.[21] *Sed magis amica veritas*: despite his admiration for much of de Lubac's theology, Journet's criticisms of its defects could be fierce, especially when it came to the Jesuit's defence of Teilhard de Chardin, whom Journet accused of compromising the doctrine of creation *ex nihilo*.[22]

In the late 1960s, Journet and Maritain, on the one hand, and de Lubac and Balthasar, on the other, came to the conclusion that the Second Vatican Council was the occasion, without being the cause, of one of the most devastating intellectual and spiritual crises in the history of the church. Maritain said that the disease of neo-Modernism made the Modernism of the turn of the century look like 'hay-fever'.[23] In a review of Balthasar's response to the crisis, Journet quotes a lecture delivered by de Lubac in 1967 in which he says that 'the signs are on the increase of a spiritual crisis of a kind that has only rarely shaken the Church'.[24] Journet shows himself to be in fundamental agreement with Balthasar's own diagnosis of the post-conciliar sickness ('the loss of continuity with Christianity as it has been understood up to now'), and of the remedy required (the rediscovery of martyrdom as the definitive Christian attitude towards the world). On martyrdom he says, very much in the spirit of Balthasar himself, 'God is not content with a cordial Thank You. He wants to recognize His Son in Christians.'[25]

During the pontificate of Paul VI, Balthasar, Congar, and de Lubac were drawn into co-operation with the magisterium. Journet applauded this new work, in the service of Peter, of the erstwhile *avant-gardistes*. For example, in 1971 he welcomed de Lubac's article in *L'Osservatore Romano*, on the meaning of the phrases, 'particular Churches' and 'local Churches', as an 'important and masterly clarification'.[26]

WHO IS THE CHURCH?

Holding Fast to Mother Church

In a letter written for Journet's eightieth birthday, Pope Paul VI praised his friend's 'bond of love and fidelity with the Church'. He uses the words of St Augustine to illustrate Journet's 'way of thinking and working': 'Let us love the

[21] JMC, iv.355.   [22] Boissard, *Charles Journet*, 326–31.
[23] Cf. Jacques Maritain, *The Peasant of the Garonne*, trans. Michael Cuddihy and Elizabeth Hughes (London: Chapman, 1968), 5–6.
[24] Journet, 'Cordula ou l'épreuve décisive', *Nova et vetera*, 43 (1968), 147–54 (147).
[25] 'Cordula ou l'épreuve décisive', 149.
[26] Journet, 'Églises particulières et Églises locales', *Nova et vetera*, 46 (1971), 58–60 (58).

Lord our God; let us love His Church. Him let us love as Father, her as Mother; Him as Lord, her as Handmaid, for we are the Handmaid's sons.'[27] The Pope's text is well chosen. Like Augustine, Journet thought of the church as a person—Mother and Handmaid—in relation to other persons: the Three Divine Persons, and the human person of the Blessed Virgin Mary.

Journet once told his friend Fr (later Cardinal) Cottier that he owed his vocation as an ecclesiologist to St Catherine of Siena, Dante, and Humbert Clérissac, OP.[28] Now, in each of these authors the church appears as a kind of person, at once historically incarnate and eternally transcendent. St Catherine's mission, after all, was by her tears to wash the face of Christ's Bride, disfigured by the sins of its members. Seventy years before St Catherine, Dante was dazzled by the beauty of the church personified in the Blessed Virgin and Beatrice, but repelled by the crimes of the church's supreme pastors. As for Father Clérissac, it was his posthumously published book, *Le mystère de l'Église*, which has a whole chapter on the personality of the church, that brought Charles Journet and Jacques Maritain together in a friendship that would last over fifty years. In 1920, Journet wrote out of the blue to Maritain to thank him for his preface to Clérissac's book: in those few pages, he said, 'there is more true Thomism than in many volumes, and for me they have been like a grace of supernatural light'.[29]

Applying the Term 'Person' to the Church

Journet recognizes that the church is not a person in the same sense in which a man is a person. The term 'person' is at once too strong and too weak: too strong because, whereas the human person is 'a physical, substantial whole, and incommunicable in his ontological constitution', the church is 'a moral, accidental whole, uniting in herself innumerable physical persons'; too weak, because 'the human person belongs to the natural order, while the Church is a whole depending on grace'. Journet concludes that we should call the church a 'mystical' person 'to signify both the attenuations and the enhancements by which the word "person" becomes applicable to her'.[30] As a person, it is real, not fictional, collective rather than individual, supernatural, not merely natural.[31] The church is a person, not in separation from the persons and souls who are its

[27] 'Lettre de Sa Sainteté Paul VI au Cardinal Journet pour son quatre-vingtième anniversaire', *RevTh*, 71 (1971), 197.

[28] Georges M.-M. Cottier, OP, 'L'œuvre de Charles Journet (1891–1975)', *Nova et vetera*, 50 (1975), 242–58 (251).

[29] JMC, i.35.

[30] Charles Journet, *L'Église du Verbe incarné: Essai de théologie speculative*, ii, Sa structure interne et son unité catholique (part 2) (EVI 2/1) (Paris: Éditions Saint-Augustin, 2000), 1, 264.

[31] Cf. EVI 2/1, 799–843.

members, and yet somehow by transcending them: in one respect, *we* are the church, but in another, *it* stands above us, or rather embraces and protects us: 'The name "Bride", which belongs to [the church], is something very different from a metaphor. The reality it denotes is a mystery of faith, the mystery of a supernatural, multitudinous person, who is ontologically subsistent, and who transcends the personality of each of her members'.[32]

The Person of the Church and the Person of Christ

'The Church', says Journet, 'is something of Christ (*quelque chose du Christ*).'[33] When Saul is struck down on the road to Damascus, the risen Lord tells him, 'I am Jesus whom you are persecuting' (Acts 9.5), as if Christ and Christians are so much one that to attack the disciples is to strike against the Master. This doctrine of the mystical union of Christ and his church is at the centre of Pauline theology: 'You are all one (*heis*, one person) in Christ Jesus' (Gal. 3.28). The church is the Body of which Christ is the Head and Christians the members (c.f. Eph. 4.15; Col. 1.18). Christ and his church, the Bridegroom and the Bride, are one flesh (c.f. Eph. 5.28–33), like a building held together by its cornerstone (c.f. Eph. 2.20). Summarizing the Apostle, St Augustine coins the phrase 'the Whole Christ' (*totus Christus*), made up of Head and members, and reads the Psalms as the antiphonal chants of that one, mystically composite Christ.[34] St Thomas Aquinas unfolds the same doctrine: 'The head and members form as it were a single mystical person (*quasi una persona mystica*).'[35] And Bossuet sums up the whole tradition when he says, in words loved by Journet, that the church is 'Jesus Christ poured out and communicated (*répandu et communiqué*)'.[36]

Here, then, is the first sense in which the church is a person: somehow the church *is* Christ. But, without further precisions, this identification leads to serious errors, in which, as Pope Pius XII says, Christ and Christians are so confused that divine attributes are given to man and Christ is made 'subject to error and the human proclivity for evil'.[37] It is to protect the truth from such deformity that Journet makes a series of distinctions concerning the church's identification with Christ.

---

[32] Cited in Michel Cagin, 'Le mystère de l'Église: En relisant le livre du Père Clérissac', *Nova et vetera*, 66 (1991), 28–48 (33n).

[33] Journet, *Vérité de Pascal: Essai sur la valeur apologétique des 'Pensées'* (Saint-Maurice: Éditions Saint-Augustin, 1951), 257.

[34] For texts, see E. Mersch, SJ, *The Whole Christ: The Historical Development of the Doctrine of the Mystical Body in Scripture and Tradition*, trans. John R. Kelly, SJ (London: Dobson, 1938), 384–440.

[35] *ST*, 3a.48.2 ad1; Blackfriars, liv.78–9.

[36] EVI 2/1, 259n.   [37] *DS* § 3816.

The name 'person' belongs to Christ on His own and to the Whole Christ, Head and Body, in two different ways. When . . . we proclaim that the Whole Christ is one single person, that in no way extends the Hypostatic Union to the [Mystical] Body and members of Christ. We say, then, that, unlike Christ on His own (*Christ seul*), who is a person in the strictest sense, the Whole Christ is a person in a loose sense, that is, as a 'mystical' person.[38]

Referring to Pius XII's statement in *Mystici Corporis Christi* that the church is, 'as it were, another person of Christ',[39] Journet argues that there are not two persons, Christ and the church, but one person, Christ, 'considered, on the one hand, in His *individual* body, which is united to Him substantially, . . . and, on the other hand, in a social, collective, *Mystical* Body, which is united to Him'. He concludes, as Pope Pius does, that we avoid any confusing of Christ with the church by opposing the church to Christ as Bride to Bridegroom: '[T]hen there will indeed be two distinct persons, but that is to pass from the *biological* comparison to the *nuptial* one.'[40] Only the nuptial comparison can reconcile the two complementary truths, namely, that the church is in one aspect a different thing from Christ, and in another identical with him. Christ loves the church with a husbandly heart (c.f. Eph. 5.5), and the church, in its members, loves its head with the heart of a bride. Thus, says Journet, hidden deep within the church on its earthly journey, are 'souls that merit, in the noblest and purest sense, the great name of brides of Christ, of Christ taken in His entirety, with His humanity supporting His divinity'.[41] This collective realization of the bridal grace and love of the church is personal in the Blessed Virgin: in her the church as devoted Bride is a real, individual person.

According to Journet, Christ is both the '*redemptive* mystical personality of the Church' and its '*efficient* mystical personality'. He explains this distinction by referring to the two movements of Christ's human operations: ascending from world to God, descending from God to world. First, Christ, true God and true man in one person, as man offers to God a sacrifice whose merit and satisfactory value are infinite; in this ascendant way, Christ is the *redemptive* mystical personality of the church. Second, Christ, true God and true man in one person, as God uses the human nature united to himself as an instrument for pouring out divine gifts upon human beings; in this descendant way, Christ is the efficient mystical personality of the church.[42] The incarnate Word in the human nature proper to him, not the Father or the Holy Spirit, consummated the ascendant mediation on Calvary. By contrast, in the descendant media-tion, the whole Trinity, using the now glorified humanity of the Son as an instrument, forever communicates the fruits of his sacrifice in and through the

---

[38] EVI 2/1, 265.   [39] *DS* § 3806.   [40] EVI 2/1, 265n.
[41] EVI 2/1, 572.   [42] Cf. EVI 2/1, 344–5.

church, his Body: its glowing source (*foyer*) was Calvary, 'but its rays were to reach all subsequent generations in time, as they come into existence'.[43]

Although it surpasses our own poor acts of worship and petition, Christ's ascendant mediation is not intended to abolish ours; on the contrary, it 'provoke[s] them, arouse[s] them, draw[s] them into its wake': 'Consequently, we must say that the whole Church forms with Christ but a single mystical person, adoring, offering, beseeching.'[44] As regards Christ as efficient mystical personality of the church in his acts of descendant mediation, Journet reminds us that the whole Trinity is the 'supreme principal cause' of these acts, and the sacred humanity the instrumental cause. However, Christ's human nature is an instrument in a unique sense: it is a living instrument, 'the most free, the most loving, the most sensitive that has ever been created', and it is also united in person to the Word as what St Thomas calls an 'exceptional instrument of the divinity', and it can effect our salvation 'by its own power'.[45] Thus, under the motion of the divine omnipotence, the humanity of Christ pours out on men the overflowing fullness of his riches in order to make them like him and give them a share in his kingship, priesthood, and holiness. By this threefold 'influx', the church, Christ's Mystical Body, is brought into being.[46] As man, then, Christ is the 'instrumental efficient personality' of the church.[47]

The Person of the Church and the Person of the Holy Spirit

Human persons are made up of body and soul. So it is, by analogy, with the person of the church: according to the Fathers and Doctors, the soul informing the Mystical Body is the Holy Spirit. This motif, taken up by the Popes and the Second Vatican Council,[48] receives systematic exposition in Journet's writings. The Holy Spirit, he says, is the *uncreated soul* of the church, both by efficient causality and indwelling. Properly speaking, it is the whole Trinity that is the first efficient cause of the church, but by appropriation it is the Holy Spirit: by his influence, 'He moves, fills, and unites the Church'.[49] Likewise, though the whole Trinity indwells the church as in a temple, 'we can also speak, by appropriation, of the indwelling of the Holy Spirit, because of love's likeness to Him, the love that attracts the presence of the Divine Persons into the loving soul'.[50] The *created soul* of the church is the effect of the Trinity's (or Holy Spirit's) efficiency and indwelling: Charity, grace, and glory.[51]

---

[43] Cf. EVI 2/1, 409–10.   [44] EVI 2/1, 369–70.   [45] Cf. EVI 2/1, 417.
[46] Cf. EVI 2/1, 420.   [47] Cf. EVI 2/1, 417–48.   [48] Cf. *LG* § 7.
[49] Journet, 'De la personnalité de l'Église', *RevTh*, 69 (1969), 192–200 (193).
[50] EVI 2/1, 849.
[51] On the relation between the Church's uncreated soul and created soul, see EVI 2/1, 882ff.

Journet goes beyond the traditional understanding of the Holy Spirit's mission in the church as its soul by arguing that he himself is the church's person, its 'extrinsic and efficient personality'. '[I]f He covers [the church] with His powerful, infallible, and permanent protection, He becomes, by that fact, *the subject to whom her advances, her successes, her conquests must be attributed.*'[52]

There is no contradiction in saying that the efficient personality of the church is, in one way, the incarnate Word and, in another, the Holy Spirit. Strictly speaking, it is the Triune Godhead that is the principal efficient cause of all that the church is, its supreme efficient personality; the Holy Spirit has that role, as already explained, by appropriation. What is exclusive to Christ is the human nature united to him in person, and in that respect he is the instrumental efficient personality. The church, Mystical Body and Bride of the incarnate Word, stands thus at the heart of the Trinity, at the intersection, so to speak, of the missions, visible and invisible, of the Son and the Spirit.[53]

The Church's Personal Realization: The Blessed Virgin Mary

As the Fathers of the Second Vatican Council did in the eighth chapter of *Lumen Gentium*, Charles Journet saw the church in Mary and Mary in the church.

> Christ-conforming grace, which vivifies and fashions the whole church from within, flourishes in the Virgin, albeit in a unique manner. In consequence, *speaking properly, we must say that Mariology is a part of ecclesiology*: it is that part of ecclesiology which studies the church in its most excellent and for ever unequalled point. Mary is the purest and most intense realization of the church.[54]

In placing Mariology within ecclesiology, Journet does not intend to diminish the grandeur of the Mother of God, reducing her to a mere symbol or cipher. Mary is not only the extrinsic form of the church, a moral example or model, but also, says Journet, the church's 'intrinsic, modalizing form', shaping it into what and who it is.

> Within the Church, she is the form in which the Church is fulfilled as Bride, in order to give herself to the Bridegroom. The more the Church resembles the Virgin, the more she becomes Bride; and the more she becomes Bride, the more she resembles the Bridegroom; and the more she resembles the Bridegroom, the more she resembles God.[55]

---

[52] EVI 2/1, 798.   [53] Cf. EVI 2/1, 760–86.
[54] EVI 2/1, 667–8.   [55] EVI 2/1, 727.

Journet describes sanctifying grace as 'Christ-conforming', because it over-flows from Christ the Head to his members and shapes them inwardly into his likeness. Now, this grace of Christ is communicated to his Blessed Mother, from her Immaculate Conception onwards, in a unique way:

> As it comes forth from the side of Christ, the grace that forms the Church in Christ's likeness, Christ-conforming grace, is poured out in a privileged manner on the Virgin and in a general manner on other Christians.[56]

Likewise, if the church has a 'collective co-redemptive mediation' in co-operation with its Head, the Blessed Virgin has a 'primary and universal co-redemptive mediation'. Mary's mediation of grace, in dependence upon her son, is 'absolutely universal': it extends to all men and women of all time, obtains for them all the graces deriving from the redemptive work of Christ, and is therefore 'anterior and enveloping in relation to the co-redemptive mediation of the Church'. 'The Virgin's mediation is, consequently, the point to which the Church's mediation tends without ever attaining it, just as a curve tends towards its asymptote.'[57]

Here, too, is the point to which Journet's ecclesiology tends. What has seized his heart in the church is its assimilation to Mary, its supreme member, model, and Mother. 'The whole Church is Marian.'[58]

The Personality of the Church According to the *Ressourcement* School

The personality of the church was a preoccupation not only of Journet and Maritain, but of the exponents of *ressourcement*.[59] All of them show respect for Journet's work: for example, Balthasar describes *L'Église du Verbe incarné* as 'the fullest treatise of ecclesiology in our time'.[60] Moreover, their picture of *la personne Église*, in its main outline, is similar to Journet's: they refuse to make it into an eternally and separately existing hypostasis in the manner of Origenism and Gnosticism;[61] they show that there is 'a certain relation of mystical identity between [the church] and [Christ]';[62] they find in the nuptial theme the guarantee of a union without confusion between the persons of

---

[56] EVI 2/1, 668.   [57] EVI 2/1, 692.   [58] EVI 2/1, 720–31.

[59] See Hans Urs von Balthasar, 'Who is the Church?' ('Who'), in *Explorations in Theology*, ii, Spouse of the Word, trans. A. V. Littledale, Alexander Dru *et al.* (San Francisco: Ignatius Press, 1991), 143–91; *Theo-drama: Theological Dramatic Theory, vol. 3, The Dramatis Personae: The Person in Christ*, trans. Graham Harrison (San Francisco: Ignatius Press, 1992), 339–60; Yves Congar, OP, 'La personne "Église"', *RevTh*, 71 (1971), 613–40. The theme runs through the whole of de Lubac's *The Splendour of the Church* (London: Sheed & Ward, 1956).

[60] Balthasar, 'Who', 155.

[61] Cf., Balthasar, *Theo-drama*, 344–5.

[62] De Lubac, *Splendour*, 152.

Christ and the church;[63] they strive to 'establish a balance between the Christocentric and pneumatocentric explanatory principle of the Church';[64] they refuse to romanticize the church, nor do they forget its visibility and hierarchical structure;[65] and they all find in the Blessed Virgin the 'excellent personal realization of the Church's, indeed all mankind's, response to God's offer of a spousal covenant'.[66]

There are also disagreements between Journet and the *ressourcement* school. For example, Congar asks whether Journet's distinction, in relation to Christ as the church's mystical personality, between the 'ascending' movement of supplication (and merit) and the 'descending' movement of efficiency, is an 'entirely happy' one, since it is in danger of reducing Christ's person in his sacred humanity to a mere psychological centre of knowing and willing.[67] The answer would seem to be that it is the ontological person of the eternal son who makes merit and supplication, even though he does so in his humanity, not in his divinity, and in virtue of the created grace and charity that fill his human soul. The sanctifying grace communicated by the Head to the members ('Christ's grace as head of the church')[68] is, as Journet insists, 'filial', granting us adoption as God's sons, but only because 'the grace of Christ as an individual man'[69] is, first of all and most fundamentally, *filial* grace, because it is the grace proper to the one who by nature and from all eternity is the Father's only-begotten son.[70]

CONCLUSION: TOWARDS AN ECCLESIOLOGICAL APOLOGETICS

Despite their differences, Journet and the theologians of *ressourcement* had a single inspiration, a perception of that transcendent beauty of the church which the sins of its members cannot destroy. In a different way from the treatises of the Counter-Reformation, theirs were apologetic ecclesiologies.[71] 'The voice of Tradition', writes de Lubac, 'has continually called on me to look up into the "heavenly Jerusalem", whose beauty has taken a daily firmer hold

---

[63] See Balthasar, 'Who'.   [64] Cf. Balthasar, *Theo-drama*, 345.

[65] Cf. de Lubac on 'The Two Aspects of the One Church', *Splendour*, 55–86.

[66] Congar, 'La personne "Église"', 640.

[67] Cf. 'La personne "Église"', 627n.

[68] Cf. *ST*, 3a.8; Blackfriars, xlix.52–3.

[69] Cf. *ST*, 3a.7; Blackfriars, xlix.4–5.

[70] As Journet says: '[T]he created grace was *filial*. It was the grace of the only Son of the Father; it was, as it were, an effect of the eternal filiation in the soul of Christ' (EVI 2/2, 453).

[71] On this aspect of Congar's ecclesiology, see Gabriel Flynn, *Yves Congar's Vision of the Church in a World of Unbelief* (Aldershot/Burlington VT: Ashgate, 2004).

on me.' But he insists that it is not a dream, nor does he seek it as a 'refuge from everyday monotony and the burden of existence'. On the contrary, he finds it 'at the very heart of earthly reality, right at the core of all the confusion and all the mischances which are, inevitably, involved in [its] mission to men'. Now he seeks to share his vision with others, 'especially my fellow priests'.[72]

Journet's ecclesiological vocation was also born out of love for the church contemplated as a person in the purity of its union with Christ. Arriving in Rome in September 1965 for the third session of the Council, he went to pray before the tomb of St Catherine of Siena at Santa Maria sopra Minerva. That evening he put down his thoughts in a notebook: 'At the Minerva, St Catherine and her love for the Church. It is the Church as she is—holy—that she loves, to whom her heart goes out.' 'Those few words,' says Guy Boissard, 'thrown hastily onto paper, sum up the central intuition that guided [Journet] in the research he conducted over many years in order to investigate more deeply the theology of the Church.'[73] Like St Catherine, Journet was realistic about the moral frailty evident in the church in its wayfaring state. However, he consistently argued that, though the church is 'not without sinners', it itself is 'without sin', in the truth it teaches, the grace it imparts, and in those of its members who love Christ with its own bridal heart.[74] And this undiminished beauty of the *una sancta* exists most perfectly, not in abstraction, but concretely and personally in a woman of flesh and blood, now glorified: in Mary, says Journet, are 'recapitulated and summed up all the riches that the Church, taken as distinct from Christ, taken as the Bride of Christ, could offer successively down the ages of faith: all the splendours, all the purity, all the heart-rending sorrow and compassion'.[75] For the greater love of Jesus, Mary in the church has stolen his heart.

---

[72] De Lubac, *Splendour*, p. ix.   [73] Boissard, Charles Journet, 297.
[74] See Journet, *Théologie de l'Église* (Paris: Desclée de Brouwer, 1958), 236–9.
[75] *The Church of the Word Incarnate*, trans. A. H. C. Downes (London: Sheed & Ward, 1955), pp. xxx–xxxi.

9

Humani Generis and Nouvelle Théologie

Joseph A. Komonchak

INTRODUCTION

Humani Generis[1] was issued in order to deal with 'some false opinions threatening to undermine the foundations of Catholic doctrine'. That some such document was in the works had been widely rumoured for some time, its issuance apparently designed to end a decade-long period of public theological controversy, the most serious since the Modernist crisis of the early twentieth century. It was widely interpreted as threatening the movements of theological recovery and renewal that are the subject of this volume. In what follows, we will consider the historical background to *Humani Generis*, assess its contents and reception, and outline the consequences for leading *ressourcement* theologians of this last effort by Pius XII to hold everything together.

FIRST SIGNS OF TROUBLE

After two decades of relative quiet, two articles appeared around the year 1930 which sought to put the Modernist crisis into perspective. Marie-Dominique Chenu saw it as the latest in a series of crises that have marked the history of theology, analogous to the challenge posed by the introduction of Aristotelianism in the thirteenth century.[2] The Modernist crisis was simply a normal crisis of growth brought about by the introduction of historical method, what we might call the rise of historical consciousness. Bruno de

---

[1] Pius XII, *Humani Generis*: Encyclical Letter Concerning Some False Opinions Threatening to Undermine Catholic Doctrine (12 August 1950), *AAS* xlii (1950), 561–78. ET available at <http://www.vatican.va/holy_father/pius_xii/encyclicals/documents/hf_p-xii_enc_12081950_humani-generis_en.html>.

[2] M.-D. Chenu, 'Le sens et les leçons d'une crise religieuse', *VI*, 13 (1931), 356–80.

Solages traced the reasons for the widespread character of the crisis to the poverty of clerical education in the nineteenth century, expressing the fear that, since that formation had not notably improved in quality, a new crisis could be possible.[3]

The two articles were a sign that scholars were beginning to hope that the worst of the anti-Modernist repression was over and that it might be safe once again to address questions that had not so much been addressed and answered as forced underground. This theological rebirth was part of a general revitalization of Catholic thought in the 1930s, a decade whose multiple crises (in economics, politics, international relations, etc.) demanded that Catholics accept their responsibility to offer the world something more than the discredited individualism of liberalism and the collectivism of the three forms of totalitarianism which were flourishing in its place. That this new sense of historic responsibility had consequences for the doing of theology was a view held by several French theologians at work during the 1930s, among them the Dominicans Chenu, Yves Congar, and Louis Charlier, and the Jesuits Yves de Montcheuil, Henri de Lubac, and Pierre Teilhard de Chardin.[4]

In the mid-1930s, Chenu began a series of essays on theology in which he called into question the primacy of the theological conclusion and began to insist that theologians regard the life of the church as a primary *locus theologicus*. This in particular required them to be alert to what he would later call 'signs of the times', so that a theology present to its age would enable the church to be present, incarnate in its various milieux.[5] Late in 1937 Chenu published a series of talks he had given on how philosophical and theological studies were being carried out at Le Saulchoir, where he was Regent of Studies.[6] He noted how, from having been at the centre of intellectual life at the thirteenth-century universities, Dominicans had increasingly emigrated to the margins of cultural life. In place of the emphasis St Thomas had put on *inventio*, they had become content, as had theologians in general, with adding a few more conclusions to a system of syllogisms. At Le Saulchoir, as opposed to many institutions, philosophical and theological studies were alive and fresh, respecting the autonomy of the necessary auxiliary disciplines, drawing immediately upon spiritual participation in the mystery of God, and alert and present to the needs of the day.

---

[3] Bruno de Solages, 'La crise moderniste et les études ecclésiastiques', *Revue apologétique*, 51 (1930), 5–30.

[4] See my 'Returning from Exile: Catholic Theology in the 1930s', in Gregory Baum (ed.), *The Twentieth Century: A Theological Overview* (Maryknoll NY: Orbis, 1999), 35–48.

[5] See in particular 'Position de la théologie', *RSPT*, 2 (1935), 232–57.

[6] Chenu, *Une école de théologie: le Saulchoir* (Kain-les-Tournai/Étiolles: Le Saulchoir/Casterman, 1937); re-issued as *Une école de théologie: le Saulchoir*, eds. G Alberigo, É Fouilloux, J Ladriére, J.-P. Jossua (Paris: Cerf, 1985).

Chenu's book was considered something of a manifesto by many members of his own community, and was certainly so read by Dominicans elsewhere, most importantly in Rome. Early in February 1938, he was called to Rome and forced to sign ten propositions that reveal both the stunning incomprehension of his Roman readers and the concerns that drove their criticism, particularly the unchanging nature of doctrinal truths and the role of Thomas Aquinas' contribution to making theology a demonstrable science, based on scripture and tradition.[7]

1. Dogmatic formulas state absolute and immutable truth.

2. True and certain propositions, whether in philosophy or in theology, are firm and not at all fragile.

3. Sacred Tradition does not create new truths; one must instead firmly maintain that the deposit of revelation, that is, the complex of divinely revealed truths, was closed at the death of the last apostle.

4. Sacred Theology is not some spirituality which has found instruments adequate to its religious experience; it is rather a true science, by God's blessing acquired through study, whose principles are the articles of faith as well as all the revealed truths to which the theologian adheres by at least unformed divine faith.[8]

5. The various theological systems are not simultaneously true, at least with regard to points on which they disagree.

6. It is a glorious thing that the Church considers the system of St Thomas to be quite orthodox, that is, quite in conformity with the truths of faith.

7. It is necessary to demonstrate theological truths by Sacred Scripture and Tradition and to explain their nature and intimate meaning by the principles and doctrine of St Thomas.

8. Although properly a theologian, St Thomas was also properly a philosopher; for that reason his philosophy does not depend for its intelligibility and truth on his theology, and it states truths that are absolute and not merely relative.

9. It is quite necessary for a theologian, in his scientific work, to make use of the metaphysics of St Thomas and diligently to follow the rules of dialectics.

---

[7] For Chenu's travail, see Fouilloux, 'Le Saulchoir en procès (1937–42)', in *Une école*, 37–59; and 'Autour d'une mise à l'Index', in *Marie-Dominique Chenu: Moyen Âge et modernité*, Les Cahiers du Centre d'études du Saulchoir, 5 (Paris: Centre d'Etudes du Saulchoir, 1997), 25–56.

[8] See Yves Congar, *Journal d'un théologien, 1946–1956*, ed. Étienne Fouilloux (Paris: Cerf, 2000), 330.

10. In speaking about other writers and doctors one should use respectful moderation in one's style of speech and writing, even when they are found to be defective on some matters.[9]

A year of relative quiet came to an end when Chenu was informed in January 1939 that Rome was unhappy with Yves Congar's book *Chrétiens désunis*. This time the work was censured for augmenting the role of experience at the expense of dogma, which was relativized as a result. The following five propositions were identified as being problematic:

1. Instead of adherence to the dogmatic formulas proposed by the Church *propter auctoritatem Dei revelantis*, Christian faith is the common religious experience of Christians, experience of the *value of the Christian life* and of the *exigencies* of the Mystical Body of Christ which must always be perfected in accord with the needs of the times.

2. That is why, when individual religious experience goes astray and falls into error, it must be *corrected* by the criterion *of the common religious experience of authentic Christians*, which is something always alive, complete, which renews everything in accord with the needs of the times, rather than by the dogmatic formulas, which are always a partial, incomplete, often too harsh and rigid expression of the common experience.

3. Dogmatic formulas, although always true and always to be maintained in the same sense, *remain ever relative*, in virtue of a two-fold relativity, historical and metaphysical; thus they are always imperfect and so 'radically fragile' that they are relatively true rather than absolutely true.

4. The dogmatic formulas which are a 'conceptualization of religious experience' or a way of expressing this living and complete experience by fixed and always defective concepts.

5. The religious experience of Protestants, although it is deficient and mixed with many errors, *preserves aspects and tendencies of genuine Christian life, particular tendencies which are found in less lively a fashion in the Church*. The latter, by the conversion of Protestants, would become not only quantitatively but also qualitatively richer and more catholic.[10]

Things became more complex still with the publication in September 1938 of Louis Charlier's *Essai sur le probléme théologique*. Charlier agreed with Chenu about the rigidity of post-Tridentine scholasticism and the need for complementarity between speculative and positive theology, but disagreed

---

[9] See Chenu, *Une école*, 35. Author's translation.
[10] See Fouilloux, 'Autour d'une mise à l'Index', 38.

with him over Aquinas' view of the scientific character of theology. The work, soon withdrawn from circulation, was the object of criticism.[11]

On the feast of St Thomas Aquinas, 1940, Mariano Cordovani, OP, gave an important address in which it is not hard to see references to the views of these French and Belgian theologians and a reflection of the concerns at the Holy Office. Cordovani described several views that were suspect: a 'subjective consideration of dogma' as 'an expression of the religious experiences of the faithful'; 'a psychological and historical relativism' that 'pervades certain books that are presented as programmes for reform and in which it is impossible to find the revealed ontological truth'; present religious experience as the only source and criterion for theological progress; tradition as creative; the idea 'that theology is a vague spirituality that has found modes of expression adequate to its religious experience'; an exaggerated mysticism in views of the church; the view that things lacking in the Church can be found in schismatic churches; the idea that dogmatic definitions impoverish and harden revealed truth; mistaken views of the finality of marriage. Cordovani insisted that he favoured a healthy freedom in theological research:

> I do not at all approve of that hunting passion that goes off in search of someone else's errors for the sake of the thin satisfaction of finding faults in a colleague . . . But . . . thoughtlessness and arrogance . . . truly bring mockery upon a theologian who neglects the deposit of revelation, ignores the documents of the Church's magisterium, and . . . thinks he has a right to import into the temple of theology methods which literary critics sometimes allow themselves, but which a master in divinity never may.[12]

Things remained fairly quiet until 4 February 1942, when Chenu learned that *Le Saulchoir* and Charlier's *Essai* had both been placed on the Index. The closest thing to an official explanation of the Roman action was an article by Pietro Parente, which found the two authors guilty of ridiculing scholasticism for its conceptualism and syllogistic, deductive method; for compromising the stable and immutable character of theological formulas; for mistaken views of the development of doctrine and of tradition. He then introduced the phrase that would have a great future in the next decade: 'Thus it is clear that this *new theology* . . . offers nothing certain and sure that can provide a basis for constructing a new doctrine more in accord with today's needs.'[13] Chenu was removed from Le Saulchoir and Charlier forbidden to teach.

---

[11] For this wider context, see R. Guelluy, 'Les antécédents de l'Encyclique "Humani Generis" dans les sanctions romaines de 1942: Chenu, Charlier, Draguet', *Revue d'Histoire Ecclésiastique*, 81 (1986), 421–97; Jürgen Mettepenningen, 'L'Essai de Louis Charlier (1938): Une contribution à la nouvelle théologie', *RThL*, 39 (2008), 211–32.

[12] Mariano Cordovani, 'Per la vitalità della teologia cattolica', *Ang*, 17 (1940), 133–46.

[13] Pietro Parente, 'Nuove tendenze teologiche', *L'Osservatore Romano*, 9–10 February 1942; republished in Latin in *Periodica*, 31 (1942), 184–8; my translation. For a good account of the whole affair, see Fouilloux, 'Le Saulchoir en procès'.

ANOTHER STORM GATHERS

By the late 1930s, three publishing initiatives had been planned and initiated in order to promote a renewal of theology. Yves Congar founded Unam Sanctam, a series of monographs devoted to ecclesiology and Christian re-union. Among its first volumes were his *Chrétiens désunis*; a translation of Johann Adam Möhler's *Die Einheit in der Kirche*; and de Lubac's *Catholicisme: les aspects sociaux du dogme*. Questions about all three works were to be raised in Rome. French Jesuits, led by de Lubac and Daniélou, embarked upon two publishing projects, a series of translations of works by the Fathers of the Church, *Sources chrétiennes;*[14] and a monograph series, *Théologie*. By 1946 ten volumes had appeared in the *Sources chrétiennes* series and eight in the *Théologie* series, among them Bouillard's doctoral dissertation, *Conversion et grâce chez S. Thomas d'Aquin*, Daniélou's book on Platonism and mystical theology in Gregory of Nyssa, and de Lubac's *Corpus Mysticum* and *Surnaturel*.

With the Second World War over, the debate about theological method might have been resumed in any case; but the excitement of liberation gave greater impetus to reflections on the responsibilities of Christian thinkers. In April 1946, Daniélou gave voice to this excitement in an essay which, intentionally or not, had all the appearance of a manifesto and a call to action.[15] He began by noting the contemporary intellectual elite's renewed interest in Christianity and search for a living theology present in the world of thought. Theology's lack of cultural *engagement* was a consequence of the Modernist crisis and its aftermath. The severe crackdown was necessary: 'It was a matter of warding off the dangers created by Modernism', he wrote, adding then a comment that annoyed a good number of people: 'Neo-Thomism and the Biblical Commission were these guard-rails. But it is quite clear that guard-rails are not responses.'[16]

Theology faced three challenges: it had to treat God as subject and not as object; to respond to contemporary experience; and to engage the whole person in committed action. 'Theology will be living only if it responds to these aspirations.' The first mark of contemporary religious thought was 'a renewed contact with its sources in the Bible, the Fathers of the Church, and the liturgy'.[17] This would repair the rupture between scripture and theology. In particular, he urged a recovery of the way in which the Fathers read the Scriptures, especially their figurative interpretation of the Old Testament. Such

[14] See Fouilloux, *La collection 'Sources chrétiennes': Editer les Péres de l'Eglise au XXe siécle* (Paris: Cerf, 1995).
[15] Daniélou, 'Les orientations présentes de la pensée religieuse', *Études*, 249 (1946), 5–21.
[16] 'Les orientations présentes', 5–7.
[17] 'Les orientations présentes', 7.

a recovery relied on a retrieval of patristic sources, where '[the Fathers] are not simply the real witnesses of a past that is gone; they are also the most relevant nourishment for people today because we find in them again precisely a certain number of categories which are those of contemporary thought and which scholastic theology had lost'.[18] Finally, the liturgical renewal was transforming liturgy into 'the place for man's encounter with the Mystery of God';[19] a further illustration of the concern that theology be in touch with life.

If theology were to engage contemporary thought, it would have to widen its horizons and face the 'two abysses, historicity and subjectivity'. 'It is very clear,' he continued, 'that such categories are foreign to scholastic theology. Its world is the immobile world of Greek thought in which it was its mission to incarnate the Christian message.'[20] Furthermore, 'to be living, theology has to take account of the needs of souls, to be animated by a spirit of apostolate, to be totally engaged in the work of building up the Body of Christ'.[21] This requires theology and spirituality to renew contact, particularly important for the lay vocation, a theology of marriage, and for Christian temporal and political *engagement*. Daniélou concluded on a grand note:

> Such are the broad lines of the task that now lies before Christian thought. . . . Preceding generations have accumulated materials; it is time now to build. For this people must arise who join a profound sense of the Christian tradition, and a life of contemplation, which gives them an understanding of the mystery of Christ, to a keen sense of the needs of their time and a burning love for the souls of their brethren—people who, the tighter they are bound by the inner bond of the Spirit, the more free they are with regard to all humanity.[22]

Daniélou's article was read as a challenge at the Dominican province of Toulouse's studium, stable of *Revue thomiste*.[23] The young editor, Marie-Michel Labourdette, saw Daniélou's article as 'a declaration of war' on Thomism and decided to respond to it. In August 1946 he circulated the abstract of an article entitled 'La théologie et ses sources'. Labourdette noted the inauguration of the two new series, *Sources chrétiennes* and *Théologie*, and observed the important role that de Lubac and Daniélou were playing in both. He had high praise for the project of making works of the Fathers more widely available and special praise for one of the monographs published in the second series, Jean Mouroux' *Sens chrétien de l'homme*. But Labourdette believed that in both series one could perceive an intention to call into question the great progress made when theology had achieved scientific status during the Middle

---

[18] 'Les orientations présentes', 10.
[19] 'Les orientations présentes', 12.   [20] 'Les orientations présentes', 14.
[21] 'Les orientations présentes', 17.   [22] 'Les orientations présentes', 21.
[23] See further Fouilloux, 'Dialogue théologique?' in S.-T. Bonino (ed.), *Saint Thomas au XXe siécle*, Actes du colloque du Centenaire de la *Revue Thomiste* (Paris: Centre National de Livre-Saint Paul, 1994), 153–95.

Ages and particularly in the work of Aquinas. He sensed a depreciation of scholastic theology and feared a double relativism, both historical and subjectivist. He cited as illustrative a statement made towards the end of Bouillard's *Conversion et grâce*: 'Une théologie qui ne serait pas actuelle serait une théologie fausse.'

While Labourdette's article posed serious challenges, it has to be said that it was written respectfully and intelligently, as a serious theological critique: just what theologians should offer one another. Labourdette was proposing a theological conversation, not an intervention of authority. He refused to accept Garrigou-Lagrange's contentious article for the *Revue thomiste*—which instead had to be published in *Angelicum*—and in the middle of the conflict he wrote to him:

> The doctrinal crisis is serious, and [in France] we are in a difficult battle, rather different from the one you wage in Rome. The vast majority is against us, and they are often the elements who are the most active, the most alive, and, so far as one can judge, the most generously Christian. There is one thing that we absolutely have to avoid, or risk losing all credibility: giving the impression that we are appealing, to settle the debates, to Roman authority. Yes, authority has to be exercised. Perhaps it has done so too late. Others may have that duty. Our role, for the sake of the truth, is to defend it by the sole forces of our intelligence and our good reasons. . . . [I]t would be catastrophic if Thomism could only defend itself by recourse to authority. I believe that the *Revue thomiste* has this mission of defending Thomism by itself and by its intrinsic force alone.[24]

In the summer of 1946 Pope Pius XII had occasion to address delegates of two religious orders as they gathered in Rome for general meetings at which to elect superiors general. While in his speech to the Dominicans, the Pope was content with a forceful reminder of the need to follow Aquinas' method, doctrine, and principles in both philosophy and theology, to the Jesuits he made a remark that was widely quoted:

> A lot has been said, not always with sufficient reflection, about a 'new theology' which, in a constantly developing world, would itself also be in constant development, always en route and never arriving anywhere. If such a view were thought legitimate, what would happen to the immutable Catholic dogmas and to the unity and stability of faith?[25]

There is circumstantial evidence that Garrigou-Lagrange was responsible for this passage; in a letter to Labourdette written shortly before the papal discourses, he said: 'Fr Daniélou's article in last April's *Études* appears to be the manifesto of this new theology [*théologie nouvelle*] . . . But here [in Rome]

---

[24] Labourdette to Garrigou-Lagrange, 2 April 1947, quoted in 'Correspondance Étienne Gilson–Michel Labourdette', *RevTh*, 94 (1994), 479–529 (498).
[25] *AAS*, xlii (1950) 385–9.

people are closely watching the whole movement, which is a return to Modernism . . .'[26]

De Lubac's notes during the 1946 General Congregation reveal the tense atmosphere. The Pope's remarks about 'new theology' were widely understood to be aimed at French theologians; rumours were spreading that he himself was particularly the target; it was known that Bouillard's book had already been the subject of a formal doctrinal investigation; it was rumoured that Garrigou-Lagrange was preparing a very critical attack.[27] De Lubac and the other Jesuits read Labourdette's article in this atmosphere, which explains why their response, approved by their superiors, was so vigorous. De Lubac was the principal author of this reply, which appeared early in 1947 as a collective response from the five Jesuits who felt themselves indicted: de Lubac, Daniélou, Bouillard, Fessard, and Balthasar.[28] It rejected his charge that there was a kind of new school forming, defending the positions against charges of doctrinal or subjectivistic relativism, and arguing that there was room within the church for different theological schools.

The Jesuits' response was so vigorous that one can wonder whether any real theological dialogue would have been possible; but all possibility was erased by the almost simultaneous publication early in 1947 of Garrigou-Lagrange's notorious article, 'La nouvelle théologie où va-t-elle?'[29] Now they confronted, not a relatively young and unknown critic, but a man who for almost half a century had been a fierce defender of orthodoxy and foe of people suspected of heresy; he was also an adviser to the Holy Office, where his views were thought to carry great weight.

Garrigou-Lagrange answers his question in two places in the article: 'And where is this new theology going to head with the new masters who inspire it? Where is it heading if not down the road to scepticism, fantasy, and heresy?'[30] 'Where is the new theology heading? It is returning to modernism.'[31] He identifies the new theology with Bouillard's by now notorious statement: 'A theology that is not relevant or contemporary (*actuelle*) would be a false theology',[32] which he reads in the worst possible light, as logically entailing that the theology of Aquinas and the dogmatic formulations of Trent are now false because no longer contemporary. He finds this based in a Blondelian notion of truth, which saw it not as conformity with reality but as conformity with one's

[26] Garrigou-Lagrange to Labourdette, 17 July 1946, quoted in Fouilloux, 'Dialogue théologique?', 170n.
[27] Henri de Lubac, *At the Service of the Church*, trans. Anne Elizabeth Englund (San Francisco: Ignatius Press, 1993), 250–7.
[28] Labourdette, 'La théologie et ses sources', *RSR*, 33 (1946), 385–401.
[29] Réginald Garrigou-Lagrange, 'La nouvelle théologie, où va-t-elle?', *Ang*, 23 (1946), 126–45. The article did not appear until the beginning of February 1947.
[30] 'La nouvelle théologie', 134.   [31] 'La nouvelle théologie', 143.
[32] 'La nouvelle théologie', 126.

subjective life. Garrigou-Lagrange then illustrates the new views with highly selective references to de Lubac's *Surnaturel*,[33] Chenu's *Le Saulchoir*,[34] a book review by Fessard,[35] Daniélou's article,[36] and unpublished articles, by Teilhard de Chardin and Yves de Montcheuil, which had been circulating.[37]

Garrigou-Lagrange's 'atomic bomb' had the effect of so frightening the Jesuit superiors in Rome that they refused to allow the indicted Jesuits to reply to it; and they began to indicate reservations about their French colleagues, in particular the tone and content of their response to Labourdette. The Jesuits were permitted to prepare private replies to Garrigou-Lagrange which were then sent to Rome, apparently for private use in defending the accused. Garrigou-Lagrange became acquainted with Bouillard's reply and made it the target of criticism in a new article.

Some efforts to mediate in the disputes were undertaken, notably by Bruno de Solages, and other figures became involved in the controversies, particularly over the question of the possibility of distinct theologies, a discussion which anticipates what since Vatican II we have discussed under the rubric of pluralism in theology. Whereas Bouillard's book was the principal object of concern at the beginning of the controversy, de Lubac's views, as expressed in the brief doctrinal appendix in *Surnaturel*, soon came to dominate. Many readers, and not only in Rome, could not see how de Lubac's repudiation of the hypothesis of 'pure nature' did not compromise the gratuity of the supernatural order. In September 1947 the Jesuit Father General, Janssens, had *Surnaturel* reviewed by four Jesuit censors.[38]

Fouilloux is correct in noting that no real theological dialogue was possible because the Jesuits were kept under very tight rein by their superiors. In addition, as early as January 1947, there were rumours that 'a kind of Syllabus is being prepared, one whole part of which is devoted to a certain "new theology"'.[39] On 15 March 1948, Cordovani published an article in *L'Osservatore Romano* in which he referred to Pius XII's talks to the Jesuits and Dominicans and regretted that the Pope's call 'for a more scientific and less arbitrary study of theology' had not been better heeded.[40]

Perhaps in response to this exhortation, on 8 September 1948, Janssens sent out norms for studies in philosophy and theology at Egenhoven and Leuven.[41]

---

[33] 'La nouvelle théologie', 132.
[34] 'La nouvelle théologie', 134.   [35] 'La nouvelle théologie', 133.
[36] 'La nouvelle théologie', 133.   [37] 'La nouvelle théologie', 135–7.
[38] For their evaluations, see de Lubac, *At the Service of the Church*, 259–64.
[39] *At the Service of the Church*, 275.
[40] Cordovani, 'Truth and Novelty in Theology', *American Ecclesiastical Review*, 119 (October 1948), 241–3.
[41] See *Acta Romana Societatis Jesu*, 11/4 (1949), 480–9. There is such a coincidence between the emphases in these norms and those of *Humani Generis* as to make one wonder whether the drafter of the norms was not well acquainted with what was being prepared for Pius XII.

These seem to show some influence of the theological controversies under way, warning against theological views, 'however brilliant and useful they may seem' which depart from the sense of the Church. They remind the Jesuits that knowledge of the deposit of the faith requires long and hard preparation and that it would be quite wrong for someone who has neglected it to think himself called 'to construct new systems in which the very notions of dogma, revelation, inspiration, original sin, the divine knowledge would without any serious basis in the Tradition assume a character and interpretation till now unknown'. After recalling that respect for the Church's teaching authority must include the ordinary magisterium, the norms warn against the growing disrespect for scholastic theology and authors, lest a twofold magisterium, one orthodox, for public consumption, one less orthodox and underground, develop in houses of formation. Similar rules were also given for education in philosophy. Aquinas was to remain their chief mentor, alongside modern philosophers who did not deviate from scholastic philosophy. Students were also to be given clear and correct ideas on the relationship between faith and philosophy and to be taught that rationality did not need supplementing with intuition.

In the spring of 1949 Edouard Dhanis, SJ, carried out an official visitation of Fourviére, during which he prepared a memorandum reminding the faculty of their duties to the magisterium.[42] After the publication of *Humani Generis*, Teilhard de Chardin reported the rumour that 'the entire avalanche was triggered by a report from Danis (*sic*)... The General supposedly found it so "appalling" that he had to hand it over to the Pope (?!). Whence the execution of Fourviére and the Encyclical.'[43]

The 'execution of Fourviére' anticipated the encyclical by a couple of months. In May 1950 de Lubac was informed that he would have to leave the faculty; later that month, the removal from Jesuit libraries and destruction of copies of Émile Delaye's *Qu'est-ce qu'un Catholique* was ordered; he too had to leave.[44] On 14 June, three further Jesuits—Bouillard, Alexandre Durand, and Pierre Ganne—were told to leave Fourviére. When Bouillard asked for an explanation, he was told that the Father General's letter said they had not taken proper note of the Pope's warning to the Society, to the criticisms of their views by eminent theologians, or to his personal warnings.[45] According to de Lubac's protest letter, he had accused them of 'pernicious errors on essential points of dogma! Errors, he adds, in which I have been obstinate,

---

[42] See Fouilloux, *Une Eglise en quête de liberté: La pensée catholique française entre modernisme et Vatican II (1914–1962)* (Paris: Desclée de Brouwer, 1998), 290.

[43] Quoted in de Lubac, *At the Service of the Church*, 301.

[44] *Acta Romana Societatis Jesu*, 11/6 (1950), 852.

[45] Henri Bouillard, *Vérité du christianisme* (Paris: Desclée de Brouwer, 1989), 405–6, citing Bouillard's diary.

despite the most authoritative warnings'.[46] In his own letter to the Society, published in 1951, Janssens admitted that these actions were taken in the knowledge that the Pope intended to intervene.[47] It is possible that he acted before the encyclical appeared so that the removals would not appear to be the consequence of the papal intervention.

HUMANI GENERIS

Unfortunately, we do not know who wrote or collaborated in the writing of the encyclical. Congar was told by the Dominicans of Bologna that Parente was one of the writers[48] and from a conversation with Fr Charles Boyer, drew the impression that he and Parente had been involved, but Fouilloux says that Boyer formally denied the claim.[49] De Lubac quotes Fr Pierre Charles' denial that he had anything to do with it: 'If I had drafted it, it would be in better Latin.' De Lubac also cites a hypothesis sent to him by a priest in Rome in March 1951 that 'three amalgamated drafts can be distinguished . . . : a "malevolent" document was the original basis for it; a first reshaping gave a "more malevolent" document; the encyclical resulted from another reshaping, by "a man of very good will . . .", who might have been "some Benedictine"'.[50] Perhaps some credit can be given to this hypothesis from the comment that Congar heard that 'it was the Abbot General of the Benedictines who wrote the encyclical's paragraph with regard to Fr. Daniélou'.[51] I have found no evidence about Garrigou-Lagrange's involvement, but certain sections of the encyclical sound very much like him. Other theologians working in Rome, Gagnebet, Dhanis, and Guy de Broglie, SJ, should also be considered possible authors.[52]

Some commentators contrasted it with Pius X's *Pascendi, Humani Generis* being far more moderate in tone, in the care with which it gave directives, in the balance it showed between the rejection of errors and the acceptance of

---

[46] De Lubac, *At the Service of the Church*, 293–5.

[47] See *Woodstock Letters*, 80 (1951), 291. On the eve of *Humani Generis*' publication, Congar's Father General told him that had he not been there, the French Dominicans would have suffered the same fate; *Journal*, 164.

[48] Congar, *Journal*, 169.

[49] *Journal*, 173.

[50] De Lubac, *At the Service of the Church*, 299. Giacomo Martina has a similar view. See, 'The Historical Context in Which the Idea of a New Ecumenical Council was born', in René Latourelle (ed.) *Vatican II: Assessment and Perspectives Twenty-Five Years After (1962–1987)*, i (New York: Paulist Press, 1988) 3–73 (32).

[51] *Journal*, 179.

[52] *Journal*, 213–14.

elements of truth, and in its encouragement to research,[53] and care not to condemn named individuals.[54]

The influence of successive authors may, as Aubert suggests, explain why there is no clear and coherent structure or plan to the encyclical.[55] Weigel concludes that 'an order of uninterrupted logical continuity has not been widely recognized, for those who made skeleton outlines were at variance with each other'.[56] Aubert suggests the following division: Introduction on principal contemporary errors; then errors in theology, in philosophy, and with regard to the relation between faith and the positive sciences. This is also the structure Fenton's outline discerned, and it has some basis in the typography of the *AAS*.[57]

Humani Generis begins with a description of 'the principal trends' of the day: evolution, existentialism, historicism, which 'overthrow the foundation of all truth and absolute law', an 'imprudent "eirenicism"', neglect of the magisterium; in sum, the dangers of separation from the Church's teaching authority.[58]

Turning first to theological errors, some seek to weaken the significance of dogmas and free them from ancient terminology and concepts, returning to biblical and patristic language. This would improve ecumenical conversations and enable theologians to address modern needs and to make use of 'concepts of modern philosophy, whether of immanentism or idealism or existentialism or any other system', and highlight doctrinal development.[59]

The Pope's judgement is severe: this not only leads towards 'dogmatic relativism'; it already contains it. Terminology may vary, and the Church cannot be bound to every ephemeral philosophy, but it is wrong to abandon traditional concepts, 'based on principles and notions deduced from a true knowledge of created things', used and sanctioned in ecumenical councils. In addition, 'contempt for terms and notions habitually used by scholastic theologians leads of itself to the weakening of... speculative theology, a discipline which these men consider devoid of true certainty because it is based on theological reasoning'.[60] Clearly referring to the views of Bouillard and de Lubac, these paragraphs remind one of Garrigou-Lagrange's articles. If he had any part in writing *Humani Generis*, I would place it here.

A second area of error concerns the magisterium, which 'in matters of faith and morals must be the proximate and universal criterion of truth for all

---

[53] See Gustave Weigel, 'Gleanings from the Commentaries on *Humani generis*', TS, 12 (1951), 520–49 (529).

[54] See Congar's reports in his *Journal*, 166.

[55] Roger Aubert, '*Humani generis*', in *Dictionnaire d'histoire et de géographie ecclésiastique*, s.v., 334–9.

[56] Weigel, 'Commentaries', 534.   [57] *AAS*, xlii (1950) 561–78.

[58] *HG* § 5–7, 10–12.   [59] *HG* § 14–15.

[60] *HG* § 16–17.

theologians'. Papal teaching about 'the nature and constitution of the Church' is abandoned in favour of 'a certain vague notion which they profess to have found in the ancient Fathers, especially the Greeks', and since popes do not seek to judge theological disputes, they feel able to go back to the ancient sources, in the light of which the recent magisterium is to be explained.[61] The Pope's judgement is that while it is true that the popes leave some questions open, there are some things once open that are now closed. There follows a famous paragraph:

> Nor must it be thought that what is expounded in Encyclical Letters does not of itself demand consent, since in writing such Letters the Popes do not exercise the supreme power of their Teaching Authority. For these matters are taught with the ordinary teaching authority . . . and generally what is expounded and inculcated in Encyclical Letters already for other reasons appertains to Catholic doctrine. But if the Supreme Pontiffs in their official documents purposely pass judgment on a matter up to that time under dispute, it is obvious that that matter . . . cannot be any longer considered a question open to discussion among theologians.[62]

Recourse to the sources of divine revelation is always necessary, because it is the theologians' role to show how doctrine 'is to be found either explicitly or implicitly in the Scriptures and in Tradition'. These sources are inexhaustible, and theological speculation without them. But theology is more than history, for its teaching office gives authoritative interpretations of the deposit of faith. 'The most noble office of theology is to show how a doctrine defined by the Church is contained in the sources of revelation.'[63]

Finally, Pius XII turns to errors concerning the interpretation of scripture. Some want to restrict its inerrancy to faith and morals; others try to interpret the Bible apart from the analogy of faith and church tradition. Some want to substitute literal sense with 'symbolic or spiritual' sense, particularly in interpreting the Old Testament, 'today a sealed book'. (This would appear to be aimed in particular at Daniélou.) All depart from the magisterium on biblical interpretation.[64]

There follows a rather lengthy list of problems that have arisen in consequence of these errors.[65] It shows no particular order, nor how these errors follow from those more fully exposed. So confused and confusing is it that, here again, one might think of Garrigou-Lagrange.

The next section turns to errors in philosophy, beginning with praise of the ability of properly-trained reason, based on the 'sound philosophy' of earlier ages and endorsed by the magisterium, to prove God's existence and the foundations of Christian revelation, to discover the natural law, and to promote understanding of revealed mysteries. The Church leaves much in

---

[61] *HG* § 18.   [62] *HG* § 20.   [63] *HG* § 21.
[64] *HG* § 22–3.   [65] *HG* § 25–8.

philosophy to free discussion, but not such basic principles, which may be elaborated and restated, but not denied, as truth is unchanging. Hence it demands that seminarians be instructed 'according to the method, doctrine, and principles of' Aquinas, and deplores this philosophy being scorned as outdated and rationalistic. Some claim that an absolutely true metaphysics is impossible, as 'reality, especially transcendent reality, cannot better be expressed than by disparate doctrines . . .'; traditional philosophy may be 'useful as a preparation for scholastic theology', but 'hardly offers a method of philosophizing suited to the needs of modern culture'. Some therefore are turning to 'philosophies of all kinds, ancient and modern, oriental and occidental' implying that 'any kind of philosophy or theory, with a few additions and corrections if needed, can be reconciled with Catholic dogma'.[66]

All these errors, which can have bad effects in theology, would have been avoided had people acknowledged the magisterium, 'which by divine institution has the mission not only to guard and interpret the deposit of divinely revealed truth, but also to keep watch over the philosophical sciences themselves', to protect Catholic dogma.[67]

The final section turns to faith and the sciences, first admitting that the Church must take modern sciences into account, but that this applies only to 'clearly proved facts' and not to 'hypotheses'. Caution is needed when 'the doctrine contained in Scripture or in Tradition is involved' with 'hypotheses'.[68] The Pope then applies this to the question of evolution, which could only be true of the origin of the human body; souls are immediately created by God. It must be balanced with faith and dogma, especially with regard to polygenism and the teaching of the church on original sin.[69]

Turning to history, the Pope deplores certain overly free interpretations of the historical books of the Old Testament, particularly the first eleven chapters of Genesis. These are clearly symbolic but nevertheless 'pertain to history in a true sense', although this requires expert study. While it can be granted that popular narratives have made their way into the Scriptures, they should not be thought equivalent to extravagant ancient myths.[70]

The encyclical ends with the Pope enjoining bishops and superiors general to take great care that 'these various opinions not be advanced in schools, conferences or writings of any kind and not be taught to either clergy or faithful'. Teachers must observe these norms, striving to advance what they teach without transgressing the limits in the encyclical, addressing new questions as they arise prudently and cautiously. They should not indulge in 'a false "eirenicism", that the dissident and erring can happily be brought back to the bosom of the Church, if the whole truth found in the Church is not sincerely taught to all without corruption or diminution'.[71]

[66] *HG* § 29–32.   [67] *HG* § 34.   [68] *HG* § 35.
[69] *HG* § 36–7.   [70] *HG* § 38–40.   [71] *HG* § 41–3.

IMMEDIATE CONSEQUENCES

In an internal address, the Jesuit Father General noted the controversy, speaking of the Society's having been the object of the 'solemn warning' of Pius XII in 1946 in which 'he urged those who were apparently teaching a "New Theology" to return to humility and prudence'. Because the problem was a result of 'too great a deviation from Scholastic philosophy', he had undertaken to reform the system of teaching. But things were more difficult when it came to theological reform:

> Admonitions, both public and private, were administered time after time. Censures were invoked. Works which were being circulated in manuscript form were suppressed. Some of our men were forbidden to write on specified subjects. Several books, which could not have been given approval, were condemned.... It was obvious, once a thorough visitation...had been made, that the evil had rooted itself so deeply in the members of the Society—and more especially in others outside the Society—that the ordinary remedies at the disposal of the General would not cure this evil.

Hence the Holy See 'took the business in hand' and prepared the encyclical. 'Would that some of Ours', Janssens concluded, 'had not strayed from the wise norms set down in our Institute.' He was in effect declaring Jesuits to be guilty of crimes of which the encyclical had not named them perpetrators.[72]

On 25 October 1950, Janssens ordered several books and articles[73] to be removed from libraries to which younger Jesuits had access. Permission could be given for them to be consulted only 'if the errors or ambiguities are pointed out which in them are opposed to the teaching of the Encyclical *Humani generis*'.[74]

On 11 February 1951, Janssens sent the Society a letter, longer and, it could be argued, more severe on the Jesuits than *Humani Generis* itself. The encyclical had named no names, but Janssens begins by saying that it 'envisions principally a rather complex intellectual movement in which some of Ours have taken part and even played leading roles.' He includes a long exhortation to obedience to the encyclical and its norms and notes that he has had to do so 'because I have learned from several facts that it is opportune for me to be insistent; some among you need to be instructed by their superior and father'.

---

[72] See *Woodstock Letters*, 80 (1951), 213–15.

[73] Bouillard, *Conversion et grace*, 'Notions conciliaires et analogie de la Vérité' (*RSR*, 35 (1948), 251ff.), 'L'intention fondamentale de Maurice Blondel et la théologie', (*RSR*, 36 (1949), 321f), 'L'idée chrétienne du miracle' (*Cahiers Laënnec*, 8 (1948), 25–37); Daniélou, *Dialogues*, 'Les orientations présentes'; de Lubac, *Surnaturel, Corpus Mysticum, De la connaissance de Dieu*, 'Le mystère du surnaturel' (*RSR*, 36 (1949), 80ff); de Montcheuil's *Pages religieuses de Maurice Blondel* and *Leçons de Christ*; Le Blond, 'L'analogie de la Vérité: Réflexions d'un philosophe sur une controverse théologique' (*RSR*, 34 (1947), 129ff).

[74] *Acta Romana Societatis Jesu*, 11/6 (1950), 882–3.

He continued with his own interpretation of what he thought the encyclical said or implied with regard to doctrinal relativism, where Bouillard and de Lubac are clearly intended; to philosophical issues, including the possibility of an 'absolutely true metaphysics'; to proofs of the existence of God, of the fact of revelation, and of the credibility of Christianity; to the freedom of God in creating; to the immediate creation of the human soul; to the gratuity of the supernatural order, at some length, clearly with de Lubac's views in mind; to the notion of original sin and to polygenism; to the real presence and transubstantiation, where he is upset that some Jesuits hold the symbolic view; to the identity between the Mystical Body and Catholic Church; to the enduring value of scholastic philosophy and theology; and to the interpretation of the Bible. To these he even adds a few points of doctrine concerning eschatology, which had not been raised in *Humani Generis*.

Janssens' letter, which has received surprisingly little analysis, is remarkable not only for its assumption of a guilt not explicitly laid at the feet of the Society of Jesus, but also for the effort made to explicate the significance of the teachings of *Humani Generis* and to make these explanations binding also on members of the Society. Where the encyclical was sober and careful, Janssens' letter is nervous and sweeping. He seems concerned to exclude or to prevent any kind of attempt to evade the force of the Pope's words. He has made himself not only the interpreter of the Pope but the enforcer within the Society of the consequences of the papal teaching. His letter concludes: 'I order Ours to conform themselves, in word and writing, to the decisions on doctrinal matters enunciated in this letter', adding 'I am aware . . . that my predecessors have never promulgated such extensive prescriptions on doctrinal matters. But none of them was ever in such circumstances—that an Encyclical of the Supreme Pontiff would condemn so many dangerous or erroneous opinions threatening to become contagious in the Society.'[75]

LATER SIGNIFICANCE

Over the four years of the controversy there had been rumours that a new *Syllabus* or a new *Lamentabili* would be issued; and indeed the rumour persisted even after the appearance of the encyclical that a list of condemned propositions would soon be published.[76] No such document ever appeared. When the Theological Commission began preparing texts for Vatican II, it made ample use of *Humani Generis*, particularly in its draft *De deposito fidei*

---

[75] *Woodstock Letters*, 313, 314.   [76] Congar, *Journal*, 177.

pure custodiendo, which addressed many doctrinal problems. It also prepared a new formula for the profession of faith, never used, which concludes:

> I also profess without doubt all the other things defined and declared by the Ecumenical Councils and especially by the Council of Trent and the First Vatican Council, particularly with regard to the jurisdictional primacy and infallible magisterium of the Roman Pontiff; and I also condemn and reject whatever is condemned and rejected in those Councils and in Encyclicals, namely in *Pascendi* and *Humani generis*.

In the Vatican II documents, *Humani Generis* is cited a total of six times: three times in the Decree on Priestly Formation (§ 15, 16), once in the Declaration on Christian Education (§ 11), and once each in the Constitutions on the Church (*LG* § 8) and on Divine Revelation (*DV* § 10). Four of the six references occur in two minor documents, therefore, and they are cited in support of the role of Thomism in Catholic education and formation.[77]

CONCLUSION

Reading *Humani Generis* today, one is struck first by the difference between its method and style and the style and method of the encyclicals of Pius XII's successors. It reads as if every single sentence or even every single clause might be intended or rightly interpreted to supply the major premise for a new syllogism leading to a new theological conclusion. In fact, this is how it was interpreted in certain theological circles during the decade after its appearance when its implications for specific scholastic questions were debated.

One is also struck by the encyclical's dogmatic and peremptory character. The Pope was handing down judgements (which he expected to be accepted) for which he felt no great need to supply reasons. The encyclical was one of the last efforts to hold back a tide that was calling into question the near-monopoly in theology enjoyed by scholastic method, language, principles, and concepts. It was followed by efforts made during the preparation of Vatican II to enforce the teachings of the encyclical and to insist that its norms for seminary education in philosophy and theology be maintained. The Council chose another kind of language for its documents, and its norms with regard to seminary education departed significantly from those

---

[77] For the much more modest role assigned to Thomism at the Council, see my 'Thomism and the Second Vatican Council', in Anthony J. Cernera (ed.), *Continuity and Plurality in Catholic Theology: Essays in Honor of Gerald A. McCool, S.J.* (Fairfield CT: Sacred Heart University Press, 1998), 53–73.

in force before Vatican II. In any case, within a very short time after the Council, the scholastic monopoly was shattered and a bewildering variety of methods, languages, systems, etc. were available for the doing of theology, including a new *intellectus fidei* with the philosophical resources of other cultures.

10

Analogy of Truth: The Sacramental Epistemology of *Nouvelle Théologie*[1]

Hans Boersma

NOUVELLE THÉOLOGIE AS RESSOURCEMENT OF A SACRAMENTAL ONTOLOGY

The French renewal movement of *nouvelle théologie* remains, in some ways, an enigma. Questions remain about what constituted the theological *raison d'être* of the Jesuits from Lyon-Fourvière and the Dominicans from Le Saulchoir.[2] This enigma is especially noteworthy considering the influence that the movement has had on Catholic theology, particularly through the Second Vatican Council. Part of the problem is the fact that these theologians hardly formed a distinct school of thought.[3] Theologians associated with the Fourvière scholasticate—Henri de Lubac (1896–1991), Jean Daniélou (1905–74), Henri Bouillard (1908–81), and Hans Urs von Balthasar (1905–88)—as well as those linked with the Saulchoir studium—Marie-Dominique Chenu (1895–1990) and Yves Congar (1904–95)—shared common interests, to be sure. But they did not set out to establish a particular theological system or school. Another reason for the difficulty in locating these thinkers on the theological map is the remarkably negative assessments that many of them gave of

[1] I am grateful to the Association of Theological Schools and the Henry Luce Foundation for appointing me as Henry Luce III Fellow in Theology for 2007–8, which has allowed me to use a year-long sabbatical to reflect on the sacramental ontology of *nouvelle théologie*. I very much appreciate the comments of my colleague, Bruce Hindmarsh, on an earlier draft of this essay.
[2] The *nouvelle théologie* movement is usually identified by these two theological training centres, though we may want to include the Louvain theologians, René Draguet (1896–1980) and Louis Charlier (1898–1981). Cf. Robert Guelluy, 'Les Antécédents de l'encyclique "Humani Generis" dans les sanctions Romaines de 1942: Chenu, Charlier, Draguet", *Revue d'histoire ecclésiastique*, 81 (1986), 421–97.
[3] The theologians involved wanted to return to the sensibilities of the great tradition rather than start a new school of thought. The very term '*nouvelle théologie*' was one that they generally disavowed. I adopt it simply because of its common academic usage.

post-conciliar developments in the Catholic Church. De Lubac, Daniélou, and Balthasar all expressed themselves negatively—sometimes sharply so—about the changes after Vatican II, even though these would have been unthinkable without the impact of *nouvelle théologie*. Even Congar, although largely positive about the changes, expressed words of caution at times.[4] The establishment, in 1971, of the journal *Communio* reflected the growing unease of a number of the former 'rebels'.[5] It is not easy to identify a group of theologians that hardly formed a distinct school of thought and who were often reticent about the developments that they themselves appeared to have put in motion.

It is nonetheless possible to remove some of the enigma surrounding *nouvelle théologie*. Although we may not be able to speak of a distinct school of thought, this does not mean we cannot identify shared theological concerns. And while the reactions of many of the *nouveaux théologiens* to post-conciliar changes were indeed remarkable, it is possible to give a theological explanation for this change in attitude. But the prerequisite for dealing with *nouvelle théologie*'s enigma is that we deal with these theologians on their own terms. It may be tempting to locate *nouvelle théologie*, historically, between the Modernist Crisis of the early twentieth century and the theological pluralism of the post-Vatican II period. The Modernist Crisis, with its turn to historical critical exegesis (Alfred Loisy (1857–1940)) and to subjective human experience (George Tyrrell (1861–1909)), was the cause of great upheaval within Catholicism during the first decade of the twentieth century.[6] The movement was condemned in 1907 by Pope Pius X's decree, *Lamentabili Sane Exitu* and by his encyclical, *Pascendi Dominici Gregis*, in which he unequivocally rejected the agnosticism, immanentism, and relativism of Modernism, itself the 'synthesis of all heresies'.[7] The freedom of exploration and the theological pluralism following Vatican II may seem like a belated victory for the Modernist movement. The ecclesiastical climate between 1907 and 1960 made it difficult for history and experience to function as theologically meaningful categories. The condemnation of Modernism ensured that theologians were careful not to give the impression that they were returning to the 'historicism' and

[4] Cf. Jean Puyo (ed.), *Jean Puyo interroge le Père Congar: 'Une vie pour la vérité'*, Les Interviews (Paris: Centurion, 1975), 156–60.

[5] Although de Lubac was one of the founders of *Concilium* in 1965, he broke with it in order to join Hans Urs von Balthasar and Joseph Ratzinger in setting up the *Communio* journal in 1972.

[6] Cf. Gabriel Daly, *Transcendence and Immanence: A Study in Catholic Modernism and Integralism* (Oxford: Clarendon, 1980); Pierre Colin, *L'Audace et le soupçon: La Crise du modernisme dans le catholicisme français 1893–1914* (Paris: Desclée de Brouwer, 1997).

[7] Pius X, Syllabus condemning the Errors of the Modernists (3rd July 1907), *ASS* xl (1907), 470–8. ET available at <http://www.papalencyclicals.net/Pius10/p10lamen.htm>. *Pascendi Dominici Gregis*. Encyclical Letter on the Doctrines of the Modernists (8 September 1907), *ASS* xl (1907), 593–650, (632), §39. ET available at <http://www.vatican.va/holy_father/pius_x/encyclicals/documents/hf_p-x_enc_19070908_pascendi-dominici-gregis_en.htm>.

'subjectivism' of the Modernist movement. *Nouvelle théologie* may thus appear as the one theological movement during this time period that was not afraid to speak out, as the one exception to the rule of an overall submission to a climate of fear. Thus, the theological trajectory would run from Modernism, via *nouvelle théologie*, to post-conciliar pluralism.

This historical account is not without warrant. It is true that the *nouveaux théologiens* were the one major group of scholars that were not afraid to speak up, sometimes at great personal cost.[8] *Nouvelle théologie* indeed had the same theological opponent that Modernism had faced: the intellectualism of neo-Thomism which, thanks to Pope Leo XIII's encyclical, *Aeterni Patris* (1879), had become the semi-official voice of Catholicism. This neo-Thomist establishment did suffer its most serious defeat at the Second Vatican Council, a loss that seems irreversible considering the indebtedness of Popes John Paul II and Benedict XVI to *nouvelle théologie*.[9] And the neo-Thomist confidence in the ability of discursive reason to access and possess theological truth was not overly hospitable to the theological pluralism that characterized the years following the Council. Thus, if one were to describe a history of the decline of neo-Thomism, it would be quite appropriate to begin with Modernism and move, via *nouvelle théologie*, to the Second Vatican Council.

But it is, of course, possible for two quite disparate groups to face the same opponent. To give a historical account of the demise of neo-Thomism is not the same as to present a theological discussion of what motivated *nouvelle théologie*. In particular, the view of *nouvelle théologie* as a Modernism *redivivus* leaves unexplained the enigma of the remarkable change in attitude of most of the *nouveaux théologiens* during the post-Vatican II years. One could perhaps argue that, faced with the consequences of their thinking, a number of them drew back and adopted a reactionary demeanour. There might be a psychological explanation for this—many Catholics found the liturgical, doctrinal, and social developments difficult to process—but the explanation fails to convince. That most of the *nouveaux théologiens*, battle-hardened and seasoned scholars, would suddenly repudiate the consequences of their own theology seems unlikely. Indeed, my reading of these theologians has confirmed for me that we need to look deeper for an adequate interpretation of *nouvelle théologie*.

We may want to begin with the other factor that renders the movement enigmatic—the fact that it is not a distinct school of thought. Without wanting to go back on this assertion, I do believe it is necessary to qualify it. There was,

---

[8] For a historical account of the controversies, as well as for further literature, see Hans Boersma, *Nouvelle Théologie and Sacramental Ontology: A Return to Mystery* (Oxford: Oxford University Press, 2009), Ch. 1.

[9] For a discussion of Ratzinger/Benedict XVI as a *ressourcement* theologian, see the chapter by Lewis Ayres, Patricia Kelly and Thomas Humphries in this volume.

I believe, a theological sensibility that the *nouveaux théologiens* shared.[10] To get at this shared sensibility, we may begin with the fact that *nouvelle théologie* is also known as the *ressourcement* movement. The latter term is theologically more substantive, as it points to the movement's return to the church Fathers and the later medieval tradition—including, in the case of Bouillard and Chenu, St Thomas Aquinas. This return to the 'great tradition' was, in part, an anti-neo-Thomist move. The scholastic approach of the neo-Thomist manualist tradition worked with a view of theology that assumed that theo-logical discourse was able to capture adequately and comprehensively the revealed data in a system of thought by making use of syllogistic argumenta-tion. The *ressourcement* of the Church Fathers and the Middle Ages was an attempt to go beyond such a 'dialectical' theological method in favour of a more 'symbolic' approach.[11] The *ressourcement* of St Thomas was intended, at least in part, to show up the inadequacies of the 'rationalist' neo-scholastic interpretation of the Angelic Doctor in favour of a more 'poetic' view of the nature of truth claims.[12] This return to the tradition lay at the very heart of *nouvelle théologie*, while, by contrast, we look in vain for a similar *ressource-ment* among the earlier Modernists. Different sensibilities appear to have characterized the two movements.

Nouvelle théologie was, more than anything else, a return to mystery: created realities were sacraments (*sacramenta*) that pointed to and participated in spiritual mysteries or sacramental realities (*res*). The *nouveaux théologiens* looked to the great tradition—and in particular to the Eastern Church Fathers—to regain this sense of mystery, the loss of which they blamed partly on the regnant school of neo-Thomism. In the great tradition they saw an approach to scripture, to tradition, and to the church that was sacramental in outlook. To recover the mystery of scripture, it was important not to remain at the literal or historical level, but instead to move on to the various spiritual levels of interpretation. To appreciate the mystery of the tradition, one had to follow the Spirit's guidance of the development of the initial faith deposit towards the plenitude of truth. And to enter into the mystery of the church, one had to partake of the eucharistic body of Christ, which made present the

---

[10] My use of the word 'sensibility' has been triggered by Graham Ward's use of the term to describe the movement of Radical Orthodoxy. Cf. James K. A. Smith, *Introducing Radical Orthodoxy: Mapping a Post-Secular Theology* (Grand Rapids MI: Baker Academic, 2005), 63–70.

[11] Henri de Lubac opposed these two terms in *Corpus Mysticum: The Eucharist and the Church in the Middle Ages: Historical Survey*, trans. Gemma Simmonds with Richard Price and Christopher Stephens (eds.), Laurence Paul Hemming and Susan Frank Parsons (London: SCM, 2006), 221–47.

[12] I am thinking here of Pierre Rousselot's interpretation of Thomas, arguing that for Thomas, theology functioned like 'a logical poem, better at charming someone who already believes than useful for controversy'; see *Intelligence: Sense of Being, Faculty of God*, trans. and ed., Andrew Tallon, Marquette Studies in Philosophy, 16 (Milwaukee WI: Marquette University Press, 1998), 130.

unity of the ecclesial body of Christ and so the fullness of Christ himself. Scripture, tradition, and church were mysteries whose various levels were sacramentally hinged together: the literal to the spiritual sense of scripture, the initial deposit to the full flowering of the tradition, and the eucharistic structure of the church to the unity of its life. In a similar way, all of existence— nature and the supernatural—was connected by way of an overall sacramental ontology. People's real lives—and thus history and experience—were God's chosen means to make himself present. The mystery of God's presence could be known in and through human history and human experience.

These various ways in which the sacramental ontology of *nouvelle théologie* unfolded need not detain us any further.[13] I will focus instead on the nature of human discourse, which *nouvelle théologie* also regarded as sacramental in character. Human language was a suitable means to make present the eternal truth of divine mystery—a mystery which, at the same time, eluded the human grasp. The *nouveaux théologiens* established this sacramental view of truth by expanding the traditional Thomist doctrine of 'analogy of being' (*analogia entis*) from the area of ontology to that of epistemology.[14] Just as one could say that creaturely *being* participated in God's being, so also creaturely *truth* participated in God's truth; at the same time, both divine being and divine truth infinitely transcended human being and human truth.[15]

An analogical or sacramental epistemology was bound to cause offence. On the one hand, an equivocal view of truth claims would take exception to the insistence that such claims were, in a real sense, adequate, that they truly made present the divine mystery. This, we could say somewhat anachronistically, was the Modernist objection to the sacramental view. For George Tyrrell, truth and experience were two unconnected categories.[16] Human experience, which he regarded as revelatory in character, reached far beyond the theological concepts that surrounded this experience. Edward Schillebeeckx sums up Tyrrell's view by commenting: 'The two aspects of the act of faith—the aspect of experience and the conceptual aspect—were ... according to Tyrrell, completely separate. The conceptual aspect was simply an extrinsic, symbolic, and pragmatic protection for the real core of faith (the so-called revelation in time consisting in this conceptual aspect).'[17] Tyrrell, in other words, separated

---

[13] See Boersma, *Nouvelle Théologie and Sacramental Ontology, passim.*

[14] Agnès Desmazières, 'La "nouvelle théologie", prémisse d'une théologie herméneutique? La controverse sur l'analogie de la vérité (1946–1949)', *RevTh*, 104 (2004), 241–72.

[15] Cf. the statement of the Fourth Lateran Council that 'between the Creator and the creature so great a likeness cannot be noted without the necessity of noting a greater dissimilarity between them', DS § 806.

[16] See especially George Tyrrell (alias Hilaire Bourdon), *L'Église et l'avenir* (1903); George Tyrrell, *Through Scylla and Charybdis; or, The Old Theology and the New* (London: Longmans, Green, 1907).

[17] Edward Schillebeeckx, *Revelation and Theology*, ii. *The Concept of Truth and Theological Renewal*, trans. N. D. Smith (London: Sheed & Ward, 1968), 12. Cf. Aidan Nichols, *From*

religious experience and conceptual truth claims.[18] On the other hand, a univocal view of truth claims would be offended by the relativism that the sacramental approach seemed to imply. This was the standard neo-Thomist charge against *nouvelle théologie*. Several of the neo-Thomists took umbrage at *nouvelle théologie*'s appeal to an 'analogy of truth' (*analogia veritatis*) and were troubled by the weakened stability of truth claims that this seemed to imply.[19] Réginald Garrigou-Lagrange (1877–1964), in particular—that 'sacred monster of Thomism' as he has been called[20]—expressed his astonishment at *nouvelle théologie*'s abandonment of the correspondence theory of truth (*adaequatio rei et intellectus*).[21] Neo-Thomist conceptualism was much more confident than *nouvelle théologie* of the human ability to access truth and to express it in entirely adequate terms.

PRECURSORS TO *NOUVELLE THÉOLOGIE*'S SACRAMENTAL EPISTEMOLOGY

Nouvelle théologie's sacramental ontology was profoundly influenced by Maurice Blondel (1861–1949), Pierre Rousselot (1878–1915), and Joseph Maréchal (1878–1944). Blondel, a philosopher from Aix-en-Provence, argued in his 1893 dissertation, *L'Action*, that although philosophy must take its starting-point in human action, we could not but be struck by our actions' inability to reach the ultimate purpose of their desires. The inner dynamism of our actions could never reach its final goal and would always remain frustrated

Newman to Congar: The Idea of Doctrinal Development from the Victorians to the Second Vatican Council (Edinburgh: T&T Clark, 1990), 132–5.

[18] Alessandro Maggiolini observes that Tyrrell 'could not admit that our statements about God have an authentically analogical character. In this way, *Pascendi*'s charge of agnosticism does indeed apply to Tyrrell', 'Magisterial Teaching on Experience in the Twentieth Century: From the Modernist Crisis to the Second Vatican Council', trans. Andrew Matt and Adrian Walker, *Communio*, 23 (1996), 225–43 (235–6).

[19] Among Garrigou-Lagrange's essays related to the controversy, see especially, 'La nouvelle théologie, où va-t-elle?' *Ang*, 23 (1946), 126–45; 'Nécessité de revenir à la définition traditionnelle de la vérité', *Ang*, 25 (1948), 185–98. See also Marie-Michel Labourdette and Marie-Joseph Nicolas, 'L'Analogie de la vérité et l'unité de la science théologique', *RevTh*, 47 (1947), 417–66.

[20] Richard Peddicord, *The Sacred Monster of Thomism: An Introduction to the Life and Legacy of Reginald Garrigou-Lagrange* (South Bend IN: St Augustine's, 2005), 2. Cf. Aidan Nichols, *Reason with Piety: Garrigou-Lagrange in the Service of Catholic Thought* (Naples FL: Sapientia Press of Ave Maria University, 2008).

[21] See Garrigou-Lagrange, 'La nouvelle théologie', 130; 'Nécessité de revenir'; *De gratia: Commentarius in Summam Theologicam S. Thomæ I^{ae} II^{ae} q. 109–14* (Turin: Berruti, 1947), 328–9, n. 2; *Reality: A Synthesis of Thomistic Thought*, trans. Patrick Cummins (St Louis MO: Herder, 1950), 381. Cf. Étienne Fouilloux, *Une Église en quête de liberté: La Pensée catholique française entre modernisme et Vatican II (1914–1962)*, Anthropologiques (Paris: Desclée de Brouwer, 1998), 31.

and unfulfilled. According to Blondel, human beings longed for the moment of truth, when their actions would finally correspond to the mind's ultimate aim. That is to say, the purpose of life lay in the truth of full correspondence between mind and action. At that point, Blondel made the daring comment: 'The abstract and fanciful *adæquatio rei et intellectus* [correspondence of reality and intellect] gets replaced by the legitimate methodical investigation, the *adæquatio realis mentis et vitae* [real correspondence of mind and life].'[22]

Pierre Rousselot, another influential figure behind *nouvelle théologie*, explicitly applied the doctrine of *analogia entis* to epistemology. His 1908 Sorbonne dissertation, *L'Intellectualisme de saint Thomas*, essentially outlined the various ways in which discursive reasoning was, for Thomas, a deficient and imperfect mode of arriving at intellectual knowledge.[23] The instruments of human reason—concepts, sciences, systems, and symbols—were means by which the intellect tried to deal with its own deficiencies.[24] These instruments of reason were merely 'substitutes' for pure ideas.[25] With regard to concepts, Rousselot took his starting-point in the Thomist doctrine of analogy.[26] This doctrine should induce in us conceptual humility: 'No notion is truly common to God and creature, so no notion is attributed to God *as is*.'[27] Thomas, explained Rousselot, had recognized that human concepts were unable to grasp the essence of a material object's individual particularity, so that the human intellect was forced to impose general concepts on particular objects.[28] For example, while people might rightly use the general concept of *humanitas* to describe both Socrates and Plato, the human intellect was unable to describe the true essence of Socrates and Plato individually. Strict correspondence between intellect and object remained elusive in this life. Drawing on this interpretation of Thomas, Rousselot himself went a step further and concluded that *all* human knowledge—not just knowledge of God and of angels— remained analogical in character.[29]

The approach of Joseph Maréchal, a philosopher from Louvain, was similar to that of Blondel and Rousselot. Maréchal was convinced that the human intellect could not, in totalizing fashion, grasp the essence of God. For Maréchal, the doctrine of analogy meant that one could only come to know

---

[22] Maurice Blondel, 'Le Point de départ de la recherche philosophique', *Annales de philosophie chrétienne*, 151 (1906), 337–60; 152 (1906), 225–49 (235). Cf. also Blondel, *L'Action: Essai d'une critique de la vie et d'une science de la pratique* (Paris: Alcan, 1893); ET, Blondel, *Action (1893): Essay on a Critique of Life and a Science of Practice*, trans. Olivia Blanchette (Notre Dame IN: University of Notre Dame Press, 1984), 283.

[23] Pierre Rousselot, *L'Intellectualisme de saint Thomas* (Paris: Alcan, 1908); ET, Rousselot, *Intelligence*.

[24] *Intelligence*, 55, 70.

[25] In four subsequent chapters, Rousselot discussed the 'substitutes' of the concept, of science, of systems, and of symbols; *Intelligence*, 86–167.

[26] *Intelligence*, 69–77.   [27] *Intelligence*, 76.

[28] *Intelligence*, 80–1.   [29] *Intelligence*, 87–8.

God by means of material objects and hence in very inadequate ways. St Thomas had stated that the divine names 'do say what God is; they are predicated of him in the category of substance, but fail to represent adequately what he is'.[30] Maréchal, in the fifth volume of *Le Point de départ de la métaphysique* (1926), concluded from this that one had to distinguish between affirmations and representations. One has to do justice both to the fact that the names of God did signify the divine substance itself and to the fact that the names of God nonetheless fell short in their representation of him. Thus, said Maréchal, the 'signification of those divine attributes, that is to say, the objective value that the affirmation confers on them in its judgement, relies on a conceptual "representation" that is very inadequate, because it is borrowed from our experience of creatures'.[31] Human representations were linked to material objects and so could never get beyond analogical predication.

The epistemology of Blondel, Rousselot, and Maréchal limited the absolute character of human truth claims. Blondel did so by starting with human action and by relating the nature of truth directly to human experience. Rousselot went about it by downplaying the ability of discursive reasoning. And Maréchal did it by insisting on a distinction—allegedly going back to Thomas himself—between affirmations and representations. All three assigned much greater importance to temporal history and human experience than neo-Thomism had done. The impact that their affirmation of history and experience had on *nouvelle théologie* might seem to give credence to an interpretation of *nouvelle théologie* as a second Modernist stage. Before drawing premature conclusions, however, I want to turn to some of the proponents of *nouvelle théologie* themselves—to Henri Bouillard, Marie-Dominique Chenu, Louis Charlier, and Hans Urs von Balthasar—since they all made reference to the analogous character of truth, sometimes in direct dependence on Blondel, Rousselot, and Maréchal.

NOUVELLE THÉOLOGIE AND THE ANALOGY OF TRUTH

The character of truth was an issue that featured particularly in discussions surrounding doctrinal development. The neo-Thomist 'logical' theory limited

---

[30] *ST*, 1a.13 ad.2, Blackfriars iii.54–5.
[31] Joseph Maréchal, *Le Point de départ de la métaphysique: Leçons sur le développement historique et théorique du problème de la connaissance*, v. *Le Thomisme devant la philosophie critique* (Louvain/Paris: Museum Lessianum/Alcan, 1926), 234. For the most prominent passages in English, see Maréchal, *A Maréchal Reader*, trans. and ed., Joseph Donceel (New York: Herder and Herder, 1970).

doctrinal development to conclusions correctly drawn either from the revealed deposit or from already existing Catholic doctrine.[32] *Nouvelle théologie*, drawing particularly on the Tübingen school of Johann Adam Möhler (1796–1838) and Johann Evangelist Kuhn (1806–87), took a 'theological' approach to doctrinal development, according to which doctrine organically developed from the initial Christological deposit of faith.[33] Christian doctrine and, therefore, theological truth systems, developed over time through the guidance of the Spirit and the decisions of the magisterium.

Marie-Dominique Chenu, in his 1937 *Une école de théologie: Le Saulchoir*, dealt both with the nature of theology and the implications for doctrinal development.[34] He appealed to the Tübingen school for his anti-intellectualist take on theology, and he was obviously apprehensive of the 'autonomous' logic of systematic constructs and of appeals to a 'catalogue of propositions filed in some Denzinger'.[35] For Chenu, doctrinal development was the application of the basic sacramental principle that one could only know God in a human manner (*modum cognoscentis*) and that the word of God came to us in human words:

> If the economy of revelation develops in time, if therefore faith finds its authentic expression in statements that are connected to history, the particular instance—which is all it is—of development of doctrine to the interiority of the new economy, in the life of the Church, does not worry the theologian: it is normal, and here the law of the Incarnation becomes manifest.[36]

Chenu recognized that these comments opened the door to a degree of relativism.[37] But, he maintained, it was merely the relativism inherent in the nature of human language. Chenu used the doctrine of analogy to insist both on the truthfulness of human discourse and on its inadequacy. Appealing to his renowned predecessor, Ambroise Gardeil (1859–1931), Chenu insisted on the 'doctrine of analogical knowledge': 'With such a radical source of relativity, the historical contingencies and psychological complexities of dogmatic formulas can be considered in a level-headed way.'[38]

---

[32] For nuances within the neo-Thomist perspective, see Gezinus Evert Meuleman, *De ontwikkeling van het dogma in de Rooms Katholieke theologie* (Kampen: Kok, 1951), 31–51; Herbert Hammans, *Die neueren katholischen Erklärungen der Dogmenentwicklung* (Essen: Ludgerus-Verlag Hubert Wingen KG, 1965), 119–73; Nichols, *From Newman to Congar*, 136–94.

[33] Jan Hendrik Walgrave describes the logical and theological approaches to doctrinal development as follows: 'A theory of development is called "logical" because according to it the process of development is simply described in terms of logical inference and the criterion of its truth is the logical test, whereas the qualification *theological* means that the process is conceived of as partaking of the character of mystery that is proper to the object of theology, and that the criterion of its truth does not properly consist in a logical verification but in a charismatic decision accepted by faith.' *Unfolding Revelation: The Nature of Doctrinal Development* (Philadelphia PA/London: Westminster/ Hutchinson, 1972), 165.

[34] See Marie-Dominique Chenu, *Une école*, 129–50.

[35] *Une école*, 132.   [36] *Une école*, 139.

[37] *Une école*, 135, 140.   [38] *Une école*, 140.

A year later, Louis Charlier, a Dominican theologian from Louvain, published his *Essai sur le problème théologique*.[39] For Charlier, too, the sacramental character of doctrinal development showed up in the fact that theological language was analogical in character. According to Charlier, one should look at the revealed deposit (*donné révélé*) not just from a 'conceptual' angle, but also from a 'real' point of view. Theology, which was faith in action,[40] had the task of moving through concepts and formulas in order to reach the reality (*res*) of faith.[41] Since the church, according to Charlier, was an 'integral part of the mystery of Christ', there could be 'real development' and 'real progress', for the growth of the church went accompanied by growth of the entire mystery of God.[42] Like Chenu, Charlier used the doctrine of analogy to insist both on the truthfulness of human discourse and on its inadequacy. The former accounted for the similarity, while the latter expressed the infinite dissimilarity between human language and the eternal reality (*res*) to which it referred. 'Here below', Charlier maintained, 'God "informs" our spirit of the revealed deposit through the intervention of human words: authentic and official notification, sealed by God in certain signs of the given reality; true expression, undoubtedly, but inadequate to the reality which it can only translate analogically.'[43] Human language was sacramental in character, and the doctrine of analogy was for Charlier the way to express this sacramental understanding of truth.[44] On this view, the intellect could never claim to grasp the fullness of divine truth. To discern the magisterium's role, therefore, 'Denzinger does not suffice'.[45] The logical view of doctrinal development went wrong by ignoring the 'relativism of the analogy of knowledge and the historical relativism of temporal conditions'.[46] As a result, Charlier insisted on appropriately valuing the 'human contingencies' of particular time periods, which shaped the 'formulation' of Christian thought.[47] In short, also for Charlier, the doctrine of analogy underpinned his epistemology.

The publication in 1944 of Henri Bouillard's *Conversion et grâce chez S. Thomas d'Aquin* became the occasion for sharp debate, involving a number of the Fourvière faculty.[48] Bouillard's book was controversial because of its

---

[39] Louis Charlier, *Essai sur le problème théologique*, Bibliothèque Orientations: Section scientifique, 1 (Thuillies: Ramgal, 1938). Charlier's views on development of doctrine are discussed in Meuleman, *De ontwikkeling van het dogma*, 70–5; Hammans, *Die neueren katholischen Erklärungen*, 180–5.

[40] *Essai*, 75.

[41] *Essai*, 66. As a result, Charlier insisted that 'before anything else, the theologian must have a keen sense of the mystery of God' (*Essai*, 154).

[42] *Essai*, 70.   [43] *Essai*, 68.

[44] Cf. *Essai*, 156.   [45] *Essai*, 77. Cf. *Essai*, 165.

[46] *Essai*, 80.   [47] *Essai*, 80.

[48] Cf. Karl-Heinz Neufeld, 'Fundamentaltheologie in gewandelter Welt: H. Bouillards theologischer Beitrag', *ZkT*, 100 (1978), 417–40; Étienne Fouilloux, 'Dialogue théologique? (1946–1948)', in Serge-Thomas Bonino (ed.), *Saint Thomas au XXᵉ siècle*, Actes du colloque

historical approach to Thomas's theology, which seemed to his opponents simply a way to circumvent the Angelic doctor's authority.[49] When Bouillard seemed to question Thomas's understanding of transubstantiation and of elevating grace, this appeared to the neo-Thomists to be the beginning of the slippery slope of Bouillard's relativism, which was at bottom a return to Modernism.[50]

Underlying Bouillard's alleged relativism was his understanding of truth. Bouillard insisted that it was 'the law of the Incarnation' that permanent divine truth was only accessible by way of contingent human notions.[51] Well aware that this might cause the neo-Thomists to accuse him of relativism, Bouillard clarified by making a distinction between the absolute character of affirmations, on the one hand, and the contingent or relative character of human notions or representations, on the other hand:

> History thus manifests at the same time the relativity of notions, of schemes in which theology takes shape, and the permanent affirmation that governs them. It is necessary to know the temporal condition of theology and, at the same time, to offer with regard to the faith the absolute affirmation, the divine Word that has become incarnate.[52]

Thus, by adopting Maréchal's distinction between affirmations and representations, Bouillard insisted *both* on the absolute character of eternal affirmations *and* on the relativity of historically contingent theological representations and systems through which these affirmations came to expression. Bouillard wanted to safeguard the validity and significance of both.[53]

Bouillard was no doubt pleased to encounter the link between the doctrine of analogy and the nature of the truth claims of Christian doctrine in Jean-Marie Le Blond's 1947 defence on his behalf, in an essay entitled 'L'Analogie de

---

du Centenaire de la *Revue Thomiste* (Paris: Centre National de Livre-Saint Paul, 1994), 153–95; Jürgen Mettepenningen, 'Truth as Issue in a Second Modernist Crisis? The Clash between Recontextualization and Retrocontextualization in the French-Speaking Polemic of 1946–47', in M. Lamberigts, L. Boeve, and T. Merrigan (eds.), *Theology and the Quest for Truth: Historical and Systematic Theological Studies*, BETL 202 (Louvain/Leuven: Presses Universitaires de Louvain/Peeters, 2007), 119–42.

[49] Particularly controversial was Bouillard's comment that a 'theology that is not up to date [*actuelle*] is a false theology' (*Conversion et grâce chez S. Thomas d'Aquin: Étude historique*, Théologie 1 (Paris: Aubier, 1944), 219). Cf. the reactions by Garrigou-Lagrange, 'La Nouvelle théologie', 126, 129; 'Les notions consacrées par les Conciles', *Ang*, 24 (1947), 217–30. Cf. Bouillard's response on this point in 'Notions conciliaires et analogie de la vérité', *RSR*, 35 (1948), 251–71 (255–6).

[50] Cf. Garrigou-Lagrange's comment, 'Où va la nouvelle théologie? Elle revient au modernisme'; 'La nouvelle théologie', 143.

[51] Bouillard, *Conversion et grâce*, 220.

[52] *Conversion et grâce*, 220–1.

[53] Garrigou-Lagrange saw in Bouillard's distinction a return to Blondel's view of truth as *adaequatio mentis et vitae*; 'La nouvelle théologie', 129–30.

la vérité' ('The Analogy of Truth').[54] This essay provides an interesting entry into the issues at stake in the debate surrounding *nouvelle théologie*. While Le Blond judiciously did not name any of the antagonists by name, he made an obvious reference to the difficulties in which Bouillard found himself. Le Blond posited a link between the doctrine of analogy of *being* and the notion of analogy of *truth*, a link he believed ought to 'make people guard against hasty judgements and summary condemnations'.[55] Le Blond made the case that if one accepted an analogy of proportionality between names applied to God and to human beings, then such an analogy should apply not just to the concept of being, but also to the transcendentals of truth, goodness, and unity, since these transcendentals were 'basically being itself in its relationship to intelligence, appetite, and self-possession'.[56] The result of this identification of truth, goodness, and unity with being itself was that the doctrine of analogy applied to all of them: 'The thesis of the analogy of truth is, in effect, no less compelling than that of the analogy of being. The truth is not univocal; there is, shall we say, a subsistent truth that is absolute, which is God himself in his simplicity, God as he knows himself and knows in himself all things.'[57] All other truths, the Rector of the House of Philosophy at Mongré concluded, had to be 'complex and deficient', just as all human beings were complex and deficient.

By insisting on an 'analogy of truth', Le Blond posited a similarity between ontology and revelation. In both cases, simplicity and fullness could be found only in God. Human being and human truth were only analogous being and analogous truth. This allowed theological statements to share in the truth, since they manifested 'a tendency to the absolute'.[58] Le Blond's distinction between absolute, simple truth and contingent, complex truths echoed Bouillard's differentiation between affirmations and representations:

> This position of the absolute, which precisely gives our true affirmations their own character, accounts for the *form* of our knowledge, in an affirmation that reaches the infinite and for which the various representations supply the limiting *matter*; the latter unveils the ideal and the domain of the spirit in this fundamental, implicit affirmation of the absolute, which supports all its acts.[59]

---

[54] Jean-Marie Le Blond, 'L'Analogie de la vérité: Réflexion d'un philosophe sur une controverse théologique', *RSR*, 34 (1947), 129–41. For a neo-Thomist response, see Labourdette and Nicolas, 'L'Analogie de la vérité'. For discussions of Le Blond's essay, see John Auricchio, *The Future of Theology* (Staten Island NY: Alba, 1970), 311–14; Thomas G. Guarino, 'Fundamental Theology and the Natural Knowledge of God in the Writings of Henri Bouillard', Ph.D. thesis (Catholic University of America, 1984), 32–7. For a critical assessment of Le Blond's position, see John F. X. Knasas, *Being and Some Twentieth-Century Thomists* (New York: Fordham University Press, 2003), 166–72.

[55] 'L'Analogie de la vérité', 129.
[56] 'L'Analogie de la vérité', 130.
[57] 'L'Analogie de la vérité', 130.
[58] 'L'Analogie de la vérité', 131.
[59] 'L'Analogie de la vérité', 131.

Le Blond's essay placed Bouillard's terminology of 'affirmation' and 'representation' within the context of a Thomist doctrine of analogy, which included not just analogy of being but also analogy of truth. And Le Blond did not shy away from the consequences: even the Thomist synthesis itself could not 'be equal to the subsistent Truth, and cash in all [its] riches'.[60] The implication of Le Blond's analysis was, of course, that if one were to make the mistake of identifying the truth with a particular historical theological synthesis, one would fall into the trap of univocity, mistaking limited, historical representations for eternal, absolute affirmations.[61]

In 1947, Hans Urs von Balthasar entered on a discussion of 'Truth as Participation' in his book, *Wahrheit der Welt*.[62] Balthasar, too, referred to the doctrine of *analogia entis* as a way to introduce an 'analogy of truth'. The Thomist view of a 'real distinction' among creatures between essence and existence had been the basis for the doctrine of analogy of being and for a participatory ontology. Balthasar argued that this 'real distinction' was applicable not just to ontology but also to epistemology. It was equally necessary to make a real distinction between essential and existential *truth*:

> If the identification of essence and existence is impossible in creatures, then the coincidence of existential and essential truth must be equally impossible. This inference is so simple and evident that one has to wonder why the philosophical systems based on the *realis distinctio* in creaturely being are not equally radical in considering creaturely truth in terms of this distinction.[63]

Balthasar, like the other proponents of *nouvelle théologie*, moved from analogy of being to analogy of truth.

Balthasar was, of course, well aware of the consequences of his 'analogy of truth'. As a result, he argued for a sacramental understanding of human truth claims. On the one hand, he did not shy away from asserting the provisional and dialogical character of human truth claims. The tension between essence and existence within human truth claims, asserted Balthasar, 'rules out precisely the sort of systematization that has not been opened up to the historical varieties in which truth unfolds in the course of tradition...'[64] With this unveiled jab at neo-Thomism and other rationalist approaches to doctrine,

---

[60] 'L'Analogie de la vérité', 133.
[61] Le Blond repeatedly pressed the charges of univocity ('L'Analogie de la vérité', 130, 138, 140) and of Cartesian rationalism ('L'Analogie de la vérité', 138, 141). There is little doubt that he had in mind Garrigou-Lagrange from the Angelicum in Rome, as well as the Toulouse Dominicans.
[62] Hans Urs von Balthasar, *Wahrheit der Welt* (Einsiedeln: Benziger, 1947). This book later became the first volume of his *Theologik*. ET, von Balthasar, *Theo-Logic: Theological Logical Theory*, i. *Truth of the World*, trans. Adrian J. Walker (San Francisco: Ignatius, 2000).
[63] *Theo-Logic*, i.250.
[64] *Theo-Logic*, i.250.

Balthasar insisted that worldly truth was just as mutable as worldly being.[65] Human propositions and truth systems could be related 'in thousands of ways, with myriads of overlappings, affinities, and derivations'.[66] On the other hand, none of this should paralyse the truth seeker, for the doctrine of analogy meant that that 'individual, partial truths' really did contain truth.[67] The human mind was not 'shut up in finitude'. The very recognition of the relative character of human truth implied that our relative truths participated in the greater truth of God: 'To perceive the limit of worldly truth means to apprehend concomitantly and tacitly what lies beyond it.'[68] Thus, Balthasar believed that an analogical understanding of truth avoided both neo-Thomist rationalism and what he called 'vitalist' irrationalism.[69] The reason for Balthasar's relative confidence was his sacramental understanding of human truth claims, with creaturely intelligence bearing 'an intrinsic impress and seal of God's infinite truth'.[70]

CONCLUSION

The approach of *nouvelle théologie* was not so much a *via media* as an attempt to connect—in sacramental or analogical fashion—what had been separated by Modernists and neo-Thomists alike. From the perspective of *nouvelle théologie*'s sacramental ontology, both Modernist equivocity and neo-Thomist univocity failed to recognize the sacramental character of human discourse.[71] The former erred through its meagre, symbolic view, which lost sight of the actual presence of the divine mystery in human language. The latter went astray by its massive insistence on real presence, forgetting the spiritual character of human speech and the infinite mystery of divine truth which human discourse aimed to make present. Using the influential terminology of Maurice Blondel, we could say that the Modernists fell into a 'historicist' understanding of truth—where the reach of truth claims was entirely relative and unable to transcend the limits of human history and experience; while the

---

[65] *Theo-Logic*, i.251.   [66] *Theo-Logic*, i.252.
[67] *Theo-Logic*, i.252.   [68] *Theo-Logic*, i.252.
[69] *Theo-Logic*, i.252. Cf. David C. Schindler, 'Towards a Non-Possessive Concept of Knowledge: On the Relation between Reason and Love in Aquinas and Balthasar', *Modern Theology*, 22 (2006), 577–607.
[70] *Theo-Logic*, i.252.
[71] Cf. Bouillard's comment: 'If one and the same revealed truth is expressed in different systems (Augustinian, Thomist, Suarézian, etc.), the various notions that one uses to translate it are neither "equivocal" (or else one would no longer speak of the same thing), nor "univocal" (otherwise all the systems would be identical), but "analogous", that is to say that they express the same reality in a different way' ('Notions conciliaires', 254). Cf. Thomas G. Guarino, *Foundations of Systematic Theology* (New York: T&T Clark, 2005), 239–53.

neo-Thomists lapsed into an 'extrinsicist' view of truth—where conceptual truth claims were absolute in nature and unconnected to human history and experience.[72] Thus, the way to resolve the enigma of *nouvelle théologie* is not to place it on the historical trajectory from Modernism to post-conciliar pluralism. Rather, by grounding itself in the traditional doctrine of analogy, *nouvelle théologie* presented a sacramental epistemology that offered to the modern world a theological recovery of mystery.

---

[72] See especially Maurice Blondel, *Histoire et dogme* (La Chapelle-Montligeon: Libraire de Montligeon, 1904); ET, *The Letter on Apologetics and History and Dogma*, trans. and ed., Alexander Dru and Illtyd Trethowan (Grand Rapids MI: Eerdmans, 1994).

11

Nouvelle Théologie: Four Historical Stages of Theological Reform Towards Ressourcement (1935–1965)

Jürgen Mettepenningen

INTRODUCTION

'The originality of twentieth-century Catholic theology', is how the French Jesuit Bernard Sesboüé rightly describes the *ressourcement* movement.[1] One of the latter's components, the so-called *nouvelle théologie*, made an important contribution to it, although A. N. Williams called its proper name a paradox, for it concerns no 'new' theology but a return to the oldest sources of faith, theology, and Catholicism.[2] Nonetheless, the leading circles of the Roman Catholic Church originally did not like the movement because its endeavour was combined with heavy criticism towards neo-scholasticism. After some thirty years, however, the Council Fathers of Vatican II did accept its central features.

First, I present some characteristics of the movement in order to make *nouvelle théologie*'s endeavour clear within its theological context. Second, I give a survey of the development of the four consecutive phases of the *nouvelle théologie*, each representing another facet of it. Finally, some closing considerations aim to nuance the division into four phases and to present the *nouvelle théologie* as a very important link within the development of the broader *ressourcement* movement.

---

[1] Cf. Bernard Sesboüé, *La théologie au XXe siècle et l'avenir de la foi: Entretiens avec Marc Leboucher* (Paris: Desclée de Brouwer, 2007), 11.

[2] A. N. Williams, 'The Future of the Past: The Contemporary Significance of the *Nouvelle Théologie*', *IJST*, 7 (2005), 347–61 (348).

DESCRIPTION

Presenting a portrait of *nouvelle théologie* is a difficult and delicate affair. While '*nouvelle théologie*' is to be understood as a cluster concept and the dedicated expression for a theological movement, the originally negative connotations surrounding it, and the fact that its representatives were not always eager to identify themselves with the movement, make it difficult to provide an unambiguous description of it. Nevertheless, I am convinced that without the following three characteristics, little, if anything, can be said about *nouvelle théologie*.[3]

The first essential characteristic of *nouvelle théologie* is its original entrenchment in French-speaking territories (France and Belgium). As a consequence of French anti-clerical politics at the beginning of the twentieth century, the French Dominicans of the Parisian province were resident in Le Saulchoir, located in Kain, a small village near Tournai in southern Belgium. Only in the second half of the 1930s did they move back to Paris, some ten years after the return of the French Jesuits from Hastings in England. The study houses of both the Dominicans (Le Saulchoir) and the Jesuits (Lyon-Fourvière) should be seen as the originating centres for the *nouvelle théologie*, as discussed below.

The endeavour to ascribe a worthy place to history within Catholic theology is a further characteristic feature of *nouvelle théologie*. Up until this juncture, Roman texts constituted the background and determined the degree of openness to history. In practice, this implied that theologians took these texts as their point of departure, arriving by way of deduction at new faith insights that were completely compatible with existing and familiar tenets of the magisterium's articulation of the faith (cf. the combination of both the so-called Denzinger theology[4] and conclusion theology; in other words, a theology

---

[3] On the *nouvelle théologie* and its theological-historical background, see Christoph Frey, *Mysterium der Kirche, Öffnung zur Welt: Zwei Aspekte der Erneuerung französischer katholischer Theologie*, Kirche und Konfession, 14 (Göttingen: Vandenhoeck & Ruprecht, 1969); Jean-Claude Petit, 'La compréhension de la théologie dans la théologie française au XXᵉ siècle: Vers une nouvelle conscience historique: G. Rabeau, M.-D. Chenu, L. Charlier', *Laval théologique et philosophique*, 47 (1991), 215–29; Petit, 'La compréhension de la théologie dans la théologie française au XXᵉ siècle: Pour une théologie qui réponde à nos nécessités: la nouvelle théologie', *Laval théologique et philosophique*, 48 (1992), 415–31; Étienne Fouilloux, *Une Église en quête de liberté: La pensée catholique française entre modernisme et Vatican II (1914–1962)*, Anthropologiques (Paris: Declée de Brouwer, 1998); Jürgen Mettepenningen, *Nouvelle Théologie—New Theology: Inheritor of Modernism, Precursor of Vatican II* (London/New York: T&T Clark, 2010). On *nouvelle théologie*'s systematic-theological importance, see for example Hans Boersma, '*Nouvelle Théologie' and Sacramental Ontology: A Return to Mystery* (Oxford: Oxford University Press, 2009).

[4] The concept 'Denzinger theology' is also used by Franco Giulio Brambilla in his interesting article entitled '*Theologia del Magistero* e fermenti di rinnovamento nella teologia cattolica', in G. Angelini and S. Macchi (eds.), *La teologia del Novecento: Momenti maggiori e questioni aperte*, Lectio, 7 (Milan: Glossa, 2008), 189–236.

centred around its method of reaching Denzinger-compatible conclusions via a logically correct reasoning built on Catholic and non-disputable premises). *Nouvelle théologie*'s representatives, however, considered the time to be more than ripe to abandon such closed thinking and to resist such an unworldly notional system that was determined to preserve itself, whatever the cost.

A third characteristic feature can be added at this juncture, namely, the appeal of a positive theology: the search for the building blocks of theology in an exploration of the sources of faith (Bible, liturgy, and patristics). The representatives of *nouvelle théologie* attached as much importance to this positive theological method as to the speculative method. In their opinion, the all-embracing speculative theology—more specifically its reduction to neo-scholasticism—had lost contact with reality to such a degree that a corrective manoeuvre had become necessary to overcome the rupture. The practice of speculative theology had deduction at its core, while positive theology arrived at its insights by way of induction. Against the background of a handbook tradition, the republication of many prominent commentaries on Thomas, and the magisterium's assertive reaction to the Modernists, the magisterium opted for neo-scholasticism rather than positive theology. The representatives of *nouvelle théologie*, however, supported the complementarity of both theological approaches—i.e., a positive-speculative theology. The word order is similarly important at this juncture: valid contributions to Catholic theology can only be made on the basis of thorough and critical source analysis. One must first examine the building blocks before one can build.

DEVELOPMENT

Four phases can be distinguished within the development of *nouvelle théologie*: Thomistic *ressourcement*, theological *ressourcement*, the internationalization of the movement, and its assimilation during the Second Vatican Council. This overview thus covers a period of around thirty years, from the 1930s to Vatican II.

FIRST PHASE

During the first phase, members of the Dominican order were the initiators of *nouvelle théologie* and its most important representatives. From 1935 onwards, three French Dominicans—Yves Congar, Marie-Dominique Chenu, and Henri-Marie Féret—and two of their Belgian *confrères*—Louis Charlier and Dominicus De Petter—presented their insights, which came to be considered as 'new' because they were not in line with the Roman view on orthodoxy.

They were reacting against the rupture between faith and theology. Four elements can be postulated as the central contributions to *nouvelle théologie*'s first phase.

First, on 18 January 1935, Yves Congar, professor at Le Saulchoir, published an opinion piece in the Catholic newspaper, *Sept*, on 'The Deficit of Theology'.[5] Congar used the piece to formulate his critique of the practice of theology, which had become little more than a technical matter and had long lost sight of its relationship with the faith and life of ordinary men and women. He compared neo-scholastic theology to a 'wax mask': an expressionless face, lacking any genuine connection with reality. Congar called for a theology rooted in faith and life.

Second, Chenu likewise published an article on the 'Position of Theology'.[6] This contribution served as a blueprint for the third chapter of Chenu's book, *Une école de théologie: Le Saulchoir*, which appeared *pro manuscripto* in 1937.[7] For Chenu, theology was 'faith *in statu scientiae*' or 'faith in its intellectual mode', and the framework within which a theologian functioned was much broader than that provided by neo-scholasticism.[8]

Third, around 1935, Congar, Chenu, and Féret were planning to write a kind of history of Roman Catholic theology of the West.[9] The project of these three Saulchoir professors aimed to describe theology's historical development with special attention to its relationship with cultural contexts and spiritual life—so with the reality of life and faith. Being heirs to the thought of Ambroise Gardeil and Marie-Joseph Lagrange, these 'three musketeers' called for a reformation of theology:[10] theology has to be centred around the living faith, not around a 'dry' system based on Thomistic commentaries from the sixteenth and seventeenth centuries. Although the project has never been realized, the work of each of them is characterized by its underlying statement that theology is rooted in reality and cannot be understood without taking both its roots of faith and cultural context into account.

---

[5] Yves Congar, 'Déficit de la théologie', *Sept*, 18 January 1935.

[6] Marie-Dominique Chenu, 'Position de la théologie', *RSPT*, 24 (1935), 232–57.

[7] Chenu, *Une école de théologie: le Saulchoir* (1937); reissued as *Une école* (1985); Ch. 3, 'La Théologie', 129–50. Given the fact that the book was not commercially available, only one review exists, penned by Franz Stegmüller: 'Review of "*Une école de théologie*"', *TR*, 38 (1939), 48–51.

[8] Chenu, 'Position de la théologie', 233; *Une école*, 145.

[9] Cf. Michael Quisinsky, *Geschichtlicher Glaube in einer geschichtlichen Welt: Der Beitrag von M.-D. Chenu, Y. Congar und H.-M. Féret zum II. Vaticanum*, Dogma und Geschichte, 6 (Berlin: LIT, 2007). For the text of the plan, see 47–53.

[10] Chenu alludes here to Ambroise Gardeil, *Le donné révélé et la théologie*, Bibliothèque théologique, 4 (Paris: Cerf, 1909). Chenu provided a foreword to the second edition (Chenu, 'Préface pour la deuxième édition', in Gardeil, *Le donné révélé et la théologie*, 2nd edn., 1932, pp. vii–xiv). For the expression the 'three musketeers', see *Henri-Marie Féret: Dominicain: 1904–1992*, unpublished pamphlet of the '*Groupe évangélique*' (Paris, 1992), 3.

Finally, in 1938, Louis Charlier published his *Essai sur le problème théolo-gique*.[11] Although Charlier had not studied at Le Saulchoir, his ideas were remarkably similar to those of Chenu. A professor at Louvain's Dominican study house, Charlier's work caused something of a stir and was the subject of a considerable number of reviews.[12] The joint relegation of Chenu's work and Charlier's book to the church's Index of Prohibited Books in February 1942[13] marked the end of the first phase of the *nouvelle théologie*.[14] It should be noted, nevertheless, that both works were written independently of each other. Archival research reveals that Rome's waning irritation with regard to *Le Saulchoir* was rekindled by Charlier's *Essai* and the attention it had received in reviews.[15]

It was within the context of the relegation of both works to the Index that the expression '*nouvelle théologie*' was used for the first time, namely by Pietro Parente, considering its representatives as a kind of *novi heretici*.[16] Parente argued that both works had brought neo-scholasticism into discredit with their (exaggerated) interest in experience, the subject, religious sentiment, and the notion of development. In the same spirit, the superiors of the Louvain Dominican convent—where Charlier had taught—considered it appropriate to deprive Dominicus De Petter of his teaching assignment in 1942. De Petter had caused something of a stir in 1939 with the publication of his article on 'Implicit Intuition' in the first issue of *Tijdschrift voor Philosophie* (a periodical he had founded) in which the anti-neo-scholastic tone was difficult to ignore.[17] Johan Van Wijngaerden has rightly pointed out that the sanction-ing of De Petter can only be understood correctly against the background

[11] Louis Charlier, *Essai sur le problème théologique*, Bibliothèque Orientations: Section scientifique, 1 (Thuillies: Ramgal, 1938).
[12] Cf. Mettepenningen, 'L'*Essai* de Louis Charlier (1938): Une contribution à la *nouvelle théologie*', RThL, 39 (2008), 211–32.
[13] Cf. *AAS* 34 (1942), 37. See also Fouilloux, 'Autour d'une mise à l'Index', in *Marie-Dominique Chenu, Moyen-Âge et modernité*, Les Cahiers du Centre d'études du Saulchoir, 5 (Paris: Cerf, 1997), 25–56.
[14] The idea that *nouvelle théologie* evolved in a number of phases is also supported by Tarcisus Tshibangu, Rosino Gibellini, and Étienne Fouilloux, although the dates of each phase differ from scholar to scholar. Cf. Tarcisus Tshibangu, *La théologie comme science au XXème siècle* (Kinshasa: Presses universitaires, 1980), 79–110; Rosino Gibellini, *Panorama de la théologie au XXᵉ siècle*, Initiations, 2nd edn. (Paris: Cerf, 2004), 186–96; Fouilloux, *Une Église en quête de liberté*, 193–300. While Fouilloux appears to suggest that the movement consisted of three phases, he does not discuss the third phase explicitly, cf. Fouilloux, '"Nouvelle théologie" et théologie nouvelle (1930–1960)', in Benoît Pellistrandi (ed.), *L'histoire religieuse en France et Espagne*, Collection de la Casa Velázquez, 87 (Madrid: Casa de Velázquez, 2004), 411–25.
[15] Cf., for example, Chenu's letter to Henri-Dominique Gardeil, 28 February 1939, in the 'Archives de la Province dominicaine de France'; there 'Corr Chenu Février 1939', 2. Chenu writes that the Dominicans experience internal conflict because the younger generation wanted to free itself from the prevalence of Thomism. He notes in the margins: 'Je présume que l'incident Charlier (Louvain) est à l'origine de cette recrudescence'.
[16] Pietro Parente, 'Nuove tendenze teologiche', *Osservatore Romano*, 9–10 February 1942, 1.
[17] Dominicus-Maria De Petter, 'Impliciete intuïtie', *Tijdschrift voor Philosophie*, 1 (1939), 84–105.

of the sanction issued against his *confrère* and fellow community member, Charlier.[18]

The aforementioned so-called *nouveaux théologiens* or 'new theologians' of the period 1935–42 reacted against neo-scholasticism by insisting on a return to the historical Thomas, a demand that fitted well within the emerging historical interest in the Middle Ages characteristic of the time. In other words, instead of referring to authoritative commentaries on Thomas from the sixteenth and seventeenth centuries, they wanted to refer to Thomas himself. In this regard, the first phase can be identified with a Thomistic *ressourcement*, whereby the thirteenth-century Thomas took pride of place over the (neo-) scholastic Thomistic system. However, neo-scholasticism could not be abandoned completely—such would imply the dismissal of the accepted foundations of orthodoxy and, more than likely, one's own dismissal. Rather, it was supplemented in an initial step before proceeding to a second step towards a theological *ressourcement*.

SECOND PHASE

In *nouvelle théologie*'s second phase, the Dominicans withdrew into the background and the Jesuits took the lead. The beginning of this phase can be related to a trilogy of publications written by three Jesuits, heirs to Léonce de Grandmaison and Pierre Rousselot. The first of these was Henri Bouillard's reworked doctoral dissertation, published in 1944 under the title *Conversion et grâce chez Saint Thomas d'Aquin*.[19] In the book's concluding observations, Bouillard writes that 'a theology which is not related to contemporary life, is a false theology'.[20] Such statements could only be interpreted as an attack on neo-scholasticism. The second publication was an article by Jean Daniélou, published in 1946 in *Études* under the title 'Les orientations présentes de la pensée religieuse'.[21] Daniélou was not only explicit in arguing that Thomism had a relative value, but he also insisted that a return to the triptych of Bible, liturgy, and patristics was to be preferred above a theology that owed its existence to a single medieval theologian. The commotion that followed the article caused his removal as editor of *Études*. The third publication, which

---

[18] Johan Van Wijngaerden, 'Voorstudie tot het denken van E. Schillebeeckx: D.M. De Petter o.p. (1905–1971): Een inleiding tot zijn leven en denken. Deel 1: Een conjunctureel-historische situering', MA thesis (Louvain, 1989), 114–17.

[19] Henri Bouillard, *Conversion et grâce chez S. Thomas d'Aquin: Étude historique*, Théologie, 1 (Paris: Aubier, 1944). Bouillard defended his doctoral dissertation in 1941.

[20] *Conversion et grâce*, 219.

[21] Jean Daniélou, 'Les orientations présentes de la pensée religieuse', *Études*, 79 (1946), 5–21.

appeared in the same year, was Henri de Lubac's *Surnaturel*.[22] Based on a historical study, de Lubac wanted to 'present a sort of essay in which contact between Catholic theology and contemporary thinking could be restored', as he formulated the aim in his memoirs.[23] De Lubac did not hesitate to pepper his overview with barely concealed critiques of neo-scholasticism.

The desire of these three and other Jesuits (among them Yves de Montcheuil[24]) to inject theology with a new lease of life and its associated return to the sources of the faith inspired them to establish the series *Sources chrétiennes* and *Théologie*, in 1942 and 1944, respectively. Both series were based at the house of studies maintained by the order in Fourvière, near Lyon, even though as a professor at Lyon's Institut Catholique, Henri de Lubac was not a member of its staff, and Daniélou lived in Paris. It took little time for Fourvière and the series to be seen as *nouvelle théologie*'s vehicles, with de Lubac as the central figure.[25] Bearing in mind the commotion caused by *Surnaturel*, Fergus Kerr argues that this book brought about the greatest crisis that twentieth-century Thomism—and perhaps even Catholic theology of the preceding century as a whole—had ever faced.[26] The fact that *Surnaturel* considered grace, (neo-)scholasticism, Augustinianism, and *ressourcement* justifies Kerr's statement.

This second phase is built on the first in the sense that the Thomistic *ressourcement* served as its precursor and ongoing foundation. The second phase can be described as a theological *ressourcement*: a return to the sources of faith. As a consequence, the magisterium and its orientation towards neo-scholasticism were forced deeper into the shadows. Via the integration of the historical perspective, theology was called upon to cross the boundaries of a closed meta-historical Thomism, a meta-historical 'magisteriumism', and a meta-historical orthodoxy to a historically oriented, open Thomism, and a source theology.

---

[22]   Henri de Lubac, *Surnaturel: Études historiques*, Théologie, 8 (Paris: Cerf, 1946).

[23]   De Lubac, *Mémoire sur l'occasion de mes écrits* 2nd edn. (Namur: Culture et Vérité, 1992 (1989)); Œuvres complètes, 33 (Paris: Cerf, 2006), 34.

[24]   Cf. Sesboüé, *Yves de Montcheuil (1900–1944): Précurseur en théologie*, Cogitatio Fidei, 255 (Paris: Cerf, 2006).

[25]   On de Lubac and the difficulties he was confronted with at the time, see Bernard Comte, 'Le Père de Lubac, un théologien dans l'Église de Lyon', in Jean-Dominique Durand (ed.), *Henri de Lubac: La rencontre au cœur de l'Église* (Paris: Cerf, 2006), 35–89, esp. 73–81; Fouilloux, 'Autour d'un livre (1946–1953)', in Durand (ed.), *Henri de Lubac*, 91–107, esp. 93–5. For a more general study, see Joseph A. Komonchak, 'Theology at Mid-Century: The Example of Henri de Lubac', *TS*, 51 (1990), 579–602. Also n. 27 below.

[26]   Fergus Kerr, *After Aquinas: Versions of Thomism* (Malden MA: Blackwell, 2002), 134. The conference 'Surnaturel: une controverse au Cœur du thomisme au XXᵉ siècle' took place in 2000 and its proceedings appeared in *RevTh*, 109 (2001), 5–351. Reference can also be made at this juncture to John Milbank, *The Suspended Middle: Henri de Lubac and the Debate concerning the Supernatural* (Grand Rapids MI/Cambridge: Eerdmans, 2005).

De Lubac, Daniélou, and the Fourvière Jesuits met with stiff opposition, which caused a polemic (which we will not discuss here) with Réginald Garrigou-Lagrange at the helm.[27] In February 1947, he published his article 'La nouvelle théologie où va-t-elle?',[28] the text of which contained his answer: *nouvelle théologie* is a new kind of Modernism. He considered Daniélou's article to be programmatic of the *nouvelle théologie* and—unimpeded by anachronism—the books of Bouillard and de Lubac its results. Of greater importance, however, was Garrigou-Lagrange's belief that the weapons used in the past to suppress Modernism should be used once again to suppress *nouvelle théologie*.[29] Finally, the polemic culminated in Pope Pius XII's promulgation of *Humani Generis* (1950). This encyclical can be understood as Rome's final serious defence of neo-scholasticism as a normative framework determining the orthodoxy of theology. The contents of *Humani Generis* ran parallel to *Pascendi Dominici Gregis*, the 1907 encyclical in which Modernism was condemned. *Humani Generis*, however, says nothing about *nouvelle théologie*; although it is clear that the encyclical's rejection of several 'new' tendencies had this particular movement in mind.[30] In the months before and after *Humani Generis*, the General of the Jesuits, the Belgian Jean-Baptiste Janssens, took several disciplinary measures against Fourvière, its professors, and de Lubac.[31]

THIRD PHASE

After the second phase (1942–50), which concluded in the same way as the first, with Roman censure, *nouvelle théologie* found itself sailing into new waters, this time beyond the borders of France. The third phase concerns the period from *c*.1950 to the eve of the Second Vatican Council, a phase

---

[27] On the polemic, see Fouilloux, 'Dialogue théologique? (1946–1948)', in Serge-Thomas Bonino (ed.), *Saint Thomas au XXe siècle*: Actes du colloque du Centenaire de la *Revue Thomiste* (Paris: Centre National de Livre-Saint Paul, 1995), 153–95; Aidan Nichols, 'Thomism and the *Nouvelle Théologie*', *The Thomist*, 64 (2000), 1–19; Agnès Desmazières, 'La *nouvelle théologie*, prémisse d'une théologie herméneutique? La controverse sur l'analogie de la vérité (1946–1949)', *RevTh*, 104 (2004), 241–72; Mettepenningen, 'Truth as Issue in a Second Modernist Crisis? The Clash between Recontextualization and Retrocontextualization in the French-Speaking Polemic of 1946–47', in Mathijs Lamberigts, Lieven Boeve, and Terrence Merrigan (eds.), *Theology and the Quest for Truth: Historical- and Systematic-Theological Studies*, BETL, 202 (Louvain/Leuven: Presses Universitaires de Louvain/Peeters, 2006), 119–41.

[28] Réginald Garrigou-Lagrange, 'La nouvelle théologie où va-t-elle?', *Ang*, 23 (1946), 126–45.

[29] The concept of 'retrocontextualization' was first used in my article 'Truth as Issue in a Second Modernist Crisis?', 141.

[30] The encyclical does not mention *nouvelle théologie*, although it condemns thirteen matters it refers to as 'new'. There was clearly little to misunderstand: the *nouvelle théologie* had been rejected. Cf. Fouilloux, '"Nouvelle théologie" et théologie nouvelle (1930–1960)', 414, n. 13.

[31] See Mettepenningen, *Nouvelle Théologie—New Theology*, 101–13.

characterized by the internationalization of the *nouvelle théologie*. For example, *nouvelle théologie* pressed on in the Netherlands, with scholars such as Edward Schillebeeckx[32] and Piet Schoonenberg,[33] and—albeit to a lesser extent—in the German-speaking world with the likes of Karl Rahner[34] and Hans Urs von Balthasar.[35] In the English-speaking world *nouvelle théologie* became known due to articles by Philip J. Donnelly, Cyrill Vollert, Gustave Weigel, and David L. Greenstock.[36] Moreover, *nouvelle théologie* became a worldwide phenomenon through the interest of bishops in the work of de Lubac and other aforementioned theologians.[37] In France, however, *nouvelle théologie* was as good as paralysed in the 1950s; although there are some who defend the hypothesis that the work of the worker-priests should be understood as *nouvelle théologie*'s pastoral component.[38] Nonetheless, *nouvelle théologie* could enter without any problem into other French-speaking areas, such as, for example, Canada.[39] The internationalization of the movement

[32] Cf. Mettepenningen, 'Edward Schillebeeckx: Herodero y promotor de la *nouvelle théologie*', *Mayéutica*, 78 (2008), 285–302.

[33] Cf. Mettepenningen, 'Christus denken naar de mensen toe: De *nouvelle théologie* christologisch doorgedacht door Piet Schoonenberg', *Tijdschrift voor Theologie*, 46 (2006), 143-60. Schoonenberg's doctoral dissertation is the most comprehensive Dutch language representation of the French debate. He does not hesitate to express his sympathy for *nouvelle théologie*'s endeavour, especially Charlier's vision. Such sympathy did not square with the prevailing wind in Rome at the time and Schoonenberg was not granted permission to publish. Sixty years later, however, the dissertation finally went to press: Piet Schoonenberg, *Theologie als geloofsvertolking: Het proefschrift van 1948*, eds. Leo Kenis and Jürgen Mettepenningen, Documenta Libraria, 36 (Louvain: Faculteit Godgeleerdheid/Maurits Sabbebibliotheek/Peeters, 2008).

[34] Cf. Sesboüé, *Karl Rahner*, Initiations aux théologiens (Paris: Cerf, 2001), 193–5.

[35] Cf. Rudolf Voderholzer, 'Die Bedeutung der sogenannten *Nouvelle Théologie* (insbesondere Henri de Lubacs) für die Theologie Hans Urs von Balthasars', in Walter Kasper (ed.), *Logik der Liebe und Herrlichkeit Gottes: Hans Urs von Balthasar im Gespräch* (Ostfildern: Matthias Grünewald, 2006), 204–28.

[36] Philip J. Donnelly, 'The Gratuity of the Beatific Vision and the Possibility of a Natural Destiny', *TS*, 11 (1950), 374–404 (already in 1947, Donnelly wrote two articles on *nouvelle théologie*: *TS* 8 (1947) 471–91, 668–99); Cyril Vollert, '*Humani Generis* and the Limits of Theology', *TS*, 12 (1951), 3–23; Gustave Weigel, 'The Historical Background of the Encyclical *Humani Generis*', *TS*, 12 (1951), 208–230; David L. Greenstock, 'Thomism and the New Theology', *The Thomist*, 13 (1950), 567–96.

[37] We mention here, as an example, Claude Rolland, Bishop of Antsirabé (Madagascar), who, as an alumnus of Le Saulchoir, asked Chenu to be his personal advisor during Vatican II. On the influence of de Lubac, see, for example, de Lubac, *Carnets du Concile*, ed. L. Figoureux, i (Paris: Cerf, 2007), 7–104; Karl Heinz Neufeld, 'In the Service of the Council: Bishops and Theologians at the Second Vatican Council (for Cardinal Henri de Lubac on His Ninetieth Birthday)', in R. Latourelle (ed.), *Vatican II: Assessment and Perspectives, Twenty Years After (1962-1987)*, i (New York: Paulist Press, 1988), 74–105 (88–95).

[38] See, for example, Wolfgang W. Müller, 'Was kann an der Theologie neu sein? Der Beitrag der Dominikaner zur *nouvelle théologie*', *Zeitschrift für Kirchengeschichte*, 110 (1999), 86–104 (103).

[39] See, for example, the French translation of an article by the Swiss theologian Thomas Deman: Thomas Deman, 'Tentatives françaises pour un renouvellement de la théologie', *Revue de l'Université d'Ottawa*, 20 (1950), 129*–167* (orig.: 'Französische Bemühungen um eine Erneuerung der Theologie', *TR*, 46 (1950), 64–82).

provided a support base at Vatican II, a constitutive part of a theological *aggiornamento* which made the assimilation of the *nouvelle théologie* in the universal church possible. Nonetheless, it should be noted as an aside that *nouvelle théologie* was not well received everywhere during the 1950s: Spain, for example, had few, if any, representatives.[40]

FOURTH PHASE

The fourth phase of the *nouvelle théologie* is to be situated during the Second Vatican Council itself, which ultimately appropriated *nouvelle théologie*'s central features. The dogmatic constitution *Dei Verbum* can be singled out in this regard for containing definite echoes of these features, and the pastoral constitution *Gaudium et Spes* pointed out that theology 'should pursue a deep knowledge of revealed truth, while not disregarding the connection with its own day, so that it can help those educated in the various disciplines to gain a fuller knowledge of the faith'.[41]

Several of *nouvelle théologie*'s representatives were present during Vatican II as *periti* (Congar, de Lubac, Daniélou) or as personal advisors to one of the Council Fathers (Chenu, Féret, Schillebeeckx). Viewed from the perspective of the Council, Michael Quisinsky has described the role of Congar, Chenu, and Féret as that of pioneers, particularly with respect to the integration of history within theology.[42] It is in this sense that Bruno Forte rightly and accurately describes Vatican II as 'the Council of history'.[43] Indeed, the deposition of Roman neo-scholasticism and the assimilation of the *nouvelle théologie* allow us to speak, as Peter Eicher suggests, of the rehabilitation of Chenu, Congar, and de Lubac during the Council.[44]

In the final analysis, the Council transformed the negative connotations associated with *nouvelle théologie* into positive connotations which reflected positively on its various representatives, several of whom were made cardinals (Daniélou in 1969, de Lubac in 1983, Congar—sadly late—in 1994, and Balthasar in 1988, although he died before the ceremony of elevation).

[40] Cf. Fouilloux, 'La "nouvelle théologie" française vue d'Espagne (1948–1951)', *Revue d'histoire de l'Église de France*, 90 (2004), 279–93.

[41] *Gaudium et Spes*, pastoral constitution of Vatican II, 7 December 1965, Tanner, ii, 1112.

[42] Cf. Quisinsky, *Geschichtlicher Glaube in einer geschichtlichen Welt*.

[43] Bruno Forte, 'Le prospettive della ricera teologica', in Rino Fisichella (ed.), *Il Concilio Vaticano II: Recezione e attualità alla luce del Giubileo* (Milan: San Paolo, 2000), 419–29 (423).

[44] Cf. Peter Eicher, 'Von den Schwierigkeiten bürgerlicher Theologie mit den katholischen Kirchenstrukturen', in Karl Rahner and Heinrich Fries (eds.), *Theologie in Freiheit und Verantwortung* (Munich: Kösel, 1981), 96–137 (101).

CONCLUSIONS

The phased division of *nouvelle théologie* as has been presented should not be interpreted rigorously. Indeed, some considerations are necessary to nuance the division and, in so doing, to show something of the complexity of research surrounding *nouvelle théologie*.

First of all, it should be mentioned that history is not a beautiful line with clear distinctive consecutive phases. So, for example, *Humani Generis* did not put an end to the theological reform movement, and archive material reveals a lively correspondence between the representatives of Le Saulchoir and Fourvière beyond the borders of the phases, containing shared advice, commentary, and critique.[45] Moreover, Henri-Marie Féret can be understood as a bridge figure. The year in which his *L'Apocalypse de Saint Jean* was published—1943, beyond the 1942 'boundary'[46]—demonstrates this. Roger Aubert rightly described this work as the starting point of a polemic surrounding the so-called '*théologie de l'histoire*'.[47] Henri Bouillard, too, who studied grace from the perspective of Thomas Aquinas, can also be considered to be a bridge figure.

Second, it remains important to recognize that several of the aforementioned theologians denied the fact that they were representatives of *nouvelle théologie*. In his *Situation et tâches présentes de la théologie* (1967), Yves Congar states that he was frequently confronted with the impossibility of defining *nouvelle théologie* in the period between 1946 and 1950.[48] For Congar, such a definition would have been as much a fancy as *nouvelle théologie* itself. In 1975, Congar repeats a comparison he made in 1950: *nouvelle théologie* is like a monster that does not exist, although its traces can be found wherever we look.[49] In 1985, de Lubac likewise described *nouvelle théologie* as a 'myth', as something that never existed.[50] Indeed, his conviction in this regard dates back as far as 1947, when he wrote in an 'examination of conscience' on his theological endeavours that he lacked the temperament to be a reformer, that he was even less inclined to the task of a renewer, and that

---

[45] Cf. the letters of Congar and Chenu (in the 'Archives de la province dominicaine de France', Paris) and of de Lubac (in the 'Archives françaises de la Compagnie de Jésus', Vanves).

[46] Henri-Marie Féret, *L'Apocalypse de saint Jean: Vision chrétienne de l'histoire*, Témoignages chrétiens (Paris: Corrêa, 1943). Here Féret provides, among other things, an explanation and interpretation of history based on Revelation.

[47] Cf. Roger Aubert, 'Discussions récentes autour de la Théologie de l'Histoire', *Collectanea Mechliniensia*, 33 (1948), 129–49.

[48] Congar, *Situation et tâches présentes de la théologie*, Cogitatio fidei, 27 (Paris: Cerf, 1967), 14.

[49] Cf. Congar's letter to Emmanuel Suárez, 16 January 1950, in the 'Archives de la province dominicaine de France', there 'Corr Congar, Janvier 1950'; Jean Puyo (ed.), *Jean Puyo interroge le Père Congar: 'Une vie pour la vérité'*, Les Interviews (Paris: Centurion, 1975), 99.

[50] De Lubac, *Entretiens autour de Vatican II: Souvenirs et Réflexions*, Théologies, 2nd edn. (Paris: France Catholique/Cerf, 2007 [1985]), 12.

he had never promoted *nouvelle théologie*.[51] Similarly, de Lubac's *confrère* Bouillard argued in 1947 along similar lines that 'the creation of a *théologie nouvelle* was not something to which he pretended', a conviction he was to repeat with vehemence some three years later.[52] We thus have statements from three prominent protagonists in which it is made clear that *nouvelle théologie* is difficult to delineate or define, and that its very existence can even be called into question.

In addition to the previous consideration, we state, however, that nowadays the existence of *nouvelle théologie* is no longer debated. There is no question any more about its existence, but rather about its contents. Here, on this level too, we have to recognize that there still is no agreement, which has of course to do with the origins of the term '*nouvelle théologie*' itself. The content of the concept depends on how one understands and takes into account the original negative meaning given by the magisterium, which focuses on the contributions of every single theologian. In general, we can state that the theologians mentioned here should all be considered representatives of the *nouvelle théologie* for a certain time, from the perspective of some of their contributions, within the specific theological-historical context of their time. Because of the Roman rejection of *nouvelle théologie* before Vatican II, people like Congar, de Lubac, and Bouillard refused to proclaim themselves as its representatives.

It is obvious that *nouvelle théologie* was centred around a *ressourcement*: a return to the sources of faith, theology, and Catholicism. In so doing, it was reacting against a specific way of doing theology which had become normative since the Modernist crisis. Ironically enough, the adherents of such a neo-scholastic theology, who aimed to combine a Denzinger theology and a conclusion theology, accused the representatives of a 'source theology' of being 'new modernists', i.e., new representatives of 'the collection of all heresies', as Pope Pius X described Modernism in 1907.[53] Nonetheless, when we consider *nouvelle théologie* from the perspective of the Modernist crisis, we find that most of its representatives are not inheritors of the thought of so-called Modernists, but rather of a 'third group' of theologians. Indeed, next to Modernists and anti-Modernists, there were several thinkers who wanted to go beyond the polemic. Jesuits such as Léonce de Grandmaison and Pierre Rousselot, and Dominicans like Ambroise Gardeil and Marie-Joseph Lagrange, are to be considered as important 'predecessors' of Chenu, Congar, Féret, Bouillard, Daniélou, and de Lubac. Having said that, *nouvelle théologie* is to be considered as the heir to the endeavour of people who had tried to be

---

[51] Cf. de Lubac, *Mémoire sur l'occasion de mes écrits*, 270.

[52] Bouillard, *Vérité du christianisme*, Théologie (Paris: Desclée de Brouwer, 1989), 401, 406.

[53] Pius X, *Pascendi Dominici Gregis*. Encyclical Letter on the Doctrines of the Modernists (8 September 1907), *ASS* xl (1907), 593–650 (632). ET available online at <http://www.vatican.va/holy_father/pius_x/encyclicals/documents/hf_p-x_enc_19070908_pascendi-dominici-gregis_en.html>.

true Thomists, true theologians, and true bridge-builders between faith, Catholicism, and the modern sciences.

Taking *nouvelle théologie* into consideration means that we need to recognize its four phases, each of them representing a different facet of it. Although during all its phases the representatives had shared an uneasiness about neo-scholasticism, they all shared the plea for a renewed appreciation of the 'first sources' of faith, theology, and Catholicism, namely (via) patristics, Bible, and liturgy.

12

Ressourcement and the *Enduring* Legacy of Post-Tridentine Theology

Christopher Ruddy

[Chenu and I] came to deep agreement, both on this mission [of bringing to fruition in the Church what was good in Modernism's appeals and concerns] and on the necessity of 'liquidating' 'Baroque theology.' [...] We began a dossier on this theme. ... Some months ago, at the beginning of [19]46, I said to Father Chenu that our dossier had become pointless since the 'Baroque theology' was being liquidated every day and the Jesuits were among its most ferocious liquidators ...[1]

INTRODUCTION

The assigned title of this paper may suggest a task similar to squaring a circle. The *ressourcement* movement, in its various practitioners and emphases, was united in the conviction that the theology that emerged after the Council of Trent—and especially in the neo-scholastic revival from roughly 1850 to 1950—was adequate neither to the fullness of Christian tradition nor to the demands of modern life. Hans Urs von Balthasar, for instance, dismissively spoke of his seminary training in 'sawdust Thomism', rescued only by friendships with mentors Erich Przywara and Henri de Lubac.[2] De Lubac himself wrote of '[a] certain scholastic conservativism, which claimed in all good faith to be tradition itself, [that] was alarmed at any appearance of novelty. A kind of so-called "Thomist" dictatorship, which was more a matter of government than intellectuality, strove to stifle any effort toward freer thought.'[3]

---

[1] Yves Congar, *Journal d'un théologien: 1946–1956*, éd. Étienne Fouilloux (Paris: Cerf, 2001), 24.
[2] See Edward T. Oakes, *Pattern of Redemption: The Theology of Hans Urs von Balthasar* (New York: Continuum, 1994), 2–3.
[3] Henri de Lubac, *At the Service of the Church: Henri de Lubac Reflects on the Circumstances that Occasioned His Writings*, trans. Anne Elizabeth Englund (San Francisco: Communio Books/ Ignatius Press, 1993), 47.

If, then, the *ressourcement* movement, for all of its internal variety, had a common *bête noire*, it was a post-Tridentine theology held to be mired in a polemical mixture of defensiveness, aggression, ahistoricism, a fixation on ecclesiastical authority (or the lack thereof), and a rather modern neo-scholasticism draping itself in the trappings of timeless tradition. This is the 'Baroque theology' derided by Congar, a theology he allows may also be called a 'theology of the Counter-Reform' or even 'post-Tridentine theology, although the Council of Trent plays little role in this theology which, at a certain moment in history—in the seventeenth, eighteenth, and nineteenth centuries—was identified with the Society of Jesus'.[4] Congar further specifies the content of this theology, focusing particularly on the relationship of faith and reason and on ecclesiology:

> [F]aith was not defined—as in Saint Thomas—as the adhesion of the intellect to the Truth of God, but as submission to its authority. You see the difference: on one side, a logic of light, of the vitality of intellect; on the other side, a logic more militaristic, more moralistic, much more external to the relationship of God and man.
>
> For Father Chenu, as for myself, theology is essentially a promotion of faith in human reason more than a submission of reason.
>
> [...] In ecclesiology, this theology insists a great deal on the hierarchical aspect. It places the pope at the summit of a pyramidal vision, in a somewhat militaristic spirit. In sacramental theology, it insists on the famous *ex opere operato*, that is to say, on the degree of efficacy of the sacraments, the conditions of their validity. Again, an overly external view which I have always done my best to counter.[5]

Congar and Chenu were, of course, leaders of the theological movement that came to be known as *nouvelle théologie*—an originally derisive term applied to it by Roman opponents such as Pietro Parente and Réginald Garrigou-Lagrange. These 'new theologians' differed markedly in theological interests (e.g., ecclesiology, epistemology, exegesis, liturgy), social location (e.g., the Jesuit Fourvière, in Lyon, and the Dominican Le Saulchoir in Belgium and then France[6]), and even temperament (e.g., Chenu's exuberance contrasted sharply with Congar's sobriety, even dourness). Nevertheless, they shared a belief that only a comprehensive recovery of the breadth and depth of

---

[4] Jean Puyo (ed.), *Jean Puyo interroge le Père Congar: 'Une vie pour la vérité'*, Les Interviews (Paris: Éditions du Centurion, 1975), 46. Congar immediately adds that he intends no reference to the 'stupid animosity' between Jesuits and Dominicans, which he considers a thing of the past, and that he has many Jesuit friends such as de Lubac. Congar's *Journal d'un théologien*, though, indicates that he considered the Jesuits prone to authoritarianism; in contrast to the Dominican emphasis on truth and its prophetic demands, they promote the 'safe' and the 'prudent', all in service to centralized authority; see, for example, 89–90.

[5] Puyo (ed.), *Jean Puyo interroge le Père Congar*, 46–7.

[6] See Henry Donneaud, 'Le Saulchoir: une école, des théologies?' *Gr*, 83 (2002), 433–49; Étienne Fouilloux, 'Une "école de Fourvière"?' *Gr*, 83 (2002), 451–9. Both articles helpfully differentiate significantly different eras of leadership and theological approaches within these two institutions.

the Christian tradition could provide the resources for an effective engagement with, and evangelization of, the modern world; *ressourcement,* in other words, drives *aggiornamento.* Such engagement had been hindered by what de Lubac called a 'separated theology' that, in its bifurcated conception of nature and grace, both reflected and reinforced divisions between the sacred and the secular.[7] An overarching goal of *nouvelle théologie* thus was, in the words of the prophet Isaiah, to 'repair the breaches' that had developed over centuries within Catholic life and thought between nature and grace, speculative and positive theology, theology and spirituality, and church and world, among other binaries.[8] Vatican II can be read, rightfully, as the ecclesiastical vindication of these efforts to repair the breaches.

One unfortunate, and unintended, side-effect of this vindication, though, has been the creation of a new breach within the church's history and theology: that between pre- and post-Vatican II Catholicism. Both 'knockers'—who regard some or much of Vatican II's teaching as a disastrous break with the past—and 'boosters'—who regard some or much of Vatican II as a liberating break with that same past—can miss what Benedict XVI has called the 'hermeneutic of reform', which, over against a 'hermeneutic of discontinuity and rupture', places real discontinuity in a broader, deeper framework of real continuity.[9] It would be a strange *ressourcement,* after all, that simply regarded centuries of thought as a new Dark Ages or that reduced complex eras and theologies to brief, sometimes dismissive summaries in textbooks.

My thesis in this essay is that a proper understanding of both *ressourcement* and Vatican II must take account of the enduring relevance of post-Tridentine theology, both to post-Vatican II Catholicism and to Vatican II itself. If Vatican II helped integrate post-Tridentine theology into broader Catholic tradition, perhaps one contemporary task is to ensure that such integration continues today, at a time when the newness of Vatican II has, for some, tended to obscure or even dismiss the old that the Council took great care to affirm. The fine balance achieved at Vatican II can be maintained only by continuing to hold together the old and the new. Post-Tridentine theology thus has an enduring, if admittedly secondary, relevance for both the reception of Vatican II and *ressourcement* itself.

---

[7] De Lubac's *Surnaturel* is the *Magna Carta* of the attempt to overcome such separation; for a brilliant account see Joseph A. Komonchak, 'Theology and Culture at Mid-Century: The Example of Henri de Lubac', *TS,* 51 (1990), 579–602.

[8] Denys Turner sees *nouvelle théologie* as marked by a desire to 'restore lines of continuity' in the practice of theology and 'above all the instinct to make and remake *connections*'. 'Guest Editorial', *IJST,* 7 (2005), 343–4.

[9] Pope Benedict XVI, 'Christmas Greetings to the Members of the Roman Curia and Prelature' (22 December 2005), *AAS* xcviii (2006), 40–53. ET available at <http://www.vatican.va/holy_father/benedict_xvi/speeches/2005/december/documents/hf_ben_xvi_spe_20051222_roman-curia_en.html>. The terms 'knockers' and 'boosters' are borrowed from Charles Taylor, *The Ethics of Authenticity* (Cambridge MA: Harvard University Press, 1991).

This essay has three parts. First, I survey various efforts to name the centuries after the Council of Trent, culminating in a definition of 'post-Tridentine theology'. Second, I examine ecclesiology as an exemplar of this theology, particularly in its emphases on ecclesial (especially papal) authority and institutional visibility. Third, I offer concluding reflections on the enduring legacy, for good and for ill, of post-Tridentine theology. This essay is precisely that, a 'try' that sketches the key concerns and continued relevance of post-Tridentine theology, aware that theology can never rest secure in its inheritance, but, mindful of the Parable of the Talents, must wisely and shrewdly transform these talents into still-greater treasure.

THEOLOGY AFTER TRENT

We must accept the multiplicity of names not as a postmodern celebration of diversity but as a recognition of the futility of the quest for the perfect name.[10]

Naming involves distinctions and, often, judgements. Think, for example, of the political and religious resonances of 'Derry' and 'Londonderry' in Northern Ireland. A name not only reflects identity but can also shape and construct it, as with the conferral of a new name upon entering into religious life or the forcible imposition of European names upon African slaves. Naming the centuries after Trent is no different, and the term 'post-Tridentine' is deceptively clear. It is important therefore to clarify its meaning.

John O'Malley's *Trent and All That* analyses five common names given to Catholicism in the centuries following Trent: 'Counter Reform/Counter Reformation', 'Catholic Reform/Catholic Reformation', 'Tridentine Reform/Tridentine Age', 'Confessional Age/Confessional Catholicism', and 'Early Modern Catholicism'.[11]

'Counter Reform' or 'Counter Reformation', in his judgement, expresses well the anti-Protestant thrust of the period and captures the *Sturm und Drang* involved in such intense religious conflict. If emphasizing 'many aspects of the

---

[10] John W. O'Malley, *Trent and All That: Renaming Catholicism in the Early Modern Era* (Cambridge MA: Harvard University Press, 2000), 125.
[11] Like Congar, O'Malley also speaks of 'Baroque Catholicism'. He notes Werner Weisbach's *Der Barock als Kunst der Gegenreformation* (1921), which spoke positively of Baroque art as, in O'Malley's words, 'a genuine expression of Counter-Reformation spirituality—heroic, mystical, turbulent, ascetic, erotic' (35). Weisbach's generally positive assessment, however, was soon overtaken by Benedetto Croce's dismissal of the Baroque as representative of the decadence of Counter-Reformation Catholicism. Given Croce's immense intellectual influence in Italy and beyond, it is possible that his work shaped Congar and other theologians. O'Malley cites, in particular, Croce's *Storia dell'età barocca in Italia: Pensiero, poesia e letteratura, vita morale* (Bari: G. Laterza, 1929), and his 'Controriforma', *La Critica* 22 (1924), 325–33.

Catholic reality after about mid-[sixteenth]-century, particularly for those decisions, institutions, and mind-sets that Catholic officialdom, lay and clerical, deliberately set in motion in order to oppose Protestantism or to fence Catholics off from it', 'Counter Reformation' nonetheless 'attributes too much to top-down causality' and tends to envision Catholic leaders as acting independently of their surrounding cultures.[12] The term also forces everything into its framework of opposition. The Jesuits, for instance, were founded not to combat Protestantism but to help souls and to be missionary—even if such combat soon became an integral part of their identity, for better and for worse.

'Catholic Reform' or 'Catholic Reformation', by contrast, emphasizes that ecclesial reform was not merely a reaction to the Protestant Reformation, but grew out of a tradition of reform that dated back to the eleventh century, intensified with the Council of Constance (1414–18), and culminated in Trent's efforts to reform the church by first reforming its clergy—the Pope, the other bishops, and pastors. If somewhat more reserved about the positive achievements of Trent's reform than Hubert Jedin, O'Malley judges it to be reasonably successful, especially given its massive scope. These two terms, moreover, highlight the deep continuities between pre- and post-Protestant Reformation Catholicism. One drawback to this term is its tendency to conflate reform and renewal: where reform tends to work 'from the outside to the inside',[13] and was understood to refer primarily to the enforcement of clerical discipline, renewal tends to work 'from the inside out' and deals with matters of the heart and of spirituality. Philip Neri and Ignatius Loyola fall in this latter category, even if their labours helped advance church reform in this narrower sense.

'Confessional Catholicism' or 'Confessional Age'—more recent terms—describe well the control, order, discipline, clarity, boundaries, and distinctiveness of Catholicism (and of Lutheranism and Calvinism) in the aftermath of the Protestant Reformation. 'In the seventeenth century', O'Malley writes, 'the confessionalizing impulse was to the social, political, and ecclesiastical order what Descartes's "clear and distinct ideas" were to philosophy'.[14] Confessionalism, however, suffers from the same 'top-down' tendencies as other terms and tends to obscure Catholicism's continuity with its past. Most of all, its focus on social control and disciplining causes it to lose sight of the consolations of religion. It can handle 'the bleakness of moral codes' and 'the brutality of religious wars', but not 'the sublime, the self-transcending, the wondrous'.[15] Baroque art, O'Malley notes, 'painted more visions of heaven than of hell'.[16]

---

[12] *Trent and All That*, 129.
[13] *Trent and All That*, 133.
[14] *Trent and All That*, 137.
[15] *Trent and All That*, 140.
[16] *Trent and All That*, 120.

O'Malley's preferred term is 'Early Modern Catholicism'. Acknowledging its blandness and generality, he sees these qualities as strengths. It is an umbrella capable of embracing the other names as well as a broader time-frame. Where the other terms tend towards 'top-down' views of ecclesial life and emphasize either change or continuity, 'early modern Catholicism' is particularly strong in accounting for 'history from below' (particularly the role of women, both lay and religious), and for both change and continuity. Catholicism in this era was not simply an actively reforming clergy and a passive, malleable laity, but a more complex interplay of reform, renewal, and devotion—an interplay that both influenced, and was influenced by, broader historical, cultural, and political forces.

One additional name that O'Malley discusses, before arguing for 'Early Modern Catholicism', is 'Tridentine Reform' or 'Tridentine Age'. He readily grants its strengths: its recognition of the Council's pervasive impact on its time, unparalleled by any other event or person, save Martin Luther; its acknowledgement, unlike 'Catholic Reform', of change and a certain disconti-nuity, even in the midst of continuity; the far-reaching influence on Catholic life of Trent's renewal of parish life and creation of the seminary system; and its ability to encompass a broad time-span (from the mid-sixteenth century to the seventeenth century and 'in certain palpable ways even into the mid-twentieth.')[17] But O'Malley also notes the limits of 'Tridentine Reform' and 'Tridentine Age', particularly given the Council's relative silence on three subsequent major developments: the emergence of the papacy as 'almost the essence of Catholic self-definition', despite the 'great irony' that Trent was nearly silent on the one issue that both Catholics and Protestants agreed needed reform;[18] the expansion of missionary activity, despite Trent's com plete silence on the subject; and the burgeoning of 'active' female religious life, despite conciliar legislation requiring the cloistering of female religious.

It should be apparent, in view of O'Malley's work, that 'post-Tridentine theology' cannot be understood simply in chronological or causative terms. Although Trent set forth a doctrinal and disciplinary agenda for Catholicism that decisively shaped its life and thought from 1563 (the close of Trent) to 1869 (the opening of Vatican I) and even 1962 (the opening of Vatican II), not everything that happened in those centuries can be linked directly to Trent. One thinks, for instance, of the different theological visions and concerns of the Tübingen School or of John Henry Newman. Komonchak likewise cau-tions that describing pre-Vatican II Catholicism *in globo* as 'post-Tridentine' does not account sufficiently for the ecclesial and theological changes brought about by Catholicism's engagement with modernity: e.g., bureaucratization, centralization of power in Rome, greater ecclesiastical control over intellectual

---

[17] *Trent and All That*, 135.
[18] *Trent and All That*, 136, 132.

life, the formation of a 'counter-society' mentality in which the church felt itself at once under siege from secularizing political and intellectual forces and yet confident in its ability to propose a positive alternative to that secularization of public life.[19]

Trent, like any council, must be understood therefore not only in its intentions, but also in its subsequent interpretation and implementation, which may not always be consistent with those intentions. The post-Tridentine era sometimes exhibits, for instance, a certain hardening of Trent's suppleness. Jedin offers an arresting image: where the Council Fathers intended Trent's doctrinal definitions to serve as boundary-stones that would demarcate Catholic teaching on disputed matters, these boundary stones often became 'barbed wire acting as a barrier to all free movement' and helped turn the post-Tridentine church into a Counter-Reformation church, closed at times to the encounter and the dialogue that Trent at its best had tried to foster.[20] Giuseppe Alberigo distinguishes similarly between Trent and Tridentinism, praising the former for theological creativity and pastoral vigour, while criticizing—somewhat one-sidedly—the latter for its ecclesiastical uniformity, aggrandizing expansion of papal authority, and cultural isolation.[21] And, yet, the traffic could move both ways, as when the nineteenth-century Roman School both affirmed papal authority to a degree that far exceeded Trent and yet developed a more properly theological ecclesiology that, inspired by Johann Adam Möhler and others in the Tübingen School, drew upon scripture and the Fathers. The post-Tridentine era resists reductive summaries.

'Post-Tridentine theology', therefore, is not a perfect or a comprehensive name, but it does allow one to identify key, enduring, defining characteristics of the period between Trent and Vatican II. If Trent was concerned primarily with defining doctrine and renewing discipline in response to the Protestant reformations, then post-Tridentine theology may be defined as a body of thought drawing out the implications of that doctrine and discipline, most often in response to external challenges, even as it went beyond the scope of Trent's teaching. It has at least two major stages: an initial response to the Protestant reformations from the mid-sixteenth to mid-seventeenth centuries, and a later, neo-scholastic response to various intellectual and political revolutions of the eighteenth and nineteenth centuries. It is a theology shaped by controversies whose method grew increasingly abstract and deprived of a

---

[19] Komonchak, 'Modernity and the Construction of Roman Catholicism', *Cristianesimo nella Storia*, 18 (1997), 353–85.

[20] Hubert Jedin, *Crisis and Closure of the Council of Trent: A Retrospective View from the Second Vatican Council*, trans. N. D. Smith (London: Sheed & Ward, 1967), 164.

[21] Giuseppe Alberigo, 'From the Council of Trent to "Tridentinism"', in Raymond F. Bulman and Frederick J. Parrella (eds.), *From Trent to Vatican II: Historical and Theological Investigations* (New York: Oxford University Press, 2006), 19–37.

---

substantive historical and scriptural grounding. But it also exhibited clarity and rigour of thought, a systematic character well-suited for the formation of an educated clergy, and an emphasis on elaborating distinctive Catholic teaching on such matters as justification and the hierarchical nature of the church. This complex, enduring legacy of post-Tridentine theology is perhaps nowhere more evident than in the field of ecclesiology.

ECCLESIOLOGY AS EXEMPLIFYING POST-TRIDENTINE THEOLOGY

My vision of the Church [displeased Rome]. It challenged the pyramidal, hierarchicized, juridical system put in place by the Counter-Reform. [...] Rome did not appreciate any more that I advocated a return to the sources.[22]

Post-Tridentine theology finds no more visible expression than in its ecclesiology. From the close of Trent to the opening of Vatican II, Catholic ecclesiology focused primarily on several key themes, each developed in response to the dual challenges of the Protestant Reformation(s) and of the political and intellectual revolutions of the late eighteenth and nineteenth centuries: the church's authority in matters religious and political, the papacy, ecclesial visibility and institutions, the necessity and distinctiveness of the ordained priesthood, the objectivity of the sacraments, a quantitative catholicity emphasizing universality in time and space, and an apologetic focus on the four notes of the church (unity, holiness, catholicity, and apostolicity). This twofold reaction is exemplified, respectively, by the writings of the Italian Jesuit Cardinal Bellarmine (1542–1621) and the nineteenth-century Roman School, respectively.

Bellarmine is today known best—and sometimes only—for his definition of the church as 'the group of men and women brought together by the profession of the same Christian faith and by communion in the same sacraments under the governance of legitimate pastors, especially of the one vicar of Christ on earth, the Roman Pontiff', as well as for his statement that 'the church is a group of men and women as visible and palpable as is the group of the Roman people or the Kingdom of France or the Republic of Venice'.[23] These definitions clearly incline towards the 'totally external view' of post-Tridentine ecclesiology decried by Congar in his interview with Jean Puyo. Congar argues

---

[22] Puyo (ed.), *Jean Puyo interroge le Père Congar*, 102.
[23] Robert Bellarmine, *De controversiis christianae fidei adversus huius temporis haereticos*, Book III, Chapter 2, *Opera Omnia* II (Naples, 1856), 75.

elsewhere that Bellarmine's ecclesiology is 'dominated' by the concern of 'being able to say where and what the true Church is'.[24]

Bellarmine's definition thus excludes those who do not profess the Christian faith (he lists Jews, Muslims ['Turks'], pagans, heretics, and apostates), those who do not share in the same sacraments (catechumens and excommunicates; the former are not admitted to participation in the sacraments, the latter dismissed from it), and those who do not submit to legitimate pastors (schismatics 'who have faith and the sacraments'). Komonchak has noted, moreover, that Bellarmine's use of apparently 'spiritual' terms such as *communio* and *commercium spirituale* is entirely formalistic, lacking in theological, material substance; even here, the emphasis falls on externality and submission to authority.[25] I would add that Bellarmine's ecclesiology lacks comprehensiveness (although, in fairness, *De Controversiis* was intended to be inherently topical rather than global in its concerns), as well as adequate theologies of the laity (*De Laicis* is a treatise on church-state matters, devoid of any consideration of the laity's identity and mission in the church) and of the Holy Spirit.

Bellarmine's externality, however, has its virtues. External exclusivity pairs with a surprising internal inclusivity. His definition of the church and its visibility makes no attempt to read hearts or to judge anyone's faith. Harsh to those without and constricted in its ability to recognize invisible or incomplete belonging, Bellarmine's ecclesiology is nonetheless merciful and forbearing to those within the fold. He explicitly includes as members 'reprobates, the wicked, and the ungodly'.[26] This externality, for its obvious flaws, can be a useful theological and pastoral corrective to perennial temptations to sectarianism and Donatism.

The style of Bellarmine's theology is also commendable. Clearly affirming papal authority (if not sufficiently so for Pope Sixtus V, who decried Bellarmine's constraints on the papacy's temporal authority), as well as Catholic teaching on the sacraments and salvation, he does so dispassionately, with a minimum of polemical rancour and with a sensitivity to history and patristic sources lacking in his more scholastic contemporaries such as Francisco Suárez and Domingo Bañez.[27] Such measure is all the more commendable, given the enormous, unprecedented challenges posed by the Protestant reformations. One may rightly see Bellarmine, then, as representative of a post-Tridentine theology that at its best confirmed Catholic faith and responded intelligently and constructively, if limitedly, to challenges.

---

[24] Congar, *L'Église: de saint Augustin à l'époque moderne* (Paris: Cerf, 1970), 372.
[25] Komonchak, 'Concepts of Communion. Past and Present', *Cristianesimo nella Storia*, 16 (1995), 321–40 (324–5).
[26] Bellarmine, *De controversiis*.
[27] John Patrick Donnelly, 'Introduction', in John Patrick Donnelly and Roland J. Teske trans. and ed., *Robert Bellarmine: Spiritual Writings* (New York/Mahwah NJ: Paulist, 1989), 14.

Nearly three centuries after Bellarmine wrote *De Controversiis*, the
Roman School responded to an even deeper challenge: where the Protestant
Reformation(s) wished to mend Christianity, the Enlightenment and the
eighteenth- and nineteenth-century European political revolutions sought to
end it. And, within Catholicism, various movements such as Febronianism
and Josephism had raised anew the spectre of conciliarism and national
churches as challenges to papal authority.[28] Hermann Pottmeyer has written
of the 'three traumas' affecting 'papal Rome' in the nineteenth century:
the *ecclesial* trauma of conciliarism and Gallicanism, the *political* trauma of
state-controlled churches, and the *intellectual-cultural* trauma of rationalism
and liberalism.[29]

Theological responses to these traumas varied. The Tübingen School
offered the most nuanced engagement with the intellectual challenges of
modernity, particularly in Möhler's ecclesiological integration of modern
philosophical (Schelling, Hegel) and religious (Schleiermacher) thought with
a scriptural and patristic *ressourcement*.[30] The Ultramontanism represented
by Joseph de Maistre and Félicité Lammenais chose resistance and counter-
attack, by contrast, and held the papacy to be the only secure bulwark against
the ecclesial, political, and intellectual revolutions of the time:

> Christianity rests entirely on the pope, so that the principles of the political and
> social order . . . may be derived from the following chain of reasoning: there can be
> no public morality and no national character without religion, no European
> religion without Christianity, no Christianity without Catholicism, no Catholi-
> cism without the pope, no pope without the sovereignty that belongs to him.[31]

Under the influence of Ultramontanism and the pontificates of Gregory
XVI and Pius IX, Catholicism became increasingly identified with the Pope's
authority and even with his very person. At the extreme, this identification of
the church and the Pope passed over into the identification of the Pope and
Christ, in forms both 'softer' (e.g., the effective restriction of the title 'Vicar of
Christ' to the Pope, while the other bishops were regarded as 'vicars of the
Pope') and 'harder' (e.g., devotion to 'the three white things': the eucharistic
host, Mary, and the Pope; or, admittedly atypical, the belief, according to an
early-twentieth-century Canadian bishop, that 'the pope is the second mode of

---

[28] See William Henn, *The Honor of My Brothers: A Brief History of the Relationship between
the Pope and the Bishops* (New York: Herder & Herder, 2000), 131–6.

[29] Hermann J. Pottmeyer, *Towards a Papacy in Communion: Perspectives from Vatican
Councils I & II* (New York: Herder & Herder, 1998), 36–50.

[30] See Thomas F. O'Meara, 'Between Schelling and Hegel: The Catholic Tübingen School', in
Romantic Idealism and Roman Catholicism: Schelling and the Theologians (Notre Dame IN:
Notre Dame, 1982), 138–60. Also Grant Kaplan, *Answering the Enlightenment: The Catholic
Recovery of Historical Revelation* (New York: Herder and Herder, 2006).

[31] Joseph de Maistre, 'Letter to the Count of Blacas', in *Correspondance* iv (Lyon, 1821), 428,
cited in Pottmeyer, *Towards a Papacy in Communion*, 53–4.

the real presence of Jesus Christ in the Church').[32] It must be acknowledged, however, that for all of its intransigence, Ultramontanism also evinced a deep commitment to the good of all humanity. Rejecting 'the dream of a church closed in on itself, on its own power', many leading Ultramontanists allied themselves with the oppressed and the marginalized of society. Cardinal Manning of Westminster's unstinting support for workers and labour unions, for instance, found unprecedented support in the charter of Catholic social teaching, *Rerum Novarum*, Pope Leo XIII's 1891 encyclical.[33]

The Roman School offered a more supple response than did the Ultramontanists and their descendants. Based in the mid-nineteenth century at the Jesuit-run Roman College, its leading representatives were Giovanni Perrone, Carlo Passaglia, Clemens Schrader, and Johann Baptist Franzelin. All were influenced by Möhler and his recovery of the Fathers, but were more sympathetic to the later, more Christological ecclesiology of his *Symbolik* than to the earlier, more pneumatological cast of *Einheit in der Kirche*. The dominant ecclesiological characteristics of the Roman School are twofold. The first is a clear affirmation of ecclesial authority and structures, particularly of papal primacy and infallibility. Schrader, and especially Franzelin, exercised significant influence at Vatican I. The second is a resolutely theological grounding of ecclesiology, with a decidedly Christological and incarnational foundation; the church as the mystical body of Christ is their key image. A passage from Franzelin's *Theses de Ecclesia Christi* (1887) exemplifies these two points:

> The Church is an image of Christ, its Founder and Head, in its inmost constitution, by which it expresses itself in a likeness to the Incarnate Word. As Christ is the God-man, the Word made flesh, so his Body, the Church, in its members, in its hierarchy, in its sacraments and institutions consists of a twofold element, an external element that of itself is human and visible, and an internal element that is divine and invisible and by which the human element is informed and elevated and thereby formally constituted as *ecclesiastical*.[34]

The Roman School's main flaw, however, was its failure to integrate fully the visible and the invisible dimensions of the church. It unwittingly and unwillingly fell prey to a kind of ecclesiological Nestorianism, in which the two dimensions exist side-by-side, but also effectively separate and unsuccessfully united. Its robustly Christological vision of the church had little effect on its largely formalistic, Bellarminian treatment of the church's visibility.[35] Put

---

[32] J. M. R. Tillard, 'Théologies et "devotions" au pape depuis le Moyen Âge. De Jean XXIII à ... Jean XXIII', *Cristianesimo nella Storia*, 22 (2001), 191–211 (197).
[33] Tillard, 'Théologies et "devotions"', 207.
[34] J. B. Franzelin, *Theses de Ecclesia Christi* (Rome: Typographia Polyglotta, 1887), 324, in Komonchak, 'Concepts of Communion', 327.
[35] See Komonchak, 'Concepts of Communion', 327–30.

perhaps too simply, the Roman School held *that* the two dimensions were integrated, but was unable to explain *how* they were integrated.

The Roman School's ecclesiology had a lasting influence up to Vatican II.[36] Schrader and Franzelin contributed to *Pastor Aeternus*, while the renewal of the theology of the church as the mystical body of Christ was deepened through the exegetical labours of Émile Mersch and others. This renewal reached its ecclesiastical apogee in 1943 with the publication of Pius XII's encyclical, *Mystici Corporis Christi*, drafted largely by the Jesuit Sebastian Tromp. The preparatory draft of Vatican II's *De Ecclesia* betrayed a more unilaterally institutional ecclesiology, but, even on the eve of Vatican II, the manualist tradition was not monolithic. In 1955, for instance, Timoteo Zapelena of the Gregorian University devoted the first four theses of his *De Ecclesia Christi* to a discussion of the Kingdom of God, taking care to show that the Kingdom is at once eschatological and incarnational, an interior reality and a visible society under the governance of the Roman Pontiff.[37]

Thoroughly Christological and desirous of integrating the church's visible and invisible dimensions, the Roman School thus helped point the way to Vatican II, and one may hear its echoes in *Lumen Gentium*:

> The one mediator, Christ, established and constantly sustains here on earth his holy church, the community of faith, hope, and charity, as a visible structure through which he communicates truth and grace to everyone. But, the society equipped with hierarchical structures and the mystical body of Christ, the visible society and the spiritual community, the earthly church and the church endowed

---

[36] See Étienne Fouilloux, 'Les théologiens romains à la veille de Vatican II', in *Histoire et théologie: Actes de la Journée d'études de l'Assocation Française d'histoire religieuse contemporaine sous la direction de Jean-Dominique Durand* (Paris: Beauchesne, 1994), 137–60.

[37] See Timotheus Zapelena, *De Ecclesia Christi: Pars Apologetica* (Rome: Gregorian University, 1955). Congar's *Journal d'un théologien* records his back-to-back meetings on 17 May 1946 with both Zapelena and Tromp at the Gregorian University. He writes of his agreement with Zapelena's position that the church was founded at Pentecost, rather than at the Cross, as Tromp held (87). And, in words that cohere with this paper's critique of post-Tridentine understandings of ecclesial visibility and membership, Congar writes, 'Tromp is in reaction against everything that would limit, from a more theological, Christological, or pneumatic point of view, the [church's] perfect identity with the visible institution. This is why he critiques very strongly the idea that the church would already be established at the Incarnation, at Christmas, or even at the Annunciation. The Greek Fathers take a hammering from him.... Tromp reacts against the scholastic (Thomist) and patristic idea that the mystical body = wherever the grace of Christ (*de gratia capitis*) reaches. This seems to him not to recognize the necessity, in the joining of members to the Body, of hierarchical and visible elements.' Perhaps Tromp's resistance here helps make sense of *Humani Generis*' warning against certain forms of ecclesiological *ressourcement*: 'What is expounded in the Encyclical Letters of the Roman Pontiffs concerning the nature and constitution of the Church, is deliberately and habitually neglected by some with the idea of giving force to a certain vague notion which they profess to have found in the ancient Fathers, especially the Greeks. The Popes, they assert, do not wish to pass judgement on what is a matter of dispute among theologians, so recourse must be had to the early sources, and the recent constitutions and decrees of the Teaching Church must be explained from the writings of the ancients' (*HG* §18).

with heavenly riches, are not to be thought of as two realities. On the contrary, they form one complex reality comprising a human and a divine element. For this reason the church is compared, in no mean analogy, to the mystery of the incarnate Word. (*LG* § 8)

THE ENDURING LEGACY OF POST-TRIDENTINE THEOLOGY

The hermeneutic of discontinuity risks ending in a split between the pre-conciliar Church and the post-conciliar Church. It asserts that the texts of the Council as such do not yet express the true spirit of the Council. It claims that they are the result of compromises in which, to reach unanimity, it was found necessary to keep and reconfirm many old things that are now pointless.[38]

What, then, is the *enduring* legacy of post-Tridentine theology? For some *ressourcement* theologians, its legacy might be summed up as an exhausted project, if an understandable and perhaps even necessary one. At best, such Tridentinism—'a system which took in absolutely everything', in Congar's words, 'of theology, ethics, Christian behaviour, religious practices, liturgy, organization, Roman centralization, the perpetual intervention of Roman congregations in the life of the Church, and so on'[39]—did what it had to do, but its time has now passed. More severely, it failed to respond constructively and thoroughly to the religious, political, and cultural challenges of its time. Congar's monumental *L'Église*, for instance, is marked by a sustained critique of post-Tridentine Catholicism's obsession with ecclesial power and authority and of its imperious conception of church-state relationships. As noted above, his diaries rail against the centralizing, authoritarian 'system' he believed to be at work in the Society of Jesus and in the Vatican, in contrast to Dominican ideals of consensual governance and the disinterested, even prophetic quest for truth.[40] The limits of post-Tridentine theology and ecclesiology can be seen in the very titles of Congar's major works: *Divided Christendom, Lay People in the Church, True and False Reform in the Church, The Mystery of the Temple, Tradition and Traditions, I Believe in the Holy Spirit*. Each title is a proverbial shot across the bow announcing the 'liquidation' of the Baroque theology that

---

[38] Pope Benedict XVI, 'Christmas Greetings'.

[39] Congar, *Fifty Years of Catholic Theology*, ed. Bernard Lauret (Philadelphia: Fortress Press, 1988), 3–4. Congar quickly adds, though, that Vatican II took great care to connect its teaching to both Trent and Vatican I. He mentions here Giuseppe Alberigo's distinction between Trent and Tridentinism.

[40] See n. 3 above; also Alberto Melloni's good, but sometimes one-sided, article, 'The System and the Truth in the Diaries of Yves Congar', in Gabriel Flynn (ed.), *Yves Congar: Theologian of the Church* (Louvain/Grand Rapids MI: Peeters/Eerdmans, 2005), 277–302.

Congar desired from the early years of his theological labours. At Vatican II 'the ontology of grace or the reality of Christian existence was given priority or primacy in regard to social organization or juridical structure'.[41] For the *ressourcement* movement, the legacy of post-Tridentine theology is as that which has been overcome or at least superseded, a reminder at once of the dangers of controversy-driven thought and of the achievements of Vatican II.

There is much merit in this view. The limits of post-Tridentine ecclesiology are evident, especially when compared to the achievements of the *ressourcement* theologians. Most important is its lack of a thoroughly eucharistic ecclesiology. Post-Tridentine ecclesiology clearly holds that the church makes the Eucharist, but devotes much less attention to the no less foundational truth that the Eucharist makes the church. The development of an adequate eucharistic ecclesiology was catalysed by the twentieth-century Orthodox renewal begun at St Sergius in Paris, and by the work of *ressourcement* theologians such as Congar and especially de Lubac.[42] One sees the fruits of their labours—along with those of Louis Bouyer and others associated with the modern liturgical movement—in Vatican II's affirmation that the eucharistic sacrifice is 'the source and the culmination of all Christian life' (*LG* § 11), as well as in the theological vision of Pope John Paul II's final encyclical, *Ecclesia de Eucharistia*. Similarly, post-Tridentine ecclesiology lacks an adequate theology of the local church, of the missionary nature of the church, and of episcopal collegiality (particularly the relationship between *sub Petro* and *cum Petro*).[43] These pre-Vatican II absences—and others such as ecumenism, pneumatology, and a theology of the laity[44]—are still felt, even and perhaps especially in the ongoing reception of Vatican II's teaching on these subjects.

I would argue, however, that there is another, more positive legacy of post-Tridentine theology, particularly of its ecclesiology. This enduring legacy can be found in those post-Tridentine elements which Vatican II intentionally and fruitfully recontextualized in the framework of the church's broader tradition, but which have sometimes been de-emphasized or even marginalized in the

---

[41] Congar, *L'Église*, 473.

[42] De Lubac, *Corpus Mysticum: l'eucharistie et l'Église au Moyen Âge. Étude historique* (Paris: Aubier, 1944); ET, *Corpus Mysticum: The Eucharist and Church in the Middle Ages: Historical Survey*, trans. Gemma Simmonds with Richard Price and Christopher Stephens, eds. Laurence Paul Hemming and Susan Frank Parsons (Notre Dame IN: University of Notre Dame Press, 2007). See also Paul McPartlan, *The Eucharist Makes the Church: Henri de Lubac and John Zizioulas in Dialogue* (Edinburgh: T&T Clark, 1993); and '*Ressourcement*, Vatican II and Eucharistic Ecclesiology', Ch. 25 in this volume.

[43] See Ruddy, *The Local Church: Tillard and the Future of Catholic Ecclesiology* (New York: Herder and Herder, 2006).

[44] Trent itself affirmed the priesthood of all believers, but neither the Council nor post-Tridentine theology did much to develop a theology of the common priesthood or to tie the common priesthood to the church's eucharistic and missionary dimensions; see Nelson H. Minnich, 'The Priesthood of All Believers at the Council of Trent', *The Jurist*, 67 (2007), 341–63.

decades since the Council.[45] A serious challenge today is to read Vatican II in the light of the Christian tradition as a whole—and not vice-versa—and so to come to a deeper understanding of precisely how Tridentine and post-Tridentine emphases on, say, Christ's real presence in the Eucharist or the qualitative difference between the baptismal and ordained priesthoods contribute to Vatican II's teaching. This is the challenge set forth by Pope Benedict in his now-famous Christmas Address to the Roman Curia in 2005: a 'hermeneutic of reform' that seeks to discern continuity of principle amidst discontinuity of application and context.

One particular area of contemporary importance is the Christocentrism of post-Tridentine ecclesiology, particularly in the Roman School. Vatican II set forth a robustly Trinitarian ecclesiology (e.g., *LG* § 2–4; *Ad GD* § 2–4), in which the missions of Son and Spirit lovingly serve the Father's plan for humanity and all creation. Christ remained at the conciliar centre—the title of *Lumen Gentium* refers not to the church, but to Christ—but that centre was amplified to embrace a fuller and more explicitly Trinitarian perspective. In the post-conciliar era, both one-sidedly horizontal (in the laudable intent to affirm the dignity of all the baptized) and pneumatic (with the laudable intent of discerning the divine presence in all Christians and even in other religions) ecclesiologies have some-times disturbed the Council's finely-wrought integration of Christology and pneumatology. In a contemporary context, *Dominus Iesus*, whatever limits it may have, was right to affirm the unique and universal salvific role of Christ, the inseparable bond between the saving work of Christ and of the Holy Spirit, and the church's unique and universal mediation of that salvation.[46] Surely a con-temporary theological task is to discern the shape of God's presence beyond the visible bonds of the church, but it must always recall the Christocentrism that lies at the heart of Catholic faith, not least at Vatican II. As Congar wrote, genuine *ressourcement* consists not in a restoration or a repristination of the past, but in a 'recentering on Christ and his paschal mystery'.[47]

Post-Tridentine theology, moreover, has certain enduring formal or stylistic dimensions. I will mention here only three: method, pastoral concern, and reasoned engagement. First, post-Tridentine theology worked within a shared, if narrow, scholastic framework that made possible a common theological conversation. R. R. Reno, in a critique of the 'heroic generation' of Congar, de Lubac, and Lonergan, among others, distinguishes between exploratory and standard theologies.[48] Exploratory theology is 'creative and personal. It is born out of a loyalty to doctrine, but it is not ecclesially normative.' It cannot

---

[45] For the influence of Trent on Vatican II's teachings, see Komonchak, 'The Council of Trent at the Second Vatican Council', in Bulman and Parrella (eds.), *From Trent to Vatican II*, 61–80.
[46] See Robert Imbelli, 'The Reaffirmation of the Christic Center', in Stephen J. Pope and Charles Hefling (eds.), *Sic et Non: Encountering Dominus Iesus* (Maryknoll NY: Orbis, 2002), 96–106.
[47] Congar, *Vraie et fausse réforme dans l'Église*, Unam Sanctam, 20 (Paris: Cerf, 1950), 338.
[48] R. R. Reno, 'Theology After the Revolution', *First Things*, 173 (May 2007), 15–21.

provide a 'baseline' for teaching or pastoral life. Standard theology is 'more pedestrian', 'not rejecting and beginning afresh but instead refining and renewing through careful additions, adjustments, and adumbrations of what has been long taught'.[49] Reno reckons that *ressourcement* theology tended to undercut the very standard theology that made its own labours possible. Today, he argues, Catholic theology is suffering from that absence of a common framework and language. The church, he concludes, 'need[s] a period of consolidation that allows us to integrate the lasting achievements of the Heroic Generation into a renewed standard theology'.[50] I am more sceptical than Reno about the possibility of a new standard theology, but surely theological formation cannot be reduced to a survey of different theological methods from which one may select according to personal prefer-ence. Any community that lacks a common language, however limited, will be literally idiotic.

Second, post-Tridentine theology was deeply pastoral, even if differently so from Vatican II. Trent, according to Jedin, aimed 'to strengthen those who had remained faithful to the Catholic Church and to clarify and reaffirm their faith, not win the Protestants over'.[51] The Council did so through clarifying contested doctrines and enforcing tighter discipline, especially of bishops and pastors. Exhortation alone was not sufficient; 'teeth' were needed to uproot deep-seated abuses, especially financial ones among bishops.[52] Such clarity and definition are relevant again today in light of the changing signs of the times. The sociologist Christian Smith has noted the frightening religious inarticulacy of American teenagers and young adults. This inarticulacy has devastating consequences for church life, for 'articulacy fosters reality'.[53] What is left unarticulated is, to some degree, non-existent or at least deprived of force. To return to an earlier point, the life of the church as a whole and in its members suffers when it loses a common language and when the vocabulary of faith is no longer used or understood by its members. If Trent created the seminary system to form the educated clergy needed to respond to the challenges of its time, a similar effort is needed today to form the theologically educated laity needed to meet the challenges of contemporary life.

Finally, post-Tridentine theology, despite its often apologetic and contro-versial cast, can show that honest, forthright engagement of differences need not be divisive or unecumenical, but rather a condition for dialogue. Jedin, we have seen, viewed Trent's doctrinal decrees as boundary stones, marking off

[49] Reno, 'Theology After the Revolution', 17–18.
[50] 'Theology After the Revolution', 21.
[51] Jedin, *Crisis and Closure of the Council of Trent*, 165.
[52] O'Malley, 'Trent and Vatican II: Two Styles of Church', in Bulman and Parrella (eds.), *From Trent to Vatican II*, 301–20 (307).
[53] Christian Smith with Melissa Lundquist Denton, *Soul Searching: The Religious and Spiri-tual Lives of American Teenagers* (New York: Oxford University Press, 2005), 268.

territory but allowing for passage. That these stones became barbed wire after Trent, as Catholics and Protestants alike 'withdrew to hedgehog positions of defence',[54] should remind us today of the dangers of divisive, if often comfortable, ideological isolation. The example of Bellarmine shows the possibility of reasoned engagement in the midst of fierce disagreement.

The enduring legacy of post-Tridentine theology, then, can be found in its oft-neglected contributions to Vatican II, which were not simply tactical concessions to the conciliar 'minority', but expressions of a fundamental continuity in faith and doctrine. The *ressourcement* movement rightly saw the limits of post-Tridentine theology, but Vatican II integrated that theology's enduring insights into the broader Christian tradition recovered by the *ressourcement* theologians. A sad irony in present-day Catholicism is that those who see Vatican II as a liberating break from pre-conciliar benightedness can wind up becoming unwitting prisoners of that past, trapped in its fixation on ecclesial power, where one group's gain is the other's loss. Ecclesiology is too often reduced to ecclesiastical political science. Chapter 3 ('The Church is Hierarchical') of *Lumen Gentium* dominates much ecclesiological reflection to the exclusion of the Constitution's later chapters on holiness and eschatology, while Chapter 2 ('The People of God') is subjected to a reactive protest against hierarchy, rather than being read as the historical unfolding of the mysterious reality set forth in Chapter 1 ('The Mystery of the Church'). Post-Vatican II Catholicism needs more than ever the Council's integration of the best insights of post-Tridentine theology with the Great Tradition; a *ressourcement* sketched by the historian Eamon Duffy:

> The clerical authoritarianism of the Church of the 1950s now looks what it was, a drastic and distorted overdevelopment of the Church's historical particularity at the expense of other equally important dimensions, like the role of prophecy or the dignity of the laity.... But if we believe in the reality of revelation, and if we believe that the Church is entrusted with it, then we have to give a concrete meaning and form to that confidence. We cannot indefinitely postpone our obedience and response to the truth, as it seems to me many forms of liberal Protestantism tend to do. If the Church has the gospel of truth, *someone, somewhere*, has to be trusted to say what it is, and to call on us to receive it. That process seems to me now more complex and less simplistically hierarchical than we imagined in 1950, but the essence of what we believed in 1950 seems to me both true, and precious. A Church without real authority is not the Church at all. We receive and proclaim the Catholic faith which comes to us from the apostles, we do not invent it...[55]

---

[54] Jedin, *Crisis and Closure of the Council of Trent*, 164.
[55] Eamon Duffy, 'Confessions of a Cradle Catholic', in *Faith of Our Fathers: Reflections on Catholic Tradition* (London: Continuum, 2004), 11–19 (19).

Part II

Central Figures of the *Ressourcement*

13

Marie-Dominique Chenu and Le Saulchoir: A Stream of Catholic Renewal

Janette Gray, RSM

INTRODUCTION

Marie-Dominique Chenu, OP (1895–1990) was the precursor of the great between-the-wars theologians who initiated the *ressourcement* which led to Vatican II. From the early 1920s he promoted studies of Thomas Aquinas in his intellectual and social context: the philosophical-theological renaissance that flowered in Paris from the twelfth to the thirteenth centuries. Chenu is the least known of the Catholic reformers. His student and colleague, Yves Congar, OP, and another of his students, Edward Schillebeeckx, OP, are much more acclaimed. Even his Jesuit contemporaries, Henri de Lubac and Jean Daniélou, have received more recognition. Yet Chenu was crucial in the historical retrieval of theological sources which led to the pejoratively named *nouvelle théologie*. Coined by their Vatican censors, this blanket term covered the parallel but not identical projects of the war-time theology faculties of the Jesuits at Fourvière in Lyon and the Dominicans at Le Saulchoir, initially in Kain-lez-Tournai outside Tournai in Belgium, then after 1937 in Étiolles near Paris. Their efforts were implicitly condemned in Pope Pius XII's 1950 encyclical, *Humani Generis*.[1]

Chenu's theology originated within the limits of Pope Leo XIII's endorsement of neo-scholastic Thomism as the 'universal theology' for Latin Catholicism in 1879, and the proscription of any tendencies to theological 'Modernism' by Pius X.[2] The analytical scholasticism that was so exclusively

---

[1] Pius XII, *Humani Generis*: Encyclical Letter Concerning Some False Opinions Threatening to Undermine the Foundations of Catholic Doctrine (12 August 1950), *AAS* xlii (1950), 561–78. ET available at: <http://www.vatican.va/holy_father/pius_xii/encyclicals/documents/hf_p-xii_enc_12081950_humani-generis_en.html>.

[2] Leo XIII, *Aeterni Patris*: Encyclical Letter on the Restoration of Christian Philosophy (4 August 1879), *Acta Leonis XIII*, i (1881), 255–84. ET available at: <http://www.vatican.va/

enshrined was defined by its propositional content and deductive method. Chenu labelled this 'modern scholasticism', to flag his belief that its true paternity was Enlightenment rationalism, not unbroken continuity with medieval Thomist thought.[3] For Chenu this late scholasticism reduced theology to a propositional apologetics that took on the rationalist style of the modernity it sought to combat. In *Une école de théologie: le Saulchoir*, his manifesto for a reformed theological curriculum, he commented:

> In today's method, it is a logical formalism which triumphs to the detriment of curiosity, and so the medieval 'disputation' approach is substituted with 'scholastic exercises', which are only a parody of dialectic.[4]

Its consequent solipsism relegated theology to the margins of the contemporary world.[5] Instead Chenu proposed an innovative theological *rapprochement* with contemporary thought in order to overcome this marginalization. He found authorization for this in the example of Thomas Aquinas in the thirteenth century. Chenu's *ressourcement* began with diachronic study of Thomas's full opus in its context which showed the extent of the 'modern scholastic' deviation from Thomas's theology. This was later published as *Towards Understanding St Thomas* in 1950.[6] It revealed the scope of Thomas's engagement with his contemporary context and the recently recovered Aristotelian philosophy. This contrasted Thomas's theology with the systematized digest form of the manual theology of the early twentieth century.[7]

---

holy_father/leo_xiii/encyclicals/documents/hf_l-xiii_enc_04081879_aeterni-patris_en.html>; Pius X, *Pascendi Dominici Gregis*. Encyclical Letter on the Doctrine of the Modernists (8 September 1907), *ASS* 40 (1907), 593–650. ET available at: <http://www.vatican.va/holy_father/pius_x/encyclicals/documents/hf_p-x_enc_19070908_pascendi-dominici-gregis_en.html>; see Roger Aubert, 'The Modernist Crisis and the Integrist Reaction', in R. Aubert, J. Bruhls, and J. Hajjar (eds.), *The Church in a Secularised Society*, trans. Janet Sondheimer (New York/ London: Paulist/Darton, Longman & Todd, 1978), 198–203.

[3] When commenting on its origins, Chenu also called this 'baroque scholasticism'; see Chenu, *Une école*, 155. *Une école de théologie: Le Saulchoir* (Kain-lez-Tournai/Étiolles: Le Saulchoir, 1937); re-issued as *Une école de théologie: Le Saulchoir*, eds. G. Alberigo, É. Fouilloux, J. Ladrière, J.-P. Jossua (Paris: Cerf, 1985); and Chenu, 'Ratio superior et inferior. Un cas de philosophie chrétienne', *RSPT*, 29 (1940), 84–9 (84).

[4] *Une école*, 156. Chenu also termed this neo-scholasticism or neo-Thomism as 'thomisme de séminaire' and 'thomisme régénéré par le kantisme'.

[5] Chenu, 'Aux origines de la "science moderne"', *RSPT*, 29 (1940), 206–17 (210); and 'Ratio superior et inferior', 88; cf. Michael J. Buckley, SJ, *At the Origins of Modern Atheism* (New Haven: Yale University Press, 1987), 341–2, 344–7, particularly 357.

[6] *Toward Understanding Saint Thomas* (Chicago: Henry Regnery, 1964). Originally published as *Introduction à l'étude de Saint Thomas d'Aquin* (Montreal/Paris: Institut d'études médiévales/ Vrin, 1950).

[7] A further reductionist treatment of Aquinas was introduced with 'the *Philosophia perennis* of the "Twenty-Four Theses"' in 1914. The author of this digest was G. Mattiussi, SJ, a disciple of L. Billot, SJ (1846–1931), who was the influential theologian at the Gregorian University. Chenu, *Un théologien en liberté: Jacques Duquesne interroge le Père Chenu* (Paris: Le Centurion, 1975), 31.

Chenu's understanding of the *ressourcement* was not one of 'returning to the sources' as historical scholarship for its own sake (not 'antiquarian' as Congar later commented), but as drawing from these sources to delineate Aquinas' theological method and his contemporaries from its 'modern-scholastic' analytical strait-jacket. Then twentieth-century theology could see ways, reflected in the techniques and critical approaches practised in the past, to engage with contemporary theological and philosophical issues, with what Chenu termed 'a new freshness'.

SOURCES OF THE STREAM: 'IN THE ROMAN CURRENT'[8]

Chenu's supervisor for doctoral studies at the Angelicum in Rome was Réginald Garrigou-Lagrange, OP (1877–1964), an eminent exponent of the analytical scholasticism that Chenu later came to reject. Garrigou-Lagrange had formerly taught at Le Saulchoir from 1904 to 1909 and presided at the Angelicum from 1909 to 1959. He had introduced his own 'return to the sources' by promoting the study of St John of the Cross, which reinstated mystical theology into the theological curriculum of the Angelicum, after an absence since the Enlightenment. Chenu valued this 'grand master' for his learning and generous patronage, despite judging that Garrigou-Lagrange was unashamedly ignorant of history and its importance for doctrine and theology.[9] While Chenu's thesis, entitled 'On Thomas' Contemplation: psychological and theological analysis of contemplation', was influenced by Garrigou-Lagrange's focus on spirituality, it deviated from his method by applying the New Testament exegete M.-J. Lagrange, OP's historical method to Aquinas.[10] To Garrigou-Lagrange's annoyance, Chenu also explored Aquinas against the wider context of his medieval contemporaries, the twelfth- and thirteenth-century Franciscans.[11]

Much of Chenu's lifelong concern to assert the crucial necessity for the study of the medieval sources in their historical context had its foundation in this study of Aquinas. While Garrigou-Lagrange's concern was aroused, Chenu's brilliance so won over his teacher that on completion of his doctorate

---

[8] Chenu in Olivier de la Brosse, *Le Père Chenu: la liberté dans la foi* (Paris: Cerf, 1969), 37.

[9] Chenu, 'Regard sur cinquante ans de vie religieuse', in C. Geffré (ed.), *L'hommage différé au Père Chenu* (Paris: Cerf, 1990), 259–68 (262); Chenu, *Un théologien en liberté*, 38.

[10] *Un théologien en liberté*, 49.

[11] C. G. Conticello, *'De Contemplatione* (Angelicum 1920). La thèse inédite de doctorat du P. M.-D. Chenu', *RSPT*, 75 (1991), 363–422 (364–5). Later Chenu summarized this material into the section on Thomas 'The Contemplative' in his favourite work, *Aquinas and His Role in Theology* (College ville MN: Liturgical Press, 2002) [*St Thomas d'Aquin et la théologie*, Paris: Editions du Seuil, 1959], 35–62.

he was invited to assist Garrigou-Lagrange in teaching at the Angelicum.[12] Garrigou-Lagrange's disappointment that Chenu declined his invitation is judged by Congar and the historian Fouilloux as igniting his later antagonism towards Chenu. Even so, Chenu continued to draw on Garrigou-Lagrange's *ressourcement* of mystical theology and the restoration of spirituality to theological study on his return to teaching at Le Saulchoir. Chenu later noted that he and Garrigou-Lagrange were working from very different understandings of theology and spirituality.[13] Fergus Kerr, OP describes Garrigou-Lagrange's work as 'all too much like the exposition, highly abstract and syllogistic, of a set of quasi-Euclidean theorems'.[14] Yet this methodological difference seems to have been patent only to the young Chenu and not to Garrigou-Lagrange, since shortly after his return to Le Saulchoir, in late 1921, Garrigou-Lagrange again unsuccessfully requested that Chenu join him at the Angelicum.[15] Perhaps this invitation was an attempt to divert Chenu's scholarship away from the more innovative academy of Le Saulchoir; this would appear to be supported by Garrigou-Lagrange's vehement opposition after the publication of *Le Saulchoir* in 1937.

'A FISH TO WATER': LE SAULCHOIR

From the early part of the twentieth century, under the leadership of Ambroise Gardeil, OP (1905–1911), Le Saulchoir was a centre for textual scholarship with a reputation for an historical criticality then uncommon outside the Tübingen School and the work of Johann Möhler, given the 'anti-Modernist' repression.[16] Chenu returned to Le Saulchoir, like 'a fish to water' he said.[17] There he taught the history of Christian doctrines and became steeped in the historical vicissitudes of doctrine which dictated the direction of his future theology. Chenu emphasized that this was not the 'history of dogma', because doctrine allowed for more historical elucidation than 'dogma' without

---

[12] Yves Congar, 'Hommage au Père M.-D. Chenu', *RSPT*, 75 (1991), 361–504 (361).

[13] *Un théologien en liberté*, 38–40.

[14] Fergus Kerr, OP, *Twentieth Century Catholic Theologians: From Neoscholasticism to Nuptial Mysticism* (Oxford: Blackwell, 2007), 12.

[15] André Duval, OP, 'Aux origines de l'"Institut historique d'études thomistes" du Saulchoir (1920 et ss.). Notes et Documents', *RSPT*, 75 (1991), 423–48 (438).

[16] Gardeil was Regent of Studies from 1894, when the *studium* was still located in France at Corbara, then at Flavigny, before the move to Belgium in 1904; see Jean-Pierre Jossua OP, 'Le Saulchoir: une formation théologique replacée dans son histoire', *Cristianesimo nella storia*, 14 (1993), 99–124 (101–2); Aubert, *Le problème de l'acte de foi: Données traditionnelles et résultats des controverses récentes* (Louvain: Universitas Catholica Lovaniensis, 1945), 587–600.

[17] Duval, 'Aux origines', 437.

the inevitable condemnation for relativism.[18] As Yves Congar his student, colleague and friend later commented:

> It was the history of doctrine where he exposed us to finding the truth of history, that is the drama where one takes the part of each side of a problem and poses what its understanding and misunderstandings involve. . . . One then lived the issues as a problem-solving exercise.[19]

Fostered by the team-approach to the study of the primary sources at Le Saulchoir, Chenu quickly learned the historical skills that equipped him for his breakthrough study contextualizing Aquinas' theology in 'La théologie comme science au XIIIᵉ siècle' in 1927.[20] His object was to situate Aquinas in the theological ferment of his time and stress the revolutionary nature of his contribution, as a signal to theologians in the early twentieth century that they too should engage with contemporary philosophy and social issues. The radical intention at the origins of Chenu's work in the history of doctrine is most evident in a story told of his early days at Le Saulchoir. Congar recalled an encounter with Chenu, where they conspired to undertake the elimination of 'modern-scholasticism':

> One day, chatting at the entrance of the old Saulchoir, we found ourselves in profound accord—at once intellectual, vital and apostolic—on the idea of undertaking a 'liquidation of baroque theology'. This was a moment of intense and total spiritual union. We elaborated a plan and distributed the tasks among ourselves. I still have the dossier that was begun then. . . . It was not a question of producing something negative: the rejections were only the reverse of aspects that were more positive. . . . What would a little later be called 'ressourcement' was then at the heart of our efforts. [21]

While Congar claimed this was not 'revolutionary', he and Chenu were soon censured and Chenu was removed from his post as Regent of Studies at Le Saulchoir by Gillet, the Master General of the Dominicans, 'for recommending a return to the sources'. Congar later made a crucial distinction that this was not a 'mere detached, scholarly reconstruction nor a futile attempt at what [he] calls "repristination".'[22]

Before these events, in 'What is theology?' ('Position de la théologie', 1935), Chenu intensified his historical critique of 'modern scholasticism'.[23] He

---

[18] *Un théologien en liberté*, 48.

[19] Congar, 'The Brother I have Known', *The Thomist*, 49 (1985), 495–503 (495).

[20] Chenu, 'La théologie comme science au XIIIᵉ siècle: Genèse de la doctrine de Saint Thomas', *Archives d'histoire doctrinale et littéraire du moyen âge*, 2 (1927), 31–71. Later revised in an unpublished manuscript in 1943, then republished in an expanded version in 1957 as *La théologie comme science au XIIIᵉ siècle* (Paris: Librairie Philosophique J. Vrin, 1957).

[21] Congar, 'The Brother I have Known', 499. See further Gabriel Flynn's essay in this volume.

[22] Congar, *Vraie et fausse réforme dans l'église*, Unam Sanctam, 20 (Paris: Cerf, 1950), 337.

[23] Chenu, 'Position de la théologie', *RSPT*, 24 (1935), 258–67. ET 'What is Theology?', in *Faith and Theology*, trans. Denis Hickey (Dublin: Gill, 1968), 15–35.

insisted that Revelation and the Incarnation are manifested in the theological working of human reason, thereby situating theology within the historical framework given by these doctrines. He recalled the principle founded on Augustine by Thomas Aquinas, 'Cognita sunt in cognoscente secundum modum cognoscentis' (*ST* 2a2ae 1 ad 2): that the human means of inquiry is as constitutive of faith and theology as of other human knowledge.[24] The article also attacked the extreme rationalism of 'modern scholasticism' and the separation of faith and reason that this had engendered, advocating instead their coherence and critical correlation in theology: 'If a human truly could know God, he would know God humanly.'[25] For Chenu, human subjectivity was therefore integral to theology and faith because it is only through our humanity that we meet God.[26] Theology is constructed on *both* the revelatory 'given' and the philosophical 'construct'.[27] Chenu asserted that theology required the historical 'return to the primary experiences' to test the value of any deduced or abstracted propositions. Only a *ressourcement* of the experiential and historical sources of theology could overcome the stagnation produced by a concentration on the deduction of abstract formulations.[28] Positive and speculative theology could no longer be maintained separately.[29]

Here Chenu situated the construction of theology in terms of the historical consciousness of modernity. In order to explain how the 'construct' always remains secondary to Revelation, Chenu pointed to the role of historical development in theology, effectively serving to correct 'the ineffectiveness of speculation', concluding that Christian theology is ontologically historical. Historical method is apposite to a faith founded on Revelation in history, whereas philosophical methods were more appropriate to an order of essences and timeless laws. This represented a direct attack on the prevailing theological preoccupation with examining eternal causes. Chenu's understanding of historical development admitted the influence of Bergsonian and Hegelian evolutionary views of history, but he does not also adopt their determinism. To support his claim, Chenu introduced an analogy between the correlation of historical and theological method and the Incarnation of Christ, 'just as Christ assumed human nature'.[30] This recurrent 'theandric principle' he advanced as the continuation of Ireneaus' theology of the 'recapitulation in Christ'.[31] Enlisting first Aquinas and then Augustine as prototypes of historically grounded theology, Chenu concluded that the historical 'givens' of Revelation,

---

[24] Chenu, 'What is Theology?', 19; *La théologie comme science au XIIIe siècle*, 71, 70 n.1.
[25] 'What is Theology?', 19. Chenu repeats this aphorism in *Une école*, 137.
[26] 'What is Theology?', 22–5.
[27] 'What is Theology?', 16.
[28] 'What is Theology?', 23.
[29] Chenu, 'Préface', in C. Geffré, OP (ed.), *Un nouvel âge de la théologie* (Paris: Cerf, 1972), 9.
[30] 'What is Theology?', 27.   [31] *Un théologien en liberté*, 81.

which herald the economy of salvation, manifest also as components for the construction of theology.[32]

> But the theologian works on history. His 'givens' are neither the nature of things nor their eternal forms, but events according to a *plan* [*économie*] and events are always tied to time as limbs are connected to a body, independent of an order of essences. This is the *real* world not the abstraction of the philosopher.[33]

Chenu completed his map of the 'position' of theology by providing a demonstration of history as a locus for theological reflection. While registering the danger of reduction to either 'anthropocentrism' or 'theocentrism', Chenu refused the false dichotomy of humanism opposed to theology as too simplistic. In a sweep through the historical 'drama' of two renaissances, Chenu contrasted 'the thorough spiritual correlation' of Aquinas' response to the Aristotelian humanism of his time, with the degenerate 'scholasticism's' inability to correlate critically with subsequent revolutions in human thought. He regretted the absence of 'another Aquinas' in the subsequent history of doctrinal conflict and development and considered that Aquinas' 'theological humanism' succeeded in integrating faith and reason with that critical curiosity that marks true humanism.[34]

This article drew less attention from the Dominican authorities in Rome than *Le Saulchoir*, although its critique severed any further accommodation by Chenu to 'modern scholasticism'. Chenu's particular version of '*la nouvelle théologie*' marked a thorough reform of previous theological method. While de Lubac's *Catholicisme* and *Surnaturel* opened the central doctrines to the breadth of the patristic and other non-Thomist sources, Chenu's contribution reformed even this methodology, turning 'the return to the sources' from a positivist retrieval into a dynamic resourcing for constructing contemporary theology.

FINDING THE SOURCES: A SCHOOL OF THEOLOGY

In *Le Saulchoir*, Chenu's theological project expanded to a critique of the current Dominican theological curriculum. Chenu combatively outlined the programme he proposed for Le Saulchoir as necessarily grounded in critical doctrinal history, the study of other philosophers since Aquinas, and a priority on biblical exegesis. The manifesto's target was the prevailing manual-style theology of 'modern-scholasticism' as taught at the Angelicum. In contrast,

---

[32] 'What is Theology?', 28.
[33] 'What is Theology?' 27.
[34] 'What is Theology?', 34.

Chenu advocated an historical reading of Aquinas that related his works to his times, and which demanded of current theology a similar immersion in the pastoral and philosophical concerns of the '*present* reality'. He charged that:

> This beautiful intellectual style of Saint Thomas is not a pure form; it is born, it is real life, it attains its perfection in matter, and therefore in time, in kind, in a context, in a body. It is good Thomism that makes history of Thomist thought, seeing his soul united to his body.[35]

For Chenu the priority was on recognizing the temporality of theology, and its own integral mission—not of sacralizing history but of restoring the sense of the innovation of the gospel to our everyday understanding of faith. The starting point for Chenu is that history is *within* theology, not extrinsic to it, nor related to it merely as a 'new' methodology, nor some ideological or alien imposition. Theology is historically located because of Revelation; its task is to unfold the meaning of this Revelation for each new age, so, he asks, how can theology therefore be exempt from the historical approach to truth?[36] Chenu was concerned to awaken theology to its historical character, but he was equally determined not to subsume Revelation to history, nor history to theology. Commitment to the autonomy of secondary causes was integral to his reading of the move in twelfth- to thirteenth-century theologies from the earlier allegorical and typological interpretations of the world and nature to that of a more historical understanding.[37] While he would stipulate that history is not equivalent to Christian Revelation, he nevertheless insisted that 'sacred history' was not a super-addition to other history. The origins of Chenu's interest in the historical status of Christian theology and the use of an historical method to re-awaken this were the recently re-visited debates about the development of doctrine. Despite its limited initial influence, Newman's *Essay on the Development of Christian Doctrine* injected an historical and psychological perspective into the debate by recognizing the historical contingency of doctrine while avoiding falling into a doctrinal relativism or historicism.[38]

Consistent with the official theology's obsession with what Chenu called 'a rigid concept of the immutability of dogma' was its defensiveness against the sense of rapid political and social change affecting post-First World War Europe.

---

[35] *Une école*, 173.   [36] *Une école*, 134–5.

[37] Chenu developed this in 'Nature and Man: The Renaissance of the Twelfth Century', in his *Nature, Man, and Society in the Twelfth Century* (Toronto: University of Toronto Press, 1997), 1–48, originally published as 'Le Nature et l' homme. La Renaissance du XIIᵉ siècle', *La Théologie au Douzième Siècle* (Paris: Vrin, 1957), 19–51.

[38] John Henry Newman, *Essay on the Development of Christian Doctrine* (London: James Toovey, 1846), cited in *Une école*, 117, 140; also 'La raison psychologique du développement du dogme d'après Saint Thomas' (1924), in *La Parole de Dieu I: La Foi dans l'intelligence* (Paris: Cerf, 1964), 52–8 (57–8, n. 3).

That many of these other theologians were also committed to the reactionary political agenda of *Action française* and Mussolini's Fascism is significant.[39] The pervasive attitude in these circles was that of nostalgia for a lost past, focused on a reductionist reading of the 'order' of medieval Christendom, in the style of an ecclesial 'Pre-Raphaelite' nostalgia. Beyond the more politically committed reactionaries, there was a broader intellectual reaction to modernity and its totalitarianisms as represented by Nicholas Berdiaeff, who exercised extensive influence on French Catholic thought and its intellectuals. Berdiaeff viewed the collapse of European civilization in World War I and the Bolshevik revolution as a series of disasters resembling the 'collapse' of the Roman Empire and the subsequent barbarian invasions of civilization. He called for 'a new Middle Ages' which would restore a social order on top of the ruins of liberalism and against communism.[40] Chenu recognized that challenging the established theological methodology was the key to unlocking this alliance and its appropriation of the medieval era. His strategy in *Le Saulchoir* was to meet this 'negative conservatism stuck in routinely defending untenable positions' and 'a state of siege'[41] on its own terms, by recovering the not-so-tranquil reality of the 'Age of Faith'. As the scholastic period *par excellence* it presented an obvious Trojan horse for historical-critical investigation, under the guise of examining Thomist theology. This allowed Chenu to demonstrate how such idealistic appropriation of the past was inadequate in theological and historical terms.[42]

Chenu noted that the 'menace' to the church and theology posed by the critical epistemological turn of the late nineteenth century had parallels in 'many revivals, according to the cycles of culture, in Western Christianity', recognizable by the intensity of the 'defensive reactions' these also generated.[43] Chenu's use of 'the cycles of nature' here is not reference to a cyclical ahistoricity, but rather alludes to an historical passage of time, avoiding obvious historicist resonances. His true historical understanding is elaborated:

> The world of the historian unfolds in time; it is something successive, irreversible, according to the eras that are stages on the road to a destiny, in a series of discreet events, and not in an eternal return of generations and corruptions, as Aristotle said.[44]

---

[39] Joseph Komonchak, 'Theology and Culture at Mid-Century: The Example of Henri de Lubac', *TS*, 51 (1990), 579–602 (601–2); André Laudouze, OP, *Dominicains français et Action Français: 1899–1940. Maurras au Couvent* (Paris: Les Éditions Ouvrières, 1989), 217.

[40] Nicholas Berdiaeff, *Un nouveau Moyen Âge* (Paris: Plon, 1927), cited in Yvon Tranvouez, *Catholiques d'abord: Approches du mouvement catholique en France (XIXᵉ–XXᵉ siècle)* (Paris: Les Éditions Ouvrières, 1988), 115–16. Cf. also Étienne Borne's criticism of the delusion of slavishly copying the Middle Ages in 'Pour refaire une chrétienté', *VI*, 44 (1936), 353–6 (355), cited in Tranvouez, 124–5.

[41] *Une école*, 116, 122.   [42] *Une école*, 125.

[43] *Une école*, 117.   [44] 'What is Theology?', 27.

Although Chenu often referred to a recurring theme of different eras re-awakening (*réveil*) to the gospel, he portrayed these as 'ruptures' not the return of a cycle. Rather, he identified this as a '*conjoncture*', the *Annales* historical school's concept of the concurrence of different pressures for change, as different levels and sectors of a society become conscious and receptive to change. Although he was influenced early by the *Annales* method of historical research,[45] Chenu departed from its rejection of the 'event' in its search for the continuities that are hidden by classical historiography.[46] While using their detailed study of social records, Chenu also emphasized the importance of the 'event' that 'ruptures' with the presumed continuities in doctrinal history.[47] His focus on the 'event' is primarily theological: it reveals the historical currents and subtle changes that the ecclesial ideology of immutability had otherwise disguised.[48] Chenu wrote later that he was concerned with the authoritarian tendency in scholastic theology that 'detemporalized the Word of God into an abstract ideology manipulated by magisterial power'.[49] In a later work, *Aquinas and his Role in Theology*, Chenu recognized in acute periods of change a historical convergence that revealed the powerful 'rupture' of the gospel in human affairs: 'The return to the gospel brings about a break with debilitating institutional structures as well as with inappropriate personal behaviour.'[50]

Beside this historical sense is his eschatological understanding of the convergence between human aspirations for good and the gospel vision, which saw God's 'economy' already being realized in history and contemporary affairs. Because of the Incarnation, ordinary human affairs are not only a progressive unfolding of time, in the determinist sense of Hegel's teleological theory of history. Human history is not equivalent to Revelation but divine reality is manifested in material and human reality. Hence Christianity is less a timeless unchanging institution, fixed in the theocratic conventions of 'the Constantinian era', than the proclamation of a Revelation about God's dealings with humanity in history, and God's hopes for humanity now and into the future. In daily human affairs there emerges a new historical consciousness:

---

[45] Chenu, 'Post-scriptum', *Une école*, 176. Cf. Braudel's use of '*conjoncture*': 'a sense of connection between diverse but simultaneous phenomena' in Peter Burke, *The French Historical Revolution: the Annales School 1929–89* (Cambridge: Polity Press, 1990), 112.

[46] Chenu was one of the first subscribers to *Annales*; see Jean-Claude Schmitt, 'L'Œuvre médiéviste du Père Chenu', *RSPT*, 81 (1997), 395–406 (396).

[47] Chenu used the tax lists of the booksellers in Paris (1275? and 1303) and Bologna (1289) to determine the required texts at these universities and the courses and publications of the professors at that time: *Toward Understanding St Thomas*, 83, nn. 6–7.

[48] There is interesting resonance here with the disputed category of 'event' in the recent historiography of Vatican II. For a useful introduction to the salient issues, see Nicholas Lash, 'What Happened at Vatican II?' in his *Theology for Pilgrims* (London: Darton, Longman & Todd, 2008), 240–8; also Lash, 'In the Spirit of Vatican II', *Theology for Pilgrims*, 253–84.

[49] 'La théologie en procès', in *Savoir, faire, espérer: les limites de la raison* (Brussels: Facultés Universitaires St Louis, 1976), 691–6 (693).

[50] *Aquinas and His Role in Theology*, 9.

for Chenu, history itself was revelatory for theology.[51] He identified parallels between the watershed evangelical awakening of the twelfth century, the eighteenth-century Enlightenment, and breakthroughs in the history of Western thought in the late nineteenth and twentieth centuries. The parallel was not only in the dramatic turns these 'ruptures' marked, but in the challenges they made to the preaching of the gospel, and the subsequent reforms they demanded of the church. Principally these were shifts from a sacral world view to one which engaged the church to bridge the separation between the sacred and the secular. Chenu regarded such separation as dualism rendered illegitimate by the Incarnation.[52]

This *ressourcement* in *Le Saulchoir* established the historical condition of Christianity: that history is the place of revelation, creation is open to grace, and faith is the human experience of God's revealed presence participated in through the Incarnation. It is this combination of history and faith that Chenu describes as the basis of Christianity: the 'theandrism' of the Incarnation, in the human experience of faith, and in the life of the church.[53]

DRINKING FROM THE STREAM:
RETURN TO THE SOURCES

For Chenu, 'returning to the sources' was integral to his theology of history:

> The return to the sources is to history what the return to principles is to philosophy [*spéculation*]: the same spiritual power, the same rejuvenation, the same fertility; and the one vouches for the other.[54]

Yet this was not the historicist approach of the Modernist controversy. Chenu was emphatic from this early stage that the need to acknowledge its historical condition was crucial to the recovery of Thomist theology for the twentieth century from the rationalist modifications of the 'Baroque scholasticism': *'the status of the theological disciplines on which we live is that of the sixteenth–seventeenth centuries, not that of the medieval Summas'*.[55] Chenu therefore distinguished his analysis from that of the nineteenth- and twentieth-century commentators of this 'modern' Thomism:

---

[51] Chenu, 'The History of Salvation and the Historicity of Man in the Renewal of Theology', in L. K. Shook (ed.), *Renewal of Religious Thought*, 1 (New York: Herder and Herder, 1968), 153–66 (163–4).

[52] *Une école*, 116.

[53] Geffré, 'Le réalisme de l'Incarnation dans la théologie du Père M.-D. Chenu', *RSPT*, 69/3 (1985), 389–99 (390).

[54] *Une école*, 127.   [55] *Une école*, 129. (Chenu's emphasis.)

Revelation itself is endowed with human shades according to the times in
which it appeared. Saint Thomas would not be completely explained by
Saint Thomas himself, and his teaching, so high and so abstract itself is not
absolute, independent of the times during which it emerged and which have
sustained it.[56]

Chenu also distinguished this from a merely positivist archaeology:

> This was not then a simple curiosity, an archaeological quest, which might have
> been applied as well to other fields. The fruit of this conviction was that under-
> standing a text and a doctrine is inseparable from knowing the background in
> which it emerged because the insight that produced them is encountered in the
> context—literary, cultural, philosophical, theological, spiritual—in which they
> took shape.[57]

The crucial element of this recovery of Thomas in terms of his context was to
unshackle his theology from those over-analysed twentieth-century studies
that failed to acknowledge the distance between them and the thirteenth
century. It was necessary to acknowledge these differences in order to recognize, too, the very different problems facing theologians in the twentieth
century, instead of uncritically imposing the deracinated Thomism onto that
from which it was totally estranged.[58] There he challenged not only the prevailing teaching of Thomist theology but also the changelessness claimed by the
contemporary Catholic Church.

> [T]he paradoxical phenomenon that periodically arises in the Church and that is
> always disconcerting to the establishment, whether yesterday or today—the more
> that new ecclesial initiatives are spiritually and apostolically liberated, the more they
> become connected to the world, its economy, its culture, and its aspirations, touching
> not only the influential apparatus of the unversity, but other social forces as well.[59]

The significance of *Le Saulchoir* was in its comprehensive rejection of the
established Thomism. While he was building on the historical 'return to the
sources' that had distinguished Le Saulchoir, like the critical biblical studies of
the *École biblique*, Chenu's innovation challenged the nexus of the Dominican
theological identity based in Thomism and the Roman Catholic Church's
immutable identity partly preserved through this Thomism. To adjust
Thomas's teaching historically was therefore to critique the totalized structures
that had been built on this Thomism.

Although the short pamphlet, *Le Saulchoir*, was not widely distributed, it
drew immediate denunciation from the Dominican authorities in Rome for
promoting Modernism and overturning Thomism. Chenu was summoned
there by his superiors and forced to recant, then removed from the position of

---

[56] *Une école*, 125–6.   [57] *Une école*, 125.
[58] *Une école*, 170.   [59] *Aquinas and His Role in Theology*, 74.

Regent of Studies at Le Saulchoir and 'exiled' to Paris.[60] The curriculum at Le Saulchoir was gutted of any historical methodology by order of the disciplinary Visitor, Garrigou-Lagrange. While his reprimand was a Dominican affair, *Le Saulchoir* was later placed on the Index of Forbidden Books in 1942 without any prior warning. This was part of a wider condemnation of suspect theologians by Rome.[61] The scandal of this condemnation astounded Chenu's Jesuit contemporaries, who were not censured at this stage. Jean Daniélou wrote to Henri de Lubac: 'The affair of Chenu is odious, as if there is nothing more urgent to condemn.'[62]

IN CONCLUSION: 'RETURNING' OR 'SOURCING'?

Chenu did not limit his research to only going back to the 'sources', rather he understood *ressourcement* as starting at the source to follow the flow of theology into the present reality. His theological project involved 'engagement' with present reality on its terms, not those of the theology of previous centuries. Chenu himself regarded this distinction in *ressourcement*, between going backwards or forwards in the study and use of historical sources, as important to his own work. He observed that: 'We indulge in "restorations" rather than a "renovation"'.[63] In this sense he is like Matthew's scribe bringing together the old and the new.[64] In his own words:

> Let that spirit move, and it is a new world that is enthusiastically uncovered from under the old forms, with man in the midst of it all and revealed to himself for his own regeneration.[65]

---

[60] *Un théologien en liberté*, 120. The alarm raised by the pamphlet was amplified when the students at the Angelicum thunderously applauded a favourable seminar on its proposals. See Féret's letter to Chenu (22 March 1937), cited in Étienne Fouilloux, 'Autour d'une mise à l'Index', in Guy Bedouelle, OP (ed.), *Marie-Dominique Chenu: Moyen-Âge et Modernité* (Paris: Le Centre d'Études du Saulchoir, 1995), 25–56 (32–3, nn. 3, 1.)

[61] This included the dismissal of Dominicus De Petter, OP (1905–71) and condemnation of René Draguet, both of Leuven, and the condemnation of Louis Charlier, OP's book, *Essai sur le problème théologique*, Bibliothèque Orientations: Section scientifique, 1 (Thuillies: Ramgal, 1938); cf. R. Guelluy, 'Les antécedents de l'encyclique "Humani Generis" dans les sanctions romaines de 1942: Chenu, Charlier, Draguet', *Revue d'histoire ecclésiastique*, 81 (1986), 421–97; also Philip Kennedy, *Schillebeeckx* (London: Chapman, 1983), 44–5.

[62] 'Lettre 5 mars 1942', *Bulletin des amis du Cardinal Daniélou*, 2 (1976), 64, cited in E. Fouilloux, *La Collection 'Sources Chrétiennes': Éditer les pères de l'Église au XXᵉ siècle* (Paris: Cerf, 1995), 41, n. 2.

[63] Chenu, 'The History of Salvation', 155.

[64] I owe this observation to Gerald O'Collins, SJ, in a private conversation.

[65] Chenu, *Toward Understanding St Thomas*, 30.

It was this theological dimension to his historical studies that incurred some negative assessment by the French historian Jacques le Goff.[66] Chenu was also concerned with the unity and dynamic in the church's tradition that shows God is also revealed as much through contemporary reality: 'The mystery is in history. The Church is in the world.' [67]

The stream that Chenu navigated was a radical renewal of the theology and life of the Catholic Church of the early twentieth century. The 'return to the sources' involved renewal to an evangelical 'awakening', which he termed the 'freshness' of the gospel. Chenu's theology demanded contemporary recognition of the 'incarnational presence' of the gospel as real in the world: 'to be able to think out my faith within the urgency of human change, that is to create in my theological reflection a force of surprising renewal'.[68] Chenu anticipated the *ressourcement* movement's rejection of the narrower post-Tridentine tradition enshrined in 'modern-scholastic' theology. He wanted to reunite the modern and pre-modern; not to Christianize the Enlightenment project but to awaken the church and its theology to God's presence and activity in the contemporary world, instead of relegating anything of divine consequence to the past or an atemporal 'otherness'. He repeatedly exclaimed: 'God speaks today!'[69] Fergus Kerr and Giuseppe Alberigo welcomed as timely the republication of Chenu's *Le Saulchoir* in 1985 precisely because his theological method overcomes the recent recurrence of the opposition between *ressourcement* and reform.[70]

---

[66] 'Even where their analyses are as luminous, as penetrating as are those of Père Chenu or Père de Lubac, which have deepened historical understanding, they are dependent on a *parti pris* (in the best sense of the phrase).' Jacques Le Goff, *Medieval Civilisation* (Oxford: Blackwell, 1996), 344. He described Chenu's scholarship more favourably in 'Le Père Chenu et la société médiévale', *RSPT*, 81 (1997), 371–80.
[67] Chenu, 'The History of Salvation', 160.
[68] *Un théologien en liberté*, 70.
[69] Chenu, 'La Théologie en procès', 694.
[70] Kerr, 'Chenu's Little Book', *New Blackfriars* 66 (1985), 108–12 (112); also Alberigo, 'Christianisme en tant qu'histoire et "théologie confessante"', in *Une école*, 11–34 (12).

14

Ressourcement, Ecumenism, and Pneumatology: The Contribution of Yves Congar to *Nouvelle Théologie*[1]

Gabriel Flynn

INTRODUCTION

Yves Congar (1904–95) is among the most prominent of the renowned generation of *ressourcement* theologians, associated principally with the Jesuits of Lyon-Fourvière and the Dominicans of Le Saulchoir, Paris. An indefatigable 'résistant' to Nazi philosophy and ideology, a proud soldier of the French Republic, and a prisoner of war in the camps of Colditz and Lübeck from 1941–4, he was elevated to the College of Cardinals by Pope John Paul II on 26 November 1994 and buried with full military honours on 26 June 1995. His theological corpus has been lauded for its breadth, brilliance, and lucidity. His theology of ministry, theory of tradition, and mature ecumenism have, however, been criticized by commentators. Congar proposed a wide-ranging programme of reform that unintentionally set the Roman Catholic Church on its head and changed its relationship with the world forever. He viewed himself as a man of ideas,[2] but it is his idea of reform that dominates his entire *œuvre* and constitutes his most important and original contribution to theology.

The Second Vatican Council, called 'Congar's Council' by the American theologian Cardinal Avery Dulles, SJ (1918–2008), became the battleground for reform, one in which he achieved unparalleled success. As he writes: 'I was filled to overflowing. All the things to which I gave quite special

[1] I wish to thank Professors Henry Donneaud, OP, and Richard Lennan, for helpful comments on an earlier draft of this chapter.

[2] Yves Congar, 'Loving Openness Toward Every Truth: A Letter from Thomas Aquinas to Karl Rahner', *Philosophy and Theology*, 12 (2000), 213–19 (215). Unless otherwise stated, translations from the French are by the author.

attention issued in the Council: ecclesiology, ecumenism, reform of the Church, the lay state, mission, ministries, collegiality, return to sources and Tradition.'[3] By virtue of his achievement at that Council, and his extensive contribution to the advancement of the twin objectives of renewal in Christian theology and reform in the churches, he merits a pre-eminent place among the great Christian thinkers and religious leaders of the twentieth century.

In this essay, I assess Congar's contribution to *ressourcement* in the context of that movement's complex relationship with the *nouvelle théologie*. By reflecting on his ecumenism and pneumatology, I endeavour to show that his contribution in these fields, effectively spanning his entire career, would not have been possible without a return to the sources. It should be noted at the outset that Congar was not a speculative theologian. In 1985, he wrote: 'I am not a philosopher. I lack philosophical training and a philosophical spirit.'[4] Essentially, he was a careful researcher who took notes assiduously, all the while engaged in a vigorous search for truth. As he writes:

> When I was a young Dominican, I took over the motto of St Hilary which St Thomas Aquinas had first made his own (*Contra Gentes* 1, 2) and which was reproduced on his statue, in the house of studies at Le Saulchoir: 'Ego hoc vel praecipuum vitae meae officium debere me Deo conscius sum, ut eum omnis sermo meus et sensus loquatur' (*De Trin.* I, 37; PL 1, 48 C), 'For my own part, I know that the chief duty of my life is that all that I say and all that I feel speaks God.'[5]

THE EMERGENCE OF A GREAT THINKER

I begin by briefly considering the historical influences that shaped his thought. From the outset, Congar found himself at the centre of a stream of renewal that flowed from Le Saulchoir, the Faculties of Theology and Philosophy of the Dominican Province of France. That exacting 'school of theology',[6] in exile in Kain-la-Tombe near Tournai in Belgium during the period of his theological studies (1926–31) because of the anti-clerical legislation of the French Third Republic, but after 1937 located in Étiolles near Paris, provided him with an ideal of the religious and intellectual life. It was here that he came under the enduring influence of Marie-Dominique Chenu, OP (1895–1990). Congar's admiration was unbounded. In Chenu, his master and friend, he perceived a man of ideas and action, of history and theology, of truth and faith. He made

---

[3] Congar, 'Reflections on being a Theologian', trans. Marcus Lefébure, *New Blackfriars*, 62 (1981), 405–9 (405). See Congar, *Mon journal du Concile*, ii., ed. Éric Mahieu (Paris: Cerf, 2002), 511.

[4] Congar, 'Letter from Father Yves Congar, O.P.', trans. Ronald John Zawilla, *Theology Digest*, 32 (1985), 213–16 (215–6).

[5] Congar, 'Reflections on being a Theologian', 406.

[6] Marie-Dominique Chenu, *Une école*.

his own the words of Étienne Gilson, 'A Father Chenu—there is only one such every hundred years!'[7] Following Chenu, Congar pursued a strongly historical approach to theology, while also seeking to rediscover the ancient sources of the Tradition, thus placing him with those *nouveaux théologiens* who were deeply committed to *ressourcement*. An important element of the *nouvelle théologie* was the endeavour to place history within the theological endeavour. As Congar remarks: 'More and more I am combining theology with history.'[8]

Chenu awakened in him an awareness of the historical dimension of reality,[9] and, as Congar acknowledges, also provided the motivation for some of his most important theological endeavours: 'Father Chenu, an incomparable inspiration to a whole generation of young Dominicans, spoke to us on one occasion of the "Faith and Order" Movement during his course on the history of Christian doctrine, as he also spoke of the Lausanne Conference and of Möhler.'[10] In an interview given in 1975, Chenu states that he and Congar effected a rediscovery of Johann Adam Möhler (1796–1838), the German ecclesiastical historian and theologian of the church. Möhler, and the Roman Catholic School of Tübingen, had introduced a principle of renewal into nineteenth-century theology with a conception of faith which integrates its historical, psychological, and pastoral dimensions.[11] Chenu suggested Möhler as a possible model for a Roman Catholic contribution to ecumenism and, accordingly, Congar embarked on his study of church unity. Writing in 1970, he affirms the influence of Möhler: 'Möhler can even today be an animator (*éveilleur*). That is what he was for me for more than forty years.'[12] In the same brief article,[13] he notes how Möhler moves from a pneumatological approach to the church in *Die Einheit*,[14] to a profoundly Chalcedonian, Christological position in *Symbolik*.[15] An opposite development can be observed in Congar

---

[7] Congar, 'The Brother I have known', trans. Boniface Ramsey, *The Thomist*, 49 (1985), 495–503 (503); ET of 'Le frère que j'ai connu', in Claude Geffré *et al.* (eds.), *L'hommage différé au Père Chenu* (Paris: Cerf, 1990), 239–45 (244).

[8] Congar, *Dialogue between Christians: Catholic Contributions to Ecumenism*, trans. Philip Loretz (London: Geoffrey Chapman, 1966), 44; ET of *Chrétiens en dialogue: contributions catholiques à l'oecuménisme*, Unam Sanctam, 50 (Paris: Cerf, 1964), p. lvi.

[9] Jean-Pierre Jossua, *Le Père Congar: la théologie au service du peuple de Dieu*, Chrétiens De Tous Les Temps, 20 (Paris: Cerf, 1967), 19.

[10] Congar, *Dialogue between Christians*, 3; *Chrétiens en dialogue*, pp. xi–xii.

[11] Jacques Duquesne (ed.), *Jacques Duquesne interroge le Père Chenu: 'un théologien en liberté'*, Les Interviews (Paris: Centurion, 1975), 55. See further Michael J. Himes, *Ongoing Incarnation: Johann Adam Möhler and the Beginnings of Modern Ecclesiology* (New York: Crossroad, 1997).

[12] Congar, 'Johann Adam Möhler: 1796–1838', *Theologische Quartalschrift*, 150 (1970), 47–51 (50–1).

[13] Congar, 'Johann Adam Möhler 1796–1838', 50.

[14] Möhler, *Die Einheit in der Kirche oder das Prinzip des Katholizismus* (Mainz: Grünewald, 1925).

[15] Möhler, *Symbolik oder Darstellung der dogmatischen Gegensätze der Katholiken und Protestanten nach ihren öffentlichen Bekenntnisschriften*, i (Cologne: Hegner, 1960).

whose major study on the Holy Spirit, *Je crois en l'Esprit Saint*,[16] is the fruit of the latter part of his career. The contribution of Möhler and the Tübingen School helped to prepare for the ecclesiological renewal of the twentieth century. The most decisive element in that renewal, however, was a deepening in the interior life of the church, especially with reference to the person of Christ. In this regard, Congar lauds the Irish theologian Columba Marmion, OSB (1858–1923), Abbot of Maredsous, Belgium: 'Is it not remarkable that one of the most read works since the war, one of those which contributed most to foster the beginnings of this ecclesiological renewal, was the work of Dom Marmion, so fully Christological and liturgical?'[17]

Congar's life's work concerned the articulation of a complete theology, through the study of the totality of Catholic doctrine, for the benefit of the church and the advancement of its mission in the world. In a short essay written in 1937, Congar shows how the realization of his rich hopes for the church depends on a new engagement with the sources of Christianity: 'Everywhere we get a sense that it would be of great profit in our pastoral ministry and would allow Christianity to spread to a far greater extent throughout the world, if the concept of the church were to recover the broad, rich, vital meaning it once had, a meaning deriving wholly from the Bible and Tradition.'[18]

Congar was convinced that the image presented by the Catholic Church is crucial for the evangelization of the modern world and determines, to a large degree, the chances for the reunion of the Christian Churches.[19] In order to transcend the juridical idea of the Catholic Church, Congar, together with his colleagues Chenu and Henri-Marie Féret (1904–92), embarked on an enterprise to eliminate 'baroque theology',[20] a term that they coined to describe the theology of the Catholic Reformation.[21] The accomplishment of this goal was an important reason for the foundation of the Unam Sanctam collection, which was to become an ecclesiological and ecumenical library running to

---

[16] Congar, *I Believe in the Holy Spirit*, trans. David Smith, ii (New York/London: Seabury/Geoffrey Chapman, 1983), 19–20; ET of *Je crois en l'Esprit Saint*, new edn., ii (Paris: Cerf, 1995), 32–4.

[17] Congar, 'Autour du renouveau de l'ecclésiologie: la collection "Unam Sanctam"', *VI*, 51 (1939), 9–32 (11).

[18] Congar, 'Pour une théologie de l'Église', *VI*, 52 (1937), 97–9 (98).

[19] Congar, 'The Council in the Age of Dialogue', trans. Barry N. Rigney, *Cross Currents*, 12 (1962), 144–51 (146, 149–50); ET of 'Vœux pour le concile: enquête parmi les chrétiens', *Esprit*, 29 (1961), 691–700 (694, 697–9).

[20] See Jean Puyo, (ed.), *Jean Puyo interroge le Père Congar: 'une vie pour la vérité'*, Les Interviews (Paris: Centurion, 1975), 45–6.

[21] See Congar, *Martin Luther sa foi, sa réforme: études de théologie historique*, Cogitatio Fidei, 119 (Paris: Cerf, 1983), 79. See further, Martin F. Larrey, 'Towards a re-evaluation of the Counter-Reformation', *Communio*, 7 (1980), 209–24; John W. O'Malley, *Trent and All That: Renaming Catholicism in the Early Modern Era*, 2nd edn. (Cambridge MA: Harvard University Press, 2000), 119–43.

77 volumes. This series, dedicated to the restoration of the genuine value of ecclesiology by means of a return to the ancient sources of scripture and tradition, prepared the way for Vatican II.[22] Its aim was to present a multi-faceted study of the mystery of the church while, at Congar's insistence, 'always keeping in mind its organic unity'.[23] Congar was able, under the auspices of this new series, to harness the reforming energies of some of the most brilliant French and European theologians. The prospectus announcing the launch of Unam Sanctam in *La Vie intellectuelle* of November 1935 said that the idea for the collection was born of a double observation:

> On the one hand, in fact, when one reflects on the great Catholic problems of life and development, of modern unbelief or indifference, lastly of the reunion of separated Christians, one is led to think that an improvement of the present state of things, in so far as it depends on us, supposes that a notion of the Church that is broad, rich, living, full of biblical and traditional sap, penetrates Christianity: firstly the clergy, then the Christian elites, then the entire body. On the other hand, an incontestable renewal of the idea of the Church manifests itself on all sides.... *Unam Sanctam* aims to provide a better knowledge of the nature or, if you like, of the mystery of the Church.[24]

Congar's memoirs of the events of the 1930s, a tumultuous decade for Catholic intellectuals in France, reveal a profound unity in his three great projects: the renewal of ecclesiology (Unam Sanctam), the renewal of theo-logy (*ressourcement*), and the articulation of Catholic principles of ecume-nism, projects that brought him into direct conflict with high-ranking Vatican officials. At the same time in Germany, Karl Rahner (1904–84) was engaged in a similar battle against the defensive and narrow systems of neo-scholasticism which had stifled creativity in Catholic theology and effectively consigned it to the margins of contemporary society.

CONGAR AND *RESSOURCEMENT*

The return to the sources (*ressourcement*) was part of a dynamic and contro-versial movement for reform in French theology, dating from the early part of the twentieth century. It reached a dramatic high-point in the period during and following the Second World War.[25] In the 1940s and 1950s, the

---

[22] See Congar, 'Reflections on being a Theologian', 405.

[23] See Patrick Granfield, *Theologians at Work* (New York/London: Macmillan/Collier-Macmillan, 1967), 252.

[24] Congar, *Dialogue between Christians*, 24, n. 14; ET of *Chrétiens en dialogue*, p. xxxiv, n. 11.

[25] For a comprehensive treatment of the *ressourcement*, see Roger Aubert, *La Théologie Catholique au milieu du XXe siècle* (Tournai: Casterman, 1954).

ressourcement helped to liberate Protestants from tired liberalism or oppressive fundamentalism, while also freeing Catholics from neo-scholasticism.[26] Protestant neo-orthodox theologians, most notably Karl Barth (1886–1968), who called for a return to the Bible, also contributed to the Catholic *ressourcement*, by showing Catholics that it is possible to read the Bible in ways which are faithful both to the historic faith and to the methods of historical criticism.[27] The power of the movement for a return to the sources was, however, most evident on the Catholic side. Henri de Lubac (1896–1991) and Jean Daniélou (1905–74), the editors of *Sources chrétiennes*, were the leading practitioners of *ressourcement*, while Congar and Chenu represented a strongly historical approach to theology. Scholars are indebted to Congar and Daniélou, both of whom consider the same question of the present orientations in religious thought.[28]

Congar defines *ressourcement* as 'a new examination of the permanent sources of theology: the Bible, liturgy, the Fathers (Latins *and Greeks*)'.[29] The return to the sources was not just an archaic reproduction of the early church; rather, it concerned the understanding of the Fathers in their own context and the application of the pure and full vision of Christianity, expounded by them, to the church in the modern era. Congar considers the Fathers of the church as the normal spiritual *milieu* of the theologian:

> Unfortunately, the Fathers remain exterior to the thought of many modern theologians: they are invoked from the outside. . . . For Möhler, the knowledge of the Fathers is a means of being united with their spirit, and this communion itself is not properly speaking a *means*, because it is the communion with Christianity in its concrete, purest and fullest reality. Like the company of parents and brothers in the bosom of the family, the company of the Fathers is more than a means, it is a spiritual *milieu*, the *milieu* of the normal life of the theologian.[30]

The central issue, in Congar's view, concerns the construction of a complete theology capable of synthesizing the inspiration and research associated with *ressourcement* and combining it with a rediscovery of the decisive elements of the traditional treasure. These include the doctrine of the mystical Body, the theology of the Mass and of the liturgical mystery, eschatology, and *agapè*. The *ressourcement* embraces some of the liveliest aspects of the work of theology: faith, the Word, the church, and anthropology. A complete theology of this

---

[26] See George Lindbeck, 'Ecumenical Theology', in David F. Ford (ed.), *The Modern Theologians: An Introduction to Christian Theology in the Twentieth Century*, ii. (Oxford: Blackwell, 1995), 255–73 (258).
[27] Lindbeck, 'Ecumenical Theology', 258–9.
[28] Congar, 'Tendances actuelles de la pensée religieuse', *Cahiers du monde nouveau*, 4 (1948), 33–50; Jean Daniélou, 'Les orientations présentes de la pensée religieuse', *Études*, 249 (1946), 5–21.
[29] *La Foi et la Théologie*, Théologie dogmatique, 1 (Tournai: Desclée, 1962), 271.
[30] 'L'Esprit des Pères d'après Moehler', *Supplément à la 'Vie Spirituelle'*, 55 (1938), 1–25 (2).

nature, with its new techniques of research, exegesis, and criticism should 'be at the service of openness, of contact with the world *of Others*: missiology; ecumenism; pastoral [theology]'.[31] An important advantage of *ressourcement*, and one that is perhaps more relevant today than in Congar's time, is that it contributed to overcoming certain dissociations between theology and spirituality, research and pastoral work.[32]

Congar outlines his personal commitment to *ressourcement* in precise terms: 'In everything I have always been concerned to recover the sources, the roots. I am firmly convinced: a tree strikes deep roots and cannot rise to heaven except to the extent those roots hold firmly to the soil of the earth.'[33] Congar worked consistently for a reform of the church that would proceed by way of a return to the sources; this sort of reform is nothing other than a rediscovery of the deepest tradition.[34] In his view, however, *ressourcement* could only be accomplished by way of a *recentrement* (re-centring on Christ), thereby effecting 'a return to the essential, to Jesus Christ, especially in the central mystery of Easter'.[35] The combination of *ressourcement* and *recentrement* was important in his ecclesiology. It provided the insight that enabled him to deal with the important and difficult question of the relationship between the church and the world—a relationship that Congar defined in such a way as to avoid the dangerous error of either being subordinate to the other.

Congar borrowed the idea of a return to the sources from the poet and social critic Charles Péguy (1873–1914),[36] as well as from the liturgical changes inaugurated by Pope Pius X.[37] He was also influenced by Möhler, whom Congar praises for his efforts to live as perfectly as possible in communion with the spirit of the Fathers: 'But Möhler does not *use* the Fathers in order *to prove conclusions*; he seeks *to live* and, by communion with their spirit, to find as perfect as possible a communion with their thought and with their life.'[38] The path of church reform by way of a return to the biblical and patristic roots was pursued not only by Congar, but also by Daniélou, de Lubac, Joseph Ratzinger (1927–), and Rahner, to mention the most important theologians. The achievement of these scholars, seen by the Lutheran George Lindbeck as 'tradition-minded but not traditionalist renewers of theology',[39]

---

[31] Congar, *La Foi et la Théologie*, 272. See further, Marc Lienhard, *Identité confessionnelle et quête de l'unité: Catholiques et protestants face à l'exigence œcuménique* (Lyon: Éditions Olivétan, 2007).

[32] Congar, *La Foi et la Théologie*, 271–2.

[33] 'Letter from Father Yves Congar, O.P.', 215.

[34] *Vraie et fausse réforme dans l'Église*, Unam Sanctam, 20 (Paris: Cerf, 1950), 43.

[35] 'Il faut construire l'Église en nous', *Témoignage Chrétien* (7 July 1950), 1.

[36] Yves Congar, 'Le prophète Péguy', *Témoignage Chrétien* (26 August 1949), 1.

[37] Congar, 'Autour du renouveau de l'ecclésiologie', *VI*, 51 (1939), 11.

[38] Congar, 'L'Esprit des Pères d'après Moehler', 12.

[39] Lindbeck, 'Ecumenical Theology', 258.

was made possible by their deep knowledge of scripture and the Fathers and by their abiding respect for and appeal to traditions earlier than those of the Middle Ages and the Catholic Reformation.

The origins of the programme of reform and renewal that was at the heart of the *ressourcement* may be traced to certain elements in Roman Catholic Modernism.[40] An ambivalent term, 'Modernism' was first used by its Roman opponents to describe an extreme that should be avoided, a crisis, and ultimately a condemned position. It refers to a definite movement of thought within the Roman Catholic Church that began about 1900 and ended soon after its condemnation in 1907.[41] It would, of course, be misleading to refer to Modernism as a single coherent doctrine.[42] The most important factors in the rise of the Modernist movement in France were the introduction and use of the results and methods of biblical criticism, as well as new philosophical ferments.[43] Congar defines Modernism briefly as 'the introduction into the Church of historical critical methods, and their application to the religious sciences, with often insufficient philosophical foundations'.[44] He

[40] For a history of modernism, see J. Rivière, 'Modernisme', in A. Vacant, E. Mangenot, and É. Amann (eds.), *Dictionnaire de théologie catholique*, x. part ii, cols. 2009–47 (Paris: Letouzey and Ané, 1929); Pierre Colin, *L'audace et le soupçon: la crise du modernisme dans le catholicisme français, (1893–1914)* (Paris: Desclée de Brouwer, 1997); Étienne Fouilloux, *Une Église en quête de liberté: la pensée catholique française entre modernisme et Vatican II (1914–1962)*, 2nd edn. (Paris, Desclée de Brouwer, 2006); Darrell Jodock (ed.), *Catholicism Contending with Modernity: Roman Catholic Modernism and Anti-Modernism in Historical Context* (Cambridge: Cambridge University Press, 2000); Marvin Richard O'Connell, *Critics on Trial: An Introduction to the Catholic Modernist Crisis* (Washington DC: Catholic University of America Press, 1994); O'Malley, *What Happened at Vatican II* (Cambridge MA: The Belknap Press of Harvard University Press, 2008); David G. Schultenover, SJ (ed.), *The Reception of Pragmatism in France & the Rise of Roman Catholic Modernism: 1880–1914* (Washington DC: Catholic University of America Press, 2009); Schultenover, *A View from Rome: On the Eve of the Modernist Crisis* (The Bronx NY: Fordham University Press, 1993); Alec R. Vidler, *A Variety of Catholic Modernists* (Cambridge: Cambridge University Press, 1970); Gerard Loughlin, 'Catholic Modernism', in David Fergusson (ed.), *The Blackwell Companion to Nineteenth-Century Theology* (Oxford: Wiley-Blackwell, 2010), 486–508; Oliver P. Rafferty, SJ, (ed.), *George Tyrrell and Catholic Modernism* (Dublin: Four Courts Press, 2010); Claude Tresmontant, *La Crise moderniste* (Paris: Éditions du Seuil, 1979).

[41] See Gabriel Daly, OSA, *Transcendence and Immanence: A Study in Catholic Modernism and Integralism* (Oxford: Clarendon Press, 1980); Roger D. Haight, 'The Unfolding of Modernism in France: Blondel, Laberthonnière, Le Roy', *TS*, 35 (1974), 632–66 (633); Ernesto Buonaiuti, 'The Future of Catholicism', in Claud Nelson and Norman Pittenger (eds.), *Pilgrim of Rome: An Introduction to the Life and Work of Ernesto Buonaiuti*, 1st edn. (Welwyn, Herts: Nisbet, 1969), 102–4 (102); George Tyrrell, *Medievalism: A Reply to Cardinal Mercier* (Tunbridge Wells: Burns & Oates, 1994) 158; Jan Hulshof, 'The Modernist Crisis: Alfred Loisy and George Tyrrell', trans. Theo Westow, *Concilium*, 113 (1978), 28–39 (28–30).

[42] See Bernard M. G. Reardon (ed.), *Roman Catholic Modernism* (London: Black, 1970), 10.

[43] See Congar, *A History of Theology*, trans. and ed., Hunter Guthrie, SJ (New York: Doubleday, 1968), 190–1; ET of 'Théologie', in A. Vacant, E. Mangenot, and É. Amann (eds.), *Dictionnaire de théologie catholique*, xv. part i, cols. 341–502 (col. 440) (Paris: Letouzey and Ané, 1946). See further Congar, *La Foi et la Théologie*, 270.

[44] Puyo (ed.), *Jean Puyo interroge le Père Congar*, 38.

views the response of the Catholic Church to Modernism as shallow and 'purely negative'.[45]

Congar acknowledges that Modernism stimulated debate among Roman Catholic thinkers on the problems of revelation, the nature and method of theology, and the precise nature of tradition. He also refers to certain difficulties which he sees as a direct result of Modernism.[46] One of the factors that gave rise to the Modernist crisis was the lack of complete correspondence between the Catholic Church's doctrines and the historical and critical study of the documentation used as their basis. It was this factor, according to Congar, which led to an erroneous distinction, and indeed an opposition between dogma and history. Modernist thinkers claimed the right to treat the conclusions drawn from the historical study of the documentary sources of Christianity independent of the dogmatic statements of the magisterium. Congar, like the French philosopher Maurice Blondel (1861–1949), views the separation of dogma from history as unnecessary: 'To oppose the data of history and the statements of dogma was to make an unwarranted separation between the two elements of a single reality with an essentially religious nature. It amounted to judging this reality by inadequate criteria, without doing justice to its nature and its demands.'[47]

The manner in which distinctions were made by the Modernist theologians gave rise to other difficulties which Congar describes as follows: 'One of the misfortunes of the Modernists was that they did not know how to distinguish theology and dogma. Certainly at that time the distinction for all practical purposes was not as clear as it is today. This was one of the benefits of the Modernist crisis.'[48] Congar further elucidates this somewhat obscure but important point by arguing that the Modernists, in their legitimate efforts to avoid any confusion between the absolute of faith or Revelation and the theology of St Thomas, or the theology of the thirteenth century in general, wrongly separated revelation and dogma from all properly speculative content on which theology lives and without which it no longer exists as theology.[49]

Congar studied the Modernist thinkers as part of his preparations to teach an introductory course in theology at Le Saulchoir.[50] He was concerned that his generation should rescue for the church whatever was of value in

---

[45] Puyo (ed.), *Jean Puyo interroge le Père Congar*, 36.

[46] See Congar, *Tradition and Traditions: An historical and a theological essay*, trans. Michael Naseby and Thomas Rainborough (London: Burns & Oates, 1966), 216; ET of *La Tradition et les traditions: essai historique* (Paris: Fayard, 1960), 265–6. See also Congar, *La Tradition et les traditions: essai théologique* (Paris: Fayard, 1963).

[47] Congar, *Tradition and Traditions*, 216; ET of *La Tradition et les traditions: essai historique*, 265–6. See Maurice Blondel, 'Histoire et dogme', *La Quinzaine*, 56 (1904), 145–67, 349–73, 433–58.

[48] *A History of Theology*, 191; ET of 'Théologie', col. 440.

[49] *A History of Theology*, 191; ET of 'Théologie', col. 440.

[50] The substance of this course is to be found in his *La Foi et la Théologie*.

Modernism. He wanted Catholic theology, first, to benefit from the application of the historical critical method to Christian data and, second, to give greater attention to the concerns of the experiencing subject. Congar also recognized the aspiration in the Modernist movement that Catholic theology would remain closely connected to its sources:

> Modernism with considerable acuteness set before Catholic theology the twofold problem, first, of its homogeneity, when taken in its scientific and rational form, with Revelation, and second, of its relation to its positive sources, henceforth subject to historical and critical methods, viz., the Bible, ancient and progressively developing traditions and institutions.[51]

The condemnation of Modernism had an immediate effect. On 3 July 1907, the Holy Roman and Universal Inquisition issued the decree *Lamentabili Sane Exitu* which listed the errors that were believed to be threatening the church. On 8 September of the same year, Pope Pius X published the encyclical *Pascendi Dominici Gregis* which presented a systematic account of the new errors and the measures to be taken against those who held them. The repressive enforcement of *Pascendi* in seminaries and throughout the Catholic world, by means of the anti-Modernist oath, effectively brought the whole Modernist movement to a halt within a few years.[52] Legitimate dissatisfaction in the theological world did not disappear, however, simply because it could not be openly expressed.

Future generations of Catholic theologians would take up again the challenge of modernity, the question of the relationship of the Gospel to the world, and the task of reclaiming the sources of the Christian faith. One of the developments in French theology in the period following the condemnation of Modernism and before the publication of *Humani Generis* (1950) was the widespread portrayal of the church as a theandric union of all Catholics with Christ.[53] Although this new view of the church did not entail a denial of the juridical model, nevertheless, by the end of the 1930s, a new militancy emerged in favour of the spread of what has been described as 'vitalism'. This was due, in part, to the impact of factors that ranged from the description of the church as the Mystical Body in the 1920s and later to the influence of certain French theologians who became convinced, as a result of their contact

---

[51] *A History of Theology*, 192; ET of 'Théologie', col. 441.

[52] See Pius X, *Pascendi Dominici Gregis*. Encyclical Letter on the Doctrine of the Modernists (8 September 1907), *AAS* xl (1907), 593–650; *Lamentabili Sane Exitu*. Syllabus condemning the Errors of the Modernists (3 July 1907), *ASS* xl (1907), 470–8. ET *Encyclical Letter (Pascendi): on the Doctrines of the Modernists to which is added the decree (Lamentabili) of July 4, 1907, on Modernist Errors* (London: Catholic Truth Society, 1937); Owen Chadwick, *A History of the Popes 1830–1914* (Oxford: Clarendon Press, 1998), 346–59.

[53] Congar, *The Mystery of the Church: Studies by Yves Congar*, trans. A. V. Littledale, 2nd edn., rev. (London: Geoffrey Chapman, 1965), 27; ET of *Esquisses du mystère de l'Église*, new edn., Unam Sanctam, 8 (Paris: Cerf, 1953), 26.

with non-believers through the resistance movement, that the only way to attract non-Catholics into the Church was through its presentation in terms of the vital and the organic.[54]

CONGAR AND THE *NOUVELLE THÉOLOGIE*

The efforts of Congar, Chenu, de Lubac, and the other reforming theologians to form connections between the church and the world, to re-establish contact with the young generation, and to make the church more attractive to non-believers, gave rise to a theological movement that came to be known, in the first instance by its opponents within the Catholic Church, by the pejorative term *nouvelle théologie*.[55] Not surprisingly, given the prevailing atmosphere of fear and condemnation, Congar, like de Lubac, rejected the appellation *nouvelle théologie* as false.

The *nouvelle théologie* proposed a new examination of all historical theological resources, seeking in them resources for the renewal of theology. In distancing themselves from the term *nouvelle théologie*, as well as from the view that it constitutes a movement, proponents prudently sought to refute the assertion that it constituted a return to Modernism. Nonetheless, subjects that had already emerged in the Modernist debate constituted important aims of the *nouvelle théologie*, including the call for theological renewal; the need to move beyond scholasticism; the necessity of closer links with the contemporary world; a concern for a return to the Fathers of the church; and a clarification of the link between nature and grace. There were also political and psychological elements involved in the debate.[56] The epithet *nouvelle théologie* corresponds to a theology that is concerned to know the tradition, as opposed to a purely scholastic and repetitive theology. The conception of tradition proposed by the *nouvelle théologie*, far from being traditionalist, in the sense of a repetition of the recent past, is concerned rather with the unity of the ever living tradition. This is precisely Congar's position.[57]

[54] Congar, 'Letter from Father Yves Congar, O.P.', 214.

[55] Gustave Weigel, 'The Historical Background of the Encyclical *Humani Generis*', TS, 12 (1951), 208–30 (219–20). For Congar's response to Weigel's negative assessment of the '*nouvelle théologie*' see Congar, 'Bulletin de théologie dogmatique', *RSPT*, 35 (1951), 591–603 (596, n. 12).

[56] See Giacomo Martina, 'The Historical Context in Which the Idea of a New Ecumenical Council Was Born', in René Latourelle (ed.), *Vatican II: Assessment and Perspectives Twenty-Five Years After (1962–1987)*, i (New York: Paulist Press, 1988), 3–73 (31).

[57] See *Tradition and the Life of the Church*, trans. A. N. Woodrow, Faith and Fact Books, 3 (London: Burns & Oates, 1964), 144–55; ET of *La tradition et la vie de l'Église*, 2nd edn., Traditions chrétiennes, 18 (Paris: Cerf, 1984), 117–25.

Two groups of French theologians, one Jesuit and the other Dominican, became synonymous with the *nouvelle théologie*.[58] They were the Jesuit trio, Daniélou, de Lubac, and Henri Bouillard, and a corresponding Dominican trio, Chenu, Congar, and Féret. In the period 1945–50, a lively debate ensued between the Jesuit and Dominican proponents of the *nouvelle théologie* and leading Dominicans of the Toulouse province, notably, Marie-Michel Labourdette, the editor of *Revue thomiste*, as well as Réginald Garrigou-Lagrange of the Angelicum in Rome, whose polemical article on the doctrinal crisis had been declined by Labourdette on behalf of *Revue thomiste*.[59]

As early as 1946, Pope Pius XII had expressed his concerns regarding the *nouvelle théologie* to representatives of both the Dominicans and the Jesuits, warning against an attack on the fundamental tenets of Roman Catholic doctrine. In an atmosphere of suspicion and controversy, Pius XII rejected the *nouvelle théologie* in 1950 with the publication of *Humani Generis*. The encyclical warned that certain schools of thought had fallen into 'relativism' in doctrinal theology. The 'innovators' were accused of displaying 'contempt of scholastic theology' as well as false interpretation of scripture and some specific theological errors. In France, *Humani Generis* was seen as referring to certain currents of theological thought there and although no-one was named in the encyclical, some individuals, notably de Lubac and Congar, felt deeply wounded. Congar read the papal document very attentively, having been advised by Emmanuel Suárez, then Master of the Dominican Order (1946–54), that there were things in it which concerned himself. Congar denied, however, that either he or anyone in his ecumenical milieu ever practised a bad 'irenicism'.[60]

By the summer of 1953, the worker-priest movement (*prêtres-ouvriers*)[61] which Congar had supported, was also known to be in the balance. In February 1954, Congar was summoned to Paris and, together with his collegues Chenu, Féret, and Pierre Boisselot, the Director of Éditions du Cerf, was dismissed from his post at Le Saulchoir.[62] At his own suggestion, Congar went

---

[58] Weigel, 'The Historical Background of the Encyclical *Humani Generis*', 217; see further, Fouilloux, *La Collection 'Sources Chrétiennes': éditer les Pères de l'Église au XXᵉ siècle* (Paris: Cerf, 1995), 115–6.

[59] See Labourdette, 'La Théologie et ses sources', *RevTh*, 46 (1946), 353–71; Labourdette, 'La Théologie, intelligence de la foi', *RevTh*, 46 (1946), 5–44; Garrigou-Lagrange, 'La nouvelle théologie où va-t-elle', *Ang*, 23 (1946), 126–45. See, further, Fouilloux, *Une Église en quête de liberté*, 112–9.

[60] See Puyo (ed.), *Jean Puyo interroge le Père Congar*, 106–13.

[61] See Congar, 'Dominicains et prêtres ouvriers', *La Vie spirituelle*, 143 (1989), 817–20 (819). See further, Gregor Siefer, *The Church and Industrial Society: A survey of the Worker-Priest Movement and its implications for the Christian Mission*, trans. Isabel and Florence McHugh (London: Darton, Longman & Todd, 1964); François Leprieur, *Quand Rome condamne: Dominicains et prêtres-ouvriers* (Paris: Cerf, 1989).

[62] Thomas O'Meara, ' "Raid on the Dominicans": The Repression of 1954', *America*, 170 (1994), 1–8.

into exile in Jerusalem. Then, in November 1954, he was assigned to Black-friars, Cambridge. It was only through the kind offices of Bishop Jean Weber of Strasbourg that Congar was allowed to return to France in December 1956 to continue his work which he describes as 'that of an inner renewal, ecclesio-logical, anthropological and pastoral'.[63]

The clash between the defenders of traditionalism and the innovators continued to characterize theology during the preparations for Vatican II and extended, amidst divisive controversy, into the conciliar and post-conciliar periods. The unresolved tensions of the Council between the priesthood of the faithful and the ordained priesthood, the old and new liturgies, and the drama of religious liberty continue to reverberate today. What is required, is a 're-reception' of Vatican II, a claim already made by Congar elsewhere, and illustrated in *Mon journal du Concile*. Such a re-reception will be successful to the extent that it seeks to realize the original reform programme of the Council, with due regard for present difficulties, and a greater awareness of the sensi-bilities of those who view themselves as the successors of the old minority at the Council.

ECUMENISM AND PNEUMATOLOGY: FRUITS OF *RESSOURCEMENT*

Congar is perhaps best known for his contribution to ecumenism. The focus of Congar's ecumenical theology can be expressed in the following relevant points.[64] First, Congar views the Catholic principles of ecumenism in the context of the *ressourcement*. In 1959, in a text originally published in Ger-man, he proposed a wide-ranging programme of theological study, with the objective of deepening ecumenical dialogue:

A whole new chapter will have to be written on the fruit already gathered or made possible by the *Revertimini ad fontes!* advocated by Pius X. One can only hope for an intensification of work and ecumenical dialogue on all the following subjects, the crucial character of which the above exposé was designed to demonstrate: Christology (and also Mariology); redemption and creation, the will and the wisdom of God (analogy of faith and the analogy of being); the economy of salvation and communication or gift (*koinonia*). The kingship of Christ; the

---

[63] *Dialogue between Christians*, 44; ET of *Chrétiens en dialogue*, p. lvi.

[64] See Flynn, *Yves Congar's Vision of the Church in a World of Unbelief* (Aldershot/Burlington VT: Ashgate, 2004); Flynn, 'Cardinal Congar's Ecumenism: An "Ecumenical Ethics" for Recon-ciliation?', *LS*, 28 (2003), 311–25; Jossua, 'L'œuvre œcuménique du Père Congar', *Études*, 357 (1982), 543–55; Joseph Famerée, ' "Chrétiens désunis" du P. Congar 50 ans après', *NRT*, 110 (1988), 666–86; Joseph Famerée and Gilles Routhier, *Yves Congar* (Paris: Cerf, 2008).

relation of his kingship to the world and to the Church; people of God and Body of Christ. What the authority is which Christ wields in his Church, in the midst of the world. The theology of: formal visibility of the Church, apostolicity, era of the Church, tradition, baptism, eucharist and Church. The Church as an institution and God's 'actualism' (institution and event).[65]

Second, ecumenism is an ethical imperative for Christians. The acceptance of an anti-ecumenical or a pre-ecumenical state by any Christian denomination is tantamount to a rejection of Christ's call to unity. And since disunity is a grave obstacle to belief in God, it would be both contradictory and disingenuous for Christians to remain immured to the Gospel vision of unity and the concomitant moral obligation to engage in dialogue. Congar, in fact, identifies a decisive link between unbelief, as a consequence of the division of Christendom, and the significance of ecumenism for the future of the Catholic Church in a hostile world.

> Historically, the divisions among Christians, the fiercely cruel wars carried out in the name of dogmatic differences, are largely responsible for the genesis of modern unbelief (Herbert of Cherbury, Spinoza, the *Philosophes* of the eighteenth century). Concretely, the division among Christians is a scandal for the world. The world is exonerated, to a degree, from the duty to believe.[66]

Third, as noted by Congar's *confrère* Jean-Pierre Jossua, OP, ecumenism is ever a matter of 'following the little star of hope!'[67] Congar had regular meetings during the inter-war period with professors of the Institut Saint-Serge, the Orthodox Faculty of Theology in Paris, including Georges Florovsky, Sergei Bulgakov, and Leo Zander.[68] Boris Bobrinskoy, Dean of the Institut Saint-Serge, in his address on the occasion of the launch of *Mon journal du Concile* in Paris on 27 September 2002, paid tribute to Congar in the name of the Orthodox Church. His remarks are germane since they attribute to Congar a seminal role in the genesis of the *ressourcement*:

> Father Congar has permanently marked this century and has inspired a theological and spiritual fermentation around the mystery of the one Church and of the division of Christians. I can say that the Orthodox theological renewal owes much to him and likewise the liturgical renewal at Solesmes or Maria-Laach, or the patristic renewal at 'Sources chrétiennes'.[69]

---

[65] *Dialogue between Christians*, 356–7; ET of *Chrétiens en dialogue*, 434–5.
[66] Congar, 'The Council in the Age of Dialogue', 148; ET of 'Vœux pour le concile: enquête parmi les chrétiens', 696.
[67] Jossua, 'In Hope of Unity', trans. Barbara Estelle Beaumont, OP, in Flynn (ed.), *Yves Congar: Theologian of the Church* (Louvain/Grand Rapids MI: Peeters/Eerdmans, 2005), 167–81 (181).
[68] See Boris Bobrinskoy, 'Le P. Yves Congar et l'orthodoxie', *Istina*, 48 (2003), 20–3.
[69] Bobrinskoy, 'Le P. Yves Congar et l'orthodoxie', 20.

Turning briefly to pneumatology,[70] it is noteworthy that Congar situates the Fathers in the service of the Holy Spirit: 'It is the Spirit of the Lord who has filled their word and has revealed himself, in them, a spirit of wisdom and understanding.'[71] The success of the *ressourcement* depended in large measure on the development of a pneumatological ecclesiology, an important achievement of Vatican II. As Congar comments: 'A new theology, or rather a new programme of "ministries", giving the Church a new face that is quite different from the one that the earlier pyramidal and clerical ecclesiology presented, has developed since the Second Vatican Council.'[72] The publication of his acclaimed work *Je crois en l'Esprit Saint* may then be viewed as Congar's final contribution to *ressourcement*. But it would be a mistake to conclude that he came late to the Holy Spirit. When Congar began work on his *magnum opus* in pneumatology, he had already written eighteen or nineteen articles on the Spirit. I wish to discuss three elements of what he calls a 'total pneumatology'[73] that are pertinent to the present discussion.

First, in Congar, the unity of Christology and pneumatology is a prerequisite for the development of a healthy pneumatology.

> There is no separation of the activity of the Spirit from the work of Christ in a full pneumatology. . . . A pneumatology of this kind, however, goes beyond simply making present the structures set up by Christ; it is the actuality of what the glorified Lord and his Spirit do in the life of the Church.[74]

The clear benefits of a Christological pneumatology are to be found in the liturgical life of the church and in the celebration of the sacraments. It is hardly surprising, therefore, that Congar sees 'the introduction of epicleses into the new Eucharistic prayers' as '[t]he most important achievement of the Council in this sphere'.[75]

Second, Congar's pneumatology requires what he refers to as a 'pneumatological anthropology' and a 'pneumatological ecclesiology'. The integration of these two elements helped to redress a lacuna in the Catholic theology of the

---

[70] See Marc Fierens, 'L'Esprit Saint et la Liturgie dans la pneumatologie de Congar', *Questions Liturgiques*, 66 (1985), 221–7; Isaac Kizhakkeparampil, *The Invocation of the Holy Spirit as Constitutive of the Sacraments according to Cardinal Yves Congar* (Rome: Gregorian University Press, 1995); Elizabeth Teresa Groppe, *Yves Congar's Theology of the Holy Spirit* (Oxford: Oxford University Press, 2004); Patrick Mullins, 'The Spirit Speaks to the Churches: Continuity and Development in Congar's Pneumatology', *LS*, 29 (2004), 288–319; James Hanvey, 'In the Presence of Love: The Pneumatological Realization of the Economy: Yves Congar's *Le Mystère du Temple*', *IJST*, 7 (2005), 383–98.

[71] Congar, 'L'Esprit des Pères d'après Moehler', 25.

[72] *I Believe in the Holy Spirit*, trans. David Smith, i (New York/London: Seabury/Geoffrey Chapman, 1983), 170; *Je crois en l'Esprit Saint*, new edn., i.232.

[73] Congar, 'Pneumatology Today', *The American Ecclesiastical Review*, 167 (1973), 435–49 (449).

[74] *I Believe in the Holy Spirit*, i.157; ET of *Je crois en l'Esprit Saint*, new edn., i.217.

[75] *I Believe in the Holy Spirit*, i.170; ET of *Je crois en l'Esprit Saint*, new edn., i.231.

Holy Spirit and provided the basis for a renewed ecclesiology.[76] In his 'pneumatological ecclesiology', Congar moves from a view of the Spirit as an animator of church structures to seeing the Spirit as co-institutor of the church. As he comments: '[I]t is most important that the action of the Spirit should be recognized and a trinitarian design be given to ecclesiology. . . . To accept a trinitarian model for the Church means to accept and justify its nature as a community of persons.'[77] For Congar, therefore, '[t]he Church receives the fullness of the Spirit only in the totality of the gifts made by all Her members'.[78] In 1967, he expressed his agreement with the anthropological approach of Rahner and Schillebeeckx, who attempt to study God in light of modern anthropology. 'The most important work today is to show the unity between theology and anthropology.'[79] Although Congar did not construct an anthropology similar to his ecclesiology, his awareness of the importance of the unity between the human and the divine, the church and the world, conditioned his theological outlook.

Third, Congar's 'pneumatological ecclesiology' is viewed by some scholars as providing a point of departure for dialogue between Christianity and other religions.[80] The development of such a dialogue based on Congar's contribution is, however, deeply challenging given his defence of the Catholic Church's universal mediatory role in salvation.[81]

Nonetheless, his pneumatology, garnered from the *ressourcement* and dependent on it, is a respectful response to the Orthodox claim of 'Christomonism' in the Catholic Church.

CONCLUSION

Congar recounts with profound irony the words of Martin-Stanislas Gillet, sometime Master of the Dominican Order: 'You are being reproached for

---

[76] See Groppe, *Yves Congar's Theology of the Holy Spirit*, 85–137.

[77] 'Pneumatology Today', 446.

[78] 'Pneumatology Today', 443.

[79] See Granfield, *Theologians at Work*, 249.

[80] See Dermot A. Lane, 'Pneumatology in the Service of Ecumenism and Inter-religious Dialogue: A Case of Neglect?', *LS*, 33 (2008), 136–58 (142–58).

[81] See Congar, *This Church That I Love*, trans. Lucien Delafuente (Denville, NJ: Dimension Books, 1969), 59; Congar, *Cette Église que j'aime*, Foi Vivante, 70 (Paris: Cerf, 1968), 61; also Congar, 'Non-Christian Religions and Christianity', in Mariasusai Dhavamony (ed.), *Evangelisation, Dialogue and Development: Selected Papers of the International Theological Conference, Nagpur (India) 1971*, Documenta Missionalia, 5 (Rome: Gregorian University Press, 1972), 133–45 (134). See further Flynn, *Yves Congar's Vision of the Church in a World of Unbelief* (Aldershot/Burlington VT: Ashgate, 2004), 37–47; also Terrence Merrigan, 'The Appeal to Yves Congar in Recent Catholic Theology of Religions: The Case of Jacques Dupuis', in Flynn (ed.), *Yves Congar: Theologian of the Church*, 427–57.

recommending a return to the sources.'[82] The fundamental concerns of *nouvelle théologie*, exemplified in Congar's contribution to the return to the sources, include the essential unity of theology, necessary recourse to history, and the application of ancient sources to contemporary problems. There is no doubt, and the point has been made by others, that the *ressourcement* continues to command attention and respect in academic theology and, perhaps more fundamentally, remains relevant to the pastoral life of the churches today. Congar, in fact, places the *ressourcement* at the centre of the apostolic, pastoral life of the church, a point he illustrates as follows:

> I conclude that the theological treatise on the church is today the real centre of intellectual effort, at once apostolic and theological. [...] The present ferment in religious thought is characterized by a renewal in the sources, by a return to the sources. This return to the sources is more living than dialectical, immersed in pastoral and apostolic problems, centred on the human situation and the problem of the church.[83]

---

[82] 'The Brother I have known', 500; 'Le frère que j'ai connu', 242.
[83] 'Tendances actuelles de la pensée religieuse', 41–2.

15

Henri de Lubac: Looking for Books to Read the World

David Grumett

As a child, Henri de Lubac was a voracious reader. He tackled Dostoevsky aged ten, soon followed by Claudel and Péguy, and was continually searching for new books to devour.[1] In September 1929, however, on assuming his appointment as Professor of Fundamental Theology in the Catholic Theological Faculty of Lyon, he quickly found that resources were limited. In his memoirs, he recalls:

> In the loft where I was lodged, which was lit by a little skylight, I had not a single book. The Fourvière library was scarcely accessible: it had no room at that time where one could work, and none of the books could be checked out; the library of the Catholic Faculties was miserable: two dusty rooms in an old, shaky main building with a little bit of everything. Fortunately I discovered a treasure in the attic of Saint Joseph's day school, in the beautiful, old-fashioned quarters located over the chapel: a library, particularly of literature, which had long been neglected but which contained several tiers of theology well furnished with old books.[2]

As this excerpt intimates, de Lubac did not restrict his reading to theology. Nourished on works of literature and philosophy, as well as both classic and modern theologians, his *œuvre* was founded on several disciplinary engagements. A key inspiration was Maurice Blondel's philosophy of action.[3] This was in turn informed partly by readings of Aquinas and Augustine on such topics as the synthesizing role of the will in the act of faith, and the relation of faith to scientific understanding, as Michael A. Conway has shown.[4]

---

[1] Georges Chantraine, *Henri de Lubac*, i. *De la naissance à la démobilisation (1896–1919)* (Paris: Cerf, 2007), pp. iv, 170–1.

[2] Henri de Lubac, *At the Service of the Church: Henri de Lubac Reflects on the Circumstances that Occasioned his Writings*, trans. Anne Englund Nash (San Francisco: Ignatius, 1993), 16.

[3] Antonio Russo, *Henri de Lubac: teologia e dogma nella storia. L'influsso di Blondel* (Rome: Studium, 1990).

[4] Michael A. Conway, 'From Neo-Thomism to St. Thomas: Maurice Blondel's Early Encounter with Scholastic Thought', *EphThl.*, 83 (2007), 1–22; also Conway, 'A Thomistic Turn?

Nevertheless, Blondel's enterprise was primarily philosophical, employing only to a limited degree what would become classic *ressourcement* methodology: returning to the great sources of Christian tradition—scripture, patristics, and the liturgy—and applying the Christian vision there presented to the modern era. Given the subject of this collection, it is on these topics that this chapter will focus.

RE-SOURCING THOMISM

In 1879, Pope Leo XIII promulgated the encyclical *Aeterni Patris*, in which he exhorted Catholic theologians to reform their teaching and apologetics in accordance with the philosophy of St Thomas Aquinas. One of Leo's reasons for commending Aquinas' philosophy was that, in his view, it synthesized all preceding Christian thought. More than any other theologian, Aquinas had performed the task of 'diligently collecting, and sifting, and storing up, as it were, in one place, for the use and convenience of posterity the rich and fertile harvests of Christian learning scattered abroad in the voluminous works of the holy Fathers'.[5]

De Lubac wished to challenge this intellectual historiography by reading and studying patristic writers anew. De Lubac states of Aquinas and the Thomism to which his work gave birth: 'I do not regard the "common Doctor" as an "exclusive Doctor" who dispenses us from the task of familiarizing ourselves with the others; and I deem it regrettable that a certain partiality, inspired by a misguided strictness and artificial controversies, should sometimes have obscured the sense of profound unity which exists among the great masters.'[6]

The collection of patristic texts assembled by de Lubac in his projects is frequently vast and sometimes diffuse. He wished, of course, to depart from the excessively systematizing presentations characteristic of the Thomism of Cajetan and Suárez, of which he had endured three years at the Maison Saint-Louis, the Jesuit philosophate in St Helier on Jersey.[7] If present-day readers find some of his writings inchoate, they should at least recognize this to be

Maurice Blondel's Reading of St Thomas', *EphThL*, 84 (2008), 87–122; Maurice Blondel, 'The Latent Sources in St. Augustine's Thought', in M. C. D'Arcy, SJ (ed.), *A Monument to St. Augustine* (London: Sheed & Ward, 1930), 317–53.

[5] Leo XIII, *Aeterni Patris*. Encyclical Letter on the Restoration of Christian Philosophy (4 August 1879), *Acta Leonis XIII* i. (1881) 255–84, § 8; 14. ET in *The Papal Encyclicals*, ed. Claudia Carlen, 5 vols. (Pierian MI: Ann Arbor, 1990), ii.17–27.

[6] De Lubac, *The Discovery of God*, trans. Alexander Dru with Marc Sebanc and Cassian Fulsom (Edinburgh: T&T Clark, 1996), 209.

[7] Chantraine, *Henri de Lubac*, ii. *Les années de formation (1919–29)* (Paris: Cerf, 2009), 119–217.

an intentional departure from procrustean alternatives. More positively, de Lubac's method of reading sources can, at its best, be termed 'historical theology'—that is, an approach to theological reasoning which traces the development of theological concepts and shifts in their meaning in order to engage them critically and creatively.[8] The French present historic tense naturally invests theological history with a sense of peculiar immediacy and relevance which, as will be seen, he feels keenly.

Historical theology was de Lubac's response to the attempt to impose a single normative pattern on Catholic theology based on the new philosophical interpretation of Thomism. His assessment of the work of Renaissance philosopher Pico della Mirandola could fairly be applied to his own: 'A stand for intellectual pluralism against the narrowness of the school. One there senses irritation at totalizing pretensions, so strong among certain contemporary Thomists that their system has become rigid and unfaithful to the spirit of its origins.'[9] De Lubac wished, in contrast with this univocal approach to the writing of theological history, to recover and engage the full breadth of patristic tradition. This was a valuable exercise both intrinsically, and because it facilitated deeper and more accurate understanding of the Thomist synthesis.

Hence for de Lubac, the first significance of neo-Thomism lay primarily in its implications for historical method. Nevertheless, before following de Lubac back to the sources, we should note his treatment of certain key themes in Aquinas' theology in *The Mystery of the Supernatural*. This is his most explicit accessible attempt to set Aquinas against the Thomist tradition which claimed him as its own. In this work, de Lubac examines the concepts of nature and natural desire, endorsing Aquinas' attempt to defend the possibility of the beatific vision in the face of the sceptical Aristotelian philosophy of his age. Contesting the separation of grace and nature, he argues that grace perfects and contains the order of nature and that God is the author of natures.[10] According to this vision, all natural and rational processes are subjected to divine grace, and nature is endowed with a desire for God intrinsic to its very being, not a desire that is arbitrary, fleeting, or superadded.[11] By elucidating these theological motifs from Aquinas, de Lubac thus unsettles neo-Thomist philosophical orthodoxy.

These are obviously Augustinian themes. Indeed, in de Lubac's work Augustine functions partly as a foil, enabling him to pose questions that might seem too contentious for the theological politics of his day, were they directed

---

[8] A. N. Williams, 'The Future of the Past: The Contemporary Significance of the *Nouvelle Théologie*', *IJST*, 7 (2005), 347–61 (353–4).

[9] *Pic de la Mirandole: études et discussions* (Paris: Aubier-Montaigne, 1974), 285.

[10] *The Mystery of the Supernatural*, trans. Rosemary Sheed (New York: Crossroad, 1998), 21, 26.

[11] *Mystery*, 58, 229.

explicitly against neo-Thomism. By re-encountering a pre-Thomist Augustine, de Lubac was thus enabled to pursue issues in the Thomist tradition, such as the grace–nature relation. As Gemma Simmonds has already shown in this collection, however, engagement with Augustine was inseparable from another afterlife of theological interpretation.

In *Augustinianism and Modern Theology*, which closely follows the first part of his earlier seminal work *Surnaturel* (as yet untranslated into English), de Lubac attacks extrinsicist understandings of grace based on readings of Augustine. Michael Baius held that grace was purely a remedy for sin, with grace becoming effective in Adam only after the Fall.[12] This anthropology might appear affirmative of the intrinsic goodness and autonomy of human nature. Nevertheless, by denying that the human soul included within itself any spiritual quality before the Fall, Baius suggested that the soul is in essence a merely psychic entity.[13] This entailed that the purpose of the postlapsarian action of grace on the soul was to strengthen the soul for ends that were purely natural. Thereby was established, de Lubac argues, an excessively juridical conception of God's relation with his creatures, with specific natural ends granted or denied as rewards for particular good or bad acts.[14] Grace thus became omnipresent but only in a strictly limited sense, its power fundamentally attenuated by translation into purely natural effects. These positions were developed to their logical conclusion by Cornelius Jansenius, who saw divine grace reigning over the ruins of a nature formerly master of itself, controlling the human will as if it were a tool.[15] He believed that only a small number of people were elected to be saved, and that these were arbitrarily chosen.

One important practical engagement with Augustinianism occurs in the realm of church–state relations. These were pertinent issues in inter-war Europe, with the 1929 Lateran Treaty finally clarifying the relation of the papacy to the state of Italy, which had been proclaimed in 1870, and the earlier 1924 encyclical *Maximam Gravissimamque* going some way to acknowledging the secularizing reforms of the French Third Republic. The ferocious anti-secularism of the First Vatican Council was in many respects a mirror-image of the 1848 secularist revolutions that had engulfed various European states. The interpretive tradition of 'political Augustinianism' stemming from *The City of God* XIV.28 had posited church and state as two entirely separate entities defined respectively by the love of God and self-love. This provided the basis for the separation of church from state and the supposed supremacy of the heavenly city (the church), defined as purely sacred, over the earthly city

---

[12] De Lubac, *Augustinianism and Modern Theology*, trans. Lancelot Sheppard (New York: Crossroad, 2000), 2–3, 13.
[13] *Augustinianism*, 22.
[14] *Augustinianism*, 32.
[15] *Augustinianism*, 68, 72.

(the state), defined as purely secular. Giles of Rome, a key proponent of this hierarchy, had employed it to justify the necessary direct authority of the papacy over all other states and rulers.

The first problem with political Augustinianism, de Lubac argues, is that Augustine did not actually support the doctrine. In fact, he usually drew a radical distinction between the concept of the church and that of the City of God. His two cities cannot, therefore, be identified with church and state respectively, but are 'mystical societies, as secretly intermixed in history as they are adverse in principle'.[16] Political Augustinianism presents, moreover, a simplistic identification of the church as sacred and the state as secular, the shortcomings of which are increasingly apparent. Modern political society has become adult, de Lubac reminds his readers, and neither seeks nor requires theological justification of its legitimacy.[17]

In the church, part of the path to adulthood involves re-engaging received interpretations of particular figures. One striking example of this is de Lubac's attempt to rehabilitate Origen, who was widely read and interpreted by Jesuit *confrères*.[18] Yet de Lubac's own treatment of him is particularly important for *ressourcement*, being focused on scriptural exegesis. Origen has frequently been marginalized in theological history, portrayed as a heretic wishing to smuggle alien pagan ideas into Christian discourse, especially by dissolving the literal truth of Christian history into allegory, so rehabilitation attempts were potentially risky. But historic heresy and blasphemy charges against Origen have rested, de Lubac argues, on misreadings and deliberate distortions. Origen's critics often focus, de Lubac points out, on his discussions of the opening chapters of Genesis, the theological meanings of which are lost if they are read purely literally.[19] By means of allegory, de Lubac contends, Origen in fact interiorizes history and elucidates its spiritual meaning, but in no way destroys that history. Indeed, his spiritualizing of history was intended to salvage the Old Testament from Christian readers who, under Marcionite influence, would reject it altogether.[20]

De Lubac is at pains to point out that Origen, far from being a contemplative disengaged from the real world, was fully a man of the church, as catechist, preacher, and defender of Christian faith. His spiritualizing exegesis

[16] De Lubac, '"Political Augustinianism?"', in *Theological Fragments*, trans. Rebecca Howell Balinski (San Francisco: Ignatius, 1989), 235–86 (251–2).
[17] De Lubac, 'The Authority of the Church in Temporal Matters', in *Theological Fragments*, 199–233 (219).
[18] Michel Fédou, 'Karl Rahner et Hans Urs von Balthasar: lecteurs et interprètes des Pères', in Henri-Jérôme Gagey and Vincent Holzer (eds.), *Balthasar, Rahner: deux pensées en contraste* (Paris: Bayard, 2005), 141–59.
[19] *History and Spirit: The Understanding of Scripture According to Origen*, trans. Anne Englund Nash with Juvenal Merriell (San Francisco: Ignatius, 2007), 19–22.
[20] *History and Spirit*, 57–8.

is rightly seen, de Lubac argues, as a missionary endeavour intended to articulate and spread Christian faith and doctrine in the face of both Judaizing and pagan pressures by appropriating their narratives and interpretive methods. In a mission context in which Old Testament texts and exegetical methods are as omnipresent as the towns and other physical landmarks around which they are constructed, it would seem difficult to identify any other starting point for the discourse of conversion.

De Lubac discusses how, for Origen, Christ sublimates and unifies the senses of scripture by making them converge on himself. The different scriptural senses all point to Christ, and the spiritual sense is ultimately the Spirit of Christ himself.[21] The inspiration of scripture brings believers to a Christ who is rooted in history by allegory, which is therefore the dogmatic sense *par excellence*. But for Origen the spiritual sense also points to a particular relation with the Holy Spirit, the Spirit of Truth who is the Spirit of Christ, which for the reader of scripture is a lived relation.[22] The spiritual sense of scripture is thus, by extension, a lived sense. Spiritual understanding always envelops and overflows what it has grasped, as well as being enveloped and overflowed by what it has not yet grasped.

De Lubac does not approach Origen uncritically, identifying a lack of curiosity about the circumstances surrounding the historical events he narrates that the modern reader might find odd. This belies, de Lubac suggests, a lack of historical imagination which prevented him from bringing the events he described alive in their concrete reality.[23] In reading Origen, de Lubac is therefore drawn back into history itself, to plumb anew its depths as the writing of Christ in the world.

READING THE WORLD THAT IS WRITTEN BY CHRIST

In several places in his *œuvre*, de Lubac quotes the following couplet: 'The letter teaches what took place, the allegory what to believe, the moral what to do, the anagogy what goal to strive for.'[24] This has led many readers to assume that he believes that the number of scriptural senses is limited to four: the literal, allegorical, tropological, and anagogical. In fact, as a result of several

---

[21] *History and Spirit*, 308.
[22] *History and Spirit*, 444–5.
[23] *History and Spirit*, 320.
[24] De Lubac, 'On an Old Distich: the Doctrine of the "Fourfold Sense" in Scripture', in *Theological Fragments*, 109–27.

distinctions and additional terms, he distinguishes in his detailed analyses at least seven different senses of scripture.[25]

The first sense is the literal: events presented as historical facts, such as the infant Christ's flight into Egypt with his parents to escape the rage of Herod. But de Lubac sees the literal sense as rather less important than have a long line of source critics and demythologizers. Scripture's foundations rest, he believes, not on its literal sense but on its historical sense, which is present throughout the scriptural text in forms like parables and proverbs as well as more straightforwardly descriptive narrative. The whole of scripture is, he argues, historical in the sense that it all contains meaningful symbols and concepts.[26] This choice of terminology might confuse some English readers, but consider that in French 'une histoire' means a story. Moreover, the term is derived from *ysteron*, i.e., to see or to gesture, suggesting that history possesses both subjective and objective connotations.[27] There is no objective standpoint from which to adjudge historical validity, because all history contains within itself an element of histrionics. Rather, the validity of historical narrative is rooted in its depth, power, and coherence, and its capacity to bring people to faith in Christ.

The historical sense of scripture roots the others and is refracted in the others. De Lubac groups all these under another two finely differentiated headings. The spiritual sense draws out the significance of the literal, such as in the previous example, in which the flight of the holy family into Egypt can be seen as prefigured by that of Israel out of Egypt. The mystical sense, in contrast, 'contains the plenitude of doctrine', and is entirely concrete and objective.[28] It is also sacramental, and de Lubac presents it using a eucharistic analogy: Christ is revealed in the breaking of bread, as in the fragmentation of his scriptural Word into its different senses in human intellect.[29]

The first of these spiritual and mystical senses is allegory. De Lubac insists that, far from being a classical distortion of true scriptural reading, allegory is authorized by both history and scripture itself.[30] Allegorical method originates, he argues, shortly before the birth of Christ (such as in the work of Philo) and has the warrant of Paul in his interpretation of Hagar and Sarah.[31] Allegory universalizes and intensifies historical facts, completing the truths of the Hebrew Bible, not superseding them—a point de Lubac reiterates in a wartime pamphlet

---

[25] For a fuller summary, see David Grumett, *De Lubac: A Guide for the Perplexed*, with foreword by Avery Cardinal Dulles, SJ (London: T&T Clark, 2007), 75–94.

[26] De Lubac, *Medieval Exegesis*, trans. Mark Sebanc (i), Edward M. Macierowski (ii, iii), 4 vols. (Grand Rapids MI: Eerdmans, 1998–), ii.41–2.

[27] *Medieval Exegesis*, ii.43–4.

[28] *Medieval Exegesis*, ii.93–4.

[29] *Medieval Exegesis*, ii.26.

[30] De Lubac, 'Hellenistic Allegory and Christian Allegory', in *Theological Fragments*, 165–96.

[31] *Medieval Exegesis*, ii.5; De Lubac, *History and Spirit*, 77–86; see Gal. 4.24–6.

challenging theological accommodations to Nazi ideology.[32] Allegory takes a range of forms including anthropomorphisms, prophecies, precepts, and the exterior dramatization of spiritual fact.[33] Crucially, it resists closure and thereby the temptation of Mary Magdalene, which was not her desire and longing for the Word but her wish to touch and possess him. De Lubac's promotion of allegory to combat demonic Nazi mythology illustrates just how deeply he believed that the imaginative, inspirational movement which spiritual scriptural interpretation requires manifests the work of the Spirit of Christ in the world and impels readers to follow his call.

Next comes the tropological sense. De Lubac defines a trope as an expression turned around to designate some object other than the one immediately intended.[34] Moral tropology is employed frequently in Christian moral discourse, but more important is mystical tropology, in which scripture becomes a mirror in which the soul's wider search for God is reflected.[35] This encompasses ethical formation and transformation in the broadest sense. Moreover, the ordering of tropology *after* allegory enables ethical reasoning to be rooted in doctrine rather than proof texts.

De Lubac is usually deeply appreciative of patristic tradition, but here sees himself as breaking with it. Moral virtue does not provide the means to faith, he suggests, but faith the possibility of a virtuous life.[36] The respective ordering of allegory and tropology is to some extent unimportant: medieval interpretation frequently passed in practice through one sense to another in no uniform order, and the senses are in any case not systematically demarcated.[37] Nevertheless, the issue of whether moral interpretation emerges directly from a historical reading of scripture or is mediated by an allegorical reading is decisive in shaping responses to questions affecting church order and life, and the church's relation to wider society. In particular, approaches which admit allegory a role in shaping interpretation are usually more sensitive to human experience and inculturation, both in ecclesiological questions and moral issues, than approaches which seek to pass immediately from a historical and literal reading of scripture to principles of applied morality.

Finally there come two anagogical, or eschatological, senses. The first of these teaches the objective doctrine of eschatology as revealed in the life of Christ, while the second draws the person of faith into contemplation. The anagogical perspective is one of the interim, neither objective nor subjective but an eternal reality presented to humankind that intimates and anticipates

---

[32] De Lubac, 'Christian Explanation of Our Times', in *Theology in History*, trans. Anne Englund Nash (San Francisco: Ignatius, 1996), 440–56 (446–7).
[33] De Lubac, *Medieval Exegesis*, ii.13–14.
[34] *Medieval Exegesis*, ii.129.
[35] *Medieval Exegesis*, ii.142.
[36] *Medieval Exegesis*, i.114–15; ii.31, 134.
[37] *Medieval Exegesis*, i.131, 121.

its final end in Christ.[38] Anagogy is the last of the senses of scripture because it shows to humans their ultimate finality, being dependent on the senses preceding it and necessarily concluding their succession. It nevertheless suffers from an 'incurable' and 'fatal' incompleteness that needs to be 'considered above all in its positive and dynamic aspect', sustained by the action of the Spirit which 'communicates to it a virtuality without limits'.[39] This transcendent dimension of eschatology expands both the world and the understanding of the God who writes that world.

In his study of Origen, de Lubac argues that proper evaluation of scripture's anagogical dimension is vital in order to prevent spiritual interpretation becoming excessively focused on private inner contemplation.[40] The corollary of this inward turn would be an 'obscuring of the social and eschatological perspective' which loses sight of the social and political eschatology delineated so strikingly in John's Revelation. Lewis Ayres has rightly pointed out that, for de Lubac, the ultimate purpose of scriptural reading is the soul's ongoing formation and transformation.[41] These need to be seen, however, in the wider social and universal context into which the Word is also incorporated. It is vital that the reading of scripture remain both within the world and for the world.

It remains unclear why de Lubac chose to subtitle his tetralogy *Les Quatre sens de l'écriture* when it presents a more complex picture, including within its pages many theologians who recognized fewer senses than four. Indeed, the enumeration has left some interpreters with the impression that de Lubac proposes an arbitrary hermeneutic.[42] Certainly, in the period 1959–64 when his study was published, the sophisticated nature of patristic exegesis was far less widely known than now. From this perspective, the 'four senses' idea marked a significant development in understanding, without the need for further complication. But the more fundamental justification of the lack of clarity is that any number of senses is ultimately unified in Christ, being distilled and enumerated merely for the contingent purposes of human understanding. For de Lubac, scriptural reading leads thus into Christology. Moreover, the New Testament is in reality not a collection of texts but the fact of Christ himself, of whom the written texts are instruments.[43] In de Lubac's understanding of the development of interpretive tradition, propositional content is secondary to the revelation of God in Christ.[44] In Christ, God

---

[38] De Lubac, *Medieval Exegesis*, ii.183, 186.

[39] *Medieval Exegesis*, ii.204–5.

[40] *History and Spirit*, 477–9.

[41] Lewis Ayres, 'The Soul and the Reading of Scripture: A Note on Henri de Lubac', *Scottish Journal of Theology*, 61 (2008), 173–90.

[42] E.g., Hans Boersma, *Nouvelle Théologie and Sacramental Ontology: A Return to Mystery* (Oxford: Oxford University Press, 2009), 164–8.

[43] De Lubac, *L'Exégèse médiévale: les quatre sens de l'écriture*, iv. (Paris: Aubier-Montaigne, 1964), 106–23; trans. in de Lubac, *Scripture in the Tradition* (New York: Crossroad, 2000), 194–217.

[44] Lewis Ayres, *Nicaea and its Legacy: An Approach to Fourth-Century Trinitarian Theology* (New York: Oxford University Press, 2006), 426–7.

reveals himself in a form that is perfectly congruent with human understanding. Furthermore, Christ is the New Testament of God to humankind, who himself teaches successive generations of Christians how scripture should be read. Several examples of Christ exercising this didactic role are to be found in Luke's Gospel, such as on the Emmaus road. Yet the literally crucial key unlocking the truth of scripture is Christ's death and resurrection. Christ is thereby the abridged or abbreviated Word, who inspires the efforts of Christians to condense and unify scripture and comprehend its meaning.[45]

Fundamentally, scripture is therefore not writing about history but a reading of the history written by God and wrought by Christ through the Holy Spirit in the world. Christian history, which for de Lubac is coeval with the entire history of the world, and the human history which forms part of this, are recorded in scripture, but are in essence real, concrete, lived history. He states: 'If salvation is social in its essence it follows that history is the necessary interpreter between God and humankind.'[46] This process of the historical interpretation of God's revelation in Christ to humankind continues through the whole of scripture:

> The reality which is typified in the Old—and even the New—Testament is not merely spiritual, it is incarnate; it is not merely spiritual but historical as well. For the Word was made flesh and set up his tabernacle among us. The spiritual meaning, then, is to be found on all sides, not only or more especially in a book but first and foremost *in reality itself*: 'We therefore need to consider the reality and not only the words; we must seek the mystery concealed here. . . .'[47] Indeed, what we call nowadays the Old and New Testaments is not primarily a book. It is a twofold event, a twofold 'covenant', a twofold dispensation which unfolds its development through the ages, and which is fixed, one might suppose, by no written account. When the Fathers said that God was its author—the one and only author of the Old and New Testaments—they did not liken him merely, nor indeed primarily, to a writer, but saw in him the founder, the lawgiver, the institutor of these two 'instruments' of salvation, these two economies, two dispensations.[48]

God is the inspirer of scripture, but more importantly the inspirer and literal author of the history which scripture recounts. Scripture is not therefore writing about history, because the writing is the history itself, but the *reading* of history. It is in the history really written in the world by God that the exegetical challenges posed by scripture will be focused, in order that scripture may give an account of that world.

---

[45] *Medieval Exegesis*, iii.136–46.
[46] De Lubac, *Catholicism: Christ and the Common Destiny of Man* (San Francisco: Ignatius, 1988), 166.
[47] Augustine, *On the Psalms* 68.2.6, in *Complete Works*, Part III, xvii.389.
[48] *Catholicism*, 169.

LITURGY

In *Corpus Mysticum*, de Lubac argues that, anciently, the sacramental body of Christ was identified primarily with the church. A gradual shift subsequently took place, he suggests, in which the sacramental body came to be identified with the historical body of Christ as transubstantiated in the Eucharist.[49] Thus over time, corporate church life tended to be displaced by the exaltation of a reified eucharistic substance. De Lubac protests: 'Eucharistic theology became more and more a form of apologetic and organized itself increasingly round a defence of the "real presence".'[50]

De Lubac recognized in various places the value of classic liturgical practices for representing the continuity of ecclesial identity across time and space. These included the *sancta*, in which a portion of bread consecrated at the previous Mass was brought to the altar and placed in the chalice, and a piece of consecrated bread from that celebration reserved in order to be returned to the altar during the following one. In another practice, the presiding bishop would despatch consecrated bread, known as the *fermentum*, from his own Mass to the titular churches of the city.[51] Moreover, de Lubac insisted in *Corpus Mysticum* that eucharistic realism guaranteed ecclesial realism. Yet despite these occasional references, he evinces no sustained interest in concrete ritual practices, even though these are inseparable from the fields of liturgy and ecclesiology he traverses.

De Lubac later recognized that he had failed to defend with sufficient vigour the objective ritual context of liturgy and ecclesiology. Were he able to complete his work again, he reflected, he would place greater emphasis on the importance of preserving Christian heritage and interior spiritual devotion.[52] Moreover, his tremendous respect for the theology of Pierre Teilhard de Chardin, who promoted a highly materialistic and mystical eucharistic vision, suggests that he might have been sympathetic to such views himself, and that expressed more systematically, these might have resolved aporia in his liturgical thought.[53] As Laurence Hemming has perceptively identified, considerable ambivalence in fact remains in de Lubac's liturgical thought.[54] It would be mistaken to see him as an uncritical ally of the liturgical reform

---

[49] De Lubac, *Corpus Mysticum*, trans. Gemma Simmonds with Richard Price and Christopher Stephens (eds.) Laurence Paul Hemming and Susan Frank Parsons (London: SCM, 2006), 256.

[50] *Corpus Mysticum*, 220.

[51] *Catholicism*, 103–4; de Lubac, *The Motherhood of the Church: Particular Churches in the Universal Church*, trans. Sergia Englund (San Francisco: Ignatius, 1982), 206.

[52] *More Paradoxes*, trans. Anne Englund Nash (San Francisco: Ignatius, 2002), 97–8.

[53] Grumett, 'Eucharist, Matter and the Supernatural: Why de Lubac needs Teilhard', *IJST*, 10 (2008), 165–78.

[54] Laurence Hemming, 'Henri de Lubac: On Reading *Corpus Mysticum*', *New Blackfriars*, 90 (2009), 519–34.

movement, but equally erroneous to claim him as a complete conservative. Like many of his *confrères*, de Lubac seemed uninterested and at times discomfited by the sacramental ontology expressed through the categories and rituals of classic Catholic liturgy. The difficulty he experienced with this whole topic is illustrated by the fact that he never felt able to complete his projected study of mysticism.[55]

IMPACT AND AGENDA

Two immediate consequences of de Lubac's research may be noted, before wider appraisal of its legacy. First is his influence over key doctoral students. Hans Urs von Balthasar records the decisive impact of their meeting in Lyon during the autumn of 1933 on the direction of his studies towards Gregory of Nyssa, Maximus the Confessor, and Origen.[56] Jean Daniélou was another, slightly later protégé, commencing studies also on Gregory with de Lubac three years later.[57]

The second immediate result is de Lubac's outstanding practical contribution to *ressourcement*: his foundation in 1940 with Daniélou of the *Sources chrétiennes* series. Early volumes were all drawn from the Greek tradition, representing either Christian humanism or a Christ-centred mysticism—a point that did not go unnoticed by contemporary critics of this Jesuit project.[58] De Lubac believed profoundly in the power of the church Fathers to inspire engaged and rigorous theology, stating: 'Every time, in the West, that Christian renewal has flourished, in the order of thought as in that of life . . . it has flourished under the sign of the Fathers.'[59] The twentieth-century patristic renewal to a very large extent made possible, he argues, the *aggiornamento*, or deep renewal of faith, manifested in the official proceedings of the Second Vatican Council.[60] This was in sharp contrast to the more radical and critical spirit pervading the church around this time, he contended, which misrepresented its achievements and tradition while itself being overcome by morbid negativism and a continual restless search for novelty.[61]

---

[55] De Lubac, *At the Service of the Church*, 112–13.

[56] Hans Urs von Balthasar, *My Work in Retrospect*, trans. Brian McNeil (San Francisco: Ignatius, 1993), 11, 89; *At the Service of the Church*, 47.

[57] Jean Daniélou, *Et qui est mon prochain?, Mémoires* (Paris: Stock, 1974), 92.

[58] Brian Daley, 'La *nouvelle théologie* and the Patristic Revival: Sources, Symbols and the Science of Theology', *IJST*, 7 (2005), 362–82 (365–9).

[59] *At the Service of the Church*, 317–18.

[60] *At the Service of the Church*, 319.

[61] De Lubac, 'The Church in Crisis', *Theology Digest*, 17 (1969), 312–25.

What have been the wider specific impacts of de Lubac's labours, especially in recent years? His engagements with Thomism and Augustinianism have helped propel theologians in the Radical Orthodoxy movement to their own rethinking of the relations between grace and nature, and the sacred and secular. Their conclusions have been more daring than de Lubac's own, but sometimes less thoroughly grounded in textual reading.[62] In contrast, his liturgical historiography, although widely influential in the liturgical modernization movement that followed the Second Vatican Council and groundbreaking for its time, now seems a little dated. Important ecclesiological lessons have been learnt from it, but he provides little discussion of the kinds of concrete liturgical, ritual, and contemplative practices with which there is currently much engagement. Yet this new awareness of the tremendous potential for both liturgy and ritual to shape church communities and aid mission, and current resurgence of interest in classical spiritual writers, testifies to the enduring impact and development of his principles.

De Lubac's extensive study of the scriptural senses remains, in contrast, largely unexplored. This is surprising, given the considerable current interest in biblical exegesis, doctrine, and their interaction. Too often, the theological exegesis of scripture becomes an enterprise in constructing hermeneutical rules and analysis. Fatally, biblical hermeneutics, even if dignified as a 'special hermeneutics', becomes a subcategory of a general hermeneutics that could be applied to any text. For Friedrich Schleiermacher, the founding father of this procedure, even New Testament hermeneutics is 'special' only in the sense that it grapples with an exceptional mixture of languages.[63] This subordination of biblical testimony to literary theory has serious consequences for his understanding of the person of Christ: Schleiermacher concludes his study of the Christian faith by suggesting that Sabellianism and even Unitarianism might be valid doctrinal positions, being more naturally posited by religious consciousness than the Athanasian 'hypothesis'.[64] Paul Ricoeur attempts to set hermeneutics on a more profitable course using narrative theory and exploring the poetic dimension of biblical texts. Nonetheless, the narrative of Christ's life, death, and resurrection then too easily becomes an existential allegory, with the import of contingent, historical events undermined by an increasing reliance on literary notions like fiction, invention, and possibility.[65] Yet as one influential interpreter of Ricoeur has critically noted, it is not the biblical text

---

[62] See Bryan Hollon, *Everything is Sacred: Spiritual Exegesis in the Political Theology of Henri de Lubac* (Eugene OR: Cascade, 2009) for excellent constructive critique.

[63] Friedrich Schleiermacher, *Hermeneutics and Criticism and other Writings*, trans. and ed. Andrew Bowie (Cambridge: Cambridge University Press, 1998), 19–20.

[64] Schleiermacher, *The Christian Faith*, trans. H. R. Mackintosh and J. S. Stewart (Edinburgh: T&T Clark, 1928), 750–1.

[65] Kevin J. Vanhoozer, *Biblical Narrative in the Philosophy of Paul Ricoeur: A Study in Hermeneutics and Theology* (Cambridge: Cambridge University Press, 1990), 275–88.

itself which names God, but the lives of those who confess the God named, whose belief is made possible by the real embodiment of Christ in the world.[66]

De Lubac leads his readers out of this reductionist captivity by resituating narrative, allegory, and imagination in the person of Christ. De Lubac shows how Christian Trinitarian orthodoxy is founded on the literal witness of Christ in the world as revealed in scripture, which describes who Christ is and has been found to be by successive generations of readers of his work in the world. Christ incorporates into himself the human soul as well as scripture, the church, and the universe itself, forging a unity of complementary relationships.

[66] James Fodor, *Christian Hermeneutics: Paul Ricoeur and the Refiguring of Theology* (New York: Oxford University Press, 1995).

16

Daniélou and the Twentieth-Century Patristic Renewal

Bernard Pottier, SJ[1]

BIOGRAPHICAL SKETCH[2]

Born in 1905, Jean Daniélou passed his *agrégation* in grammar in 1927, by which time some of his work had already proved that he was fluent in Greek. He entered the Society of Jesus in 1929, studied philosophy in Jersey, taught for two years in a college, before going to Lyon for his theological studies, where he came into contact with de Lubac, studying alongside Balthasar, with whom he discovered Gregory of Nyssa. Ordained a priest in 1938, he became chaplain to the Sorbonne and the École Normale Supérieure at Sèvres in 1941. From that moment on an intense and enthusiastic apostolate among students began for him. This passion never left him and his manner of speech would always be more adapted to student circles than to ecclesiastical ones, whose members he occasionally shocked.[3]

In 1942, he published his translation of Gregory of Nyssa's *Life of Moses* as the first volume of the *Sources chrétiennes* collection.[4] In 1943 he defended a thesis on Gregory of Nyssa,[5] was appointed editor of *Études*, and succeeded Father Jules Lebreton to the Chair of History of Christian Origins at the

---

[1] Translated from the French by Gemma Simmonds, CJ.

[2] Here I am reliant on M. Sales, SJ, F. Jacquin, and M.-J. Rondeau (eds.), 'Les étapes d'une vie et d'une œuvre', in J. Fontaine (ed.), *Actualité de Jean Daniélou* (Paris: Cerf, 2006), 219–27. See too *Jean Daniélou (1905–1974)* (Paris: Axes-Éd. du Cerf, 1975); and the annual issues of *Bulletin des amis du cardinal Daniélou*, which have appeared regularly since 1975.

[3] 'He who was so adept at "playing the game" with young people, university students and others, never knew how to play it with the clergy', Marie-Josèphe Rondeau, 'Jean Daniélou théologien', in J. Fontaine (ed.), *Actualité*, 127–54 (134).

[4] Gregory of Nyssa, *Vie de Moïse, Sources chrétiennes*, 1 (Paris: Cerf, 1944, repr. 1955, 1968, 1987).

[5] Later published in Daniélou, *Platonisme et théologie mystique: Essai sur la doctrine spirituelle de saint Grégoire de Nysse*, Théologie, 2 (Paris: Aubier, 1944, 1954).

Institut Catholique de Paris. In 1945 he wrote in the first issue of the journal *Dieu vivant*. In 1946 he published the first of his important 'Bulletins de littérature patristique et d'histoire des origines chrétiennes' in *Recherches de Science Religieuse*. That same year, he published an article in *Études* entitled 'Les orientations présentes de la pensée religieuse' which would cause quite a stir.[6] From then on his career as a teacher, researcher, and apostle was launched.

In 1961 Daniélou was elected Dean of the Theology Faculty at the Institut Catholique de Paris, where he remained until 1969. In 1962 he was appointed *peritus* at the Second Vatican Council. On 19 April 1969 he was appointed bishop and on 28 April 1969 he was created a cardinal by Pope Paul VI. He was elected to the Académie française on 7 November 1972 to replace Cardinal Tisserant, and died on 20 May 1974.

A FAMOUS TEMPERAMENT

In a private letter in 1969, he confessed:

> I am not a good enough philosopher and don't have sufficient powers of synthesis to enable me to undertake a great theological work. I am recognizing my own limits here. Historical research is much more to my taste, and I continue to do it. It is in fact what I like best, and I almost feel guilty for doing so [. . .] I feel that I ought to do something else, but I haven't the gift for it.[7]

Rondeau comments, 'Daniélou was very clear-minded about himself. But this humble admission should not be interpreted negatively. Those who have a gift for synthesis are not the only ones to deserve the name of theologian. Daniélou was a true theologian in his own way.'[8]

Daniélou was certainly a scholar, a spiritual man, and an apostle. His extremely lively intelligence and curiosity, extraordinary memory, and astonishing appetite for work allowed him to build up a body of work which not only inspired admiration but which has had an enormous influence on intellectual life to this day. But his work as a researcher and even as a teacher was not the whole of his life. On the contrary, he valued his apostolic vocation highly, and unhesitatingly honoured the words with which St Ignatius summed up the Jesuit vocation: 'the saving of souls'.

Two witnesses can be quoted to illustrate his lively temperament. He desperately irritated Congar, who did not spare Daniélou in his *Journal du Concile*.[9]

---

[6] *Études*, 79 (1946), 5–21.
[7] Quoted by Rondeau, 'Jean Daniélou théologien', 152–3.
[8] 'Jean Daniélou théologien', 153.
[9] Yves Congar, *Mon Journal du Concile*, ed. with notes, Éric Mahieu, 2 vols (Paris: Cerf, 2002).

Despite this, Congar wrote, 'Daniélou is really extraordinary. He goes far too fast, but he has an exceptional gift of presence and of getting down to essentials.'[10] Daniélou worked on the Constitution on Divine Revelation with Mgr Garronne, who wrote, 'Those hours of working together are among my best memories of the Council.'[11] He also worked with Mgr Wojtyła (Pope John Paul II, 1978–2005) editing a text on the challenge of Marxism.[12]

THE FOUNDING OF THE *SOURCES CHRÉTIENNES* COLLECTION

In 1942, even before being awarded his doctorate in theology, Daniélou had the opportunity to publish the very first volume of the prestigious *Sources chrétiennes* collection, which continues to flourish today and has become an obligatory and universal source of reference:

> The project [of this collection] was thought up and completely developed between 1932 and 1937 by Father Victor Fontoynont SJ († 1958), who was the true founder of the collection, at the point when he was prefect of studies at the Theology Faculty of Lyon-Fourvière. But the collection only saw light during the darkest hours of the war and the occupation, in 1941–2, in Lyon, thanks to Father Th. G. Chifflot, OP († 1964), who at that time was the director of the Éditions de l'Abeille in Lyon, a branch of the Éditions du Cerf in Paris. The first volumes were printed in 1942 and appeared at the beginning of 1943, under the editorship of Fathers Jean Daniélou († 1974), and Henri de Lubac SJ.[13] If, contrary to the intentions of the founder, they did not include the original text, due to the shortage of paper, the Greek text accompanied the translation of the letters of Ignatius of Antioch (n° 10) in 1945, and subsequent volumes.[14]

The first volume, which consisted of a translation, with introduction, of Gregory of Nyssa's *Life of Moses*, was preceded by a marginal note signed by the editors. The programme they sketched out was no mean thing, and bore a combative tone concerning received opinion with regard to the Fathers of the church:

> It is a case of creating a climate of understanding them, of getting acquainted with the mentality they represent, of doing away with the prejudices about them that are still current in many minds, making people believe that the Fathers are

---

[10] Congar, *Mon Journal du Concile*, i.298; quoted by Rondeau, 'Jean Daniélou théologien', 131.

[11] Quoted by Rondeau, 'Jean Daniélou théologien', 132.

[12] Cf. Rondeau, 'Jean Daniélou théologien', 130.

[13] Who has since died in 1991.

[14] Claude Mondésert, *Pour lire les Pères de l'Église dans la collection 'Sources chrétiennes'*, Foi Vivante, 230, 2nd edn (Paris: Cerf, 1988), 17.

unreadable [. . .] it seems to us that if the Fathers are difficult, it is because we are ignorant of their mindset. To us they represent a cultural domain almost as foreign as that of India or China. What we need is to shed light from within this world, to introduce it, by showing its surroundings and describing its routes and, having handed over the keys to the reader, to leave to them the pleasure of discovering the treasures which they would never otherwise have suspected.

This concern determined the different characteristics of this collection. First of all there is the choice of texts. We did not immediately fall upon the easiest, but on the most characteristic. Then we wanted to offer all the elements so that we could facilitate the fullest understanding of the text . . . [15]

Was it this youthful audacity which would later cause problems for Daniélou?

THE 1946 ARTICLE AND THE QUESTION OF *THÉOLOGIE NOUVELLE*

We have already mentioned the article which appeared in *Études* in 1946 entitled 'Les orientations présentes de la pensée religieuse'. The contemporary theologian rereading this article will find nothing further to say; but anyone recalling the context of the time can guess that the faintly polemical tone towards scholastic theology and Thomism was unlikely to please everyone. 'Censors blinded, if not hallucinated by suspicion, thought that they could read in it the scandalous word "new theology".'[16] People were certainly talking of a renewal of theology, of a new road open to theology, of a theological renewal, etc.

> Taking note of tendencies, some of which had emerged before the war, [Daniélou] invited theologians to return to the sources of Scripture, the Fathers and liturgy; to take into account the great currents of contemporary thought, particularly Marxism, with its interpretation of history, and existentialism, fascinated by the abyss of human freedom. He invited them to respond to the needs of souls, who expected of theology not atemporal speculation but a religious anthropology capable of being the bedrock of their spiritual lives and of shedding light on their moral choices in the midst of the storms of this world. Finally, he asked them to open themselves to universalism. Christianity, which up until now was *de facto* Graeco-Roman, could become incarnate within the different civilizations of the world, which would need to develop the content of revelation, each according to the resources of its culture.[17]

---

[15] Mondésert, *Pour lire les Pères de l'Église*, 19.
[16] Joseph Paramelle, 'À la découverte des Pères de l'Église avec Daniélou', in J. Fontaine (ed.), *Actualité*, 105–11 (108).
[17] Rondeau, 'Jean Daniélou théologien', 137–8.

THE BREADTH OF HIS THEOLOGICAL OUTPUT

Daniélou published more than sixty books,[18] and at least two hundred articles. There are two general bibliographies currently in existence: Valentini's, which stops at 1968,[19] and the Jesuit Fritz Frei's[20] which continues beyond Daniélou's death in May 1974.

In addition, there are two specialist bibliographies, one on Judaeo-Christianity, published in the first volume of the journal *Recherches de Science Religieuse*,[21] the other on patristics, published in the *Mélanges* presented to Daniélou in the same year, 1972, under the title *Epektasis*.[22] It is worth saying something about these two multi-authored works, which appeared only three years after he received his cardinal's hat and therefore at the same time as he was elected to the Académie française.

In 1971 *Recherches de Science Religieuse* welcomed Daniélou's twenty-fifth 'Bulletin d'histoire des origines chrétiennes', a valuable service in which Daniélou had succeeded 'Father Jules Lebreton, the editor of this Bulletin since 1921'.[23] Throughout those twenty-five bulletins, Daniélou listed more than five hundred noteworthy books, discussed in detail with an artistry which excelled in creating a dialogue between historians and theologians. When, in 1972, Father Moingt, who at the time was editor of the journal, presented the two special volumes dedicated to Judaeo-Christianity, in honour of Daniélou,[24] he explained the enthusiasm with which the nineteen invited authors, who had themselves nearly all been listed in the famous bulletins, responded spontaneously to the invitation to take part in this project. Their scholarly contributions were distributed under four headings: Nature and sources [of Judaeo-Christianity]; History and influences; the search for traces; and the Relationship with Gnosticism. These nineteen articles constitute a new inventory of our knowledge of Judaeo-Christianity, and represent a significant milestone following H. J. Schoeps's 1949 reference work, *Theologie und Geschichte des Judenchristentums*, and Daniélou's own *Théologie du judéo-christianisme* in 1958.

---

[18] Not to mention translations in various languages and several important works which he wrote in collaboration with Connolly, Boegner, Bosc, Kaplan, Jossua, Marrou, and others.

[19] D. Valentini, *La Teologia della storia nel pensiero di Jean Daniélou*, Corona Lateranensis 20 (Rome: Lateran University Press, 1970), pp. xv–cxxix.

[20] Fritz Frei, SJ, *Médiation unique et transfiguration universelle: Thèmes christologiques et leurs perspectives missionnaires dans la pensée de Jean Daniélou*, Europaïsche Hochschulschriften, Reihe 23, Thologie, 173 (Berne-Frankfurt: P. Lang, 1981).

[21] *RSR*, 60/1 (1972), 11–18 mentions eight books, twelve articles, and 144 book reviews from Daniélou's pen, all specifically devoted to Judaeo-Christianity. Daniélou principally listed works written in French, German, and English, and occasionally in Spanish and Italian.

[22] Jacques Fontaine and Charles Kannengiesser (eds.), *Epektasis: Mélanges patristiques offerts au Cardinal Jean Daniélou* (Paris: Beauchesne, 1972), 673–89. This bibliography lists more than 250 titles.

[23] Joseph Moingt, 'Avant-Propos' in *RSR* 60/1, (1972) 7.

[24] *RSR* 60/1 and 60/2 (1972).

What *Recherches de Science Religieuse* did at that time for Judaeo-Christianity, Fontaine, Kannengiesser, and some sixty other collaborators did for patristics, by publishing the magnificent work of extracts entitled *Epektasis.*

> The enthusiasm with which a great many of Jean Daniélou's colleagues and friends collaborated in this undertaking is evidence of the esteem in which patristic scholars of all opinions held his work as a researcher. In this, they understood themselves to be honouring an author whose œuvre had renewed, illustrated, promoted, and served contemporary patristic studies in an exceptional way. In this sense, such a gathering represents, in its plurality and mutual respect, a unanimous gesture.[25]

This vast work of almost 700 pages is also organized around four major subjects which suggest both the remarkable diversity and the continuity of the principal themes: Exegesis, hagiography, and liturgy; Origen and the Alexandrian tradition; Gregory of Nyssa and Christian Cappadocia; and Christianity under Theodosius. As can be seen, Gregory of Nyssa, who was always Daniélou's favourite Father, is greatly honoured. Indeed,

> the encounter between Jean Daniélou and Gregory of Nyssa was not simply a passing opportunity for a particularly successful intellectual exercise. It bound around one of the highest Christian spiritualities the diversity of his vocations and his gifts. It remained a privileged sphere of his research and he still gladly refers to it as one of the living sources of his thought and praxis.[26]

The very notion of *epektasis*,[27] which is central to Gregory, seems to characterize Daniélou's personality. 'Speed and energy of speech, passionate attention given both to people and to ideas, impatience to finish in order to move on ever further [. . .] exceptional speed of intuition.'[28]

GREGORY OF NYSSA, THE FAVOURITE

In 1944 Daniélou published the thesis that would make him a Doctor of Arts and Theology, *Platonisme et théologie mystique: Essai sur la doctrine*

---

[25] *Epektasis*, p. vi.   [26] *Epektasis*, p. v.
[27] Cf. my 'Le Grégoire de Nysse de Jean Daniélou. Réflexions autour de "Platonisme et théologie mystique"' in J. Fontaine (ed.), *Actualité*, 87–9. This notion of *epektasis* also makes possible an original approach to the relationship between *eros* and *agape*, a delicate and interesting subject if ever there was one: cf. my 'Le Grégoire de Nysse de Jean Daniélou. *Platonisme et théologie mystique* (1944): *eros* and agapè', *NRT*, 128/2, (2006) 258–73.
[28] *Epektasis*, p. v.

spirituelle de saint Grégoire de Nysse.[29] This first of his books was described
by Ivánka as *ein großartiger Wurf*, 'a master-stroke'.[30] It has to be said that it
was the ideal moment to address the subject. In fact, for some years previously
much had been published about Platonism and mysticism, and many monographs had appeared with a bearing on the authors who inspired Gregory.
Among them were:

1930	Cherniss	*The Platonism of Gregory of Nyssa*
1936	von Ivánka	*Von Platonismus zur Theorie der Mystik*
1938	Puech	*La ténèbre mystique chez le Pseudo-Denys*
1939	Dom Stolz	*Théologie de la mystique*
1942	Balthasar	*Présence et pensée: Essai sur la philosophie religieuse de Grégoire de Nysse*.[31]

But in the background we must also add something of primary importance.
Bréhier had just produced a painstaking translation of Plotinus' six *Enneads*
between 1924 and 1931;[32] de Gandillac had finished translating Pseudo-
Dionysius;[33] and, above all, Walther Völker, Daniélou's perennial German
rival, had already carved two out of the six monumental works which would
take up the thirty-five years of his academic career. In chronological order of
publication, his monographs (which were of the greatest interest to Daniélou,
who was forever watched and, as it were, haunted by the indefatigable
Wissenschaftler) were, in 1931, on Origen; in 1938, on Philo; in 1952, on
Clement of Alexandria; in 1955, on Gregory of Nyssa himself; in 1958, on
Pseudo-Dionysius; and, finally, in 1965, on Maximus the Confessor.[34] These

---

[29]   Published in Paris, by Aubier, in 'Théologie', no. 2, the first edition in 1944, and the second
edition in 1954.

[30]   Endre von Ivánka, *ZkT*, 71 (1949), 231–3 (231).

[31]   Harold Frederik Cherniss, *The Platonism of Gregory of Nyssa*, University of California
Publications in Classical Philology II, i (Berkeley: University of California Press, 1930), 1–92;
Endre von Ivánka, 'Von Platonismus zur Theorie der Mystik (Zur Erkenntnislehre Gregors von
Nyssa)', *Scholastik*, 11 (1936), 163–95; Henri-Charles Puech, 'La ténèbre mystique chez le
Pseudo-Denys l'Aréopagite et dans la tradition mystique', *Études carmélitaines*, 23 (1938),
33–53; Anselme Stolz, *Théologie de la mystique* (Chevetogne: Éd. Bénédictines d'Amay, 1939);
Hans Urs von Balthasar, *Présence et pensée: Essai sur la philosophie religieuse de Grégoire de
Nysse* (Paris: Beauchesne, 1942).

[32]   Plotinus, *Ennéades*, trans. Émile Bréhier, Collection des Universités de France (Paris: Les
belles lettres, 1924–1931).

[33]   Pseudo-Dionysius the Areopagite, *Œuvres complètes*, trans. Maurice de Gandillac, Bibliothèque philosophique (Paris: Aubier, 1943).

[34]   Walther Völker, *Das Volkommenheitsideal des Origenes*, BHTh 7 (Tübingen: Mohr, 1931);
Fortschritt und Vollendung bei Philo von Alexandrien (Leipzig: Hinrich, 1938); *Der wahre
Gnostiker nach Clemens Alexandrinus*, Texte und Untersuchungen zur Geschichte der altchrist-
lichen Literatur, Band 57 (Berlin/Leipzig: Akademie Verlag, 1952); *Gregor von Nyssa als Mystiker*
(Wiesbaden: Steiner, 1955); *Kontemplation und Ekstase bei Pseudo-Dionysius Areopagita*
(Wiesbaden: Steiner, 1958); *Maximus Confessor als Meister des geistlichen Lebens* (Wiesbaden:
Steiner, 1965).

six superb monographs more or less followed chronological order, whereas Daniélou himself went backwards in time with his three studies on Gregory of Nyssa in 1944, Origen in 1948,[35] and Philo in 1958,[36] seeming both to precede and follow Völker with regard to the same subjects.

Over thirty years, Daniélou published two books and some sixty articles (including translations and reprints) on Gregory of Nyssa. He began his career as a writer with Gregory and ended it with him in a posthumous volume. Is there anyone who knew or currently knows this Father better than he did? Despite their admiration, his colleagues were nevertheless not always in agreement with the portrait that Daniélou painted of Gregory. We need only run through some of the revisions of his thesis or later collections of articles for this to become clear.[37]

In 1945, Maurice de Gandillac dedicated twelve pages in *Dieu vivant* to an enthusiastic account of Daniélou's thesis. The challenge that Daniélou set himself, in which he thought he had succeeded, was to elucidate the 'funda-mental ambiguity (which) here appears to be that of any Christian theology rethought in a Hellenic framework'.[38] Gandillac draws our attention to the three purgative, illuminative, and unitive ways which need to be understood more flexibly than Daniélou would lead us to suppose; he agrees with his interpretation of the *agape*; he recognizes in Gregory the writer who over-comes a certain Origenist gnosis and reveals in the theology of *epektasis*, with its double movement,[39] 'a sort of original synthesis between the mysticism of "fullness" and that of "emptiness"'.[40]

Louis Gardet, the great scholar of mysticism, notably that of Islam, dedicat-ed ten pages in *Revue thomiste* to discussing *Platonisme et théologie mystique*. Following Daniélou, he considered Gregory of Nyssa to be the founder of mystical theology, for the two reasons which Daniélou had clearly proved. In Gregory, 'the intellectualist tension [. . .] within Alexandrian circles [. . .] was overcome'[41] by an affirmation of the primacy of love. Furthermore, this victory was definitive by reason of the clear manifestation of the supernatural

---

[35] *Origène*, Le génie du christianisme (Paris: La table ronde, 1948).

[36] *Philon d'Alexandrie*, Les temps et les destins (Paris: Arthème Fayard, 1958).

[37] Daniélou, *L'être et le temps chez Grégoire de Nysse* (Leiden: Brill, 1970).

[38] De Gandillac, 'À propos de Grégoire de Nysse', *Dieu vivant*, 3 (1945), 123–34 (128).

[39] *Epektasis* presupposes a double relationship with God, that of *instasis*, in which the Word inhabits the soul and that of *extasis* in which God once more escapes. God enters the soul and the soul emigrates in God. This alternation of *instasis* and *extasis*, condensed for the first time by Gregory in the word *epektasis* based on Phil. 3.13 (*epekteinomenos*), finds itself literally in the two prefixes of the word *epektasis*: *epi* marks the immanence, *ek* infers transcendence. Perhaps it is even a case of the alternation between the *agape* eventually received through grace and then of the *erōs* ceaselessly redirected to God by means of the very initiative of a God who is always greater, who is creator and seducer and who gives himself and hides in order to give himself once more.

[40] De Gandillac, 'À propos de Grégoire de Nysse', 134.

[41] Louis Gardet, 'Saint Grégoire de Nysse', *RevTh*, 47 (1947), 342–52 (346).

nature of grace (and here Gardet supports Daniélou against Festugière): 'this participation, not of nature [. . .] but of grace [. . .] belongs to the transcendence of the immanent God and the supernatural nature of the divine life within us [. . .]. This double progression was necessary in order to [. . .] consider Gregory of Nyssa as the founder of spiritual theology.'[42]

Völker[43] welcomed *Platonisme et théologie mystique* as a great book, the work of a skilled and erudite expert who was occasionally a little eccentric, but much more faithful to Gregory of Nyssa than Balthasar. Among others he admired the chapters on the spiritual senses and on *epektasis*.[44] We should note that Völker, who, as mentioned above, was a specialist in all the great spiritual writers of the first seven centuries, observed in Gregory, no doubt in contrast, some characteristics which did not strike Daniélou. Gregory, he wrote, was not fascinated by the cross of Christ, but by his resurrection; he speaks little of suffering, penance, temptations, and *apatheia*.[45] Völker thus offers us the beguiling image of a balanced and tranquil Gregory. Besides, according to him, Daniélou exaggerates Gregory's spiritual originality with regard to Origen, which he says can all already be found in the great Alexandrian, who was a true mystic. But Daniélou points out that Origen does not situate the end of the spiritual journey on the summit of Mount Sinai, but accomplishes it on the plain of the promised land.[46] So it would not be more than a 'mysticism of the teacher', according to his terrible term.[47]

Crouzel spent fifteen pages settling this difference[48] between Völker and Daniélou, incidentally taking Völker's side, while at the same time contradicting one of his crucial theories.[49] His article ended with these words: Gregory 'should not be called the founder of mystical theology, since everything that matters can already be found in Origen'.[50]

THE FAMOUS FINAL TRILOGY ON THE
FIRST CHRISTIAN CENTURIES

Daniélou's teaching at the Institut Catholique de Paris, which began in 1943 and ended in 1969, including his final five years as Dean, was the crucible of

---

[42] Gardet, 'Saint Grégoire de Nysse', 348.
[43] Völker, 'Rezensionen', *Theologische Zeitschrift*, 5 (1949) 143–8.
[44] Völker, *Gregor von Nyssa als Mystiker*, 148.
[45] *Gregor von Nyssa als Mystiker*, 273, 106, 136, and 263, respectively.
[46] Daniélou, *Origène*, 291.
[47] *Origène*, 296.
[48] Henri Crouzel, 'Grégoire de Nysse est-il le fondateur de la théologie mystique? Une controverse récente', *Revue d'ascétique et de mystique*, 33 (1957), 189–202.
[49] See my 'Le Grégoire de Nysse de Jean Daniélou', 92–3.
[50] Crouzel, 'Grégoire de Nysse', 202.

his research and his publications. The famous red notebooks, published without a date with the subtitle *Ad modum manuscripti* or 'Notes taken in my courses by students', reflect the beginning of his work. They constitute an entire chronological journey through the history of the origins of Christianity, as their titles show: 'Judaism at the time of Christ'; 'Judaeo-Christianity'; 'The Christian message and Greek thought in the second century'; 'The third century: Origen'; and 'The fourth century: Gregory of Nyssa and his background'. These texts, typed, clipped together, and copied on rough paper, containing a great many *errata et addenda*, were the origin of all that came afterwards. The first instalment would be published in 1958 under the title 'Philo'.[51] The second instalment would be corrected several times in order to end up as one of Daniélou's master works, *Théologie du judéo-christianisme*. The fourth instalment would be edited in 1948 under the title 'Origen'.[52]

But all of these were only the preparatory work towards the famous trilogy written by Daniélou and dedicated to the *Histoire des doctrines chrétiennes avant Nicée*, which we now have in the form of three volumes, with the titles, *Théologie du judéo-christianisme*; *Message évangélique et culture hellénistique*; *Les origines du christianisme latin* published in 1991.[53] Jerusalem, Athens, and Rome: the three capitals of our civilization. The Christian message would encounter each of these cultures.

It should also be said that these three volumes, even though they owe a heavy debt to didactic content, are not manuals, but their author's own theological work: they are written in defence of one or more personal theories. They are the result of a lengthy editorial history. The first, *Théologie du judéo-christianisme*, largely taken from the second red notebook, was initially published in 1958. Discussion of its reception follows below. It was followed by a translation into English in 1964, which included several revisions, and an Italian edition in 1974, over which Daniélou took great care, to the extent that it can be said to be a second, revised and corrected, edition. This 1974 Italian edition was completely reworked by friends and colleagues of Daniélou: Mme Boulnois, Fr Paramelle, SJ and Mme Rondeau, a team of first-class scholars.

The second volume, *Message évangélique et culture hellénistique*, was first published in 1961, and reprinted in 1991. The authors most frequently discussed are Clement of Alexandria, Irenaeus of Lyon, Origen, Justin, Hippolytus, and Methodius of Olympus. Daniélou stressed the extent to which the encounter with Hellenism invited Christian theology to make a stronger case for its rational demands. He showed the capital importance in the second

---

[51] Daniélou, *Philon d'Alexandrie*.   [52] Daniélou, *Origène*.

[53] Daniélou, *Théologie du judéo-christianisme*, 2nd edn, with a preface by M. J. Rondeau (Paris: Desclée/Cerf, 1991); *Message évangélique et culture hellénistique* (Tournai: Desclée et Cie, 1961, 2nd edn. 1991); *Les origines du christianisme latin* (Paris: Desclée/Cerf, 1978, 2nd edn. 1991).

century of Middle Platonism, and, during the second and third centuries, that of the gnosticism which developed in Greek circles on the foundation of an earlier heterodox Judaism.

The third volume, *Les origines du christianisme latin*, appeared posthumously in 1978 with the help of two of Daniélou's collaborators, who followed the instructions he had left behind. It revolves around the figure of Tertullian who, while completely fluent in Greek, was himself profoundly Latin. Daniélou tries to show that there are original Latin texts, which come from a Judaeo-Christian context independent of Greek literature, before and after Tertullian.

Fr Orbe notes that,

> Only a wise mind, open to a variety of currents of thought, with a great flexibility and power of assimilation, living in continuous familiarity with the sources and the latest publications, adding to a great richness of observation an aptitude for establishing the relationship between very varied contributions, could have the courage to conceive of and create a work along lines at one and the same time so simple and so innovative.[54]

In this first, most original, work of his trilogy, which relied on the many publications of his predecessors which he continued to edit for *Recherches de Science Religieuse*, Daniélou came to formulate a new definition of Judaeo-Christianity as a truly Christian way of thinking which does not imply a link with the Jewish worshipping community, but expresses itself in the framework borrowed from Judaism, in particular with regard to the apocalyptic; in other words, an ancient Christianity of Semitic structure which produced a specific literature around 150 CE. Many specialists opposed this definition, which seemed to them to be too simplistic and sweeping; nevertheless Daniélou had put his finger on a reality which existed and which had not been identified as such. His work gave him an impressive consistency and thus illustrated a most remarkable and hitherto unknown or poorly interpreted form of the encounter between the Christian message and a given culture. Judaeo-Christianity was therefore not a matter of a few marginal Jews making room in their beliefs for Jesus (Schoeps's position), but a purely Christian phenomenon. If this was the case, Harnack's *History of Dogma*, which makes no room for it, suffers from a crucial lacuna, which leads him to his famous erroneous theory that Christian theology was born of the encounter between the evangelical message with Greek philosophy. No, Christian theology did not begin with the Apologists! Daniélou restored to us an entire sector of ancient Christian thought.

The manifestation of this very specific Christian theology—visionary, symbolic, iconological, and unconceptual—favoured the transmission of faith by a less intellectual route. The archaeological, iconographical, and liturgical (rites and sacraments) traditions are capable of adequately articulating the

---

[54] Quoted by M. Fédou, 'Le judéo-christianisme selon Daniélou', in J. Fontaine (ed.), *Actualité*, 43–56 (43). For other specialist judgements on this work, see *Théologie du judéo-christianisme*, i (1991), 10, n.1.

revelation of God in Jesus Christ. The fourth and final part of the work in question (after sources, the intellectual context, and doctrine), deals with institutions and is subdivided into baptism, Eucharist, Christian community, and personal holiness. It is here, especially, that the practice of Christianity, and in particular liturgy and sacraments, offers us theological and properly doctrinal riches which Daniélou, like no other, was able to emphasize.

> Daniélou's cherished theory, which was borne out by all the Fathers, that Christian teaching is carried out primarily at the heart of the liturgy, whose signs and texts should be noted, has regained favour over the last few decades. [. . .] it is a teaching that is authentically theological but not conceptual, authentically spiritual, but not affective. This more contemplative approach to the Christian mysteries could bring us a certain *ressourcement* with regard to homiletics and catechesis.[55]

AN ASTONISHING KNOWLEDGE
OF MIDDLE PLATONISM

'Daniélou, who had a considerable knowledge of the philosophical currents of the late Empire, was skilled in clarifying arguments and uncovering influences', wrote Rondeau.[56] In my opinion, this is faint praise. Daniélou was completely *au fait* with the work of Witt, Andresen, Waszink, Grant, Alfonsi, Theiler, and others, and knew how to take advantage of it. In many of his articles, he exploited, as it were, a family tree of the different Neo-Platonist schools, for which he had a particular sensitivity and a detective's flair. Starting with Ammonius Sakkas, that common master of Alexandria who abandoned Christianity, he distinguished three lines: first, that of Origen. Second, that of Longinus, who began in the school of Athens, where an Aristotelianizing neo-Platonism was taught. Basil of Caesarea certainly studied there, and handed on what he learned to his brother Gregory of Nyssa; this line stretched as far as Hierocles and unlike him, was not anti-Christian. Finally, that of Plotinus, Porphyry, Iamblichus, and Proclus, to mention only the most important, but among whom would later be included the Emperor Julian, and the heretics Aetius and Eunomius. Each of these three branches provoked a development in the heritage of the master, in a coherent but different way. It touches, for example, on the question of emanationism which would become strongly marked in Plotinus' branch, and would become subordinationism in Origen.[57]

---

[55] Rondeau, 'Préface', *Théologie du judéo-christianisme*, 12.
[56] Rondeau, 'Jean Daniélou théologien', 148.
[57] Cf. Daniélou, 'Grégoire de Nysse et le néo-platonisme de l'école d'Athènes', *Revue des études grecques*, 80 (1967), 395–401.

But it equally concerns philosophy of language,[58] or the argument concerning the nature of the soul,[59] or the different conceptions of metempsychosis,[60] which has an impact on Christian discussion about the resurrection.

Finally, we should add to this the persistent and powerful influences of Epicureanism, Stoicism, and Manichaeism. Daniélou's panoramic erudition allowed him to stress that certain theological conflicts within Christianity repeated the conflicts between philosophical schools which were current at the time, which for Christians were replete with implications about faith itself.

CONCLUSION

I have left to one side dozens of works and articles by Daniélou which have no direct bearing on patristics, but rather on his pastoral concern to enter into dialogue with his contemporaries, or on his theological reflection as a whole (as for example his *Essai sur la théologie de l'histoire* of 1953).

Blessed with an exceptional intelligence and temperament, Daniélou also found himself in and knew how to benefit from extremely favourable circumstances: a *kairos* for writing on Gregory of Nyssa, another *kairos* for investigating Judaeo-Christianity, with the discoveries of Nag Hammadi and the Dead Sea. He published the first volume in the *Sources chrétiennes* collection and wrote in the first issue of *Dieu vivant*. But it was not only a question of luck. It was also a question of his massive work of reading and writing, illustrated by his *Bulletins* in *Recherches de Science Religieuse*.

The result was that he made us love all these texts, through an approach which was intelligent but non-intellectual, spiritual in the best sense, demonstrating the beauty of learning at the service of faith, prayer, and liturgy.

---

[58] Cf. Daniélou, 'Eunome l'Arien et l'exégèse néo-platonicienne du Cratyle', *Revue des études grecques*, 69 (1956), 412–32.

[59] Cf. in the same line Enrico Peroli, 'Gregory of Nyssa and the Neoplatonic Doctrine of the Soul', *Vigiliae Christianae*, 51 (1997) 117–39.

[60] Cf. Daniélou, 'Metempsychosis in Gregory of Nyssa', in *Orientalia christiana analecta. The Heritage of the Early Church: Essays in Honor of the very Reverend G.V. Florovsky* (Rome: Pontificium Institutum Studiorum Orientalium, 1973), 227–43.

17

Henri Bouillard: The Freedom of Faith[1]

James Hanvey, SJ

INTRODUCTION

Henri Bouillard (1908–81) was a member of the '*cercle de Fourvière*', that group of French Jesuits whose teaching, writing, and research, though controversial until the Second Vatican Council, nevertheless prepared the ground for it and helped to shape the theology which underpinned its vision.[2] He was also part of that pre-conciliar theological movement which came to be known as *nouvelle théologie*.[3] Though Bouillard is not as well known in the Anglo-Saxon world as *confrères* such as de Lubac, Rondet, Gaston Fessard, and Daniélou, his contribution to Catholic theology, especially the revision and development of 'fundamental theology' remains significant. His work is important not only for its considerable scholarly achievements, but for the method that he forged through a rigorous engagement with the tradition, especially Thomas, and with contemporary religious and secular thinkers.[4] With the publication of

---

[1] My gratitude to Dr F. Laishley, SJ, who read a draft of this essay and made valuable suggestions and helpful corrections.

[2] For a concise discussion of the issues surrounding the *cercle de Fourvière* cf. Karl H. Neufeld, SJ, 'La Théologie fondamentale dans un monde transformé', in Karl H. Neufeld, SJ (ed.), *Vérité du Christianisme, Henri Bouillard* (Paris: Desclée de Brouwer, 1989), 359–90, esp. 359–69.

[3] Cf. The key elements of the movement critically described as *la nouvelle théologie* were set out as a positive programme to respond to the secularization of France by Jean Daniélou in 'Les orientations présents de la pensée religieuse', *Études*, 249 (1946), 5–21. Réginald Garrigou-Legrange, OP attacked Bouillard and Teilhard de Chardin in 'La Nouvelle Théologie: où va-t-elle?', *Ang*, 23 (1946), 129–45. See too his important 'Vérité et immutabilité du Dogme', *Ang*, 24 (1947), 124–39. Cf. H. Rondet, 'Nouvelle Théologie', in Karl Rahner (ed.), *Sacramentum Mundi* (New York: Herder, 1964) iv.234–6, for a very guarded treatment. For Bouillard's reaction see the notes from his journal and letters at the time in *Vérité du Christianisme*, 399–408. One should also note de Lubac's tribute to Bouillard's exemplary religious obedience ('sa soumission exemplaire'), in 'Témoignage de P de Lubac', *Vérité du Christianisme*, 413–14.

[4] With the exception of major and extensive works on Karl Barth and Maurice Blondel, much of Bouillard's work is a series of penetrating studies of those who shaped contemporary secular and theological thought. See, for example, Bouillard's meetings with Heidegger chronicled by

Humani Generis[5] he, together with others at Lyon-Fourvière, was removed from his post and forbidden to teach or to publish. These years of silence, however, were not wasted. During them, the work which Bouillard was able to accomplish represents a significant contribution to Catholic and Protestant theological and philosophical thought. Further, much of his thinking informs key aspects of the teaching of Vatican II.

In a church now so decisively formed by the Council it is not easy to appreciate the issues that made the *nouvelle théologie* so controversial. It is certainly not a sobriquet that those reckoned to be its representatives would have chosen for themselves. Indeed, many, like Bouillard understood themselves to be working within a tradition and recovering it. This was especially true of their *ad fontes* approach with the founders of Christian discourse such as Augustine and Thomas. Change is not inimical to a faith that seeks understanding but is a sign of its life. Indeed, it is necessary if it is to accomplish its mission of making Christ, who is Lord of history, known within it. To achieve this entailed a critique of the presuppositions and methods of the prevailing neo-scholasticism. To the critics of the *nouvelle théologie* it opened the way to relativism and subjectivism, thereby weakening the credibility of Christian faith and the objectivity of its truth.[6]

These are obviously important questions but they risk being seen as part of an abstract internal academic dispute unless we place them in a wider context. Bouillard possessed an acute sense of his culture as well as an evangelical motive. He was aware that the church was living in a new century, not only conditioned by the ravages of war, but also with a sophisticated secularism. To say something to the unbeliever, and to reconstruct a new Christian humanism which could do justice to human freedom without in any way compromising or diminishing the offer and the need of grace, was the urgent task. How were the Christian believer and the church to meet this new world and engage it? How to help the secular world understand itself as already living in and from the presence of the divine mystery; a presence which is not a threat but an invitation to communion? Bouillard's concern was to trace the

R. Scherer, in 'Besuch bei Heidegger', *Wort und Wahrheit*, 2 (1947) 780–2; Karl H. Neufeld, 'Comment parler de Dieu: Henri Bouillard, 1908–1981' in *Vérité du Christianisme*, 25–7; and his study of the philosopher Éric Weil, 'Philosophie et Religion Dans L'Œuvre Éric Weil', *Vérité du Christianisme*, 233–316.

[5] Pius XII, *Humani Generis*. Encyclical Letter Concerning some False Opinions Threatening to Undermine the Foundations of Catholic Doctrine (12 August 1950), *AAS*, xlii (1950), 593–630. ET available at <http://www.vatican.va/holy_father/pius_xii/encyclicals/documents/hf_p-xii_enc_12081950_humani-generis_en.html>.

[6] In addition to Garrigou-Lagrange's criticisms in 'La Nouvelle Théologie', cf. M.-Michel Labourdette, 'La Théologie et ses sources', *RevTh*, 46 (1946), 353–71; and the anonymous response from the Fourvière Jesuits, 'Théologie et ses sources: résponse aux Études critiques de la Revue thomiste (mai-août) 1946', *RSR*, 33 (1946), 385–401.

dynamic nature of that relationship without ever compromising the unique event of Christ.

> By logic of faith we mean, of course, the logic of free adherence to the Christian mystery. It lies in the correspondence between the gospel message and the logic of human existence, this correspondence being perceived and freely acknowledged... the logic of the faith is not reducible to the logic of human existence; indeed its full content is not revealed until one freely surrenders to it.[7]

CONTROVERSY AND THE INCARNATIONAL LOGIC OF THEOLOGY

Leo XIII's 1876 encyclical *Aeterni Patris*[8] was concerned to determine the correct relationship between reason and faith, arguing the necessity of a philosophy in 'accord with the Catholic faith' that also laid the foundation for theology. Aquinas' synthesis of reason and faith was to be the basis for a renewal of seminary training and Catholic thought, providing fit remedies for the intellectual turmoil of the time[9] and providing the conceptual grammar and language of orthodox faith. This is the context in which we need to read Bouillard's early work, *Conversion et grâce chez S. Thomas d'Aquin*, published in 1944.[10] Although offered as an 'étude historique', it is much more; it exposes the problems of the dominant ahistorical scholastic approach to Thomas, and shows that Aquinas did not understand his own thought in any static way but was open to change and development. The possibility that truth may change and evolve is condemned as Modernist. 'Truth is no more unchangeable than man, since with him, in him, and by him it is evolved.'[11] This explains both Bouillard's challenge, and the force of the charges against *nouvelle théologie*.

---

[7] Bouillard, *The Logic of Faith* (London: Sheed & Ward, 1967), 3–4; ET of *Logique de Foi*, 1964.

[8] Leo XIII, *Aeterni Patris*. Encyclical Letter on the Restoration of Christian Philosophy (4 August 1879), *Aacta Leonis XIII*, i (1881), 255–84. ET available at <http://www.vatican.va/holy_father/leo_xiii/encyclicals/documents/hf_l-xiii_enc_04081879_aeterni-patris_en.html>.

[9] *AP*, § 1, 17, 25ff.

[10] It was published as the first volume in the series *Théologie* by the faculty at Fourvière, having been prepared as his doctoral dissertation under Charles Boyer for the Gregorian University, Rome, in 1940; cf. Neufeld, 'La Théologie fondamentale dans un monde transformé', 370 ff. For an illuminating discussion on Modernism, see Michael F. Reardon, 'Science and Religious Modernism: The New Apologetic in France, 1890–1913', *The Journal of Religion*, 57/1 (1977), 48–63.

[11] *Veritas non est immutabilis plus quam ipse homo, quippe quæ cum ipso, in ipso et per ipsum evolvitur.* Cf. *DS* § 2058. Also the Antimodernist Oath, '*ideoque prorsus reicio haereticum commentum evolutionis dogmatum, ab uno in alium sensum transeuntium, diversum ab eo, quem prius habuit Ecclesia....*' *DS* § 2145.

The primary object of Bouillard's study was to examine Thomas's teaching on grace and the freedom of the act with which one turns to God.[12] He uncovered a significant difference between the way Aquinas speaks of justification in his commentary on the Sentences and his approach in the *Summa*, and argued that this is explained by Aquinas' discovery of the condemnation of semi-Pelagianism at the Council of Orange, in the light of which he modifies his teaching. This may seem to be a fairly straightforward matter of historical and textual research but it raised deeper questions about the method and assumptions of Thomas's thought and the neo-scholastic edifice built around it. If Aquinas can be shown to have altered his position, not only does that show that his own thought has a fluidity and responsiveness to new discovery, it also shows that his thought, too, must be read within its context. Widening this point, Bouillard argues that the formulas used to express this constant truth of faith must necessarily be contingent and subject to revision. Indeed, it is the very structure or law of the Incarnation that its truth is to be found in the contingencies of history.[13] In other words, the truths of faith are never given in a pure state; just as we are historically conditioned, so are our theological speech and thought, hence we must develop adequate hermeneutical categories and methods to recognize this if we wish to faithfully speak and represent them. As Eileen Scully observes, 'Bouillard's intention in *Conversion et grâce* was not simply to undertake a first level historical investigation in order to reconstruct the external facts of what had taken place; far more importantly he set out to discover the *meaning* of history, once reconstructed.'[14] However, as well as deepening understanding, this hermeneutic also has problems; but Bouillard is clear that if theology does not pursue this path it risks being false.[15]

Bouillard distinguishes between the constancy of Christian truth and the contingencies of expression and thought, allowing him to negotiate a *via media* between the danger of relativism (Modernism) and the false security of a rigid neo-scholasticism. However, it not only allows for the fact of pluralism given the historical character of all thought, it goes further and makes it a necessity. Nevertheless, this should not threaten the possibility of a universal truth, but it should make us attend to the many forms that truth may take and its complexity.[16] To draw a parallel with science: Newtonian physics

---

[12] 'L'object de notre étude n'est donc pas la psychologie de la foi, ni le rôle de la lumière de grâce dans l'acte de foi, mais le rapport que soutient avec la grâce l'acte libre par lequel l'homme se tourne vers Dieu...', *Conversion et grâce*, 2.

[13] *Conversion et grâce*, 220.

[14] Eileen Scully, *Grace and Human Freedom in the Theology of Henri Bouillard* (Bethesda MD: Academia Press, 2007), 69.

[15] *Conversion et grâce*, 223, 216, 219; 'Une Théologie qui ne serait pas actuelle serait une Théologie fausse.'

[16] Cf. Neufeld, 'La Théologie fondamentale dans un monde transformé', 371.

works well at one level but is also superseded by Einstein's theory of relativity. This does not necessarily produce relativism; rather, it suggests an argument against it: we would not bother to change our theories if we did not think that the new theory was closer to the truth.[17]

The other important dimension that emerges from Bouillard's *Conversion* is his perception that theology, even when it deals with the constant truths of faith, must be grounded in human experience and subjectivity. In a later work, Bouillard quotes Gabriel Marcel with approval, '*quand nous parlons de Dieu, n'oublie pas que c'est nous qui parlons*'.[18] A theology which separates nature and grace in such a way that the human autonomy is devalued will not be able to respond to the contemporary world—especially the secular world—which so prizes that autonomy. These ideas required a subtle grasp of the hermeneutic relationship between the historicity of human existence and expression and the incarnational reality of Christian truth, which was beyond the possibility of the neo-scholastic system and its presuppositions espoused by Garrigou-Lagrange and others at the time. Yet, if one also takes seriously the 'situatedness' of human thought and action, then it is understandable that Bouillard's conclusions, which expressed the revisionary programme of the *nouvelle théologie*, should be met with resistance by an ecclesial culture that valued certainty and stability. These were values that it could offer a world shattered by conflict and an exhausted European culture emerging from the trauma of totalitarianism into the bleak grey dawn of a new 'cold' war.

KARL BARTH, DIALOGUE, AND HUMAN EXPERIENCE

Perhaps it was hoped that after *Humani Generis*, Bouillard would not only be silenced, but prevented from any further creative work. In fact, this 'desert time' was important and productive. In his study of Karl Barth, Bouillard found a major dialogue partner even more challenging than the rationalism of the neo-scholastic tradition.[19] Barth is the great theologian of God's freedom.

[17] Even at this early stage we can see that Bouillard's thought is theologically oriented by the dynamic (*loi*) of the Incarnation which is the governing element in a hermeneutic of the historical character of human existence. It is a feature that runs through the works of all of the theological architects of Vatican II.

[18] Bouillard, *Connaissance de Dieu* (Paris: Aubier 1967), 83; cf ET, *Knowledge of God*, trans. Samuel D Fermiano (New York: Herder and Herder, 1969), 28.

[19] Bouillard's major study of Barth was presented for the degree of *doctorat d'état* at the Sorbonne and published in two volumes, i. *Genèse et evolution de la Théologie dialectique*; and ii. *Parole de Dieu et existence humaine, 1 & 2*, Théologie 38–9 (Paris: Aubier, 1957). See too Neufeld, 'Karl Barth et le catholicisme', in *Vérité du Christianisme*, 101–16.

God is the one who loves in freedom attested in his sovereign act of revelation, Jesus Christ. This act seeks and creates fellowship with us and it reveals to us our own condition before God. We have no access to him—for God is only as he gives himself to be known in his revelation. God's absolute freedom is both the condition and guarantor of his total otherness and the very possibility of his being God '*pro nobis*'. Only in the act of revelation can we know that God's freedom is his triune life encountered by us as grace. Yet, having allowed God's act to be our presupposition and ground, then we come to understanding its intelligibility, its inner coherence and rationale, which later in the *Church Dogmatics*, Barth calls God's Wisdom.[20]

For Barth, grace is never an abstract reality or concept but is always the personal concrete encounter with the God who elects to be with us and for us in Jesus Christ. This grace is objectively Jesus Christ and subjectively (within us) the Holy Spirit: the grace by which we know him and respond in obedience to his Word. When we have grasped this, already itself a grace, then we understand that this is an utterly unique act. In other words, there cannot be any pre-existing metaphysical category or system which can condition or determine God's freedom or give access to him. Any claim to know him independently of God's revelation or prior to it must be false. When we see this, we not only grasp the liberation—epistemological, ontological, and existential—that is given to us, we also grasp that God cannot be known truly in any other way. Thus, God's freedom comes to ground our freedom which is itself the gift of his grace. Theology cannot compromise with the ontological and epistemological consequences of this truth which cannot be preceded by any a *priori* condition in us but must always precede a *posteriori* God's act.[21] What is at stake is the freedom of theology itself precisely to be 'Theo-logy' and therefore speak truly of the grace in which it stands. Only when theology proceeds in this way does it serve the church and bear witness to the Word that has been addressed to it.

Barth's theology, written in the most dramatic, vigorous expressionist German, is far from the style and system of Catholic neo-scholasticism. It is a deliberate rejection of both neo-Kantian Liberal Protestantism and a Schleiermachian tradition of trying to ground openness to the Divine in the constitution of human consciousness and subjectivity. Yet the majesty of Barth's theology is no 'neo-orthodox' retreat from the world. It is a theology

---

[20] Barth, *Church Dogmatics II.1. The Patience and Wisdom of God*. Revised Study Edition (London: T&T Clark, 2009) (*CD*).

[21] This is the fundamental thesis that determines the whole of Barth's opus. It is set out in Volume 1 of the *CD* but is treated most clearly and succinctly in *CD* ii.1, § 28, 'The Being of God as the One who Loves in Freedom'. For an abbreviated English translation of the second volume of Bouillard's study, see *The Knowledge of God*. One of the best studies of freedom in Barth remains John Macken's *The autonomy theme in the Church Dogmatics: Karl Barth and his critics* (Cambridge: Cambridge University Press, 1990).

that has deep social and political concerns; precisely as a theology of freedom it protests against all political and social idolatry, as the Barmen Declaration of 1934 demonstrates.[22]

The question of the epistemological and ontological status of human nature in the light of revelation which Barth raises in such an acute form is critical for Catholicism, its practice as well as the philosophical and theological traditions that articulate it. It maps out a radical alternative to the Catholic theologians of the *nouvelle théologie*, a central part of whose concern was the construction of a Christian humanism in response to the challenges of the Enlightenment and secular modernity. Their aim was to do this without compromising the reality of grace.

In his study of Barth, Bouillard eschews polemicism; he approaches both as 'student' and an honest enquirer. His method is characterized by the hermeneutics of generosity and in a spirit of an ecumenical Christian search for the truth.[23] That Bouillard should engage Barth is not only an example of his own Christian freedom and generosity, given that Protestantism was regarded as heretical, it is a demonstration of his own method.

There are three aspects which are central to Bouillard (and Catholicism) identified in this encounter: the possibility of natural knowledge of God, the *analogia entis*, and the proofs for the existence of God.[24] At first glance, these may appear rather limited and academic, but they expose the deeper question of Barth's understanding of the relationship between grace and nature; the human capacity for God and the role of human freedom and experience in response to the Divine initiative—all familiar themes of Bouillard's work.

At the heart of Bouillard's criticism of Barth lies the problem of human freedom. In Bouillard's view, Barth's emphasis on the absoluteness of God's freedom threatens to negate human freedom. To do this is not only to destroy what is human, but raises problems for the very nature of grace itself. Grace heals and elevates human nature; it does not evacuate or instrumentalize it.[25] Previously, as we have seen, Bouillard had argued, against neo-scholasticism, that the *praeambula fidei* entail a desire for the supernatural. Using the resources provided by Rousselot's work on Thomas and Blondel's analysis of human action, Bouillard was able to give an account of that natural desire for

---

[22] Pius XI also produced a rejection of National Socialism, *Mit brennender Sorge*. Encyclical Letter on the Church and the German Reich (14th March 1937), *AAS*, xxix (1937), 145–67. ET available at <http://www.vatican.va/holy_father/pius_xi/encyclicals/documents/hf_p-xi_enc_14031937_mit-brennender-sorge_en.html>.

[23] Hans Küng did not share this view; cf. Henri de Lubac, 'Zum katholischen Dialog mit Karl Barth', *Dokumente*, 14 (1958), 448–54.

[24] Bouillard's treatment of Barth's objections to the *analogia entis* may be found in abbreviated form in *The Knowledge of God*, 124–6.

[25] In this regard, Bouillard argues that modern Protestantism (Barthian) and certain forms of Catholicism are different aspects of the same heresy. Cf. 'Karl Barth et le catholicisme', 104–6.

God. This is what Barth rejected: it opened the way to the danger of natural theology and the possibility of knowing God by a route other than revelation.[26] Indeed, the persistence of natural theology was a symptom of the sinfulness of humanity and its false epistemology. It perpetuated the destructive illusion that we can have autonomy from God's grace. With ringing and trenchant tones Barth writes:

> God comes forward Himself to be man's Saviour. This presupposes, and it is already proclaimed a truth of divine judgement, that man cannot be helped in any other way. It is not merely that man lacks something which he ought to be or to have or to be capable of in relation to God. He lacks everything. It is not merely that he is in a dangerous and damaged state, but in his being towards God he is completely finished and impotent. He is not only a sick man but a dead one. It was because the world was lost that Christ was born.[27]

In line with this, Barth must also reject proofs of God's existence which, in the words of Vatican I, 'can be known with certainty from created things, by the natural power of human reason'.[28] The one exception that Barth is prepared to make is Anselm's 'ontological proof'. In his view, the 'proof' arises out of faith while deploying reason in its service; it does not constitute reason as an alternative possibility.[29] Anselm's proof plays an important role in Barth's own thought leading him to develop the *analogia fidei* as an alternative to the *analogia entis*—a Catholic idolatry which he rejects on the same grounds as natural theology.

Against Barth's radical rejection of a 'natural theology' Bouillard argues that God's revelation does not create a world or a history anew, it already presupposes and is homogenous with it:

[26] I discuss the significance of Blondel below, but Pierre Rousselot, SJ (1878–1915) was also significant for Bouillard and the professors of Fourvière. *L'Intellectualisme de Saint Thomas*, originally a thesis for the University of Paris, the most complete edition of which was published in 1936 (Paris: Beauchesne) and 'Les Yeux de la foi', (*RSR*, 1 (1910), 241–59, 444–75) represent a major attempt to break out of the neo-scholastic Thomism of the time. Cf. Gerald McCool, *From Unity to Pluralism: The Internal evolution of Thomism* (New York: Fordham University Press, 1989), 39–58; the book offers a useful context for Catholic thought leading up to the Council. See too, Aidan Nichols, *From Newman to Congar. The Idea of Doctrinal Development from the Victorians to the Second Vatican Council* (Edinburgh: T&T Clark 1990), 195–213; and Avery Dulles, *A History of Apologetics* (New York: Corpus, 1971), 210–12.

[27] *CD* 1.2., 57–8ff, which is also directed at Emil Brunner; *CD* 1.16. 187ff. Also Karl Barth, *Natural Theology—Comprising Nature and Grace by Professor Dr Emil Brunner and the reply No.1 By Dr Karl Barth* (London: The Centenary Press, 1946); H. Bouillard, 'The Problem of Natural Theology as seen by K. Barth and R. Bultmann', *The Logic of Faith*, Ch. 5, 89–114.

[28] First Vatican Council, Dogmatic Constitution on the Catholic Faith, *Dei Filius*, Ch. 2, in Tanner, ii.806.

[29] Karl Barth, *Fides Quaerens intellectum: Anselms Beweis der Existenz Gottes im Zusammenhang seines theologischen Programms* (Munich: Chr. Kaiser Verlag, 1931), 63.

How could we discern the action of God in them (God's acts) if our spiritual being did not possess the power of knowing God, of the Absolute, whose presence is perceptible in our heart of hearts, bore no relation to the God of whom the Bible speaks?...Unless we had a pre-existing apprehension of God (however implicit), we should have no reliable principle to guide us in recognising a divine revelation in a particular event; there would be nothing to justify us in stating that the God of the Bible was, beyond all doubt, our God.[30]

Moreover, our very understanding of scripture and the witness to faith also requires that we have the structures of meaning and the rational capacity to understand them. Otherwise, 'nothing would remain but to read the scriptures and remain silent'.[31]

Barth, of course, had already anticipated this objection in his understanding of the self-attesting nature of the event of revelation. But Bouillard's point is more nuanced. He argues that knowledge of God by faith allows for two possibilities: first, by revelation and grace, and second, as a possibility that is immanent in reason itself. They are not on the same level, nor does it imply that reason can make good any deficiency in the former or substitute for it.[32] According to Bouillard, they function in a different but related way: '... one is conditional on an *event*, and the other is an *a priori*. The former conditions faith as an *event*; the latter conditions it as regards *meaning*.'[33] It is an important distinction which does not imply that natural knowledge of God delivers knowledge of the Trinity etc., but it does point to the way in which natural knowledge of God discloses to us the possibility and ground of our own existence as orientated to the supernatural. In other words, there is a pre-existing apprehension of what we may later come to know as God given in what it is to be human.[34]

According to Bouillard, and critically against Barth, the possibility of 'natural theology' and the role of human subjectivity are also present in Anselm's 'ontological proof'.[35] Bouillard points out that Anselm would not recognize a distinction between dialectic, or reason, and faith. It is faith that makes reason necessary, not the reverse. Not only is Anselm concerned to prove that God exists, he desires to show how such a proposition is true. In other words, he seeks to show that faith possesses a rationality that is universally valid for believer and unbeliever alike. To say that God does not exist is to

---

[30] Bouillard, 'The Problem of Natural Theology', 109; *Knowledge of God*, 27.

[31] *Knowledge of God*, 35.

[32] *Knowledge of God*, 28. 'The natural knowledge of God is not then a sufficient condition for the knowledge of faith' (29).

[33] 'The Problem of Natural Theology', 109.

[34] Cf. *Knowledge of God*, 60; 28.

[35] Cf. *Knowledge of God*, Part II, 'The Proof for the Existence of God'. A very useful exploration of Barth and Bouillard's study of Anselm is Vincent G. Potter, 'Karl Barth and the Ontological Argument', *The Journal of Religion*, 45/4 (1965), 309–25.

think the unthinkable. Yet there is more at stake here, because faith requires not only intellectual assent but consent. What makes the difference is not only revelation but a living faith that consents to it. For the believer, Anselm's argument is compelling and meaningful, but for the unbeliever it remains an empty formal exercise. Bouillard holds that Anselm's recognition of this is found in his *Epistola de Incarnatione Verbi*, Chapter 2, where he argues that we need the personal experience of God to bring our understanding alive. It is the Augustinian principle of *credo ut intelligam*. It may appear as if Bouillard has arrived at a position at least similar to Barth if not the same as it. The central point for Bouillard is that the structure of Anselm's argument is both philosophical and theological; the *intellectus fidei* is incorporated into a rational endeavour.[36]

For Bouillard, Anselm gives an important lead in showing that, even for the unbeliever, reason can shape a true idea of God. He accepts, however, that faith is a living relationship; it cannot be an agreement with logic or propositions only. Faith is the living personal relationship which takes place between God and the human person, and as such it is mediated in human existence and history, 'the relationship between man and God is not simply that about which there is truth, but that through which there is truth concerning man and God'.[37] The lived reality of faith creates a hermeneutic.

> But note that these signs are not the middle term in a line of reasoning that would inevitably lead to the conclusion that God has actually revealed himself. They are the place or juncture in which we experience, the transparency (so to speak) in which we perceive, the revelation God is making to us. ... We do not reason from the signs to the revelation; we read the revelation in the signs.[38]

For Bouillard, whenever we are confronted with 'the logic of faith' we are also confronted with the meaning of our own existence and purpose. There is always a call to 'conversion'. This is not a loss of liberty or reason but it uncovers that their fulfilment lie in the relationship of faith and in the act of adoration. Here reason and faith describe a life which lives in freedom and love: 'Liberty is the image of God; it recognises him in the act through which it consents to become his image. Its internal logic becomes evident in its openness to salvation.'[39]

---

[36] Bouillard, *The Knowledge of God*, 75ff; Potter, 'Karl Barth and the Ontological Argument', 315. For useful background to the significance of 'reason' or 'dialectic' in medieval thought, and the significance of Anselm as an innovator in its use within theology, see Edward Grant, *God and Reason in the Middle Ages* (Cambridge: Cambridge University Press, 2001), 53–6.

[37] *The Knowledge of God*, 95.

[38] *The Logic of Faith*, 17.

[39] *Knowledge of God*, 95. For a comprehensive and challenging exposition and defence of Barth cf. T. F. Torrance, 'The Problem of Natural Theology in the Thought of Karl Barth', *Religious Studies*, 6/2 (1970), 121–35, especially his critical appreciation of Bouillard's argument (134–5)

HUMAN FREEDOM AND DIVINE PRESENCE,
THE LOGIC OF EXISTENCE

One of the distinguishing characteristics of Bouillard's thought is its willing-ness to engage with other thinkers and systems.[40] Heidegger and Weil are examples of secular philosophical minds which attracted his attention, but Bouillard is also indebted to Christian philosophers such as Gabriel Marcel and especially Maurice Blondel. Marcel is important for the ways in which he is able to articulate and ground the situatedness of human existence and uncover its rationale in 'a mysticism of presence'.[41] In developing a Christian existentialism and also offering a critique of Sartre, Marcel develops the idea of our participation in the mystery of being. Whereas Sartre largely understands freedom in terms of autonomy expressed in choice, Marcel stresses the whole phenomenon of participation.[42] Indeed, it is the very relational nature of our freedom that discloses being and is recognized as mystery, 'mystery … is something in which I am involved; its essence, therefore, is not entirely in front of me. It is as if in that particular zone the distinction *in me* and *in front of me* loses significance.'[43] For Bouillard, this is the way in which the human person already lives within the supernatural which is not something accidental to human existence but grounds it in freedom and love. Marcel's position does not demand adherence to Christianity but it does prepare the way for it.[44]

Maurice Blondel is, perhaps, the most significant contemporary thinker for Bouillard, and his thought exercises the most influence on his work. This is well evidenced by the number of essays on Blondel that Bouillard produced during his career.[45] In his seminal philosophical work, *L'Action* and later in the controversial *Lettre sur l'apologétique*, Blondel develops what was to become known as the 'method of immanence'. As Bouillard explains, Blondel begins with the question that Christianity itself poses: If its claims are true then they must be reflected in human nature:

[40] As well as Barth and Bultmann, Bouillard also offered studies on Kierkegaard and Schleiermacher. Cf. 'Faith According to Kierkegaard', Part II.3 of *The Logic of Faith*; 'Liminare: Schleiermacher', *Archives de philosophie*, 32 (1969) 5–8; and *Vérité du Christianisme*, 85–8.
[41] *The Logic of Faith*, 144–6. It is also attractive to Bouillard because of the openness of Marcel's system of thought. Cf. *The Logic of Faith*, 159.
[42] Bouillard, 'Le mystère de l'être dans la pensée de Gabriel Marcel', in *Logique de Foi* 149–67 (163–4). Cf. J. Maritain, *Du Régime Temporel et De La Liberté* (Paris: Desclée de Brouwer, 1934); Jean Mourroux's influential *La Liberté chrétienne* (Paris: Aubier, 1966), originally published as a study, *Sens chrètien de l'homme*, 1946.
[43] *The Logic of Faith*, 151, citing Marcel.
[44] *The Logic of Faith*, 154.
[45] Cf. his major study, *Blondel et le christianisme* (Paris: Seuil 1961); ET: *Blondel and Christianity*, trans. James M. Somerville (Washington: Corpus Books, 1969). The most succinct treatment is in *The Logic of Faith*, 161–185.

[T]he obligation imposed from without must be paralleled by the existence within
of a need and the urge to satisfy it and the expectation or the hope that it will be
satisfied. If it is necessary for man to accept the supernatural proclaimed in the
Christian message, man's being must surely have some sign upon it to show that
this is so.[46]

It should be possible to discover this through reflection upon ourselves and
our acts. This is the proper work of philosophy; even though philosophy can
and must retain its own autonomy, it can also uncover the conditions for a
genuine understanding of the *humanum* which is already orientated to Christian life and truth. Through his complex analysis of the human action, and the
difference between what we intend (*volonté voulante*) and what we actually do
(*volonté voulue*), Blondel opens the way for the supernatural. In our experience of this difference we are constantly immersed in the reality of our finite
existence; we are always discovering that we are not and cannot be self-
sufficient. To attain our end we need resources beyond those which we can
provide from ourselves. This 'crisis' requires of us a realization—noetic and
practical—that we draw from a source 'from which springs the very dialectic
whose whole purpose is to bring us back to it'.[47] In this way Blondel exposes
the paradox of human existence: 'the *indispensible* condition for the consummation of human action is *inaccessible* to human action'.[48] Thus emerges from
our reflection and in our experience what Bouillard, interpreting Blondel,
names 'the undetermined supernatural'.[49] Philosophy can at least show its
logical necessity, but our actual response in faith confirms it in history and
existence. 'Blondel's philosophy paves the way for the Christian faith, because
it discloses that the internal logic of human action is, fundamentally, identical
with the internal logic of Christianity.'[50]

It would be an easy misreading of Blondel to think that if the supernatural is
necessary then we have made it natural, thereby undermining its character as
grace. Bouillard's defence of Blondel is important because it is clearly a defence
against the critics of his own position. The necessity of the supernatural does
not undermine the freedom of God's self-gift because it does not require that
God *ought* to give himself, rather that the human person ought to accept it.
Although God is not compelled to reveal himself, the presence of the supernatural means that the possibility of our receiving it is already given. Moreover, the very fact that Blondel has uncovered the logic of finite existence—
that we cannot provide for ourselves the conditions of our own fulfilment—
means that we must also recognize that revelation cannot originate with us. It

---

[46] Bouillard, *The Logic of Faith*, 166.
[47] *The Logic of Faith*, 173, 174, citing Blondel.
[48] *The Logic of Faith*, 166.
[49] *The Logic of Faith*, 179.
[50] *The Logic of Faith*, 181.

can only originate in God. There is always for Bouillard, as for Blondel, the necessity of faith which opens us to the full understanding of this. Philosophy does not absolve us of the *fiat* of faith, freely responding to the offer that God makes of himself. Philosophy can never substitute for the personal relationship that faith is.[51]

A central concern for *ressourcement* theologians was to find a theology adequate to the intellectual and cultural situation of contemporary European society. In Blondel, Bouillard recognized that he had found a Christian philosopher whose intention was like his own: to say something meaningful to those who feel they can no longer believe.[52] When we regard the various strands of Bouillard's thought over the years, we can see the way in which this was always a central concern. It also gives coherence to the wide range of his dialogue with contemporary thinkers. For this reason, Bouillard's thought is significant in the development of the school of fundamental theology which has come to replace the pre-conciliar apologetics.[53] Ultimately for him, as for the other theologians of the *ressourcement*, faith is always a *credere in Deum*— a movement of love, a living relationship which cannot be reduced to an adherence to propositions important though they may be in articulating the structure of that movement.[54] This is why, even within the academic analysis and discussion, there is also a sense of a spiritual vision, an aesthetic, which aims to captivate the heart as well as the mind. This explains how there is coherence, not only in Bouillard's thinking, but in his living out of a sacrificial obedience to religious and ecclesiastical authorities. In the Council, especially in the Constitutions *Dei Verbum* and *Gaudium et Spes*, Bouillard could recognize that his work had been received.[55]

---

[51] Bouillard, *The Logic of Faith*, 180.

[52] Bouillard, *Comprendre ce que l'on croit* (Paris: Aubier, 1971), 9, 97ff. Also supported by Karl Rahner's observations at a conference given in Paris in 1965: 'la théologie d'aujourd'hui et de demain devra se faire théologie du dialogue avec les hommes qui ne pensent pas pouvoir croire.' 'La situation actuelle de la théologie en Allemagne, conférence donnée à Paris le 28 février 1965', in *Recherches et Débats*, 1965 (cahier 51), 224.

[53] Cf. Claude Geffré, *Un Nouvel âge de la théologie* (Paris: Cerf, 1972); Jean-Pierre Torrell, 'New Problems in Fundamental Theology in the Postconciliar Period', in René Latourelle and Gerald O'Collins (eds.), *Problems and Perspectives in Fundamental Theology* (New York: Paulist Press 1982), 11–22. In this regard, Bouillard's works stand comparison with Rahner and Lonergan. Cf. Bernard Lonergan, *Insight: A Study in Human Understanding* (London: Darton, Longman & Todd, 1958); *Method in Theology* (London: Darton, Longman & Todd, 1972) for his reservation about Bouillard's position in *Conversion*; *Grace and Freedom: Operative Grace in the Thought of Thomas Aquinas, The Collected Works of Bernard Lonergan*, eds. Frederick E. Crowe and Robert M. Doran (Toronto: University of Toronto Press, 2005), 25–6, n. 17.

[54] Cf. Henri de Lubac, *Méditation sur l'Eglise* (Paris: Aubier, 1953), 25. Scully summarizes Bouillard's indebtedness: to Blondel, heteronomy as the true condition for autonomy; to Marcel, faith's participation in mystery; and to Kierkegaard, faith as relationships between persons. *Grace and Human Freedom*, 163.

[55] Cf. Bouillard's discussion of Vatican II's recovery of the wider and deeper tradition of the church's teaching on revelation which, he argued, had been obscured by Vatican I, in 'Révelation

SOME CONCLUDING OBSERVATIONS

Vatican II is, by any standards, an extraordinary council in the history of the whole church.[56] Its effects still continue to shape the life of the Catholic Church, especially in its relations with other faiths and the contemporary secular world. In many ways it represents a paradigm shift in theology and ecclesial life. Like any such shift, it creates a sense of disorientation as well as new possibilities. The church is, I believe, still in the process of appropriating the Council, which must include a better understanding of the theological vision out of which they come. This requires less rhetoric about a naive polemical distinction between the hermeneutics of continuity and discontinuity and a deeper grasp of the dynamic hermeneutic of *ressourcement*. The study of Bouillard's work together with the other theologians of the *ressourcement* movement provides us with an understanding of the ideas that inform the Council and the method and theology that is still necessary for its appropriation. Without this, we risk misreading the Council, distorting its achievements, and failing to use the resources it provides in meeting the challenges that continue to face the church on its journey in and through history.

It is clear that the working out of the relationship between nature and grace which enriches and deepens our account of human subjectivity and historical existence underlies much of the Council's teaching. We can see the ways in which Bouillard and others prepare the ground for this. If modernity is marked by a turn to the subject, the anthropocentric turn, it is evident that the thinkers who inform the Council gave the church the resources to meet this turn on its own terms. If the human subject really applies reflective reason to his or her own intellectual, personal, and social acts, if he or she really makes the journey into their own consciousness and existence, then they will encounter neither a solipsistic self nor the ultimate *aporia* of a chance existence. They will come to the mystery of their own finitude, not a barren limit which frustrates human desire, but precisely the movement which opens to an infinite personal Love in whose image they are made; they will come, in one way or another, to the person of Jesus Christ and the mystery of the church. With the Enlightenment, the Catholic tradition recognizes that reason is an indispensable tool in uncovering this truth. But it also recognizes that reason itself must stand in the presence of a Truth which it cannot measure or exhaust.

---

et Histoire', *Vérité du Christianisme*, 183–98. The two essays, 'Le Sens de l'apologétique', *Bulletin du comité des études de la Compagnie de Saint-Suplice*, 35 (1961), 311–26; and 'Plan d'un cours d'apologétique', *Bulletin du comité des études de la Compagnie de Saint-Suplice*, 35 (1961), 449–52 (both reproduced in *The Logic of Faith*), read remarkably like the agenda for the work of the Council, an agenda to which it responds in a number of its major Constitutions.

[56] Cf. John W. O'Malley, *What Happened at Vatican II* (Cambridge MA: Harvard University Press, 2008).

In Vatican II the church completes the work of Vatican I precisely by responding to the Enlightenment and secular modernity. It develops a conceptual sophistication and recovers a theological richness to engage the questions of modernity and show where its search must proceed. In doing so, the Council opens up possibilities for new humanism which is grounded in Christ, committed to rationality and the possibility of object truth, while embracing the complexity of human historicity. In such a way can it respond to the questions of post-modernity, recognizing what is worth preserving in its insights and those of modernity as well. With such a task, the church can show itself as offering the deepest service to humanity in conserving and deepening our understanding of what it is to be human. It can ground human freedom intellectually and existentially in history, and show how the human subject is a genuine agent in creating culture in pursuit of the lasting human good, which also cherishes and conserves the creation confirmed and sanctified by the Incarnation and Resurrection. The theology that informs the Council, like the Council itself, is a work in progress. *Ressourcement* is not a position achieved but a task to be undertaken. Above all, it offers a theology which is imbued with an awareness of the immanence of God in the world, secured by the Incarnation of Christ and the indwelling Spirit.

Not only in its explicit teaching but in the theological vision that informs it, the Council offers a self-understanding that is not simply about our historical situatedness but about our vocation to create a history that truly reflects the truth of our nature. The universal call to holiness is a call to sanctify history with our lives lived in loving obedience to God's will made known in Christ. It indicates, too, the way in which the church's soteriological mission has concrete consequences in building and renewing those social, political, and international structures which can sustain human flourishing. The drama of our freedom has a purpose. It is given that we may accept the invitation to life that awaits us. In Bouillard's words, 'the true fulfilment of liberty consists of communion with God. "For all things are yours", says St Paul, "whether the world or life or death or the present or the future, all are yours; and you are Christ's; and Christ's is God's." (I Cor. 3:21–3).'[57]

---

[57] Bouillard, *The Logic of Faith*, 56.

18

Balthasar and *Ressourcement*: An Ambiguous Relationship

Edward T. Oakes, SJ

INTRODUCTION

Any discussion of Hans Urs von Balthasar's debt to the *ressourcement* movement of French Catholic theology in the middle of the twentieth century must first take into account the rich irony embedded inside this controversial movement, indeed inside the very word itself. The French coinage *ressourcement* is best translated into English by the phrase 'return to the sources'. Now, at first glance it would seem that no activity could possibly be more traditional, even traditiona*list*, than a return to the sources *of* the very tradition that traditionalists claim to be defending. After all, what good is tradition if those who live inside it are unfamiliar with its sources?

The irony, of course, is that the opponents of this new attention to the sources of Christian tradition accused its advocates of representing something not traditional at all but rather something *newfangled*. Hence their accusation that *ressourcement* was really, deep-down, *une nouvelle théologie*, and for that reason to be suspected of implicit affinities with Modernism. ('Modern' is itself a word rooted in the Latin word for recent or new; and once this so-called Modernism was condemned as a heresy, accusations that a theology was 'new' could be difficult to shake off.) The situation is certainly peculiar: by calling for a *ressourcement*, the advocates of this movement clearly signalled their *intention* to be traditional; but they were *perceived* by their opponents as innovators. How did things come to such a pass?

This debate, as it happens, was but one skirmish in a centuries-long battle over how Western civilization should come to terms with its past, a debate that flared into literal warfare during the French Revolution. In the decades leading up to that epochal event, a fierce—though for a while, entirely academic—debate arose between defenders of ancient cultural norms and those of a modernity just coming into view. This was the famous *querelle entre les anciens et les modernes* that animated French culture for a good part of the eighteenth century.[1] In the early days of the French Revolution this debate was re-cast in the now conventional terms of left and right, from the accident that the Girondists (who advocated a moderate, property-based revolution) sat to the right of the main aisle in the French National Assembly, with the Jacobins (who wanted to abolish the monarchy entirely) to the left.

Labels such as Girondist and Jacobin do not carry much resonance today, but the contemporary idioms for left and right—liberal and conservative—do very much continue to resonate, often with confusing effect. As protean as these terms surely are, their respective etymologies can begin to highlight the fundamental difference between these two points of view: their different evaluations of the past, that is, of tradition. 'Liberal' is rooted in the Latin word *liber*, 'free', here meaning a desire to be free from the past. ('Progressive' also implies the same thing, since it refers to a progress towards the future, that is, away from the past.) 'Conservatives', of course, want to conserve at least some aspects of the past.

The question, though, is *which* past is one trying to flee or conserve? And that question brings us to the heart of our question: why did *ressourcement* provoke such opposition from those who claimed for themselves the traditionalist mantle? To answer that question, it helps to cast a brief glance away from theology as an academic discipline for a moment and look first at debates raging inside religious, cultural, and political conservatism, broadly conceived.

THE PROJECTS OF CONSERVATION

Catholic traditionalists of the Chesterbelloc school, for example, point to the Middle Ages, especially the thirteenth century (that 'most glorious of centuries'[2]), as the high point from which later history represents a sad decline. T. S. Eliot represents the Anglo-Catholic sub-species of this affinity for the past, only he located the Golden Age in the seventeenth century, the age of the Metaphysical Poets, when churchmen like Lancelot Andrewes and Archbishop Laud governed an Established Church of dignified and majestic worship and from which Romanticism brought about a sad decline.

Political varieties of conservatism often appeal to the nineteenth century, when *laissez-faire* capitalism reigned and technology came into its own,

---

[1] See Joan DeJean, *Ancients against Moderns: Culture Wars and the Making of a Fin de Siècle* (Chicago: University of Chicago Press, 1997); also Hyppolyte Rigault, *Histoire de la querelle des anciens et des modernes* (Paris: Adamant, 2001).

[2] As in James Joseph Walsh, *The Thirteenth, Greatest of Centuries* (New York: Catholic Summer School Press, 1912).

apotheosized in the Crystal Palace exhibition hall built in London in 1850. Unfortunately for those who like these protean terms to stay put, *this* kind of conservatism often goes under the name of 'liberalism' in Europe (because its advocates want to keep the economy 'free' of governmental interference), whereas in America liberals are usually understood as advocates of more governmental regulation of the economy. But some of those erstwhile pro-government liberals, at least in America, noted the failure of the welfare state to conquer poverty and its attendant pathologies and thereby earned the name of 'neo-conservatives'. Thus, to some old-style conservatives, new converts to the cause can seem like a Trojan horse, since these neo-conservatives might be less than forthright in defence of ancient norms over modern ones.

This taxonomy, sketchy as it necessarily is, helps us to understand why the *ressourcement* movement was perceived by anti-Modernist theologians like Réginald Garrigou-Lagrange and other neo-Thomists (the neo in that appellation is telling) as an innovation: because over against the hard-won clarities of the manual Thomists, which had been hammered out in the fight against Modernism, this new attention to Christian sources *did* strike them as something new—and threatening.[3]

HISTORICAL AND ABSOLUTE TRUTH

At its deepest level, the debate over (theological) Modernism in late nineteenth- and early twentieth-century Catholic theology centred on the role of history over the perennial truth of revelation.[4] Here is the problem: if what revelation reveals is true absolutely, how can that absolute truth be true of one

---

[3] 'Crucial was the fact that nineteenth-century Catholic historiography generally did not deal with Christian origins.' John Ratté, *Three Modernists* (New York: Sheed & Ward, 1967), 11. Crucial, too, was the condemnation of so-called 'Americanism', which in its technical meaning refers to a canonical 'heresy' that attempted to hand control of American parishes to a lay board. But its broader meaning extends to a suspicion of American culture *tout court*, particularly of its own home-grown philosophy of pragmatism, which was perceived by its European opponents as a philosophy that defined truth as a mere coping mechanism. Recent research has uncovered the French Modernists' debt to American pragmatism: see David G. Schultenover, SJ (ed.), *The Reception of Pragmatism in France & the Rise of Roman Catholic Modernism: 1880–1914* (Washington DC: Catholic University of America Press, 2009). See also his *A View from Rome: On the Eve of the Modernist Crisis* (The Bronx NY: Fordham University Press, 1993), 39–61.

[4] 'Modernism could fairly be defined as the attempt to synthesize the basic truths of religion and the methods and assumptions of modern thought, *using the latter as necessary and proper criteria*. ... And since Christianity is an historical religion, claiming that certain alleged historical events are of vital significance for the relations of God and men, a special problem will be that of determining the historicity of its original traditions by the light of historical criticism.' Bernard M. G. Reardon, *Roman Catholic Modernism* (Stanford CA: Stanford University Press, 1970), 9, emphasis added.

era and not of another? If the doctrine of the Immaculate Conception, for example, was a matter of debate in the thirteenth century (with Thomas Aquinas denying it), but infallibly defined in the nineteenth, what does that say about its eternal truth value?

John Henry Newman, who did so much to alert the theological world to the historical development of doctrine—and who, for just that reason, was regarded with corresponding suspicion by anti-Modernists in the early twentieth century—caught the problem exactly in his sermon 'Faith and Doubt' delivered soon after his reception into the Catholic Church:

> I must insist upon this: faith implies a confidence in a man's mind, that the thing believed is really true; but, if it is once true it never can be false. If it is true that God became man, what is the meaning of my anticipating a time when perhaps I shall not believe that God became man? This is nothing short of anticipating a time when I shall disbelieve a truth....If at present I have no doubt whatever about it, then I am but asking leave to fall into error; if at present I have doubts about it, then I do not believe it at present, that is, I have not faith. ... I may love by halves, I may obey by halves; I cannot believe by halves: either I have faith, or I have it not.[5]

Against this initially plausible defence of the perennial truth of revelation, however, other considerations came to the fore, especially historical studies in the changes in world views from one era of history to another, such as the shift from geocentrism to heliocentrism in the seventeenth century. An examination of these shifts led scholars to see that it would have been impossible for, say, Thomas Aquinas to have been a heliocentrist in the thirteenth century, especially given his reverence for the authority of Aristotle's physics. Then the question naturally arose: to what extent, then, is Thomas to be understood solely within the framework of the medieval world view shared by all his contemporaries (and one correlatively impossible for moderns to share) in contrast to those perennial truths he managed to enunciate?

One fascinating skirmish in this battle concerns the attempt by the French Dominican Marie-Dominique Chenu to set up a programme of studies for young Dominicans in their priory in Le Saulchoir, a programme specifically designed to study Thomas's thirteenth-century roots and presuppositions, a plan of studies that was placed on the Index of Forbidden Books at the instigation of Chenu's fellow Dominican, Garrigou-Lagrange.[6] This episode

[5] Newman, 'Faith and Doubt', *Discourses Addressed to Mixed Congregations* (London: Longmans, Green, 1916), 216–17.
[6] The story is told by Fergus Kerr, *Twentieth-Century Catholic Theologians: From Neoscholasticism to Nuptial Mysticism* (Oxford: Blackwell, 2007), 17–33. Chenu's book placed on the Index was Le *Saulchoir* (1937), reprinted as *Une école* (1985) among whose provocative statements is this one: 'The institution and the doctrine are closely allied with one another, in the inspiration that carried the one and the other into a new age' (*Une école*, 149; author's translation).

highlights how at least some anti-Modernists saw that any historicization of a perennial philosopher and theologian like Aquinas would be deeply threatening to their anti-Modernist project.[7] This is why they held that any undue attention to original sources preceding (or even coinciding with!) the medieval synthesis of Thomas constituted, for them, an innovation: because it threatened to make perennial truth relative to the age in which it was formulated. Thus, a 'conservative' (and certainly a traditional) return to the sources came to be seen as a stalking horse for Modernist relativization.[8]

BALTHASAR AMIDST THE *RESSOURCEMENT*

Hans Urs von Balthasar (1905–88) finds himself caught in this same bind: on the one hand, many liberal theologians see him as too conservative, precisely for rooting his thought in the sources of the tradition,[9] while on the other he is regarded with deep suspicion by many Catholics on the traditionalist right for

---

[7] And not without good reason either: 'Since the 1920s some of the most creative theologians of the day, mostly French Jesuits teaching at Lyon, and their pupils had begun to rediscover the older Church Fathers, in particular Greek Fathers such as Clement of Alexandria, Origen, and Gregory of Nyssa, but also Augustine. Theologians such as Henri de Lubac and Hans Urs von Balthasar were able to write theological treatises displaying a depth but also a liveliness almost unknown for a century because—without thereby in any way denying the importance of Thomas—they had studied and written about these older theologians, who were certainly much less systematic than Aquinas but much closer to the words of Holy Scripture than were his writings. All in all, then, considering the ecclesiastical side of the development, it may have been not so much the influence of modern philosophy that called Thomism into question but rather the return to Scripture and the rediscovery of the relevance of the classical Fathers of the Church.' Nicholas Lobkowicz, 'What Happened to Thomism? From *Aeterni Patris* to *Vaticanum Secundum*', *American Catholic Philosophical Quarterly*, 69 (1995), 397–425 (416). Thus, *nouvelle théologie* was in no sense anti-Thomist, but it did threaten a certain *kind* of Thomism: 'If the *nouvelle théologie* is in any sense a movement, therefore, it cannot simply be characterized as anti-Thomist, much less as some sort of Jesuit ambush on Thomism.... [Its target was] a monolithic *neo*-Thomism which had become as remote from contemporary concerns and the needs of the twentieth-century church as it was arguably distant from the spirit of Thomas himself.' A. N. Williams, 'The Future of the Past: The Contemporary Significance of the *Nouvelle Théologie*', *IJST*, 7 (2005), 347–61 (349).

[8] This same accusation continues to be voiced: 'Thomistic philosophy has passed from being nourished upon historical reflections to being devoured by them.... The retreat of Thomism from the cultural arena began the day that the primacy of philosophic *eros* and *habitus* was suppressed as secondary to historical learning.' Steven A. Long, 'Nicholas Lobkowicz and the Historicist Inversion of Thomistic Philosophy', *The Thomist*, 62 (1988), 41–75 (42, 55). The clash between the Lobkowicz and Long articles neatly captures what is at stake in this issue of perennial truth vs. history.

[9] 'For many years he has done battle with a sharp tongue against certain post-conciliar trends in the Church in order to uncover in them numerous hidden ambiguities and inclinations which would "lighten the ballast of what is Christian".' Medard Kehl, 'Hans Urs von Balthasar: A Portrait', in Medard Kehl and Werner Löser (eds.), *The Von Balthasar Reader*, trans. Robert J. Daly and Fred Lawrence (New York: Crossroad: 1982), 1–54 (4).

his alleged innovations, such as his holding out hope for universal redemption and for his theology of Christ's descent into hell on Holy Saturday. Prescinding from these particular issues, at least this much can be said about his relation to the past: unlike so many self-styled traditionalists, he actually knows the tradition.[10]

Under that rubric, Balthasar can be regarded as perhaps the premier representative of the *ressourcement* school. First of all, he studied his pre-ordination theology in the late 1930s at the French Jesuit theologate at Lyon-Fourvière under Jesuit scholars, especially Henri de Lubac, who were at the time beginning their renowned series *Sources chrétiennes*, from which came the moniker *ressourcement*.[11] But even as a theology student awaiting ordination to the priesthood—and young scholar though he was—he was publishing his own monographs on Origen, Gregory of Nyssa, and Maximus the Confessor. Furthermore, his publishing firm *Johannes Verlag* later went on to publish de Lubac's complete works in German translation, most of them prepared by Balthasar himself.[12]

For these and other reasons, no competent scholar would wish to deny Balthasar's deep debt to the *ressourcement* theologians, especially de Lubac. He certainly was not shy in dismissing traditionalists' accusations that *ressourcement* meant something new and therefore nefarious, just because it appeared to be new to them.[13] Once that is conceded, though, the real question becomes

---

[10] 'One may call his attitude "conservative" in the sense that he attempts to "conserve" a tradition which he, unlike so many who claim the title, thoroughly knows.' Louis Dupré, 'Hans Urs von Balthasar's Theology of Aesthetic Form', *TS*, 49 (1988), 219–318 (315).

[11] 'In Lyons during my theological studies, it was the encounter with Henri de Lubac that decided the direction of my studies.' Balthasar, *My Work in Retrospect*, trans. Brian McNeil (San Francisco: Ignatius Press, 1993), 89.

[12] 'We were a fine group [at Lyon], resolute and exposed, and it was clear to us from the beginning that the bastions of anxiety that the Church had contrived to protect herself from the world would have to be demolished; the Church had to be freed to become herself and open to the whole and undivided world for her mission. For the meaning of Christ's coming is to save the *world* and to open for the whole of it the way to the Father.... This passion rallied us young theologians in Lyons (Fessard, Bouillard, Daniélou and many others) around our older friend and master Henri de Lubac, from whom we gained an understanding of the Greek Fathers, the philosophical mysticism of Asia and the phenomenon of modern atheism; to him my patristic studies owe their initial spark. For patristics meant to us a Christendom that still carried its thoughts into the limitless space of the nations and still trusted in the world's salvation. At that time, I conceived the plan of a closely woven trilogy on the writings of Origen, Gregory of Nyssa and Maximus the Confessor, of which unfortunately only fragments were completed. This passion made the radiance of de Lubac's *Catholicisme* a fundamental book for us, and I translated it shortly afterward.' Balthasar, *Retrospect*, 48–9.

[13] 'De Lubac's work [*Catholicism*] was a tapestry, a composition formed of selections from unknown Church Fathers and from the great theology of the saints—actually the oldest theology, which could only appear as *nouvelle théologie* to certain reactionaries. And as for his *Surnaturel*, for which he had to languish in the *Caves du Vatican* for decades, it was nothing else but the simple recovery of an important aspect of Augustine and Aquinas.' Balthasar, *Test Everything, Hold Fast to What Is Good: an Interview with Hans Urs von Balthasar by Angelo Scola*, trans. Maria Shrady (San Francisco: Ignatius Press, 1989), 14.

what exactly Balthasar drew from the *ressourcement* theologians and above all what use he made of their legacy.

BALTHASAR AS THE EXEMPLARY
RESSOURCEMENT THEOLOGIAN

Perhaps the first point to note is that Balthasar had no patience for that dreamy nostalgia that sees in the return to sources the solution to all problems in modern theology. In fact, he disdained such daydreaming. I do not mean to imply that other prominent exponents of *ressourcement* theology were themselves vapidly nostalgic towards the Christian past. But in Balthasar one finds far more explicit warnings against romanticizing the era of the Church Fathers, as here:

> The greatest and for later times the most decisive and consequential encounter [between Hellenism and Christianity] took place in Alexandria, especially in that greatest genius, next to Augustine, of the patristic era: Origen. We can no longer deny that in his case and despite his unbending will to be and to remain an authentic Christian, not only the outer words but also the basic forms of Hellenism had penetrated into the inner realm of Christianity and to a great extent established itself there from then on because of the unique influence of this giant of the spirit.... It is not so much a question of certain individual doctrines that worked their way inside (such as, for example, his doctrine of the pre-existence of souls), which could easily be declared heretical upon their enunciation, as it was much more a question of the inner space of the spirit, a whole tissue of assumptions from time immemorial that are not easy to get hold of, an atmosphere, a formal methodology.[14]

Origen could be condemned easily enough because his Platonism led to explicit doctrines clearly at odds with the biblical world view. But for Balthasar, the problem was more pervasive than that, and shows up in the way that some Fathers shy away from the radical meaning of the incarnation, especially the Alexandrians.

> The incarnation is almost looked on by the Alexandrians as a 'distortion' of the purely spiritual into its polar opposite, matter, a distortion that was necessary for pedagogical and salvation-historical reasons in order to capture the distance of the material world from God and gradually lead it back to the realm of the spiritual and divine by a reverse movement. Origen's myth of the pre-existence of souls and his idea that the material world is a consequence of the fall of sin shows this conceptual schema (that in many places is muffled and only latently present)

---

[14] Balthasar, 'Patristik, Scholastik, und Wir', *Theologie der Zeit*, 3 (1939), 65–104 (85).

in its most bare-faced and, as such, in its most heterodox form. But even where this myth is quite lacking, as in Clement, Athanasius, Gregory of Nyssa, and Maximus, the direction their thought takes towards it is still present. In this schema the incarnation must appear as something provisional and transitional. The resurrection of the flesh, formally confessed and maintained, appears like a disturbance of the systematic lines and usually was subtilized in one or another form.[15]

What is so fascinating about this passage is that Balthasar criticizes some of the very figures to whom he had already devoted important monographs in his years at Fourvière. He also shows a similar caution towards de Lubac's theology of grace, a point insufficiently noted by most Balthasar scholars. Now, Balthasar never developed a specific doctrine of grace and nature,[16] so one must cull both his debt to and his divergence from de Lubac by taking note of some remarks he made in passing to drive home other points. As to the basics of de Lubac's own doctrine, Balthasar certainly voices his assent, but often with important nuances, as here:

> With *Surnaturel*, a young David comes onto the field against the Goliath of the modern rationalization and reduction to logic of the Christian mystery. The sling deals a death blow to this giant, but Goliath's acolytes seize upon the champion and reduce him to silence for a long time. *Not entirely without justification.* The work, pieced together from many disparate preparatory studies, is not completely rounded out.[17]

No one doubts that when de Lubac published *Surnaturel* in 1946, he irrevocably altered the Thomist understanding of grace. Even more, he changed Thomism itself, which now gives Thomas priority of place over his later commentators by embedding him in the patristic tradition he knew so well. Finally, and most crucially, the human person is now seen as inherently open to the supernatural. No longer is grace seen as 'topping out' nature, like icing atop a layer cake. Unfortunately, de Lubac had made his case so convincingly that problems soon followed in his overpowering wake, which is perhaps what Balthasar meant by claiming that *Surnaturel* is not fully rounded out. For after Vatican II, grace came to be seen as so intrinsic to the human person that the supernatural gifts of revelation and the church and its sacraments seemed, at best, merely symbolic reminders of an already realized redemption.

Writing over a decade before the opening of that epochal council, that is, in his seminal ecumenical classic, *The Theology of Karl Barth*, Balthasar spotted

---

[15] Balthasar, 'Patristik, Scholastik, und Wir', 87–8.

[16] In my first interview with him in 1983 when I was beginning research on my doctoral dissertation in Basel, he told me, *Ich habe keine Gnadenlehre*: 'I have no doctrine on grace.'

[17] Balthasar, *The Theology of Henri de Lubac: An Overview*, trans. Joseph Fessio, SJ and Michael Waldstein (San Francisco: Ignatius Press, 1991), 63; emphasis added.

the central difficulty in de Lubac's position and even affirmed that Karl Rahner (usually perceived as Balthasar's main rival in post-Vatican II Catholic theology) was essentially correct in his assessment of de Lubac's fatal ambiguity.[18] True enough, both Balthasar and Rahner agree with the central result of de Lubac's research:

> Rahner begins by agreeing with most of de Lubac's basic positions. Yes, we must reject the older 'extrinsicism' that made grace seem like some accidental appendage of a nature already well constituted in itself. Rejected too, as religiously dangerous, was the presupposition that one could in the concrete order neatly divide the realm of nature from that of grace.[19]

But there lurks a problem in this verdict that there is no such thing as pure nature in the concrete order, a verdict shared by nearly everyone familiar with this debate, including Garrigou-Lagrange![20] But as Garrigou-Lagrange was well aware, the point can be overstressed, leading to further antinomies down the road; and on that point, if on no other, Balthasar and Rahner are agreed too, with Garrigou-Lagrange, and against de Lubac:

> But Rahner is anxious to avoid the ultimate conclusions that de Lubac draws from these premises. He asks: Is man's inner orientation to grace so constitutive of his 'nature' that the latter (as pure nature) cannot be conceived apart from grace, and thus that the concept of pure nature is unusable? Can grace then still be seen as undeserved? If we make this connection between a nature fulfilled only by grace and grace itself, then Rahner feels we have levelled the two orders, somehow making grace a requirement of nature. Why? Because we have fused the gratuity of creation and the gratuitous grace of God's self-revelation of the divine

---

[18] 'The question is simply whether de Lubac's theory, certainly Catholic in its basic intention, can hold up when all its implications are thought through to their logical conclusion. And so we see Catholic theology necessarily moving towards a reflection on de Lubac's theses. While most Catholic theologians who caviled at de Lubac's intentions misconstrued and distorted his starting point, *Karl Rahner*, it seems, was the only one to subject his thought to a competent, careful, informed critique.' Balthasar, *The Theology of Karl Barth: Exposition and Interpretation*, trans. Edward T. Oakes, SJ (San Francisco: Ignatius Press, 1992), 297–8.

[19] Balthasar, *Barth*, 298.

[20] 'All theologians agree that this state of pure nature never existed.' Réginald Garrigou-Lagrange, OP, *Grace: Commentary on the* Summa Theologica *of St. Thomas, Ia IIae, q.109–14*, trans. by the Dominican Nuns of Corpus Christi Monastery of Menlo Park, California (St Louis MO: B. Herder, 1952), 23. Nor, for that matter, did de Lubac, despite what his critics claimed, deny the *theoretical* possibility of pure nature: 'It is said that a universe might have existed in which man, though without necessarily excluding any other desire, would have his rational ambitions limited to some lower, purely human, beatitude. *Certainly I do not deny it.* But having said that, one is obliged to admit—indeed one is automatically affirming—that in our world *as it is* this is not the case.' De Lubac, *The Mystery of the Supernatural*, trans. Rosemary Sheed with additional translations of non-French portions by John M. Pepino (New York: Crossroad, 1998), 54; emphasis added. In other words, the differences between Garrigou-Lagrange and de Lubac all took place within the confines of commonly agreed-upon first principles. And for an added fillip of surprise, Balthasar once called Pius X's condemnation of Modernism 'generally justified' in his article 'Peace in Theology', *Communio*, 12 (1985), 398–407 (402).

intimacy, which is still undeserved even according to the presuppositions of creation.[21]

These words proved to be prophetic, as the neuralgia of liberal Catholic theology in the wake of Vatican II has shown. To be fair, de Lubac later came to see the harm done to the church by false interpretations of his own works on grace:

> People now talk about the Church more than they experience her. They chatter on about questions of faith more than they live its mystery. Thus there results in many cases, even today, this sleepwalking, this lack of commitment, this absence of an instinctive reaction [to defend the Church], indeed this secret complicity, in the face of certain destructive actions.[22]

Balthasar, however, does more than just lament. His own careful assessment of de Lubac, coupled with his own distinctive theology of the nature/grace dialectic, also points to a possible resolution of this knotty and difficult problem. He does this by seeing nature not just as a contrasting concept to grace but also as a *parable* of grace. Nature, in other words, is far more dynamic than it comes across as being in the usual tractates on grace, including de Lubac's. There is, however, one significant exception in the neo-Thomist tradition to this generally bloodless portrayal of nature. I am referring to the work of a nineteenth-century theologian not much read today, Domenico Palmieri, who opens up an important vista in this passage:

1. Every act of conceding that something is 'necessary' in nature belongs to an infinite hierarchy of *gradations*, of which each one can seem like a 'grace' to the other, narrower gradations.

2. The *de facto* immense *wealth* of creation, for example, of the animals and plants ordered to man, has a specific 'graced' character as such.

3. Much that corresponds to human nature in general is not meant for each individual—for example, bodily and mental integrity, prosperity, and so on—especially since certain natural laws exclude the possibility that each isolated individual can partake of all these goods. They are thus, for the individual [who is lucky enough to possess them in prosperity], 'grace' in a preeminent way.

4. God could have ordered the world in many other different ways: that he chose *this* total arrangement that furnishes so much beneficence to the individual as well as to the whole can certainly be characterized as a 'grace'.

---

[21] Balthasar, *Barth*, 298.
[22] De Lubac, *L'Église dans la crise actuelle* (Paris: Cerf, 1969), 18. For a fuller account of de Lubac's dismay at certain post-Vatican II trends, see Christopher J. Walsh, 'De Lubac's Critique of the Post-conciliar Church', *Communio*, 19 (1992), 404–32.

5. Finally the whole environment, necessarily ordered to an innate dynamic as such, is *de facto* and constantly contingent and so has a 'gracious' character to it in all its details.[23]

In other words, in the real world as we experience it, 'natural gratuity' is present everywhere. From this there opens out the extraordinary vista of Balthasar's five-volume *Theo-Drama* as well as his numerous shorter essays in a kind of theological literary criticism, ranging all the way from careful analyses of Shakespeare's *Measure for Measure* to an essay on the plays and poetry of Bertolt Brecht.[24]

CONCLUSION

A full analysis of the aforementioned sources for Balthasar's theology would burst the bounds of this essay,[25] but that fact itself is the best conclusion: Balthasar is such an important *ressourcement* theologian because he was able, with his remarkable erudition, to draw on nearly all the sources of the Christian tradition, literary, philosophical, and theological. In that regard, for all his careful distinctions, explicit disagreements with de Lubac, and his own unique positions, he must be regarded as the twentieth century's premier *ressourcement* theologian.

---

[23] Balthasar, *Barth*, 277–8; the numbered points are drawn from Domenico Palmieri, *Tractatus de gratia divina actualis* (Gulpen: M. Alberts, 1885), 7–8.

[24] On *Measure for Measure*, see *Theo-Drama*, i. *Prolegomena*, trans. Graham Harrison (San Francisco: Ignatius Press, 1988), 466–78; on Brecht, 'Bertolt Brecht: the Question about the "Good"', *Explorations in Theology* iii. *Creator Spirit*, trans. Brian McNeil, CRV (San Francisco: Ignatius Press, 1993), 413–59. On the often neglected topic of Balthasar's literary criticism, see Ed Block, 'Balthasar's literary criticism', in Edward T. Oakes, SJ and David Moss (eds.), *The Cambridge Companion to Hans Urs von Balthasar* (Cambridge: Cambridge University Press, 2004), 207–23.

[25] A recent volume that goes into these sources in rich detail is Walter Kardinal Kasper (ed.), *Logik der Liebe und Herrlichkeit Gottes: Hans Urs von Balthasar im Gespräch*, Festgabe für Karl Kardinal Lehmann zum 70. Geburtstag (Ostfildern: Matthias-Grünewald-Verlag, 2006).

19

Louis Bouyer and the Unity of Theology

Jake C. Yap

In his funeral eulogy for the French Oratorian priest and theologian Louis Bouyer (1913–2004), the late Jean-Marie Lustiger, Cardinal-Archbishop of Paris, made public a little-known fact: during the pontificate of Paul VI, the pope wished to confer the red hat on Bouyer. The theologian politely declined the cardinalate, stating that, given his theological 'bad reputation' in France, the honour would doubtless bring 'too many complications' to the Holy Father. Thus, Bouyer's outstanding role in Catholic theology, Cardinal Lustiger lamented, remained hidden by the 'singularity of his person and the originality of his genius'.[1]

Louis Bouyer is not totally unknown. In two theological fields in particular, he has carved out a reputation, namely, the history of Christian spirituality, and liturgy. But it is another matter to recognize his contribution in other areas of theology, and when one takes the time to do so, one realizes with wonder that his is a theology of astonishing depth and breadth. His books, covering numerous theological topics, manifest a broad range of interests as well as an exceptional grasp of the material, both sacred and secular. His literary style is characterized by a kind of forceful clarity and perspicacity. His prose is frequently breathtaking, even when he is most ferociously adversarial, but especially when he is most inspired simply to proclaim the gospel. His role in the French *ressourcement* movement, his contribution to the recovery of the treasures of traditional Christian teaching, his ecumenism, his doctrinal synthesis accomplished in a manner both lucid and erudite, what James Connolly calls 'a classical example of the French technique of *haute vulgarisation*',[2] his campaign to restore spirituality to theology without compromising theological rigour—all this indicates a theologian of major importance.

---

[1] For the full text, cf. 'Homélie à l'occasion des funérailles du Père Louis Bouyer', see *Communio*, (French ed.), 30/1 (2005), 177.

[2] James M. Connolly, *The Voices of France: A Survey of Contemporary Theology in France* (New York: Macmillan, 1961), 64.

CONVERT AND ECUMENIST

Born in 1913 into French Lutheranism, Louis Bouyer was ordained a pastor in 1936. Three years later, he was received into the Roman Catholic Church, studied for the priesthood, and received holy orders in 1944. From 1947 to 1962, he taught at the Institut Catholique de Paris, giving his final courses there just before the opening of the Second Vatican Council. Although he was never a *peritus* at Vatican II, he served the Council in other capacities: in 1960 he was a consultor for the Preparatory Commission for studies and seminaries; in 1964, a consultor for the application of the liturgical reform. In 1969 and again in 1974 he was a member of the Pontifical International Theological Commission.

Though a Roman Catholic for most of his adult life, Bouyer never repudiated his Protestant beginnings and had nothing but gratitude towards those mentors and authors who influenced him. The works of Ramsey among Anglicans, of Cullmann, Jeremias, Riesenfeld, and Mowinckel among Protestants, and of Bulgakov, Lossky, and Florensky among the Orthodox, were not only intellectually and spiritually exciting for him but 'veritable sources'. He said in an interview in 1979:

> If I have drawn above all from the Catholic tradition such as it has been expressed in the Latin Church, if I owe much to the rediscovery (in our modern times, notably by Etienne Gilson) of St Thomas Aquinas in particular, I owe yet more to the Fathers and to Scripture. But what has helped me the most to understand the Fathers and Scripture are the works of Protestant, Anglican and Orthodox authors. [...] I am totally at ease with the Orthodox, Anglicans or Protestants who have a true ecumenical spirit, those who rediscover that catholicity which is not one sect among others ... but truly *the* truth tending towards all its plenitude.[3]

In this statement we find three marks of his theological enterprise: *ressourcement*, catholicity, and ecumenicity.

Bouyer is recognized today as a *ressourcement* theologian of great stature and significance. Marcellino D'Ambrosio places him squarely among 'some of the greatest names in twentieth-century Catholic scholarship' such as de Lubac, Daniélou, Balthasar, Congar, and Chenu.[4] It is to be noted that most, if not all, of the theologians he cites would not, strictly speaking, be considered 'original' thinkers; indeed, it is by the very nature of *ressourcement* that the accent is on the foundational sources of the Christian faith: above all Sacred Scripture, then

---

[3] Louis Bouyer, *Le métier de théologien: entretiens avec Georges Daix* (Paris: Editions France-Empire, 1979), 163. All citations in this chapter are from this edition. A new edition, considerably supplemented with additional material, is published by Ad Solem (Geneva: 2005).

[4] Cf. Marcellino D'Ambrosio, '*Ressourcement* theology, *aggiornamento*, and the hermeneutics of tradition', *Communio* 18 (1991), 530–55 (531). Fergus Kerr, in his *Twentieth Century Catholic Theologians: From neoscholasticism to Nuptial Mysticism* (Oxford: Blackwell, 2007), does not devote a chapter to Bouyer but pays tribute to him in a brief footnote on p. 10.

the church Fathers and the sacred liturgy. For Bouyer, these three are united under the rubric of 'mystery', a key term which runs through many of his books like a silver thread and which is also the title of one of his last books.[5] Μυστηριον in Saint Paul is the secret plan of God for human salvation, hidden in ages past but now revealed in Jesus Christ through the church (cf. Eph. 3.9–11). In a word, Christ is the Mystery (Col. 1.27). For Bouyer, theological *ressourcement* brings to light this saving mystery as it is revealed in Sacred Scripture, interpreted and explained by the Fathers, and celebrated in the liturgy.[6]

'LE PROBLÈME FONDAMENTAL DE LA THÉOLOGIE'

What are the dominant theological questions and concerns of Louis Bouyer, as his numerous writings might suggest? In a 1979 interview published as *Le métier de théologien*, Bouyer mentions that in reading the Russian Orthodox theologian, Sergei Bulgakov, he discerned an intuition of what he would suggest is the fundamental problem of theology—*the relationship between God and creation*. On the one hand, there is 'the life of God which he has in himself from all eternity, and which is manifested in the Trinity'; on the other, there is creation, especially the highest of God's creation which is human beings, 'considered not only as produced by him but as called to return to him, to enter into a relationship with him and to live in a participation in his own life'.[7] This perspective would bear fruit in his two trilogies.

Between 1957 and 1982, Louis Bouyer published six books which constitute his veritable *magnum opus*. These are topically related to one another in sets of three, hence, trilogies. There is, first of all, an 'economic trilogy', concerned with creation in three successive levels or aspects: a so-called 'supernatural anthropology', *The Seat of Wisdom* (1957); a 'supernatural sociology', *The Church of God* (1970); and a 'supernatural cosmology', *Cosmos* (1982).[8] The

---

[5] Bouyer, *Mystérion: Du Mystère à la mystique* (1986), ET *The Christian Mystery*, trans. Illtyd Trethowan (Edinburgh: T&T Clark, 1990).

[6] Of significance are Bouyer's first three major books: each represents one of the three main 'sources' of the French *ressourcement* project: a commentary on *The Fourth Gospel* (1938) shows the primary importance Bouyer attaches to scripture; a study on Athanasius' theology in *L'Incarnation et l'Église: Corps du Christ dans la théologie de saint Athanase* (Paris: Cerf, 1943) is his major patristic volume; and his celebrated *Le Mystère Pascal: (Paschale Sacramentum). Méditation sur la liturgie des trois derniers jours de la Semaine Sainte* (Paris: Cerf, 1945) is his first foray into liturgics.

[7] Bouyer, *Le métier*, 188. Bouyer seems to echo a sentiment earlier expressed by Karl Barth who, in 1946, declared that '[t]he subject of theology is the history of the communion of God with man and of man with God', thus summing up in outline form his *Kirchliche Dogmatik*. See Barth's *Dogmatics in Outline*, trans. G. T. Thomson (New York: Harper & Row, 1959), 5.

[8] Background source-material and Bouyer's personal reflections on the trilogies may be found in *Le métier*, 187 ff.

overarching theme of this trilogy is the consideration of the Creator-creature relationship from a micro to a macro perspective: the anticipation and perfection of that relationship in one particular individual (Mary) as the 'supreme example' of creation as intended by God, to its collective expression in the 'whole of conscious creation eschatologically assembled' (the Church), and finally to all spiritual and material creation (the 'world', Gk κοσμος).[9] This first trilogy leads to a more 'properly theological' one, 'oriented to the divine object itself',[10] 'in the sight of God within the faith',[11] considering in turn each of the three persons of the Godhead: *The Eternal Son* (1974), *The Invisible Father* (1976), and *Le Consolateur* (1980).

Back to Bouyer's central theological concerns: If his entire enterprise may be described as focusing above all on the relationship between God and humanity, this leads to articulating *how* this relationship takes place. The answer for Bouyer is astonishingly simple: it is through the 'Word of God'. Here one meets a key term of vast Bouyerian significance, for 'Word of God' is Bouyer's *primary motif for describing how that relationship is possible and how it is to be characterized: as creative, salvific, and unitive.* Most of Bouyer's books are directly or indirectly concerned with the divine Word.

> The sources of theology can appear very simple at first sight: it is essentially the Word of God. Only the Word of God is presented to us, not by means of two sources, Scripture and Tradition, but by means of a complexity of approaches, which is nevertheless organically one, from one unique source.[12]

This statement undoubtedly links Bouyer's *ressourcement* project with his desire to recover the full biblical and traditional meaning of the 'Word'. Finally, a third thematic concern of Bouyer's theology is this: *the goal of the divine-human relationship, or the result of the divine intervention in human history, is divine adoption.* Human beings are made 'sons in the Son'. In his books, Bouyer returns again and again to this theme by means of many other similar terms or images: recapitulation, divinization, the wedding-feast of the Lamb, or more simply, union with God. He says, for example: 'The Word of God is communicated to the Church in a vision inseparable from entering vitally into union with God the Father.'[13] Aidan Nichols, reviewing Bouyer's *The Invisible Father*, notes the centrality of this theme in his theology. As Nichols writes: 'The doctrine of adoptive divine filiation lies at the heart of Bouyer's triadology: Cyrillism in modern exegetical guise.'[14]

---

[9] Bouyer, *Le métier*, 191–2.   [10] *Le métier*, 192.
[11] Bouyer, *The Church of God, Body of Christ and Temple of the Spirit*, trans. Charles Underhill Quinn (Chicago: Franciscan Herald Press, 1982), p. xiv.
[12] Bouyer, *Le métier*, 212.
[13] *Le métier*, 212.
[14] Cf. Nichols' review in the *Irish Theological Quarterly*, 66 (2001), 81–2 (82).

The remainder of this chapter will examine the unity of theology as exemplified by Louis Bouyer. How did this French theologian undertake the unification of the great themes and tasks of Christian theology?

THE WORD OF GOD

All of Bouyer's interpreters have noted the preponderant use of the Word-motif which constitutes an integral part of and shapes his overall theological vision. As Jan Chaim puts it: 'The undisputed merit of Louis Bouyer...is that of having been one of the first theologians to have glimpsed the necessity of deepening the theology of the Christian Mystery with that of the Word of God.'[15] Before the theological renewal of the twentieth century, the manualist tendency was to subsume the 'Word of God' under the general rubric of *De Revelatione*. For Bouyer, this despoils the former of its biblical richness and treats the latter as only 'things to be learned' from God. Throughout his writings, Bouyer will return almost untiringly to this refrain: that God gives his Word in order that he might be 'known', not conceptually or merely intellectually, but in the biblical sense of the most intimate of relationships. The goal of God's Word, he says, is 'not simply the communication of a truth, but the communication of life'.[16] But perhaps the most important reason why Bouyer underscores the Word-motif is that, for him, the 'one many-splendoured mystery' of the Christian faith is Jesus Christ, the Word of God *par excellence*, who is God's total and indeed 'only possible' revelation to humanity.[17]

In brief, the theologian has in mind three interrelated referents for the 'Word of God': divine revelation, Sacred Scripture, and Jesus Christ. These are inseparably connected and share a unique historical progression. The Word first makes its appearance as the gratuitous and unexpected self-revelation of God in the history of Israel. It traverses uncounted years of living contact with

[15] Jan Chaim, *La Dottrina Sacramentale di Louis Bouyer*, Ph.D. thesis (Pontifical Gregorian University, 1984); published excerpts Rome: Pontifical Gregorian University, 1984), 69. Cf. also, among others, Richard William Walling, 'Metamorphosis of the Sacred: Christian Liturgy and the Mystery of the Incarnation in the Work of Louis Bouyer' (unpublished Ph.D. thesis, Catholic University of America, 1990); Karin Heller, *Ton Créateur est ton époux, ton rédempteur: contribution à la théologie de l'Alliance à partir des écrits du R. P. Louis Bouyer, de l'Oratoire* (Paris: Editions Téqui, 1996); and more recently, Davide Zordan, *Connaissance et mystère: l'itinéraire théologique de Louis Bouyer* (Paris: Editions du Cerf, 2008). Cf. also Jake Yap, '"Word" and "Wisdom" in the Ecclesiology of Louis Bouyer' (Unpublished D.Phil. thesis, University of Oxford, 2003).

[16] Bouyer, *Le métier*, 54.

[17] Bouyer, *The Eternal Son: A Theology of the Word of God and Christology* (Huntington IN.: Our Sunday Visitor, 1978), 13, 16.

the Jewish people in the oral tradition of the prophets, before finally being written down and subsequently venerated as Israel's Sacred Scriptures. Then appears the Word's definitive historical realization; as the Christian scriptures put it: 'Long ago God spoke to our ancestors in many and various ways by the prophets; but in these last days he has spoken to us by a Son' (Heb. 1.1), a Son whom the same scriptures designate as *the* Word of God, full of grace and truth, shining forth with the glory of the Father (Jn 1.14). Bouyer's account not only articulates a 'history of the Word' but also what one might call a 'pre-history': the Word as the Trinitarian Second Person 'perfectly resembling and of one substance with the Father'.

Bouyer's theology of the Word is extremely robust. It is, if one may say so, full-bodied and muscular, bursting with life and extraordinary vitality. One feels that his account is celebrative, joyous, transfixed with wonder at the richness, power, grandeur, and infinite mercy of condescending divine love. Consider the following passage:

> We need to add that, in the traditional conception, first Jewish and then Chris-
> tian, the reading of the sacred text is never a simple 'lesson' in the sense in which
> we understand the word today. It cannot be reduced, that is, to the merely
> didactic, to a form of instruction, like that given in a class or a seminar. The
> reading of the divine Word in the Church is necessarily a celebration: in the
> simple proclamation of His Word to the world, God is glorified. [. . .] It is a Word
> which of itself calls for sacred song: which is not to be uttered by any but pure lips,
> lips which express the holy joy, the religious fear of a heart that is not only
> believing and submissive, but adoring.[18]

One discerns here not only the theologian speaking but the believer and worshipper. The Catholic Bouyer is also the child of his Protestant upbringing who holds the Word of God to his heart—a religious instinct which should of course be catholic in the universal sense.

Thus, in an important way, Bouyer's Word-theology is in the service of what he considers one of the church's primary actions, namely worship and adoration of God. At the same time, it is a hermeneutical prolegomenon to other, more foundational doctrines, for example, his Christology and ecclesiology.

THE CHRISTIAN MYSTERY

Bouyer's theology of the Word is incomplete and diminished without an account of the 'mystery' which comprises its essential content. As already noted above, Bouyer capitalizes on the Pauline μυστηριον which is none other

---

[18] Bouyer, *Introduction to Spirituality*, trans. Mary Perkins Ryan (New York: Desclée, 1961), 41.

than 'Jesus Christ and him crucified' (1 Cor. 2.2). It is this evangelical 'mystery' which for Bouyer constitutes the primary content, core and climax of the divine Word itself. Then, as the next step in a continuum, it is in the Christian liturgy that the mystery of Jesus Christ is actualized and contemporized, made available to Christians and to the church today. Bouyer's theological vision follows the progression 'Word-Mystery-Liturgy'.[19]

In all likelihood drawing from Karl Barth's theology of the Word of God, Bouyer depicts the progression of divine revelation precisely as the presence- and power-filled action of God throughout the history of Israel. In so doing, Bouyer claims that he is simply recovering the biblical notion of Word with its powerful 'personalist realism', by this presumably meaning the Word's power to make present the person of the divine speaker.[20] He is adamant that this does not occur in a merely incremental fashion, as if by a 'multiplied complexity of more and more diverse propositions', but rather by the 'deepening of truths, very simple and very rich', which were given from the very beginning and which make up a unified whole.[21] He compares the divine Word's evolution to a musical theme enriching itself continually by taking on new harmonies, 'to the point where it finally takes possession of our whole mental and spiritual universe'.[22] And now, the music has reached its crescendo.

'When I came to you, brothers and sisters,' wrote St Paul to the community in Corinth, 'I did not come proclaiming the mystery of God to you in lofty words or wisdom. For I decided to know nothing among you except Jesus Christ, and him crucified' (1 Cor. 2.1–2). This Pauline single-mindedness constitutes, for Bouyer, not only the content of the apostle's personal preaching, but the very secret (μυθίηριον) of the divine wisdom, which is God's eternal plan of salvation for his creation. In the same epistle Paul scoffs at the 'wisdom of the world' which the divine wisdom has exposed to be what it truly is—foolishness.

> Has not God made foolish the wisdom of the world? For since, in the wisdom of God, the world did not know God through wisdom, God decided through the foolishness of our proclamation, to save those who believe. For Jews demand signs and Greeks seek wisdom, but we preach Christ crucified, a stumbling block

---

[19] Readers and admirers of his books and writings on the Christian liturgy must take note of this theological framework; Bouyer's lively sense of the liturgy arises from his robust appreciation of the divine Word. Cf. for example, *Liturgical Piety* (Notre Dame IN: University of Notre Dame Press, 1955). This edition was published the following year in Britain as *Life and Liturgy*, and as an abridged French translation, *La vie de la liturgie*.

[20] Bouyer, *Dictionary of Theology*, trans. Charles Underhill Quinn (New York: Desclée, 1965), 468.

[21] Bouyer, *The Meaning of Sacred Scripture*, trans. Mary Perkins Ryan (Notre Dame IN: University of Notre Dame Press, 1958), 224.

[22] *The Meaning of Sacred Scripture*, 224.

to Jews and foolishness to the Greeks, but to those who are the called, both Jews and Greeks, Christ the power of God and the wisdom of God. (1 Cor. 1.20–4)

For Paul, as for all subsequent bearers of the Word of God, the apostolic preaching will consist in that 'secret and hidden [wisdom of God], which God decreed before the ages for our glory' and has now 'revealed to us through the Spirit' (1 Cor. 2.7, 10). For 'he has made known to us the mystery of his will, according to his good pleasure that he set forth in Christ, as a plan for the fullness of time, to unite all things in him, things in heaven and things on earth' (Eph. 1. 9–10). This self-same mystery, 'hidden throughout the ages and generations but has now been revealed' is nothing short of 'Christ in you, the hope of glory' (Col. 1.26, 27).

In other words, a straight line runs through Bouyer's theology of the *Word*, and finds its climax in the evangelical *mystery*, which is its core and content. The mystery is 'only to be grasped through a theology of God's Word, and as the very summit of that theology.'[23] It is God's Word *par excellence*,[24] 'the final word the Word of God had to speak to us'.[25] However, the line does not end there, but continues on to the *liturgy*. It is in the liturgical life of the church that the mystery is proclaimed, celebrated, and perpetually actualized. Of this crucial interrelationship Bouyer writes:

> The divine Word presents the Mystery to us as the substance of our faith. But it is in the sacraments that it causes us effectively to participate in it and that faith can make our own the Mystery here proclaimed. [...] The Word of God illuminated in the tradition of the Church is concentrated in the Mystery: Christ and His cross. But, in the Church, the Mystery is not merely proclaimed. Rather, with the very authority of God, it is proclaimed as present. It is then represented, rendered present for us, in us. It is for the sacraments to apply to us this permanent presence and actuality of the Mystery.[26]

In this last sentence, Bouyer uses a word, 'actuality', which is pregnant with meaning and ecumenical value. Elsewhere he wrote that it is the 'imperishable actuality of the cross which allows the sacramental mystery to be renewed indefinitely'.[27] The French *actualité* does not simply mean 'reality'; it denotes a matter of present interest and current impact. This statement puts the accent on the ever-saving reality of an *ephapax* event: the death of Christ on a bleak mound of dirt outside Jerusalem on a day when even the sun hid its light (Mt. 27.45) has become the source of inexhaustible light and life for all creation ever since. In Bouyer's horizon, actualism is a recurring motif. As a theological

[23] *Liturgical Piety*, 105.   [24] *Liturgical Piety*, 101.
[25] Bouyer, *The Word, Church and Sacraments in Protestantism and Catholicism*, trans. A. V. Littledale (New York: Desclée, 1961), 77.
[26] Bouyer, *Introduction to Spirituality*, 105.
[27] Bouyer, *The Paschal Mystery: Meditations on the Last Three Days of Holy Week*, trans. Sister Mary Benoit (London: Allen and Unwin, 1951), 43.

term it is especially prominent at the intersection of his account of the mystery and of the liturgy, as the following passage is but one example: 'Of this mystery the liturgy forms the setting. It is in the liturgy that it remains perpetually actual, perpetually living and conscious.'[28] Behind this is, of course, Bouyer's concern that the mystery, for all its 'everlasting validity', does not remain a dead letter, a thing of the past, having no link whatsoever with the present or with the people of this age. It is for this reason that the church is commissioned to preach the Word, which is equivalent to saying, to proclaim the mystery or the gospel. He writes:

> [As] God's gift of Himself proclaimed by Christ the Word became by means of His Cross the actual reality of that new creation in this world of ours, so the Word of the Cross has to be proclaimed through the Church by those whom Christ has sent, in order to speak through them to all generations, so that God may effectively be all in all.[29]

THE LITURGY IN THE CHURCH

The Christian μνθίηριον is the saving reality at the very heart of the Word of God. This mystery is no mere message, but a veritable power to save. To consider it otherwise, to regard either mystery or Word as simply instruction or information, is to diminish their presence- and power-filled actuality. If Bouyer's theology of the Word insists on one thing, it is precisely this. However, the actuality of the mystery needs to find its habitat or setting, its rightful place, in the liturgy of the Christian people which is itself the heir of the Jewish liturgy.[30] This is why Bouyer says that the mystery is 'accomplished' in the liturgy. He can mean by this, as he says elsewhere, the simple fact that the liturgy 'places this Mystery within us'.[31] Moreover, St Paul has specified where the mystery is to be proclaimed: 'For as often as you eat this bread and drink the cup, you proclaim the Lord's death until he comes' (1 Cor. 11.26). Hence Bouyer hails the Eucharist as 'the *situs* of the Mystery, of its ever-active presence in the Church'.[32]

Perhaps one of Bouyer's most audacious statements is as follows: 'Since [the] liturgy is predominantly the coming down of God's Word to us, it is

---

[28] Bouyer, *The Meaning of the Monastic Life*, trans. Kathleen Pond (London: Burns & Oates, 1955), 173.

[29] *Liturgical Piety*, 107.

[30] Cf. Bouyer, 'Liturgie juive et chrétienne', in Lancelot Sheppard (ed.), *Le Culte en Esprit et en Vérité* (Paris: Desclée et Cie, 1966), 45–62.

[31] *Introduction to Spirituality*, 125.   [32] *Liturgical Piety*, 158.

fundamentally a liturgy of the Word.'[33] This is obviously true of the first part, he says, but 'the Mass is equally a liturgy of the Word in the second part', what is now called the Liturgy of the Eucharist. And the chief reason he gives is that, since the time of Augustine, the sacrament could be understood as a *verbum visibile*, a word made visible (and necessarily so) by sacred actions and concrete realities. For Bouyer, because the sacrament is *verbum*, it performs what the Word says it does.

This perspective is both theologically sound and ecumenically valuable. It makes possible a rapprochement of two powerful Christian intuitions: the actualistic understanding of 'Word' in Protestantism (via Barth), and the actualistic understanding of 'sacrament' in Catholicism. According to him, the mystery is actualized in the liturgy, not only in the second part (the Liturgy of the Eucharist) which, according to Catholic sacramental theology, is the locus of the re-presentation of the saving mystery of Christ's sacrifice, but also in the *first* part (the Liturgy of the Word) where the mystery is also actualized and made present.[34]

In short, Word and sacrament make a happy marriage in Bouyer, who truly has an ecumenical goal in mind: he wishes to demonstrate the implausibility of opposing Word to sacrament, and thus to hammer another nail into the coffin of a supposed polarity between the Protestant 'churches of the Word' and the Catholic 'church of the sacrament'. It is worthwhile noting that Bouyer can be ecumenical *because* he is evangelical. Conversely, since his starting point is the full gospel of the Christian mystery (that is, because he is evangelical), his approach cannot help but be ecumenical.

CHRISTIAN SPIRITUALITY IN THE HEART OF THE WORLD

In the liturgy, the ecclesial community continually celebrates Christ's presence and re-presents his saving act. While Bouyer places the liturgy (or more broadly, worship) squarely at the centre of ecclesial life, he also envisions that through it the divine life would be introduced into the whole of the Christian's existence, irradiating into the world at large. To a great extent, this is accomplished by means of the spiritual life or the spirituality of the Christian believer.

---

[33] Bouyer, *Liturgical Piety*, 29.
[34] Though commonplace today, the idea that Jesus Christ is present in power when the scriptures are read and the gospel preached was preserved much more in Protestantism and probably owes its place in Vatican II's *Sacrosanctum Concilium* §7 to liturgical *ressourcement*.

For Bouyer, Christian spirituality is grounded precisely in the historical fact of a God who has taken the first step to reveal himself to human beings. All Christian spirituality finds its indestructible *raison d'être* on this unshakeable basis:

> No Christian spirituality worthy of the name can exist where the conviction has been weakened that God, in Christ, has made Himself known to us by His own words, His own acts, as Some One. The whole spiritual life of Christians is aroused and formed by the fact that, as they believe, God has spoken to us and that His living Word has been made flesh amongst us. In other words, in Christianity, the spiritual life does not start from a certain conception of God, not even from the idea that He is a personal God, but from *faith*, the faith which is proper to Christianity: that is, the assent we give to the Word of God, to that Word which is made known to us, which is given to us in Christ Jesus.[35]

Christian spirituality is therefore the authentic spiritual life which gives an affirmative response to the divine Word. In typical Bouyerian fashion, the accent is again placed on the primacy of the Word, and then on the appropriate human and ecclesial actions it inspires. Once again, Bouyer's readers must remember that his writings on spirituality, even if they are ostensibly 'historical surveys', have for their purpose an invitation to the reader to 'go and do likewise'. In other words, a pastoral or hortatory goal motivates his numerous works on spirituality.

Dom Illtyd Trethowan, reviewing Bouyer's *The Church of God* (1970), praises it for not simply being a 'brilliant and powerful theological achievement' but also for its 'clarion call to genuinely Christian living'.[36] Yves Congar, Bouyer's contemporary, similarly notes that the latter's 'profound perception and conviction' is the connection (*lien*) between theology and spiritual experience.[37] These comments illuminate a vital conviction which drives Bouyer: the inseparability of theology and spirituality. For Bouyer, a spirituality that is not grounded in correct doctrine would become easy prey to either shallowness or fanaticism, while a theology that is not prayed, not doxological, would be dry and barren.

For this reason, Bouyer is critical of a classic of devotional writing like *The Imitation of Christ*.

> A spirituality [like that of the *Imitation*] which holds theology in contempt and, in a flush of false humility, thinks itself able to exist without it *ipso facto* gives a blessing to a theology the principles of which will now be confined to narrow

[35] *Introduction to Spirituality*, 6–7.
[36] Cf. Trethowan's review in *The Downside Review* 89/296 (July 1971), 250–4 (254).
[37] Cf. Congar's review of Bouyer's *Le Consolateur* in 'Chronique de Pneumatologie', *RSPT*, 64/3 (1980), 445–9 (446).

rationalism and which will show itself incapable of expressing the mystery while being all too adroit in travestying and emptying it.[38]

In contrast to this, it is the mark of the true giants of Christian spirituality—whether a Protestant like Johann Arndt or a Catholic like John of the Cross—that theirs is a solid 'spiritual theology', that is to say, 'intrinsically theological by the very fact that it is constructed wholly from spirituality, and remaining at the heart of the latter'.[39]

THE UNITY OF THEOLOGY

In *The Meaning of Sacred Scripture* (French original: *La Bible et l'Évangile*, 1952), Bouyer compares the progress of the divine Word through human history to a musical theme enriching itself continually by taking on new harmonies, 'to the point where it finally takes possession of our whole mental and spiritual universe'.[40] This too can be an apt metaphor for how Bouyer conceives of theology, both its nature and its task. At the age of 66, still at the height of his powers, Bouyer spoke at length about the craft of theology (*métier théologique*) and the role of the theologian:

> The theologian needs to present together Christian truth in such light that it illumines the situation in which contemporary men (taken individually or in the sense of the whole Church) find themselves. Consequently, the theologian certainly needs to make a constructive effort, which he can do only personally. [...] It is only an individual who could arrive at a synthesis which is a real synthesis. Moreover I believe that a theological synthesis can be done only in a triple exchange: firstly, the living Tradition of the Church grasped through its entire history in reference to its source in the Word of God; secondly of course, the life of the contemporary Church and its problems; and thirdly, the contemporary culture, from whose problems Christian truth of all time is necessarily inseparable.[41]

Put more succinctly, theology aims to interpret the Word of God in the light of the church's own experience and the experience of the rest of humanity.[42] This guarantees a unity and coherence in the theological venture, theology itself becoming as it were a bridge between God and creation, between

---

[38] Bouyer, *The Invisible Father: Approaches to the Mystery of the Divinity*, trans. Hugh Gilbert (Petersham MA/Edinburgh: St. Bede's/T&T Clark, 1999), 279.
[39] Bouyer, *Women Mystics*, trans. Anne Englund Nash (San Francisco: Ignatius, 1993), 124.
[40] *The Meaning of Sacred Scripture*, 224.
[41] *Le métier*, 45.
[42] *Le métier*, 46.

revelation and faith, the 'properly theological' and the 'economic'. Again one is reminded here of his two trilogies.

Because Bouyer sees theology's task or 'job' as essentially that of interpreting the Word of God in the light of the church's own experience, this is to say that theology must be *ecclesial*, that it cannot be divorced from the believing community from which, within which, and for which it exists. 'Eliminate the Church, and Christianity will be no more than a dream which each one lives in his own way, and Christ will be no more than a myth.'[43] Even more vigorously he says:

> This is why I believe that there is no graver condemnation which can be placed on the work of a theologian, however ingenious, than when one says that his work allows us to know his thinking. The work of a true theologian must allow us to know, not *his* thinking, but the *Noûs Christou*, the mind of Christ, which the *mens Ecclesiae*, the mind of the Church, alone transmits to us and keeps alive for us.[44]

Finally, for Bouyer, true theology must be *mystical*. By 'mystical', he means its origin in the mystery of Christ. 'Progress in theology,' he says, 'even when it is authentic, would nevertheless be something quite questionable if it did not always bring us back to the essential, that is to say, to the mystery of Christ, always more profoundly assimilated and lived.'[45] Faced with a theology that is not in any way 'mystical', Bouyer says (somewhat whimsically) that the disappointment will be so acute that one feels like repeating the words of Mary Magdalene, 'They have taken away my Lord and I do not know where they have put him.'[46] Once theology has reached such a state, it would have to do two things: 'take up dieting' and 'get more exercise'.[47] This means that theology would need to unburden itself of those (mostly philosophical) presuppositions which hamper its authentic development, and it would also need to apply itself more rigorously to the full Gospel message, one that entails suffering, martyrdom, asceticism, and above all, the cross. It must keep on directing people to the cross, to the Christian mystery *par excellence*.

Thus, the theological continuum one perceives in Louis Bouyer (Word-Mystery-Liturgy-Church-Spirituality-Theology) comes full circle. There is a unity in theology founded in the Word of God, a unity which, in the final analysis, simply reflects the unity of the Christian life. Beyond all construals, what is most profound in Bouyer's vision is also what is most simple: that the Trinitarian God is truly, as scripture affirms, wise and good and loving beyond imagination. And, in a way that the creature can only dimly begin to grasp,

---

[43] *Le métier*, 131.

[44] *Le métier*, 208–9.

[45] *Le métier*, 216.

[46] Bouyer, *The Invisible Father*, 280. The actual reference here is to Suárezian theology, but the sentiment seems apropos to other kinds of theology as well.

[47] Bouyer, *Le métier*, 299–300.

God has included it in his divine life, first by creating it, then by saving it. At the end of time, on the threshold of eternity, the creature will find itself forever united with God. This is what Bouyer affirms most of all, and his theology, his 'hymn of praise' to the Almighty, is meant to be, in the end, doxological, in praise of the divine Word.

Part III

Ressourcement as a Threefold Programme of Renewal

20

The Renewal of Biblical Studies in France 1934–1954 as an Element in Theological *Ressourcement*

Benedict T. Viviano, OP

BACKGROUND

French Catholics have had their work cut out for them. In France's Golden Age under Louis XIV (1643–1715) there were simultaneously two sorts of thinkers: Cartesian rationalists valuing clear and distinct ideas, and historical-critical philologists like Richard Simon (1638–1712). His pioneer biblical criticism was anything but clear and distinct. It was sunk in the mud of historical and literary particularity, not to mention the confusion of religious variety. Among his many titles to honour are his early struggles for the right of French Jews to receive respect and understanding.[1] This muddy confusion opened him to the simplistic salvos of the great bishop Jacques-Bénigne Bossuet (1627–1704), learned in patristics. As a result of Simon's harassment, leadership in biblical studies passed out of the hands of Catholics for a long time. The debate between Simon and Bossuet foreshadowed the twentieth-century conflict between Daniélou-de Lubac and de Vaux. The suppression of the Jesuits (1773) did not help Catholic biblical studies.

We need make only one point about the mid-nineteenth century: when conservative scholars (Catholics, Protestants, Orthodox Christian, and Jewish)

---

[1] Paul Auvray, *Richard Simon (1638–1712)* (Paris: Presses Universitaires de France, 1974); Jean Steinmann, *Richard Simon et les origines de l'exégèse biblique* (Paris: Desclée de Brouwer, 1960); Sascha Müller and Rudolf Voderholzer, *Richard Simon (1638–1712), Exeget, Theologe, Philosoph und Historiker: eine Biographie* (Würzburg: Echter, 2005); cf. my review, 'Rezensionen-*Richard Simon (1638–1712). Exeget, Theologe, Philosoph und Historiker. Eine Biographie*', *Freiburger Zeitschrift für Philosophie und Theologie*, 54/1 (2007) 275; Lothar Lies, '*Fundamentaltheologie—Kritik und Theologie. Christliche Glaubens- und Schrifthermeneutik nach Richard Simon (1638–1712)*', *TR*, 103/4 (2007), 302; Paul Hazard, *European Thought in the Eighteenth Century* (London: World, 1953).

hesitated to embrace the newer critical theories about the Pentateuch, the
Psalter, the Gospels, and the Epistles of Paul, they usually did so in good
conscience and with sincerity. The theories were not yet sufficiently tested.
This sincerity was not the case in the twentieth century.[2]

With Pope Leo XIII (1878–1903), a new era began: the Holy See spoke with
a new voice, of positive teaching and encouragement, instead of condemnations and lamentations. This voice expressed itself in a series of encyclical
letters, the basic goal of which was a general revival of Catholic cultural and
intellectual life. It began in 1879 with a letter on the renewal of Catholic
philosophy and theology, especially, but not exclusively, through the study of
Thomas Aquinas. It continued with the opening of the Vatican library to
researchers of different denominations and with letters on the value of historical and biblical studies. It culminated in a famous encyclical on social questions (recognizing, for example, the right of workers to form unions and the
right to a just wage), as well as an effort to persuade French Catholics to
support the Third Republic (1870–1940). This meant giving up their sterile,
doomed policy of trying to restore a Bourbon, legitimist, absolute monarchy.
This nostalgic monarchism is well illustrated in Henry James's early novel
The American (1877), as well as in the novels of Marcel Proust. Leo's well-
intentioned shift in policy, expressed by Cardinal Lavigerie's 'toast' to the
Republic in Algiers, was not accepted at the time by France's aristocratic Catholic
elite. It was put on hold by the bitter disputes occasioned by the Dreyfus Affair, as
well as by the rejectionist policies of the *Action française* movement.[3]

But before the dawn was seen to be in part false, a French Dominican
named Marie-Joseph Lagrange (1855–1938) enjoyed a thirteen-year period of
glory and success. His Christian name was Albert, and he had trained as a
lawyer in Paris, a useful *métier* when he later found himself in trouble, and as
an Orientalist in Vienna. Oriental studies helped him with the Bible as well as
with the new discoveries from Mesopotamia (Iraq): the Code of Hammurabi,
the Gilgamesh epic, and the creation account, Enuma Elish. These needed to
be integrated into the study of biblical law and of the biblical accounts of the
creation of the world and of the primeval flood.

Lagrange had been asked by his superiors to open a school of biblical studies
in Jerusalem, on property the Dominican order had bought a few years earlier.
He opened the school in 1890. Here he hoped to re-examine the Bible in the
light of the new comparative material. He launched the quarterly *Revue*

[2] This is the view of Norbert Lohfink, *Katholische Bibelwissenschaft und historisch-kritische
Methode* (Kevelaer: Butzon und Bercker, 1966).

[3] Adrien Dansette, *Religious History of Modern France* (New York: Herder & Herder, 1961);
J.-D. Bredin, *The Affair* (New York: Braziller, 1986); Eugen Weber, *Action Française: Royalism
and Reaction in Twentieth-Century France* (Stanford CA: Stanford University Press, 1962);
B. T. Viviano, 'The Church in the Modern World and the French Dominicans', *Freiburger
Zeitschrift für Philosophie und Theologie*, 50 (2003), 512–21.

biblique in 1892, and a commentary series, *Études bibliques*, soon thereafter. The journal quickly earned respect in the learned world, due to its regular publication of newly discovered inscriptions, found in the fields of Ottoman Palestine and Jordan. Seminarians interested in ideas devoured the *Revue* as bringing in a fresh theological tone. Priests of various dioceses and religious orders were happy to collaborate, as were lay scholars. Best of all for a devout Religious who wanted to work for the good of the Church, for thirteen years Lagrange enjoyed the favour of Pope Leo XIII. As a 'fair-haired boy', he was showered with signs of favour. His school church was elevated to the rank of a basilica. Such success to be sure evoked some measure of jealousy and hostility.

With the election of Pius X (1903–14) the ill winds blew stronger. Jesuits were ordered to halt all collaboration with Lagrange. A rival biblical institute was set up in Rome (1909) by Leopold Fonck, SJ. Lagrange's brilliant doctoral student, Rev. Joseph Bonsirven, was denied his doctorate in Rome. With the papal documents *Pascendi Dominici Gregis* and *Lamentabili*,[4] biblical studies were frozen in place. A timid thaw began around 1935, for which the death of Fonck, along with the signing of the Lateran accords (1928–9) prepared the way. The deaths of Cardinals Pietro Gasparri and Rafael Merry del Val in 1935 removed further obstacles to progress.[5]

THE RENEWAL, PHASE ONE (1935–1943)

The rise of fascist and totalitarian regimes and their eventual defeat or disintegration can be understood as perhaps the last gasps of the Baroque absolutist model of government. The Baroque model is pre-modern, satisfying for the politically immature. During its Western twilight, glimmers of the next step could be seen in the French Church. In the midst of the Second World War, the important encyclical on biblical studies, *Divino Afflante Spiritu*,[6] was

---

[4] Pope Pius X, Encyclical Letter *Pascendi Dominici Gregis. Encyclical Letter on the Doctrines of the Modernists* (8th September 1907), *AAS* xl (1907), 593–650. ET available at <http://www.vatican.va/holy_father/pius_x/encyclicals/documents/hf_p-x_enc_19070908_pascendi-dominici-gregis_en.html>. *Lamentabili Sane. Syllabus Concerning the Errors of the Modernists*, (3 July 1907). *ASS* xl (1907), 470–8. ET available at <http://www.papalencyclicals.net/Pius10/p10lamen.htm>.

[5] F.-M. Braun, *The Work of Père Lagrange* (Milwaukee: Bruce, 1963); M.-J. Lagrange, *Père Lagrange: Personal Reflections and Memoirs* (New York: Paulist Press, 1985); Bernard Montagnes, *The Story of M.-J. Lagrange: Founder of Modern Catholic Bible Study* (New York: Paulist Press, 2006); *M.-J. Lagrange: une biographie critique* (Paris: Cerf, 2004); Tomáš Petráček, *Le père Vincent Zapletal O.P. (1867–1938): portrait d'un exégète catholique*, Studia friburgensia, Series historica, 6 (Fribourg: Academic Press, 2007).

[6] Pope Pius XII, Encyclical Letter *Divino Afflante Spiritu* on Promoting Biblical Studies (30 September 1943), *AAS* xxxv (1943), 297–325. ET available at <http://www.vatican.va/holy_father/pius_xii/encyclicals/documents/hf_p-xii_enc_30091943_divino-afflante-spiritu_en.html>.

released by Pius XII. In addition to its encouraging tone, a return to Leo XIII, it conceded the key point for which Lagrange had pleaded and on which he had published in 1903, forty years earlier, namely, that there are many literary genres in the Bible, not just one. This seems banal, but the issue at stake was whether everything in the Bible was literally, historically, true or not. Besides history, the other main genres in the Bible are law, prophecy, wisdom, and praise. Present in the Bible are also edifying fiction (e.g., part of Jonah) and the re-use in purified form of Ancient Near-Eastern myths (e.g., in Genesis 1, Daniel 7, Psalm 29, Revelation 12). The deeper point is that the Bible was not necessarily inerrant in matters (geography, astronomy, chemistry) not directly related to human salvation. That point was not conceded until 1965.[7]

Another significant event of the war years was the publication in 1942 of the Louvain professor Canon Lucien Cerfaux's *Theology of the Church according to St. Paul.*[8] It was published in the Unam Sanctam series, started not long previously by Yves Congar, as the vanguard in the renewal of ecclesiology. His book balanced the then current obsession of regarding the Church as the body of Christ, with other Pauline ecclesial models, notably the Church as the people of God and the Church in relation to the future Kingdom of God. In doing so he anticipated by a year the encyclical letter on the church as the body of Christ, *Mystici Corporis Christi,*[9] in turn informed by the studies of Émile Mersch, who was killed in 1940, and by Sebastian Tromp. The letter represented an ecclesial step forward, but it did not give a full picture of the biblical data. Cerfaux was supported by the systematic theology of M. D. Koester;[10] their studies would be integrated into the Vatican II Constitution on the Church, *Lumen Gentium.*

THE RENEWAL, PHASE TWO (1944–1954)

Even hardened secular observers noticed that a revival of Catholic intellectual life took place in the period 1944–54. It involved a certain conjunction of

---

[7] *DS* § 3829–31.

[8] Lucien Cerfaux, *La théologie de l'Église suivant saint Paul*, Unam Sanctam, 10 (Paris: Cerf, 1942); ET: *The Church in the Theology of St. Paul* (New York: Herder & Herder, 1963).

[9] Pope Pius XII, Encyclical Letter, *Mystici Corporis Christi*. Encyclical Letter on the Mystical Body of Christ (29th June 1943), *AAS* xxxv (1943), 195–248. ET available at <http://www.vatican.va/holy_father/pius_xii/encyclicals/documents/hf_p-xii_enc_29061943_mystici-corporis-christi_en.html>.

[10] Mannes Dominikus Koster, *Ekklesiologie im Werden* (Paderborn: Bonifacius-Druckerei, 1940), reprinted (Mainz: Grünewald, 1971) under the title *Volk Gottes im Werden*; Piotr Napiwodski, *Eine Ekklesiologie im Werden* (published on the server of Fribourg University, 2005).

Christ and culture, a new harmony of faith and reason.[11] Fear of the worker-priest experimental collaboration with communist trade unions led the CIA to support a work by the respected sociologist, Raymond Aron, *The Opium of the Intellectuals*, which denounced this alliance.[12] The curtain came down on this brief honeymoon period with a papal condemnation of the worker-priest movement and its theologians in 1954.[13] The synthesis had fallen victim to the Cold War. People thought the drama was over. And then came the death of Pius XII, the election of John XXIII, and the convocation of the Second Vatican Council. The working of the Holy Spirit in the Church could be and often is resisted (Acts 7.51), yet it continues underground and has occasional eruptions that are visible and palpable.

With regard to biblical studies, too, the pace quickens in this period. First, a new series in biblical theology was launched: *Lectio Divina*, accompanied by two other series: *Cahiers Sioniens* and the first fascicles of the *Bible de Jerusalem*. The first and third of these projects are still going strong today. The second, the *Cahiers*, rendered great service in its day by showing the complementary lights shed on the Bible by the Christian, Jewish, and Islamic traditions of interpretation. This took place especially in a series of collective volumes on some of the great biblical personalities: Abraham, Moses, and Elijah.

Second, a magisterial development occurred. Catholic school teachers and intellectuals had for a long time been troubled by how to present the origins of the world and of humankind in a way which took into account both the biblical narratives of Genesis 1–3 and the views of modern science (the evolution of the species, the great antiquity of the planet, the descent of man from lower primates). The Jesuit palaeontologist, Pierre Teilhard de Chardin (1881–1955), was pushing from behind the scenes for the freedom to publish his hypotheses on the phenomenon of man and on the goal of the universe (the Omega point), but met with consistently firm opposition from Rome. His allies, Jean Guitton and Mgr Bruno de Solages, tried their best. Other scholars wanted to publish on Genesis. The encyclical *Divino Afflante Spiritu* was insufficient as support for an imprimatur. On 16 January 1948 a letter was released by the secretary of the Biblical Commission, Jacob Voste, OP, who had been a student of Lagrange. The letter was addressed to the Cardinal Archbishop of Paris, Emmanuel Suhard. It assured him and concerned scholars that Genesis 1–3 should now be addressed with all the resources of modern science and critical scholarship.

---

[11] See Janet Flanner, *Paris Journal 1944–1965*, ed. William Shawn (New York: Atheneum, 1965), 121–2, 213, 239, 251, 263, 294; cf. Tony Judt, *Past Imperfect: French Intellectuals, 1944–1956* (Berkeley CA: University of California Press, 1992).

[12] Raymond Aron, *The Opium of the Intellectuals* (Garden City NY: Doubleday, 1957) (French original *L'opium des intellectuals* (Paris: Calman Levy, 1955)).

[13] François Leprieur, *Quand Rome condamne: Dominicains et prêtres-ouvriers* (Paris: Plon-Cerf, 1989).

There then appeared in quick succession a commentary on Genesis by Joseph Chaine (Lyon);[14] a study of the first sin as the presumption of moral autonomy by Canon Joseph Coppens (Louvain);[15] and a study of Genesis and modern science by Canon Charles Hauret (Strasbourg).[16] As for poor Teilhard, his work could only be published after his death in 1955.[17] In America, books on Genesis in this spirit were published by Bruce Vawter[18] and J. L. McKenzie.[19]

On the whole, these works did not affect the general public as other events and publications did, such as the revelation, in 1945, of the full horror of the Nazi genocide (the Shoah), symbolized by Auschwitz. This, combined with the establishment of the State of Israel in 1948, led Christians of all denominations gradually to reassess their thinking, teaching, and prayers about Jews and Judaism. At the same time, two events of major significance for biblical theology did impinge on the public imagination.

The first was the discovery of the Dead Sea Scrolls at caves on the sides of Wadi Qumran by an Arab shepherd boy. Thanks to the sensationalist evaluation of the find by the archaeologist W. F. Albright, and the literary presentation by the critic Edmund Wilson (initially in the *New Yorker* magazine), the discoveries unleashed a firestorm of excitement and interest, drawing in academics, churches, synagogues, mosques, and governments. It increased interest in the Hebrew Bible, the inter-Testamental period, the origins of Christianity and monasticism (Jewish monks had become barely conceivable after Freud's pan-sexualism, although the record was already there in Philo and Josephus). The discovery increased confidence in the reliability of the Hebrew manuscript tradition, since it included two complete leather scrolls of the longest of the writing prophets, Isaiah, which strongly supported the medieval manuscript tradition. To be sure, fragments of other passages from the Hebrew Bible, e.g., Jeremiah and 1 Samuel, showed greater variety and at times greater proximity to the Septuagint or Old Greek translation.

Such a discovery needs to be crystallized around a person, and in this case, that person was the French Dominican and director of the French archaeological school in Jerusalem, Roland de Vaux. He looked the part: wiry and

---

[14] J. Chaine, *Le livre de la Genèse*, Lectio divina, 3 (Paris: Cerf, 1951).

[15] J. Coppens, *La connaissance du bien et du mal et le péché du paradis: contribution à l'interprétation de Gen., II–III* (Louvain: E Nauwelaerts, 1948).

[16] C. Hauret, *Origines de l'univers et de l'homme d'après la Bible (Genèse I–III)* (Paris: J Gabalda, 1950, rev. ed. 1952); ET: *Beginnings: Genesis and Modern Science*, trans. John F. McDonnell (Dubuque IA: Priory Press, 1955; rev. ed. 1964).

[17] P. Teilhard de Chardin, *Le phénomène humain* (Paris: Seuil, 1955); ET: *The Phenomenon of Man*, trans. Bernard Wall (London: Collins, 1959).

[18] B. Vawter, *A Path through Genesis* (New York: Bruce, 1956); Vawter, *On Genesis* (Garden City NY: Doubleday, 1977).

[19] J. L. McKenzie, *Myths and Realities: Studies in Biblical theology* (Milwaukee WI: Bruce, 1963); *The Two-Edged Sword* (Milwaukee WI: Bruce, 1956).

bearded, he combined active on-site digging with published scholarship, spirituality with humour, faith with reason, ability in both Arabic and Hebrew, Gallic flair with accented English. The media made him a star and the University of Harvard gave him a visiting professorship in 1963.[20]

This is not the place to tell the whole long and complex story of the Scrolls.[21] But one clarification might be helpful in the present context. There is a distinction to be made between the *site* of the discovery of the Scrolls (involving archaeological exploration) and the publication of the *texts* of the Scrolls, involving palaeography, Semitic philology, and all the elements of interpretation: literary analysis, structure, history, and theology. De Vaux was involved in both aspects. As far as archaeology is concerned, once Israel's war of independence was over, the sites of both Qumran and the École biblique were in Jordanian or West Bank Palestine. It was quickly agreed that the excavation should be a joint project of the British and French archaeological schools in Jerusalem. But the director of the British school had suddenly become the head of the Jordanian antiquities authority based in Amman, and, as he was not free to share the work, leadership fell by default to de Vaux, although he had not sought this responsibility.

So it was too with the publication of the texts. Given the complexity and size of the task, and the worldwide interest it had acquired, it was decided early on that the responsibility for the editing should lie with an international, inter-denominational team. Unfortunately, due to the sensibilities of the Jordanian authorities, Jewish scholars could not then be included. At the time, this was not considered a problem, since the Israelis had just acquired the main body of intact scrolls and had enough to do editing them. Things changed again after 1967, when the West Bank was overrun by Israel. De Vaux was appointed editor-in-chief of the fragmentary texts (mostly from Caves 4 and 11) and head of the team for Oxford University Press. This arrangement worked for a while, but personality problems within the team and de Vaux's untimely death in 1971 slowed the pace of publication down. Only recently have all the fragments been published in careful editions. But in those first heady years, in the late 1940s and 1950s, the Scrolls gave a powerful impetus to the biblical *ressourcement*.

De Vaux was clearly riding too many horses at the same time, as he became the key figure in the second major event of biblical significance that affected the general public. This was the publication of the *Bible de Jérusalem* in one

---

[20] Edmund Wilson, *The Scrolls from the Dead Sea* (New York: Oxford University Press, 1955); enlarged editions 1969, 1978; Jeffrey Meyers, *Edmund Wilson: a Biography* (Boston: Houghton Mifflin, 1995).

[21] Early accounts include those by J. T. Milik, *Ten Years of Discovery in the Wilderness of Judea*, Studies in Biblical Theology, 26 (London: SCM, 1959); F. M. Cross, Jr., *The Ancient Library of Qumran* (Garden City NY: Anchor, 1961); John Trever, *The Dead Sea Scrolls: A Personal Account* (Grand Rapids MI: Eerdmans, 1978).

volume in 1955. This project had begun ten years earlier with a series of
fascicles covering the entire Bible, and with extensive introductions and notes,
as well as a fresh translation from the original Hebrew and Greek, a translation
which could at times benefit from the new readings provided by the Qumran
manuscripts. This Bible and its notes were soon translated into the main
Western languages. The English version was published in 1966 as *The Jerusalem Bible.*[22]

This Bible was reaping the harvest of sixty-five years of scholarship in
Jerusalem, at the École biblique, and elsewhere in the French Catholic world.
It represented a collaborative effort by the many different streams of Catholic
clergy: Dominicans and Jesuits in the lead, followed by members of many
other religious orders and diocesan priests. This in itself represents an 'internal
ecumenical' breakthrough, astonishing when one considers the animosities of
the past. Many distinguished laymen contributed to the literary quality of the
work, such as Étienne Gilson and Henri-Irénée Marrou.

The *Bible de Jerusalem*, with its fresh approach and its elegant production,
was a best-seller from the start. It provided the Catholic renewal with an
up-to-date Bible. The notes included a mild version of the documentary
hypothesis concerning the sources of the Pentateuch (Julius Wellhausen and
Hermann Gunkel, among others), stated in a calm, serene tone that did not
frighten readers. (Lagrange had already tried to promote the documentary
hypothesis in 1898.) However, the *Bible de Jerusalem* was less successful in its
introduction to the synoptic Gospels, because it failed to present clearly the
commonly accepted two-source solution to the synoptic problem, the relationship of the Gospels to one another and to their sources. Through a
collaboration between a Dominican scholar (Raymond-Jacques Tournay), a
Jesuit musician (Joseph Gelineau), and a Jewish poet (Raymond Schwab), its
Psalter was soon being sung around the world. Recordings of this collaborative
Psalter won phonograph prizes. An English reviewer declared the *Jerusalem
Bible* to be the best Bible in the world at the time.

This translation also had an impact on Protestant editions of the Bible.
Liberal French Protestants had produced an intelligent, annotated version in
the first part of the century, the *Bible du Centenaire*, in three large, expensive,
and impractical volumes, thus selling few copies. The editors wanted it to be
reproduced in a cheap, compact version by the Bible Society. This however
could not be done because the rules of the society did not allow notes. The
Catholics had no such rules. When Oxford University Press learned of the

---

[22] See the contribution by O. T. Venard, OP, 'The Cultural Backgrounds and Challenges of *La
Bible de Jérusalem*', in Philip McCosker (ed.), *What is it that Scripture Says? Essays in Biblical
Interpretation, Translation and Reception in Honour of Henry Wansborough OSB* (London:
T&T Clark, 2006), 111–34; François Laplanche, *La crise de l'origine: La science catholique des
Évangiles et l'histoire au XXe siècle* (Paris: Albin Michel, 2006).

plans to translate the *Bible de Jerusalem* into English, they rushed into print their own annotated Bible (1965) to preserve their share of the market. Oxford University Press was not bound by the rules of the Bible Society. But the *Centenaire* had been the forgotten pioneer.

Although the *Jerusalem Bible* is often used in worship, it is important to understand that it is in no way an official Bible. It is a private initiative, undertaken by a publisher, Éditions du Cerf, and a school, the École biblique. School and publisher, both Dominican institutions, had always operated within the Church; the Bible has always carried the imprimatur. Winning the discreet but real support of the Vatican had been a triumph for de Vaux's diplomatic charm. The effect on individual spiritual lives is incalculable.

We may add a few additional remarks on the contribution of the French scriptural *ressourcement* to Vatican II. First, the studies on the inspiration of scripture by Pierre Benoit, OP, [23] themselves nourished by Thomas Aquinas and Lagrange, made a sharp distinction between inspiration and revelation. Thus all scripture is inspired by God, but only parts contain divine revelation, in the sense of religious truths which are unattainable by reason alone. This distinction supported the distinction made at the Second Vatican Council between inspiration and inerrancy. That is: all scripture is inspired, but only those truths revealed for the sake of our salvation are necessarily inerrant, free from error. Other statements, e.g., of geography, history, or astronomy, can be erroneous (*DV*, § 11). Second, Benoit also contributed biblical support for the declaration on religious freedom (*Dignitatis Humanae*),[24] mainly through the parable of the wheat and the weeds (Mt. 13.24–30). Finally, Albert Gelin provided a valuable gift to Christian spirituality with his little book on the poor and the afflicted (*anawim, aniyyim*) in the Bible.[25]

SCRIPTURE AND PATRISTICS

Among the masters of the *ressourcement*, alongside Chenu and Congar, Louis Bouyer and Albert Gelin, were the Jesuits Henri de Lubac and Jean Daniélou, both of whom were known for their great knowledge of the church Fathers.

---

[23] Paul Synave, *Prophecy and Inspiration: A Commentary on the* Summa Theologica (New York: Desclée, 1961); Benoit, *Aspects of Biblical Inspiration* (Dubuque IL: Priory Press, 1965); UK edition, *Inspiration and the Bible* (London: Sheed & Ward, 1965); Benoit, *Jesus and the Gospel*, i (New York: Herder and Herder, 1973), 1–10.

[24] J. Hamer and Y. Congar (eds.), *La Liberté religieuse: declaration Dignitatis humanae personae: texte latin et traduction française*, Unam Sanctam, 60 (Paris: Cerf, 1967), esp. 205–13 (P. Benoit).

[25] A. Gelin, *The Poor of Yahweh* trans. Kathryn Sullivan (Collegeville MN: Liturgical Press, 1964); French original *Les Pauvres de Yahvé* (Paris: Cerf, 1953).

But at times their relationship to professional biblical scholarship was troubled, precisely because of their love of the Fathers. This requires a word of explanation.

First of all, it goes without saying that all Catholic exegetes accept and presuppose the whole long tradition of Christian interpretation of scripture which begins with the Fathers. On this point there is no dispute. The debate turns rather on developments that have occurred since the Fathers, especially since 1450 or since 1800. Must these developments be rejected out of hand because they are not all found in the Fathers? Again, is it legitimate to have a direct access to scripture, to analyse and to discuss it, without always passing through the views of the Fathers? In their enthusiasm for the Fathers, de Lubac and Daniélou at times give the impression that the answers to these two questions are yes and no, respectively. These answers have provoked disagreement.

In trying to understand these issues, it is important to have some chronology clearly in mind. For example, de Lubac's best known work, *Catholicism: The Social Aspects of Dogma*, was first published in 1938, when the author was 42.[26] The whole aim of the book is to try to correct an unhealthy Christian individualism, an individualistic turn taken by St Augustine.[27] This is a praiseworthy goal. The book made a contribution to the Vatican II Constitution on the Liturgy, especially on the Eucharist. (The footnotes were at times taken over in their entirety.) But in chapter six, on the interpretation of scripture, the book manifests a romantic enthusiasm for some of the more far-fetched, fanciful, and forced patristic interpretations, which goes beyond prudent limits. There is much of beauty and virtue in this chapter, especially on the harmony of the two Testaments and on the firm rejection of Marcionism. There is also an awareness that patristic exegesis can be excessive and abusive. Yet de Lubac manifests impatience with the literal sense that could easily violate sound exegetical method. Why is this?

Allow me to offer some explanations. First, the chronology shows that the book was written before *Divino Afflante Spiritu* and Voste's letter. De Lubac and Daniélou were both formed and began writing in the era when *Pascendi* and *Lamentabili* reigned as the official line. As Jesuits with the fourth vow of special obedience to the Holy See, they both felt bound in conscience to keep to this line. They were victims, one could say, of their *'sentire cum ecclesia'*— thinking with the Church—understood as the Holy See. They did not yet benefit from the encyclical's openness to different genres, and its goal, for exegetes, of recovering the original human author's intention. To escape from a childish historicization of everything, they took refuge in patristic allegory

---

[26] H. de Lubac, *Catholicisme*, Unam Sanctam 3 (Paris: Cerf, 1938); ET *Catholicism*, trans. Lancelot C. Sheppard (London: Burns & Oates, 1950); esp. Chs. 3 (on the sacraments) and 10 (on the present situation).
[27] Gerhard Lohfink, *Jesus and Community*, trans. John P. Galvin (New York: Paulist, 1984).

and typology. Second, they did not expect that the Holy See would change its course. Père Lagrange may have died in 1938 in the same despair, after his article on the Old Testament patriarchs was turned down by the censors for the fifth time. Third, de Lubac and Daniélou had not yet clearly broken with the sterile politics of Bourbon restoration (*Action française*); this break occurred after France's defeat by Germany, when the Vichy government of Marshal Henri Philippe Pétain (1856–1951) began to collaborate in the deportation of Jews to the extermination camps. Fourth, they felt it was sufficiently bold at the time to break with the Maurrasian Thomism that prevailed in some Roman universities and French seminaries, in favour of a renewal through the Fathers. That was risky enough. Fifth, any academic field of specialization tends to think that it is the most important one. Once the two had made the choice for patristics, it was natural that they should try to promote it. There had been a strong French tradition (at the Sorbonne and elsewhere) of patristic scholarship at least since the Maurist Benedictines of the seventeenth century, with their access to the royal Greek type-fonts to print their editions of the Fathers. Interest in patristic study increased and there were many dissertations on the Fathers. Moreover, it was repugnant to French national pride simply to copy the conclusions of German research. Besides, they were involved in an ecumenical collaboration with the Russian Orthodox theologians centred at the Institut Saint-Serge in Paris. The Fathers represented common ground. So for these five reasons, I suggest that de Lubac and Daniélou were not quite at home with modern exegesis.

At their most extreme, de Lubac and Daniélou adopted a somewhat antagonistic tone. For example, they both defended an allegorical interpretation of the Good Samaritan (Lk. 10.25–37) as the originally intended, authentic meaning.[28] Not content with this, Daniélou insinuated that, since this interpretation was so deeply rooted in the tradition of the Church, this interpretation was the true meaning of the parable, going back to Jesus himself, or at least to the 'elders' cited by Origen. There was no freedom not to accept it. The Jesuit scripture scholar, Joseph A. Fitzmyer, in his fine commentary on Luke, brushes this interpretation aside as fanciful and remote from the text in

---

[28] De Lubac, *Catholicisme*, 168; ET *Catholicism*, 100; Cf. de Lubac, *Catholicisme* 462–4. 'Ainsi nous apparaît-il que la tradition patristique ancienne nous donne l'interprétation véritable de l'ensemble de la parabole (462)... [L]a tradition est unanime à voir dans le Bon Samaritain la figure du Christ (463)... Ainsi voyons-nous en quel sens il est vrai de voir dans l'exégèse patristique du Bon Samaritain la tradition authentique de la parabole (464)...' The three terms 'véritable', 'unanime', and especially 'authentique' can be read, by those who are sensitive to dogmatic language, as though they are meant to take on a juridical sense of moral/doctrinal obligation. But both Daniélou and de Lubac express themselves rather carefully. Cf. J. Daniélou, 'Le bon Samaritain', *Mélanges bibliques rédigés en l'honneur d'André Robert* (Paris: Bloud & Gay, 1957), 457–65; *Bible et Liturgie: la théologie biblique des sacrements et des fêtes d'après les Pères de l'Église*, Lex Orandi, 11 (Paris: Cerf, 1951); ET: *The Bible and the liturgy*, trans. Michael A. Mathis (Notre Dame IN: University of Notre Dame Press, 1956).

context. In his history of pre-modern exegesis,[29] de Lubac also adopts a rather aggressive tone. The allegorical interpretation of the Old Testament is a necessary and obligatory part of the tradition and cannot be ignored, on pain of loss of communion with the tradition.

My comments on this view will be based on my own experience of living in Jerusalem for twelve years, trying to understand the Hebrew Bible as a Christian, and observing how the rabbis present that Bible to their own people. The first thing I learned is that the Pentateuch is more important in classical Jewish liturgy and life than is the rest of the Hebrew canon. If you cannot make sense out of it, the door is closed to the Jewish faith and to the nourishment of our own Christian faith. Second, I came to understand that the Pentateuch is not history in the same sense that the succession narrative is history (2 Samuel 9–20; 1 Kings 1–2). It is something else: a mixture of history, myth, legend, poetry, and law. It is about the birth of a nation. It contains a constitution of a state. And it is a great book of religious revelation. Only a complex reading approach will do justice to its complexity. Third, when one reads the Sabbath sermons of modern orthodox rabbis like Pinchas Peli, one realizes that they are desperate to find meaning anywhere. Historical criticism, the rabbinical and Christian traditions, philosophy, psychology, science, literature—all are placed at the service of the great and difficult task of making the Torah meaningful to people today, especially to people of good will.[30]

Given this experience, one is more disposed to give de Lubac a favourable hearing, despite his excesses. This is especially true because of two points he makes. First, the Fathers used allegory not for all the books of the Old Testament but only or primarily for the Pentateuch and the Song of Songs. This is good and appropriate news, because, even if every word of Wellhausen were divinely inspired, his words would not suffice for a full, rounded, intellectually, aesthetically, and spiritually satisfying understanding of the Pentateuch. It suffices to read him to be convinced of that fact. He simply did not write commentaries on the Torah (although he did on the minor prophets and the Gospels). So here de Lubac's defence of allegory is appropriate. Second, de Lubac argues that if we do not accept non-literal, 'spiritual' senses of scripture, much of the Old Testament, and particularly the Pentateuch, becomes spiritually unavailable to the faithful. This seems true to me.

[29] De Lubac, *Histoire et esprit: l'intelligence de l'Écriture d'après Origène*, Théologie 16 (Paris: Aubier, 1950); de Lubac, *Exégèse médiévale*, 4 vols. Théologie 41, 42, 59 (Paris: Aubier, 1959, 1961, 1964); parts of these have been translated: *The Sources of Revelation* trans. Luke O'Neill (New York: Herder & Herder, 1968); *Medieval Exegesis: the four senses of Scripture*, trans. Mark Sebanc (i), E.M. Macierowski (ii, iii) (Grand Rapids MI: Eerdmans/Edinburgh: T&T Clark, 1998–).
[30] W. G. Plaut (ed.), *The Torah: A Modern Commentary* (New York: Union of American Hebrew Congregation, 1981); Pinchas Peli, *Shabbat shalom: a renewed encounter with the Sabbath* (Washington DC: B'nai B'rith Books, 1988); *Torah today: a renewed encounter with scripture* (Washington DC: B'nai B'rith Books, 1987).

A small example may suffice. In Exod. 15.27; cf. Num. 33.9 we read: 'Then they came to Elim, where there were twelve springs of water and seventy palm trees, and they encamped there by the water.' Even if this is literally, historically true, it does not say much, by itself, to the modern reader. It comes as no surprise, then, that the Fathers interpret the twelve springs as the preaching of the twelve apostles, and the seventy palm trees as the seventy pagan nations of the world to whom they are sent to preach (or the seventy elders of Lk. 10.1, 17). It is no wonder that Philo and the rabbis said something similar about the twelve tribes and the seventy nations, since some meaning is better than none.[31]

Nevertheless, reading the Fathers on scripture will not solve all of our exegetical problems. De Vaux said this tersely, politely, firmly in his review of Daniélou's book on Origen.[32] To be sure, Origen was a genius. He was often better than some of the childish, apologetic literal-mindedness of the nineteenth century. But we must still have the courage to bite the historical-critical (often German Protestant) bullet before we can have a credible word of our own to say.

In our own day, a spirit of discontent with modern exegetical methods is noticeable among both younger Jewish and Christian scholars.[33] The French *ressourcement* theologians can, then, still be of service. Our weakness as Catholics remains the fact that we are still deficient in good full-scale commentaries on the Old Testament, especially on the Pentateuch. Perhaps the long delayed publication of Père Lagrange's commentary on Genesis will help to open up the dam.[34] Christoph Dohmen's commentary on Exodus may be a sign of better things to come.[35]

---

[31] Daniélou, *Sacramentum futuri: études sur les origines de la typologie biblique* (Paris: Beauchesne, 1950), ET: *From Shadows to Reality: Studies in Biblical Typology of the Fathers*, trans. Wulstan Hibberd (Westminster MD: Newman, 1960), 172–4.

[32] R. de Vaux, *Revue biblique*, 57 (1950), 140–1.

[33] J. D. Levenson, *The Hebrew Bible, the Old Testament, and historical criticism: Jews and Christians in biblical studies* (Louisville KY: Westminster/John Knox Press, 1993); Markus Bockmuehl, *Seeing the Word: Refocusing New Testament Study* (Grand Rapids MI: Baker Academic, 2006).

[34] The first step towards this has been taken by the publication of Lagrange's article on the Patriarchs, in Guy Couturier (ed.), *Les Patriarches et l'histoire: autout d'un article inédit du père M.-J. Lagrange*, Lectio divina, hors-série (Paris: Cerf, 1998).

[35] C. Dohmen, *Exodus 19–40*, Herders theologischer Kommentar zum Alten Testament (Freiburg im Breisgau: Herder, 2004). See also B. S. Childs, *The Book of Exodus: A Critical Theological Commentary* (Philadelphia: Westminster, 1974); W. H. C. Propp, *Exodus 1–18*, Anchor Bible 2a (New York: Doubleday, 2000); *Exodus 19–40*, Anchor Bible 2b (New York: Doubleday, 2006).

21

Ressourcement and the Renewal of Catholic Liturgy: On Celebrating the New Rite

Keith F. Pecklers, SJ

INTRODUCTION

In order to understand *ressourcement* in terms of the liturgical renewal launched at Vatican II, it is essential to consider the historical context out of which the conciliar liturgy emerged. Thus, beginning with a presentation of eighteenth- and nineteenth-century foundations for liturgical renewal, we shall consider the role which the twentieth-century liturgical movement played in calling the Roman Catholic Church to a recovery of its liturgical sources. We will then examine how that movement was ratified at the Second Vatican Council (1962–5) with the call to 'full, conscious, and active liturgical participation', and the eventual implementation of the new rite through the work of the International *Consilium*. The chapter will conclude with a brief reflection on the current state of liturgical affairs forty-five years on. What I wish to affirm from the outset is that the success of the liturgical renewal can only be understood when viewed within its wider collaboration with the biblical, ecumenical, and patristic movements. At the end of the day, each of those movements shared a common agenda: plumbing the depths of the church's apostolic and patristic origins so as to assist the mystical Body of Christ in its renewal and fresh discovery of its mission.

EIGHTEENTH- AND NINETEENTH-CENTURY FOUNDATIONS

In the eighteenth century, ancient sacramentaries and the *Ordines Romani* were discovered, studied, and published, thanks to the work of scholars such as

Cardinal Giuseppe Tomasi (†1713).[1] This desire to return to the sources also found support at the level of the Magisterium. Pope Benedict XIV exhibited a keen interest in liturgical renewal through recovering the church's liturgical foundations and in 1741, he established a commission to propose liturgical changes and launch a reform. In his 1742 encyclical *Certiores Effecti* he emphasized the importance of the lay faithful receiving communion from the Eucharist consecrated at that particular Mass and not distributed from the tabernacle—a problem which continues in our own day, two hundred and sixty years later.[2]

One notable attempt at liturgical renewal is found in the Synod of Pistoia held in 1786 under the leadership of the Bishop of Pistoia-Prato, Scipio de Ricci (†1810). Inspired by Jansenism, the Synod called for a return to the pristine liturgy of the early church. It affirmed the independence of diocesan bishops to govern their own dioceses and that such governance should take place with the approval of the diocesan synod of clergy. This had been the position of the Gallican articles of 1682.

Interestingly, one finds quite a resemblance between the liturgical agenda at Pistoia and what was proposed two centuries later at Vatican II. But the late eighteenth century was a different age. Lacking proper catechesis on the part of the clergy and faithful, and without the various ecclesial movements which paved the way for Vatican II, the Synod was bound to fail, and indeed it did. With the promulgation of the Papal Bull *Auctorem fidei* in 1794, Pius VI condemned the eighty-five propositions of the Synod of Pistoia either as heretical, false, or scandalous, depending on which number was in question.[3] Bishop de Ricci had been deposed four years earlier in 1790 and died in exile in 1810.

Faithful to its desire to return to patristic sources, the Synod advocated the active liturgical participation of the faithful, introducing use of the vernacular; eliminating Masses taking place simultaneously in the same place; the centrality of the Sunday and parochial Eucharist at which the parish priest should always preside, proclaiming the Eucharistic Prayer in a loud, clear voice so that members of the congregation could be more spiritually engaged within it. Echoing Benedict XIV's plea, it decreed that communion given to the faithful should be consecrated at that same Mass and not taken from the tabernacle. Baptismal preparation was recommended for parents and godparents and baptisms should appropriately take place at the Easter Vigil. Moreover, couples preparing for the Sacrament of Matrimony should also be given proper catechetical preparation.[4]

---

[1] See I. Scicolone, *Il Cardinale Giuseppe Tomasi di Lampedusa e gli inizi della scienza liturgica*, Cultura cristiana di Sicilia, 6 (Palermo: Instituto superiore di scienze religiose, 1981).

[2] Pope Benedict XIV, *Certiores Effecti*, Bull. Rom. Bened. XIV, XIV, 1.213–213.

[3] Pope Pius VI, *Auctorem Fidei*, Bull. Rom. Cont., 9.395–418.

[4] See C. Lamioni, ed., *Il Sinodo di Pistoia del 1786* (Rome: Herder, 1991); Keith F. Pecklers, 'The Jansenist Critique and the Liturgical Reforms of the Seventeenth and Eighteenth Centuries', *Ecclesia Orans*, XX/3 (2003), 325–38.

In 1832, Prosper Guéranger re-founded the French Benedictine monastery of Solesmes which had been suppressed during the French Revolution. In the tradition of the great European monasteries as centres of spiritual, cultural, and educational renewal, Guéranger desired to assist the French church in returning to its true foundations through a recovery of the Roman Rite properly celebrated. Influenced by Jansenism and Gallicanism, the church in France had resisted implementation of the Decrees of the Council of Trent and this was especially evident in the realm of worship.[5] Indeed, by the eighteenth century, ninety of the one hundred and thirty-nine dioceses in France had their own distinct liturgy, and in some dioceses, such as Versailles and Beauvais, there were as many as nine Breviaries and Missals.[6] French bishops viewed their approval of liturgical changes as similar to that of their predecessors who had exercised the same power in approving the study and revision of earlier liturgical texts.[7] For his part, Guéranger lamented the fact that such liturgical diversity deprived the faithful of drinking deeply from the church's wellspring and thus advocated a liturgical practice at Solesmes which adhered strictly to the Tridentine Roman Rite, basing much of his own research, however, on medieval foundations rather than patristic ones.[8]

Ressourcement within Catholic liturgical renewal owes a great deal to the theological scholarship of the nineteenth-century Tübingen School, particularly the recovery of the theology of the church as the Mystical Body of Christ. Twentieth-century liturgical reformers were keenly aware that the credibility and eventual success of their efforts would depend largely upon their ability to posit their call to liturgical renewal within a solid theological framework. Indeed, throughout the 1930s and 1940s, liturgical pioneers were often criticized by their peers for limiting their concerns to the aesthetics of liturgy—the kind of vestments worn, for example—elements which were considered peripheral to the more fundamental mission of the church. But a careful reading of their writings reveals quite a different reality.

German Romanticism recovered interest in the church's past with careful attention to the social dimension of Christianity as an antidote to the individualism which its proponents found operative within the Reformation and the Enlightenment. The work of ecclesiologists of the Tübingen School grew naturally within such a context, leading to a new and richer understanding of the nature of the church through a return to the sources. Johann Michael

---

[5] For a survey of the neo-Gallican liturgies, see F. Ellen Weaver, 'The Neo-Gallican Liturgies Revisited', *Studia Liturgica*, 16 (1986–7), 62–5.

[6] Olivier Rousseau, OSB, *The Progess of the Liturgy* (Westminster MD: The Newman Press, 1951), 24.

[7] J. F. De Percin De Montgaillard, *Du droit et du pouvoir des évêques de regler les offices divins dans leurs diocèses* (Paris: n.p., 1686).

[8] Cuthbert Johnson, *Prosper Guéranger (1805–1875): A Liturgical Theologian* (Rome: Pontificio Ateneo S. Anselmo, 1984), 147–89.

Sailer (†1832) emphasized Christian worship's anchor both as the foundation and centre of the church's life that forms the faithful into an organic society.

Johann Adam Möhler (†1838) brought this theology to full stature, arguing that worship held the responsibility of assimilating in an interior manner the doctrine and theology that the church had articulated externally. Unlike Sailer's emphasis on the church as a society, Möhler chose the image of a community. This vision of the baptized was a far cry from the institutionalized image of the church in the nineteenth century. The divine life was communicated by the apostles not to individuals, but to brothers and sisters who were incorporated into that same body of Christ. Thus, the Tübingen movement would come to lay the ecclesiological foundations for a renewed understanding of the church and its worship, and eventually influenced Vatican I's *Dogmatic Constitution on the Church* in which the proposed draft began, 'The Church is the Mystical Body of Christ'. Had that Council not been interrupted, it is certainly plausible that this doctrine would have held sway much earlier than when it was officially introduced in 1943 during the Pontificate of Pope Pius XII.[9]

THE TWENTIETH-CENTURY LITURGICAL MOVEMENT

Proponents of the twentieth-century liturgical movement found a natural resonance with what had evolved at Tübingen in the mid-nineteenth century, as they began to probe some of those same apostolic and patristic sources regarding church worship. But even despite the efforts at Tübingen and an awareness of the recovery of Mystical Body theology at the First Vatican Council, twentieth-century liturgical reformers had their work cut out for them as they attempted to promote their agenda. In fact, when liturgical pioneers argued that we are all members of the mystical body of Christ, their detractors suggested that such affirmations were quite suspicious since they seemed to ignore the church's hierarchical structure. Shrewdly, they rephrased their affirmation: 'The Church is the mystical Body of Christ, *albeit hierarchically ordered.*' Other critics of the liturgical movement suggested that the pioneers' insistence on the communal dimension of worship was a subtle attempt to deny the real presence of Christ in the Blessed Sacrament. Such debates would play out in various ways both in Europe and North America until the promulgation of Pius XII's two landmark encyclicals, *Mystici Corporis Christi* in 1943, and *Mediator Dei* in 1947, both of which essentially gave

---

[9] Enrico Cattaneo, *Il Culto Cristiano in Occidente* (Rome: CLV, 1992), 458–9.

credence and further impetus to what the liturgical pioneers had been advocating for twenty or thirty years.

Be that as it may, the fundamentally Pauline understanding of the church as
the Mystical Body of Christ offered the necessary theological framework that
the liturgical pioneers desired as they sought to return to the liturgical sources.
Worship necessarily implied social responsibility towards the wider body of
Christ within the world and thus, they advocated a recovery of the link
between liturgy and *diakonia*. Already in the First Apology of Justin Martyr
(†165) which offers an extraordinarily detailed albeit simplistic account of the
dominical eucharistic structure in mid-second-century Rome, reference was
made to the collection for needier members of the community. Importantly, it
was the same president of the liturgical assembly who both led the prayer of
that local church and was responsible for the distribution of goods to those
most in need.

Twentieth-century liturgical reformers also relied on St Augustine's reflections on the Mystical Body of Christ as it gathered for the celebration of the
Eucharist: 'So if it's you that are the body of Christ and its members, it's the
mystery meaning you that has been placed on the Lord's table; what you
receive is the mystery that means you.'[10] In the year 426 Augustine wrote
about the opening rite of the Eucharist on Easter Day:

> 'I advanced towards the people. The church was full, and cries of joy echoed
> throughout it: "Glory to God!", "God be praised!" No one was silent; the shouts
> were coming from everywhere. I greeted the people and they began to cry out
> again in their enthusiasm. Finally when silence was restored, the readings from
> sacred scripture were proclaimed.'

As Cabié, from whom this quotation is taken, comments,

> This participative worship was further exhibited by the procession with the gifts
> as the faithful brought forth the bread which they had baked and wine which they
> had made, along with an offering for the poor.[11]

It was precisely this sort of participation at the Sunday Eucharist that had been
lost over the centuries and represented that which the twentieth-century
liturgical pioneers sought to recover.

Ressourcement within Catholic worship was given significant direction in
1909. Curiously, the occasion was a Catholic labour conference in Malines at
which the Belgian former industrial chaplain and then Benedictine monk of
Mont César, Lambert Beauduin, delivered an important lecture entitled '*La*

---

[10] Augustine of Hippo, 'Sermon 272. On the Day of Pentecost to the *Infantes*, on the
Sacrament', in Augustine, *Complete Works*, Part III, vii. 300.
[11] Robert Cabié, *The Church at Prayer II: The Eucharist* (Collegeville MN: The Liturgical
Press, 1992), 50; see, too, 78–9.

vraie prière de l'Église'. Beauduin based his talk on Pius X's first *Motu Proprio* published six years earlier in 1903 on the subject of sacred music, *Tra le sollecitudini*, in which the Pope spoke of liturgy as the church's most important and indispensible source:

> Since we have very much at heart that the true Christian spirit be revived in all possible ways and that it be maintained among all the faithful, it is above all necessary to provide for the holiness and dignity of the sacred places where precisely the faithful gather to draw this spirit at its primary and indispensable source, that is, active participation in the sacred mysteries and in the public and solemn prayer of the Church.[12]

As the majority of conference participants were heavily involved in the social apostolate and labour movements, Beauduin explored what it might mean for the Belgian church to rediscover Catholic worship as the source of the church's social mission. To some degree, the important social encyclical of Leo XIII, *Rerum novarum*, gave impetus to a greater understanding of the church's social mission which flows from the Eucharist. The problem was that worship and the church's social outreach were often seen as two distinct realities which could not intersect. The beauty of the Tridentine Mass would lift the mind and heart to God as the church gathered, and congregants would leave the often mundane world of daily life to experience heaven on earth in the transcendent experience of Catholic worship; there, they would find the strength to return to the world and carry on. It was precisely the separation of those two distinct worlds that troubled Beauduin. He lamented the fact that the liturgy of the day deprived the faithful of drinking from that deeper source as nourishment for the Christian mission.

Thanks to Beauduin's efforts, Mont César soon became a centre for liturgical renewal. In various liturgical conferences and study weeks, Beauduin led participants back to the liturgical sources of the early church to discover the ways in which the liturgy offered the true spiritual source for Christian social activism.[13] Early on in his liturgical mission, Beauduin remarked, 'What a shame that the liturgy remains the endowment of an elite; we are aristocrats of the liturgy; everyone should be able to nourish himself from it, even the simplest people: we must democratize the liturgy.'[14]

Beauduin's biographer recalled his enthusiasm at the realization that it is in the Eucharist that the church takes on flesh. Beauduin once rushed into class

---

[12] *ASS* xxxvi (1904) 331, cited in J. Neuner and J. Dupuis (eds.), *The Christian Faith in the Doctrinal Documents of the Catholic Church* (New York: Alba House, 1982), 34. ET available at <http://www.vatican.va/holy_father/pius_x/motu_proprio/documents/hf_p-x_motu-proprio_19031122_sollecitudini_it.html>.
[13] See Raymond Loonbeek and Jacques Mortiau, *Un Pionnier Dom Lambert Beauduin (1873–1960): Liturgie et Unité chrétiens* 2 vols (Louvain-La-Neuve: Collège Érasme, 2001).
[14] Quoted in Sonya A. Quitslund, *Beauduin: A Prophet Vindicated* (New York: Newman Press, 1973), 16.

immediately after Mass and proclaimed enthusiastically to his students: 'I've just realized that the liturgy is the center of the piety of the Church!'[15] Consistent with his other concerns, Beauduin was bothered by the fact that Pius X's decree on frequent Communion in 1905, *Sacra Tridentina Synodus*, failed to stress the reality that Communion was an integral part of the Mass itself.[16] He wondered, for example, why more solemnity and attention were given to eucharistic adoration and benediction than to Mass itself.

Belgium was hardly the only country engaged in a recovery of the church's liturgical tradition. At the same time that Beauduin was working, the German Benedictine Abbey of Maria Laach was emerging as a centre for liturgical research and writing, focused largely on the study of early source material. Encouraged by his abbot, Ildefons Herwegen (†1946), Odo Casel (†1948) made a significant contribution to liturgical science and specifically liturgical theology. Over a thirty-year period from 1918 until his untimely death in 1948, Casel wrote hundreds of articles and books which influenced liturgical renewal around the globe. Most famous was his text *Das cristliche Kultmysterium*, in which he argued that the Christian sacraments had their foundations in the Greek mystery religions. Despite the limits of Casel's research, his interpretation unearthed the symbolic richness of the liturgical life as it expresses the church's self-identity as the Mystical Body of Christ.

In 1918, Casel joined fellow monk Cuniber Mohlberg and the Italo-German diocesan priest Romano Guardini (†1968), with the collaboration of Franz Dölger and Anton Baumstark, in launching a three-part series of publications all focused on returning to the liturgical sources: *Ecclesia Orans, Liturgiegeschichtliche Quellen*, and *Liturgiegeschichtliche Forschungen*. The periodical *Jahrbuch für Liturgiewissenschaft* followed in 1921 and two years later, Romano Guardini published his important work *Vom Geist der Liturgie*, which became a classic text in liturgical spirituality. The monks of Maria Laach gave significant attention to Orthodox liturgical sources, where there was much to be received, since the Orthodox Church had been far more successful at preserving its patristic foundations.[17]

The historian of the liturgical movement, Olivier Rousseau (†1984), noted how the Eastern churches played their own role in the western liturgical movement. This was largely due to French contact with Russian Orthodox immigrants who had arrived there following the Bolshevik Revolution of 1917. Unlike the Western churches, the Orthodox Church had preserved the liturgical spirit of the early church and thus had much to offer pioneers of the liturgical revival in the West who wished to return to the liturgical sources. For

---

[15] Quitslund, *Beauduin*, 16.
[16] Pope Pius X, *Sacra Tridentina Synodus* S. Congregatio Concilii, *Sacra Tridentia Synodus*, *ASS*, xxxviii (1905), 400–6.
[17] See Rousseau, *The Progress of the* Liturgy, 139–48.

the Orthodox, everything was considered through the lens of liturgy. In the words of Rousseau: 'Her piety was never separated from her official prayers, to which she has always remained uniformly faithful.'[18]

In Austria, the Augustinian Canon Pius Parsch (†1954) pursued an integrative approach in his return to the sources. Both through his scholarship and pastoral activity at the small church of St Gertrude near his monastery of Klosterneuburg, Parsch recovered the sense of the Eucharist as a sacrificial meal in which the entire community actively participated while recognizing its connection to the wider body of Christ throughout the world.[19] What emerged was an Austrian movement focused on a common goal of both biblical and liturgical re-sourcing which served the renewal of the church at its very core, rather than treating liturgy in isolation. Such renewal was promoted through the publication in 1923 of *Das Jahr des Heiles*, a commentary on the Missal and Breviary for the entire liturgical year, and the establishment of the journal *Bibel und Liturgie* in 1926, promoting a wider knowledge of the Bible among Catholics in the context of the liturgy.[20]

The Second World War had its own effect on the liturgical renewal both in raising serious questions on the role of faith amidst the tragedy of war and in stirring a greater desire for more profound worship. This was especially the case in Germany, where liturgical pioneers such as Hans Anscar Reinhold and Johannes Pinsk became strong opponents of the Third Reich both in their writing and preaching. Offering a French response to those pressing questions of the day, Dominicans Pie Duployé and Aimon-Marie Roguet founded the Centre de Pastoral Liturgique in Paris in 1943 with the launching of the journal *La Maison-Dieu* two years later in 1945.

The integration of the liturgical movement with the evolving biblical, patristic, and ecumenical movements continued to bear fruit not only in Austria, but also in other European countries and in North America.[21] All social movements begin at the local level and gradually come to be ratified at the official level after much effort, and this was certainly the case with the liturgical movement. It was not until Pius XII's encyclical on the sacred liturgy in 1947, *Mediator Dei*[22]—the first encyclical on liturgy in the history of the

---

[18] Rousseau, *The Progress of the Liturgy*, 140.
[19] See Pius Parsch, *Volksliturgie Ihr Sinn und Umfang* (Würzburg: Echter, 2004).
[20] See Roman Stafin, *Eucharistie als Quelle der Gnade bei Pius Parsch* (Würzburg: Echter, 2004).
[21] See Pecklers, *The Unread Vision: The Liturgical Movement in the United States of America 1926–1955* (Collegeville MN: The Liturgical Press, 1998); also Bruno Bürki and Martin Klöckener, *Liturgie In Bewegung—Ein Movement* (Freiburg/Geneva: Universitätsverlag/Labor et Fides, 2000).
[22] Pius XII, *Mediator Dei*. Encyclical Letter on the Sacred Liturgy (20 November 1947), *AAS* xxxix (1947), 521–95. ET available at <http://www.vatican.va/holy_father/pius_xii/encyclicals/documents/hf_p-xii_enc_20111947_mediator-dei_en.html>.

church—that the liturgical movement was actually legitimated and made credible.

Before discussing the liturgical reforms of Vatican II, it is important to mention the International Liturgical Congress at Assisi held in 1956, which in many respects paved the way for the Council's Preparatory Commission on the Liturgy. Of course, Assisi was not the only important congress held in the 1950s. Such international meetings began at Maria Laach in 1951, followed by Odilienberg in 1952, Lugano in 1954, and gathered together liturgical scholars and members of the hierarchy along with missionaries from far flung corners of the globe. There, a network of contacts and resources grew and the liturgical movement was no longer a mere lobbying effort registering limited success. Indeed, the Assisi Congress was convoked by the Prefect of the Congregation of Sacred Rites, Cardinal Gaetano Cicognani, who presided over the meeting, and all 1,400 delegates were received by Pope Pius XII in a private audience at the end of the week. Thus, the Assisi convocation represented a certain coming of age for the liturgical movement.

THE LITURGICAL REFORMS OF THE SECOND VATICAN COUNCIL

On 25 November 1959 Pope John XXIII announced the Second Vatican Council and a Preparatory Commission on the Liturgy was established with Cardinal Cicognani as President (succeeded by Cardinal Arcadio Larraona in 1962) and Annibale Bugnini, CM (†1982) as Secretary. Not surprisingly, it was the Assisi roster that assisted in selecting members for the liturgical commission. The collaboration of liturgical scholars in the 1950s had led to consensus on several key areas: the need to recover the rich theology of worship whose heart was the paschal mystery of Christ; the pastoral dimension of worship as had been evident in the early church which would necessarily include worship in the vernacular; and attention to the church's worship in relation to its mission within the world—a subject that would lead to questions concerning cultural adaptation, especially in mission lands. It is not surprising that the general orientation of the schema that would eventually lead to the Council's Constitution on the Sacred Liturgy closely resembled the fundamental goals of the liturgical movement.[23]

Commenting on this fact, the Benedictine liturgical scholar, Anscar Chupungco, wrote: 'It can be said that through these pastors and liturgists the

---

[23] For a thorough treatment of the work of the Preparatory Commission and the formulation of *Sacrosanctum Concilium*, see Annibale Bugnini, *The Reform of the Liturgy 1948–1975* (Collegeville MN: The Liturgical Press, 1990).

liturgical movement entered the Council hall.'[24] Chupungco's words are quite significant, I believe, for what we have considered in terms of the return to the sources at Tübingen in the nineteenth century and in the liturgical movement in the twentieth, makes it abundantly clear that Vatican II was as much a point of arrival as a point of departure. In other words, if it were not for the scholarly research that had been undertaken as discussed earlier in this chapter, and the seeds thereby sown, the renewal launched by Vatican II would have been anaemic at best. This was true, of course, not only in terms of the liturgical movement but in all of the movements for renewal together.

The Preparatory Commission prepared a schema which included areas that required both theological reinterpretation as well as ritual revision: the mystery of the liturgy in relation to the church's life and mission; the celebration of the Eucharist with particular attention to a recovery of clerical concelebration; the Liturgy of the Hours; sacraments and sacramentals; revision of the liturgical calendar; the use of Latin; liturgical formation; liturgical participation of the lay faithful; linguistic adaptations to different cultures and peoples; the simplification of liturgical vestments; sacred music and art. Essentially, the schema endeavoured to treat the full measure of the church's liturgical life and, with few emendations, that text was presented to the Council Fathers as the Constitution on the Liturgy. Some, at least, were pleased that the Constitution on the Liturgy was the first document to be examined, for the subject of liturgy was not complicated and could be treated expeditiously! In reality, discussions lasted from 22 October to 13 November 1962 in the course of fifteen general congregations lasting about fifty hours with 328 oral interventions and 297 written proposals.[25]

On 4 December 1963, at the end of the Council's second session, the Constitution on the Sacred Liturgy, *Sacrosanctum Concilium*, was presented in its final form, passed the general vote by a wide margin of 2,147 to four, and was then promulgated by Paul VI who had only been elected Pope on 21 June. Throughout the text, *Sacrosanctum Concilium* represented a fundamental desire to return to the sources. *SC* § 14 articulates the need to renew the liturgy so that the faithful might 'be led to take a full, conscious and active participation in liturgical celebration. This is demanded by the nature of the liturgy itself; and, by virtue of their baptism, it is the right and the duty of the Christian people . . .'

The scope of the liturgical reform was perhaps most clearly expressed at *SC* § 34 which stated that, in being restored to their pristine beauty, 'the rites should radiate a rich simplicity; they should be brief and lucid, avoiding pointless repetitions; they should be intelligible to the people, and should

---

[24] Anscar J. Chupungco, '*Sacrosanctum concilium*: Its Vision and Achievements', *Ecclesia Orans* XIII/3, (1996), 495–514 (498).

[25] Chupungco, '*Sacrosanctum concilium*', 498.

not in general require much explanation'. It was precisely 'rich simplicity' which had characterized the Roman Rite as it grew from the fifth to the eighth century before it came into contact with the more dramatic, poetic, and wordy Gallican Rite whose elements gradually crept into the Roman Rite over the centuries.[26]

SC § 50 is equally explicit:

> ... [T]he rites, in a way that carefully preserves what really matters, should become simpler. Duplications which have come in over the course of time should be discontinued, as should the less useful accretions. Some elements which have degenerated or disappeared through the ill effects of the passage of time are to be restored to the ancient pattern of the fathers, insofar as seems appropriate or necessary.

Sacrosanctum Concilium also recovered the importance of liturgical theo-logy and spirituality with special emphasis on the Christological centre of all Christian worship (*SC* § 7). Sacred Scripture was likewise restored as the source for all liturgical renewal with patristic theology and practice as its guide and inspiration. Most importantly, since liturgy is to be 'high point and ... source' of the Church's life (*SC* § 10), the assembly's 'full, conscious, and active participation' within the liturgy was to be an essential goal of all liturgical formation.

The Constitution reflects a patristic understanding of pastoral governance on matters liturgical, exercised in a spirit of collegiality. There is an underlying sense that liturgical issues pertaining to the local church are best dealt with by episcopal conferences or even diocesan bishops themselves (*SC* § 22). This was a far cry from the Tridentine emphasis on liturgical centralization located in what was then called the Congregation for Sacred Rites, founded in 1588. Theological justification for such liturgical de-centralization was found in the fact that the diocesan bishop is empowered to shepherd that local church and not merely serve as a sort of district representative or middle-manager; thus the bishop or episcopal conference should have the authority to make appro-priate liturgical decisions.[27]

Throughout the Constitution we find a careful balance between tradition and progress. *SC* § 23 states:

> In order that healthy tradition can be preserved while yet allowing room for legitimate development, thorough investigation—theological, historical and pas-toral—of the individual parts of the liturgy up for revision is always to be the first step. The general laws regarding the structure and intention of the liturgy should also be taken into account, as well as the experience stemming from more recent

---

[26] See Edmund Bishop, 'The Genius of the Roman Rite', in *Liturgica Historica: Papers on the Liturgy and Religious Life of the Western Church* (Oxford: Clarendon Press, 1962 [1918]), 1–19.
[27] *SC* § 41; Chupungco, 507–8.

liturgical renewal and from the special concessions that have, from time to time, been granted. Finally, changes should not be made unless a real and proven need of the church requires them, and care should be taken to see that new forms grow in some way organically out of the forms already existing.

Thus, in some respects, the document serves as a *via media*. For example, despite popular misconceptions, the Council did not completely abolish Latin. Indeed, the translations of post-conciliar liturgical texts (prayers, readings, and blessings) begin with the original Latin text (called the *editio typica*, the 'typical edition') and from there the text is carefully translated into the vernacular. With the publication of Pope Benedict XVI's Apostolic Letter *Summorum Pontificium*[28] in July 2007 granting wider usage of the Tridentine Rite, I spent a good deal of time explaining to journalists that it was not the Latin Mass that the Pope was restoring, since it has always been permissible to celebrate the New Rite in Latin. Rather, it was the Tridentine form of the Latin Mass, which is a very different matter.

At the same time, however, *Sacrosanctum Concilium* was much more than a compromise document. In some places, the Constitution calls for revision of liturgical rites and their corresponding liturgical texts. Regarding the Order of Mass, for example, it was to be revised in such a way 'that the specific ideas behind the individual parts and their connection with one another can be more clearly apparent, and so that it becomes easier for the people to take a proper and active part (*SC* § 50). On the subject of cultural adaptation—what would later come to be called 'liturgical inculturation'—*SC* § 40 states, 'However, in some places or some situations, there may arise a pressing need for a more radical adaptation of the liturgy . . .'

THE INTERNATIONAL *CONSILIUM* AND THE IMPLEMENTATION OF THE NEW RITE[29]

If members of the Preparatory Commission and the Council Fathers found their task to be daunting, the greater challenge was yet to come. The reforms would need to be implemented and the universal Church would need to be formed and catechized in a new worship style and language. The *Consilium ad*

---

[28] Benedict XVI, *Summorum Pontificium*: Apostolic Letter motu proprio on the use of the Roman Liturgy prior to the reform of 1970 (7 July 2007), *AAS* xcviv (2007), 777–81. ET available at <http://www.vatican.va/holy_father/benedict_xvi/motu_proprio/documents/hf_ben-xvi-motu-proprio_20070707_summorum-pontificum_lt.html>.

[29] On the *Consilium* and its work see Archbishop Piero Marini, *A Challenging Reform: Realizing the Vision of the Liturgical Renewal*, eds. Mark R. Francis, CSV, John R. Page, Keith F. Pecklers, SJ (Collegeville MN: The Liturgical Press, 2007).

exsequendam constitutionem de Sacra Liturgia was formed by Pope Paul VI in January 1964, with Cardinal Giacomo Lercaro of Bologna as President and Annibale Bugnini, CM as Secretary. Commenting on those appointments, Former Papal Master of Ceremonies, Archbishop Piero Marini wrote:

> The discreet appointment of Lercaro and Bugnini . . . was essential for the success of the reform. These appointments made by Paul VI demonstrated not only the open-mindedness on the Pope's part but also a fair degree of courage. Lercaro enjoyed greater prestige internationally than in Italy. Within the Roman Curia and beyond, he was often seen as being too progressive . . . As for Bugnini, his appointment was truly a vindication, since it was only one year before that he had been sidelined by the Curia. From that moment on, he would remain at the helm of the liturgical reform of Vatican II until 1975, when the Congregation for Divine Worship was restructured.[30]

In order to properly launch the reform, the *Consilium* published several important documents: the First Instruction, *Inter Oecumenici* of 1964, on the orderly carrying out of *Sacrosanctum Concilium*; the 1965 Letter, *Le renouveau liturgique*, on furthering the liturgical reform; the Second Instruction, *Tres abhinc annos*, and Letter, *Dans sa récente allocution*, which dealt with issues regarding the reform—both published in 1967; and finally the 1969 Instruction *Comme le prévoit*, on liturgical translation into local languages. The Congregation for Divine Worship issued the Third Instruction *Liturgicae instaurationes* in 1970 on the orderly carrying out of the Liturgy Constitution.

From its inception, the *Consilium* was charged with the task of revising existing liturgical books so that they were in harmony with the directives of the Council. Even more important would be the editing and revision of the Latin post-conciliar liturgical books which would then be translated into vernacular languages by regional commissions. The *Consilium* also worked on composing liturgical texts such as three new Eucharistic Prayers in 1968. Despite its efforts, however, ongoing tensions remained with the Congregation for Divine Worship which gradually limited the *Consilium*'s authority and influenced the liturgical autonomy of respective episcopal conferences in the task of implementation. As early as February 1964, just a few months after the promulgation of *Sacrosanctum Concilium*, the bishop members of the French Liturgical Commission stated in a letter to several dicasteries of the Roman Curia that they found themselves frustrated by those who would restrict the authority of episcopal conferences given to them by Vatican II.[31]

Both the *Consilium* and Congregation for Divine Worship existed to facilitate implementation of the liturgical reforms on the international level, but the greater challenge would be implementation on the local or regional levels. For

---

[30] Marini, *A Challenging Reform*, 12.
[31] See Marini, *A Challenging Reform*, 168–70.

example, the Holy See initially found it difficult to understand why the churches of Latin America could not use the same vernacular liturgical books as the church in Spain. But linguistic issues—not to mention historic and cultural ones—soon made it clear that there were too many variances to support just one translation in Castilian Spanish from the Latin *editio typica*.

Reforming the liturgy in a post-conciliar church was part of a much larger agenda that would work in tandem with an overall renewal of the church's life. Unlike its Tridentine form, Vatican II worship was to reach out widely to embrace all of God's world. Liturgy, then, was necessarily concerned about life outside of the sanctuary walls: human liberation, justice and mercy for the poor and oppressed, dialogue with other Christians and with non-Christian believers.

THE LITURGICAL RENEWAL FORTY-FIVE YEARS ON

As we reflect back on the Second Vatican Council, the renewal of Catholic worship and the New Rite which was a product of the Reform, it must be said that we are in a far better place today than we were prior to Vatican II. The liturgy has been returned to the people of God to whom it rightly belongs by virtue of their baptism. At the same time, a great deal happened very quickly in a short period of time. For example, an English translation of the Latin Missal of Paul VI was produced in a record four years. In some cases, liturgical changes were introduced without understanding why. Indeed, many bishops returned home from the Council enthusiastic about the prospect of a renewed liturgical life, but felt largely unprepared for the task of implementation. For some, the implementation of the new rite unleashed a freedom and zeal for liturgical creativity which the church had not known for centuries. Much of this experimentation of the 1960s and 1970s emerged at the grassroots level, and it must be said that a good deal of the 'liturgical creativity' of those years left much to be desired. In fact, the sort of experimentation which marked those early years after the Council was not what the architects of the liturgical reform had in mind at all. Of course, mistakes were made in the implementation of the liturgical reforms, but it was done as well as was possible at the time by those who were most directly involved in the process.[32] Nonetheless, it must also be admitted that the results around the globe have been largely uneven. Even today, the kind of liturgical participation and careful preparation envisaged by the Council exhibited in a proper

[32] See Robert F. Taft, SJ, 'Return to our Roots: Recovering Western Liturgical Traditions', *America*, 198/18 (May 26–June 2, 2008), 10–13.

implementation of the new rite is barely visible in some countries, while it is abundantly present in others.

Forty-five years on, we have made good progress in recovering the link between liturgy and ecclesiology, but there is much work that remains to be done. We have yet to plumb the riches of our sources and to understand at a profound level what liturgical participation actually demands of the assembly if we take our worship seriously. Some progress has also been registered in recovering worship's transcendent dimension and the non-verbal symbolic richness that Christian liturgy offers, but in many places our post-conciliar celebrations remain too loquacious and idiosyncratic, for example, when presiders and preachers call more attention to themselves than to Jesus Christ whom Vatican II calls the 'chief liturgist' and whose paschal mystery lies at the heart of every liturgical celebration.

CONCLUSION

In December 2007, at Archbishop's House in Westminster, London, Archbishop Piero Marini launched the book already cited here, *A Challenging Reform*. In the course of his remarks he made a rather bold statement: 'The future of liturgy is the future of the church.' The following morning during a press conference on the book's publication, he expanded on what he meant by those words:

> . . . Celebrating the liturgy is itself the primordial source of renewal in the church. We learn the liturgy by celebrating it. The more we succeed at celebrating the liturgy, the more we'll live the Christian life fully and the more we'll succeed in transforming the church. The great ideals of the church are in crisis today in part because there's a crisis in the liturgy. The great ideals of ecumenism, of internal reform of the church, are all connected. The crisis of the liturgy places in crisis these other great values, because the Council wanted to confront these challenges of the mission of the church, of reform, of dialogue with the world, by beginning with the liturgy. If the liturgy is the source and summit, then we foster in the liturgy the kind of life we need to meet these great goals.[33]

Marini's words are a strong reminder of the vision of worship which Vatican II unleashed—a vision deeply bound up with the wider mission of God's church and with God's mission in the world. Forty-five years after the promulgation of *Sacrosanctum Concilium*, we have barely scratched the surface in implementing the liturgical reforms desired by the Council.

---

[33] Archbishop Piero Marini, Interview with John L. Allen, Jr., Archbishop's House, Westminster, London, 15 December 2007. Available at <http://www.natcath.com/mainpage/specialdocuments/marini_interview.pdf, 6>.

22

Knowing God in History and in the Church: *Dei Verbum* and '*Nouvelle Théologie*'

Brian E. Daley, SJ

INTRODUCTION

> We make ourselves a place apart
> Behind light words that tease and flout,
> But oh, the agitated heart
> Till someone find us really out. . . .
>
> But so with all, from babes that play
> At hide-and-seek to God afar,
> So all who hide too well away
> Must speak and tell us where they are.[1]

Revelation, as Robert Frost reminds us in his early poem of that title, is a fundamental part of the way persons relate to each other. Personal relationships begin in knowing, in the mutual recognition that leads to communication and friendship; but because our inner selves are so easily concealed, the initiative lies always with the one known. And to say that we, as persons, are made in the image of God is to remind ourselves (among many other things) that our contact with God, too, begins in mutual knowing—a knowing that God must initiate, form, and complete—and that it, too, is meant to end in friendship.

Four decades on, the Second Vatican Council's Dogmatic Constitution on Divine Revelation, *Dei Verbum,* may not strike us as particularly radical. To conceive of our knowledge of God primarily in terms of a personal response of

---

[1] Robert Frost, 'Revelation', from *A Boy's Will* (1913), in Frost, *Collected Poems, Prose and Plays* (New York: Library of America, 1995), 27–8.

obedience to the self-disclosure of a tri-personal God, who is still fully engaged in our history to 'speak and tell us who he is', probably seems close to obvious. So may the Constitution's encouragement to read scripture within the human contexts and literary forms in which it was originally composed; or its attempt to integrate the text of scripture into the larger context of the church's tradition of interpretation, preaching, teaching, and worship as a single, continuous, and living expression of God's self-disclosure in the fleshly terms of human history. To understand the radical importance of this document, then, it is necessary to recognize how controversial it was in its time, how revolutionary its style, its assertions and omissions, and how near it came, in earlier drafts, to being abandoned to the wastebasket.

DEI VERBUM AND THEOLOGY
AS KNOWLEDGE OF GOD

Dei Verbum is not simply an essay on one discrete theological locus. It is a foundational statement about theology itself: about what it means to 'know' God, what is involved in human speech about God, and how that speech is rooted in God's free initiatives in speaking to us. It is also about the church: how the church teaches us to know and speak of God, how the church comes to certainty about what it will teach and how it will teach it. Historically, *Dei Verbum* marks the end of a long debate within Catholicism about the methods and presuppositions of manualist scholasticism. At the same time, it is an acknowledgement of the legitimacy of the more historically conscious, spiritually and liturgically oriented, and existentially focused style of thought, marked by the call to 'return to the sources' in the scriptures and the Fathers, which in the 1940s and 1950s had been pejoratively branded as 'the new theology'—*la nouvelle théologie*.[2]

Conceptually, the roots of the controversy lay in the transformation of Christian theology in the late twelfth century, from the largely contemplative practice of the monastic schools, rooted in the liturgical cycle and patristic exegesis, to a place among the 'sciences' in the emerging universities. In the *Posterior Analytics*, Aristotle had described 'science' ($\dot{\epsilon}\pi\iota\sigma\tau\dot{\eta}\mu\eta$) as an organized body of knowledge, in which phenomena are arranged according to a chain of causal explanations, reaching back deductively to ever-more-general, universally acknowledged principles.[3] Thomas Aquinas, in the first

---

[2] See Brian Daley, '*La nouvelle théologie* and the Patristic Revival: Sources, Symbols, and the Science of Theology', *IJST*, 7/4 (2005), 362–82.

[3] *Posterior Analytics* I, 2 (71b8–72b4). On the scholastic understanding of theology as a science in this sense, from the Middle Ages until the twentieth century, see Tarcisse Tshibangu,

question of the *Summa Theologiæ*, offers an influential description of organized Christian learning and teaching (*sacra doctrina*)—what we would call theology—as an Aristotelian science: it follows the rules of logic to draw its conclusions, but its principles are based on a limited share of God's own knowledge of himself and creation, communicated to humanity in the 'data' of revelation and shared most fully by the saints in heaven.[4] The science of theology, in Thomas's view, considers many particular things, but the formal object is simply God, and all the details of Christian teaching are of theological concern 'insofar as they have reference to God as their origin'.[5] This conception of theology as a science capable of comprehensive study in a university was the basis of what became known as 'scholasticism', theology developed in and for the 'schools'.

In the controversies that followed the Reformation, Catholic and Protestant scholasticism took on a more polemical edge, colouring their development of theology's rational conclusions by their needs to defend respective ecclesial positions. Catholic theology stressed the structures and role of church authority, and the legitimacy of practices and beliefs lacking obvious roots in scripture; Protestant scholasticism stressed the primacy of the Word of God in church organization and worship, and distanced itself from any aspects of Catholic teaching lacking biblical warrant. By the nineteenth century, the European Enlightenments had largely displaced Protestant scholasticism with more subjective, historically contextualized modes of theological reasoning. A number of influential Catholic theologians, too—the 'Tübingen School' in Germany, for instance—attempted to articulate the reasonableness and coherence of faith in somewhat similar ways. The principal Catholic response, however, to the secularizing thrust of nineteenth-century politics and intellectual life was the revival of scholasticism, bringing a new stress on the rational plausibility of Catholic teaching as a deductive system, and on the necessity of the Catholic Church as the guardian and herald of truth. For many neo-scholastic Catholic theologians, the deductive process led, like a science, from the principles revealed in scripture and in the cherished unwritten traditions to the dogmas which the church eventually proclaimed with certainty to the faithful.[6] To do theology was to participate in the church's officially sanctioned system of reasoned discourse about God.

Théologie positive et théologie speculative: Position traditionnelle et nouvelle problématique (Louvain: Publications universitaires, 1965). For developments in theology as a discipline in the twelfth century, see Marie-Dominique Chenu, *La théologie au douzième siècle* (Paris: Vrin, 1957); for theology as a science, see Chenu, *La théologie comme science au XIIIe siècle* (Paris: Vrin, 1943).

[4] *ST* 1a 1.6, Blackfriars, i.20–35; also 1a 1.1, Blackfriars, i.4–9.

[5] *ST* 1a 1.7, Blackfriars, i.24–7 (adapted).

[6] E.g., 'The nature of dogma and that of our mind make possible only one single process in dogmatic evolution: the dialectic process, or the process of reasoning.' M. M. Tuyaerts, OP,

At the end of the nineteenth century, however, other voices were increasingly heard, critical of the scholastic model for being overly conceptual, even rationalistic in its understanding of how humans come to know God. Besides the explicitly historical approach of the Tübingen school and the Anglican convert John Henry Newman, the German neo-scholastic Matthias Joseph Scheeben (1835–88) offered a version of scholastic argument stressing the spiritual, even mystical experience of the believer as the fullness of human knowledge of God. But most mainstream Catholic theologians found such attempts seriously inadequate. The main critique levelled against the so-called 'Modernists' at the turn of the century, in fact, was that their emphasis on the inner, spiritual significance and historical context of religious doctrines had effectively robbed traditional Christian teaching of any claim to scientific objectivity.[7] In the charged climate of the first few decades of the twentieth century, Catholic theologians who objected to the scholasticism taught in the seminaries had to emphasize that their alternative approaches were not meant to question the full truth of the church's affirmations, or to deny scientific status to theological reflection on the 'sources' of faith.

FRESH MOVES IN EARLY- TO MID-TWENTIETH-CENTURY CATHOLIC THEOLOGY

It was in this challenging milieu that a number of gifted theologians—mainly French Jesuits and Dominicans—in the 1920s and 1930s began to offer a vision of theology that differed subtly but radically in its spirit, method, and style from the dominant version of scholasticism. A good glimpse of this new approach appeared in Marie-Dominique Chenu's dense and synthetic 1935 article 'Position de la Théologie'.[8] For Chenu, theology is not simply a deductive system of propositions based on the assumptions of faith. It is,

---

L'Évolution du Dogme: Étude théologique (Louvain: Nova et Vetera, 1919) 236; cited by Henri de Lubac, 'The Problem of the Development of Dogma' (1948), *Theology in History*, trans. Anne Englund Nash (San Francisco: Ignatius Press, 1996 [1990]), 248–80 (249), originally published in *RSR*, 35 (1948), 130–60.

[7] For example, George Tyrrell, the English Jesuit expelled from the Society and suspended from priestly ministry on suspicion of modernist tendencies, wrote to his friend, Baron Friedrich von Hügel, on 10 February 1907, that he understood the original Christian narrative as 'a work of inspired imagination, not of reflection and reasoning... The whole has a spiritual value as a construction of Time in relation to Eternity. It gives us the *world* of our religious life. But I do not feel bound... to determine prematurely what elements are of literal, and what of purely symbolic value—which is the core of historic fact and which of idealization...' in Maude D. Petre (ed.), *George Tyrrell's Letters* (London: Fisher and Unwin, 1920), 57–8.

[8] For ET, see, 'What is Theology', in Chenu, *Faith and Theology*, trans. Denis Hickey (New York: Macmillan, 1968), 15–35.

rather, the reflective form of believing; a kind of self-conscious, questioning contemplation of God as he reveals his transcendent reality to us in the scriptures and the life of the church. Theology, for Chenu, is not simply reasoning about the church's teachings, but the mind's engagement with its own conversion, its anticipation of eschatological vision. Yet theology is always radically historical in its way of reasoning about God, because God has revealed himself to human beings in contingent events and particular persons and words within human history; as a result, in a certain sense it defies deductive reasoning. Chenu writes that, unlike the philosopher,

> the theologian works with a history. His 'data' are not the natures of things, or the timeless forms; they are events, corresponding to an *economy*, whose realization is bound to time ... The *real* world is this one, not the abstraction of the philosopher. The believer, the believing theologian, enters by his faith into this plan of God; what he seeks to understand, *quaerens intellectum*, is ... a series of absolute divine initiatives, whose essential trait is to be without a reason ... the sweet and terrible contingency of a love which needs give no account of his benefits or his refusal to benefit.[9]

As a result, the theologian always contemplates both the events and persons of the biblical narrative and the practices and proclamations of the ordered Christian community:

> The theologian ... has no object apart from the *auditus fidei*, of which the historian, working in the light of faith, gives him the content—not simply a catalogue of propositions arranged by some Denzinger or other, but living material, in its full abundance ...[10]

Chenu's vision of sacred science was not something he had concocted on his own; it expressed a sense of the character and task of theology that had been growing steadily, if quietly, for several decades, encouraged not least by earlier members of the Dominican faculty of Le Saulchoir: Ambroise Gardeil, Antoine Lemonnyer, and Pierre Mandonnet. For his part, Chenu's younger *confrère* at Le Saulchoir, Yves Congar, was to become one of the great pioneers of Catholic ecumenism, and would contribute in an unparalleled way to the renewal of the Catholic Church's understanding of itself as a living, historical community formed by the presence of the Holy Spirit.

In 1937, Congar's Jesuit contemporary, Henri de Lubac—a young professor at the Jesuit faculty of Fourvière in Lyon—published his own first book, *Catholicisme*,[11] in a new series on the Church, Unam Sanctam, newly founded

---

[9] 'Position de la théologie', *RSPT*, 25 (1935), 232–57 (247) (author's translation).
[10] 'Position de la théologie', 245.
[11] *Catholicisme: Les aspects sociaux du dogme* (Paris: Cerf, 1937). ET (4th edn.), *Catholicism: Christ and the Common Destiny of Man* trans. Lancelot C. Sheppard and Elizabeth Englund (San Francisco: Ignatius, 1988). All references are to this translation.

by Congar. *Catholicisme* represents a plea for a more socially active, genuinely corporate understanding of the church as Christ's Body.[12] This sense of the church owed much to the foundational work of the Belgian Jesuit Émile Mersch (1890–1940), who had published several important monographs on the church centred on the eucharistic and biblical image of the Body of Christ—a revolutionary change of perspective in the years after the Modernist controversy.[13] De Lubac's awareness of historical development, and of the riches offered by a careful reading of patristic texts, was also influenced by the work of preceding French Jesuit theologians such as Léonce de Grandmaison (1868–1927)[14] and Jules Lebreton (1873–1956).[15]

Throughout his career, de Lubac recognized that the revival of a more inclusive sense of the church and the rescue of theology from 'the bitter fruits of individualism',[16] from anti-modern and anti-Protestant polemics and rigid clerical institutionalism, was intimately connected with the retrieval of a more lively, historically aware understanding of the long tradition in which the church lives: more specifically, with the recovery of an appreciation for the spirit and style of patristic biblical exegesis. Even in *Catholicisme* de Lubac displays the intuition that would later lead him to become the first modern scholar to take patristic biblical exegesis seriously,[17] as embodying a grasp of God's saving engagement in history that modern exegesis, with its predominating concern for uncovering the 'original intention' of the author or redactor, has often lost from view. The driving force of early Christian exegesis, de Lubac realized, is a comprehensive view of the narrative of human history, as

[12] *Catholicism*, 314–17.

[13] See Mersch, *Le corps mystique du Christ: Études de théologie historique*, i and ii (Leuven: Museum Lessianum, 1933); *Théologie du corps mystique* (Brussels: Éditions Universelles, 1949). De Lubac's own monumental study of the development of the phrase 'mystical body' up to the thirteenth century is really an elaborate, theologically reflective documentation of the implications of Mersch's work in the light of Pius XII's encyclical *Mystici Corporis Christi* (June 29, 1943): *Corpus Mysticum: l'Eucharistie et l'Église au Moyen Âge: Étude historique* (Paris: Aubier, 1949). ET, *Corpus Mysticum: The Eucharist and the Church in the Middle Ages: Historical Survey*, trans. Gemma Simmonds with Richard Price and Christopher Stephens, eds. Laurence Paul Hemming and Susan Frank Parsons (London: SCM, 2006).

[14] See his posthumously-published *Dogme chrétien: sa nature, ses formules, son développement* (Paris: Beauchesne, 1928); and *Jésus Christ: sa personne, son message, ses preuves* (Paris: Beauchesne, 1928). Himself occasionally suspect of Modernism, Grandmaison tried to sketch an approach to the doctrinal tradition that was both attentive to normative content and open to genuine growth in conceptuality and understanding.

[15] See de Lubac's penetrating, posthumously published essay, 'La doctrine du Père Lebreton sur la Révélation et le dogme d'après ses écrits antimodernistes', *Théologie dans l'histoire* (Paris: Desclée de Brouwer, 1990), ii.108–56. As professor at the Institut Catholique de Paris, Lebreton was constantly in the spotlight of bishops and theologians on the lookout for traces of Modernism.

[16] *Catholicism*, 319.

[17] See *Histoire et esprit: l'intelligence de l'Écriture chez Origène*, 2nd edn. (Paris: Cerf, 2002 (1950)); and *Exégèse médiévale* i–iv (Paris: Aubier, 1959–64); ET *Medieval Exegesis* trans. Mark Sebanc (i), Edward M. Macierowski (ii, iii), 4 vols. (Grand Rapids MI: Eerdmans, 1998–).

beginning with God's creation and finding its goal and inner meaning in the incarnation of the Word, an embodiment of God in human terms that the church, in the power of the Holy Spirit, still strives to grasp and to witness.

The ability to read older narratives and fragments of prayer and prophecy in the light of the present situation of a people struggling to believe, to incorporate earlier textual strata into later ones and to see in the result a revelation of God's continuing fidelity to his promises, was what enabled Israel to give form, through the centuries, to its own biblical canon. In the light of Jesus' resurrection and the event of Pentecost, Jesus' disciples were able to take this complex Jewish canon and to see in the whole of it an even more radiant meaning, reflected from the life and person of Christ. And as the church of the first three centuries continued this struggle of reception and interpretation, it came to recognize a still larger collection of texts and traditions as its canonical narrative. To see Old Testament and New as a single, continuous book, formed from many layers and parts, and to interpret the whole of it as pointing to the final salvation of the world in Christ, involved a constant labour of preaching and study, a continuing inheritance of earlier interpretive traditions. In the process, Christian scripture came to be contextualized as the textual skeleton of a living tradition of hearing and responding to God's revealing Word; and the church, through its processes of appointing authorized teachers and leaders, itself was formed into a living community of faith around text and interpretive traditions. Scripture, tradition, and teaching church form and define one another.

Seasoning his argument with ample references, de Lubac insists throughout *Catholicism* that the Bible, as the Fathers understood it, can never be simply taken as a book of information about ancient Israelite religion or the experiences of Jesus' followers, any more than it can be taken as a guide for the private moral and spiritual instruction of pious individuals. It is a book that tells a single, coherent narrative of creation, fall, and redemption that is fulfilled in Christ and awaiting final realization in the life of the church.[18] It is the story of the growth to eschatological perfection of the Body of Christ.

> In the interpretation of the Old Testament the aspect of historical fulfillment and that of the social community, two aspects that practically coincide, are of prime importance.... The law of 'spiritual intelligence' is the very law of all spirituality, which is never authentic and trustworthy save only as it is not an individualist way, but a spiritualization of the liturgy—an application, that is, to the life of the soul of the Church's life-rhythm. For one and the same essential mystery permeates the whole of Scripture and liturgy, apart from which there is no participation in the mystery of God.[19]

---

[18] *Catholicism*, 169–70.

[19] *Catholicism*, 215. On the connection, in de Lubac's theology, between patristic figural exegesis and the renewal of the church, see Susan K. Wood, *Spiritual Exegesis and the Church*

It is no coincidence, then, that both the Dominicans at Le Saulchoir and the Jesuits at Fourvière—pupils and *confrères* of Chenu, such as Congar and Irénée Henri Dalmais, or of de Lubac, such as Jean Daniélou, Hans Urs von Balthasar, and Henri Bouillard—identified the renewal of theology and the church's life and liturgy, in the years following World War II, with an abandonment of the methods of handbook scholasticism, and a 'return to the sources' with a new emphasis on biblical and patristic studies. One of the clearest expressions of this was the establishment by de Lubac and Daniélou, in 1943, of a new series of annotated French translations of the Fathers, entitled *Sources chrétiennes*. The very title was a challenge to scholasticism, which had long spoken of two distinct 'sources' of the dogmatic principles behind the science of theology: scripture and non-scriptural tradition. Here complete works—not just excerpts containing dogmatic ideas—were offered; the first twenty to appear all came from the Greek Fathers, little used in Western scholastic theology, and almost all of the first thirty volumes contained works of a spiritual, liturgical, or exegetical character.

While post-Reformation Catholic seminary teaching had generally relied on textbooks, organized along scholastic lines of tracts and theses, and had used scriptural and patristic texts in a secondary, proof-text way, the proponents of this 'new' approach were insisting that the best way to enter the theological tradition was by reading classical works, in their entirety, seeking to understand them in their own context. As Chenu had urged in his programmatic description of the new 'school' of theology being developed at Le Saulchoir, students needed to be exposed to the complete, original works of the great Christian saints and doctors—Thomas's *Summa*, rather than a modern digest of Thomism, but also the main works of Augustine, Anselm and Bonaventure: 'the real work needs to be done not on surrogates . . . but on fresh documents, for which their inexhaustible richness truly merits the name "sources".[20] A prefatory note included in the first volume of *Sources chrétiennes* (1943), clarified the aims of the series:

> It is intended to put at the disposal of the educated public complete works of the Church Fathers . . . [who] represent for us a cultural realm almost as distant as that of India or China. What we need to do is to explain that world from within . . . and then to hand the keys over to the reader, leaving him or her the pleasure of discovering treasures that he or she would not otherwise have guessed exist.[21]

---

in the Theology of Henri de Lubac (Grand Rapids MI: Eerdmans, 1998). On the logic and assumptions of patristic exegesis, see Daley, 'Is Patristic Exegesis Still Usable? Reflections on Early Christian Interpretation of the Psalms', *Communio* 29/1 (2002) 181–216; also John O'Keefe and R. R. Reno, *Sanctified Vision: An Introduction to Early Christian Interpretation of the Bible* (Baltimore MD: Johns Hopkins University Press, 2005).

[20] *Une école de théologie: le Saulchoir*, 127.

[21] 'Note liminaire du no.1 de la Collection', republished in Claude Mondésert, *Pour lire les Pères de l'Église dans la Collection 'Sources Chrétiennes'* (Paris: Cerf, 1988), 19. Compare

The 'sources' now being made available, in other words, were not images and concepts woven into a systematic tapestry of recent making, not integrated and prefabricated systems of religious ideas, but separate worlds, linked by the tradition of faith and the reception of the church, while remaining distinct in time and place, culture and language. To the notion of theology as a science was now added a concrete, positive appreciation of evolution, and a recognition that orthodox teaching may have different concerns and forms at different points of the church's life.

One might best characterize the new approach, offered by Chenu and Congar, de Lubac and Daniélou and their colleagues, by saying they were proposing a new strategy for reading theological texts. Their point was that if theology was to move beyond a sterile, self-referential rationalism, and to be a source of renewal for the church as a whole, the diverse classic texts of the entirety of the Christian tradition ought to be read as widely as possible. Theology needed to read not just texts concerning the 'great ideas' of the dogmatic tradition, but also liturgical and spiritual texts, and must give primacy of place to the sacred text of scripture, and its tradition of interpretation. It needed to read theological sources contemplatively, rather than argumentatively or simply in search of dogmatic *loci*; and with a sense of each text's historical context, within a theological tradition that is still under way, still seeking a deeper understanding of the inexhaustible Mystery disclosed to faith. Finally, it needed to read these theological sources 'in the church': with a conscious awareness of the rootedness of theology in the life of the community as Christ's Body, sent under the Apostles and their successors to be salt of the earth and light of the world. For de Lubac and Daniélou, especially, the inspiration behind this changed intellectual model for the 'science' of theology was clearly patristic biblical interpretation in which the scriptures, received as telling a single story whose climax and fullness is Christ, were analysed and preached to the church with all the linguistic and rhetorical refinement late antiquity could muster.

REACTIONS

To many theologians of a more traditional scholastic bent, especially within the Dominican order, this new perspective on theology's 'sources' seemed subversive and dangerous. In a long review article, discussing both *Sources chrétiennes* and a new series of historically-oriented monographs inaugurated by the Jesuits of Fourvière, Marie-Michel Labourdette, a professor at the Dominican faculty of Toulouse, remarked that 'the whole problem of

Daniélou's influential, somewhat inflammatory article, 'Les orientations présentes de la pensée religieuse', *Études*, 79 (1946), 5–21 (esp. 11).

theology, and its ambition to form itself into knowledge in the proper sense, is posed here'.[22] Although he did not expressly discuss the question of the 'sources' of theology, Labourdette perceived that both the method and the content of the theological vision offered by these works was significantly different from that of the scholastic tradition, at least in its recent form. Their emphasis on historical context, continuity and change within tradition, and the integral connection of theological knowledge with worship and the life of faith all shifted the focus from the strictly cognitive understanding of theology that was at the heart of scholasticism. Labourdette writes ruefully:

> The idea of speculative truth, expressing in its own right a relationship of conformity between an utterance and things, is thus twisted towards a very different meaning: that of sincerity of witness and expression, of authenticity in the formulation of experience. The interest of a philosophy or of a theological synthesis . . . will no longer be the value of its doctrine as a transmission of permanent truths.[23]

With its emphasis on inductive, historically contextualized study and on a serious engagement with the symbolic thought-forms of patristic biblical exegesis and spiritual doctrine, this new approach to theology seemed to suggest a flight from objectivity, an avoidance of systematic thinking, a rejection of the clarity of reasoned argument about God and God's works, in favour of trendy social thinking and the pursuit of spiritual relevance. It seemed to be slipping again into the vague subjectivism associated with the philosophy of Maurice Blondel (often tagged 'immanentism'), or into the historical relativism of the Modernists. In the process, too, the role of the church's magisterium as the final arbiter of theological truth appeared to be in danger.

Others also sensed potential danger in this new approach. Chenu's essay on the programme of study at Le Saulchoir was censured by his superiors in 1937, and placed on the Index of Forbidden Books in February 1942. In an article published in *L'Osservatore Romano*, Mgr Pietro Parente (a professor of theology at the Lateran University and a definitor in the Holy Office) explained that Chenu's book had been suppressed because it was dismissive of the scholastic method and of the value of its conclusions, and implied a sympathy with such Modernist notions as the constant evolution of dogma and the primacy of religious feeling over reason. Although his article was written in Italian, Parente explicitly referred to Chenu's work, and that of a Belgian *confrère*, as representing '*la nouvelle théologie*'—the first published appearance of a French phrase that was to become emblematic of a revolution in perspective destined to dominate the Catholic theology of the late twentieth century.

---

[22] 'La théologie et ses sources', *RevTh*, 46 (1946), 353–71 (356).
[23] 'La théologie et ses sources', 367.

Tension continued to grow between representatives of this new perspective and the exponents of traditional scholasticism, into the 1950s.[24] For a time, at least, Pope Pius XII seems to have shared the concern that Chenu, de Lubac, and their younger colleagues were a threat to the church's theological tradition and teaching role. In one week in September 1946, the Pope addressed the 29th General Congregation of the Jesuits and the General Chapter of the Dominicans and used the occasion to denounce the 'new theology' being promoted in 'some quarters' as undermining the Catholic commitment to teaching unchanging truth.[25] On 12 August 1950, the Pope issued his encyclical *Humani Generis*, which was mainly concerned to reaffirm the permanence of Catholic dogma, and the theological systems that articulated it, as formulations of immutable truth. Among the dangerous tendencies of the time, the encyclical opposed the idea of evolution, as applied both to the cosmos and to Christian teaching, as a kind of historicism opposed to the objective truth-value of the scriptures and the magisterium, and rejected as 'false eirenism' (the encyclical's term for ecumenism) the new emphasis on scriptural and patristic studies that might open avenues to greater understanding with other Christians, but implied a rejection of the scholastic method. No names were mentioned in the encyclical, but Jesuit and Dominican superiors took the letter as an official rejection of the 'new theology'. De Lubac was removed from all teaching responsibilities at Fourvière and never returned to the classroom. Congar, Bouillard, and others were later also forbidden to teach for a time. Teilhard de Chardin was sent to New York, where he had few contacts and died, in a kind of intellectual exile, on Easter Sunday, 1955.

RAPPROCHEMENT AND THE EVOLUTION
OF *DEI VERBUM*

In subtle, often invisible ways, the attitude of the official church changed rapidly in the years between *Humani Generis* and the opening of the Second Vatican Council. While manual scholasticism remained the dominant vehicle

---

[24] See the influential series of highly critical articles by Réginald Garrigou-Lagrange, of the Angelicum in Rome: 'La nouvelle théologie ou va-t-elle?' *Ang*, 24 (1947) 124–39; 'Necessité de revenir à la définition traditionelle de la vérité', *Ang*, 25 (1948) 185–98; 'L'immutabilité du dogme selon le concile du Vatican et le relativisme', *RevTh*, 49 (1949), 309–32; 'Le relativisme et l'immutabilité du dogme', *RevTh*, 50 (1950), 219–46. Garrigou-Lagrange's argument is that truth is free of historical mutability, and that the task of theology, as a science, is to draw valid conclusions from the dogmas already formulated from the data of divine revelation, as conveyed in scripture and unwritten tradition. His main intended opponents appear to be Maurice Blondel, in philosophy, and Pierre Teilhard de Chardin.

[25] For the Pope's address to the Jesuits and Dominicans, see, respectively, *L'Osservatore Romano* (18 September 1946) and *L'Osservatore Romano* (22–23 September, 1946).

of theological teaching in the Roman universities and curial documents, Congar, de Lubac, and their colleagues rapidly gained a following among theologians and bishops in other parts of the world. Congar was even invited to be a consultant for the preparatory Theological Commission for the Council. Still, the drafts or *schemata* prepared for the Council by the Commission continued to embody a style of theology which, as Congar remarked, differed little from that of the documents of Vatican I. It was only during the conciliar debates themselves that the change of theological perspective associated with the 'new theologians' was embraced as the dominant style in which the church's magisterial tradition was to be expressed.

This is nowhere more visible than in the evolution of the Council's document on revelation, *Dei Verbum*. In response to a general invitation to theological faculties and curial congregations to submit suggestions for the coming Council's agenda, the Holy Office—under the prefecture of Cardinal Alfredo Ottaviani—drew up an ample list of subjects. Urging that the coming Council explicitly reject such rampant modern errors as evolutionism and relativism, along with the philosophical traps latent in immanentism, existentialism, and phenomenology, the document suggested the Council affirm, in its teaching on divine revelation and the church's magisterium, 'a genuine notion of essential truth, on which both the natural and supernatural order rests', and in the process offer a 'vindication of scholastic theology against the hidden assaults of the New Theology'.[26] Other groups, too, were convinced that the coming Council needed to deal seriously with fundamental questions of revelation, scriptural inspiration and interpretation, written and unwritten tradition as the sources of theology, the connection between the Bible, theology and the church's teaching office, the new interest in the Bible among the laity, and Pope John XXIII's concern to promote understanding with other Christian Churches. Whether one wanted to confirm traditional Catholic approaches, or reshape them in deliberately ecumenical and modern terms, the question of revelation and its sources must lie at the centre of any fruitful discussion.[27]

A draft for a document on revelation, drawn up by advisors to the Preparatory Theological Commission in the winter of 1961, was sent to all the bishops in the summer of 1962, immediately prior to the Council's first session. In the words of Joseph Ratzinger, now Pope Benedict XVI, it 'amounted to a canonization of Roman school theology'.[28] Although it strongly encouraged

---

[26] 'Proposal of the Holy Office' (1960) in *Acta et Documenta Concilio Oecumenico Vaticano II Apparando* i.iii (Vatican: Typis Polyglottis Vaticanis, 1960), 4, 9.

[27] The best discussion remains René Latourelle, *Theology of Revelation* (New York: Alba House, 1966), esp. 181–309 and 453–88.

[28] Ratzinger, 'Dogmatic Constitution on Divine Revelation: Origin and Background', in Herbert Vorgrimler (ed.), *Commentary on the Documents of Vatican II*, iii (New York: Herder and Herder, 1969), 155–66 (159). See, too, the chapter by Lewis Ayres, Patricia Kelly, and Thomas Huruphries in this volume.

the study of scripture as a principal source of doctrine,[29] and even approved the relatively new Catholic practice of encouraging the laity to read the Bible regularly,[30] it continued to insist that the scriptures and non-scriptural tradition form two distinct 'sources' of faith and doctrine.[31] It continued:

> Let no one, then, dare to suggest that tradition is of lesser value, or to deny credence to it. For even though Sacred Scripture, since it is inspired, offers us a divine instrument for expressing and illustrating the truths of faith, its meaning still cannot be surely and fully understood, or even explained, by any other means than by tradition. In fact, tradition and only tradition is the way by which certain revealed truths—especially those pertaining to the inspiration, canonicity and integrity of the whole of Scripture and each of its holy books—become clear and are known to the Church.[32]

The draft also emphasizes strongly the 'historical and objective truth of the facts of the life of our Lord Jesus Christ, as they are narrated in the Holy Gospels',[33] and insists on the total inerrancy of all the books of Scripture, 'since the divine inspiration, by itself, necessarily excludes and rejects all error on any subject, religious or profane, just as it is necessary that God, the supreme Truth, cannot in any way be the author of error'.[34]

Behind these familiar affirmations lay a distinctly cognitive understanding of divine revelation: in the course of history, God has communicated information about the real state of things, which we could not otherwise have known. Some of this is contained in the inspired writings of scripture, which God has 'inwardly stirred and moved' human beings to write so as to convey the relevant ideas;[35] the rest is contained in the 'divine tradition . . . which the Apostles received either from the mouth of Christ or at the prompting of the Holy Spirit'.[36] Scripture's mode of communicating the divine message is by inspired writing, then, while tradition's is by hearing and preaching; both are to be taken at face value, as humanly accessible information about God and his works.

Like the data of empirical science, the information divine revelation offers is to be intellectually analysed and processed, and used to increase our comprehensive knowledge of reality grounded in God. Although the ecclesial culture and theological context in which this understanding of revelation is articulated is a

---

[29] See the *relatio* of Salvatore Garofalo, *ASSCOVII*, i.iii (Congregatio Generalis 19), 29–30. All references are the author's translation.

[30] 'Schema constitutionis dogmaticae de fontibus revelationis, caput v', 27, *ASSCOVII* i.iii.24–5.

[31] 'Schema constitutionis dogmaticae de fontibus revelationis, caput i', 4, *ASSCOVII*, i.iii.15–6.

[32] 'Schema constitutionis dogmaticae de fontibus revelationis, caput i', 5, *ASSCOVII* i.iii.16.

[33] 'Schema constitutionis dogmaticae de fontibus revelationis, caput iv', 21, *ASSCOVII* i.iii.22. See also the remarks of Achille Cardinal Liénart on the schema, i.iii.32–4.

[34] 'Schema constitutionis dogmaticae de fontibus revelationis, caput ii', 12, *ASSCOVII* i.iii.18.

[35] 'Schema constitutionis dogmaticae de fontibus revelationis, caput ii', 8, *ASSCOVII* i.iii.17; 36 n. 2.

[36] 'Schema constitutionis dogmaticae de fontibus revelationis, caput ii', 4, *ASSCOVII* i.iii.15.

world away, in one sense, from the culture and context of the conservative evangelical emphasis on biblical inerrancy, in another sense they are strikingly similar: both have their roots in the realistic common-sense epistemology of the Enlightenment; both assume God's revelation is primarily a communication of information we would otherwise not have that can be used for deductive conclusions; neither is particularly interested in the historical context of the original biblical texts, or in the epistemic implications of the fact that God is an unknowable Mystery.

The draft was finally introduced for discussion, by Cardinal Ottaviani, at the nineteenth General Congregation of the Council's first session, on 14 November 1962. It immediately became engulfed in controversy. In Ratzinger's words, discussion of the document 'took place in an atmosphere of restless theological ferment and sometimes almost risked being overwhelmed by it'[37]—precisely because what was at stake were the most fundamental issues of how God and the human mind can communicate with each other. After a vote on whether or not to continue discussion of the draft failed to give a clear result, Pope John XXIII removed the text on 21 November, and gave it to a new drafting committee composed of members of Cardinal Ottaviani's Commission and Cardinal Bea's Secretariat for Christian Unity. This new committee produced a second draft during the winter and spring of 1963, which carefully avoided most of the controversial issues in the earlier version— especially the ecumenically sensitive question of the 'double source' of church teaching. Many now found this second draft so vague as to say nothing of substance. In fact, it was so heavily criticized during the second session of the Council that many thought the best plan might be simply to let the whole subject slip from view,[38] but Pope Paul VI, in his closing remarks at the end of the second session, included the completion of a document on revelation as one of the main tasks of the next conciliar period.

A new 'mixed' subcommission of bishops and experts—including some of the most distinguished theologians and biblical scholars of the time[39]—set to work again in the winter and spring of 1964, completing a wholly new draft by the beginning of June, which now largely reflected the *nouvelle théologie* perspective. Although debate on the new draft in the Council's third session, from 28 September to 6 October 1964, also became heated at times, it was clear that all but a small core of theologically traditional bishops were in favour of using it as the basis for a final conciliar document.[40] Suggestions for

---

[37] Ratzinger, 'Dogmatic Constitution on Divine Revelation', 155.

[38] See Ratzinger, 'Dogmatic Constitution on Divine Revelation', 162.

[39] The subcommittee included, among others, Yves Congar, Aloys Grillmeier, Karl Rahner, Joseph Ratzinger, Otto Semmelroth, and the secretaries of the Theological Commission, Sebastian Tromp and Gérard Philips. See Ratzinger, 'Dogmatic Constitution on Divine Revelation', 162.

[40] Hanjo Sauer, 'The Doctrinal and the Pastoral: the Text on Divine Revelation', in Giuseppe Alberigo and Joseph Komonchak (eds.), *History of Vatican II* iv (Leuven/Maryknoll: Peeters/ Orbis, 2003), 195–231.

emendation were submitted throughout the third session and a newly revised text circulated on 20 November 1964. This draft was again discussed at the start of the fourth and final session of the Council, 20–22 September 1965, and new, specific emendations (*modi*) submitted and worked into the text. A group of some 250 conservative bishops submitted a common letter, urging the Commission to clarify the notions of the material distinction of scripture and tradition, and the inerrancy and historical reliability of scripture, in the traditional sense proposed in the original draft. The drafting committee made further modifications in the text that satisfied most of the critics, so that the entire document was finally approved on 18 November 1965, with 2,344 bishops voting *placet* and only 6 *non placet*.

The document had come on a long journey and shows the scars of frequent emendation and collective authorship. Nevertheless, it offers a view of God's self-disclosure in history, and of human speech and thought about God, which in many ways realizes the desire of the 'new' theologians of the mid-twentieth century to free the church's understanding of its teaching activity from the grip of anti-Protestant, anti-secularist polemics, and to plunge it again into the language and logic of preaching, narrative and symbol, in which it had first come to birth in the age of the Fathers.

DEI VERBUM, THE DISTINCTIVE FEATURES

What was 'new', then, in *Dei Verbum* as it finally won the approval of the Council Fathers? We cannot provide a detailed analysis of the document here, but can at least underline a few of its distinctive features.

1) Revelation as God's Action

From its opening chapters, *Dei Verbum* treats revelation as a verbal noun, an activity of the ever-mysterious and ever-present God in human history, rather than as a body of information to be studied. In the Prologue, for instance, the Council takes as a kind of epigraph the opening verses of the First Letter of John, to describe its own teaching activity: 'We proclaim to you the eternal life which was with the Father and was made manifest to us—that which we have seen and heard we proclaim also to you, so that you may have fellowship with us' (1 John 1.2–3).[41]

---

[41] *DV* §1, Tanner, ii.971.

The first section of the document reflects further on this personal, historical character of revelation: it is not simply a matter of ideas, or even of words, but 'unfolds through deeds and words bound together by an inner dynamism'.[42] God's personal involvement in creation since the beginning, particularly in the sacred history of Israel, is thus the heart of the revelatory process, and reaches its fullness in the life and person of Christ, 'who is in himself both the mediator and the fullness of all revelation'.[43] Drawing on the theme of divine friendship with humanity, a theme enunciated as far back as Clement of Alexandria and particularly beloved by Thomas Aquinas, the text presents God's self-disclosure as an act primarily intended to draw the human race into a new relationship of intimacy, of knowledge experienced as love.[44]

2) Two Sources or One?

The most hotly debated part of *Dei Verbum* was Chapter 2, dealing with the sources of God's self-revelation. Many bishops and *periti* (theological advisors) wanted the Council to reaffirm and elaborate on the scholastic distinction briefly stated by the Council of Trent, that the 'truth and teaching' revealed by God is 'contained in written books and in unwritten traditions, which were received by the apostles from the mouth of Christ himself'.[45] Others, concerned to move beyond this traditional point of controversy with Protestants over the sufficiency of scripture for the church's teaching, were eager that scripture be placed within the broader historical context of ongoing tradition and reception, in a privileged location but not in isolation from the church's continuing reflection and proclamation. Again, it was this second approach which largely prevailed in the final redaction. Here God's revelation, which has come to its full, inexhaustible personal expression in Christ, is seen as being proclaimed first of all by the Apostles Christ commissioned.[46] This

---

[42] *DV* § 2, Tanner, ii.972.

[43] *DV* § 2, Tanner, ii.972, citing Augustine, *De catechizandis rudibus* 4.8, *CCSL* 46.128.

[44] *DV* § 2, Tanner, ii.972. De Lubac points out that in the discussion of the third (1964) draft, some thought it excessive to speak of God as addressing the human race as 'friends', and suggested replacing this with 'sons and daughters'. The Council preserved this more affective phrasing, drawn from John 15.12–15, suggesting God's gracious decision to elevate humanity, in Christ, to a level of relationship more equal to himself. See de Lubac, *La revelation divine* (Paris: Cerf, 1983), 37–8. See Clement of Alexandria, *Stromateis* 7.2.5; 7.3.19; 7.3.21; 7.11.62; 7.11.68; 7.12.79 (*GCS* xvii, ed. O. Stählin (Leipzig: 1909), 6, 14, 15, 45, 49, 56); Aquinas, *Commentarius in III Sent.* 27.2 (*Opera Omnia* ix, ed. S. E. Fretté and P. Maré (Paris: Vivès, 1873), 431–2); *Summa Contra Gentiles* 4.54.5 (trans. Charles J. O'Neil (Garden City NY: Image Books, 1957), 230–1); *Quaestiones Disputatae de Virtutibus in Communi* 1.5.5 (*Opera Omnia* xiv, ed. S. E. Fretté (Paris: Vivès, 1875), 192); *ST* 2a2ae 23.1, Blackfriars, xxxiv.5–9; 2a2ae 25.1–2, Blackfriars, xxxiv.81–7.

[45] Council of Trent, Session 4, First Decree: acceptance of the sacred books and apostolic traditions (8 April 1546), Tanner, ii.663. See also Vatican I, *Dei Filius* § 2, Tanner, ii.806.

[46] *DV* § 7, Tanner, ii.973–4.

apostolic witness, which is carried on in the church by the bishops who have succeeded the Apostles as authoritative teachers, has taken two forms: 'in a special way' in the written testimony of scripture, but also in the broader phenomenon of 'sacred tradition'.[47] What is distinctive here is that scripture and the tradition not explicitly contained in scripture are both seen as part of a larger, ongoing process of proclamation, reception, and interpretation located within the church, as the structured, divinely guided body of believers. In a statement clearly echoing the theological style of Chenu, Congar, and de Lubac, *Dei Verbum* depicts revelation as a living chain of communication, rather than as a twofold body of information:

> This tradition which comes from the apostles progresses in the church under the assistance of the Holy Spirit (an allusion to Vatican I, *Dei Filius* 4). There is growth in understanding of what is handed on, both the words and the realities they signify. This comes about through contemplation and study by believers, who 'ponder these things in their hearts' (see Lk. 2:19, 51); through the intimate understanding of spiritual things which they experience; and through the preaching of those who, on succeeding to the office of bishop, receive the sure charism of truth. Thus, as the centuries advance, the church constantly holds its course towards the fullness of God's truth, until the day when the words of God reach their fulfilment in the church.[48]

The Council here offers Catholic theology a new answer to the old question about revelation's sources. In the context of the church's continual meditation on the Word of God, *Dei Verbum* insists, 'sacred tradition and scripture are bound together in a close and reciprocal relationship. They both flow from the same divine wellspring (*scaturigine*), merge together to some extent, and are on course towards the same end',[49] and together, as the Constitution later adds, 'investigate, by the light of faith, all the truth that is stored up in the mystery of Christ'.[50]

3) Understanding of scripture

As part of this understanding of revelation as situated within the church's living tradition of reception and interpretation, *Dei Verbum* turns to the difficult questions of the inspiration and inerrancy of scripture. Taking up another phrase of Vatican I (*Dei Filius* 2), it reminds us that the books of the Bible, 'were written under the inspiration of the Holy Spirit and therefore have God as their originator: on this basis they were handed on to the church'.[51] Like the tradition that interprets scripture, the divine 'authorship' of the canonical texts does not compete with their human authorship in particular

---

[47] *DV* § 7, Tanner, ii.973–4.   [48] *DV* § 8, Tanner, ii.974.
[49] *DV* § 9, Tanner, ii.974.   [50] *DV* § 24, Tanner, ii.980.   [51] *DV* § 11, Tanner, ii.975.

cultures at particular times. 'God has spoken through human agents to humans', the document observes, quoting Augustine's *City of God*.[52] So the truth communicated in scripture is the truth God wished to reveal in this human, historical way, 'for the sake of our salvation'.[53] To understand scripture correctly, readers must pay close attention to language and texts, to literary genres within their original cultures, looking for 'that meaning which a biblical writer intended and expressed . . . by means of such literary genres as were in use at his time.'[54] Similarly, Christian readers must read scriptural texts not simply from the perspective of historical reconstruction, but as part of a unified sacred narrative, 'in the light of the same Spirit through whom it was written.'[55] Scriptural interpretation in the church relies on all the tools of modern historical criticism, but may not simply rely on them, to do its job.

4) Word and Symbol

Unlike other Vatican II documents that show the influence of *la nouvelle théologie*—notably the Constitution on the Church, *Lumen Gentium*—*Dei Verbum* makes relatively little explicit allusion to the writings and exegetical practice of the church Fathers as the inspiration for its new perspective on revelation and biblical interpretation. Readers of scripture are encouraged to study the Fathers and the liturgy in order 'to attain . . . an ever deeper understanding of holy scripture'[56] but there is—surprisingly—little else explicitly referring to the biblical interpretation of the Fathers, despite the renewed interest in figural exegesis stimulated in the 1940s by de Lubac and his followers.

Still, *Dei Verbum*'s approach to God's revealing Word bears the marks of a hermeneutical reorientation that would lead Catholic biblical study, and the rest of Catholic theology, on a journey, still under way, away from the literalism and rationalism of scholastic proof-texting and deductive argument, towards a new ability to live, reason, and worship intelligently in a world of life-giving signs. In one passage, for instance, the Constitution tellingly compares the church's veneration for the scriptural text with its veneration of the Lord's eucharistic body, referring to 'the one table of God's word and Christ's body'.[57]

Here the scriptural text points not just to ideas otherwise unavailable about the hidden God. Scripture, like the Eucharist, is at heart sacramental; it invites us to share God's life, as the written, 'fleshly' part of a much wider tradition of

---

[52] *DV* § 12, Tanner, ii.976, alluding to *De Civitate Dei* 16.6.2, *CCSL* 48.507.
[53] *DV* § 11, Tanner, ii.976.
[54] *DV* § 12, Tanner, ii.976, alluding to Augustine, *De Doctrina Christiana* 3.18.26, *CCSL* 32.93; Augustine, *Complete Works*, Part I, xi.181.
[55] *DV* § 12, Tanner, ii.976.
[56] *DV* § 23, Tanner, ii.979.
[57] *DV* § 21, Tanner, ii.979.

teaching and interpretation realized continually at the heart of the church, which is itself Christ's Body. Tradition, scripture, and the magisterium all find their place within a church that is not simply a social structure, but—in the words of *Lumen Gentium*—'the kingdom of Christ already present in mystery',[58] 'the visible sacrament of this saving unity' to which God invites all nations.[59] Scripture, tradition, and magisterium are structural principles of a single, divinely constituted world of life-giving signs, uniting us with God through Christ in the Spirit. In teaching Christians to think by the logic of signs once again, as well as by the logic of deduction, the 'new theologians' of the twentieth century had taught us to read scripture and human history as the church Fathers had read them for centuries, and to find in that contemplative, imaginative awareness of text and event a new key to what the church really is. Forty years after *Dei Verbum*, we are still struggling to read the signs, and to share in the life they promise.

[58] *LG* § 3, Tanner, ii.850.   [59] *LG* § 9, Tanner, ii.856.

Part IV

Ressourcement and 'the Church in the Modern World'

23

Ressourcement and the Retrieval of Thomism for the Contemporary World

Stephen M. Fields, SJ

INTRODUCTION

It has been argued that no tension existed between the *ressourcement* move-ment and the thought of St Thomas. This claim has some merit, at least from the perspective of the *ressourcement*. Marcellino D'Ambrosio argues, for instance, that for the Dominicans of Le Saulchoir and the Jesuits of Lyon-Fourvière the real enemy of contemporary theology was neo-scholasticism. Lacking a historical sense, its 'excessive preoccupation with clarity and sys-tematization' made it 'oblivious to human subjectivity', even as it caused a '"rupture between theology and life"'.[1] These deficiencies led to the irony that, for the *ressourcement*, the chief antagonists of Thomas were his interpreters. John of St Thomas, Cajetan, Suárez, and Banez, for example, enjoyed a hegemony in the Tridentine church that prevented an authentic retrieval of the Angelic Doctor.[2] Aquinas' own genius, the *ressourcement* opined, con-stituted a kindred spirit. Like the Fathers of the church whom the movement pledged to revive, Thomas 'held theology, spirituality, and pastoral practice in a dynamic and vital unity', even as he maintained a dialogue with the currents of his time.[3] As such, he served as a paradigm of the movement's goal: to diagnose accurately contemporary problems in order to solve them by

---

[1] Marcellino D'Ambrosio, '*Ressourcement* theology, *aggiornamento*, and the hermeneutics of tradition', *Communio*, 18 (1991), 530–55 (534–6), citing M.-D. Chenu, 'Position de la théologie', *RSPT*, 24 (1935), 232–57 (244), and Jean Daniélou, 'Les orientations présentes de la pensée religieuse', *Études*, 249 (1946), 1–21 (6, 14).

[2] See D'Ambrosio, '*Ressourcement* theology', 543, citing Étienne Gilson, 8 July 1956, *Letters of Étienne Gilson to Henri de Lubac*, trans. Mary Emily Hamilton (San Francisco CA: Ignatius Press, 1988), 23–4, 33 n.6.

[3] D'Ambrosio, '*Ressourcement* theology', 546–7.

creatively drawing on Christianity's living tradition.[4] The criticism levelled against the *ressourcement*, therefore, by the Dominicans Labourdette and Garrigou-Lagrange—that it rejected Thomism—would appear to be self-serving.[5] In failing to distinguish between Aquinas himself and outmoded Thomist accretions, they exculpated themselves from a fresh retrieval of the thirteenth century's inspiration.

Yet, the polemic between these two parties runs deeper, certainly from the perspective of the neo-Thomists. Aidan Nichols notes that Maritain, for instance, even while endeavouring to remain faithful to the spirit of Thomas, contended that the *ressourcement* was introducing a new anti-intellectualism into theology.[6] Others feared that the rejection of the scholastic method portended a return to Modernism.[7] A wave of 'historical and doctrinal relativism' could be undammed if the correspondence of the mind to the object known were replaced as the criterion of truth with the correspondence of the mind to life.[8] Labourdette argued not only that Thomism contains the resources for a theology of event and history, but that its metaphysics is 'quite simply, true'.[9] It followed for him that the job of Thomas's interpreters was not merely to retrieve his spirit but to integrate issues of contemporary import into his universal verity.[10]

The tension between these two parties over how to understand Aquinas came to a head in 1950 with the promulgation of Pius XII's *Humani Generis*.[11] Prior to it, de Lubac had undertaken a fresh study of the natural desire for God in Thomas and a wide range of other sources. Cajetan had denied the supernatural end of this desire as authentically Thomist.[12] According to de Lubac, however, this end appears throughout the Angelic Doctor's corpus, including in this important instance: 'the rational creature, which can attain the perfect good of happiness, but needs the Divine assistance for the purpose,

---

[4] Compare D'Ambrosio, '*Ressourcement* theology', 545, citing Yves M.-J. Congar, *Vrai et fausse réforme dans l'église*, Unam Sanctam, 20 (Paris: Cerf, 1950), 337.

[5] D'Ambrosio, '*Ressourcement* theology', 551.

[6] Aidan Nichols, OP, 'Thomism and the Nouvelle Théologie', *The Thomist*, 64 (2000), 1–19 (7).

[7] Nichols, 'Thomism', 2, citing letter of Réginald Garrigou-Lagrange, 17 July 1946. See also Étienne Fouilloux, 'Dialogue théologique? (1946–1948)', in Serge-Thomas Bonino, OP (ed.), *Saint Thomas au XXᵉ siècle*, Actes du colloque du Centenaire de la *Revue Thomiste* (Paris: Centre National de Livre-Saint Paul, 1994), 170.

[8] Nichols, 'Thomism', 10–11, referring to Garrigou-Lagrange, 'La nouvelle théologie, où va-t-elle?', *Ang*, (1946), 126–45.

[9] Nichols, 'Thomism', 12–13, citing M.-M. Labourdette, OP, and M.-J. Nicolas, OP, 'L'analogie de la verité et l'unité de la science théologique', *RevTh*, 55 (1947), 417–66.

[10] Nichols, 'Thomism', 13–14.

[11] Pius XII, *Humani Generis*: Encyclical Letter Concerning some False Opinions Threatening to Undermine Catholic Doctrine (12th August 1950), *AAS* xlii (1950), 561–78. ET available at <http://www.vatican.va/holy_father/pius_xii/encyclicals/documents/hf_p-xii_enc_12081950_humani-generis_en.html>.

[12] Henri de Lubac, *The Mystery of the Supernatural*, trans. Rosemary Sheed (New York: Herder and Herder, 1967), 11–12.

is more perfect than the irrational creature, which is not capable of attaining this good, but attains some imperfect good by its natural powers'.[13] While endeavouring to see the meaning of texts such as this clearly, de Lubac also lent his ear to the dynamic metaphysics sounded by Maurice Blondel and echoed in Pierre Rousselot and Joseph Maréchal. He thus revolutionized post-Tridentine theology by directly challenging the incoherence lodged in the core of the theory of pure nature. On the assumption that '[a] nature is an essence which *rests content* with the good that is proportionate to it', the pure nature theory posited that grace alters the natural end of human beings.[14] Suarez, for instance, supposed that as punishment for original sin God withdraws humanity's supernatural finality.[15] As a riposte, de Lubac pointed out that, because a being's end necessarily dictates its structure, an end cannot be changed without modifying the entire species.[16] In consequence, the supernatural order is not properly inferred from the natural. On the contrary, '[i]t is not nature...which requires grace; it is rather grace which...calls into being spiritual creatures to receive it'.[17] In other words, it is not possible to envisage 'a concrete nature in existence prior to or without its supernatural finalization'.[18] Congenially intrinsic to nature, grace is no extrinsic conferral, which could make it seem an alien imposition, however much the adage 'gratia perfecit naturam' be insisted upon.

As Joseph Komonchak points out elsewhere in this volume, the encyclical claimed that the gratuity of the supernatural is destroyed by '[o]thers' when they say that God 'cannot create intellectual beings without ordering and calling them to the beatific vision'.[19] It did not, however, name de Lubac explicitly, and this quotation constitutes its unique mention of the supernatural's gratuity. Moreover, de Lubac's position does not advance the censured position. In fact, he wanted to maintain God's double gratuity: in offering the beatific finality on the one hand, and in creating a nature capable of enjoying it on the other.[20] Nonetheless, the response to the encyclical by the

---

[13] *ST* 1a2ae.5.2 ad 2; in de Lubac, *Mystery*, 198.

[14] Charles Boyer, 'Nature pure et surnaturel dans le *Surnaturel* du Père de Lubac', *Gr*, 28 (1947), 279–95 (291), in de Lubac, *Mystery*, 196–7.

[15] Francisco Suarez, *De gratia*, prolog. 4, c. 1, n.5, *Opera omnia*, vol. 7 (1857), 18; in de Lubac, *Mystery*, 89.

[16] De Lubac, 'Le mystère du surnaturel', *RSR*, 36 (1949), 94–5; cited in Stephen J. Duffy, *The Graced Horizon: Nature and Grace in Modern Catholic Thought* (Collegeville MN: Liturgical Press, 1992), 76.

[17] Anton C. Pegis, 'Nature and Spirit: Some Reflections on the Problem of the End of Man', *Proceedings of the American Catholic Philosophical Association* 23 (1949), 7–9, summarizing de Lubac; in Duffy, *Horizon*, 70, n.9.

[18] Duffy, *Horizon*, 70.

[19] *HG* 26. See further Joseph A. Komonchak's chapter, '*Humani Generis* and *nouvelle théologie*', Ch. 9 in this volume, 149f.

[20] For a criticism of this double gratuity, although one that seems lacking in force, see Duffy, *Horizon*, 79–80.

Jesuit Superior General, John Baptist Janssens, apparently bore in mind de
Lubac's Blondel-inspired critique of Cajetan. Janssens, taking upon himself the
prerogative of further specifying the pope's meaning, declared to his Order in
an official letter: 'Henceforth, [Jesuit theologians] will not say that the thesis
that a spiritual creature could have been not destined to supernatural beatitude
is simply an interpretation of dogma by means of a defective philosophy.'[21]
Needless to say, *Humani Generis*, together with the Jesuits' response, cast a
pall over de Lubac's approach to Thomas. As a result of this, Karl Rahner,
although holding with de Lubac that only the one concrete order of grace
actually exists, developed the 'supernatural existential', which maintains
humanity's natural end, at least as a theoretical possibility.[22]

The polemic between Thomism and the *ressourcement* reveals two issues of
initial concern to the subject of this chapter. The first deals with integrating
patristic insights about subjectivity and event into a sound metaphysics.[23] For
all its acquired anachronisms, Thomism, Nichols rightly observes, has long
held pride of place as the reliable hermeneutic of Christianity.[24] It has done so,
I would further contend, precisely because it possesses a doctrine of analogy
sufficiently broad and flexible to integrate subjectivity and event into a synthesis of nature and grace. Analogy is the keystone that coherently links God
(as self-manifesting transcendence), the human person (as fallen and justified), and the material cosmos that, as St Paul says, 'has been groaning in
labour pains' while awaiting its deliverance (Rom. 8.21–2). It is precisely this
strength of Thomism that dovetails with our second issue. Taking a lead from
de Lubac as the maestro of nature and grace, it is time to sound new harmonies
that have been too stilled by *Humani Generis*. To these we shall soon give ear
after rehearsing a preliminary score.

THE NARRATIVES OF MODERNITY

In light of the *ressourcement*, outlining a plan to retrieve Thomism for contemporary thought requires a working definition of what is usually called modernity. Two main strains of analysis present themselves. The first finds clear
expression in Nietzsche, who views the modern project as homogeneously
developing from the origins of mind in the West. Any solution to modern
problems must therefore entail a radical reworking of the roots of thought and

---

[21] John Baptist Janssens, 'A Letter of Very Rev. Father General on the Encyclical "Humani
Generis" (11 February 1951)', *Woodstock Letters* 80 (1951), 291–316, at 299–300; see also
Komonchak's chapter in this volume, 147.
[22] See Karl Rahner, *Foundations of Christian Faith: An Introduction to the Idea of Christianity*,
trans. William V. Dych (New York: Seabury Press, 1978), 126–33.
[23] Nichols, 'Thomism', 18.   [24] Nichols, 'Thomism', 19.

culture.[25] By contrast, the second strain sees modernity as the result of a disintegration of this homogeneity.[26] Following this strain, Louis Dupré's account offers the advantage of an especially nuanced hermeneutics. Focusing on a careful diagnosis of modernity's complex causes, it is laudably reticent of offering a critique of a project that it considers unfinished.[27]

Dupré argues that modernity results from a realignment of three components that constitute the origins of the West's ontotheological synthesis: the noetic human subject as the interpreter of reality, the extra-subjective cosmos, and the transcendent source of both. A crucial shift occurred when fourteenth-century humanists, such as Dante and Petrarch, articulated what has come to be validated as modernity's defining principle: 'Mind stands in a creative relation to that physical reality on which it in other respects depends.'[28] Until this time, the intelligibility of the objective world, crystallized in the notion of form, had assumed priority over the human knower.[29] Aesthetics, for instance, was essentially mimetic. Transcendence, whether understood as the infinite Good, the Prime Mover, or a personal God, obtained either in an immediate or a causally necessary relation with the objective forms of the world received by the subject. With the aggressive assertion of the prerogatives of subjective ingenuity over mind's more passive assimilation of the objective cosmos, a new view of scepticism was introduced. It became, not an aberration, but, as Newman regrettably opines, the normal progression of human reason.[30] Thus d'Holbach, placing God in the eighteenth-century dock, could utter a belief echoed with little emendation by today's popular pundits: 'To discover the true principles of morality, men have no need of theology, of revelation, or of gods.... They have only to commune with themselves, to reflect upon their own natures.'[31] Scepticism has been broadened and reinforced, moreover, by modern developments in empirical science that highlight nature's spontaneous capacity for emergent novelty. These have further

[25] Louis Dupré, *Passage to Modernity: An Essay in the Hermeneutics of Nature and Culture* (New Haven CT: Yale University Press, 1993), 5, referring also to Heidegger, Derrida, and Rorty.

[26] *Passage to Modernity*, 5, referring to Hans Blumenberg, Eric Voegelin, and Alisdair McIntyre.

[27] *Passage to Modernity*, 5–6.

[28] Dupré, *Passage to Modernity*, 249–50, 252.

[29] Dupré, *Passage to Modernity*, 18ff.

[30] John Henry Newman, *Apologia pro Vita Sua* (New York: Doubleday, 1956), 336.

[31] Baron Paul d'Holbach, *Common Sense: or Natural Ideas Opposed to Supernatural* (New York, n.p., 1795), 8–9; originally *Le bon sens: ou idées naturelles opposées aux idées surnaturelles* (Amsterdam, n.p., 1772). See Sam Harris, *The End of Faith: Religion, Terror, and the Future of Reason* (New York/London: W. W. Norton, 2004), Chs. 1–2; Richard Dawkins, *The God Delusion* (London: Bantam Press, 2006), Chs. 5–9; Christopher Hitchens, *God Is Not Great: How Religion Poisons Everything* (London: Atlantic Books, 2007), Chs. 13, 15–16.

strained the credibility of form as the link between transcendence and the knowing subject.[32]

The upshot is that modernity can be defined as the growing distance among the intrinsically linked elements of the West's intellectual infrastructure. Elevating subjective creativity has led to a double doubt: about God, and about the structured intelligibility of the cosmos. Even post-modernism, contends Dupré, constitutes but a moment within what is rightly the modern. It remains dependent on subjectivity.[33] Derrida, for instance, even while sundering the link between language and objective reference, subsumes language into writing.[34] This can hardly be viewed as anything other than a quintessential act of creative mind. Still evolving, therefore, modernity has yet to establish a final synthesis among the attenuated elements that make it up.[35]

ARTICULATING NATURE AND GRACE FOR MODERNITY

Our considerations up to this point show that the nexus between subjectivity, transcendence, and the events of the cosmos constitutes the structure of modernity, on the one hand, and the core of the relation between the *ressourcement* and Thomism, on the other. Our overview of the polemic between these last two schools of thought pointed us towards the relation between nature and grace as the means of developing their continuing dialogue. It follows, therefore, that our task now becomes formulating a view of this relation that can address modernity's attenuation of its three structuring components. Four elements emerge from our considerations as requisite for any such synthesis. First, human creativity should assume a priority, because it is modernity's defining aspect. Second, a credible analogy should be established between this creativity, transcendence, and cosmic events. Third, this analogy should be sufficiently differentiated so as to embrace complexity and specialization in both human and cosmic creativity. (In other words, the distance among the components attenuated by modernity should be respected even as it is breached.) Fourth, transcendence should be demonstrated as the ground of human creativity and events, not alien to or distant from them.

We will now outline a synthesis based on these elements. It will begin by discussing Edward Schillebeeckx's study of Max Seckler's neglected

---

[32] Dupré, *Passage to Modernity*, 250.   [33] *Passage to Modernity*, 250.

[34] Jacques Derrida, *Of Grammatology*, trans. Gayatri Chakravorty Spivak (Baltimore MD: Johns Hopkins University Press, 1976), 6–7.

[35] Dupré, *Passage to Modernity*, 252.

retrieval of the instinct of faith in St Thomas.[36] Schillebeeckx contends that it 'surpasses everything [on the subject] that we have hitherto been offered'.[37] Then, after assessing Seckler's contribution to our synthesis, we will turn for further insights to St Augustine's *Confessions*.

THE INSTINCT OF FAITH

In analysing the instinct of faith in Thomas, Seckler, as Schillebeeckx points out, emphasizes the creativity of the human spirit. The instinct constitutes a moment within the differentiated unity of God's free will. As 'the divine impulse which prompts…us to believe', it is 'suited to bring about activity' in life.[38] For Thomas, the instinct lodges within the structure of the divine 'creative act'.[39] This one act is, at the same time, the means by 'which all creatures are flowing out from God' and 'the principle of their return to God'.[40] Within this act, 'one and the same grace', says Thomas, 'both calls [nature to faith] and justifies [nature in faith].[41] According to Seckler, this call, even as associated with grace, is seen by Thomas as belonging to nature. If these claims can be warranted, it follows that the subject's creativity, precisely as freely human, is linked intrinsically to the free revelation of God in Jesus Christ.

Seckler grounds his demonstration by linking revelation and value. The instinct represents the subjective action of grace moving the human heart (mind and will) to apprehend the objective value of revelation as it comes externally to the person.[42] The intrinsic goodness of this object attracts the subject precisely because the subject possesses a potential to be attracted. A congeniality thus obtains between divine and human actions—between, in other words, divine and human goodness, grace, and nature. The potential to be attracted to revelation is not, in the first instance, an explicitly articulated experience. It obtains as a formal, *a priori* predisposition. Nonetheless, once activated, it is capable of reflexive explication as conscious experience.[43] As a natural pre-disposition, the instinct grounds the subject's ability to respond to

---

[36] Max Seckler, *Instinkt und Glaubenswille nach Thomas von Aquin* (Mainz: Matthias-Grünewald-Verlag, 1961), as discussed in Edward Schillebeeckx, OP, *Faith and Revelation*, trans. N. D. Smith, 2 vols. (New York: Sheed and Ward, 1967–8), i.30–75.

[37] *Faith and Revelation*, i.32.

[38] *Faith and Revelation*, i.30, 33.

[39] Schillebeeckx, *Faith and Revelation*, i.33.

[40] Schillebeeckx, *Faith and Revelation*, i.34, citing a similar reading in Henri Bouillard, *Conversion et grâce chez S. Thomas d'Aquin: Étude historique*, Théologie 1 (Paris: Aubier, 1944).

[41] Schillebeeckx, *Faith and Revelation* i.52, citing ST 1a2ae. 113 ad 2.

[42] Schillebeeckx, *Faith and Revelation*, i.37.

[43] Schillebeeckx, *Faith and Revelation*, i.38.

any objective value. As an inner motive or prompt to faith as value, the instinct admits of an analogical potential capable of embracing the divine revelation freely offered in history.[44] This analogy embraces all of the following qualities of the instinct: 'a tendency of the human spirit itself'; 'the beginning of the entire act of faith';[45] 'the grace that invites us to believe'.[46] In sum, Seckler, following de Lubac's inspiration, sees Thomas endowing the act of creation as such with a supernatural potential. This is fully realized only in the beatific vision, the human person's one and only end.[47] Given human freedom, however, this end is by no means necessarily realized by any human being.

NATURE AND GRACE IN THE INSTINCT OF FAITH

The key issue raised by Seckler's analysis concerns the precise relation in the instinct between nature and grace. In order to explain this, a first question needs to be addressed. It expresses the nub of the criticism also levelled against de Lubac.[48] Does Seckler's position exact grace and so undermine its gratuity? Does it, in other words, fall into semi-Pelagianism by holding that 'the natural desire of salvation is already the seed of salvation'?[49] On the one hand, his exposé makes it clear that nature is perfected by grace when the Gospel, apprehended as a value, is accepted as the supreme good. It could appear that revelation would not be exacted, therefore, because its advent in history is utterly gratuitous.[50] Were it not to appear, other values would have to fill its gap, and humanity would be left ultimately unfulfilled.[51] It might be argued, on the other hand, that if this were the case, then God would have fashioned a creature whose end he could have withheld fulfilling. If so, God's goodness would be compromised. It would seem, in consequence, that if Seckler's position is to avoid this conclusion, it would have to concede that nature does seem to exact a supernatural end. In other words, if God's goodness is to be upheld, Seckler would seem to confer on humanity a natural claim to the Beatific Vision.[52]

---

[44] Schillebeeckx, *Faith and Revelation*, i.40, referring to Seckler, *Instinkt*, 110, citing *ST* 2a2ae.2.9.
[45] Schillebeeckx, *Faith and Revelation*, i.40 referring to Seckler, *Instinkt*, 110.
[46] Schillebeeckx, *Faith and Revelation*, i.33.
[47] Schillebeeckx, *Faith and Revelation* i.41, referring to Seckler, *Instinkt*, 128–9.
[48] See Duffy, *Graced Horizon*, 77f. and de Lubac, *Mystery*, 68f.
[49] Duffy, 'The Problem of Nature and Grace', 34. See also Karl Rahner, 'Concerning the Relationship Between Nature and Grace', *TI*, i. *God, Christ, Mary and Grace*, trans. Cornelius Ernst, OP (London: Darton, Longman & Todd, 1961), 297–317 (310, n.1).
[50] Schillebeeckx, *Faith and Revelation*, i.47.
[51] Schillebeeckx, *Faith and Revelation*, i.44–5.
[52] See Duffy, *Horizon*, 33.

In answer to this objection, Seckler would reply that redemption should be seen as a continuation of creation.[53] Conversely, creation should be seen as a function of God's free, primordial plan of redemption. Schillebeeckx does not further explain these claims but I would defend them by the following argument.[54] Because God is infinitely self-present, it cannot be said that God decides first to create and then, once the Fall occurs, secondly to redeem. On the contrary, God's eternally free intention to create must be understood as foreseeing the Fall, and hence as including within it the intention to redeem. The free intention to create in light of its consequences embraces, therefore, the gratuity to redeem (and vice versa). Redemption and creation are reciprocally entailed. If it seems from human nature's having one supernatural end that grace is exacted, this is an appearance, not the reality. God's infinite goodness is vindicated by his primordially free decision to create. In other words, it may seem that God owes us revelation, because without it our end would remain unfulfilled. But the truth is that God owes us nothing but what he has intended freely and primordially. This is the fulfilment of creation in the redemption, and conversely, the beginning of the redemption in creation. These claims cannot be made *a priori*, but only *a posteriori*. They are evident only in light of the revelation that, in fact, has been freely posited in history.

A second question raised in Seckler concerns whether the instinct belongs to the order of nature or of grace. On the one hand, he affirms that Thomas identifies the instinct of faith with the natural desire for the Absolute that is ontologically prior to conscious intellection and volition.[55] On the other hand, in keeping with the continuity of creation and redemption, he argues that the instinct cannot be characterized as belonging distinctly to either, nor as a medium between them. It is '*of grace, without actually being grace*'.[56] By this, Seckler seems to mean that the human person as created receives, in and through the instinct, not sanctifying grace, but prevenient grace. This predisposes the person to accept the revelation that, in an explicit act of faith, justifies and sanctifies. In other words, the 'spiritual core' of the person constitutes 'a *promise of* [sanctifying] *grace*'.[57] This promise is the divine movement that 'sets up in man the inner dimension of return' in grace to the God of creation.[58] To hold otherwise would replace reflection on the concrete reality of humanity with moot speculation about an end that never

---

[53] Schillebeeckx, *Faith and Revelation*, i.47.
[54] Based on Rahner, 'Salvation', *Sacramentum Mundi*, trans. Cornelius Ernst and Kevin Smyth (London: Burns & Oates, 1970), v.430b.
[55] Schillebeeckx, *Faith and Revelation*, i.42.
[56] Schillebeeckx, *Faith and Revelation*, i.50, citing Seckler, *Instinkt*, 213.
[57] Schillebeeckx, *Faith and Revelation*, i.48.
[58] Schillebeeckx, *Faith and Revelation*, i.48, citing Seckler, *Instinkt*, 178; 51; 64, citing *In I Sent.* Dd. 14, 15.

obtained in historical nature; and this, claims Seckler on the heels of de Lubac, is alien to Thomas.[59]

A CONTEMPORARY THOMISTIC SYNTHESIS
OF NATURE AND GRACE

Let us now assess Seckler's contribution to our overriding goal. This requires us to outline a synthesis of nature and grace that incorporates the four elements needed to retrieve Thomism for contemporary thought. Let us begin with the first element and evince the other three from it. It stipulates that priority be given to a defining hallmark of modernity, human creativity. This is precisely Seckler's point of departure. He locates the instinct of faith in the 'cradle' of nature as an anthropological *a priori*.[60] The fecund source of intellection and volition, it generates a range of psychological phenomena, such as wonder and questioning, the seed beds of novelty.[61] In Thomas, says Seckler, the instinct grounds human religiosity.[62] It intrinsically links divine and human creativity, such that human freedom, even while contingent upon divine freedom, retains its own integrity.

This link between the human and divine that Seckler finds in Thomas is doubly justified. On the one hand, the instinct lodges within the divine continuum of creation and redemption. This integral act ensues from God's primordial decision. While historically extroverted, it is made in free love from all eternity. The instinct constitutes the pivot harnessing the emanation of creation to its redemptive return. As such, the instinct discloses nature to be a redemptive vocation that awaits a fulfilment that cannot be deduced. On the other hand, the instinct does not compromise human freedom. Just as no necessity obtains in revelations being given, so none obtains in its being accepted. Free human choice can either fulfil the instinct by accepting Christ as the supreme value, or it can seek satisfaction in a host of secondary goods (or evils). The acceptance of revelation becomes the highest act of creativity that the human person can effect. Intellection and volition become moments within the circumncession of nature's *a priori* and grace's value. Freedom binds these into an aesthetic whole. It establishes a new synthesis that bears the marks of Thomas's definition of beauty: the intrinsic symmetry and harmony of form that structure the possession of truth and goodness (*ST* 1a.39.8; 2a2ae.142.2). In the wedding of divine and human freedom, grace perfects

---

[59] Schillebeeckx, *Faith and Revelation*, i.49–50, citing Seckler, *Instinkt*, 207; see also Dutty, Horizon, 74.

[60] Schillebeeckx, *Faith and Revelation*, i.53.

[61] Schillebeeckx, *Faith and Revelation*, i.52.

[62] Schillebeeckx, *Faith and Revelation*, i.53.

the form of human nature that it has, from the outset, prepared to be perfected.

The link established by Seckler's anthropology between divine and human freedom is fused by understanding grace itself as an analogy. Reaffirming Thomas, Seckler claims that 'one and the same grace both calls and justifies'.[63] It therefore follows that prevenient and sanctifying grace are integrally distinct, not equivocally disjoined. Whereas only sanctifying grace justifies, prevenient grace is oriented towards sanctifying grace as its proper end, goal, and perfection. Coumingled with nature, prevenient grace embraces human freedom even as it is embraced by it. Furthermore, if grace is analogous, then nature is analogous.[64] As the subject of prevenient and sanctifying grace, nature serves as the substratum of grace's analogy. Moreover, it follows that nature and grace, as such, are analogous. Both originate in the Logos, who is the self-same source of their similarity and distinction. Echoing the Prologue to John's Gospel, for instance, Irenaeus says that the Word, through whom all things came to be, 'in an invisible manner contains all things created, and is inherent in the entire creation'. As Word, he 'governs and arranges all things'. As Incarnate, the Word recapitulates or 'sum[s] up in Himself all things' in heaven and on earth.[65] Created, presided over, and incarnated by the Logos, nature cannot be absolutely alien to the life of grace. The Word refashions from within what he himself primordially fashioned and conservingly guides.

THE DISTINCTION IN RELATION BETWEEN NATURE AND GRACE

The fundamental difference between nature and grace turns on nature's radical otherness to God.[66] Nature is finite, contingent, dependent on time and space, and historical. On this account, the Council of Nicaea, in decisively parting company with Origen, posits no intermediary between divinity and creation except God's intelligent freedom. Brought forth *ex nihilo*, nature possesses no entitlement, of itself, to the life of grace.[67] Hence, as Seckler

---

[63] Schillebeeckx, *Faith and Revelation*, i.52, citing *ST* 1a2ae.113.8 ad 2.

[64] See Balthasar, *Theology of Karl Barth: Exposition and Interpretation*, trans. Edward T. Oakes (San Francisco: Ignatius Press, 1992), 281.

[65] Irenaeus, *Against the Heresies*, in *Ante-Nicene Fathers*, i, trans. and ed. Alexander Roberts and W. H. Rambaut (Peabody MA: Hendrickson Publishers, 1996 (Edinburgh, 1868–9)), 315–567 (546–8).

[66] See Balthasar, *Theology of Karl Barth*, 267.

[67] See Andrew Louth, *The Origins of the Christian Mystical Tradition from Plato to Denys* (Oxford: Oxford University Press, 1981), 75–7.

observes, a formal distinction obtains between the natural desire for God and the instinct of faith, even though they are materially the same.[68] Although formally distinct, they nonetheless possess the same supernatural object. This claim entails no contradiction. As Blondel shows, for instance, a purely philosophical analysis of the natural desire warrants humanity's supernatural end, however impotent philosophy finds itself in further trying to specify it.[69] From its perspective, theology can assert that the natural desire is an instinct for the faith that reveals the beatific vision as the person's end. Preveniently graced from the outset, nature has been rendered capable of being sanctified and justified in the continuum that embraces both creation and redemption.

As the vehicle of grace, nature might even be termed grace's sacrament, if by sacrament we mean an outward, empirical sign intrinsically mediating a hidden reality that it contains. Thomas uses instrumental causality to explain the sacraments. This notion can be useful, as long as distinctions are made that spare the freedom innate in both nature and grace. An instrumental cause exercises two powers. On the one hand, the 'power of the instrument' designates the innate activity that the cause exercises in virtue of its defining form. On the other hand, the 'instrumental power' designates the activity that it receives from a principal agent. The power of the instrument assumes instrumental power when the principal agent transfers to it a form that this agent possesses. When this transfer obtains, the instrumental power is incorporated into the finality of the activity intended by the agent.[70] Accordingly, it could be said that nature's innate freedom is the power of the instrument ensuing from its divinely created otherness. This freedom is commingled with grace, both prevenient and sanctifying, and thus assumes an instrumental power. When this commingling obtains, a formal unity between the innate freedom of nature and grace results. This unity is directed towards the realization of a common finality, the beatific vision, which is the end of the human person.

The key question, of course, concerns how human freedom retains its innate freedom when it becomes, in and through grace, an instrumental power. This problem becomes less intractable when human nature is seen as oriented towards its single supernatural end. Limited by finitude and flawed by sin, nature nonetheless implicitly participates in grace from the beginning Precisely where, in the existential and psychological order, nature and grace join as an instrumental power capable of effecting humanity's final end can never be specified. 'Our actual nature is *never* "pure" nature', rightly claims Rahner.[71] '[No] slice of "pure nature" [exists] in this world', echoes Balthasar.[72] One may

---

[68] Schillebeeckx, *Faith and Revelation*, i.58.

[69] Henri Bouillard, 'Philosophy and Christianity in the Thought of Maurice Blondel', in *The Logic of the Faith* (New York: Sheed & Ward, 1967), 161–85 (179–80).

[70] James S. Albertson, 'Instrumental Causality in St. Thomas', *New Scholasticism*, 28 (1954), 409–35 (412, 419, 424, and *passim*).

[71] Rahner, 'Nature and Grace' (1959), *TI*, iv, trans. Kevin Smyth (Baltimore/London: Helicon Press/Darton, Longman & Todd, 1966), 165–88 (183).

[72] Balthasar, *Theology of Karl Barth*, 288.

just as well ask where in the waters of baptism the physical cleansing ends and the spiritual character begins. The instrumental cause does not forfeit its formal power of the instrument when it becomes an instrumental power. Nor, then, does human freedom.

In conclusion, Seckler shows us how to integrate creativity into what might be called an analogy of freedom. At its core lies the instinct of faith. It is the point where human freedom, as innately derived from nature's radical otherness to God, meets the continuum of God's eternal freedom to create and redeem. As preveniently graced, human creativity originates as an instrumental power oriented towards the justifying revelation of Christ. As the supreme value, the Incarnation recapitulates what the Logos has primordially prepared it to receive. Accordingly, Seckler's recovery of freedom in Thomas accounts for the release of the existential potential of human subjectivity. Where freedom obtains, the spontaneity of wonder, restlessness, and questioning emerge. Where these flourish, the complex novelty of human and cosmic events results. Such novelty can neither be anticipated nor deduced. If nature is grace's sacrament, these events can lay an implicit claim to grace.

Under Schillebeeckx's guidance, we have seen how Seckler weaves into a synthesis the four elements required to retrieve Thomism for contemporary thought: creativity, analogy, complexity and differentiation, and transcendence as nature's ground. But our task cannot end here. We are also called upon to retrieve Thomism in light of the *ressourcement*. Accordingly, Seckler's analogy needs extending more deliberately into the events of the cosmos. History and the phenomena investigated by the empirical sciences constitute two broad classes of events. We will restrict our examination to history. In so doing, we will next look for inspiration in Augustine's *Confessions* and thus bring Thomas into dialogue with a patristic source.

HISTORY IN THE PERSPECTIVE OF AUGUSTINE'S *CONFESSIONS*

In order to integrate into history the analogy of freedom grounded in the instinct of faith, let us first evince a definition of history from *Confessions*. Fundamentally, history is the nexus of events created by the actualization of human deliberation and freedom in time and space. Events are spontaneous. Resisting predictability, they nonetheless embody intelligibility and purpose. As the products of choice, however, they are conditioned by the primal fall and so also manifest sin and absurdity. Created by responsible agents, history itself is free. Moreover, it is sacramental in the sense previously defined. It is constituted by empirical media that intrinsically mediate a hidden reality. In other words, history's nexus of events implicitly holds vestiges of human rationality and volition that await discernment and articulation. Explicating these in his personal history occupies Augustine's entire work in *Confessions*. But Augustine does not undertake this hermeneutics merely to gain a more complete self-understanding. For him, history manifests a purpose more profound than any human rationality and freedom. It is the locus of God's provident intelligence and spontaneous love. Whereas human effort can cause history to degenerate into base loves, the divine work, active in the midst of depravity, is always redemptive.

As sacramental, history emerges in *Confessions* as complex and differentiated. On the one hand, it consists of what might be called a 'natural' level: its implicit content of human intelligibility and freedom available for the hermeneutical work of rational explication unaided by the grace of faith. On the other hand, it consists of what might be called a 'graced' level: the redemptive work of God, active in the heart of nature, that faith makes accessible to reason. Almost any of the numerous anecdotes with which Augustine weaves the intricate tapestry of his spiritual journey would serve to illustrate these levels. As one example, let us take Augustine's account of his boyhood experiences of moral and physical evil.

The natural level of this aspect of Augustine's history becomes explicit when he uses memory, understanding, and will, the three powers of the soul, to recall and analyse the corporal punishment he received at school. These events, first recollected in vivid detail, describe the 'wretchedness' Augustine 'suffered', and his 'rough roadway' of 'heavy labor and pain' that 'terrify'.[73] Having exercised memory, he proceeds to exploit the faculty of understanding. Plumbing the irony implicit in the events, he wryly observes: '[W]e loved to play, and we were punished by adults who nonetheless did the same themselves.'[74] This second power of the soul defines, but does not resolve, the moral problem raised by memory: the unjust inflicting of pain. Will, soul's third power, effects a resolution. As reason's dynamic appetite, will inspires understanding to develop a theodicy that not only validates God's justice, but finds the grace of his saving love.

It is will, then, that causes the transition from history's natural to its graced level. Will grounds a communication with God based on mutual friendship. Addressing God, Augustine says: Although 'I begged you ... not to let me be beaten', yet, 'you did not grant my prayer'.[75] Augustine's deliberate trust in God's silence in the face of his earnest entreaty vindicates God's goodness. This vindication integrates the soul's three powers into a new synthesis in grace. Augustine is now enabled to recall more poignantly, to understand

---

[73] *Confessions*, i.9, in Augustine, *Complete Works*, Part I, i.48–9.
[74] *Confessions*, i.9, in Augustine, *Complete Works*, Part I, i.49.
[75] *Confessions*, i.9, in Augustine, *Complete Works*, Part I, i.49.

more deeply, and to loathe more intensely his own sin, and that of his oppressors. The final resolution of the anecdote's irony finds expression in a prayer for God's 'mercy', together with a request that God 'free' all those bound hostage by 'follies'.[76] In short, history's deepest meaning resides in the grace working in nature's core. This meaning is discerned only by reason enlightened in faith. When enlightened, reason advances the redemption of history by calling upon, submitting to, and cooperating with the Providence already active in history.

But a deeper reading of *Confessions* shows that no purely natural level of history exists. For Augustine, the source of human rationality, and hence the source of the soul's three powers, is by no means self-sufficient, but is grounded in the soul's own vital source. A subtle dialectic early in the work leads Augustine to affirm that any relationship with the saving God can obtain, not principally because God lodges in him, but first and foremost because he is lodged in God. Paradoxically constituting a transcendence as absolute as his immanence, God is the centre of Augustine's being, more intimate to him than he to himself.[77] The powers of the soul flow forth from this intimacy, which consequently constitutes the wellspring of human rationality. Most importantly, always and everywhere, God for Augustine is never the object of a purely natural speculation. On the contrary, not an impersonally emanating first cause, God is the One who feeds 'Israel for ever with the food of truth', even as he leads the individual soul to take on the 'light burden' of 'Christ Jesus, my helper and my redeemer'.[78] Thus, memory, understanding, and will are implicit sacraments of grace. A loving Providence, the God of Christian revelation, sustains them, even as they belong to nature that, as created, is other than God.

Furthermore, like the soul's powers, history is an implicit sacrament of grace. On the one hand, as we have seen, history is constituted by the active objectivation in time and space of the soul's three powers. Because these flow from Providence's loving intimacy, it follows that wherever history manifests truth, goodness, beauty, and love, God is implicitly present. On the other hand, as we have also seen, history evinces an explicit level of grace that can be articulated when the soul's three powers are consciously synthesized in faith. Different from the implicit grace that grounds and sustains the soul's three powers, the divine friendship consciously nourished in prayer explicitly discloses to reason the activity of the redeeming God in history. It discloses to Augustine's faith enlightened reason, for instance, the ineluctability that drew him to Christ. The events of his life thus constitute a unified pattern. This allows Augustine

[76] *Confessions*, i.9, in Augustine, *Complete Works*, Part I, i.50.
[77] *Confessions*, i.2, in Augustine, *Complete Works*, Part I, i.40.
[78] *Confessions*, ix.10, in Augustine, *Complete Works*, Part I, i.227; ix.1, in Augustine, *Complete Works*, Part I, i.209.

to see that the action of Providence in history does not compromise human freedom, but actually fulfils it.

CONCLUSION

Confessions complements and extends Seckler's understanding of the instinct of faith in Thomas. First, Thomas and Augustine both understand human rationality as a sacrament of grace. In Thomas, the sacramental relation between nature and grace, both prevenient and sanctifying, can be explained by instrumental causality. The same might be affirmed of Augustine. Only in retrospect, for instance, does Augustine see that what he thought was the 'natural' use of the three powers of his soul was in fact harnessed by an implicit grace leading to the conversion he consummates in an explicit act of faith. Can we not then identify this implicit grace in Augustine with the prevenient grace that, according to Thomas, envelopes the natural desire for God? In both thinkers, human freedom never loses its integrity when commingled with grace. On the contrary, it is fulfilled in a divine end, even as it is inspired and driven by a divine impulse. In both, therefore, the transcendent is the immanent source and summit of human creativity.

On the other hand, Augustine shows us how the transcendent can be extended into history. If history is the extroversion in events of human intelligence and freedom; and if these faculties, created in nature as other than God, are nonetheless infused with prevenient grace; then history is as sacramental as human rationality. This claim in no sense affirms that either the human person or history exacts a supernatural end. This end is given in the Incarnation. It cannot be deduced; it alone makes justifying grace available. Still, as both Thomas and Augustine aver, a divine agency preveniently sustains both the human person and history. It guides them to claim their proper fulfilment, faith in Christ (or the desire for it).[79] Sin and depravity are always possible. But even as Augustine demonstrates the transcendent to be the source of history, he extends the analogical link between nature and grace that Seckler finds in Thomas. History incarnates both prevenient and sanctifying grace. As the substratum of both, history is analogous. It is linked to its transcendent source through the agency of human intelligence and freedom, from which events spring. As such, history can be investigated by a variety of hermeneutics, philosophical and theological.

---

[79] Council of Trent, Decree on Justification (13 January 1547), Ch. 4, in Tanner, ii.672.

In conclusion, a dialogue between the ressourcement and Thomism yields benefits for contemporary thought. First, just as the rumours of John Partridge's death were greatly exaggerated when Jonathan Swift published his hoax obituary, so are the rumours of modernity's passing. In fact, what is called postmodernism only proves modernity's vigour. Both are parasitic on the creativity of the human subject. By its nature, this creativity arises in the subject's perception of value. Moreover, it is driven towards the realization of value in action. As a guide amidst the myriad delusions vying for humanity's choice of values, grace makes possible a union with the highest and most authentic of values. It does this in two senses that have wide ramifications for the destiny of our species. As prevenient, grace embraces the very origins of intelligence and will. It constitutes them as a transcendent vocation. Although nothing created can fulfil it, this vocation, albeit ineluctable, can be freely refused. However hidden, the creating Logos is acting to redeem the person in the depth of subjectivity. But this action is not justification. As sanctifying, grace aligns human creativity with Christ. It endows what is only an implicit vocation with the concrete potential of fulfilment. Opening the person to a decisive change in consciousness, the Incarnation offers the reciprocity of friendship between the finite seeker of value and value's infinite representation. In turn, this friendship bolsters creativity. Widening understanding and enhancing perception, it shows us the final meaning of history's triumphs and failures, both personal and communal.

No wonder, then, that St Ignatius Loyola boldly affirms that the 'Creator [acts] immediately with the creature, and the creature with its Creator and Lord'.[80] He underscores the paradox that 'the way down [into the person is] the way up to God'.[81] Even before we deliberately enter into a relationship with the God of grace, God's saving grace has freely entered into a relationship with us. Prevenient grace fashions human freedom into a seed of divine value that only the divine value incarnate can nurture into bloom.

---

[80] David L. Fleming, *A Contemporary Reading of the Spiritual Exercises: A Companion to St Ignatius' Text* (St Louis MO: Institute of Jesuit Sources, 1980), 'Fifteenth Annotation', 12.

[81] Dupré, 'Ignatian Humanism and Its Mystical Dimension', *Communio*, 18 (1991), 164–82 (181).

24

Ressourcement and Vatican II

Gerald O'Collins, SJ

Enriching the work and achievements of the Second Vatican Council (1962–5), various currents of *ressourcement* theology, concerned to rediscover forgotten or neglected dimensions of the great tradition found in the scriptures, the Fathers of the church, and the liturgy, flowed together: for instance, the biblical movement, the ecumenical movement, the liturgical renewal, the patristic renewal (championed, in particular, by those who had launched the *Sources chrétiennes* series), and the renewal of Thomism.[1] Some of those who led *ressourcement* theology (for instance, Marie-Dominique Chenu, OP, Yves Congar, OP, Jean Daniélou, SJ, Henri de Lubac, SJ, and Karl Rahner, SJ) became *periti* or expert-consultants who collaborated closely with the bishops in producing the conciliar texts.[2] In his diary entry on the eve of the closing of the Council, 7 December 1965, Congar listed what he had contributed—either as initial drafter or as editor of emendations subsequently proposed by the bishops—to eight of the sixteen documents issued by the Council.[3]

In tackling the impact of *ressourcement* theology on Vatican II, we can examine first what some conciliar texts say about the need to retrieve valuable

---

[1] In this present volume see chapters on the renewal of biblical studies (B. T. Viviano); on contributions to ecumenism (G. Flynn, P. D. Murray, J. Webster, and A. Louth); on the renewal of the liturgy (K. F. Pecklers); on the patristic retrieval (B. Pottier); and on the renewal of Thomism (F. A. Murphy and S. Fields).

[2] In this present volume see chapters on Chenu (J. Gray); on Congar (G. Flynn, J. Komonchak, J. Mettepenningen, and P. D. Murray); on Daniélou (B. Pottier); and on de Lubac (D. Grumett). Some might query the inclusion of Rahner among the leaders of *ressourcement*, but see the chapter by R. Lennan. Rahner often refrains from citing particular biblical and other sources; yet repeatedly one can add precise references that support what he proposes—e.g., to take one example among very many—on the theology of the death and resurrection of Jesus (*Foundations of Christian Faith*, trans. W. V. Dych [New York: Seabury Press, 1978], 264–85).

[3] Congar, *Mon journal du concile*, 2 vols. (Paris: Cerf, 2002), ii.511. On this diary see the review by G. Flynn, *Louvain Studies*, 28 (2003), 48–70; and J. J. Scarisbrick, 'An Historian's Reflections on Yves Congar's *Mon Journal du Concile*', in G. Flynn (ed.), *Yves Congar: Theologian of the Church* (Louvain: Peeters Press, 2005), 249–75.

sources in the tradition that should revitalize the church's teaching and practice. Second, we will describe a roadblock which initially hindered that retrieval from shaping the teaching of the Council: the widespread manualist theology, exemplified by textbooks published in Rome and the *Sacrae Theologiae Summa* authored by a number of Spanish Jesuits. Third, we investigate how *ressourcement* theologians worked with the bishops in challenging, revising, and replacing draft documents prepared by the 'manualists'. Sampling Vatican II texts will illustrate the way these texts frequently embodied some major and minor themes developed by *ressourcement* theology.

REFERENCES TO *RESSOURCEMENT* BY VATICAN II

Those who scour the sixteen documents of Vatican II for *explicit* references to *ressourcement*, or the return to the sources, will find something to report. The clearest endorsement of *ressourcement* comes in the Decree on the Appropriate Renewal of Religious Life (*Perfectae Caritatis*, 28 October 1965). The decree emphasizes that 'an appropriate renewal of religious life comprises *both* a continual return to the sources of the whole Christian life and to the original inspiration of the institutes *and* their adaptation to the changed conditions of the times'. Starting from the 'supreme rule', 'the following of Christ proposed in the Gospel', the decree then spells out five principles for this renewal, which should be 'promoted under the impulse of the Holy Spirit and the guidance of the Church' (§ 2; italics mine).[4]

Apropos of the life of prayer for religious, the decree recommends that they should 'draw from the fitting sources of Christian spirituality'. That means drawing not only from the Eucharist but also from daily contact with 'the Sacred Scripture, so that by reading and meditating on the divine scriptures they might learn the surpassing knowledge of Jesus Christ (Phil. 3: 8)' (§ 6).[5]

On the same day that *Perfectae Caritatis* appeared, Vatican II also promulgated the Decree on the Training of Priests (*Optatam Totius*). It proposed a thoroughgoing revision of ecclesiastical studies, which involved seminarians studying biblical languages, Latin, and the liturgical language of their own rite. Knowing the original languages of 'Sacred Scripture and Tradition' will facilitate their access to the sources and free them from the sometimes misleading medium of translation (§ 13). Those who teach theology are directed to use a

---

[4] Both here and later, I provide my own translation of Vatican II documents, but without spending time on repeatedly justifying my preferences.
[5] On the return to the sources in *Perfectae Caritatis*, see F. Wulf, 'Decree on the Appropriate Renewal of the Religious Life', in H. Vorgrimler (ed.), *Commentary on the Documents of Vatican II*, trans. W. Glen-Doepel *et al.* (London: Burns & Oates, 1968), 301–70 (329, 333, 335–6, 348).

genetic method (see below), which begins by drawing on the riches of scripture, the patristic tradition, and best medieval authors as foundational for
Catholic faith and doctrine (§ 16).

Three weeks later, in its Dogmatic Constitution on Divine Revelation (*Dei
Verbum*, 18 November 1965), Vatican II called on all Christians, and not
merely members of religious institutes, to be 'nourished and ruled by Sacred
Scripture', 'the pure and perennial source of spiritual life' (§ 21; see § 25). The
day before the Council concluded, it exhorted priests, in the Decree on the
Ministry and Life of Priests (*Presbyterorum Ordinis*, 7 December 1965), to
return to the same biblical source: their 'sacred knowledge' should be 'drawn
from reading and meditating on the Sacred Scripture'. This knowledge should
also be 'fruitfully nourished by the study of the Holy Fathers and Doctors of
the Church and other monuments of Tradition' (§ 19).

Two other documents also presented a creative return to biblical and
traditional sources as the route to renewal in the life of the church. Thus the
Constitution on the Sacred Liturgy (*Sacrosanctum Concilium*, 4 December
1963) prescribed that texts set to music should be 'drawn especially from
Sacred Scriptures and from liturgical sources' (§ 121). Apropos of the special
position of the Eastern Churches, the Decree on Ecumenism (*Unitatis Redintegratio*, 21 November 1964) earnestly recommended that Catholics should
'access more often the spiritual riches of the Eastern Fathers which lift the
whole human person to contemplate divine matters' (§ 15).

While *Perfectae Caritatis* leads the way in spelling out what *ressourcement*
involves, five other Vatican documents emphasize how a creative return to the
sources will revitalize the church's teaching and practice. Without ignoring
other sources that should be retrieved (liturgical sources, the writing of the
Fathers and Doctors of the Church, and, in particular, 'the spiritual riches of
the Eastern Fathers'), the conciliar documents repeatedly stressed the need to
return to the scriptures, the pre-eminent source for Christian faith and life.

THE CHALLENGE OF THE MANUALISTS

A sense of how the pre-conciliar manuals of theology worked can sharpen our
appreciation of what *ressourcement* theology stood for and had to contend
with when Vatican II was being prepared and began.[6] Manualist theology,
which belonged to what many identify as 'neo-scholasticism', was embodied in
some of the nine drafts distributed (seven in August and two in November
1962) to the bishops attending the Council. Two of those drafts, or 'schemata',

[6] See J. Wicks, 'Theology, Manualist', in R. Latourelle and R. Fisichella (eds.), *Dictionary of
Fundamental Theology* (New York: Crossroad, 1996), 1102–5.

involved the manualist approach in a special way: on the moral order (*De Ordine Morali*, largely prepared by a sub-commission led by Franz Xavier Hürth, SJ, who filled out a sketch composed by Sebastian Tromp, SJ)[7] and on the church (*De Ecclesia*, largely prepared by Marie-Rosaire Gagnebet, OP,[8] and Tromp, under the watchful eye of Cardinal Alfredo Ottaviani, the head of the Theological Commission).[9]

One might characterize manualist theology as (1) 'regressive' in method, (2) conceptualist rather than historical and biblical, (3) legalistic and worried about errors, (4) non-liturgical, and (5) non-experiential. Let me take up in turn those five characteristics.

1. The Regressive Method

The 'regressive' method began with whatever was the present teaching of the pope and bishops and returned to the past in order to show how this teaching was first expressed in the scriptures, developed by the Fathers and Doctors of the Church, and deployed in official teaching. Manualist theologians read the sources but only in the light of what was currently taught and believed, and with the intention of defending what came from the official teaching authority of the church and, in particular, from the pope of the time. In the words of Pius XII, 'it belongs to them [theologians] to point out how the doctrine of the living Teaching Authority is to be found either explicitly or implicitly in the Scriptures and Tradition'.[10]

Ressourcement theology used rather a 'genetic' method, a return to the sources that studied first the biblical witness and then the subsequent history of doctrinal development. By starting from the scriptures and the Fathers, it tracked, along the lines of John Henry Newman's view of doctrinal development, the living tradition and what it embodied for growth and change in church teaching and practice.

---

[7] See J. A. Komonchak, 'The Struggle for the Council during the Preparation of Vatican II', in G. Alberigo and J. A. Komonchak (eds.), *History of Vatican II* (Maryknoll NY: Orbis Books, 1995), 167–356 (246–51).

[8] But see the chapter in this volume by H. Donneaud on Gagnebet's work in retrieving Thomas Aquinas' understanding of theology as a science.

[9] Komonchak, 'The Struggle for the Council', 285–300, 311–13.

[10] Pope Pius XII, encyclical letter *Humani Generis*: Encyclical Letter Concerning some False Opinions Threatening to Undermine Catholic Doctrine (12 August 1950), *AAS* xlii (1950), 561–78. ET available at <http://www.vatican.va/holy_father/pius_xii/encyclicals/documents/hf_p-xii_enc_12081950_humani-generis_en.html>, § 21. This encyclical was widely and correctly understood to repudiate the *ressourcement* approach of the so-called *nouvelle théologie* of French Dominicans and Jesuits.

2. Conceptualist

Largely indifferent to the claims not only of historical consciousness but also of the critical biblical scholarship (that was encouraged by the 1943 encyclical of Pius XII, *Divino Afflante Spiritu*,[11] and that went beyond lifting 'proof texts' from the scriptures and studied them in the full context), the manualists at their worst seemed to imagine that concepts had been transmitted unchanged from one generation of church teachers and theologians to another. Ignoring the political, social, and cultural developments of the modern world, they claimed 'unprejudiced' access to an objective order and dealt with eternal truths and general laws, from which they felt justified in deducing particular applications. Thus the draft document *De Ordine Morali* drew commands and prohibitions from universal principles of morality, while largely neglecting the central role of love that the New Testament proposes as giving a specifically Christian orientation to life.

3. Legalistic

A legalistic mentality prompted the manualists to assign a wide range of 'notes' or qualifications to theological propositions. In decreasing importance, these 'notes' ran from the highest level 'of defined faith' to the least authoritative, 'offensive to pious ears'. The propositions they had crafted allowed manualist authors to indulge in syllogistic deductions and, inevitably, to condemn errors of every kind, often a series of such abstractions as agnosticism, atheism, humanism, materialism, relativism, and subjectivism.

This legalistic mentality was also highly juridical, concerned (in manuals of ecclesiology) with the validity of the sacraments and the supreme jurisdiction of the bishops and pope. Congar, de Lubac, and other *ressourcement* theologians privileged the sacramental character of the whole church rather than the juridical approach of what Congar called 'hierarchology'.[12]

4. Non-Liturgical

Following the seven fundamental principles and sources, or '*loci theologici*', enumerated by Melchior Cano, OP (1509–60), manualists made no room for

---

[11] Pope Pius XII, Encyclical Letter *Divino Afflante Spiritu* on Promoting Biblical Studies (30 September 1943), *AAS* xxxv (1943), 297–325. ET available at <http://www.vatican.va/holy_father/pius_xii/encyclicals/documents/hf_p-xii_enc_30091943_divino-afflante-spiritu_en.html>.

[12] See Hans Boersma, '*Nouvelle Théologie' and Sacramental Ontology: A Return to Mystery* (Oxford: Oxford University Press, 2009), 242–87; P. McPartlan, *The Eucharist Makes the Church: Henri de Lubac and John Zizioulas in Dialogue* (Edinburgh: T&T Clark, 1993).

liturgy and liturgical sources as an important and even essential 'locus' for theology. De Lubac's principle, 'the Eucharist makes the Church',[13] was alien to their theological imagination. By making the liturgy the theme of their first officially approved document, *Sacrosanctum Concilium*, the bishops at Vatican II were, one might say, endorsing the principle of 'the liturgy makes the Council'. They ranked the study of liturgy and liturgical sources among 'the principal courses' for programmes of theology (§ 16). Among the texts promulgated in the Council's final session, *Dei Verbum*, when recognizing 'the divine Scriptures, taken together with Sacred Tradition, as the supreme rule of faith' (§ 21), specifically mentioned the study of only two items belonging to 'tradition': 'the Fathers, both of the East and the West, and *the sacred Liturgies*' (§ 23; italics mine). Much pre-Vatican II manual theology paid little more than lip-service to the Fathers and none at all to liturgical sources.[14]

5. Non-Experiential

The Gospel of John, the letters of St Paul, the *Confessions* of St Augustine, and other classical works, established and encouraged an experiential approach to understanding and interpreting the divine-human relationship. A long line of spiritual and mystical authorities examined this relationship in the key of experience. William of Saint-Thierry (1085–1148) was one of very many Christians who explored in depth our spiritual experience. Nevertheless, two modern documents of the Catholic magisterium, *Dei Filius*[15] and *Pascendi Dominici Gregis*[16] warned, respectively, against denying that 'external signs' could lend credibility to divine revelation, against appealing only to the 'internal experience' of individuals (*DS* § 3033), and against making faith in God depend on the 'private experience' of the individual and maintaining that interior, immediate experience of God prevails over rational arguments (*DS* § 3484). This justified opposition to one-sided and partial versions of religious experience unfortunately encouraged among manualists the dangerous delusion that somehow we could encounter and accept the divine self-communication 'outside' human experience.

---

[13] Boersma, *'Nouvelle Théologie' and Sacramental Ontology*, 247–55.

[14] When citing Fathers of the Church, many manualists were content to lift proof texts from a classic anthology: M. J. Rouet de Journel (ed.), *Enchiridion Patristicum*, 23rd edn. (Barcelona: Herder, 1965). Not content with using anthologies, such leading figures of *ressourcement* theology as Jean Daniélou and Henri de Lubac were outstanding patristic scholars.

[15] First Vatican Council, Dogmatic Constitution on the Catholic Faith, *Dei Filius*, Tanner, ii.804–9.

[16] Pius X, *Pascendi Dominici Gregis*. Encyclical Letter on the Doctrines of the Modernists (8 September 1907), *ASS* xl (1907), 593–650, (632), § 39. ET available at <http://www.vatican.va/holy_father/pius_x/encyclicals/documents/hf_p-x_enc_19070908_pascendi-dominici-gregis_en.html>.

Vatican II's *Dei Verbum* was to set the record straight. Through the special history of revelation and salvation, the Israelites 'experienced the ways of God with human beings' (§ 14). In the post-New Testament life of the Church, so the Council acknowledged, their 'experience' of 'spiritual realities' has helped believers contribute to the progress of tradition (§ 8). The Council's closing document, the Pastoral Constitution on the Church in the Modern World (*Gaudium et Spes*, 7 December 1965) was nothing less than a profound reflection on the experience of the whole human family in the light of the crucified and risen Christ. It is in the light of Christ's revelation that 'the sublime calling and profound misery which human beings experience find their final explanation' (§ 13). Here and elsewhere *Gaudium et Spes* sets itself to correlate 'the light of revelation' with human experience (e.g., § 33).

Pope John Paul II proved himself an authoritative commentator on *Gaudium et Spes*. Right from his first encyclical, *Redemptor Hominis* (1979), he drew on the constitution and repeatedly reflected on human experience. His 1980 encyclical, *Dives in Misericordia*, began by appealing to collective and individual experience (§ 4) and went on to use 'experience' as a noun thirteen times and as a verb six times. His studies of phenomenologists and mystics also help explain his interest in human experience, both general and religious. But not many commentators have reflected on the theme of experience endorsed by Vatican II and then running through the teaching of John Paul II: few, apart from G. H. Williams, have drawn attention to this theme.[17]

THREE ACHIEVEMENTS OF *RESSOURCEMENT* THEOLOGIANS

After sketching five characteristics of the widespread manualist theology with which *ressourcement* theology had to contend, let me next take up three dramatic examples from Vatican II: the transformation of Catholic doctrine (1) on revelation through *Dei Verbum*, (2) on the church through *Lumen Gentium*, and (3) on divine revelation made to all human beings through *Ad Gentes*.

---

[17] G. H. Williams, *The Mind of John Paul II: Origins of his Thought and Action* (New York: Seabury Press, 1981), 115–40. See D. S. Jeffreys, 'A Deep Amazement at Man's Worth and Dignity', in T. Perry (ed.), *The Legacy of John Paul II: An Evangelical Assessment* (Downers Grove IL: IVP Academic, 2007), 37–56 (39–42); N. R. Pearcey, 'Evangelium Vitae', in Perry (ed.), *The Legacy of John Paul II*, 181–204 (201–4); K. L. Schmitz, *At the Center of the Human Drama: The Philosophical Anthropology of Karol Wojtyla/Pope John Paul II* (Washington, DC: Catholic University of America Press, 1993), 127, 134–5, 126–8.

THE DOCTRINE OF REVELATION (*DEI VERBUM*)

In August 1962, just six weeks before the Council opened on 15 October, the bishops received seven official drafts, which included a 'schema' on 'the Sources of Revelation' and another on the related topic of 'Preserving the Purity of the Deposit of Faith'. In November 1962, many of the bishops at Vatican II were to criticize strongly the first schema and a majority voted to have the document returned to the Theological Commission for rewriting. Pope John XXIII intervened to confirm the majority view and set up a new joint commission to handle the work of revision. The members of the 'mixed commission' were drawn from the Secretariat for Christian Unity and from the Theological Commission itself.[18] In its fourth and final session, the bishops were to approve the Dogmatic Constitution on Divine Revelation, *Dei Verbum*, a text that enjoys theological priority in the corpus of the sixteen documents of Vatican II. *Ressourcement* theologians played a vital role in the preparation of that final text, not only such well known ones as Daniélou, Rahner, and Ratzinger but also such lesser known ones as Pieter Smulders.[19]

Josef Frings, the Cardinal Archbishop of Cologne, asked Ratzinger, as his theological *peritus*, to evaluate the seven drafts, and then signed the response he received from Ratzinger and forwarded it to the Vatican. Ratzinger suggested that the Schema 'On Preserving the Purity of the Deposit of Faith' should be put aside. As for the draft text on 'the Sources of Revelation', it needed an opening chapter on revelation itself and should be revised to avoid pronouncing authoritatively on topics debated among Catholics. In an address to German-speaking bishops on 12 October, the day before the Council opened, Ratzinger sharply criticized the schema's version of revelation and its treatment of such controversial topics as the relationship between scripture and tradition. Ratzinger's earlier study of Bonaventure's conception of revelation had allowed him to retrieve the notion that revelation is actualized in its outcome, living faith. Divine revelation exists in living subjects, those who respond with faith.[20] In a lecture given in 1963, Ratzinger was to insist that 'revelation always and only becomes a reality where there is faith . . . revelation to some degree includes its recipient, without whom it does not exist'.[21]

---

[18] On the debate about 'the Sources of Revelation', see G. Ruggieri, 'The First Doctrinal Clash', in G. Alberigo and J. A. Komonchak (eds.), *History of Vatican II*, (Maryknoll, NY: Orbis Books, 1997), ii.233–66.

[19] On the input from these *periti* toward the genesis of *Dei Verbum*, see Jared Wicks, 'Vatican II on Revelation—Behind the Scenes', *TS*, 71 (2010), 637–50. Wicks supplies rich documentation about this work from the *periti*, a documentation which includes his own outstanding articles, not least the five articles he published on 'Pieter Smulders and *Dei Verbum*'. See further the chapters by Brian E. Daley and Lewis Ayres, Patricia Kelly, and Thomas Humphries in this present volume.

[20] On all this, see Wicks, 'Vatican II on Revelation', 641–3.

[21] 'Revelation and Tradition', in K. Rahner and J. Ratzinger, *Revelation and Tradition*, trans. W. J. O'Hara (London: Burns & Oates, 1966), 26–49 (36).

Around the time when Frings contacted Ratzinger in August 1962, the papal nuncio to the Hague, Archbishop Giuseppe Beltrami, consulted a Dutch Jesuit, Pieter Smulders, about the same seven schemas. Smulders strongly criticized the schema 'on Preserving the Purity of the Deposit of Faith' for one-sidedly presenting revelation as word (*locutio Dei*) and not recognizing that divine works also belong to the event of revelation. Word and saving deeds belong inseparably together, above all in the supreme self-manifestation of God in Jesus Christ, witnessed by 1 John 1:2–3, a text which would appear three years later in *Dei Verbum* (§ 1).[22] Through his work as a *peritus* for the bishops of Indonesia in 1962 and 1963, as drafter of a paper for the 'mixed commission' established by John XXIII in November 1962,[23] and then in 1964 as a drafter of what would become the prologue of Chapter 1 of *Dei Verbum*, Smulders played a major role in the production of the constitution and, not least, in its 'sacramental' view of divine self-revelation as occurring through inseparably interrelated 'words and works' (§ 2, 4, 14, 17).

It has been more or less conventional to assign an ecumenical origin to this way of presenting God's saving and revealing self-communication, as if the bishops and their drafters consciously wanted to combine here the language of word-of-God theologians like Karl Barth and Rudolf Bultmann with that favoured by Oscar Cullmann, Wolfhart Pannenberg, and George Ernest Wright about God's revealing and/or saving acts in history. But a year before the promulgation of *Dei Verbum*, the Council's Dogmatic Constitution on the Church had already used the scheme of 'word/work' when recalling Jesus' proclamation of God's kingdom: 'This kingdom shines out to human beings in the word, works, and presence of Christ' (*Lumen Gentium*, 5). Even more significantly, in November 1962, the language of 'words' and 'works' had already entered the making of *Dei Verbum* through the paper Smulders drafted for the mixed commission and in the paper that Daniélou produced for Cardinal Garrone (see below).

The 'sacramental' language of *Dei Verbum* applies equally to 'the economy of revelation' and 'the history of salvation' As with the administration of the sacraments, the words and deeds of persons interact to communicate God's revelation and salvation (§ 2, 4, 14). Above all in the case of Jesus himself, the words and deeds of a person convey the saving self-manifestation of God (§ 17).

Just as Ratzinger's thinking on revelation was shaped by a retrieval of St Bonaventure, the *ressourcement* theology of revelation coming from Smulders was affected not only by biblical theology but also by St Hilary of Poitiers. In the scheme of 'words and deeds' as the vehicle of revelation, Smulders, a world-class expert on Hilary, echoed his language. In the opening

---

[22] In 'Vatican II on Revelation', 643–5, Wicks summarizes the input coming from Smulders towards the final text of *Dei Verbum*.

[23] See G. O'Collins, 'At the Origins of *Dei Verbum*', *Heythrop Journal*, 26 (1985), 5–13.

article of his *Tractatus Mysteriorum*, Hilary wrote of the biblical 'words (*dicta*)' and 'facts (*facta*)' that, respectively, 'announce (*nuntiare*)' and 'express/reveal (*exprimere*)' the coming of Christ: '*et dictis nuntiat et factis exprimit*'.[24]

During the first session of the Council, various *ressourcement* theologians, such as Edward Schillebeeckx, OP, composed and circulated among the bishops critiques of the official schemas and even proposed alternate texts.[25] Rahner produced a critical *Disquisitio Brevis* on the question of scripture and tradition,[26] and together with Ratzinger offered an alternative to the schema on 'the Sources of Revelation' in their *De Revelatione Dei et Hominis in Iesu Christo Facta*, of which two thousand copies were circulated to the bishops in November just before they began discussing 'the Sources of Revelation'.[27]

Various themes from Rahner's *Disquisitio* and the draft he wrote with Ratzinger were to make their way into the final text of *Dei Verbum*: for instance, 'the magisterium is not above the word of God but serves it' (§ 10), and the refusal to adopt the manualist language of scripture and tradition being 'two sources' of revelation. After all, the Council of Trent spoke of only one source, the Gospel itself, which is equivalent to God's self-revelation in Christ. Rahner, Ratzinger, and other *ressourcement* theologians prompted the language of *Dei Verbum* about scripture and tradition coming from the same divine source, functioning together inseparably, and moving toward 'the same goal', the final revelation of God at the end of world history (§ 9).[28]

In the debate of November 1962, among the bishops who called for a radical revision of the schema on 'the Sources of Revelation' was Cardinal Gabriel Garrone of Toulouse, who then became a member of the new joint commission. To supply a fresh prologue he turned to Daniélou, who supplied a draft 'On Revelation and the Word of God' that Garrone presented to the commission on 27 November 1962. Many of the Daniélou/Garrone themes found their way into the final text of *Dei Verbum*, for instance, Christ as 'the' Revealer of the triune God.[29]

---

[24] *Traité des mystères*, 1.1, ed. J.-P. Brisson, *Sources Chrétiennes*, 19 bis (Paris: Cerf, 2005), 71.
[25] Schillebeeckx can rightly be considered a *ressourcement* theologian, given his work on, for example, revelation, theology, and the sacrament of marriage: see *Revelation and Theology*, 2 vols., trans. N. D. Smith (London: Sheed & Ward, 1967–8; a collection of pre-conciliar articles in which he retrieved themes from scripture and Thomas Aquinas); and *Marriage: Secular Reality and Saving Mystery*, 2 vols., trans. N. D. Smith (London: Sheed & Ward, 1965; orig. 1963; a work in which he retrieved themes from scripture and the history of the Church).
[26] Hanjo Sauer published this text as an appendix to *Erfahrung und Glaube: Die Begründung des pastoralen Prinzips durch die Offenbarungskonstitution des II. Vatikanischen Konzils* (Frankfurt: Peter Lang, 1993), 657–8.
[27] The text in its original Latin with a German translation was published by E. Klinger and K. Wittstadt (eds.), *Glaube im Prozess: Christsein nach dem II. Vatikanum* (Freiburg: Herder, 1984), 33–50.
[28] On the content and influence of the Rahner and Rahner/Ratzinger documents, see Ruggieri, 'The First Doctrinal Clash', 236–41; and Wicks, 'Vatican II on Revelation', 646–7.
[29] On Garrone and Daniélou, see Wicks, 'Vatican II on Revelation, 647–50.

The history of the writing of *Dei Verbum* offers a dramatic case of the close collaboration of Daniélou, Rahner, Ratzinger, Smulders, and other theologians (and biblical scholars) with the bishops in producing a text that embodies some key themes of *ressourcement* theology. Before moving to a similar example, the transformation of teaching on the church that resulted in *Lumen Gentium*, let me cite five major themes from *ressourcement* theology that *Dei Verbum* incorporated.

(a) Where manualist theology understood revelation to be the disclosure by God of otherwise unattainable truths, an increase in 'supernatural' knowledge making up the 'deposit of faith' that is 'contained in' the inspired scriptures and tradition, Chapter One of *Dei Verbum* interpreted revelation as *primarily* the personal self-revelation of the triune God in Christ, who invites human beings to enter freely into a dialogue of love. As an interpersonal event, revelation evokes a response of faith, understood as a personal commitment of the whole human being inspired by the Holy Spirit (§ 5) and not merely an intellectual assent to the truths now revealed (which the manualists stressed when interpreting faith). *Dei Verbum* presented the divine self-revelation and the history of salvation as inseparably connected and interchangeable (§ 2, 3, 4). To borrow language from St John's Gospel, the *light* of revelation brings the *life* of salvation, and vice versa.

The climax of this divine self-communication[30] and its signs came with the death and resurrection of Christ, together with the outpouring of the Holy Spirit (§ 4).[31] Through the Spirit the divine revelation given, once and for all, remains a present reality repeatedly actualized (§ 8) until the final consummation of revelation at the end of time (§ 4). Thus *Dei Verbum*, not to mention other documents of Vatican II,[32] understands revelation to be a past, present, and future reality.[33] Essentially completed (as to its 'content', the 'deposit of

---

[30] By speaking of God 'manifesting' and 'communicating' himself (*Dei Verbum*, § 6), Vatican II introduced into official Catholic teaching the language of divine 'self-communication', a term cherished by Rahner for holding together God's self-*revelation* and self-*giving* through saving grace. God's communication is not merely cognitive but constitutes a real self-communication of God that not only makes salvation known but also brings it in person. See Rahner, 'Observations on the Concept of Revelation', in Rahner and Ratzinger, *Revelation and Tradition*, 9–25 (14–15). John Paul II took up the language of divine 'self-communication' in his 1980 encyclical *Dives in Misericordia* (§ 7) and then repeatedly in his 1986 encyclical *Dominum et Vivificantem* (§ 13, 14, 23, 50, 51, 58).

[31] Manualist theology lacked such a rich, doctrinal appreciation of the revelatory and salvific impact of Christ's resurrection; they left the resurrection aside or at best reduced it to a 'proof' that lent credibility to his divine identity. Thus Jesús Solano, who wrote a standard manual on Christology that ran to 326 pages, devoted less than a page to the resurrection: *Sacrae Theologiae Summa*, vol. 3 (Madrid: Biblioteca de Autores Cristianos, 1956).

[32] On the teaching about revelation to be gleaned from other documents of Vatican II, see G. O'Collins, *Retrieving Fundamental Theology* (Mahwah NJ: Paulist Press, 1993), 63–78.

[33] On 'Revelation, Past, Present, and Future', see G. O'Collins, *Rethinking Fundamental Theology: Toward a New Fundamental Theology* (Oxford: Oxford University Press, 2011), Ch. 5.

faith' [§ 10] or the 'treasure of revelation, entrusted to the church' [§ 26]) in the past with Christ and the apostolic church, revelation is repeatedly actualized in the event of human faith until its consummation in the face-to-face encounter with God at the end. Here *ressourcement* theology tells a different story from the manuals, which limited revelation to the past and allowed only for an ongoing understanding and interpretation of such past revelation. This was to ignore what one should draw from Bonaventure (see Ratzinger above) and the logic of faith presented by John's Gospel: since faith is an encounter 'now' with God in Christ, so too must revelation be an actual, present self-disclosure of God who invites such faith. As reciprocal realities, faith and revelation occur together.

(b) Such teaching on revelation entailed a switch of language: from the manualist terminology of revealed 'mysteries' (in the plural) to the terminology of 'the mystery' or divine plan now personally disclosed in Christ (§ 2) or *reductio in mysterium* popularized by Rahner[34] and other *ressourcement* theologians. Talk of 'the mystery' forms a major *leitmotif* of *Dei Verbum*: five times this constitution speaks of 'mystery' in the singular (§ 2, 15, 17, 24, and 26) and never of 'mysteries' in the plural. The same tendency shows up in the other texts promulgated by Vatican II: the sixteen documents use 'mystery' in the singular 114 times and 'mysteries' in the plural only fourteen times. While not totally avoiding talk of 'mysteries' (see *Unitatis Redintegratio* § 11; *Optatam Totius* § 16), Vatican II preferred to retrieve the biblical language of the 'mystery' of the triune God, revealed in the history of salvation and inviting human beings into a new relationship of eternal love (Eph. 1. 9). For that matter, right from his first encyclical John Paul II exemplified the same tendency. *Redemptor Hominis* (1979) speaks fifty-nine times of 'the mystery of redemption', 'the paschal mystery', 'the mystery of Christ', and so forth, without ever using the term 'mystery' in the plural. The Pope's second encyclical, *Dives in Misericordia* (1980), uses 'mystery' thirty-nine times but 'mysteries' only twice.

(c) We have already remarked above on the 'sacramental' and historical approach that such *ressourcement* theologians as Daniélou and Smulders contributed to *Dei Verbum*. This approach understands revelation to be a living event communicated through words and deeds functioning together in the course of salvation history.

(d) The presentation of revelation as primarily an encounter with the self-communicating God put into a new context the whole debate about tradition

---

[34] Rahner, 'The Concept of Mystery in Catholic Theology', *TI*, iv, trans. K. Smyth (1960) (London: Darton, Longman & Todd, 1966), 36–73, esp. 60–73.

and Sacred Scripture. They are inseparably related in their past origin (the living word of God or divine self-disclosure), present functioning, and future goal (the final revelation to come at the end of history) (*Dei Verbum* § 9). Revelation, as a living reality, is made known by the inspired Scriptures, but cannot be 'contained in' anything, not even in the inspired Scriptures.[35]

In 1546 the Council of Trent declared 'the gospel' to be 'the source of all saving truth and conduct', adding that 'this truth and rule of conduct are contained in the written books [of the Bible] and the unwritten [apostolic] traditions' (*DS* § 1501). Despite Trent's language about the gospel (= revelation) being 'the source' (in the singular), there emerged in Catholic manualist theology the 'two-source' theory of revelation, according to which scripture and tradition are two distinct sources for revealed truths. Tradition could and does supply some truths which are not found in scripture. In other words, scripture is not merely 'formally insufficient' (= needing to be interpreted and actualized by tradition) but also 'materially insufficient' (= not 'containing' all revealed truths). This view obviously privileged a propositional notion of revelation: namely, the model of revelation as the communication of truths which would otherwise have remained hidden in God. Although *Dei Verbum* did not explicitly rule out the 'two-source theory', that theory is certainly much more difficult to maintain in the face of Vatican II's understanding of revelation as being primarily God's self-revelation and its stress on the unity between scripture and tradition.

(e) Largely the product of *ressourcement* thinking, *Dei Verbum* shows a profoundly biblical orientation. It comes as no surprise when it invites theologians to make the study of Scriptures the very 'soul' of their work (§ 24). This recommendation, taken from Leo XIII's 1893 encyclical *Providentissimus Deus*, drew on an early Jesuit tradition[36] and the practice of the best medieval theologians, which in their turn reflected the theological method of church Fathers, both Eastern and Western. The prayerful study of the Bible, both Old and New Testaments, was 'the very soul' of their teaching; their work, which ran to nearly 400 volumes in the Migne edition, could be described as one vast commentary on the scriptures.

While Catholics like Marie-Joseph Lagrange (1855–1938) carried forward critical biblical scholarship, de Lubac and other *ressourcement* figures reintroduced a 'spiritual' interpretation of the scriptures that retrieved the best of the patristic and medieval traditions. In its chapter on the interpretation of the scriptures, *Dei Verbum* endorsed both critical and 'spiritual' interpretation (§ 12).

---

[35] See Ratzinger, 'Revelation and Tradition', 35–7.
[36] See J. M. Lera, 'Sacrae paginae studium sit veluti anima Sacrae Theologiae (Notas sobre el origen y procedencia de esta frase)', in A. Vargas Machuca and G. Ruiz (eds.), *Palabra y Vida. Homenaje a José Alonso Díaz en su 70 cumpleaños* (Madrid: Universidad Comillas, 1984), 409–22.

The biblical component of *ressourcement* flowered, however, in the whole closing chapter of *Dei Verbum*, 'Sacred Scripture in the Life of the Church' (§ 21–6). Here the Council dreamed of the whole church being nourished by the Bible at every level of its existence. A prayerful knowledge of the scriptures would foster among all the baptized a living union with Christ and a life centred on him and blessed by the Holy Spirit.

Along with the five themes just described, one could scrutinize further the final text of *Dei Verbum* and note how it embodied other themes from *ressourcement* theology: for instance, a sense of biblical truth as truth 'for the sake of our salvation' (§ 11), as well as an endorsement of a three-stage scheme in the formation of the Gospels spelled out by the Pontifical Biblical Commission (§ 19), and also the pastoral tone and ecumenical spirit of *Dei Verbum*, which embodied the desires and hopes of Pope John XXIII for the work of Vatican II. Yet one should also honour Congar for having, years before, set out the pastoral and ecumenical needs of the church.[37] But let us turn next to the ways in which *ressourcement* theologians, led not only by Congar[38] but also by Gérard Philips, helped transform teaching on the church.

THE DOCTRINE OF THE CHURCH (*LUMEN GENTIUM*)

Above I recalled how Gagnebet and Tromp, under the watchful direction of Cardinal Ottaviani, led the way in preparing a draft text *De Ecclesia*. This schema of manualist inspiration highlighted the church as a hierarchical society rather than as being a mystery and the whole people of God. Following Pius XII's 1943 encyclical, *Mystici Corporis Christi*,[39] it identified the Mystical Body of Christ with the Roman Catholic Church and so used the term 'church' exclusively of the Roman Catholic Church. In the final days of the first session of Vatican II, this schema was sharply criticized by the bishops (1–6 December 1962).

Even before that, in October 1962, Cardinal Leo Jozef Suenens had asked Philips to 'revise, complete, and improve' this schema on the church.[40] As a result of the December debate, the schema was removed, and over several

---

[37] Congar, *Divided Christendom: A Catholic Study of the Problem of Reunion*, trans. M. A. Bousfield (London: G. Bles, 1938; French original 1937); Congar, *Vraie et fausse réforme dans l'Église* (Paris: Cerf, 1950).

[38] See W. Henn, 'Yves Congar and *Lumen gentium*', *Greg* 86 (2005), 563–92.

[39] Pope Pius XII, *Mystici Corporis Christi*. Encyclical Letter on the Mystical Body of Christ (29 June 1943), *AAS* xxxv (1943), 193–248, § 80. ET available at <http://www.vatican.va/holy_father/pius_xii/encyclicals/documents/hf_p-xii_enc_29061943_mystici-corporis-christi_en.html>.

[40] G. Ruggieri, 'Beyond an Ecclesiology of Polemics: The Debate on the Church', in Alberigo and Komonchak (eds.), *The History of Vatican II*, ii.281–357 (282–4).

months (February–May 1963) a new draft was prepared on the basis of a revised text authored by Philips.[41] For some weeks in the spring of 1963, Congar also worked on the revision that resulted in a new draft mailed to the bishops in the middle of the year. In that revised schema, which eventually became the final text of *Lumen Gentium* (21 November 1964), Congar worked on sections 9, 13, 16, and 17 in Chapter 2 ('The People of God') and contributed to Chapter 1 ('The Mystery of the Church').

Section 16 of Chapter 2, with its positive regard for Jews, Muslims, and others, prepared the way for *Nostra Aetate*, Vatican II's Declaration on the church's relation to non-christian religions (28 October 1965) and also for a key doctrinal principle (see below) in *Ad Gentes*, the Decree on the missionary activity of the church (7 December 1965). But it was in Chapter 1 that themes cherished by Congar and other *ressourcement* theologians came through even more clearly. In richly biblical and patristic language, that chapter emphasized the sacramental reality of the church, from which 'shines' the 'light' of Christ and which is 'the sign and instrument of intimate communion with God and of unity among the whole human race' (§ 1). A full spread of biblical images (§ 6) illuminate 'the mystery of holy Church' (§ 5), which 'subsists' (= continues to exist [fully]) in the Roman Catholic Church (§ 8) and is not simply identical with the Roman Catholic Church, as Tromp and other manualists claimed. To be sure, the meaning of 'subsists' continues to be disputed, with the Congregation for the Doctrine of the Faith offering over the years varying translations, as Sullivan has pointed out.[42] But the conclusion that the Church of God is not *tout court* identical with the Roman Catholic Church does not depend on the translation of '*subsistit*'; it emerges clearly from other passages in Vatican II documents.

Recognizing in this context how 'many elements of sanctification and of truth' are found outside the 'structure of the' Roman Catholic Church (§ 8), *Lumen Gentium* would go on to specify some of these elements: 'believing the Sacred Scripture' to be 'the norm of faith and life', belief in the Trinity, and the reception of baptism and 'other sacraments in their own Churches or ecclesial communities' (§ 15). Here the Council recognized as 'Churches' bodies of Christian not (or not yet) in union with the Roman Catholic Church. Even more specifically in its Decree on Ecumenism (*Unitatis Redintegratio* of 21 November 1964), Vatican II recognized how the principle 'the Eucharist makes the church' operates also for the Eastern Churches not in communion

---

[41] J. Grootaers, 'The Drama Continues between the Acts: The "Second Preparation" and its Opponents', in Alberigo and Komonchak (eds.), *The History of Vatican II*, ii.359–514 (399–412).

[42] For a magisterial guide to the meaning of 'subsists' in this context and some of the controversy surrounding its meaning, see F. A. Sullivan, 'The Meaning of *Subsistit in* as explained by the Congregation of the Doctrine of the Faith', *TS*, 67 (2006), 116–24; Sullivan, 'A Response to Karl Becker, SJ, on the Meaning of *Subsistit in*', *TS*, 67 (2006), 395–409; Sullivan, 'Further Thoughts on the Meaning of *Subsistit in*', *TS*, 71 (2010), 133–47.

with the Bishop of Rome: 'through the celebration of the Eucharist of the Lord in each of these Churches, the Church of God is built up and grows' (§ 15). In other words, while the Church of God continues to exist fully in the Roman Catholic Church, it also continues to exist in other churches or ecclesial communities, above all in the Eastern Churches, which enjoy almost all the elements of Christian elements of sanctification and truth.

As well as supplying the basic draft that became the eight chapters of *Lumen Gentium*, Philips played a major role, in particular, in developing Chapter 4 ('The laity') and the application of Christ's triple office (of priest, prophet, and king/shepherd) to bishops (and ordained priests) and to all the baptized. The teaching/prophetic, priestly, and pastoral/kingly office of the bishops, which had already appeared in the original schema, was further elaborated in Chapter 3 ('The hierarchical constitution of the church and in particular the episcopate'); the priestly, prophetic, and kingly role of all the baptized was introduced, above all, in Chapter 4. Philips played a major role in these two developments.[43]

Before the Council opened, both Congar and Philips had written on both the triple office and on the laity. Congar had published a classic study on the laity;[44] and in that book he dedicated Chapters 4, 5, and 6 to the way lay people share in the priestly, kingly, and prophetical (in that order) functions of Christ. In the year Vatican II opened, Philips published *Pour une christianisme adulte*, in which he expounded the three functions of the laity: 'A Priestly, Prophetic, Royal People.'[45] Yet, at the Council, neither Congar nor Philips seemed to have been involved, at least directly, with the drafting and emending of the Decree on the apostolate of the laity (*Apostolicam Actuositatem*, 18 November 1965). That document spoke of 'the priestly, prophetic and kingly offices of Christ', in which the laity 'share' (§ 2). Consecrated as a 'royal priesthood' (§ 3), they participate in 'the function of Christ, priest, prophet and king' (§ 10). Congar and Philips had encouraged such an eminently *ressourcement* theme—both of them through their publications and Philips through *Lumen Gentium*, promulgated a year earlier and containing in Chapter 4 a firm endorsement of the priestly, prophetic and kingly role of all the baptized.

In the genesis of *Lumen Gentium*, Congar had his significant role, but it was Philips who authored the initial draft, secured an entire chapter on the laity,[46]

---

[43] Two years after the Council closed, Philips published *L'Église et son mystère au IIe Concile du Vatican: histoire, texte et commentaire de la Constitution 'Lumen Gentium'*, 2 vols. (Paris: Desclée, 1967). Philips treats the threefold office of the bishops (i.254–7) and, at greater length, that of the laity (ii.31–48).

[44] Congar, *Jalons pour une théologie du laïcat* (Paris: Cerf: 1953); trans. D. Attwater as *Lay People in the Church: A Study for a Theology of the Laity* (London: Bloomsbury, 1957).

[45] Trans. E. Kane as *Achieving Christian Maturity* (Dublin: Gill, 1966), 65–93.

[46] In the Gagnebet-Tromp 1962 schema *De Ecclesia*, Philips had largely authored the chapter on the laity. He tweaked this chapter a little for the revised text adopted in March 1963 that became the new base-text for *Lumen Gentium*.

applied the scheme of 'priest, prophet, and king/shepherd' to the hierarchy and the laity, defended the collegial character of bishops (who form with the Pope an 'apostolic college' [§ 22–3]), and—more than any other expert-consultant—helped to shepherd *Lumen Gentium* through to its final form and promulgation in November 1964.[47]

Apropos of introducing into the Council's documents the *munus triplex* of 'priest, prophet, and king', Congar's hand is most visible in the decree *Presbyterorum Ordinis*. He drafted the text (with the help of Joseph Lécuyer and Willy Onclin), was involved in the revisions, and composed the moving conclusion (§ 22). In this document on the ministry and life of ordained priests, numbers 4–6 take up and spell out in detail what the introduction states: 'through the sacred ordination and mission that they receive from the bishops, priests are promoted to serve Christ the *Teacher*, *Priest*, and *King*' (§ 1; italics mine). Number 4 details what is involved in priests being 'ministers of the sacraments and the Eucharist'; and number 6 describes their role as kingly 'rulers of God's people' and 'pastors' of the Church'.

The triple office of Christ as priest, prophet, and king, in which all the faithful share through baptism and some through ministerial ordination, is a major theme of the 1964 Dogmatic Constitution on the Church and of two decrees that depended upon it and were promulgated in 1965: the Decree on the Apostolate of the Lay People and the Decree on the Ministry and Life of Priests. *Ressourcement* theology, represented by Congar and Philips, had retrieved this theme of the '*munus triplex*' from traditional and biblical sources. One can trace it back through John Henry Newman, John Calvin, Thomas Aquinas, and various Fathers of the Church to its roots in the Scriptures, both Old Testament and New Testament.[48]

DIVINE REVELATION TO ALL (*AD GENTES*)

This third section will address more briefly one further *ressourcement* theme that, thanks to Congar, found its place in the teaching of Vatican II: God's self-revelation to all people.

Sharply differing views of Christian missionary activity led to many difficulties in the drafting, discussion, and revision of *Ad Gentes*.[49] At the end, however, 2394 fathers voted yes and only four voted no—a dramatic tribute to

---

[47] See Alberigo and Komonchak (eds.), *History of Vatican II*, ii–iv, *passim*.

[48] See G. O'Collins and M. K. Jones, *Jesus Our Priest: A Christian Approach to the Priesthood of Christ* (Oxford: Oxford University Press, 2010), 1–229.

[49] See H. S. Brechter, 'Decree on the Church's Missionary Activity', trans. W. J. O'Hara, in H. Vorgrimler (ed.), *Commentary on the Documents of Vatican II*, iv (London: Burns & Oates, 1969), 87–181 (98–111).

the work of Congar and other experts in developing the Decree on the Church's Missionary Activity. He played a major role in developing the decree and, especially, in composing Chapter 1 ('Doctrinal principles'), his own work 'from A to Z', as he put it.[50] This is the longest of the six chapters that make up *Ad Gentes*, as well as including more sources (cited or referred to) in the footnotes than all the other chapters put together. 'The patristic references are particularly numerous and excellently chosen', Heinrich Suso Brechter wrote, 'whereas the following chapters quote almost exclusively from conciliar texts and papal allocutions.'[51] In a *tour de force* Congar quoted or referred to twenty-three Fathers of the Church, some of them, like Irenaeus and Augustine, more than once, retrieving remarkable texts that illuminate principles that give life to the church's missionary activity, itself based in the missionary activity of the Trinity for the salvation of human beings. Let me cite an example that concerns the divine self-revelation to all people.

To explain 'the preparation for the Gospel' (§ 3), footnote 2 quotes two passages from Irenaeus' *Adversus Haereses*: 'the Word existing with God, through whom all things were made...was always present to the human race'; hence 'from the beginning the Son, being present in his creation, reveals (*revelat*) the Father to all whom the Father desires, at the time and in the manner desired by the Father' (*Adversus Haereses*, 3. 18. 1; 4. 6. 7). Thus *Ad Gentes* aligns itself with Irenaeus in recognizing the Word as the agent of all creation (see Jn 1.1–3, 10; 1 Cor. 8.6; Col. 1.16, Heb. 1.2). Consequently the Word has 'always' been 'present to the human race', and not merely to certain groups or nations.[52]

Granted the Christological origin and character of creation, right 'from the beginning' of human history the Son has been 'revealing' the Father to human beings. In all the sixteen documents it is only here that Vatican II applies the verb 'reveal' to the knowledge of God mediated through the created world. Clearly this revelation of God through creation and 'ordinary' human history allows for endless variety, as the Son 'reveals the Father to all whom the Father desires and at the time and in the manner desired by the Father'. In contemporary terms, Irenaeus was speaking of the 'general' history of revelation (and salvation), in which from the beginning of the human story the Son of God has been revealing the Father.

The two quotations from Irenaeus highlight the universal divine activity by which the Word/Son of God was preparing people for the coming of the

---

[50] *Mon journal*, ii.511.

[51] Brechter, 'Decree on the Church's Missionary Activity', 113.

[52] From the time of Justin Martyr, this real but hidden presence of the Word *in* the created world and *to* the human race went under the name of 'the seeds of the Word' (*Ad Gentes*, § 11), another rich theme retrieved by *ressourcement* theology. See J. Daniélou, *A History of Early Christian Doctrine*, ii, *Gospel Message and Hellenistic Culture*, trans. J. A. Baker (London: Darton, Longman & Todd, 1973), 41–4.

Gospel. The use of the term 'reveal' implies the counterpart of faith: it is with true faith that human beings can respond to the initiative of the Son of God present in and through creation and revealing God to them.[53] The divine quest for all human beings takes precedence over any human quest for God. It is primarily due to this divine initiative and not to a human search that 'elements of *truth* and *grace*', which constitute 'a secret presence of God', are already found among peoples before they are evangelized and can accept Christ explicitly.[54]

The Decree on the Church's Missionary Activity echoes what had been said a year earlier in *Lumen Gentium* about those who had 'arrived at an explicit recognition of God and who, not without divine grace, strive to live an upright life': 'whatever *goodness and truth* that is found among them is considered by the Church to be a preparation for the Gospel and *given by Him who enlightens all human beings* that they may at length have life' (§ 16; italics mine). As we noted above, Congar helped shape this article of *Lumen Gentium* about God preparing people for evangelization.[55]

CONCLUSION

I have concentrated on examples from *Dei Verbum, Lumen Gentium*, and *Ad Gentes* to illustrate the way in which *ressourcement* theology, represented by Congar, Daniélou, Philips, Smulders, and others contributed to the making of the Vatican II's teaching. One could add many further examples and further names. Let me mention only three further items.

First, Chenu had retrieved, ultimately from the New Testament, the language of 'the signs of the times' (Mt. 16.3).[56] The final and longest document from Vatican II, the Pastoral Constitution on the Church in the Modern World (*Gaudium et Spes*, 7 December 1965) picked up this theme: 'the Church

---

[53] This point (a faith response to revelation made by the non-evangelized) is expressly acknowledged in the chapter for which Congar was responsible: 'in ways known to himself God can lead those who, through no fault of their own, are ignorant of the Gospel to that faith without which it is impossible to please him (Heb. 11: 6') (§ 7).

[54] *Ad Gentes* § 9, my italics.

[55] On salvation and revelation being available outside the visible church and on the church's role in the divine plan for humanity, see G. Flynn, *Yves Congar's Vision of the Church in a World of Unbelief* (Aldershot/Burlington VT: Ashgate, 2004), 39–51.

[56] See Chenu, *Le Saulchoir*; Chenu, 'Les Signes des temps', in Y. Congar and M. Peuchmaurd (eds.), *L'Église dans le monde de ce temps: Constitution pastoral 'Gaudium et Spes'* (Paris: Cerf, 1967), 205–25. Citing Mt. 16.3, Pope John XXIII introduced the theme of 'the signs of the times' in his 1962 'bull' of convocation for Vatican II, *Humanae Salutis*, and a year later in the encyclical *Pacem in Terris* (§ 126–9), but there is no evidence that the pope directly drew this theme from Chenu.

carries the responsibility of scrutinizing the signs of the times and interpreting them in the light of the Gospel' (§ 4). It is the whole 'people of God', led 'by the Spirit of the Lord who fills the whole world', who try 'to discern' in 'the events, the needs, and the longings that it shares with other human beings of our age', what 'may be true signs of the presence or of the purpose of God' (§ 11).

Second, the Decree on Ecumenism, *Unitatis Redintegratio*, included the important observation that 'there exists an order or "hierarchy" among the truths of Catholic doctrine' (§ 11). All truths of Catholic doctrine are important, but some truths (for instance, the Trinity and the incarnation) are more fundamental than others (for instance, the primacy of the Bishop of Rome). Even if Congar did not work on the drafting of that decree, he helped to originate the principle of a 'hierarchy of truths', a principle ultimately based on his retrieval of the notion of truth and truths developed by Thomas Aquinas.[57]

Third, among the pioneering works of *ressourcement* theology, de Lubac's *Catholicism*[58] stands out. It came about when Congar invited de Lubac to put together some articles into a book published by the Unam Sanctam series, directed at the time by Congar himself. Some of the language of what became a classic article in *Gaudium et Spes* (and was to be cited by John Paul II) about Christ revealing human beings to themselves and all human beings being called to the 'same destiny' (§ 22) echoed what de Lubac had written.[59]

Called by Pope John XXIII, Vatican II was the most significant religious event in the twentieth century. One generation has now passed and a second is well established since the Council ended in 1965. Its teaching is still being received and tested in the lives of believers. In major ways that teaching was shaped by theologians of the *ressourcement* movement: Chenu, Congar, Daniélou, de Lubac, Philips, Rahner, Ratzinger, Smulders, and others. They left the whole Christian Church a life-giving legacy in what they retrieved from the scriptures and the great tradition for the documents of Vatican II.

---

[57] See William Henn, *The Hierarchy of Truths According to Yves Congar, OP* (Rome: Gregorian University Press, 1987).

[58] Trans. L. C. Sheppard and E. Englund (San Francisco: Ignatius Press, 1988; French original, *Catholicisme: Les aspects sociaux du dogme* (Paris: Cerf, 1947).

[59] De Lubac, *Catholicism* (in this order) 299, 339. Paul McPartlan drew attention to this similarity in *Sacrament of Salvation: An Introduction to Eucharistic Ecclesiology* (Edinburgh: T&T Clark, 1995), 74. See also McPartlan, 'John Paul II and Vatican II', in G. Mannion (ed.), *The Vision of John Paul II: Assessing his Thought and Influence* (Collegeville MN: Liturgical Press, 2008), 45–61 (49–51).

25

Ressourcement, Vatican II, and Eucharistic Ecclesiology

Paul McPartlan

INTRODUCTION

'If the Church alone makes the Eucharist, it is also true that the Eucharist makes the Church.'[1] This statement in a footnote to the second draft of what became Vatican II's Dogmatic Constitution on the Church, *Lumen Gentium*, not only shows the intention of the Council to embrace a eucharistic ecclesiology, but also clearly indicates the influence of the French Jesuit, Henri de Lubac (1896–1991), on the emerging text.

The development of eucharistic ecclesiology in the Catholic Church in the twentieth century is strongly associated with the name of de Lubac, one of the leading pioneers of the *ressourcement* that bore fruit in many areas of the Council's teaching. In his book, *Corpus Mysticum*, first published in 1944, de Lubac coined the famous principle which serves to characterize this ecclesiology: 'the Eucharist makes the Church'.[2] He repeated and developed the principle nearly ten years later in his *Méditation sur l'Eglise* (1953),[3] a book which strongly foreshadows *Lumen Gentium*.[4] '[E]verything points to a study

---

[1] *ASSCOVII*, ii.i (1971), 251, n.57.

[2] Henri Cardinal de Lubac, SJ, *Corpus Mysticum: The Eucharist and the Church in the Middle Ages*, trans. Gemma Simmonds, CJ with Richard Price and Christopher Stephens, eds. Laurence Paul Hemming and Susan Frank Parsons (London: SCM, 2006), 88. For a study of this principle, see my *The Eucharist Makes the Church: Henri de Lubac and John Zizioulas in Dialogue*, 2nd edn. (Fairfax VA: Eastern Christian Publications, 2006 [1993]). For further treatment of eucharistic ecclesiology, see my 'Eucharistic Ecclesiology', *One in Christ*, 22 (1986), 314–31; 'The Eucharist as the Basis for Ecclesiology', *Antiphon*, 6 (2001), 12–9; *Sacrament of Salvation: An Introduction to Eucharistic Ecclesiology* (Edinburgh: T&T Clark, 1995).

[3] ET *The Splendour of the Church*, trans. Michael Mason (San Francisco: Ignatius, 1986).

[4] Both have a first chapter on the church as mystery, a final chapter on the place of Mary in the mystery of the church, and many points of contact in between. In his memoirs, de Lubac notes that, when the *imprimatur* for the Italian translation of *Méditation sur l'Eglise* was refused

of the relation between the Church and the Eucharist, which we may describe as standing as cause to each other. Each has been entrusted to the other, so to speak, by Christ; the Church makes the Eucharist, but the Eucharist also makes the Church',[5] and it was the latter point that de Lubac particularly wanted to stress: 'if the sacrifice is accepted by God and the Church's prayer listened to, this is because the Eucharist, in its turn, *makes the Church*, in the strict sense of the words'.[6]

De Lubac was urging more reflection on the formative and indeed constitutive role of the Eucharist in the life of the church. This was not a new departure, but a return to ancient patterns of thought, as the opening words of *Corpus Mysticum* make clear:

> In the thinking of the whole of Christian antiquity, the Eucharist and the Church are linked. In St Augustine,...this link is given especially particular force, and this can also be said of the Latin writers of the seventh century, eighth century and ninth century. For them, as for Augustine, on whom they are dependent either directly or through other writers, and whose formulations they endlessly reproduce, the Eucharist corresponds to the Church as cause to effect, as means to end, as sign to reality.[7]

De Lubac had given an initial exposition of this patristic teaching in his momentous first book, *Catholicism*, in 1938:

> When, with St Augustine, [our forebears] heard Christ say to them: 'I am your food, but instead of my being changed into you, it is you who shall be transformed into me', they unhesitatingly understood that by their reception of the Eucharist they would be incorporated the more in the Church.[8]

He had also pointed out, however, that there came a time when this ecclesial understanding of the Eucharist (and eucharistic understanding of the church) was lost from view.

> *O signum unitatis! O vinculum caritatis!* Gradually the doctrine was forgotten...[A] change was gradually wrought in men's habits of mind...Just as they would no longer see the spiritual reflected in the sensible or the universal and particular as

---

in Rome, 'the Italian edition appeared in Milan, under the patronage of the new archbishop, Msgr. Montini [the future Pope Paul VI, who oversaw the completion of *Lumen Gentium*], who more than once cited the work and distributed it to his clergy'. *At the Service of the Church*, trans. Anne Elizabeth Englund (San Francisco: Ignatius, 1993), 75.

[5] *Splendour*, 134. Translation amended to reflect the French, *'fait l'Eucharistie'* and *'fait l'Église'*, respectively; cf. *Méditation sur l'Eglise* (Paris: Aubier, 1953), 113.

[6] *Splendour*, 152, amended translation; cf. *Méditation sur l'Eglise*, 129 (italics in original).

[7] *Corpus Mysticum*, 13.

[8] De Lubac, *Catholicism*, trans. Lancelot C. Sheppard and Anne Elizabeth Englund (San Francisco: Ignatius, 1988), 99–100; quotation from Augustine, *Confessions* 7.10/16, *Complete Works*, Part I, i.173.

reciprocally symbolical, so the idea of the relationship between the physical body of Christ and his Mystical Body came to be forgotten.[9]

This forgetting was still a problem at the time he was writing: 'There are doubtless not a few in our day inclined to think that there is but a vague extrinsic analogy between these two meanings of the "body". That was certainly not the opinion of our forebears.'[10]

De Lubac appended to *Catholicism* a selection of fifty-five texts, two-thirds of them patristic, to begin to offer the wisdom of 'our forebears' on the Eucharist and other topics to his readers. This, of course, was but a drop in the ocean; and just a few years later, in the early years of the Second World War, he and Jean Daniélou undertook to co-edit what was to become one of the major monuments of the twentieth-century *ressourcement*, namely the series of accessible editions of complete patristic texts, *Sources chrétiennes*.[11] 'Each time, in our West, that Christian renewal has flourished, . . . it has flourished under the sign of the Fathers.'[12]

THE MEDIEVAL SHIFT

The forgetting to which de Lubac refers happened in medieval times, in the transition from patristic to scholastic theology. In *Corpus Mysticum*, he offered a helpful way of conceiving the shift that occurred. The term 'body of Christ' has three possible meanings, namely the historical body, sacramental body, and ecclesial body of Christ, respectively, all of which are profoundly inter-related in the eucharistic mystery. The Fathers were particularly occupied with the link between the second and third of these bodies, with how the Eucharist makes the church. Scholasticism was more concerned with the bond between the first two bodies, with how Christ becomes really present in the eucharistic species of bread and wine by transubstantiation through the action of the church's priests, that is, with how the church makes the Eucharist. The 'caesura' which originally stood between the first and second meanings subsequently shifted to stand between the second and third. This fact 'dominates the whole evolution of Eucharistic theories'.[13]

Eucharistic controversy, particularly surrounding the views of Berengar (*c*.1010–88), played a crucial role in the shift.[14] Up to the time of Berengar,

---

[9] *Catholicism*, 98–9; initial quotation from Augustine *In Joannem*, 26.13.

[10] *Catholicism*, 99.

[11] See *At the Service of the Church*, 50, 94–6. *Sources chrétiennes* continues to thrive, and has now published more than five hundred volumes.

[12] *At the Service of the Church*, 95–6, 317–18.

[13] *Corpus Mysticum*, 256.

[14] Walter Kasper speaks of the 'general oblivion' into which eucharistic ecclesiology fell in the wake of the Berengarian controversy: 'Church as *communio*', *Communio*, 13 (1986), 100–17 (107).

the Eucharist was widely called the 'sacrament of the body of the Lord' or the 'mystery of the body', or simply the 'mystical body', *corpus mysticum*, and the church was understood in scriptural terms simply as the body of the Lord, *corpus verum*. However, after Berengar's doubts about the real presence of Christ in the Eucharist, the term *corpus mysticum*, so expressive of the sacramental presence of the mystery of Christ and the church when rightly understood, was changed, lest it encourage such doubts, and the Eucharist itself took on the same name as the church, both being called the 'body' of Christ.[15] The dynamic interplay between the two realities was thereby lost, and as the bond between Christ himself and the Eucharist was more and more accentuated, particularly with regard to the change of the bread and wine into his body and blood, so the bond between the Eucharist and the church was neglected. The Eucharist had been 'the mystery to be understood', now it increasingly became simply 'the miracle to be believed'.[16]

Eventually, in order to distinguish between the Eucharist and the church, the adjective 'mystical' began to be applied to the 'body' when the latter referred to the church. So it was that, from around the mid-twelfth century, the *church* became the 'mystical body', in a reversal of the original usage.[17] This new meaning still survives, and de Lubac's book constituted a plea to restore not necessarily the former terminology, but certainly the understanding of the relationship between Eucharist and church that it reflected.

He lamented, moreover, that it soon became common to speak of the mystical body, i.e., the church, without reference to the Eucharist, as, for example, in what is generally regarded as the first treatise on the church, *De regimine christiano* (1301/2), by James of Viterbo.[18] This work set the pattern for primarily juridical and institutional accounts of the church, and ecclesiology and eucharistic theology increasingly grew apart. Referring to this separation, notable 'from the eleventh and twelfth centuries onwards', Joseph Ratzinger, writing at the end of Vatican II, said that it 'represents one of the most unfortunate pages of medieval theology'. 'A doctrine of the Eucharist that is not related to the community of the Church misses its essence as does an ecclesiology that is not conceived with the Eucharist as its centre.'[19] Commenting on the same 'dissociation', Walter Kasper more recently said that 'the Eucharist was individualised and the Church politicised'.[20]

The famous definition of the church given by Robert Bellarmine around 1590, shortly after the Council of Trent, well illustrates the new approach. The

---

[15] See *Corpus Mysticum*, 80.   [16] See *Corpus Mysticum*, 240.
[17] See *Corpus Mysticum*, 99–100, 104.   [18] See *Corpus Mysticum*, 114.
[19] Ratzinger, 'The Pastoral Implications of Episcopal Collegiality', *Concilium*, 1/1 (1965), 20–34 (28).
[20] Kasper, 'Eucharist—Sacrament of Unity: The Essential Connection between Eucharist and Church', *Sacrament of Unity. The Eucharist and the Church* (New York: Crossroad, 2004), 117–50 (138).

church, he said, is 'the assembly of people bound together by the profession of the same Christian faith and the communion of the same sacraments under the government of legitimate pastors, above all the one vicar of Christ on earth, the Roman pontiff'.[21] Dispute with Protestants, who maintained that the true church was invisible, led Catholics so to stress the outward structure of the church, and particularly the hierarchy, that, as Yves Congar (1904–95) later said, ecclesiology became 'hierarchology' in these controversial texts, which exercised an enduring influence on the course of Catholic reflection thereafter: 'the aspects of living depth, wherein the Church is seen as a body alive and energising throughout, were passed over in silence, if not sometimes suspected of being "not really Catholic"'.[22] 'Such great apologists as Bellarmine and Cardinal du Perron', he complained, 'say nothing of the relation of the Eucharist to the Church: yet this was central in the consciousness that medieval theology had of the mystery of the Church.'[23] Like de Lubac, Congar, writing here in 1951, wanted to restore in the church an understanding of that vital relationship.

The origins of the strongly hierarchical and centralized view of the Church held by Bellarmine can actually be traced back five hundred years before him. The pope before whom Berengar made the second defence of his views in 1079[24] was the redoubtable Gregory VII, after whom the Gregorian Reform is named. This reform, prompted by the determination to eradicate abuses such as simony and to assert the independence of the church from civil powers, was driven from Rome and inevitably resulted in a more centralized and authoritarian church.[25] Thus, at the very time when the link between the Eucharist and the church was receiving less attention, because of the need to defend the eucharistic change and the real presence of Christ, and the potential of the Eucharist to shape the church was correspondingly diminishing, other factors, juridical and institutional, came to the fore and determined its shape. From earliest times, the Eucharist had shaped the church

---

[21] Robert Bellarmine, *Disputationes de controversiis*, 4 (*De Conciliis*), Book 3, Ch. 2.

[22] Congar, *Lay People in the Church*, trans. D. Attwater (London: Geoffrey Chapman, 1965), 44–6.

[23] *Lay People in the Church*, 46, n.1.

[24] The profession of faith required of him on that occasion contained the affirmation that the bread and wine are 'substantially changed [*substantialiter converti*]' in the Mass—the first appearance of such terminology in an official magisterial text.

[25] See Congar, 'The Historical Development of Authority in the Church: Points for Christian Reflection', in John M. Todd (ed.), *Problems of Authority* (London: Darton, Longman & Todd, 1962), 119–55, particularly 136–44. It is no coincidence that the schism between Christian East and West occurred at this time also. With regard to the tragic events of 1054 and the mutual excommunications of Cardinal Humbert and Patriarch Michael Cerularius, Henry Chadwick comments: 'Cardinal Humbert's strength in his own eyes, but weakness in the view of the eastern patriarchs, ... lay in his underlying axiom that obedience to papal authority was the key to unlock all disputed matters'. *East and West: The Making of a Rift in the Church* (Oxford: Oxford University Press, 2003), 217.

into a pattern of local eucharistic communities, but a more unified model now took over. Reflecting on the twelfth-century councils which advanced the reform programme and were summoned by the pope rather than by the emperor as in former times, Eamon Duffy speaks of 'the medieval reimagining of the Church not as a communion of local churches, but as a single international organisation, with the Pope at its head'.[26] Structurally speaking, the church was now a pyramid.

Congar entitled his classic analysis of this shift 'De la communion des Églises à une ecclésiologie de l'Église universelle',[27] and tellingly characterized it elsewhere as a transition from 'an ecclesiology of the *ecclesia* to an ecclesiology of powers, from an ecclesiology of communion and holiness to an ecclesiology of the institution and of the means of salvation founded by Christ'.[28] As eucharistic doctrine and ecclesiology became separated, so were power of order and power of jurisdiction distinguished by the scholastics,[29] this distinction serving to differentiate between priests and bishops. The priesthood was the highest degree of the sacrament of order, and in this sense the priest had the 'fullness' of the sacrament of order and was the ordinary celebrant of the Mass. The Eucharist was primarily understood as the transformation of bread and wine into the body and blood of Christ, and the priest had the full power to perform this consecration.[30] A bishop was a priest with added jurisdiction, to govern the church. Presiding at the Eucharist and governing the church had become separate responsibilities, as they never were in the early church. The letters of Ignatius of Antioch, at the turn of the second century, and the *Apostolic Tradition*, with origins probably in the early third century,[31] two resources used at decisive points by Vatican II in its teaching on the Eucharist and ordained ministry, clearly show the bishop to be the one who both presides at the Eucharist and governs the church. This integration of responsibilities is a hallmark of eucharistic ecclesiology: if the Eucharist makes the church, then it follows that the prime task of the one

[26] Duffy, *Saints & Sinners: A History of the Popes*, 3rd edn. (New Haven/London: Yale University Press, 2006), 130.

[27] Congar, 'De la communion des Églises a une ecclésiologie de l'Église universelle', in Y. Congar and B. D. Dupuy (eds.), *L'Épiscopat et l'Église universelle* (Paris: Cerf, 1964), 227–60.

[28] Congar, 'L'"Ecclesia" ou communauté chrétienne, sujet intégral de l'action liturgique', in J.-P. Jossua and Y. Congar (eds.), *La Liturgie après Vatican II* (Paris: Cerf, 1967), 241–80 (261). 'The vertical lines of authority from Rome replaced the horizontal lines of communion among bishops and among churches', Avery Dulles, 'The Church as Communion', in Bradley Nassif (ed.), *New Perspectives on Historical Theology: Essays in Memory of John Meyendorff* (Grand Rapids: William B. Eerdmans, 1996), 125–39 (130).

[29] Cf. Laurent Villemin, *Pouvoir d'ordre et pouvoir de juridiction: Histoire théologique de leur distinction* (Paris: Cerf, 2003).

[30] See, e.g., St Thomas Aquinas, *ST*, Suppl., 37.2.

[31] See John F. Baldovin, 'Hippolytus and the *Apostolic Tradition*: Recent Research and Commentary', *TS*, 64 (2003), 520–42.

whose calling it is to shepherd and strengthen the local community will be to preside at its Eucharist.

With regard to the pre-Nicene church, in which such a view was axiomatic,[32] Hervé Legrand says that 'presidency of the Eucharist is seen as the liturgical, prophetic and mysteric dimension of the pastoral charge of building up the Church which is conferred in ordination'.[33] It is notable, however, that in his criticism of the scholastic development whereby one presided at the Eucharist because of personally possessed priestly powers rather than by being the ordained head of a community,[34] Legrand cites contrary evidence only from the pre-Nicene period rather than from the whole of the first millennium. In fact, the Christianization of the empire in the fourth century, the consequent huge rise in numbers of the baptized, and the division of local churches into parishes, such that the faithful now regularly attended a parish Eucharist presided over by a presbyter/priest rather than, as before, a Eucharist presided over by the bishop with his presbyters gathered round, already began to distance the bishop somewhat from the regular eucharistic life of the people and to turn him into a manager of eucharistic communities. In some ways, this was the 'thin end of the wedge' that eventually resulted in the medieval separations between power of order and power of jurisdiction, eucharistic doctrine and ecclesiology. John Zizioulas[35] considers that by turning the bishop into an administrator and implying that 'the bishop and the presbyter do not differ at all from the point of view of the eucharistic function' (this was the view held by later scholasticism, but was already maintained by John Chrysostom and Jerome) the fourth century gave rise to a whole range of problems 'with which we are still wrestling in theology'.[36]

[32] See Hervé-Marie Legrand, 'The Presidency of the Eucharist According To the Ancient Tradition', in R. Kevin Seasoltz (ed.), *Living Bread, Saving Cup: Readings on the Eucharist* (Collegeville MN: Liturgical Press, 1987), 196–221 (211).

[33] Legrand, 'The Presidency of the Eucharist', 213.

[34] See Legrand, 'The Presidency of the Eucharist', 219, with reference to Congar, 'L'"Ecclesia" ou communauté chrétienne' (e.g., 262).

[35] The seminal article that Zizioulas wrote on eucharistic ecclesiology in 1969 ('La communauté eucharistique et la catholicité de l'Eglise', *Istina*, 14 (1969), 67–88) became Ch. 4 of his *Being as Communion* (London: Darton, Longman & Todd, 1985), 143–69. Zizioulas' teacher, Georges Florovsky, wrote an article in 1929, entitled 'The Eucharist and Catholicity', in which he said: 'In the Holy Eucharist believers become the Body of Christ. And therefore the Eucharist is the sacrament of the Church.' 'The Eucharist and Catholicity', in Richard S. Haugh (ed.), *Collected Works of Georges Florovsky xiii. Ecumenism i: A Doctrinal Approach* (Vaduz: Büchervertriebsanstalt, 1989), 46–57 (48).

[36] Zizioulas, 'Episkope and Episkopos in the Early Church: A Brief Survey of the Evidence', in *Episkopē and Episcopate in Ecumenical Perspective*, Faith and Order Paper 102 (Geneva: World Council of Churches, 1980) 30–42 (38).

THE MODERN RENEWAL

Having sampled the historical analyses of some of the leading pioneers and more recent advocates of *ressourcement* and a renewed eucharistic ecclesiology, let us now see more closely how the renewal occurred. The leading idea in nineteenth-century Catholic ecclesiology was of the church as a 'perfect society', *societas perfecta,* not in the sense of moral perfection but in the sense of structural completeness. The church was fully equipped to run its own affairs. The circumstances of the time brought this idea, earlier adumbrated by Bellarmine, to the fore, and popes and theologians repeatedly used it to assert the church's independence *vis-à-vis* the state.[37] The accent was still primarily on the church's outward reality: 'Christ was seen essentially as the founder of this society rather than as its actual foundation.'[38]

Though the third chapter of the draft text on the church, *Supremi Pastoris,* which was presented to the First Vatican Council in 1870, was entitled *Ecclesiam esse societatem veram, perfectam, spiritualem et supernaturalem,* the opening chapter struck a very different and more inward note: *Ecclesiam esse corpus Christi mysticum.*[39] However, the reappearance of the latter more traditional ecclesiological idea, reflecting the patristic renewal already undertaken by Möhler, Passaglia, Schrader, Franzelin, and others, caused a certain amount of consternation among the Council Fathers,[40] for whom the overriding need was to give a clear account of the structure and public profile of the church. This idea did not seem helpful to that end. It was not at all clear what structure it would indicate for the church. To some it seemed 'apt to encourage a dangerous "imaginative exuberance" from which the hard-edgedness of doctrine might well suffer'; it was 'repellent' as something 'abstract and mystical'.[41] As things turned out, the full draft was never debated by the Council. With the Franco-Prussian war looming, its later chapters on the infallibility of the church and the primacy of the pope were reworked and prioritized, and a constitution, *Pastor Aeternus,* dealing purely with the primacy and infallibility of the pope, was promulgated. Plans to follow up this 'First Dogmatic Constitution on the Church of Christ' with a second which would supply a richer context and fill in the many gaps remained unfulfilled when the Council was suspended in October 1870.

---

[37] Cf. Congar, 'Moving Towards a Pilgrim Church', in Alberic Stacpoole, OSB (ed.), *Vatican II by Those Who Were There* (London: Geoffrey Chapman, 1986), 129–52 (132–3); also Rembert Weakland, 'Images of the Church: From "Perfect Society" to "God's People on Pilgrimage"', in Austen Ivereigh (ed.), *Unfinished Journey: The Church 40 Years after Vatican II* (London: Continuum, 2003), 78–90.

[38] Congar, 'Moving Towards a Pilgrim Church', 134.

[39] Cf. C. Martin, *Omnium Concilii Vaticani Documentorum Collectio* (Paderborn: Sumptibus et typis Ferdinandi Schoeningh, 1873), 32–54 (33–4).

[40] Cf. *Splendour,* 93–4.   [41] *Splendour,* 96.

As recently as 1934, Maurice de la Taille wrote: 'However familiar this view [of the church as Christ's body] was to the Fathers, and however central its place in St Thomas, it is not necessary that it should hold the same place in the scholastic theology of today.'[42] The scholastic theology of the day was, however, being challenged by strong forces of renewal, still inspired by Möhler, which promoted a communal and organic understanding of the church and highly valued the image of the body of Christ. 'A religious process of incalculable importance has begun', Romano Guardini (1885–1968) proclaimed in 1922; 'the Church is coming to life in the souls of men'.[43] The idea of the church as 'a legal institution for religious purposes' had held sway, he said, but now the idea of it as the *Corpus Christi mysticum* was acquiring 'a wholly new power', and the liturgy must correspondingly be understood as 'the Church at prayer'.[44]

In 1943, Pope Pius XII issued an encyclical letter on the church as the mystical body of Christ, *Mystici Corporis Christi*, a major milestone on the way to Vatican II and *Lumen Gentium*. In retrospect, however, though it drew strongly on the scriptures, it appears as a transitional text. After the pattern of its presumed drafter, Sebastian Tromp, its tendency was 'to harmonise ancient Mystical Body ecclesiology with the more recent juridical approach current in Western Catholicism since Robert Bellarmine'.[45] In other words, it tended simply to clothe the pyramid in the scriptures rather than asking whether the scriptures might indicate a model for the church different from that of the pyramid. Notably absent from the footnotes was any reference to 1 Cor. 10.17, a favourite text of Augustine in his sermons[46] and one of the primary texts for eucharistic ecclesiology, in which St Paul teaches of the mystery of one bread, one body.

In fact, the encyclical made no mention of the Eucharist until a relatively late stage, when Pope Pius said that his treatment of the union of the mystical body with its head would seem 'unfinished' without 'at least a few words' on the Eucharist.[47] Just a year later, de Lubac's *Corpus Mysticum* appeared, which

---

[42] Quoted by de Lubac, *Splendour*, 96.

[43] Guardini, *The Church and the Catholic and The Spirit of the Liturgy*, trans. Ada Lane (New York: Sheed & Ward, 1935), 11. The two books united here were *Vom Sinn der Kirche* (1922) and *Vom Geist der Liturgie* (1918). Cf. Robert A. Krieg, *Romano Guardini: A Precursor of Vatican II* (Notre Dame IN: University of Notre Dame Press, 1997), 46–90.

[44] *The Church and the Catholic*, 16, 23, 31.

[45] Cf Avery Dulles, 'A Half Century of Ecclesiology', *TS*, 50(1989), 419–42 (422).

[46] E.g. Sermons 227, 229A, 272; compare Augustine, *Complete Works*, Part III, vi.254–6; Part III, vi.269–72; Part III, vii.302–10.

[47] Pope Pius XII, *Mystici Corporis Christi*. Encyclical Letter on the Mystical Body of Christ (29 June 1943), *AAS* xxxv (1943), 193–248, § 80. ET available at <http://www.vatican.va/holy_father/pius_xii/encyclicals/documents/hf_p-xii_enc_29061943_mystici-corporis-christi_en.html>. In sharp contrast, sixty years later, Pope John Paul II's *opening words* in his 2003 encyclical, *Ecclesia de Eucharistia*, were: 'The Church draws her life from the Eucharist.' *Ecclesia de Eucharistia*.

showed in fact that the term 'mystical body' had originally referred not to the church but to the Eucharist, and that the idea of the church as the body of Christ is incomprehensible without reference to the Eucharist. Though de Lubac did not ponder the structural implications of this relationship in *Corpus Mysticum*, the implications were far-reaching. If the Eucharist makes the church, it follows, as we have seen, that the church naturally consists of eucharistic communities, as the basic cells of its life, and that the pastoral leaders of those communities preside at the Eucharist. In other words, the idea of the church as the body of Christ, which seemed at the time of Vatican I to have unclear structural implications, and was then forcibly married to a pyramidal structure by Pius XII, in fact implies a rather different structure, namely a communional structure of local churches.[48]

The one Eucharist itself unites those churches and makes them to be one church, and it likewise unites the bishops who preside at the Eucharist in their respective churches into one episcopate. It is no coincidence that the section of *Lumen Gentium* which solemnly taught, in a return to patristic understanding, that it is the bishop (not the priest) who has 'the fullness of the sacrament of order' and exercises what the Fathers called 'the supreme priesthood',[49] was immediately followed by the section giving the Council's teaching on episcopal collegiality,[50] the long awaited and necessary complement to the teaching of Vatican I on the papacy. Anticipating the teaching of the Council, de Lubac had already shown, in his *Méditation sur l'Eglise*, an appreciation of the structural implications of his earlier research, when, with reference to Ignatius of Antioch and Cyprian, he wrote:

> Each bishop constitutes the unity of his flock, 'the people adhering to its priest, cohering with the heavenly sacraments'. But each bishop is himself 'in peace and in communion' with all his brother bishops who offer the same and unique sacrifice in other places... He and they together form one episcopate only, and are all alike 'at peace and in communion' with the Bishop of Rome, who is Peter's successor and the visible bond of unity; and through them all the faithful are united.[51]

De Lubac 'put the idea of the Church in concrete terms as eucharistic ecclesiology', says Ratzinger, noting that *eucharistic* ecclesiology is fundamentally

---

Encyclical Letter on the Eucharist in its Relationship to the Church (17 April 2003), *AAS* xcv (2003), 433–75. ET available at <http://www.vatican.va/edocs/ENG0821/__P2.HTM>.

[48] See the teaching of the post-Vatican II *Catechism of the Catholic Church* (1994; revised, 1997): '"The Church" is the People that God gathers in the whole world. She exists in local communities and is made real as a liturgical, above all a Eucharistic, assembly. She draws her life from the word and the Body of Christ and so herself becomes Christ's body' (§ 752).

[49] *LG* § 21, with footnote reference to the *ApostolicTradition*, 3; Tanner, ii.865.

[50] *LG* § 22: 'The order of bishops, which succeeds the college of apostles... [is] the subject of supreme and full power over the universal church, provided it remains united with its head, the Roman pontiff, and never without its head'; Tanner, ii.866.

[51] *Splendour*, 150–1.

the same thing as *communion* ecclesiology. 'This ecclesiology of communion became the real core of Vatican II's teaching on the Church, the novel and at the same time the original element in what the Council wanted to give us.'[52]

With regard to episcopal collegiality, Ratzinger notes that it was Bernard Botte (1893–1980) who 'opened the door for the Council on this point', by his study of early liturgical orders, particularly the *Apostolic Tradition*;[53] and a full account of those whose endeavours enabled Vatican II to incorporate strong elements of eucharistic ecclesiology would certainly need also to include Botte's elder Benedictine *confrère*, Lambert Beauduin (1873–1960), who pioneered and popularized the liturgical movement from 1909, convinced, as was Guardini, that the liturgy is the body of Christ at prayer, and that all the faithful should actively participate in it.[54] Vatican II strongly endorsed these views in its Constitution on the Sacred Liturgy, *Sacrosanctum Concilium*.[55] The Jesuit Émile Mersch (1890–1940) 'devoted his life to restoring the notion of the Mystical Body as the key concept of theology',[56] and wrote that 'according to the whole of tradition, the Eucharist is the sacrament of the mystical body'.[57] In its opening survey of many images for the church, *Lumen Gentium* gave a rich account of the image of the body of Christ, and of the mystery of one bread, one body (*LG* § 7).

A crucial Orthodox influence on the council's ecclesiology must also be highlighted. Each draft of what was to become *Lumen Gentium* contains a

[52] Ratzinger, *Church, Ecumenism and Politics* (Slough: St Paul's, 1988), 7, 14. Cf. J. M. R. Tillard, *Flesh of the Church, Flesh of Christ: At the Source of the Ecclesiology of Communion* (Collegeville MN: Liturgical Press, 2001); also Dennis M. Doyle, *Communion Ecclesiology* (Maryknoll NY: Orbis, 2000). The ecclesiology of communion was nevertheless not the only one present in *Lumen Gentium*; cf. Antonio Acerbi, *Due ecclesiologie: Ecclesiologia giuridica ed ecclesiologia di comunione nella 'Lumen Gentium'* (Bologna: Edizioni Dehoniane, 1975). As Charles Moeller says, 'the two perspectives—the sacramental ecclesiology of communion of the local churches and the canonical ecclesiology of the Universal Church—did not succeed in blending into a completely harmonious synthesis'. 'History of *Lumen Gentium*'s Structure and Ideas', in John H. Miller (ed.), *Vatican II: An Interfaith Appraisal* (Notre Dame IN: University of Notre Dame Press, 1966), 123–52 (133).

[53] Ratzinger, *Church, Ecumenism and Politics*, 11–12. See Dom B. Botte, 'Holy Orders in the Ordination Prayers' and 'Collegiate Character of the Presbyterate and Episcopate', in *The Sacrament of Holy Orders* (Collegeville MN: Liturgical Press, 1962), 5–23, 75–97; also his short article, 'The Collegial Character of the Priesthood and the Episcopate', *Concilium*, 4/1 (1965), 88–90.

[54] See Lambert Beauduin, OSB, *Liturgy the Life of the Church* (Farnborough: St Michael's Abbey Press, 2002; French original, 1914), 10–11, 13, 15; also my, 'Liturgy, Church, and Society', *Studia Liturgica*, 34 (2004), 147–64. For Guardini, see Krieg, *Romano Guardini*, 79.

[55] See *SC* § 7, § 14; also *LG* § 10.

[56] Avery Dulles, *Models of the Church* (New York: Image Books, 2002), 44. Mersch wrote two volumes (1933) on the history of the idea and two volumes (published posthumously, 1944) of theological reflection on it. Both pairs were translated into single volumes: *The Whole Christ: The Historical Development of the Doctrine of the Mystical Body in Scripture and Tradition*, trans. John R. Kelly (Milwaukee WI: Bruce, 1938); and *The Theology of the Mystical Body*, trans. Cyril Vollert (St Louis MO: B. Herder, 1951).

[57] *The Theology of the Mystical Body*, 580.

footnote reference to the Russian émigré theologian, Nicholas Afanasíev (1893–1966).[58] It was Afanasíev who coined the expression 'eucharistic ecclesiology', and advocated the principle that 'where there is the eucharistic assembly, there is Christ, and there is the Church of God in Christ'.[59] There is, then, a fullness in each local church, such that, when adding them together, 'One plus one is still *one*'.[60] Afanasíev strongly contrasted 'universal ecclesiology', according to which local churches are parts of a whole and have their ecclesial existence from that whole, such that if one should break away it falls 'into an ecclesiological void'.[61] A footnote to the first draft of *Lumen Gentium* noted that the two ecclesiologies were generally attributed to the Orthodox Church and the Catholic Church, respectively, and then said strategically: 'It therefore seems very useful to show how the Catholic Church also starts from a eucharistic ecclesiology which is at the same time universalistic.'[62] In response to Afanasíev's sharp contrast between sacramental and structural unity in the church, the note indicated a belief that sacrament and structure can be reconciled: the Eucharist itself gives rise to and requires the structural unity of the local churches, and the collegial unity of the bishops, which celebrate it.

Afanasíev was again cited[63] when the second draft introduced a text[64] which, much expanded, eventually became *LG* § 26, one of the principal passages of *Lumen Gentium* from the point of view of eucharistic ecclesiology.[65] There, with notable reference to Ignatius of Antioch and Augustine, the Council taught that the bishop is the primary celebrant of the Eucharist 'from which the Church ever derives its life and on which it thrives', and that

[58] Cf. my articles, 'Eucharistic Ecclesiology', 325–7; 'Catholic Learning and Orthodoxy—The Promise and Challenge of Eucharistic Ecclesiology', in Paul D. Murray (ed.), *Receptive Ecumenism and the Call to Catholic Learning: Exploring a Way for Contemporary Ecumenism* (Oxford: Oxford University Press, 2008), 160–75 (162–3); also Hervé Legrand, 'L'ecclésiologie eucharistique dans le dialogue actuel entre l'Église catholique et l'Église orthodoxe', *Istina*, 51 (2006), 354–74 (355–9).

[59] Afanasíev, 'Una Sancta', in Michael Plekon (ed.), *Tradition Alive: On the Church and the Christian Life in Our Time* (Lanham: Rowman & Littlefield, 2003), 3–30 (18, cf 14); article first published in 1963.

[60] 'The Church Which Presides in Love', in John Meyendorff *et al.* (eds.), *The Primacy of Peter in the Orthodox Church*, trans. Katherine Farrer (London: Faith Press, 1963 [1960]), 57–110; repr. John Meyendorff (ed.), *The Primacy of Peter: Essays in Ecclesiology and the Early Church* (Crestwood NY: St Vladimir's Seminary Press, 1992), 91–143 (109).

[61] 'Una Sancta', 6–7.

[62] *ASSCOVII* i.iv (1971), 87, n. 2.1.

[63] *ASSCOVII* ii.i, 251–2, n. 57: 'Regarding the link between Ecclesiology and the Eucharist, cf also N. Afanassief'; cf. also iii.i (1973), 254.

[64] Cf. above, n. 1.

[65] Gérard Philips later said that the section of *Lumen Gentium* dealing with the bishops' work of sanctification 'contained some elements of recent development of dogma of sound theological and spiritual quality on the significance of the local Church, which is also constituted as such by the celebration of the Eucharist', 'History of the Constitution', in Herbert Vorgrimler (ed.), *Commentary on the Documents of Vatican II*, i (London: Burns & Oates, 1967), 105–37 (130).

local communities united with their bishops are properly called 'churches', reinforcing its earlier teaching that 'the principal manifestation of the Church' occurs in the Eucharist of the local church celebrated by the bishop, surrounded by his college of presbyters, with the 'full, active participation' of all the people (*SC* § 41). The council repeatedly specified that when priests preside at the Eucharist they represent the bishop (cf. *LG* § 28; *SC* § 42).

Memorably summarizing its renewed emphasis on the Eucharist, the Council taught that the eucharistic sacrifice is 'the source and culmination of all Christian life' (*LG* § 11; cf. *SC* § 10). The bishops, successors of the apostles, are its primary celebrants, and their communities are not just administrative 'dioceses' but sacramental 'churches'. The mystical body as a whole is a '*corpus Ecclesiarum*' (*LG* § 23). The council thus invited us to think again in patristic terms, both about the shape of the church and about what makes the church. 'For the point of apostolic work is that all those who have become children of God through faith and baptism can assemble together in order to praise God in the midst of the church, to share in sacrifice, and to eat the Lord's supper' (*SC* § 10).

26

The Theology of Karl Rahner: An Alternative to the *Ressourcement*?

Richard Lennan

INTRODUCTION

Convergences between the practitioners of the *ressourcement* and Karl Rahner (1904–84) are not difficult to find. What primarily connects Rahner to his contemporaries, such as Henri de Lubac (1896–1991) and Yves Congar (1904–95), is a twofold passion: to articulate a theology that would free the dynamism of Christian faith from the constraints of neo-scholasticism; and to highlight the capacity of Christian faith to address the needs and questions of 'the modern world', while also challenging the limited vision of that world.[1] In his approach to revelation, grace, and the church, which were also primary themes for the theologians of the *ressourcement*, Rahner, like his contemporaries, sought to articulate a theology that illustrated how faithfulness to the church's tradition was reconcilable with openness to new questions and to the new needs of the church's mission in the twentieth century. *And yet*...

Despite the fact that it acknowledges a community of interest between Rahner and the practitioners of the *ressourcement*, the chapter will also argue, in response to the question embedded in its title, that the particularities of Rahner's work are sufficiently distinct to identify his theology as an alternative to his contemporaries.

As the chapter will illustrate, what establishes the particularity of Rahner's theology is his methodology and his portrayal of the relationship between God and humanity, as well as the corollaries he draws from that portrayal. In a

---

[1] For a survey of how de Lubac and Congar sought to renew theology, see Maureen Sullivan, *The Road to Vatican II: Key Changes in Theology* (New York: Paulist Press, 2007), 17–22; see also Gabriel Flynn, *Yves Congar's Vision of the Church in a World of Unbelief* (Aldershot/Burlington VT: Ashgate, 2004); Hans Boersma, *Nouvelle Théologie and Sacramental Ontology: A Return to Mystery* (Oxford: Oxford University Press, 2009), 223–87; Jürgen Mettepenningen, *Nouvelle Théologie—New Theology: Inheritor of Modernism, Precursor of Vatican II* (New York: T&T Clark, 2010), 7–13.

unique way, Rahner highlighted the 'mystery' of God as central to Christian faith. As we shall see, he stressed that this quality ensured not only that God exceeded human efforts at mastery of God, but also that humanity's relationship to God was inexhaustibly dynamic, with a dynamism that Rahner identified as being constitutive of authentic Christian tradition.

The dynamism of humanity's relationship with God also shaped Rahner's understanding of the task of theology. Theology was to engage, in ever-changing historical circumstances, with the God whom we could know through revelation, especially revelation in Jesus Christ, but who was never less than inexhaustible mystery—'For theology is the historical permanence of a revelation existing in ever new encounters and transforming everything into itself, with a spatio-temporal position in time.'[2]

The theologians of the *ressourcement* similarly emphasized the dynamism of theology, as a result of their engagement with the texts of scripture and the Fathers. Nonetheless, Rahner diverged from them in that he, while not ignoring Christianity's privileged sources, sought a different theological framework for expounding the implications God's presence in human history. Rahner's framework was shaped by his interpretation of Thomas Aquinas (1225–74) and his reception of Joseph Maréchal (1878–1944) and Martin Heidegger (1889–1976), but also by his grounding in the spirituality of Ignatius of Loyola (1491–1556), which was central to his life as a Jesuit.[3]

While the influences on Rahner's theology can be named with some certainty, there is room to wonder why, for all his ecclesial focus, his years of editing Denzinger's *Enchiridion Symbolorum*, and his early publications on Origen and Bonaventure, Rahner chose to make little direct use of the Bible and the Fathers, the sources that so absorbed the energy and passion of his contemporaries between the 1930s and 1950s.[4]

---

[2] Karl Rahner, 'What is a Dogmatic Statement?' (1961), *Theological Investigations (TI)*, v, trans. Karl-Heinz Kruger (New York: Crossroad, 1983), 52.

[3] There are numerous sources that discuss Rahner's theological background; see, for example, William Dych, *Karl Rahner* (London: Geoffrey Chapman, 1992), 4–17; Thomas O'Meara, *God in the World: A Guide to Karl Rahner's Theology* (Collegeville MN: Michael Glazier, 2007), 22–7; Herbert Vorgrimler, *Understanding Karl Rahner: An Introduction to his Life and Thought*, trans. John Bowden (New York: Crossroad, 1986), 48–62; and Roman Siebenrock, '"Draw nigh to God and He will daw nigh to you" (James 4:8): The Development of Karl Rahner's Theological Thinking in its First Period', *LS*, 29 (2004), 28–48. For the influence of Ignatian thought on Rahner see particularly, Philip Endean, *Karl Rahner and Ignatian Spirituality* (Oxford: Oxford University Press, 2001); and Michael Paul Gallagher, 'Ignatian Dimensions of Rahner's Theology', *LS*, 29 (2004), 77–91.

[4] Rahner's essay on Origen was published, in French, in 1932—his first published work; a shortened form, in German, was published in 1975 and that version appeared in English as 'The "Spiritual Senses" According to Origen' in *TI*, xvi, trans. David Morland (New York: Crossroad, 1983), 81–103. The essay on Bonaventure was originally published, again in French, in 1933 and, in an expanded version, in German in 1934; the German version appeared in English as 'The Doctrine of the "Spiritual Senses" in the Middle Ages: The Contribution of Bonaventure', *TI*, xvi.104–34.

It is likely that the proper terminus of such wondering can only be the acknowledgement of Rahner's individual genius, his distinctive response to the Spirit. While that genius was singular, it was not idiosyncratic: Rahner was committed to ensuring that a focus on the church's mission in the world remained the priority of all those engaged in theological endeavours, irrespective of their particular method. This emphasis is clear in, for example, his 1961 article on 'Exegesis and Dogmatic Theology', which not only affirms the importance of biblical study for theologians, but also reminds both theologians and exegetes that their common task was to address a sceptical age: 'The intellectual of today is the spiritual child of historicism and the natural sciences—a terribly sober, careful and disillusioned man . . . This is the kind of man with whom the Church must concern herself. For this is the man of today and tomorrow.'[5]

Although it was the 'doing' of theology that absorbed Rahner's energy, he did make, later in his life, occasional forays into explicit reflection on his choices as a theologian, especially in light of criticisms directed at him. One such *apologia* appeared in 1973 as the Preface to Volume 15 of his *Theological Investigations*, which comprises essays, written primarily in the 1930s, 1940s, and 1950s, that engage with patristic analyses of the sacrament of penance. Rahner rarely offered a preface to any of his works, so the exception in this instance is notable. This particular preface served a twofold purpose: to justify the inclusion of the volume in *Theological Investigations*—its focus on a single theme set it apart from other volumes in the series, which ranged over myriad topics; to respond to a particular critique of his theological interests and methods. Regarding the latter, he wrote:

> The introduction of the volume into this series has, however—I must 'confess'—yet another reason. I am suspected by many people of being only a speculative theologian who works without reference to history and who, in some circumstances, attempts to dispel difficulties which arise in understanding statements of the Church's magisterium by the merely speculative interpretation of such statements. I am absolutely convinced that genuine Catholic theology must always proceed on the basis both of exegesis and of the history of dogmas and theology, even if it must be the free choice of the individual theologian whether, in a study of a particular point, he wishes to work 'speculatively' or 'historically'. It is possible, therefore, that the present volume will dispel the suspicion that I have no appreciation of historical theology.[6]

At the end of his life—indeed, in his final public address, which took place at a celebration for his eightieth birthday in 1984—Rahner reiterated the principles that guided his work as a theologian, making clear that his insights had their source not simply in scripture, but in the whole of God's created reality:

> If as a theologian I inquire not about an abstract concept of God, but wish to approach God directly, then absolutely nothing of what God has revealed as

---

[5] Rahner, 'Exegesis and Dogmatic Theology' (1961), *TI*, v.87.
[6] Rahner, 'Preface' (1973), *TI*, xv, trans. Lionel Swain (New York: Crossroad, 1990), p. viii.

Creator of the world, as Lord of history, should be uninteresting to me. Naturally, it could be piously claimed that everything that is necessary for my salvation is contained in Holy Scripture, and that one needs to know nothing beyond this. But if I wish to love God for God's own sake and not only for the sake of my personal salvation, then in order to find God I cannot restrict my interest to Scripture alone. Rather, everything through which God permits God's very self to be perceived in this creaturely world will be of interest to me. This is especially the case for the theologian whose task is to intellectually oppose every kind of false egoism relating to salvation.[7]

The sections of the chapter that follow, all of which draw on Rahner's writings prior to the Second Vatican Council (1962–5), will illustrate the ways in which Rahner applied that conviction to all aspects of his theological work.

RAHNER AND THE RENEWAL OF CATHOLIC THEOLOGY

As already noted, Rahner's conviction that neo-scholastic theology, which prevailed in the Catholic Church of his youth, was inadequate to the challenge of presenting the Christian faith to the modern world spurred him to seek a more satisfactory method. Reflecting in later life on the sources of his youthful frustration with neo-scholasticism, Rahner identified two key irritants. First, he rejected neo-scholasticism's constricted perspective on the method and content of theology:

It was essentially an ecclesiastical science, which preferred to use Latin; by and large it had its established, clearly defined canon of topics and problems promulgated throughout the world. Neoscholasticism resolutely worked within the framework of these topics but rarely considered that its methodology was questionable.

Secondly, he was alienated by neo-scholasticism's connection to defensive, even repressive, practices within the Roman Catholic Church, whose priority seemed to be resistance to the incursions of modernity:

One withdrew, and this withdrawal took place in a way in which courageous and genuine faith and fearful repression interacted in a peculiar way, and *this* was considered to be the authentic spirit of the Church. One tried to live as far as possible in an ecclesial autarchy.[8]

---

[7] Rahner, 'Experiences of a Catholic Theologian' (1984), in Declan Marmion and Mary Hines (eds.), *The Cambridge Companion to Karl Rahner* (Cambridge: Cambridge University Press, 2005), 306–7.

[8] Rahner, 'The Present Situation of Catholic Theology' (1979), *TI*, xxi, trans. Hugh Riley (New York: Crossroad, 1988), 71; the emphasis is Rahner's.

A primary example of Rahner's dissatisfaction with both the methodology and world view common to neo-scholasticism comes in his appraisal of the theological textbooks popular in the 1950s:

[N]o one can deny that in the last two centuries cultural and spiritual transformations have taken place which, to say the very least, are compatible in depth and extent and power to mould men's lives, with those which took place between the time of Augustine and those of the golden age of scholasticism. If we hold that theology is an endeavour of the spirit and a science which has to be of service to its own time, just as it has, or should have, grown out of its own time; and if we hold this because it has to serve salvation and not mere theoretical curiosity... then we should have expected to find at least as pronounced a difference between a theological compendium of today and one of, say, 1750, as between the *Summa Theologica* of St Thomas and the writings of Augustine.

What are the facts?... Where it is properly dogmatic theology... such a modern theological treatise in no way differs from its predecessors of 200 years ago.[9]

Noting that most of the concepts central to theological thinking—such as 'hypostasis', 'the supernatural', and 'transubstantiation'—were 'the symbols and trophies of theological achievements of past centuries', Rahner lamented that Catholic theology in the middle years of the twentieth century displayed no such creativity.[10] That dearth of originality he ascribed to the tendency of neo-scholasticism to privilege clarity at the expense of questions, even though that ordering ensured that mediocrity became the hallmark of Catholic theology.

Criticism, however, was not Rahner's principal occupation: he was a practitioner. Thus, in numerous essays written in the 1950s, he proposed an alternative analysis of key theological themes. Rahner sought a theology that opened paths to the future, a theology that was not simply alert to the new questions emerging from society, but understood that humanity's relationship to God was itself a fertile source of theological questions.

Rahner stressed that this concern for the future did not imply abandonment of the past. Indeed, paradoxically, the focus on the future enabled a proper appropriation of the past: 'For the past can only be preserved in its purity by someone who accepts responsibility for the future, who preserves in so far as he overcomes.'[11] Authentic study of the past, therefore, was to serve the present and future, rather than degenerate into archaism. This test of authenticity applied even to engagement with the church's doctrinal definitions: for Rahner, as we shall see, such definitions were to be understood as a beginning,

---

[9] Rahner, 'The Prospects for Dogmatic Theology' (1954), *TI*, i, trans. Cornelius Ernst (New York: Crossroad, 1982), 2–3.

[10] 'The Prospects for Dogmatic Theology', 4–5.

[11] 'The Prospects for Dogmatic Theology', 7.

not simply an end.[12] The task of the contemporary theologian, therefore, was to discover what might be of value for today in what came from the past— 'Anything which is merely conserved, or which is handed down without a fresh, personal exertion beginning at the very sources of Revelation, rots as the manna did.'[13]

As Rahner portrayed it, the historical nature of human existence influenced our appropriation of the doctrine of the church. One consequence of the human capacity to bridge past, present, and future was that 'neither the abandonment of a formula nor its preservation in a petrified form does justice to human understanding'.[14] More particularly, Rahner argued that since human beings did not retain, in an unaltered state, the freshness and passion evident in the initial formulation of a doctrine, there was an ongoing need for retrieval of the truth expressed in any doctrine:

> The history of theology is by no means just the history of the progress of doctrine, but also a history of forgetting... What was once given in history and is ever made present anew does not primarily form a set of premises from which we can draw new conclusions which have never been thought of before. It is the object which, while it is always retained, must ever be acquired anew, by *us*, that is, we who are just such as no one else can ever be in all history.[15]

This focus on the implications of humanity's historical existence became a characteristic element of Rahner's theology. Indeed, by means of that emphasis, Rahner established, perhaps more explicitly than did the contributors to the *ressourcement*, an anthropological grounding for the process of recovering insights from the past and applying them to the present. In part, this aspect of Rahner's theology derived from his reaction against the 'frozen' truths of neo-scholasticism. Its deeper roots, however, lay in his understanding of God, and of God's relationship to humanity. Specifically, it was the notion of God's 'mystery', Rahner's signature theme, which underpinned his conviction that theology was to be more than either a repetition of the past or a commentary on the past: theology was to express the implications of encountering the God who transcends, without negating, our doctrines of God.

Rahner's stress on God's irreducible mystery, which ran seamlessly through his theology of grace, revelation, Christology, and the church, including his approach to the church's teaching, established a theological platform to

---

[12] Although the article in which Rahner expressed this principle appeared in English as 'Current Problems in Christology' (1954), *TI*, i.149–200, the German title, in its original publication, was '*Chalkedon—Ende oder Anfang?*'; that is, 'Chalcedon: End or Beginning?' For an evaluation of Rahner's impact on the renewal of Christology within Catholic theology, see Elizabeth Johnson, *Consider Jesus: Waves of Renewal in Christology* (New York: Crossroad, 1992), 11–12.

[13] Rahner, 'The Prospects for Dogmatic Theology', 10.

[14] 'Current Problems in Christology', 150.

[15] 'Current Problems in Christology', 151–2; the emphasis is Rahner's.

support the claim that what came from the past could continue to mediate life to believers in the present, as well as the future. For Rahner, because every mediation of God, 'every truth of the God who reveals himself is given as an incitement and a way to the closest immediacy of communion with him, it is all the more an opening into the immeasurable, a beginning of the illimitable'.[16] A primary consequence of the fact that God always exceeds our grasp of God was that authentic experience of God's truth could never be merely an archival experience. In other words, scripture, doctrine, and the sacramental rites of the church did something other than provide information about God or fossilize a particular insight into God: they acted as a means of encounter with the living God.[17]

The following section of the chapter will survey the key themes of Rahner's theology in order to show both the origins and implications of his emphasis on the 'illimitable' presence of God. The survey will highlight his commitment to demonstrating that the mystery of God, which he believed was at the heart of the Christian tradition, underpinned the dynamism that was intrinsic to theology. A subsequent part of the chapter will review Rahner's focus on the historical circumstances in which the encounter with, and response to, the mystery of God takes place. That review will proceed principally through an exploration of Rahner's ecclesiology since engagement with the church's context was a major element of his publications.

THE CENTRAL THEMES OF RAHNER'S THEOLOGY

In developing his analysis of mystery as the basis for the dynamism of theology, Rahner distanced his approach from that evident in neo-scholastic texts. In the latter, whose usage, Rahner claimed, had been adopted uncritically by the First Vatican Council, 'mystery' was no more than a property of a statement, something to be properly used only in the plural (as in 'the mysteries of faith'), or applied to truths that were regarded as 'provisionally' incomprehensible.[18] For Rahner, on the other hand, mystery was not provisional, but 'authentic and primordial'. Similarly, mystery was not characteristic of defective knowing, not something to be corrected even in the beatific vision, but was 'an intrinsic constituent of the very notion of knowledge'.[19]

---

[16] 'Current Problems in Christology', 149.
[17] For Rahner's view of scripture as other than bringing an 'end' to theology, the development of faith, or the church's teaching, see Rahner, *Inspiration in the Bible* (1958), trans. C. H. Henkey, 2nd rev. edn. (rev. trans. M. Palmer) (New York: Herder and Herder, 1964), 79.
[18] Rahner, 'The Concept of Mystery in Catholic Theology' (1959), *TI*, iv, trans. Kevin Smyth (New York: Crossroad, 1982), 38–40.
[19] 'The Concept of Mystery', 42.

Rahner's multi-layered depiction of 'mystery' both accompanied and depended on his interpretation of God's revelation in history. In light of the foregoing description of Rahner's methodology, it will come as no surprise that his portrayal of revelation differs notably from the neo-scholastic emphasis on 'propositions' as the primary vehicle for our knowledge of God:

> Revelation is not the communication of a definite number of propositions, a numerical sum, to which additions may conceivably be made at will or which can suddenly and arbitrarily be limited, but an historical dialogue between God and humanity in which something *happens* and in which the communication is related to the continuous 'happening' and enterprise of God. This dialogue moves to a quite definitive term, in which the *happening* and *consequently* the communication comes to its never to be surpassed climax and so its conclusion. Revelation is a saving Happening, and only then, and in relation to this a communication of 'truths'. This continuous Happening of saving history has now reached its never to be surpassed climax in Jesus Christ: God himself has definitively given himself to the world.[20]

In order to appreciate how Rahner arrived at his particular description of revelation, we need to locate his analysis within his overall understanding of God's relationship to humanity. In short, we need to explore his emphasis on the link between the theology of grace and theological anthropology.

As early as 1939, Rahner had signalled his departure from the then-conventional theological wisdom by introducing what would become a defining theme of his work: the interpretation of grace as God's self-communication—'God communicates himself to the man to whom grace has been shown in the mode of *formal* causality, so that this communication is not then merely the consequence of an efficient causation of created grace.'[21] For Rahner, God's presence to humanity (uncreated grace) was not a 'thing' added to modify an already-complete human nature (efficient cause/created grace), nor was it simply a constituent of human nature, but was always God's free self-giving to humanity. Thus, God was the 'end' or fulfilment of humanity (quasi-formal cause): relationship to God, therefore, defined humanity.[22] That God's self-giving remained free, albeit radically dependable, underscored the 'mystery' of God that even revelation did not dissolve.

Rahner's theology of grace, with its attendant anthropology, reached its mature articulation in a series of articles that he wrote in the 1950s, largely in response to Henri de Lubac and the *nouvelle théologie*.[23] Rahner critiqued de

---

[20] Rahner, 'The Development of Dogma' (1954), *TI*, i.48; the emphasis is Rahner's.
[21] Rahner, 'Some Implications of the Scholastic Concept of Uncreated Grace' (1939), *TI*, i.334; the emphasis is Rahner's.
[22] 'Some Implications of the Scholastic Concept of Uncreated Grace', 334–7; Rahner added 'quasi' to 'formal' in order to protect God's transcendence by underscoring that the whole discussion of causality was applying human terms to God, see 330–1.
[23] In addition to the article that appears in the next footnote, the key texts on grace that Rahner published in the 1950s were: 'Thoughts on the Theology of Christmas' (1955), *TI*, iii,

Lubac for portraying human nature as complete without God, thereby not only reducing grace to being 'extrinsic' to any consideration of humanity, but also implying that God could be understood as obliged to offer that grace in order to establish a relationship with humanity.[24] As an alternative, Rahner developed another of his signature notions: 'the supernatural existential', which linked his anthropology with a portrayal of grace as the event of God's free self-communication.

In accord with his emphasis on God's formal causality, Rahner stressed that '[t]he capacity for the God of self-bestowing personal Love is the central and abiding existential of man as he really is'.[25] Such an existential not only located God at the centre of human existence, it also highlighted, against de Lubac, God's freedom and choice: 'God wishes to communicate himself, to pour forth the love which he himself is . . . And so God makes a creature whom he can love: he creates man. He creates him in such a way that he *can* receive this Love which is God himself, and that he can and must at the same time accept it for what it is: the ever astounding wonder, the unexpected, unexacted gift.'[26]

As already noted, there is an inextricable bond between Rahner's theology of grace and his theological anthropology: given the reality of grace, God's self-communication as the quasi-formal cause of humanity, it was impossible to gain a proper understanding of human beings without reference to humanity's relationship to God. In accord with ideas he developed in *Spirit in the World* (1939), his seminal work on human transcendence, Rahner understood the human being as 'a reality absolutely open upwards'.[27] Not only was the relationship to God the source of human freedom, it also provided the 'end' for that same freedom—'Man, made for mystery, must be such that this mystery constitutes the relationship between God and man, and hence the fulfilment of human nature is the consummation of its orientation towards the abiding mystery.'[28]

In short, the authentic exercise of human freedom was possible only when human beings took into account their 'obediential potential', their status

---

trans. Karl-Heinz and Boniface Kruger (New York: Crossroad, 1982), 24–34; 'The Eternal Significance of the Humanity of Jesus for our Relationship with God' (1953), *TI*, iii.35–46; 'Reflections on the Experience of Grace' (1954), *TI*, iii.86–90; 'On the Theology of the Incarnation' (1958), *TI*, iv.105–20.

[24] Rahner, 'Concerning the Relationship Between Nature and Grace' (1950), *TI*, i.297–305. For a fuller discussion of the divergences between Rahner and de Lubac see, Roger Haight, *The Experience and Language of Grace* (Dublin: Gill and Macmillan, 1979), 123–6; for an examination of textual sources used by de Lubac and Rahner see, David Coffey, 'Some Resources for Students of La *Nouvelle Théologie*', *Philosophy and Theology* 11 (1999): 367–402.

[25] 'Concerning the Relationship Between Nature and Grace', 312.

[26] 'Concerning the Relationship Between Nature and Grace', 310; the emphasis is Rahner's.

[27] 'Current Problems in Christology', 183.

[28] 'The Concept of Mystery', 49.

as a 'hearer of the word'.[29] Authentic freedom, therefore, could never be independent of our radical orientation to God—'As human we are the beings who, as finite spirits who inquire and must inquire about being, stand before the free God, affirm our freedom in the way we raise questions of being, and must therefore take this divine freedom into account.'[30]

Human freedom, moreover, was neither an abstraction nor a merely 'inner' quality: it was always freedom realized in history—'We are not simply put on a spatiotemporal stage to set out our lives. Spatiotemporality is our inner makeup, and belongs properly to us as human. Because matter is one of our essential components, we ourselves construct space and time as intrinsic components of our existence.'[31] Since human freedom's proper object was God, Rahner's insistence on history as the necessary venue for the exercise of freedom implied that God could be experienced in history.

Even though Rahner affirmed 'spatiotemporality' as a constitutive element of our humanity, the foregoing survey of his theology of grace, with its reinterpretation of causality and its analysis of the structure of human transcendence and freedom, might suggest that his approach was entirely inductive, that he was constructing a model, a concept, of how God might relate to humanity. As already indicated, however, Rahner understood his method as an attempt to explicate 'the saving Happening' of God's revelation in Christ. In other words, Rahner saw himself to be proceeding deductively, to be fashioning a theology that did justice to the primary datum of Christian faith: God's self-revelation in history, explicitly God's revelation in Jesus Christ.

Thus, Rahner viewed his emphasis on 'uncreated grace', on the depiction of God's relationship to humanity in terms of formal causality and self-communication, as consistent with the content of Scripture and the Fathers.[32] Indeed, in 'Theos in the New Testament', a significant article written in 1950, Rahner employed his ideas on grace and theological anthropology as a hermeneutical key to provide insight into the Trinitarian implications of the Bible's use of 'God'.[33] Similarly, Rahner's writings are unequivocal in affirming that the revelation of God in Jesus Christ as 'Saviour' was not simply the final chapter in the gradual process of God's self-communication, but was both the fullness of that self-communication and, more fundamentally, the act that grounded the whole history of revelation:

---

[29] Rahner, *Hearer of the Word: Laying the Foundations for a Philosophy of Religion* (1941), trans. Joseph Donceel (New York: Continuum, 1994), 54.

[30] *Hearer of the Word*, 76.

[31] *Hearer of the Word*, 112.

[32] 'Some Implications of the Scholastic Concept of Uncreated Grace', 334.

[33] Rahner, 'Theos in the New Testament' (1950), *TI*, i.79–148; see also his 'Remarks on the Dogmatic Treatise "*De Trinitate*"' (1960), *TI*, iv.77–102.

The whole movement of this history lives only for the moment of arrival at its goal and climax—it lives only for its entry into the event which makes it irreversible—in short, it lives for the one whom we call Saviour. This Saviour, who represents the climax of this self-communication, must therefore be at the same time God's absolute pledge by self-communication to the spiritual creature as a whole *and* the acceptance of this self-communication by the Saviour; only then is there an utterly irrevocable, self-communication on both sides, and only thus is it present in the world in a historically communicative manner.[34]

If the 'happening' of God's self-communication in Jesus Christ shaped Rahner as a Christian, developing a theological framework to explore and underscore that event was at the heart of his project as a Christian theologian. Accordingly, in Rahner's Christology we encounter the central theological themes of the Christian tradition—grace, revelation, Trinity. We encounter those themes, however, in a framework that highlights God's mystery, thereby departing significantly from the limited vision of neo-scholasticism. Most importantly, Rahner's approach does not simply apply a fresh coat of paint to the tradition: it recaptures the dynamism of the tradition, the dynamism rarely evident in neo-scholasticism.

Complementing Rahner's emphasis on 'mystery' as the source of that dynamism was a further element that he developed in the 1950s to elucidate how finite human beings could encounter the infinite God in history: the theology of the symbol, which became another of his trademarks.

Following Thomas Aquinas, Rahner understood the symbol as an expression of formal causality: the creation of the symbol was the self-realization of what was symbolized. The symbol, therefore, did not simply point to something else, but shared *analogia entis* with the being it symbolized.[35] Understood in the context of revelation, then, symbols were not something 'adopted' by God, much less something containing an encrypted divine message: they were the self-expression of God in human history, in a means accessible to humanity.

For Rahner, the Incarnation, since it was the 'supreme' form of God's symbolic self-communication—'The Logos is the "word" of the Father, his perfect "image", his "imprint", his radiance, his self-expression'—provided the richest insights into the constitution and function of the symbol.[36] Most particularly, Rahner argued that interpreting the Incarnation in terms of Jesus as symbol underscored that God desired to be known by human beings in a fully human way:

[T]he incarnate word is the absolute symbol of God in the world...He is not merely the presence and revelation of what God is in himself. He is also the expressive presence of what—or rather, who—God wished to be, in free grace, to

---

[34] Rahner, 'Christology within an Evolutionary View of the World' (1962), *TI*, v.175–6; the emphasis is Rahner's.
[35] Rahner, 'The Theology of the Symbol' (1959), *TI*, iv.231.
[36] 'The Theology of the Symbol', 236; the emphasis is Rahner's.

the world, in such a way that this divine attitude, once so expressed, can never be reversed, but is and remains final and unsurpassable.[37]

In addition, as a result of the Incarnation, it became possible to recognize that 'all things possess, even in their quality of symbol, an unfathomable depth, which faith alone can sound'.[38]

Rahner's stress on the symbolic reality of God's self-communication not only reinforced the centrality of mystery—'an unfathomable depth'—but also underscored the need to ensure that theology did not foreclose on such mystery by assuming to have said the last word about God. Even though God's revelation in Jesus Christ established unequivocally that God, not the world, was the source of salvation, which was 'more than the world and history', the emphasis on symbol affirmed human history, with its accompanying culture, as the indispensable venue for the encounter with God.[39] Within that history, the primary symbol of God's abiding presence and invitation to humanity was the church. Accordingly, the following section will review Rahner's understanding of the church, including the implications of its existence in history, in order to see whether the dynamism of faith is as present in this aspect of Rahner's theology as in others.

RAHNER'S VISION OF THE CHURCH

Given his stress on mystery, it follows that Rahner was unsympathetic to interpretations of the church that focused primarily on the church's juridical dimension. Accordingly, in his extended 1947 commentary on Pope Pius XII's *Mystici Corporis Christi* (1943), Rahner warned that 'ecclesiological Nestorianism' could result if the juridical apparatus of the church dominated ecclesial reflection.[40]

Even prior to his cautions about *Mystici Corporis Christi*, Rahner had stressed that: '[The] "Church" is then, *before* being the visible social organisation—even though this is its necessary expression—the social accessibility of the historico-sacramental permanent presence of the salvation reality of Christ.'[41] Indeed, as early as 1934, in what can be read as anticipating his developed theology of mystery and revelation, Rahner wrote that, through the church, 'the supernatural life... —which, at least in itself, seems to lie quite apart from the human, historical reality—appears supported by what is visible

---

[37] 'The Theology of the Symbol', 237.
[38] 'The Theology of the Symbol', 239.
[39] Rahner, 'History of the World and Salvation-History' (1963), *TI*, v.111.
[40] Rahner, 'Membership of the Church according to the Teaching of Pius XII's Encyclical *Mystici Corporis Christi*' (1947), *TI*, ii, trans. Karl-Heinz Kruger (New York: Crossroad, 1975), 70.
[41] Rahner, 'Priestly Existence' (1942), *TI*, iii.248; the emphasis is Rahner's.

and human, brought down into the earthly point of time, dependent on worldly things'.[42] In short, the depiction of the church as a means of encounter with God in history was fundamental to Rahner's ecclesiology from its earliest articulation.

In its mature form, Rahner's alternative to both the juridical view of the church and to any reduction of the church to an 'invisible' community of shared religious instincts or feelings relied on his theology of symbol. This focus emphasized that the church was best understood in sacramental terms: 'this symbol of the grace of God [the church] really contains what it signifies; that it is the primary sacrament of the grace of God, which does not merely designate but really possesses what was brought definitively into the world by Christ: the irrevocable, eschatological grace of God which conquers triumphantly the guilt of man'.[43] The church, therefore, could never be reduced to a juridical reality without obscuring its deepest identity, which derived directly from God: 'The grace of salvation, the Holy Spirit himself, is of its essence.'[44] The sacramental analysis of the church, then, enabled Rahner to navigate between the Scylla of an 'internal' or 'invisible' church, which might imply disdain for structures and doctrine, and the Charybdis of legalism, which separated those same structures and doctrines from any reference to the charisms of the Spirit.

Although there might have been a danger that the definition of the church as a sacrament could lead to either an idealized or an ahistorical portrait, one that implied a perfect church immune to the vicissitudes of history, the nuances of Rahner's presentation enabled him to avoid such an impoverished ecclesiology. Indeed, Rahner was constantly alert to the fact that 'sacrament' was not a claim to divinity for the church. Consequently, he could acknowledge that the church's responses to contemporary challenges did not always bear witness to the unequivocal triumph of grace:

Does the fact that the Church can never end up outside the truth of Christ mean also that she proclaims this truth with that power, in that topical and always freshly assimilated form one might hope for and which would make it truly salutary?...Do we not frequently (contrary to the meaning of the gospel truth) purchase the permanence of the gospel message in the Church at the price of guarding scrupulously against exposing ourselves to this 'chaos' (out of which tomorrow will be born) or, at best, by meeting it purely defensively, trying merely to preserve what we have?[45]

Indeed, two decades before Vatican II's tentative acknowledgement of the church as *semper sancta et semper purificanda*, Rahner had referred explicitly

---

[42] Rahner, 'The Meaning of Frequent Confessions of Devotion' (1934), *TI*, iii.184.
[43] 'The Theology of the Symbol', 241.
[44] 'The Theology of the Symbol', 241.
[45] Rahner, 'Dogmatic Notes on "Ecclesiological Piety"' (1961), *TI*, v.339.

not simply to 'a church of sinners', but to 'the sinful church'.[46] Significantly for this chapter's stress on Rahner's efforts to promote the dynamism inseparable from authentic reception of God's self-communication, he ascribed the particularity of the church's sinfulness not to malice or even to failures in zeal, but to a lack of trust in God's capacity to secure the future:

> [The Church] is often in the position of one who glorifies her past and looks askance at the present, in so far as she has not created it herself... it often loves the calm more than the storm, the old (which has proved itself) more than the new (which is bold and daring).[47]

This suggested that the sinfulness of the church arose from the refusal to surrender to the Spirit, even though, paradoxically, it was the Spirit who was the source of the church's life and mission.

The emphasis on the dynamism that was inseparable from the church's sacramentality flavoured the whole of Rahner's ecclesiology. His theology, therefore, never lacked a sense of the Spirit as the permanent agent of renewal for the church. In 1946, for example, he described the Spirit as 'the element of dynamic unrest if not of revolutionary upheaval'.[48]

Similarly, on the eve of Vatican II, Rahner highlighted the capacity of the Spirit to move the church in directions that were not part of the church's own planning.[49] This focus on the Spirit was crucial in enabling Rahner to hold in tension two seemingly irreconcilable claims: the charismatic nature of the church's structure as the basis of the claim to the obedience of faith:

> [The Church's] authority is not from the people, but from the grace of Christ. It derives ultimately not from a vote from below, but from investment from above.[50]

and the equally charismatic nature of all the members of the church:

> in the Church to which charismatic elements belong, subordinates are not simply those who have to carry out orders from above. They have other commands as well to carry out: those of the Lord, who also guides God's Church directly and does not always in the first place convey God's commands and promptings to ordinary Christians through ecclesiastical authorities.[51]

---

[46] The reference to Vatican II comes from *Lumen Gentium* §8; Rahner's description of 'the sinful church' can be found in 'The Church of Sinners' (1947), *TI*, vi, trans. Karl-Heinz and Boniface Kruger (New York: Crossroad, 1982), 259.

[47] Rahner, 'Thoughts on the Possibility of Belief Today' (1962), *TI*, v.16.

[48] Rahner, 'The Individual in the Church' (1946) in *Nature and Grace*, trans. Diana Wharton (London: Sheed and Ward, 1963), 79.

[49] Rahner 'Do Not Stifle the Spirit!' (1962), *TI*, vii, trans. David Bourke (New York: Crossroad, 1977), 74–5.

[50] Rahner, *Free Speech in the Church* (1953), trans. G. Lamb (New York: Sheed and Ward, 1959), 13.

[51] Rahner, *The Dynamic Element in the Church* (1958), trans. W. O'Hara (London: Herder & Herder, 1964), 70.

Rahner, of course, was not unaware of the possibility, even the likelihood, of conflict between the various expressions of the Spirit's presence in the church. Nonetheless, he maintained an unequivocal commitment to what, in his later theology, he named the 'open' church, a church willing to respond to new questions.[52] Equally, he remained hopeful that the Spirit could not only reconcile differences in the church, but also lead the church into the future via creative engagement with the challenges raised by the culture in which it carried out its mission.

Rahner's own engagement with the relationship between faith and culture, with the latter understood largely in the context of Europe, focused on the prospects for faith in a society where the customary supports for that faith had declined after the Second World War—his reflection on this theme reached its fullest development after Vatican II, when his emphasis was on the impact of 'secularization' and 'pluralism'.[53] As Rahner's theology in general aimed to underscore the dynamism inherent in Christianity, so too his analysis of the church's place in a changing world stressed that the church needed to be more than a museum-piece 'left over as a sort of atavistic remnant from the past'.[54] A particular challenge for the church, then, was to avoid being merely a sour critic of modernity—'today's Christianity often gives rise to the painful impression that it is running ... in a disgusted, critical mood behind the carriage in which the human race drives into a new future'.[55]

Living constructively in the present, however, required that the church come to terms with its existence in the 'diaspora', a key term for Rahner's analysis of the church's place in the modern world.[56] In such a situation, where church members would be a minority in society, it would be possible for the church to engage creatively with the world only if members of the church were alive with the hope that had its foundation in the Spirit:

> But might we not perhaps venture the paradox that, the more the Church is the community of those who *believe contra spem in spem* that God has done great things in them (i.e. of those who believe precisely because they accept the servant-form of the Church and help to endure it patiently to the end), the more (and really only thus) the Church will also become—precisely in this way—that *signum elevatum in nationes* of which the first Vatican Council speaks so triumphantly?[57]

[52] For the centrality of the 'open' church to Rahner's ecclesiology in the decades after Vatican II see Richard Lennan, *The Ecclesiology of Karl Rahner* (Oxford: Clarendon Press, 1995), 213–57.

[53] For an overview of Rahner's writings during this period see Richard Lennan, 'Faith in Context: Rahner on the Possibility of Belief', *Philosophy and Theology*, 17 (2005), 241–8.

[54] *Free Speech in the Church*, 47.

[55] Rahner, 'Christianity and the "New Man"' (1961), *TI*, v.150.

[56] For the foundations of Rahner's use of the 'diaspora' see, 'Peaceful Reflections on the Parochial Principle' (1948), *TI*, ii.288; 'The Christian among Unbelieving Relations' (1954), *TI*, iii.355; and *Free Speech in the Church*, 86.

[57] 'Dogmatic Notes on "Ecclesiological Piety"', 342–3; the emphasis is Rahner's.

What Rahner desired to see manifest in the church was the willingness to trust that God was not absent from unattractive historical situations. Indeed, Rahner even ventured that the circumstances of the church in the diaspora could be interpreted as a 'must', an indispensable condition, for God's salvific work.[58] For Rahner, a church whose members accepted such a situation, who continued to immerse themselves creatively in their society as an expression of their faith and hope, had much to offer the modern world, which was far from fulfilled since its technological sophistication did not guarantee happiness or prevent freedom declining into boredom and insecurity.[59]

CONCLUSION

This chapter has chronicled the key elements of Rahner's theology from his early years, the years that coincided with the period during which the practitioners of the *ressourcement* were also doing their most significant work. The review has stressed that Rahner sought explicitly to articulate a theology that, in highlighting God's self-communication to the whole of humanity and to the entire created universe, promoted creative engagement with God in response to the questions of history. Rahner's stress on 'mystery', which is underpinned by his interpretation of revelation and grace, as well as being inseparable from his anthropology, results in a theology that highlights the dynamism inherent in humanity's relationship with God. This dynamism was also central to Rahner's construal of authentic ecclesial faith. The church's faith, therefore, ought to be a vehicle enabling the Christian community to negotiate change, while not only drawing on what connected the community in the present to its past, but also maintaining its orientation to the future, to an ever-deeper encounter with the mystery of God.

Rahner's focus on 'mystery' represents, perhaps, his most significant bequest to the contemporary church. Support for that claim could come, for example, from the increased engagement in recent years with Rahner's work on Christian spirituality, which is a major venue for the application of the theology of mystery.[60] While it might surprise many who have heard only of the fabled density of Rahner's theological thinking or who share the perception that his writing is too opaque to be accessible to any but a coterie of *aficionados*, Rahner composed prayers, wrote much about prayer, and published many homilies and

---

[58] For Rahner's idea of the saving 'must' see *Free Speech in the Church*, 81; and *Mission and Grace*, i, (1959), trans. Cecily Hastings (London: Sheed and Ward, 1963), 21–7.

[59] 'Do Not Stifle the Spirit!', 75.

[60] See, for example, the re-release of Rahner's *The Mystical Way of Everyday Life: Sermons, Prayers, and Essays*, ed. Annemarie Kidder (Maryknoll NY: Orbis, 2010); as well as *Karl Rahner: Spiritual Writings*, ed. Philip Endean (Maryknoll NY: Orbis, 2004); and Harvey Egan, *Karl Rahner: Mystic of Everyday Life* (New York: Crossroad, 1998).

retreat talks. It is important to emphasize that those writings were not the work of a 'different' Rahner, not a hobby tangential to his main scholarly occupations, but simply another medium for expressing his primary theological insights. Thus, his theology of the supernatural existential is no less central to his reflections on laughter—'good laughter is a sign of love, a revelation and a school of the love of everything in God'—and sleep—'If one approached sleep . . . as an agreeable and trusting acceptance of an utterly human act, then falling asleep could be seen as relating to the inner structure of prayer, which is equally a letting-go, an entrusting one's own inner conviction to the providence of God, which one lovingly accepts'—than it is to his closely-argued analysis of grace, theological anthropology, or the history of the sacrament of penance.[61]

While the burgeoning interest in Rahner's writings on spirituality means that aspects of his work that were previously undervalued are now finding their place in the sun, this emphasis has not eclipsed the more 'traditional' study of Rahner. Indeed, Rahner's theological method, long the staple of 'Rahner studies', continues to stimulate theological debate.[62] In addition, Rahner's theology is applied to the discussion of issues that Rahner himself did not live to see emerge, such as the ecological crisis or the implications of the 'post-colonial' world.[63] Furthermore, the publication, in German, of Rahner's collected works, an English-language compilation of abstracts of his essays, and a volume of various reminiscences about Rahner not only attest to the enduring vitality of his work, but have all contributed to the ongoing prominence of Rahner within the theological community.[64]

Since Rahner understood his theology to be explicitly ecclesial in its intent, it is important to complete this essay by offering some evaluation of the potential of his theology to meet the needs of the contemporary church.

---

[61] *The Mystical Way of Everyday Life*, 180–3.

[62] See, for example, Robert Masson, 'Interpreting Rahner's Metaphoric Logic', *TS*, 71 (2010), 380–409, which is itself an engagement with three recent monographs on Rahner's sources and method. In addition, the publication of *The Cambridge Companion to Karl Rahner*, is a significant recent re-presentation of the primary themes of Rahner's theology.

[63] The work of Denis Edwards is an example of the application of Rahner's theology to discussion of ecological questions; see Edwards' *Ecology at the Heart of Faith* (Maryknoll NY: Orbis, 2006); and *How God Acts: Creation, Redemption, and Special Divine Action* (Minneapolis: Fortress, 2010); see also Hyun-Chul Cho, 'Interconnectedness and Intrinsic Value as Ecological Principles of the World: An Appropriation of Karl Rahner's Evolutionary Christology', *TS*, 70 (2009), 622–37. For an assessment of Rahner's work in the light of various 'post-colonial' themes see, Paul Crowley (ed.), *Rahner Beyond Rahner: A Great Theologian Encounters the Pacific Rim* (Lanham: Rowman and Littlefield, 2005).

[64] The publication of Rahner's *Sämtliche Werke*, which will span more than thirty volumes, was begun by Herder Verlag in 1995 and continues; for the English compilations, see Daniel Pekarske, *Abstracts of Karl Rahner's Theological Investigations 1–23*, Philosophy and Theology 14 (Charlesville: Philosophy Documentation Centre, 2002); and his *Abstracts of Karl Rahner's Unserialized Essays* (Milwaukee: Marquette University Press, 2009). For the reminiscences see, *Encounters with Karl Rahner: Remembrances of Rahner by those who knew him*, ed. Andreas Batlogg, Melvin Michalski, and Barbara Turner (Milwaukee: Marquette University Press, 2009).

At present, where there is 'a struggle within the Church about both how to understand its own life and how to express that life, and, further, the struggle orbits around the relationship of the past and the challenges of the future', Rahner's theology is unsatisfying for some within the church.[65] Indeed, as Philip Endean notes, 'an apophatic, mystical approach to theology like Rahner's' is unlikely to be congenial to those who believe that 'the Christian Church can only maintain its cohesion and identity if it develops a clearer sense of boundaries between those within and those without'.[66] Thus, those who connect 'Catholic identity' with the maintenance of a strict division between past and present, between continuity and change, and between 'the church' and 'the world' tend to baulk at Rahner.[67]

On the other hand, Rahner's theology, aligned as it is on the ongoing encounter with the mystery of God that establishes not only the possibility of holding together past, present, and future, but also the capacity to recognize the movement of the Spirit both within and beyond the church, continues to offer the church a challenging vision.[68] Rahner's work reminds us that the dynamics of the encounter with the God revealed in Jesus Christ will not always accord with our preferences, that it will call us to negotiate issues that we would rather avoid:

> our own responsibility and our own age demand that we should be spiritual. Only he who is a member of the Church *and* independent, humble, *and* daring, obedient *and* conscious of his own personal responsibility, a pray-er *and* a doer, adhering to the Church in her past *and* in her future—only such a one as this makes room for the Spirit of God at Pentecost . . . to renew the face of his own soul, to use those who are his own in order to transform the earth as well.[69]

Fortunately, in its efforts to navigate the shoals represented by the questions addressed to it today, the church does not need to make a definitive choice between the theologians of the *ressourcement* and the work of Rahner, but can draw from both, and still other sources of wisdom. If the value of the theologians of the *ressourcement*, with their emphasis on biblical and patristic renewal, is clear, it is also crucial that the contemporary church not lose sight of the hope that Rahner's theology offers, a hope grounded in the God who remains always greater while drawing us, through our everyday experiences, into a relationship that is the gateway to a transformed world.

---

[65] Lawrence Cunningham, *An Introduction to Catholicism* (Cambridge: Cambridge University Press, 2009), 252.

[66] Philip Endean, 'Has Rahnerian Theology a Future?' in *The Cambridge Companion to Karl Rahner*, 281–96 (293).

[67] The criticism that Rahner gives priority to the secular, thereby obscuring the centrality of God in human life and history, can appear in the most unexpected of places: see, for example, the negative assessment of Rahner by two prominent figures in the contemporary Catholic Worker movement in Dan McKanan, *The Catholic Worker after Dorothy: Practicing the Works of Mercy in a New Generation* (Collegeville MN: Liturgical Press, 2008), 113–15.

[68] See Paul D. Murray, 'The Lasting Significance of Karl Rahner for Contemporary Catholic Theology', *LS*, 29 (2004), 8–27.

[69] Karl Rahner, 'The Church as the Subject of the Sending of the Spirit', *TI*, vii.190–1; the emphasis is Rahner's.

27

Benedict XVI: A *Ressourcement* Theologian?

Lewis Ayres, Patricia Kelly, and Thomas Humphries

INTRODUCTION

Is Joseph Ratzinger (1927–), Pope Benedict XVI from 2005 to 2013, a *ressourcement* theologian? At a fundamental level, yes. Although he is a full generation younger than the main figures of the movement, he nonetheless shared much of their experience as twentieth-century Catholic theologians: he took inspiration from the liturgical movement of the late nineteenth and early twentieth centuries; he has been deeply influenced by the various movements of patristic retrieval that marked the second half of the nineteenth and first half of the twentieth century; he saw much of his own early agenda endorsed and promoted by the reforms of the Second Vatican Council.[1] Nevertheless, Ratzinger/Benedict is also a 'second-generation' *ressourcement* theologian. One of the ways in which the young seminarian Ratzinger came to be influenced by these earlier movements was *through* the works of the first generation of *ressourcement* figures, and throughout his career he has treated the figures of that earlier generation (especially de Lubac) as authorities rather than colleagues.

Since the beginning of the 1960s, Ratzinger has also been engaged in a long-running engagement with those who wished to embrace whole-heartedly modern historical-critical biblical methods (even as he takes many of the results of this scholarship to be an important and necessary resource for modern theology). His views about this engagement closely follow those of de Lubac about the direction of post-conciliar Catholic exegesis, but the depth of his interest in historical-critical exegesis further marks him as a member of

---

[1] Francis Schüssler-Fiorenza offers a brief but very helpful personal reminiscence of the younger Ratzinger as a *ressourcement* theologian in 'From Theologian to Pope', *Harvard Divinity School Bulletin*, 33/2 (2005), 56–62.

a younger generation. Joseph Ratzinger is also distinct from the key *ressourcement* theologians, not only in generation but also in cultural context. His interest in exegesis often also proceeds via reflection on the demands of modern (mostly German) hermeneutical theory: de Lubac himself also approached the challenge of historical-critical exegesis as a philosophical problem (following Blondel's work)—what are the limits of the knowledge that the exegete may claim?; what are their presuppositions?—but in Ratzinger we see a focused hermeneutical challenge that reflects a rather different hermeneutical tradition.[2] Similarly, Ratzinger's dissertation and *Habilitationschrift* demonstrate a concern with the character and metaphysics of history that marks him as thinking in the wake of German Romantic and Idealist concerns, concerns present in, but not at the centre of, the French theological context in the first half of the twentieth century. We might, then, view Ratzinger's work as a test case for asking what *ressourcement* theology will look like when transposed into new cultural contexts and into new times, and what challenges it faces in a new century.

Born in 1927, Ratzinger grew up in the south German Catholic heartland of Bavaria and, while he was eventually conscripted into the Hitler Youth and the German anti-aircraft forces, his family was strongly anti-Nazi.[3] He entered the seminary with his brother Georg in 1946 and eventually studied in Munich before his ordination in 1951. During his theological studies, he was introduced to the work of de Lubac, being encouraged to read *Catholicisme* and *Corpus Mysticum*. He was struck by the 'astounding historical erudition' of these works, which 'opened up the tradition of the Fathers'.[4] *Catholicisme* was 'a key reading event [which offered] a new and deeper connection with the thought of the Fathers...', while *Corpus Mysticum* gave him 'a new understanding of the unity of Church and Eucharist';[5] both works exerted

---

[2] Of course, viewing the matter thus also involves a judgement about Rahner and Balthasar: the latter provides another example (admittedly of an earlier generation) of a theologian deeply influenced by (contemporary) *ressourcement* figures and yet shaping a theology deeply influenced by German philosophical traditions; whether Rahner should be included in the *ressourcement* is an open question; cf. Richard Lennan's chapter in this volume. On de Lubac's attitude to historical-critical exegesis, see Marcellino D'Ambrosio, 'Henri de Lubac and the Critique of Scientific Exegesis', *Communio*, 19 (1992), 365–88.

[3] Much insight into his education is to be found in Joseph Ratzinger, *Milestones: Memoirs 1927–1977*, trans. E. Leiva-Merikakis (San Francisco: Ignatius Press, 1998). Ratzinger offers a perceptive analysis of the problems faced by the churches in the face of the attempts by the Nazis to control or destroy them in 'The Spiritual Basis and Ecclesial Identity of Theology', *The Nature and Mission of Theology*, trans. Adrian Walker (San Francisco: Ignatius Press, 1995), 45–72 (45–50). Arguably, it is precisely this experience of watching the Nazi attack on the church which has shaped his insistence on the need for a strong magisterium which can hold out against nationalistic attempts to turn the church into a government agency.

[4] Ratzinger, *Das neue Volk Gottes. Entwürfe zur Ekklesiologie* (Düsseldorf: Patmos-Verlag, 1969), 95 (authors' translation).

[5] Ratzinger, *Milestones*, 98.

a significant influence on his theology. The young Ratzinger was also influenced by a number of figures who had themselves influenced earlier generations of *ressourcement* theologians. Romano Guardini's short text *The Spirit of the Liturgy* was an important influence and, a little later, the work of Newman.

Ratzinger's formal philosophical and theological education was based on the neo-scholastic texts standard at the time, and he speaks of an early difficulty 'penetrating the thought of Thomas Aquinas, whose crystal-clear logic seemed to us to be too closed-in on itself, too impersonal and ready-made'. But he attributes this difficulty to the philosophy professor at the seminary who 'presented us with a rigid, neo-scholastic Thomism'.[6] His critique of neo-scholasticism would ever after follow the example of the *ressourcement* theologians, describing its 'superficial approach', and lamenting the topsy-turvy use of scripture and tradition.[7] Nevertheless, around the edges of this formal education, fellow students and some professors provided conduits for the best of work advocating for alternative approaches.

Given that he had already experienced the draw of the *ressourcement* approach and of the liturgical movement as a seminarian, it should not surprise us that Ratzinger's further academic studies took the form of two extended acts of historical investigation and recovery. He was always first and foremost a theologian rather than a historian, but the way forward lay in appropriate retrieval.

AUGUSTINIANISM

Ratzinger's doctoral dissertation, 'The People and the House of God in Augustine's Doctrine of the Church', was completed in 1953 (and unfortunately has never been translated into English).[8] Rather than summarizing the dissertation itself it will be more helpful for our purposes to note some features of the book that mark the beginning of a consistent 'Augustinian' approach in Ratzinger's theology. Ratzinger sees Augustine's notion of 'the people of God' reflecting the bishop's understanding of the Christian community as spiritually united in liturgical worship of God. 'Spiritually united' here refers to the unity of Christians in Christ's body, and his animating Spirit a unity which provides their truest reality. Thus at the very beginning of his career we see the

---

[6] *Milestones*, 44.
[7] See for example the criticism of scripture used merely apologetically in Ratzinger, 'Dogmatic Constitution on Divine Revelation', trans. William Glen-Doepel, in Herbert Vorgrimler (ed.), *Commentary on the Documents of Vatican II* (London: Burns & Oates, 1968), iii.191; iii.269.
[8] *Volk und Haus Gottes in Augustins Lehre von der Kirche* (Munich: K. Zink, 1954).

young Ratzinger subscribing to a certain Platonism, one strongly Christianized and central to patristic and medieval tradition.

Ratzinger also sees Augustine's celebration of the Christian liturgical community as the heart of an apologetic strategy against late antique Platonism. But Christianity here is presented not so much as Christian cult opposed to pagan religious cult, but as a *rational* cult or philosophy able to answer and surpass the Platonist challenge (which Augustine takes to be the most significant challenge from the Classical tradition). Ratzinger argues that Augustine presents the church community as taking up and providing more fulfilling answers to the Platonic tradition's concerns about the relationship of the material and the spiritual, and the semiotic character of material existence. Against a denigration of the material, Christianity presents an intelligible created order as revealing and leading towards the spiritual informing presence of the Word. But at the same time, the very goals of philosophy—awareness of the intelligible and purification of the soul—are taken up and rendered universally possible through the church's faith in God's redemptive drawing of us towards eternal life. The character of Christian liturgy is also able to resist Platonism's tendency to fall back towards traditional Greek and Roman religion, evident in those Platonic traditions, which saw cults requesting the aid of divine beings as part of the journey towards union with The One. Christianity overcomes this tendency through its vision of a liturgy in which the one Creator of all acts in the community, drawing the world to its consummation: Christian worship draws our hearts to Christ and through Christ to the one Father of all. Of course, Augustine's emphasis on the centrality of humility (of humanity before God, but based on the humility of Christ before the Father) also transforms ancient ethical dynamics, but in so doing the appropriate emphases of ancient religion and moral philosophy are re-ordered and consummated.

This Augustinian conception of a developing Christian culture absorbing, transforming, and giving new meaning to fallen human cultural expression remains a central feature of Ratzinger's thought and demonstrates the strong parallels between his thought and that of the earlier generation of *ressourcement* theologians. While Ratzinger has written little at length about the great controversies concerning nature and grace that were so central to de Lubac's *œuvre*, we see where his sympathies lie when we reflect on the importance he gives to Augustine's vision of the consummation of human activity in a liturgical culture of worship. The Christian tradition brings unity and consummation to human striving because it orients all human activity towards praise. At the same time, the consummation of human activity is found in recognition that as God works in the liturgy of the church, our praise finds its form through the Spirit's work among us. This Augustinian vision sees a profound unity between nature and grace, but one that is approached via the metaphysics of history and culture.[9]

At the same time, we should note further convergences that are apparent between the work of the young Ratzinger and earlier *ressourcement* emphases when we think a little more deeply about Ratzinger's conception of the relationship between the church and its Lord. Like those earlier figures, Ratzinger came to see patristic theology as offering a vital synthesis of theology and prayer: whatever else theology is, it must finally lead to union with God through contemplation and charity. 'Behind Athanasius... there stands Anthony of Egypt; behind Gregory the Great, Benedict of Nursia; behind Bonaventure, Francis of Assisi.'[10] His later writing on what he has called a 'spiritual Christology' reflects deeply on the union of God the Father and Son and does so by turning us again to patristic—and specifically Greek—sources: 'According to the testimony of Holy Scripture, the centre of the life and person of Jesus is his constant communion with the Father.'[11]

At the same time, Ratzinger tends to interpret these motifs in an Augustinian key. When Ratzinger eventually takes up the motif of communion in his ecclesiology, the heart of that motif is presented as its ability to show how the earthly communion of Christians is constituted by our sharing in communion—through Christ and in the Spirit—with the Father, and is constituted for Christ's salvific work in the world.[12] It is from this vision of communion that Ratzinger draws his ecclesial ethics. No individual becomes an *alter Christus* by experiencing union with the Father through the Spirit without also having consideration for others. The Christian must always return to the (Augustinian) twofold love of God and neighbour. Indeed, 'the Church cannot neglect the service of charity any more than she can neglect the Sacraments and the

[9] While it seems fair to call this vision 'Augustinian', it is important to note that Augustine himself may have been far more hesitant about the relationship between pre-Christian culture and the life of the church.

[10] Aidan Nichols, *The Thought of Benedict XVI* (London: Burns & Oates, 2005), 64.

[11] Ratzinger, *Behold The Pierced One: An Approach to a Spiritual Christology*, trans. G. Harrison (San Francisco: Ignatius Press, 1986), 15. This turn towards Eastern sources is a central feature of French *ressourcement* theology and may be seen reflected in the later Ratzinger/Benedict's celebration of the contribution of Origen of Alexandria and his calls for deeper Western reception of the Third Council of Constantinople (on Christology) and the Second Council of Nicaea (on icons). For an in-depth study of *ressourcement* study of patristic theology in general see Brian Daley's essay in this volume.

[12] See Tracey Rowland, *Ratzinger's Faith: The Theology of Pope Benedict XVI* (Oxford: Oxford University Press, 2008), Ch. 5; Congregation for the Doctrine of the Faith, 'Letter to the Bishops of the Catholic Church on Some Aspects of the Church Understood as Communion', (28th May, 1992), *AAS* lxxxv (1993), 838–50; ET available at <http://www.vatican.va/roman_curia/congregations/cfaith/documents/rc_con_cfaith_doc_28051992_communionis-notio_en.html>. For an excellent summary of Ratzinger's understanding of *communio* see Ratzinger, 'Communio: A Program', *Communio* 19 (1992), 436–49. At the foundation of his interpretation is Oskar Saier's famous 'Communio' in *Der Lehre des II. Vatikanischen Konzils. Eine rechtsbegriffliche Untersuchung* (Munich: Hueber, 1973).

Word', because these are inter-dependent aspects of the church which lives by the Spirit.[13] 'The Spirit, in fact, is that interior power which harmonizes their hearts with Christ's heart and moves them to love their brethren as Christ loved them, when he bent down to wash the feet of the disciples (cf. *Jn* 13:1–13) and above all when he gave his life for us (cf. *Jn* 13:1, 15:13).'[14] Reflection on the Spirit as instrumental for Christian love unites Ratzinger once again with Augustine. But if these themes unite Ratzinger to Augustine, they also reveal a common cause with and a debt to de Lubac's own Augustinian reading of the relationship between Eucharist, church, and the work of God in the world.

Although this conception of the church shows that the characteristic emphases of *ressourcement* theology surrounded and continue to surround Ratzinger's Augustinian ecclesiology, it is worth noting one of his occasional differences with de Lubac. In *The Spirit of the Liturgy*, Ratzinger summarizes de Lubac's *Corpus Mysticum*, but warns that we should not take from de Lubac any sense that late medieval developments concerning the reserved sacrament and focus on the presence of Christ in the elements are to be rejected. There is here only a difference of emphasis: de Lubac celebrates an earlier vision of Eucharist and church and laments its disappearance in the early medieval period; Ratzinger follows him, but is careful to argue for features of the post-medieval picture as a necessary supplement to any revival of the earlier model. In the first place, Ratzinger sees later devotion to the consecrated elements as an unfolding of something implicit in earlier tradition (rather than merely the result of a change away from an earlier patristic position). Second, a historical principle about tradition and the church comes into play: the very idea of such a break and such a significant failure in the church's self-understanding is rejected as denying an appropriate Christian view of the unitary history of the church. To understand why such continuity is so important to him we need to turn to another feature of his Augustinianism.

BONAVENTURE AND HISTORY

Ratzinger's *Habilitationsschrift*, the second doctorate which, in the German academic system, enables the holder to be appointed to a full university professorship, was entitled *The Theology of History in St Bonaventure*.[15] In

---

[13] Benedict XVI, *Deus Caritas Est*. Encyclical Letter on Christian Love (25th December 2005), *AAS* xcviii (2006), 217–52 § 22. ET available at <http://www.vatican.va/holy_father/benedict_xvi/encyclicals/documents/hf_ben-xvi_enc_20051225_deus-caritas-est_en.html>.

[14] Benedict XVI, *DCE*, § 19.

[15] See Nichols, 'Bonaventure and Saving History', in *Thought*, 51–65.

this dissertation Ratzinger treated Bonaventure's engagement with Joachim of Fiore in the light of how history is presented in the book of Genesis. In particular, Ratzinger calls attention to the continuity of history: 'The whole of history develops in one unbroken line of meaning, that which is to come may be understood in the present on the basis of the past.'[16] For Bonaventure—and here Bonaventure is very much an Augustinian—the unity of history is found in God's action in the created order. Augustine's account of the 'two cities'— one of this world, the other the City of God—provides an organic unity to human history by reading it as the history of fall and redemption. In *City of God*, Augustine complements this account of history with one of his most extensive accounts of how the intelligible creation reveals the glory of God and (through grace) leads the rational creation back to unity with God—a theme which then becomes central to Bonaventure's work on Genesis. All cultural striving by human beings may once again be read as either moving towards or a fallen unconscious imitation of the developing culture of Christianity. In his work on Bonaventure, Ratzinger attempted to take forward Bonaventure's account of history in order to emphasize that God's revelation is always God's action in history, not merely the delivering of a deposit of faith to the apostles. His arguments at this constructive level led to considerable criticism from his *Doktorvater*, Michael Schmaus.

Emphasis on a unitary theology of history was not only something that Ratzinger discovered in Augustine and Bonaventure: it was also central to the Tübingen theologians of the early nineteenth century and again to the Munich School of the late nineteenth and early twentieth centuries.[17] In both cases the development of a theology of history was at the service of an emergent view of the church's tradition as an organic unity. Against views which saw the development of doctrine as the unfolding of propositions logically deducible from the original apostolic deposit of faith, theologians in both these schools— and, somewhat independently, Newman—explored views of doctrinal development as involving the emergence of principles and themes which may be viewed as consonant with, and dependent on, the earliest expressions of Christianity and yet not necessary developments. These historicizing perspectives attempted to unite post-Enlightenment European philosophies of history with Christian accounts of the continuing work of Christ and Spirit in the church. Not surprisingly, these currents in Catholic thought are found also in the first generation of *ressourcement* theologians—de Lubac's magisterial essay 'The Problem of the Development of Dogma', and Congar's *Tradition and*

---

[16] Ratzinger, *Theology of History in S. Bonaventure*, trans. Z. Hayes (Chicago: Franciscan Herald Press, 1971), 8.

[17] J. von Döllinger's early work on the organic growth of tradition, O. Bardenhewer's work on the Fathers, and M. Grabmann's scholarship on scholasticism were particularly influential in Ratzinger's formation; see Nichols, *Thought*, 22–4.

Traditions—but often with less emphasis on the metaphysics of history.[18] Ratzinger's second doctorate thus both reflects his own interest in these lines of thought—an interest that will be developed through his career—and shows him attempting to link aspects of this modern account of history's unity to the Augustinian tradition.

At this point we can expand on our earlier comments about Ratzinger's uncertainty about the Thomist tradition. As we saw above, Ratzinger has noted that 'from the beginning Saint Augustine interested me very much— precisely also insofar as he was, so to speak, a counterweight to Thomas Aquinas'.[19] In his *Habilitationsschrift*, however, Ratzinger does not pit an Aristotelian-Thomist against an Augustinian-Bonaventure. Rather, he agrees that both Bonaventure and Thomas are neo-Platonizing Aristotelians who took Augustine as foundational.[20] That is, for Ratzinger, Bonaventure and Thomas do not disagree in a debate about *whether* to use Augustine or Aristotle. Rather, they disagree on *how best* to use Augustine and Aristotle. The form which Thomism took when Ratzinger was a student was unpalatable to him, but this did not lead Ratzinger to reject Thomas as a whole. For example, Michael Waldstein has argued that Ratzinger uses Aquinas' development of a Christian conception of personhood (which he develops through reflection on the relationship of the divine Father and Son) in a response to systems which developed from Kant.[21] Similarly, Ratzinger is a Bonaventurian Augustinian because of his emphasis on developing a theology of history, because of the way Bonaventure used scripture in his theology, and because of his insistence on returning to love as the basic element of Christian insight into humanity; but this does not prevent Ratzinger from praising Thomas for being the 'first person who drew out all the consequences of this article of faith [that God is Creator]'.[22] That is, Ratzinger's Augustinianism is not a rejection of Thomas, but a preference for a different mode of theology within an overall sense of the fundamental unity of the Christian tradition. Thus the slight correction we saw him make with respect to some readings of de Lubac's *Corpus Mysticum* is mirrored in his attitude to those who might see him as rejecting the importance of Thomas (even as he is unsympathetic to neo-Thomist emphases).

---

[18] See de Lubac, 'The Problem of the Development of Dogma', in *Theology in History*, trans. Anne Englund Nash (San Francisco: Ignatius, 1996), 248–80; Congar, *Tradition and Traditions* (London: Burns & Oates, 1966).

[19] Ratzinger, *Salt of the Earth: Christianity and the Catholic Church at the End of the Millennium: An Interview with Peter Seewald*, trans. A. Walker (San Francisco: Ignatius Press, 1997), 60.

[20] See the discussion in Nichols, *Thought*, 62; and Rowland, *Ratzinger's Faith*, 17–29.

[21] Michael Waldstein, 'Johannine foundations of the Church', in L. Melina and C. A. Anderson (eds.), *The Way of Love* (San Francisco: Ignatius Press, 2006), 250–65, esp. 260–1.

[22] Ratzinger, '"Consecrate them in the truth", a homily for St Thomas' day', *New Blackfriars*, 68 (1987), 112–15 (113).

THE SECOND VATICAN COUNCIL: *DEI VERBUM*

In the final two sections of this paper we turn to the Second Vatican Council and its legacy. In each case we begin by looking at Ratzinger's influence on and views of a key document from the Council—and in each case we see him taking an approach which flows organically from his earliest writing and is broadly in accord with the fundamental themes of the *ressourcement* movement. But both sections end by considering the response of Ratzinger (and Benedict) in the decades since the Council, exploring the character of the task of articulating *ressourcement* emphases in this new century.

We begin by thinking about the young Ratzinger's vision for the Council. In 1959, Ratzinger had moved from Munich, where he had taught since 1953, to Bonn, and in 1961 he was appointed theological adviser to Cardinal Frings of Cologne, later accompanying him to Rome as *peritus* for the start of the Council in 1962. At the Council, as Jared Wicks details, '[h]e helped on the Doctrinal Commission's revisions of *De ecclesia* and *De revelatione*; he assisted the Council's Commission on Missions in its early 1965 creation of what became Ch. I of *Ad gentes*; and he proposed in October 1965 a revision leading to new material in [what became] *Gaudium et Spes* no. 10'.[23]

Ratzinger's first important work was prior to the Council, 'a lecture composed by *peritus* Ratzinger and given by Cardinal Frings in Genoa on November 20, 1961, in a series on the coming Second Vatican Council'.[24] In this text, Ratzinger places the Council in its mid-twentieth-century cultural and political context, closing with 'a reflection on … the liturgical movement from which have followed fresh approaches to the Bible, the Church Fathers, and to separated Christians in ecumenical exchanges'.[25] Throughout his work at the Council he was to further this agenda.

Following the first session of the Council, the *schemata* were sent to bishops for their comments over the summer of 1962. Ratzinger's assessment for Frings, which became the Cardinal's reply, is notable in particular for its demand that 'the texts should not be treatises in a scholastic style … but should instead speak the language of Holy Scripture and of the holy Fathers

---

[23] Jared Wicks, 'Six texts by Prof. Joseph Ratzinger as *peritus* before and during Vatican Council II', *Gregorianum*, 89/2 (2008), 233–311. Some of the key pieces from the recent large body of writing are considered by Wicks in a series of review articles; see 'Review Article: New Light on Vatican Council II', *Catholic Historical Review*, 92 (2006), 609–28; 'Review Article: More Light on Vatican Council II', *Catholic Historical Review*, 94 (2008), 75–101; 'Review Article: Further Light on Vatican Council II', *Catholic Historical Review*, 95 (2009), 546–69. Ratzinger repeatedly downplays his role at Vatican II in *Salt of the Earth*, 70–5. Ratzinger's contribution to what became *Lumen Gentium* is noted by Karl Rahner, 'The Hierarchical Structure of the Church, with Special Reference to the Episcopate', in Herbert Vorgimler (ed.), *Commentary on the Documents of Vatican II* i (London: Burns & Oates, 1967), 187.

[24] Wicks, 'Six texts', 234.

[25] Wicks, 'Six texts', 235.

of the Church'.[26] In his response, Ratzinger is highly critical of all the proposed documents, although he does allow that the *schemata* on liturgy and church unity are 'much better than the others',[27] despite needing further attention. In particular, the *schema* on church unity requires careful work on the post-Reformation Churches, and, he suggests, the final document might be published in Greek, making it available to all Christians. Greek, he notes, is 'a language pertaining to the Church and venerated as an original language of Holy Scripture'.[28] From this and the final paragraph it perhaps becomes clear that the 'fresh approach' to scripture Ratzinger envisages is not primarily that of the modern historical-critical exegete, but one that enables the language of scripture (and the theological language of patristic and medieval writers understood as a commentary on scripture) to speak to Christians today, rather than being obscured by the language of the neo-Thomist manuals that he had found so uncongenial in seminary.

In addition to his advisory role to Cardinal Frings, Ratzinger was also involved in the preparation of some of the key Vatican II documents. Of particular importance for this chapter are his work on the *schema* on revelation, which became *Dei Verbum*, and his work on *Gaudium et Spes*. So far in this chapter we have said little about the character of Catholic exegesis, a central interest of Ratzinger since the days of the Council, and so we begin with *Dei Verbum*. For Ratzinger, *Dei Verbum* brought together 'three motifs': 'the new view of the phenomenon of tradition'; 'the application of critical historical methods'; and 'the biblical movement', in particular the 'new familiarity' with the sacred text which the latter has brought about.[29] Despite the difficulties encountered in the editorial process, the final text 'combines fidelity to Church tradition with an affirmation of scholarship ... [recognizing] that fidelity in the sphere of the Spirit can be realized only through a constantly renewed appropriation'.[30] Moreover, the *ressourcement* of the Bible which *Dei Verbum* enables and encourages is a 'going back [which is] at the same time, and from within, a moving forward'.[31]

In *Dei Verbum* much of the work of the *ressourcement* theologians bore fruit, and Ratzinger had done all he could to further that result. Ratzinger's particular point of departure may be seen in his address to the German-speaking bishops on the eve of the Council's opening. In this address Ratzinger insists that the references at the start of the draft *schema* prepared by the Council's preparatory committee to 'the two sources of revelation' are confused, for 'Scripture and Tradition are material principles of our knowing

---

[26] Wicks, 'Six texts', 266.
[27] Wicks, 'Six texts', 265.
[28] Wicks, 'Six texts', 265.
[29] Ratzinger, 'Dogmatic Constitution on Divine Revelation', 155, 157, 158.
[30] 'Dogmatic Constitution on Divine Revelation', 165.
[31] 'Dogmatic Constitution on Divine Revelation', 265.

revelation, not revelation itself'.[32] He suggests that for any successful discussion of revelation 'one has to speak ... of revelation in itself before saying anything about the witnesses to revelation'.[33] After the Council, Ratzinger felt that *Dei Verbum* had succeeded, primarily because it 'emphasized that both Scripture and tradition flow from the same sources', marking a return to the 'comprehensive theological view of Trent ... as compared with the superficial approach of scholastic theology [at Vatican I]'.[34] He was also clear about what had been overcome: 'the fathers were concerned with overcoming neo-scholastic intellectualism, for which revelation chiefly meant a store of mysterious supernatural teachings ...'[35]

This reference to Trent needs to be understood in the light of his detailed analysis of Trent's handling of the relationship between scripture and tradition published in 1965, during the final year of the Council's work. 'The Question of the Concept of Tradition: A Provisional Response' is an important text, revealing the core principles of Ratzinger's theology of tradition. Ratzinger suggests that we view scripture itself as the unfolding of layers of tradition and proclamation. The Old Testament consists of a series of proclamations that are also expansions and commentaries on earlier phases. The New Testament itself incorporates layers of inspired commentary. The Gospel of Christ is presented as an interpretation of the Old Testament, continuing the logic of the Old, even in the radical departure that results from the Incarnation. But the New Testament also witnesses to the proclamation and expansion of this original gospel in the apostolic community filled with the Spirit. The very structure of scripture reveals that expansive commentary under the guidance of the Spirit is the very substance of tradition. What the church comes to call its dogma, its defined belief, may then be read as an ecclesial commentary on the New Testament finding its roots in the New Testament's own commentary on itself. Tradition is thus always commentary on the Scriptures, but a commentary that is at times not 'mere exegetical interpretation', but an interpretation that occurs 'in the spiritual authority of the Lord that is implemented in the whole of the Church's existence, in her faith, in her life, and her worship'.[36] Thus, tradition as interpretation is possible because of the church's authority.

---

[32] Wicks, 'Six texts', 272.

[33] Wicks, 'Six texts', 271.

[34] Ratzinger, 'Dogmatic Constitution on Divine Revelation', 191. In the address to the bishops, he points out that Vatican I 'used this phrase as the section-title of its reaffirmation of the Council of Trent' even though 'Trent itself did not speak this way and in Vatican I's text itself this way of speaking does not occur.' Wicks, 'Six Texts', 270.

[35] 'Dogmatic Constitution on Divine Revelation', 172.

[36] See Ratzinger, 'The Question of the Concept of Tradition: A Provisional Response', in *God's Word*, trans. Henry Taylor, eds. Peter Hünermann and Thomas Söding (San Francisco: Ignatius, 2005), 65.

This account of scripture and tradition shows how deeply Ratzinger's early theology was related both to the views of scripture and tradition developed by *ressourcement* theologians, and to the conceptions of doctrinal development found in the Tübingen and Munich schools. It is also a reading of *Dei Verbum* which locates the Council's radicality in its reassertion of a patristic and medieval narrative of the continuity between scripture and tradition. At the same time, despite his optimism just after the Council, Ratzinger (like de Lubac himself) soon felt that many post-conciliar theologies of scripture failed to focus on the whole of this vision. Many instead, he felt, came to read *Dei Verbum* solely as a licence for the Catholic interpreter to take on board the full raft of historical-critical methods. Thus, since the Council, Ratzinger's work on this question has found its focus in an attempt to oppose the philosophical presumptions of an exegesis that sees itself free from presuppositions, and to suggest the contours of a truly Catholic exegetical synthesis. His particular way of portraying the current choices that face the Catholic exegete are instructive, here in a famous 1989 address:

> The debate about modern exegesis is not at its core a debate among historians, but among philosophers ... [Exegesis] cannot withdraw to the Middle Ages or the Fathers and use them as a shield against the spirit of modernity. That said, it also cannot take the opposite tack of dispensing with the insights of the great believers of all ages and of acting as if the history of thought begins in earnest only with Kant ... One does not dispose of patristic exegesis simply by labelling it 'allegorical,' nor can one set aside the philosophy of the Middle Ages by classifying it as 'pre-critical'.[37]

It is noticeable that Ratzinger (like de Lubac) sees the task before us not simply as one of turning anew to pre-modern exegesis, but of incorporating the good fruits of modernity (and here Ratzinger seems to think especially of our growing awareness of historical development, and thus of the historical circumstances that formed the background to the New Testament) with the valid fruits of Christian reading of scripture through the church's history. There is certainly continuity here between the young Ratzinger in 1965 and the older Cardinal in 1989, but there is also something of an unfinished project, and perhaps an unfinished project that faces all those who see the *ressourcement* project as vital for theological renewal in Catholic theology. A powerful theology of scripture can indeed be gleaned from across the corpus of Ratzinger/Benedict (which suggests much for the vital task of taking forward *Dei Verbum*'s account of the place of scripture and tradition in God's salvific economy), but systematic articulation of it has not been at the

---

[37] Ratzinger, 'Biblical Interpretation in Conflict: On the Foundations and the Itinerary of Exegesis Today', trans. A. Walker, in J. Granados, C. Granados, L. Sánchez-Navarro, *Opening up the Scriptures: Joseph Ratzinger and the Foundations of Biblical Interpretation* (Grand Rapids MI: Eerdmans, 2008), 1–29 (19).

forefront of his direct engagements with historical-critical exegetes.[38] Of course, one figure cannot do everything, especially when that figure plays such a prominent role in the life of the church; but perhaps one could argue that this hermeneutical focus demonstrates both the outworking of the German philosophical assumptions that we have seen elsewhere, and the need for a more sustained focus on a combination of fundamental theology and actual exegetical practice. Ratzinger's argument, that many modes of historical-critical exegesis rely on (unexamined) presuppositions that militate against truly theological readings, is both expressed in the terms of the German hermeneutical tradition and is paralleled by de Lubac's own (slightly more piecemeal) attitude. It finds, of course, many allies at the beginning of the twenty-first century. But devoting energy here—at a point where many have attacked in the past few decades—diverts attention away from what elsewhere Ratzinger himself has seen as the real need in post-conciliar appropriation of *Dei Verbum*: development of the theology of scripture that *Dei Verbum* suggests, development of the place of scripture in God's redemptive economy. Here perhaps is a task for the third generation of *ressourcement* theologians.

A further task for the next generation concerns the more careful articulation and demonstration of which practices for scriptural reading follow from or are most consonant with such a theology of scripture. This task is at once both theoretical and practical. For example, the Ratzinger/Benedict corpus is multifaceted and it may well be that his deepest contribution to the re-shaping of Catholic exegesis is to be found in his sermons and personal exegetical explorations, which are often deeply 'patristic' and yet also deeply engaged with modern exegesis. In these sermons we find hints towards a true *ressourcement* blending of approaches that opens paths for the future.[39] But in response to this corpus we must ask two sets of questions. First, is the complex performance of pre-modern exegesis, and the exploration of the history of interpretation that one finds in de Lubac's best work, best taken forward at a

---

[38] See most recently, Scott W. Hahn, *Covenant and Communion: The Biblical Theology of Pope Benedict XVI* (Grand Rapids MI: Brazos, 2009). Consideration of this persistent theme in Ratzinger's corpus is oddly missing from Rowland's *Ratzinger's Faith*.

[39] For an example of his 'patristic' style, see the sermons preached at a papal retreat in 1985, where he offers a reflection on Psalm 16 as revelatory of Christian priesthood. To show the significance of the fifth verse, 'The Lord is the portion of my inheritance and of my cup. It is you who will give back to me my inheritance', Ratzinger makes use of standard patristic techniques. First, he notes when and how the passage is used in the liturgy, subtly calling attention to the life of the Psalm within the praying community. Second, he appeals to other verses of scripture that use the same key term, 'inheritance', to create a web of meaning for this verse. Finally, he sees the fulfilment of this psalm in the priesthood of Christ. Ratzinger, *Journey Towards Easter: Retreat Given in the Vatican in the Presence of Pope John Paul II*, trans. M. Groves (Middlegreen: St Paul Publications, 1987), 151–5. His *Jesus of Nazareth*, trans. A. Walker (London/New York: Bloomsbury/Doubleday, 2007) shows him in a more detailed engagement with historical-critical scholarship, but note how significant to the volume is the relationship between New and Old Testaments.

philosophical level, or by continuing the performance of pre-modern exegesis—performing it now in a way that shows how it may be part of a continuum that does include the best of modern historical critical scholarship? How may such exegesis best be performed at both the homiletic and the academic level? Second, why is it that Ratzinger does not discuss the challenge of historical-critical exegesis via discussion of particular reading practices that should be preserved, learnt, avoided, etc.? As we become more aware of the sheer variety of historical-critical practices, does this open the possibility of such a discussion, away from the question of hermeneutics *per se*? Has the dialogue, in a Catholic context, been conducted so far with too monolithic a picture of the 'literal sense'; do historical-critical methods always investigate the same 'literal sense' as explored by patristic and medieval 'grammatical exegesis'?

THE SECOND VATICAN COUNCIL:
GAUDIUM ET SPES

With Ratzinger's very positive estimation of *Dei Verbum*, it is helpful to contrast his somewhat more critical reaction to the Pastoral Constitution on the Church in the World Today, *Gaudium et Spes*. In general terms he has sometimes expressed the view that the text is somewhat undeveloped and incomplete. A particular target of Ratzinger's criticism is what he views as the incomplete presentation of the church as the 'People of God' to be found in the document and many of those who have based their subsequent accounts of ecclesiology on this theme of *Gaudium et Spes*.[40]

After the Council Ratzinger pressed for an interpretation of the phrase 'People of God' in parallel with what he had earlier seen in Augustine: 'in Scripture [the phrase] is a reference to Israel in its relationship of prayer and fidelity to the Lord'; however, 'to limit the definition of the Church to that expression means not to give expression to the New Testament understanding of the Church in its fullness'.[41] The problem he sees with the use of 'People of God' is twofold. First, '[w]e can only agree with G. Alberigo that this way of speaking of the Church involves no small danger of sinking once more into a purely sociological and even ideological view of the Church ... by oversimplifying, externalising and making a

---

[40] See, for example, his discussion of §12, in 'The Pastoral Constitution on the Church in the Modern World. Chapter I, Part I', in H. Vorgrimler (ed.), *Commentary on the Documents of Vatican II*, trans. J. W. O'Hara (London: Burns & Oates, 1969), v.121.

[41] Joseph Ratzinger with Vittorio Messori, *The Ratzinger Report*, trans. Salvator Attanasio and Graham Harrison (Leominster: Fowler Wright Books Limited, 1985), 47. His atttitude to the reception of Vatican II should be compared to that of de Lubac. For an introduction to the latter see de Lubac, *A Brief Catechesis on Nature and Grace*, trans. Brother Richard Arnandez, FSC (San Francisco CA: Ignatius, 1984), 235–60.

catchword of a term which can only keep its meaning if it is used in a genuinely theological context.'[42] Second, he suggests that 'People of God' is used in the Old Testament to designate Israel 'only at the moment when they were addressed by God and answered his call'[43] and thus can only refer to those who are united 'from above and from within: through communion with Christ'.[44] Just as the People of God of the Old Covenant had their foundational meal and act in the Passover, so 'this new Supper is what binds together a new people of God'.[45] The metaphor of the 'People of God' thus might be taken in a way that fails to acknowledge the sacramental foundations of the church, and the sacraments 'have a Christological structure; they are the communications of Christ.[46]

> The Eucharist is the Sacrament of the Church's unity, because we all form one single body of which the Lord is the head. We must go back again and again to the Last Supper on Holy Thursday, where we were given a pledge of the mystery of our redemption on the Cross. The Last Supper is the locus of the nascent Church, the womb containing the Church of every age.[47]

Lumen Gentium describes the church as 'the universal sacrament of salvation',[48] and it is 'only against the background provided by the concept "sacrament" [that] the concept "people of God" [can] become meaningful'.[49] Indeed, Ratzinger argues, 'the Council intended the two expressions to be mutually complementary and explanatory'[50] in order precisely to avoid the very individualistic conception of faith and sacraments—'a supernatural medicine in order, as it were, to ensure only my own private health'.[51]

Once again there is a deep continuity between his early and his later work. His reactions to *Gaudium et Spes* promote a traditional Augustinian understanding of the church. It would be a mistake, however, to see this emphasis as one opposed to the reforms of the Second Vatican Council: this emphasis reflects, rather, on-going dispute about the character of that reform. In true *ressourcement* fashion, Ratzinger saw the need for a reform that would state the faith of the church in a way that would make clear its heart and its foundation in the mystery of Christ's action in the world and in the Scriptures as a witness to that mystery. The question each new generation of

[42] Ratzinger, 'Chapter I, Part I', 118.
[43] Ratzinger, *Principles of Catholic Theology*, trans. Sr Mary Frances McCarthy, SND (San Francisco: Ignatius Press, 1982), 55.
[44] *Principles*, 55.
[45] *Das neue Volk Gottes*, 79.
[46] *Principles*, 47.
[47] Homily for the closing of the 49th International Eucharistic Conference, 22 June 2008. ET available at <http://www.vatican.va/holy_father/benedict_xvi/homilies/2008/documents/hf_ben-xvi_hom_20080622_quebec_en.html>.
[48] LG § 48; cf. Tanner ii. 887.   [49] *Principles*, 45.
[50] *Principles*, 45.   [51] *Principles*, 49.

ressourcement theologians faces, however, is how to promote such reform in a way that always reveals continuity in renewal.

As an example, we can briefly explore Benedict's interventions in current liturgical practice as part of his reaction to *Gaudium et Spes*. For some commentators Benedict has initiated a 'reform of the reform', attempting to turn back the clock on the post-conciliar reforms of the Roman rite. Such a view by itself underplays the theological continuity between his early views of the liturgy and the particular reforms he has implemented or suggested, and it misses the cautious character of those reforms themselves. In the first place, it is important to see those reforms as an outworking of theological principles present since his first dissertation. Ratzinger's *The Spirit of the Liturgy* (a deliberate echo of Romano Guardini's title) emphasizes the liturgy as the high point of Christian culture—both in the sense that here the key to human culture is revealed to be our worship of God and God's descent to us enabling our worship; and in the sense that here we see the structural ways in which Christianity re-orders human culture. He insists on the character of Christian worship as sacrifice but as he does so he is careful to define sacrifice as the humble and contrite gift of love and self to God that is rendered possible by the Spirit within us. He argues, as he had done in his first dissertation, that Christian worship also has a significant cosmic dimension, showing how the liturgy shows the true function of human culture as a witness to God's construction of a symbolic cosmic order. The task of reform is never, from this perspective, to make liturgical practice more 'comprehensible' or more reflective of everyday language; it is always to make our liturgical practice reflect its core theological principles and the character of the most basic liturgical attitude towards the divine. What it has become common to describe as a 'hermeneutic of continuity' was in its initial phrasing a 'hermeneutic of reform', and the goal of faithful reform here is a constant returning to the heart of the matter that nevertheless shows the continuous presence of the Spirit in the church.[52]

But when we come to the practical programme that flows from these principles, caution must be the watchword. Hence, those who imagine Benedict to be promoting any radical change in liturgical practice are perhaps mistaken: his goal is to highlight features or modifications of liturgical practice that reveal the heart of the developing Catholic liturgical vision. As an example we might note that while he insists that the celebration of the liturgy of the Mass should always be eastward facing insofar as this orientation is symbolically towards the Cross in all its cosmic symbolic dimensions, it is the use of a

---

[52] See 'Address of his Holiness Benedict XVI to the Roman Curia Offering them his Christmas Greetings', 22 December 2005, *AAS* xcviii (2006), 40–53. ET available at <http://www.vatican.va/holy_father/benedict_xvi/speeches/2005/december/documents/hf_ben_xvi_spe_20051222_roman-curia_en.html>.

crucifix placed centrally on the altar that he recommends—a symbol that should point to the heart of the action, but one which does not involve the radical reorientation of churches and the conveying of a sense that liturgy is open to constant sudden modification. But a new set of questions then emerges for all who seek to take forward the *ressourcement* approach: what set of such subtle yet significant changes will reveal the heart of the Catholic liturgical vision? How can the meaning of such changes be explained and taught—*ressourcement* as a pastoral challenge perhaps reveals the need for new modes of on-going theological education that have so far eluded much of the Catholic world? How can the very attitude of preservation and caution be celebrated as at the heart of Catholic attention to the work of the Spirit in the church? Once again, in retrospect it may be that the character of Benedict as Pope bears as much attention as the theoretical work of his written corpus. Theology is a matter of performance as well as of speculative power, and the multi-faceted legacy of *ressourcement* figures such as de Lubac and Benedict will require much further assessment and attention if we are to see how to take this legacy into the new century.

28

Lacan's Return to Freud: A Case of Theological *Ressourcement*?

Marcus Pound

INTRODUCTION: *NOUVELLE CRITIQUE* AND THE *NOUVELLE THÉOLOGIE*

To the names associated with the *ressourcement* movement—Chenu, Congar, de Lubac, Daniélou, and, in various associated ways as explored in this volume, Jacques Maritain, Étienne Gilson, and Teilhard de Chardin[1]—one might also add the structuralist Roland Barthes (1915–80), the medievalist, sociologist, and surrealist George Bataille (1889–1962), and the French psychoanalyst Jacques Lacan (1901–81), amongst others. While not theologians, their work was nonetheless deeply indebted to the milieu of the *ressourcement* movement. The thesis under exploration here is that the influence of *nouvelle théologie*[2] can be seen to extend not just to the reforms of Vatican II, as is often suggested, nor simply by extension to the church-going masses, but more specifically to the French post-war critical theorists associated with the avant-garde. If correct, this suggested shift in our understanding of the reception of *nouvelle théologie* will impact on our reception of French post-war critical theory, thereby opening up new avenues for critical dialogue between the two.

This is not an entirely new thesis.[3] It is most strongly expressed by Bruce Holsinger in his *The Premodern Condition*.[4] Here he makes a strong case for the importance of the reception of medieval theology by those associated with

---

[1] A. N. Williams, 'The Future of the Past: The Contemporary Significance of the *Nouvelle Théologie*', *IJST*, 7/4 (2005), 347–61 (348).

[2] Although the term '*nouvelle théologie*' was initially a pejorative term for the *ressourcement* theologians, I use these terms interchangeably.

[3] See for example John Ardagh, *The New French Revolution: A Social and Economic Survey of France, 1945–1967* (London: Secker & Warburg, 1968), 379.

[4] Bruce Holsinger, *The Premodern Condition: Medievalism and the Making of Theory* (Chicago/London: University of Chicago Press, 2005), 21.

the *nouvelle critique*. Arguably, Holsinger overplays the role of the French medievalist George Bataille relative to that of *nouvelle théologie*, and in the following sections I develop his insight with special reference to Jacques Lacan, the so-called 'Christian Freud',[5] whose structural-linguistic reading of Freud did much to influence the practices of contemporary psychoanalysis. In the next section, 'Returning to Lacan', I begin by contextualizing Lacan's work within wider critical Catholic reaction to *Aeterni Patris* and disputes over the interpretative legacy of Aquinas.[6] In particular, I highlight the way Lacan's approach to the Freudian unconscious was undertaken in conversation with Aquinas and his twentieth-century commentators. In 'Psychoanalytic *ressourcement*', I explore the parallels between de Lubac's critique of extrinsicist models of nature and grace, and Lacan's critique of the prevailing ego-psychology, as well as exploring Lacan's championing of speech and revelation in the light of Gilson's return to Aquinas. By equating the ego of Freudian psychology with the Being of Greek thought, Lacan was able to utilize the theological critique of metaphysics for psychoanalytic ends. Finally, in 'Positivism', I try to make sense of why Lacan returned to theology, highlighting the role played by his anti-positivist critique to suggest that Lacan's work did not merely borrow from theology. Rather, given his anti-positivism, it makes better sense to say that it was the very shifts undertaken within the *ressourcement* movement which allowed Lacan's work to take shape in the first place. I conclude by reflecting on what all this means constructively for Catholic theology and psychoanalysis today.

HOLSINGER AND THE PREMODERN/POSTMODERN CONDITION

Bruce Holsinger has already made a convincing case regarding the 'synchronic intellectual affinities' that might be identified between the *nouvelle critique* in French philosophy and the *nouvelle théologie* within Catholic theology.[7] As Holsinger notes, French avant-garde historians may appear to 'deemphasise

---

[5] Much of Lacan's vocabulary plays upon Christian themes. Seen for example *Écrits*, trans. Bruce Fink (New York/London: W. W. Norton, 2006), 481; *The Seminar of Jacques Lacan*, bk xx: *Encore, 1972–1973*, ed. Jacques-Alain Miller, trans. Bruce Fink (New York/London: W. W. Norton, 1999), 45.

[6] Pope Leo XIII, *Aeterni Patris*. Encyclical Letter on the Restoration of Christian Philosophy (4 August 1879), *Acta Leonis XIII*, 1 (1881), 255–84. ET available at: <http://www.vatican.va/holy_father/leo_xiii/encyclicals/documents/hf_l-xiii_enc_04081879_aeterni-patris_en.html>; compare Fergus Kerr, *After Aquinas: Versions of Thomism* (Oxford: Blackwell, 2002); *Contemplating Aquinas* (London: SCM Press, 2003); also Henry Donneaud, OP, 'A hidden *ressourcement*: speculative theology according to Marie-Rosaire Gagnebet', Ch. 6 in this volume.

[7] Holsinger, *Premodern Condition*, 21.

the centrality of Catholic philosophies and theologies in the shaping of modern critical thought',[8] yet the avant-garde was preoccupied with medieval theological formations to the extent it 'merits recognition as one of the most significant epiphenomena accompanying the emergence and consolidation of so-called French theory' and may best be described as '*theoretic medievalism*'.[9]

To take an example offered by Holsinger, historians of the *nouvelle critique* make much of Roland Barthes' contribution to the epoch-making International Symposium in 1966, 'The Structuralist Controversy: The Languages of Criticism and the Sciences of Man'[10] which brought together for the first time for an American audience many of the leading figures of European structuralism. Yet barely mentioned in those accounts are Barthes's attendance at conferences such as the 1969 colloquium in Chantilly of the *Association catholique française pour l'étude de la Bible*.[11] In short, the influence of Catholic theology of the period is written out of the history of critical theory. Yet as Holsinger argues, de Lubac's *L'Exégèse médiévale* had a deep influence on Roland Barthes, in particular his structuralist analysis of the short story by Honoré de Balzac, 'Sarrasine', published under the title *S/Z*.[12] Barthes may not have directly cited de Lubac, but an earlier essay on Ignatius of Loyola and interpretation,[13] and the interpretative methodology established in *S/Z*, appear to be closely modelled on de Lubac's account of the fourfold senses of scripture,[14] such that Holsinger can conclude: 'Writing at the end of a decade breathlessly invested in its own interpretive innovations, Barthes imputes to the text the same celestial boundlessness that provided medieval exegesis with its justifying purpose.'[15]

Similarly, Georges Bataille may be the celebrated doyen of the critical theorists, and one-time associate of André Breton's surrealist movement, yet Bataille moved within a 'heterogeneous culture',[16] which included leading

---

[8] Holsinger cites Gary Gutting, *French Philosophy in the Twentieth Century* (Cambridge: Cambridge University Press, 2001), 94–8.

[9] Holsinger, *Premodern Condition*, 3.

[10] R. Macksey and E. Donato, *The Structuralist Controversy: The Languages of Criticism and the Sciences of Man* (Baltimore MD: Johns Hopkins University Press, 1972).

[11] Holsinger, *Premodern Condition*, 21.

[12] Holsinger, *Premodern Condition*, 152–94.

[13] Barthes, *Sade, Fourier, Loyola*, trans. Richard Miller (New York: Hill and Wang, 1976).

[14] According to Holsinger, Barthes initially adapted the four traditional categories: historical, allegorical, moral, anagogical, into the literal (historical), allegorical, analogical and—in place of the moral—the purely semantic interlocutions, in an earlier essay on Loyola. In *S/Z*, these are metamorphosed into five levels. The historical/literal level becomes the proairetic, allegory becomes divided into the codes of cultural and the hermeneutic, anagogy becomes symbol, and the moral yields again to the purely semantic. Holsinger, *Premodern Condition*, 181–3.

[15] Holsinger, *Premodern Condition*, 194.

[16] J. Kosky, 'Georges Bataille's Religion without Religion: A Review of the Possibilities Opened by the Publication of "The Unfinished System of Nonknowledge"', *The Journal of Religion*, 84/1 (2004), 78–87.

Catholic intellectuals, as exemplified by 'The Discussion on Sin', which contains a transcript of his discussions with the eminent *ressourcement* theologian Jean Daniélou.

If there are criticisms to be made of Holsinger it is that first, he largely restricts his intuition regarding the '*nouvelle critique*' and *nouvelle théologie* to Barthes, such that the 'synchronic intellectual affinities' between the two schools amount to little more than a revival of medievalism within philosophical thought. Second, the central figure of this revival is not a theologian as such, but the anti-theologian and author of the *Summa A/Theologia*, George Bataille. In short, the current of influence exerted by *nouvelle théologie* is downplayed in favour of Bataille's interest in medieval texts. Of course, it does not do to downplay Bataille's influence in this regard, yet Holsinger's conclusion might equally be reframed to suggest that the 'celestial boundlessness' which critical theorists imputed to their work was already inspired, received, and made possible through the work of the *nouvelle théologie*. That is, Bataille may well have propelled an interest in the medieval amongst critical theorists, but the revival of medieval texts was itself largely mediated by Catholic theologians, historians, and philosophers.

Arguably, the precedence for mutually engaged relations between the avant-garde and Catholic theologians had already been established within French cultural life following the First World War, when leading figures in French Catholic circles found themselves engaging with the very heart of France's literary and artistic avant-garde, at the vanguard of the *renaissance catholique* or *renouveau catholique*.[17] If in 1864, as Stephen Schloesser has pointed out, 'Catholicism had been defined as irreducibly anti-modernist; in 1926, it actively sought out the avant-garde',[18] perhaps best exemplified by Jacques Maritain and Jean Cocteau's jointly published *Réponse à Jean Cocteau* and *Lettre à Jacques Maritain*.[19] The publication highlights a strange precedent not matched in Germany or Italy in the same period, and sets a continuing trend for the post-war rise of critical theory.

If we have lost sight of this, it is for two reasons: the first, offered by Holsinger, is a 'peculiar hypostatization of "*theory*" as a distinct institutional formation and mode of critical engagement' within the humanities.[20] For example, reading any number of recent books on critical theory one might easily assume it lacks any connection to wider cultural and specifically theological formations.[21] The theories of Derrida or Lacan are often presented

[17] Stephen Schloesser, *Jazz Age Catholicism: Mystic Modernism in Postwar Paris, 1919–1933* (Toronto: University of Toronto Press, 2005), 4.

[18] Schloesser, *Jazz Age Catholicism*, 4.

[19] *Art and Faith: Letters between Jacques Maritain and Jean Cocteau* (New York: Philosophical Library, 1948).

[20] Holsinger, *Premodern Condition*, 9.

[21] See for example R. Harland, *Superstructuralism: The Philosophy of Structuralism and Post-Structuralism* (London/New York: Methuen, 1987).

synchronically, within the immanence of their own frameworks, which generate their own distinct terms of reference (e.g., Derrida's *differance*). The
second is a certain reticence on the side of the critical theorists themselves
to highlight their sources. Lacan, for example, having 'let slip' in an interview
that 'I got my taste for commentary from the old practice of the scholastics',
asked that it be omitted.[22]

RETURNING TO LACAN

In what follows, I wish to develop this thesis with regard to the French psychoanalyst, Jacques Lacan. Again, Holsinger has already treated Lacan and medievalism,
but his argument presents a number of problems. The thrust of Holsinger's
argument revolves around the influence of Bernard of Clairvaux and his older
contemporary, Peter Abelard, on Lacan's text. The former, Holsinger argues,
furnishes Lacan with a devotional model of pedagogical transmission; the latter
with the more combative rhetoric of the scholastic method. These poles, it is
argued, shape the ethical stylistics of Lacan's approach to psychoanalysis: devotion to Freud bordering on the religious, coupled with biting criticism of the
reigning orthodoxies of psychoanalysis. However, the references to Bernard and
Abelard are misleading. For example, Holsinger cites Lacan's devotional model of
pedagogical transmission offered up in the introduction to *The Ethics of Psychoanalysis* with reference to Bernard of Clairvaux's description of scripture as a kind
of textual food, 'to be champed, digested, and absorbed in the exegetical process.'[23]
However, not only is there no direct reference to either Bernard or Abelard in the
course of Lacan's *Seminar*, but, as Lacan himself intimates a few pages on, the very
metaphor takes its cue from Aristotle's discussion of pleasure.[24]

One way to redraw the map is to contextualize Lacan's work within wider
critical Catholic reaction to *Aeterni Patris* and the ensuing disputes over the
interpretative legacy of Aquinas. Ever since *Aeterni Patris*, Catholics had been
encouraged to seek the answers to the currents of contemporary thought
within Aquinas.[25] Thomas's ability to synthesize biblical revelation with the

---

[22] *The Seminar of Jacques Lacan*, Bk xiv: *The Logic of Phantasy*, trans. Cormac Gallagher.
Unpublished. 7.12.66.
[23] Holsinger, *Premodern Condition*, 63.
[24] *The Seminar of Jacques Lacan*, Bk vii: *The Ethics of Psychoanalysis, 1959–1960*, ed. Jacques-
Alain Miller, trans. Dennis Porter (London: Routledge, 1999), 29.
[25] See also the Papal Letter, *Jampriden* (15 October 1879); the Papal Brief, *Cum Hoc Sic*
(4 August 1880); the Papal Brief *Gravissime Nos* (December 1892), referred to by Gerald
McCool, 'Twentieth-Century Scholasticism', in David Tracy (ed.), *Celebrating the Medieval
Heritage: A Colloquy on the Thought of Aquinas and Bonaventure. The Journal of Religion,
Supplement*, 58 (1978), 198–224 (199, n.1).

intellectual currents of his day including Aristotle (Greek), Maimonides (Jewish), and Averroes (Islamic) could serve as a model for Europe, reconciling culture and Catholicism. In France, however, following on the one hand the Dreyfus affair—in which the false conviction of a Jewish artillery officer led to charges of anti-Semitism on the part of the Army, and erupted into a nationwide split between the clerical and monarchist right and the democratic left—and, on the other hand, the crisis of Modernism, Thomism had tended to become a sectarian discipline to be pitted against the 'contaminating currents of the new century', offering itself up as 'an analogue of neo-Byzantinism: an intellectual expression of eternalism'.[26]

Yet, as *Aeterni Patris* makes clear, and the French theologian de Lubac highlights, this approach was largely shaped under the influence of Cardinal Cajetan (1465–1534) and Francisco Suárez (1548–1617). Cajetan's reading of Aquinas favoured a crude dualism between nature and grace such that, given Aquinas' axioms *gratia praesupponit naturam* (grace presupposes or builds on nature) and *gratia perficit naturam* (grace perfects nature), the working assumption was that humanity occupies a realm of nature, to which is added some extra and extrinsic super-nature. Suárez's approach was to bring Aquinas into line with other scholastics, such as Bonaventure and Scotus, so as to present a unified and perennial philosophical system, an a/historical metaphysics with all the ready answers.

Reaction to *Aeterni Patris* and the model of Thomas being promoted would give rise to a wave of theological reclamations of Aquinas, both those contextualizing and historicizing his work, and those pointing to the inadequacy of the extrinicist position. It was this awareness of climate of renewal within Catholicism, I suggest, that helps us to discern some of the theological moves made by Lacan.

Lacan's public interviews may show a reticence to identify with the scholastic milieu, but he shows none of that in his seminars or conference papers. In 'The Subversion of the Subject and the Dialectic of Desire' (1960), he dates the unconscious as it appears in idealist forms of philosophy back to Aquinas.[27] In the course of Seminar XIV he interjects: 'St Thomas who, after all, has no reason not to be evoked here, in the measure that a certain way of posing the principles of being is, all the same, not without some incidence on what one makes of logic.'[28] Six years later, he would comment: 'I roll on the floor laughing when I read Saint Thomas Aquinas, because it's awfully well put together.'[29] And, in a paper given in Geneva in 1975 Lacan takes Aquinas' work *On Being and Essence* to serve in advance of his own work: 'being is not

[26] Schloesser, *Jazz Age Catholicism*, 55.
[27] *Écrits*, 676/799.
[28] *Seminar* xiv, 7.12.66.
[29] *Seminar* xx, 114.

grasped so easily, nor is essence'.[30] To this it should be added that Lacan shows more than a passing familiarity with two of the major interpreters of French Thomism in the modern period, Maritain and Gilson, admonishing his students to read the former,[31] and describing 'Monsieur Etienne Gilson' as 'someone well balanced'.[32]

Lacan's comments show a mixture of admiration and irreverence for Aquinas, but can a deeper affinity be found with the scholastic thought of Aquinas? Such a relationship has already been suggested by Richard Glejzer, Erin Labbie, and François Regnault.[33] Much of their argument centres on the specific relationship between subjectivity and language. In Glejzer's words, 'both Lacanian psychoanalysis and medieval scholasticism, [. . .] are founded upon an imperative to consider a knowledge that resists signification'.[34] What is at stake here, in Labbie's terms, is the quarrel of the universals; i.e., the ability to determine and articulate universals (e.g., goodness),[35] or in the context of Lacan, 'the real'. In Lacan's threefold scheme of the psyche—the imaginary, the symbolic, and the real—the real is, to quote Žižek:

> impossible but it is not simply impossible in the sense of a failed encounter. It is also impossible in the sense that it is a traumatic encounter that does happen but which we are unable to confront. And one of the strategies used to avoid confronting it is precisely that of positing it as this indefinite ideal which is eternally postponed. One aspect of the real is that it's impossible, but the other aspect is that it happens but is impossible to sustain, impossible to integrate.[36]

In short, the real is that element of the unconscious that cannot be accessed by conscious thought but whose presence is felt in a determining manner; so while one can presume an awareness of the real, discernible by its causal effects (not unlike Kant's transcendental deduction, but more readily discerned in the peculiar glance of an eye or a bodily inflection that incites desire), one cannot in any way specify its particular shape. In this sense the real is both universal, always at stake, evident in language, yet it remains intangible and dependent upon language. Little wonder, then, as Labbie points out, that in referring to

---

[30] 'Geneva Lecture on the Symptom', *Analysis*, 1, (1989), 15.

[31] *Seminar* xiv, 7.12.66. Lacan is referring to Maritain, *Le Paysan de la Garonne* (Paris: Desclée de Brouwer, 1966).

[32] *The Seminar of Jacques Lacan*, Bk xiii: *The Object of psychoanalysis, 1965–1966*, trans. Cormac Gallagher. Unpublished, 19.1.66.

[33] Richard Glejzer, 'Lacan with Scholasticism: Agencies of the Letter', in *American Imago*, 54/2 (1997), 105–22; Erin Labbie, *Lacan's Medievalism* (Minneapolis MN/London: University of Minnesota Press, 2006); François Regnault, *Dieu Est Inconscient* (Paris: Navarin, 1985).

[34] Glejzer, 'Lacan with Scholasticism'.

[35] Labbie, *Lacan's Medievalism*, 42.

[36] Slavoj Žižek and Glyn Daly, *Conversations with Žižek* (Cambridge: Polity Press, 2004), 71.

the nominalist/realist debates, Lacan would side with the realists following the medieval tradition of the scholastics.[37]

To clarify this relationship, one might equally take the distinction Aquinas draws between *res significata* and the *modus significandi* (the thing signified and the mode of signification), employed to carry his treatment of religious discourse. When we conjugate the verb tense of 'run': 'he ran', 'he runs', 'he will run', the same thing (*res*) is spoken about, but in three different *modi*. Aquinas employs the distinction to handle God's perfections:

> God is known from the perfections that flow from him and are to be found in creatures yet exist in him in a transcendent way. We understand perfections, however, as we find them in creatures, and as we understand them so we use words to speak of them. Therefore, we have to consider two things, in the words we use to attribute perfections to God: firstly the perfections themselves that are signified: goodness, life and the like; second, the way in which they are signified.[38]

As David Burrell explains, 'What the distinction does is call attention to the fact that we consider something from many different angles. Understanding this keeps us from confounding ourselves—but in no way promises access to the thing independent of any such angle.'[39] However, and herein lies the crucial point, when speaking of God's perfections, Aquinas employs the distinction, not so much to preserve the *res* as distinct from the *modi*, but the very opposite: 'we understand such perfections because we find them in creatures';[40] and so, as Burrell argues, in answer to the question 'how can we consider the perfections themselves [. . .] the answer of course, is that we cannot'.[41] So far, so apophatic; but not to end there. What one can do, with a twist of Kierkegaardian repetition, is note the very diversity of signification, the array of contexts in which a word is spoken, and 'let this diversity *show* us something of the thing signified'.[42] So while the distinction does not yield to any privileged access between *res* and *modi*, it nonetheless recalls to us that in speaking about God we must consider two things: the context and the 'latent' intention within the term.[43] And 'We discover this latent power not directly but indirectly, by attending to the other ways in which we put the expression

[37] Labbie, *Lacan's Medievalism*, 29. Labbie is paraphrasing Lacan, *Autre écrits* (Paris: Seuil, 2001), 327, 351. Lacan's predilection for the scholastics, as suggested by his remarks on the 'extra-ordinary good logicians' of the Scholastic period also show him to be an engaged reader of the acts of the Vatican Council, see *The Seminar of Jacques Lacan, Seminar* xii, *1964–1965: Crucial problems for Psychoanalysis*, trans. C. Gallagher. Unpublished. 7.4.65.

[38] *ST* 1a.13.3.

[39] David Burrell, *Aquinas: God and Action* (Scranton PA/London: University of Scranton Press, 2008 [1979]), 10.

[40] *ST* 1a.13.3.   [41] Burrell, *Aquinas*, 10.

[42] Burrell, *Aquinas*, 10.   [43] Burrell, *Aquinas*, 11.

to service.'[44] In short, while 'Aquinas is concerned to show what we cannot use our language to *say*, he recognises that there is no medium of exposition available other than language itself.'[45]

It is a short step from here to Lacan: all one needs to do, as Labbie in fact does, is translate Aquinas' talk about the universal perfections into the idiom of psychoanalysis, replacing Aquinas' first cause with the absent cause of the subject (what Lacan calls the *objet petit a*, the signifier of the impossibility of signification), turning Aquinas on his head such that the aim and attenuation to the split between the sign and signifier attunes one to the articulations of the unconscious, which like God, can only be approached indirectly.[46] This turn through Aquinas should also help clarify why Lacan is not best construed as an apophatic thinker like Derrida, any more than Aquinas should be: we may not be able to speak the real; but the real speaks.[47]

In sum, one might describe Lacanian psychoanalysis as a non-substantialist metaphysics, as Lacan himself implies:

> But psychoanalysis is not a religion. It proceeds from the same status as Science *itself*. It is engaged in the central lack in which the subject experiences himself as desire [. . .] it implies no recognition of any substance on which it claims to operate, even that of sexuality.[48]

In short, he draws the distinction between theology and psychoanalysis, not along the lines of a positivist account of the human subject, nor along the lines of belief, but rather the positing of substance by theology, and its lack in psychoanalysis.

PSYCHOANALYTIC *RESSOURCEMENT*

It would be wrong, however, simply to affirm the affinity between Lacan and Thomas or to present this solely in terms of Thomas's apophatic approach. The terms of the *ressourcement* debate serve well to establish the terms of Lacan's own contentions within the psychoanalytic world, and especially the International Psychoanalytical Association during the 1950s and 1960s. In the interpretation of Freud, the Association favoured the schools of 'ego-psychology'. For example, early interpreters such as Freud's daughter Anna, Harry Guntrip, or Heinz Hartmann, all argued that the self was in origin a bundle of self-seeking drives (what Freud associated with *das Es*), which should be brought into conformity through the rationalizing principle of the ego. Hence, given

---

[44] Burrell, *Aquinas*, 11.   [45] Burrell, *Aquinas*, 6.
[46] Labbie, *Lacan's Medievalism*, 17.   [47] *Seminar* xiv, 7.12.66.
[48] *Seminar* xi, 265–6.

Freud's enigmatic claim, '*Wo Es war, soll Ich werden*' [lit. 'where it was, I shall become'], the tendency was to translate it thus: 'Where the *id* was, there the *ego* shall be',[49] or, 'the *ego* must dislodge the *id*'.[50] On this reading, the aim of analysis was to assist ego in stamping out natural desire, thereby positing a split between natural desire and cultural norms. In its place Lacan offered a close reading of the original text. As he points out, Freud said neither *Id* nor *Ego*, which were Latin terms adopted by Freud's English translator with a view to giving Freud's work the ring of scientism. Moreover, as Lacan notes, Freud does not employ the objectifying article *das* to designate what the English translation calls the *Id*. With the rigour of a medievalist, Lacan unearths what is arguably a medieval sentiment within Freud's maxim, which promotes the paradoxical unity of the two: *Where it was, I shall become*, or to give it the weight of Freud, 'Here, in the field of the dream, you are at home/born.'[51]

Indeed, Lacan goes as far as to explicitly identify his criticism of ego-psychology with the loss of the scholastic principle: 'The antinomy the scholastic tradition posited as principal is here [in ego-psychology] taken to be resolved.'[52] In ego psychology, the ego is set over and against the Id (*das Es*) rather than intimately related to it.

What we discover, then, in Lacan's return to Freud is, like de Lubac, an attempt to go beyond the schematism of the id/ego or nature/grace dualism, to arrive at new ways of speaking adequately about the real [*réel*] of human experience. Lacan encapsulates this paradoxical experience in his neologism 'extimacy',[53] by which he refers to the experience of the real as 'something strange to me, although it is at the heart of me',[54] an 'intimate exteriority'.[55]

It is possible that Lacan was influenced by the French Jesuit Teilhard de Chardin's concept of *intériorité* (Lacan recounts a number of conversations he had with Teilhard, on one occasion almost reducing him to tears after Lacan had affirmed a belief in angels on the basis of scripture),[56] or Pascal's Fragment 793, where the interiority of the human is said to transcend the universe as a whole: 'All bodies, the firmament, the stars, the earth and its kingdoms, are not equal to the lowest mind; for mind knows all these and itself.' But both owe something to Augustine's theology of the interior life, where *intimum* and *summum* coincide; the distant God is a God who is most near, nearer to the human than the human person is to him/herself. Little wonder Lacan would not infrequently admonish his listeners and readers to 'become versed in Augustine'.[57]

[49] Lacan, *Écrits*, 347/417.   [50] Lacan, *Seminar* xi, 44.
[51] Lacan, *Seminar* xi, 44.   [52] *Écrits*, 675/798.
[53] *Seminar* vii, 139.   [54] *Seminar* vii, 71; *Seminar* xii, 7.4.65.
[55] *Seminar* vii, 139.
[56] *Television: A Challenge to the Psychoanalytic Establishment*, ed. Joan Copjec, trans. Jeffrey Mehlman (New York/London: W. W. Norton, 1990), 91.
[57] *Écrits*, 734/865, 742/873–4.

Lacan's appropriation of theology over and against the contemporary psychoanalytic practice of his day is affirmed in other ways too, extending to the institution of the church and the role of revelation:

> Make no mistake, people who know a little about the handling of truth are not without imprudence. They have the truth, but they teach: all power comes from God. All. That does not allow you to say that it is only the power that suits them. [. . .] That is why it is useful for the truth to be somewhere, in a strongbox. Privilege, revelation, is the strongbox. But if you take seriously *Me, the truth, I speak* [i.e., ego-psychology] this can have, alas, great disadvantages for the one who takes this path.[58]

Lacan's point is, firstly, that only when we make room for revelation—that is, a claim made upon human subjectivity that is not circumscribed by the self-certainty of the ego defences—can we take Freudian analysis seriously; and, secondly, that Freudian analysis, as interpreted by Lacan, maintains the possibility for this structural space. Of course, Lacan does not award any specific content to revelation. His concern is with the structural position it plays within theological anthropology. One can easily clarify this in relation to Kierkegaard's distinction between recollection and repetition (as Lacan himself does); or equally in relation to the work of Gilson, whose own reading of Thomas was not only contemporaneous with Lacan's, but also mediated by the current of existential thought familiar to Lacan.

Gilson's thought centred on the claim that Judaic thought introduced something new into the philosophical world of Greek thought: God was not posited as an ultimate answer to a metaphysical problem, but one who had revealed himself: I AM WHO I WILL BE [*ipsum esse*]. 'Philosophers were not able to reach beyond essences to the existential energies which are their very causes until the Jewish-Christian revelation had taught that "to be" was the proper name of the Supreme Being'.[59] Thomism was the first existentialism.

According to Gilson, early commentators, such as Augustine, understood the principle but never fully resolved 'how to express the God of Christianity in terms borrowed from the philosophy of Plotinus?'[60] They relied on 'Greek philosophical technique in order to express ideas that had never entered the head of any Greek writers'.[61]

Yet if the problem for Augustine was, as Gilson argued, that as the 'unsurpassed exponent of Christianity he never had the philosophy of his theology', forced as he was to fall back upon Greek philosophical terms,[62] the problem for Lacan is the reverse: that as the unsurpassed exponent of Freud, he never

---

[58] *Seminar* xiv, 19.6.68.
[59] Étienne Gilson, *God and Philosophy*, 2nd edn. (New Haven CT/London: Yale University Press, 2002), 65.
[60] *God and Philosophy*, 47.
[61] *God and Philosophy*, 43   [62] *God and Philosophy*, 60.

had a theology for his philosophy and hence found himself forced back onto scholastic terms.

The problem for both Gilson and Lacan was that Greek anthropology posited a tangible relation between the soul and the intellect (i.e., self-subsisting knowledge wherein reside the Platonic forms). From this perspective, the difference between soul and God was simply one of graduation: a soul is a god of a lesser degree. Accordingly, truth was immanent within human nature, merely forgotten, such that all knowledge was discovery of what one already knew: one need only remember that one was a god to be put back on the path of divinity. Hence Greek thought had no need of revelation or salvation.

'Not so in Christian metaphysics.'[63] For Gilson, Christianity's distinctive claim is that if 'the Christian God begets in virtue of his fecundity, he must be somebody else, that is another person',[64] but not another 'inferior sort of god'.[65] A distinctive line is drawn between God and creation, which underscores the need for a truth to constitute something new: revelation.

This theological distinction allows Lacan to clearly delineate his own project from the existing Freudian school. Speech implies a specular identity, in the manner of recollection, allowing for

> mediation, mediation between subject and other, and it implicates the coming into being of the other in this very mediation. An essential element of the coming into being of the other is the capacity of speech to unite us to him. [. . .]. But there is another side to speech—revelation. Revelation, and not expression—the unconscious is not expressed, except by deformation [. . .] the whole of Freud's work unfolds in the dimension of revelation, and not expression. Revelation is the ultimate source of what we are searching for in the analytic experience.[66]

This is given further weight by the interest elicited for Lacan by God's response to Moses: *Ehieh asher ehieh*. The significance of this passage lies not simply in the way God 'designates himself by the fact that he speaks'.[67] Rather,

> But it is not by that name, says Elohim to Moses, *That I revealed myself to your ancestors* [. . .] God is something one encounters in the real, inaccessible. It is indicated by what doesn't deceive—anxiety [. . .] The Greeks who did the translation of the Septuagent were much better informed than we are. They didn't translate *Ehieh asher* as *I am the one who I am*, as did Saint Augustine, but *I am the one who is.* That's not quite it, but at least it has a meaning. They thought like the Greeks that God is the Supreme Being. *I equals Being.*[68]

---

[63] *God and Philosophy*, 51.
[64] *God and Philosophy*, 52.   [65] *God and Philosophy*, 53.
[66] *The Seminar of Jacques Lacan* Bk i: *Freud's Papers on Technique, 1953–1954*, ed. Jacques-Alain Miller, trans. John Forrester (London/New York: W. W. Norton, 1991), 48–9.
[67] *The Seminar of Jacques Lacan*, Bk xvi: *From the Other to the other, 1968–1969*, trans. C. Gallagher. Unpublished. 4.6.69.
[68] *Television*, 90.

Again, such comments should be read in the light of the anti-metaphysical thrust of Lacan's work.[69] The 'I' of ego-psychology equates with the Being of Greek thought, acting as a first principle, the *causa sui*, that sustains being as a whole. In short, Lacan aimed to challenge the metaphysical structures that sustain subjectivity by challenging the Other as its locus of support.[70] Lacan's reworking is designed to shift the weight from metaphysics—with its perduring nature and stable forms—for a philosophy of becoming that can only ever be a becoming because: 'There, where he is, in his field, namely the Holy Land, there is no question of obeying anyone but him [i.e., the unconscious].'[71]

POSITIVISM

As Alexandre Leupin has pointed out, Lacan's approach rejects the evolutionary stance of Freudian psychology, a point given weight by Lacan's damming critique of positivist approaches to religion. Lacan's barb is aimed less at specific faith traditions, than at the speculative or imaginary foundations involved in comparative approaches to religions; i.e., establishing a 'common denominator of religiosity'.[72] He deems such approaches narcissistic to the extent that they seek that which remains the same within the differing traditions, thereby missing the vital injunction against idolatry that characterizes monotheistic thought: the prohibition of images, i.e., the lack upon which an individual or grouping is predicated. Hence Lacan would refer instead to religion 'in the true sense of the term—not of a desiccated, methodologised religion, pushed back into the distant past of a primitive form of thought, but of religion as we see practised in a still living, very vital way'.[73]

One should not be surprised, then, that when Lacan encounters a word such as 'grace' he admonishes his students to take seriously its specificity as a theological term: 'A notion as precise and articulate as grace is irreplaceable where the psychology of the act is concerned, and we don't find anything equivalent in classic academic psychology [. . .] they demand all of our attention in their own register and mode of expression.'[74]

And this is taken a step further in regard to psychoanalysis itself. For Lacan, psychoanalysis should pay attention to its register of expression. If, as Freud argued, the Egyptian Moses was murdered by the Hebrews he forced into exile, the memory of which was to enter a period of latency, only 'brought to light' in

---

[69] See also *Seminar* xvi, 15.169.

[70] See William Richardson, 'Psychoanalysis and the Being-question', in *Psychiatry and the Humanities: Interpreting Lacan*, vi, ed. J. Smith and W. Kerrigan (London: Yale University Press, 1983), 139–60.

[71] Lacan, *Seminar* xvi, 4.6.69.   [72] *Seminar* vii, 175.

[73] *Seminar* xi, 7.   [74] *Seminar* vii, 171.

the 'murder of Christ',[75] then Freudian psychoanalysis may be said to work within a 'Christocentric' framework.[76] And perhaps it is for this reason that Lacan would admonish his students to 'take the phrases of the Evangelists literally; if you don't it's obvious you won't understand anything'.[77]

Lacan's anti-positivism is clearly indebted to Alexandre Koyré's master-piece, *From a Closed to an Infinite World*.[78] Koyré's book fundamentally challenged many of the positivist assumptions of historiographers of science, principally the assumption that science involved a progressive unfolding of given truths, such that given a particular theory, one could always look back to discern its embryonic beginnings. Rather, in the manner now associated with Thomas Kuhn, one must understand the way knowledge works within a given paradigm—the sets of metaphysical relations which allow knowledge to work the way it does. Hence Koyré's contention, that the 'rise and growth of experimental science is not the source, but, on the contrary, the result of the new *theoretical*, that is, the new *metaphysical* approach to nature that forms the content of the scientific revolution of the seventeenth century'.[79]

On one level, Koyré's thought helps Lacan frame his contestation with the psychoanalytic institutes. Lacan is critical of the empiricist (behavioural psychology) and positivist (Jungian) assumptions at work. The former fails to take the symbolic into account; the latter, as Dylan Evans points out, wants to restore 'a subject gifted with depths', a subject with some direct, archetypal access to knowledge'.[80] On another level, it should be noted, that Koyré's influence also goes some way to explaining why Lacan thought it important to engage with theology above and beyond any particular identification. If psychoanalysis was to be fundamentally advanced, then one must attend first and foremost to the metaphysical/theological paradigm within which such a science is predetermined. And for this very reason, it does not quite do to ask what theology looks like after Lacan; rather, what is the shape of theology which allows for Lacanian psychoanalysis to take root in the first place?

From this perspective, Lacan's return to Freud might be read as one in a succession of '*retours*', not simply a return to the founding father, Freud, who was becoming increasingly left by the wayside of the developing sciences, but rather, in the spirit of *ressourcement*, a renewal of the received interpretation achieved through careful scrutiny of the historical sources, which not only testified to a period of intensity within the tradition, but redefined the nature of tradition itself—no longer the mere transmission of historical fact or

[75] Lacan, *Seminar* vii, 174.   [76] *Seminar* vii, 176.   [77] *Seminar* i, 154.
[78] Alexandre Koyré, *From a Closed to an Infinite World* (Radford: Wilder Publications, 2008).
[79] Koyré, *Newtonian Studies* (London: Chapman Hall, 1968), 6.
[80] Dylan Evans, 'Science and Truth', in *The Symptom 10*, available at <http://www.lacan.com/thesymptom/?p=59>.

revealed truth, but a repetition of the past non-identically and in different circumstances, thereby rendering it a lived tradition. Indeed, Michel de Certeau, a student and collaborator of de Lubac, and one of Lacan's inner circle, appears to make precisely this point: 'The transformation [of psychoanalysis] consists in rethinking, in terms which are no longer those of the past, the return of religious history.'[81]

In a recent paper, 'Improvisations on *Rerum Novarum*', Jacques-Alain Miller, Lacan's son-in-law and the principal authority on Lacan, refers back to the 'epoch of the *Syllabus*—the epoch of the "No!" and "the epoch of *Rerum Novarum*"'—recalling the revolution caused in the Catholic Church by *Rerum Novarum*, a 'mutation [that] permitted the Church to multiply its actions in direction of the working class' as a model for renewal within psychoanalysis.[82]

Citing the role played by Marc Sangnier, who helped create the first circle of left-wing social Catholics, Miller gives special mention to Sangnier's granddaughter, now a member of the *École de la Cause freudienne*. Why the link, if not to historically root the development of Lacanian psychoanalysis within the mileau of the wider Catholic renaissance?

TOWARDS A CONCLUSION: CATHOLICISM AND THE RETURN OF PSYCHOANALYSIS

In his address to the Rome Congress of the International Association of Applied Psychology, 1958, Pope Pius XII took the view that, in theory, any analytical system was acceptable to Catholics, given it did not contradict in any way the basic principles of Catholic philosophy and natural law.[83] In the remainder of his address Pius undertakes an exposition of what constitutes more precisely a Catholic psychological account of personality, the moral obligations of the psychologist, and more fundamentality the moral principles related to the human personality and to psychology. Much of his exposition concerns the need on the part of theories of personality to address metaphysical considerations of the human person and his/her ultimate end, along with moral responsibility in the employment of experimental psychology (prompted by the advent and use of truth serums). However, in approaching the psychological personality, Pius considers that the opinions of the

---

[81] Michel de Certeau, 'Lacan: An Ethics of Speech', *Representations*, 3 (1983), 21–39 (33).

[82] Jacques-Alain Miller, 'Improvisation on *Rerum Novarum*', available at <http://www.lacanianreview.com.br/n1/artigos2.asp#>.

[83] 'Applied Psychology: Address of His Holiness Pope Pius XII to the Rome Congress of the International Association of Applied Psychology' (10 April 1958), *AAS* 50 (1958), 268–82. ET available at <http://www.papalencyclicals.net/Pius12/P12APPSY.HTM>.

theologian and the psychologist meet on many points. He gives as his principle case the 'Universality of the "I"':

> The individual, insofar as he is a unity and indivisible totality, constitutes a unique and universal center of being and of action, an 'I' which has self-control and is the master of itself. This 'I' is the same in all psychic functions and remains the same despite the passage of time.[84]

Pius's privileging of the 'I' in this regard assumes the then prevailing ego-psychology as the basis for comparison: the *ego* shall stamp out the *id*, mastering and controlling desire. In this way the perduring nature of scholastic metaphysics was written, as it were, directly into the ego:

> The universality of the 'I' in extent and duration applies particularly to the causal bond which links it to its spiritual activities. This universal and permanent 'I', under the influence of internal or external causes consciously perceived or implicitly accepted, but always by free choice, acquires a definite attitude, and a permanent character, both in its interior being and in its external behavior.[85]

The human subject for Pius is the subject 'gifted with depths', the subject of substance, not the subject of language; the subject of imaginary wholeness rather than symbolic lack; the narcissistic 'I' which misrecognizes itself in an eternal image of promised totality. Yet as Lacan understood, the subject is not whole but split in paradoxical ways precisely by virtue of language, such that if the Holy Land is on the side of the real [*réel*], then ego-identity amounts to an aggressive idolatry.

Because Pius fails to take into account the critique of ego-psychology, unleashed by Lacan some eleven years prior,[86] he affirms, albeit implicitly, a particular version of the extrinicist model of nature/grace in which the *ego* or the Universal 'I' sits on the side of grace, mastering the *id* on the side of nature. This is not grace perfecting nature but an extrinsicist grace bringing an unruly and sinful nature into line. Yet as I have argued, this was precisely the model being concurrently criticized by the *nouvelle théologie* and which subsequently influenced Lacan's reception of Aquinas. In short, if we are to begin again to rethink the question of a Christian psychology, might we not begin with Lacan, and hence precisely in the spirit of *ressourcement*?

Referring to psychoanalysis forty-eight years later in 1998,[87] Pope John Paul II's comments were directed less towards the need for a systematic

---

[84] 'Applied Psychology'.   [85] 'Applied Psychology'.

[86] Lacan, 'The Mirror Stage as Formative of the *I* Function as Revealed in Psychoanalytic Experience', in *Écrits*, 75–81/94–100.

[87] John Paul II, 'Message to the Participants in the Course on the Internal Forum Organized by the Apostolic Penitentiary' (20 March 1998), § 5. Available at <http://www.vatican.va/holy_father/john_paul_ii/speeches/1998/march/documents/hf_jp-ii_spe_19980320_cardeal-baum_en.html>.

meta-psychology which took God and natural law into account, than towards priests who might be tempted to transform the sacrament of penance into psychoanalysis or psychotherapy. What was at stake was the role of priestly confessors, especially in the discernment of those going forward for the priesthood. Confessors have

> the very serious obligation of making every effort to dissuade from going on to the priesthood those who in confession demonstrate that they lack the necessary virtues (this particularly applies to mastering chastity, which is indispensable for the commitment to celibacy), the necessary psychological balance or sufficient maturity of judgment.[88]

John Paul II's words, unheeded in some quarters, and arriving too late, serve nonetheless as a reminder:

> The confessional is not and cannot be an alternative to the psychoanalyst's or psychotherapist's office. Nor can one expect the sacrament of Penance to heal truly pathological conditions. The confessor is not a healer or a physician in the technical sense of the term; in fact, if the condition of the penitent seems to require medical care, the confessor should not deal with the matter himself, but should send the penitent to competent and honest professionals.[89]

Psychoanalysis has an expertise: unconscious desire. So while we might concur with Pius that by its own merit psychoanalysis cannot constitute properly speaking a theology, we are reminded by John Paul II that theology is not psychoanalysis. This is not to affirm a simple opposition in which grace and nature, theology and psychoanalysis, cannot paradoxically coincide. In Lacan's work we find neither a theological psychology, nor a positivist alternative. Rather, we find a psychology which cannot be understood without taking into account theological and metaphysical presuppositions. In this regard, the articulations of Lacan, fashioned by a Catholic sensibility, can surely contribute to our comprehension of the psyche, its defensive, destructive, and creative workings. Is it not the case also then that the more we return (*retour*) to the vitality of the theological sources which underpin psychoanalysis, the more we return to the fundamentals of psychoanalysis?

---

[88] 'To the participants', § 5.   [89] 'To the participants', § 5.

29

Expanding Catholicity through Ecumenicity in the Work of Yves Congar: *Ressourcement*, Receptive Ecumenism, and Catholic Reform[1]

Paul D. Murray

The ecumenical dialogue has...compelled me to become more Christian and more catholic.[2]

[E]cumenism...by its very nature, is a movement towards accomplishment and plenitude....the purpose being to surmount a complex of conventional ideas which, far from being in the true Catholic 'tradition', represent its stagnation and attenuation. Yet, painful as such an effort is, it soon reaps its reward in the expansion of our own catholicity and in countless discoveries and enrichments.[3]

INTRODUCTION

Any intentionally comprehensive treatment of *ressourcement* would be incomplete without attending to the movement's decisive contribution to the

[1] Thanks are due to Gabriel Flynn for his advice and warm collegial conversation in the course of preparing this essay. He has been involved in receptive ecumenism (see n. 29 below) from its inception and attended both the relevant international conferences (January 2006 and January 2009); he also contributed to the lead volume (see nn. 22 and 29 below); and himself hosted a conference on the theme at Mater Dei Institute, Dublin in the summer of 2007, the papers from which were subsequently published in *LS*, 33 (2008). Thanks are also due to Ben Kautzer and Patricia Kelly for help with sourcing some of the references. An extended version of this chapter first appeared in *IJST*, 13 (2011), 249–378.
[2] Yves Congar, 'Ecumenical Experience and Conversion: A Personal Testimony', trans. Beatrice Morton, in Robert C. Mackie and Charles C. West (eds.), *The Sufficiency of God: Essays on the Ecumenical Hope in Honour of W. A. Visser 't Hooft* (London: SCM Press, 1963), 71–87 (71).
[3] Congar, 'The Call to Ecumenism and the Work of the Holy Spirit' (1950), in *Dialogue Between Christians: Catholic Contributions to Ecumenism*, henceforth *DBC*, trans. Philip Loretz, SJ (London/Dublin: Geoffrey Chapman, 1966 [1964]), 100–6 (104–5).

articulation of a Catholic theology of ecumenism, particularly in the person and work of Yves Congar (1904–95), lauded as 'the father of Roman Catholic ecumenism'.[4] There are, accordingly, five main sections to this chapter. First, attention is given to the basic fact of a relationship going beyond mere coincidence between *ressourcement* and the emergence of a Catholic ecumenism. Second, a key critical issue is identified concerning the inner coherence of Congar's ecumenical work and indication given of the reading pursued here, which finds in him a developing articulation of what has come to be referred to as receptive ecumenism. In turn, the third, fourth, and fifth sections are given over respectively to close readings of Congar's three great works of ecumenical theology: his groundbreaking 1937 study, *Chrétiens désunis*; his 1964 collection, *Chrétiens en dialogue*; and his 1982 exploration, *Diversités et Communion*.[5]

RESSOURCEMENT AND CATHOLIC ECUMENISM

The most intense period of *ressourcement* activity, the 1930s–60s, largely coincides with the period during which Catholicism began again, after the shock waves of the Modernist crisis,[6] to open to serious ecumenical engagement—in some ways picking up where the great nineteenth-century forerunner to *ressourcement*, Johann Adam Möhler (1796–1838), had left off.[7] Whilst not exclusively so, *ressourcement* energy was central to this endeavour, pre-eminently so that of Yves Congar.

In autobiographical reminiscences, Congar makes clear that his ecumenical work was rooted in a very definite sense of 'call' immediately prior to ordination in 1929, preceding and shaping all of his constructive theological work, and itself prepared for by the warm ecumenical circumstances of his early life.[8]

---

[4] W. A. Visser 't Hooft, *Memoirs* (London/Philadelphia PA: SCM Press/Westminster Press, 1973), 319, cited in Flynn, 'Cardinal Congar's Ecumenism. An "Ecumenical Ethics" for Reconciliation?', *LS*, 28 (2003), 311–25 (312). For further detail on Congar's life and work, see Ch. 14 in this volume.

[5] Congar, *Chrétiens désunis: principes d'un 'œcuménisme' Catholique* (Paris: Cerf, 1937), ET, *Divided Christendom: A Study of the Problem of Reunion*, trans. M. A. Bousfield (London: Geoffrey Bles, 1939), henceforth *DC*; *Chrétiens en dialogue: contributions catholique à l'Œcuménisme* (Paris: Cerf, 1964), ET, *DBC*; *Diversités et Communion: dossier historique et conclusion théologique* (Paris: Cerf, 1982), ET, *Diversity and Communion*, trans. John Bowden (London: SCM Press, 1984), henceforth *D&C*.

[6] See Gerard Loughlin's chapter in this volume.

[7] On Möhler and *ressourcement*, see Hans Boersma, Nouvelle Théologie *and Sacramental Ontology: A Return to Mystery* (Oxford: Oxford University Press, 2009), 41–52. For Congar's use of Möhler, see further below.

[8] Congar, *Fifty Years of Catholic Theology: Conversations with Yves Congar*, ed. Bernard Lauret, trans. John Bowden (London: SCM Press, 1988 [1987]) 77, 79; also 'Preface. The call

He was subsequently allowed to make a pair of study trips to Germany over consecutive summers in 1930 and 1931 that enabled him to engage closely with Lutheranism.[9] Thereafter, he continued to extend his circle of ecumenical friends. Following many shorter pieces, his first monograph, *Chrétiens désunis*, was devoted, as the French subtitle has it, to the 'principles of a Catholic ecumenism'—a work without precedent.

He was similarly central to various practical initiatives aimed at preparing the ground for Catholic participation in major ecumenical processes such as the 'Life and Work' and 'Faith and Order' Conferences of 1937 and 1948; endeavours frustrated by the refusal of official sanction.[10] Nor were the frustrations confined to practical matters but extended to restrictions on his ecumenical writing also.[11]

Whilst such frustrations led him to a 'turning-point'[12] that, at one level, was a move away from an explicit ecumenical focus and onto, ostensibly, more internal Catholic ecclesiological matters, such as the theology of the laity and the dynamics of Christian tradition, Congar was always clear that it represented not the relinquishing of his ecumenical concern but its focusing and deepening; not a turning away but its consequent and appropriate means of pursuit, 'Two things intimately intertwined.'[13] As he put it when reflecting back in 1963, 'It very soon occurred to me that ecumenism is not a speciality and that it presupposes a movement of conversion and reform coextensive with the whole life of all communions.'[14] Accordingly, he laid down the principles for this in his next great work, *Vraie et fausse réforme dans l'Église* (1950), and proceeded to pursue the agenda articulated there through the aforementioned particular studies, as also myriad others.[15]

Equally, for all the indisputable importance of Congar's *ressourcement*-shaped energy in promoting fresh ecumenical openings within Catholicism, it is important to acknowledge that this was neither an exclusive nor an unprecedented influence.

More or less contemporaneous with and complementary to the theological work of *ressourcement*, Congar acknowledges the 'decisive' spiritually-oriented

---

and the Quest 1929–1963' (1963), *DBC*, 1–51 (2–4); 'Letter from Father Yves Congar, OP', trans. Ronald John Zawilla, OP, *Theology Digest*, 32 (1985), 213–16 (213); 'Reflections on Being a Theologian', *New Blackfriars*, 62 (1981), 405–9 (405).

[9] *DBC*, 5–7.

[10] *DBC*, 26–8, 36–8.

[11] *DBC*, 35–6; compare 'The Catholic Church and the Ecumenical Movement on the Eve of the Amsterdam Assembly' (1947), *DBC*, 71–99.

[12] *DBC*, 38.

[13] Congar, 'Reflections', 405.

[14] *DBC*, 21; also 31, 83.

[15] See *True and False Reform in the Church*, trans. Paul Philibert (Collegeville MN: Liturgical Press, 2011). For a magisterial analysis, see Flynn, *Yves Congar's Vision of the Church in a World of Unbelief* (Aldershot/Burlington VT: Ashgate, 2004), 146–211.

contribution of the 'saintly Abbé Couturier' of Lyons (1881–1953). From the mid-1930s, Couturier single-handedly transformed the Church Unity Octave from a week of 'prayer of Catholics for the "return" of *the others*' into a genuine 'week of universal prayer for the unity of Christians', focused on the need for divinely-initiated conversion on all sides"'.[16] With this, in 1937 Courturier founded the influential Groupe des Dombes, which—rooted in his principle of 'spiritual ecumenism'—in many respects represents an unofficial precursor to later bilateral dialogues and an exemplar of the ethic of ecumenical dialogue for which Congar also called.[17]

Prior to either Courturier or Congar and standing, perhaps, as the first significant Catholic opening to ecumenical engagement since Möhler, are the remarkable Malines Conversations of 1921–5.[18] Initiated and led by Cardinal Mercier with, at least initially, tacit Roman approval, these were focused on the possibility of corporate reunion between Rome and the Church of England and gave rise to the evocative hope for a model of unity that would allow the Church of England to be 'united [with], not absorbed' by Rome; a hope that has resonance with Congar's later ecumenical writings.[19]

Allowing for these caveats, it nevertheless remains that the period of subterranean *ressourcement* activity in the middle part of the twentieth century largely coincides with the initial phase of significant, if informal, Catholic ecumenical openings. With this, the very point at which *ressourcement* theology was welcomed in from the cold after-effects of Pius XII's 1950 encyclical, *Humani Generis*, and given officially sanctioned shaping power at Vatican II coincides exactly with Catholicism's decisive entry into the modern ecumenical stream with the Council's groundbreaking 'Decree on Ecumenism', *Unitatis Redintegratio*.[20] Taken together with the 'Dogmatic Constitution on the Church', *Lumen Gentium, Unitatis Redintegratio* represents a remarkable transformation in Catholic self-understanding relative to the other Christian traditions.

[16] *DBC*, 10, 19–21; also 82–3; 'L'abbé Paul Couturier, ses intuitions, vingt-sept ans après' (1980), in Congar, *Essais œcuméniques: Le mouvement, les hommes, les problèmes* (Paris: Le centurion, 1984), 132–8.

[17] See Catherine E. Clifford, *The Groupe des Dombes: A Dialogue of Conversion* (New York: Peter Lang, 2005); also Joseph Famerée, 'The Contribution of the *Groupe des Dombes* to Ecumenism: Past Achievements and Future Challenges', *LS*, 33 (2008), 99–116; compare Congar, *D&C*, 138–9. For Congar on dialogue, see 'First, Understand' (1935), *DBC*, 296–8; also *DC*, 262; 'Les étapes du dialogue œcuménique', in Congar, *Aspects de l'œcuménisme* (Bruxelles/Paris: La Pensée Catholique/Office Général du Livre, 1962), 7–25; 'Introduction. Dialogue, Principle of Ecumenical Work, Disposition of the Human Understanding' (1963), *DBC*, 53–68.

[18] See Bernard Barlow, *A Brother Knocking at the Door: The Malines Conversations, 1921–1925* (Norwich: Canterbury, 1996).

[19] See *D&C*, 92; compare the more cautious *DC*, 164–8, 286–9, suspecting the aspiration for corporate reunion of downplaying the need for doctrinal reconciliation and ecclesial-structural conversion (291).

[20] See the chapters by Joseph A. Komonchak and Gerald O'Collins in this volume; compare *DBC*, 44; 'Letter', 215; 'Reflections', 405.

Where Catholic thinking had erstwhile been shaped—as robustly articulated in Pius XI's 1928 encyclical, *Mortalium Animos*—by the assumption of an unqualified identity between the Church of Christ and the Catholic Church and consequent espousal of the need for a one-way return of separated Christians to Rome,[21] the Council teaches more subtly that the Church of Christ 'subsists in the Catholic Church' (*LG* § 8). Whilst all the essential elements of the Church of Christ really are present in the Catholic Church, none of them are present in either perfect or exclusive form—with the possible exception, in the latter regard, of unity which is understood as needing to be lived out through communion with the See of Rome.[22] On the contrary, the Catholic Church, itself always in need of purification, *semper purificanda*, can properly appreciate and receive from the aspects of catholicity in other traditions which may be being lived there more adequately, in part, than within the Catholic Church.[23] In place of a one-way ecumenism of return to Rome—'You-come-in-ism'—here we have indicated an ecumenism of mutual growth towards full communion.

The correspondence traced here between *ressourcement* energy and Catholic ecumenical activity and their mutual flowering at Vatican II is not a matter of mere coincidence but of mutual implication in at least four ways.

First, as Congar frequently notes, the return to the sources as a means of overcoming the ossified categories of neo-scholasticism and counter-Reformation polemic and of opening Catholicism again to richer, more dynamic ways of understanding was a necessary prerequisite without which serious Catholic ecumenical activity would have remained impossible.[24] Second, the very process of *ressourcement*, of engaging afresh the sources, itself implies ecumenical scholarly interaction, most obviously with the Russian Orthodox émigré community in Paris but also with Protestant theologians.[25] Third, the characteristic scholarly ecumenical activity of overcoming distorted

---

[21] See Pope Pius XI, *Mortalium Animos*. Encyclical Letter on Religious Unity (6th January 1928), *AAS* 20 (1928), 5–16, § 10. ET available at: <http://www.vatican.va/holy_father/pius_xi/encyclicals/documents/hf_p-xi_enc_19280106_mortalium-animos_en.html>.

[22] See *LG* § 8, § 15, § 16; also *UR* § 3, § 4. For some of the debate around *subsistit*, see Murray, 'Receptive Ecumenism and Catholic Learning—Establishing the Agenda', in Murray (ed.), *Receptive Ecumenism and the Call to Catholic Learning: Exploring a Way for Contemporary Ecumenism* (Oxford: Oxford University Press, 2008), henceforth *RE&CCL*, 5–25 (22–3 n. 34); also Walter Kasper, *That They May All Be One: The Call to Unity Today* (London: Burns & Oates, 2004), henceforth *TTMABO*, 50–74 (65–8).

[23] See *LG* § 8; *UR* § 6–7, and *UR* § 4; compare Kasper, *TTMABO*, 17, 67; also n. 32 below.

[24] E.g., he writes of his 'conviction of the inseparable connection between the massive process of denudation which ecumenism demanded and the ecclesiological, pastoral, biblical and liturgical movements'. *DBC*, 21, 83; 'The Ecumenical Approach' (1957), *DBC*, 116–31 (121, 126); also *DC*, 272. Perhaps the single most significant example of this re-sourcing of Catholicism is Henri de Lubac's 1938 great work of that title: *Catholicism: Christ and the Common Destiny of Man*, trans. Lancelot C. Sheppard and Elizabeth Englund, OCD (San Francisco, CA: Ignatius, 1988).

[25] See *DBC*, 7–8, 17. See also the chapters by John Webster and Andrew Louth in this volume.

understandings of other Christian traditions by seeking both to understand them aright and to re-examine areas of historic disagreement is itself, as Congar notes, an act of historical *ressourcement*.[26] Fourth, ecumenism is an agent of *ressourcement* in a further sense, inasmuch as it offers the possibility of expanding and deepening the catholicity of any given tradition in light of the particular dimensions of catholicity lived well in other traditions.[27]

IN SEARCH OF COHERENCE IN CONGAR'S ECUMENICAL VISION

The corpus of Congar's writings stretches from within years of Catholicism's earliest openings to the ecumenical movement, to well over twenty years of mature reflection on the new possibilities and fresh challenges following Catholicism's formal ecumenical engagement at Vatican II. It is, then, hardly surprising that there are observable differences of tone—between, for example, the characteristic 'Catholic dogmatism of the time' in *Chrétiens désunis* to the much more 'open, interrogative' character of *Diversités et Communion*[28] —as also more conceptual and substantive developments across this period.

A certain amount of debate has focused here on the contrast between the central role accorded to catholicity in *Chrétiens désunis* compared with the corresponding emphasis placed on 'diversity' and 'plurality' in *Diversités et Communion*.[29] What is at issue here? Are we just dealing with a change in terminology in order to explore the same basic reality in developed terms? Or is there something more significant going on? Does the change represent the abandoning of catholicity and its distinctively Catholic vision of ecumenism in favour of a quite different perspective?

For Jossua, it is a matter of both deep continuity and 'significant evolution' that results in a 'truly dissimilar' (*vraiment dissemblable*) understanding of the search for unity, of which, it should be noted, Jossua basically approves.[30] The

[26] E.g. *DBC*, 122–3; also 45, 83, 129; 'The Encounter Between Christian Confessions—Yesterday and Today' (1958), *DBC*, 135–59 (151–3, 155); 'Historical Considerations on the Schism of the Sixteenth Century in Relation to the Catholic Realization of Unity' (1959), *DBC*, 333–57 (357); *D&C*, 142.

[27] *DBC*, 105.

[28] Jean-Pierre Jossua, OP, 'L'œuvre œcuménique du Père Congar', *Études*, 357 (1982), 543–55 (543); my translation.

[29] See Jossua, 'L'œuvre œcuménique', 552–3; compare Flynn, 'Cardinal Congar's Ecumenism, 313, 321–3; *Yves Congar's Vision of the Church*, 139–45, 219; 'Receptive Ecumenism and Catholic Learning—Reflections in Dialogue with Yves Congar and B. C. Butler', in *RE&CCL*, 399–412 (401–2, 405); also Famerée, '"Chrétiens désunis" du P. Congar 50 ans après', *NRT*, 110 (1988), 666–86.

[30] Jossua, 'L'œuvre œcuménique', 553.

continuity lies in the 'key idea' of 'a fundamental polarity between unity and internal richness'.[31] The dissimilarity lies in the respective concepts used to articulate this 'internal richness' and the very different understandings of unity they suggest.[32] Where 'catholicity', at least in the formulation given to it in *Chrétiens désunis,* 'is presented as encompassing', even 'closed', 'diversity' and 'plurality' are presented as 'open', practically to the point of bursting.[33] Intertwined with this change of tone and conceptuality is a fundamental shift in Congar's thinking about the aspiration for Christian unity.

Where *Chrétiens désunis* is characterized by a strongly Christocentric view of the visible Roman Catholic Church as *the* Church of Christ *tout simple* and hence by what amounts to a gracious articulation of the ecumenism 'of return', Congar's subsequent work was characterized by a more pneumatological understanding of the church and corresponding 'insistence on the transcendence of the mystery aimed at'.[34] In 1937, unity 'appeared as already given in the Roman Catholic Church'.[35] Consequently, whilst Congar did not view separated Christians as having to renounce anything positive in their traditions, ecumenism was nevertheless understood as a matter of one-way 'return' to the unity that has always existed in the Roman Catholic Church. In contrast, in *Diversités et Communion,* 'in strict terms unity is conceived of as future and therefore as being sought together by Christians'.[36] The pilgrim way to unity is one that all must walk. With this, in *Diversités et Communion* Congar is quite clear that whatever unity might be, it does not represent the overcoming of all differences. Rather, 'Differences in large measure remain within a restored unity'.[37]

As noted, Jossua basically shares Congar's sense of the need for a qualitative and not just quantitative expansion of the underlying notion and reality of catholicity—of the basic issue of unified multiplicity—in the direction of a more pneumatological understanding of the church.[38] In contrast, however, Flynn is considerably less sanguine about the merits of Congar's later ecumenical thinking. He finds, not evolution sustained by deep continuity, but contrast to the point of potential deleterious contradiction and even diminution. His concerns essentially relate to what he finds to be Congar's overly loose use of the notion of there appropriately being an abiding and significant diversity within any desired unity of the traditions; a concern particularly

---

[31] Jossua, 'L'œuvre œcuménique', 552.
[32] Jossua, 'L'œuvre œcuménique', 552.
[33] Jossua, 'L'œuvre œcuménique', 552.
[34] Jossua, 'L'œuvre œcuménique', 553.
[35] Jossua, 'L'œuvre œcuménique', 553.
[36] Jossua, 'L'œuvre œcuménique', 553.
[37] Jossua, 'L'œuvre œcuménique', 552.
[38] For the distinction between qualitative ('the fullness of God in Christ and the Spirit') and quantitative ('universal extension in time and space') understandings of catholicity, see Avery Dulles, SJ, *The Catholicity of the Church* (Oxford: Oxford University Press, 1987), particularly 30–47, 68–105.

focused on Congar's employment of the Lutheran-coined concept of 'recon-ciled diversity' in which Flynn hears the potential for significantly unreconciled divergences being prematurely placed alongside each other in an unstable and unreal supposed unity.[39]

Flynn's contention is that 'the shift in [Congar's] ecumenism from catholicity to pluralism/diversities entails the recognition of the division of Christendom as permanent and irreversible'.[40] Congar has succumbed 'to the temptation to accept a mere plurality of views' and thereby anomalously 'endorses an ecumenism which [he] warned against in *Chrétiens désunis*'.[41] For Flynn the solution, contrary to Congar's incautious flirtation with the problematic notion of 'reconciled diversity', is 'to formulate an ecumenical concept of catholicity that is capable of sustaining differences while also withstanding the movement towards reductionism'.[42]

For its own part, the reading conducted here concurs with this call of Flynn for, as I would express it, a sufficiently rich, robust, and dynamic understand-ing of catholicity as to be able to deal fruitfully both with the challenges posed by the continuing reality of unreconciled diversity and with the abiding importance of the proper aspiration for an intensified, enriched, and expanded unified multiplicity. It differs from Flynn's analysis, however, both in finding more positive possibilities in the notion of 'reconciled diversity' and in finding in Congar's mature work an appropriate means of seeking—perhaps without final resolution—to discern and to live the catholicity of the church as configured communion. Indeed, rather than viewing Congar's later work in terms of a radical departure from *Chrétiens désunis*, it is here viewed, for all its exploratory nature, as being of abiding significance and as representing a decisive forerunner of receptive ecumenism; itself, in many respects, a 'new name for some old ways of thinking'.[43] Three key reasons prompt this reading.

---

[39] On the origins of 'reconciled diversity', see *D&C*, 149.

[40] Flynn, 'Receptive Ecumenism', 402.

[41] Flynn, *Yves Congar's Vision of the Church*, 219 and 'Receptive Ecumenism', 402, referencing *DC*, 101; also 'Cardinal Congar's Ecumenism', 323.

[42] Flynn, 'Receptive Ecumenism', 409.

[43] Building on the relevant conciliar principles (see n. 21) and John Paul II's remarkable extension of these in his 1995 encyclical *Ut Unum Sint*, into an invitation to other Christian traditions to help re-imagine Petrine ministry, receptive ecumenism represents a fresh strategy, at the heart of which is the conviction that further progress will only be possible if the traditions switch from asking what their respective 'others' need to learn from them, to asking instead what they themselves can and must learn. As such, it seeks to embed a process of ecclesial conversion and a principle of 'dynamic integrity' at the heart of Christian ecumenical engagement. See *RE&CCL*; also Murray, 'Receptive Ecumenism and Ecclesial Learning: Receiving Gifts for Our Needs', *LS*, 33 (2008), 30–45. For Pope John Paul II's encyclical, see *Ut Unum Sint* 'Encyclical Letter on Commitment to Christian Unity' (25 May 1995), *AAS* 87 (1995), 921–82, particularly § 95–6. ET available at: <http://www.vatican.va/holy_father/john_paul_ii/encyclicals/documents/hf_jp-ii_enc_25051995_ut-unum-sint_en.html>. For the phrase 'a new name for some old ways of thinking', see William James, 'Pragmatism. A New Name for Some Old Ways of Thinking' (1907), in *The Works of William James*, I., ed. Frederick H. Burkhardt (Cambridge MA: Harvard

First and most pedestrian is that I believe the relevant texts themselves suggest such a reading: whilst there are unarguable differences in conceptual framework, tone, and even ecclesial and ecumenical vision across the writings, it is also possible to identify early, unformed anticipations of what will develop to become key later principles. As Jossua notes, far from Congar's relinquishing of the strongly Christocentric ecclesiology and catholicity of *Chrétiens désunis* being a late aberration, it was already clearly indicated in his self-critical reflections in *Chrétiens en dialogue*.[44] In turn, I am suggesting we can push further back and find initial notes—albeit as minor themes, contrary motions—even within *Chrétiens désunis*.

The second and most significant reason is that Congar himself understood his work in terms of deep continuity. For example, in the 'Preface' to *Essais œcuméniques*, having endorsed Jossua's identification of the key conceptual change from catholicity to diversity and pluralism, he immediately comments: 'And yet I have the feeling of having changed neither the faith nor the Church. I have tried hard to live my Catholic fidelity [in relation] to the two planes of the absolute and the historically relative...'[45] Allied with such a claim would be various passages in *Chrétiens en dialogue* where, in the course of reflecting back on what he considers himself to have been up to in *Chrétiens désunis*, Congar emphasizes the importance of points that might be missed on an initial reading of the work.[46]

The third, most speculative, reason for arguing for an evolving continuity of concern amidst variation of articulation and approach in Congar's ecumenical writings relates to the role of Möhler's work in his thought. As noted, from the early period of Congar's career onwards, Möhler was a key influence. From the 1930s alone we have five essays devoted to his work, some expository, others exploring Möhler's constructive significance for contemporary concerns.[47] In this period also we know that Congar wished to start the Unam Sanctam series with a new translation of Möhler's great ecclesiological work, *Die Einheit in der Kirche* (1825),[48] but was unable to do so due to delays with the translation.

University Press, 1975). For the resonance between Congar's work and receptive ecumenism, see nn. 56, 76, 77, 80, 88, 89, 95, 105.

[44] See *DBC*, 24: 89, 96.

[45] *Essais œcuméniques*, 6, my translation.

[46] See *DBC*, 21, 31, 83.

[47] See 'La pensée de Möhler et l'ecclésiologie orthodoxe', *Irénikon*, 12 (1935), 321–9; 'La signification œcuménique de l'oeuvre de Möhler', *Irénikon*, 15 (1938), 113–30; 'Sur l'évolution et l'interprétation de la pensée de Möhler', *RSPT*, 27 (1938), 205–12; 'L'Esprit des Pères d'après Moehler', *Supplément à la 'Vie Spirituelle'*, 55 (1938), 1–25; 'L'hérésie, déchirement de l'unité', in Pierre Chaillet (ed.), *L'Église est une: hommage à Moehler* (Paris: Bloud & Gay, 1939), 255–69. I am grateful to Flynn, *Yves Congar's Vision of the Church*, for many of these references.

[48] ET, Möhler, *Unity in the Church or the Principle of Catholicism: Presented in the Spirit of the Church Fathers of the First Three Centuries*, ed. and trans. Peter C. Erb (Washington DC: Catholic University of America Press, 1996), henceforth *Einheit*.

Reflecting back in 1963 he writes: 'This masterpiece, imperfect like so many masterpieces, nevertheless represented remarkably well the character and the spirit of the sort of material I hoped to supply.'[49] In turn, there are thirteen references in *Chrétiens en dialogue*, with an entire essay inspired by Möhler's *Symbolik*.[50] For its own part, *Diversités et Communion* devotes a chapter to Möhler's thinking in *Einheit*, together with providing a number of other references.[51] Here, then, we have an unquestionable line of continuity of influence. It is with conviction that he could state in 1975: 'That which Möhler did in the nineteenth century has become for me an ideal by which I wanted to be inspired to guide my own thinking in the twentieth century.'[52]

Indeed, this can be pressed further, in a fashion more directly relevant to the claim for *Diversités et Communion* giving more developed articulation, in changed context and within a different conceptual framework, to principles already present in incipient form in *Chrétiens désunis*. Here the point is that the use to which *Diversités et Communion* puts Möhler's *Einheit*—the very volume by which he had placed such store in the years immediately prior to *Chrétiens désunis* but to which, interestingly, he there makes no explicit reference—is precisely to interrogate the notion of 'reconciled diversity' that Flynn finds to be so seriously divergent from *Chrétiens désunis* and to seek to give it appropriate Catholic articulation as, effectively, the kind of principle of dynamic, ecumenically oriented catholicity for which Flynn himself calls.

It is further interesting to speculate on the asymmetry between the greater part of Congar's explicit writing on Möhler being located in the earliest period of his work, whilst his most sustained constructive use in direct relation to ecclesiological, ecumenical matters occurs in his latest writings, with no explicit reference at all in *Chrétiens désunis*. This cannot be due to an increasing familiarity with and regard for Möhler. If anything the explicit level of regard and conscious influence is higher in the earlier phase of Congar's work. I suggest that the explanation lies in it having taken time and appropriate circumstance for Congar, self-confessedly neither a speculative nor a systematic theologian, to grow into realizing the full constructive ecclesiological implications of Möhler's thought, faithfully steeped as Congar was in received Catholic self-understanding and modes of thinking even whilst seeking to engage with the ecumenical challenge.

Also significant is the fact that Congar was, in his own words, an 'occasionalist' writer: he wrote in response to specific requests, needs, and circumstances and the challenges and possibilities they presented. In this regard it is

[49] *DBC*, 24.
[50] See 'The Encounter between Christian Confessions—Yesterday and Today' (1958), *DBC*, 135–59; also 3, 24, 28, 103, 169, 342, 365.
[51] See *D&C*, 149–52; also 13, 100, 129.
[52] Jean Puyo (ed.), *Une vie pour la vérité: Jean Puyo interroge le Père Congar* (Paris: Centurion, 1975), 48, cited in Boersma, Nouvelle Théologie *and Sacramental Ontology*, 42.

interesting that his work on plurality and diversity in *Diversités et Communion* was elicited in response to the changed ecclesial and ecumenical context in which he found himself and, most particularly, by the Lutheran articulation of the suggestive notion of 'reconciled diversity'. The suggestion here is that it is not that these circumstances, this conceptual frame, prompted an incoherent fresh departure in Congar's thinking as that they provided the impetus and stimulation for him to bring to fuller articulation principles and instincts that had long been part of his overall field of ecumenical concern.

So, development we should certainly look for in Congar's ecumenical writings, but a development in service of a consistent concern to articulate and live well the catholicity of the church in the ecumenical context; a development, moreover, of which we should expect to be able to find the first incipient shoots and indications in even his most dogmatically Roman Catholic of early ecumenical writings.

REARTICULATING CATHOLICITY IN LIGHT OF ECUMENICITY IN *DIVIDED CHRISTENDOM*

Although he pulls no punches in their execution, in the 'Preface' to the English edition of *Chrétiens désunis* Congar expresses his aims in eirenic terms: to help 'enthusiasts for Œcumenism to understand the Catholic position and its demands' and to encourage 'the general body of Catholics' to 'make some effort to understand the outlook and the positions of the great non-Catholic Christian bodies'.[53] The emphasis, notably, is on promoting understanding rather than correction.

Also interesting is that the historian in him prompts him to note that the analysis of the Christian traditions that these aims imply cannot be pursued successfully at the level of theological constructs and doctrinal tenets alone—a weakness, arguably, in much bilateral ecumenism—but must 'deal with the mystery of the Church not only as a fact shown by revelation but as a concrete reality...being worked out in human life'.[54] In this Congar shows himself a counter-instance to the influential claim of Nicholas M. Healy that twentieth-century ecclesiology was dominated by conceptual-theoretical modes of proceeding insufficiently rooted in the concrete realities of church life to realize their transformative intent.[55] Similarly, he here gives first indication—subsequently emphasized more clearly in various of the essays in *Chrétiens en dialogue* (see n. 103 here)—that he anticipates, to some degree at least, what

---

[53] *DC*, pp. xiii–xiv; also 136. [54] *DC*, p. xiv.
[55] See Nicholas M. Healy, *Church, World, and the Christian Life: Practical-Prophetic Ecclesiology* (Cambridge: Cambridge University Press, 2000), 3.

becomes developed as a core principle of receptive ecumenism: that critical and constructive modes of theological analysis, the traditional preserve of historical and systematic ecclesiologists, need to be held together with pragmatic-organizational and other relevant empirical modes of analysis, the traditional preserve of practical theologians and social scientists.[56]

As was indicated in discussing Jossua's and Flynn's readings, the key organizing concept in *Chrétiens désunis* is that of catholicity. Here, for all his concern to take seriously the 'concrete reality' of the church, Congar starts out with an avowedly theological perspective—essential, he would maintain, to understanding correctly the full identity of the church's concrete reality. The point is that the church is not understood aright until understood as living with, from, and towards the life of God: 'The Church is not merely *a* Society . . . but the divine *Societas* itself, the life of the Godhead reaching out to humanity and taking up humanity into itself.'[57]

In this perspective the marks of the church are not first and foremost empirical properties brought into being by the church but properties of God shared with the church: 'The oneness of the Church is a communication and extension of the oneness of God Himself.'[58] Similarly, for all the right and proper emphasis on the quantitative dimension of the church's catholicity—on geographical and temporal extension[59]—it is the qualitative dimension of catholicity—the church's sharing in the universality, the 'gathering together in one (*unus, vertere*)',[60] of God in Christ—that is the prior, 'necessary cause of the former'.[61] This God-derived, God-impelled, God-oriented catholicity places an intrinsic dynamism at the very heart of the church in the form of 'the capacity of her principles of unity to assimilate, fulfil and raise to God in oneness with Him all men and every man and every human value'.[62] As such, 'The very idea of Catholicity involves the relation of diversity to unity and of unity to diversity.'[63] In as much, however, as this already 'exists in Christ as in its first Principle', the church's always consequential role is to make this 'manifest' and 'explicit' in the created, historical order not to bring it into being *de nuovo*.[64]

The dominant way in which Congar teases out what this consequential dynamic of the church's catholicity means in practice is in relation to geographical and cultural diversity. He speaks, for example, of 'the necessity for the Church to conform exteriorly to this differentiation and dispersion of

---

[56] *RE&CCL*, pp. xi, xiv–xv, and 'Part IV. The Pragmatics of Receptive Ecumenical Learning', 255–356; also P. D. Murray and M. J. Guest, 'On Discerning the Living Truth of the Church: Theological and Sociological Reflections on *Receptive Ecumenism and the Local Church*' in Chris Scharen (ed.), *Ecclesiology and Ethnography* (Grand Rapids, MI: Eerdmans, forthcoming).

[57] *DC*, 48–9.   [58] *DC*, 48.   [59] *DC*, 93–4.

[60] *DC*, 93.   [61] *DC*, 94; also 95; compare de Lubac, *Catholicism*, 49–51.

[62] *DC*, 94–5; also 97, 98, 101, 114, 252.   [63] *DC*, 99; also 43.

[64] *DC*, 96–7; also 98–9.

humanity'.[65] Again, 'Granted that Christ is brought to mankind *by men*, He cannot be truly made our own unless He is preached to every man in his own tongue and by his own kind. ... Therefore in every country the Church has its own background and customs, its own clergy and institutions.'[66] This embracing of 'all peoples' cannot be a matter of 'absorbing the nations and reducing them to a least common denominator' but through their 'inclusion': 'supranationalization' rather than 'denationalization'.[67] In this regard he anticipates subsequent initiatives to internationalize the Roman curia by suggesting that the cultural diversity intrinsic to catholicity needs also to be reflected 'in the central organs of unity'.[68]

At other times—and of more direct relevance to current concerns—he reflects on catholic diversity in the context of there being different spiritual 'temperaments' and traditions. In terms, for example, that could have been lifted straight from Möhler, he refers to the contrasting Pauline and Johannine traditions and draws from this the notion of there being 'in the Church different spiritual families, each "spirituality" showing varying facets of a common life in Christ'.[69] Like Möhler, however, he insists that each of these traditions needs to be 'corrected by' and held 'in communion with' each of the others.[70] For Congar, as for Möhler, heresy represents precisely 'the erection into a system of undue or partial emphasis on a particular point of view'.[71]

This notion of differing spiritual temperaments and traditions being held in Catholic communion relates closely both to Congar's concern here in *Chrétiens désunis* with an appropriately Catholic understanding of ecumenism and with his explorations of 'reconciled diversity' in *Diversités et Communion*. Whereas, however, in *Diversités et Communion* he will allow for the possibility of differing traditions bringing something of their characteristic organizational differences, appropriately reconfigured, into a genuinely reconciled and expanded Catholic communion, here Congar rejects outright Berdyaev's call for a unity 'that can be accommodated to several forms of confessional organization'.[72] His assumption is that this would necessarily reduce to the long-term continued existence of parallel separated confessional traditions that are merely spoken of as one but not in any real sense united.[73]

As, however, the existence of the Eastern Rite Catholic Churches and Catholic religious orders already indicate, this is by no means necessarily the case. It is entirely possible, as Congar himself came to recognize by *Diversités et Communion*, to think of there being diverse jurisdictions and organizational structures operating alongside each other, all in full reconciled communion

---

[65] *DC*, 103; also 108–13.   [66] *DC*, 106; also 107.
[67] *DC*, 109.   [68] *DC*, 105.
[69] *DC*, 43; compare Möhler, *Einheit*, § 35 (167–8).
[70] *DC*, 43.
[71] *DC*, 29; also 44; compare Congar, 'L'hérésie, déchirement de l'unité' (1939), 255–69.
[72] *DC*, 107.   [73] *DC* (286–93; also n. 19 here).

with the Bishop of Rome as organ and symbol of unity. Indeed, anything less is to confine the quantitative expression of catholicity to the relatively superficial level of diverse linguistic and cultural expressions and differing spiritual temperaments and traditions being sustained by a uniform organizational structure.[74] Without question, this is the limit of the vision at work in *Chrétiens désunis*.[75] What this fails to do is to attend imaginatively—and in a way that touches on directly ecclesiological matters—to the various ways in which the very organizational culture and structures of Catholicism may themselves be capable, indeed requiring, and with all integrity intact, of being expanded, reconfigured, and re-performed in the light of the alternative performance of related matters in other Christian traditions and beyond.[76] But all of this is, for now, an exercise in anticipation.

Of more immediate relevance is the fact that for all his recognition in *Chrétiens désunis* of there being an intrinsic, dynamic diversity to catholicity, he has no truck whatsoever—and, I would maintain, continued not to have even in *Diversités et Communion*—with any ecumenism that relinquishes the aim for structural unity in favour of loose mutual recognition and the treating of abiding significant differences as mere 'non-essentials'.[77] Catholic unity is fullness—the reconciled unity of all things in Christ—not the lowest common denominator of what can be agreed upon without controversy.[78] If the latter were what Congar is up to in *Diversités et Communion* then we would have to concede to Flynn that we do indeed have a real contradiction on our hands.

Similarly, it is equally questionable, for Congar, to assume that the unity and catholicity of the church are purely ahead of us, awaiting establishment through ecumenical reconciliation. On the contrary, they already genuinely exist in Christ's church, which, reflecting Catholic teaching of the time, is to be identified, without qualification, with the Catholic Church.[79] Whilst, as we

[74] Compare here the current Catholic reception of 'Anglican Patrimony' through the creation of Ordinariates for groups of Anglican clergy and laity collectively, see Pope Benedict XVI, *Anglicanorum Coetibus*. 'Apostolic Constitution Providing for Personal Ordinariates for Anglicans Entering into Full Communion with the Catholic Church' (4 November 2009), *AAS* 101 (2009), 985–6. ET available at: <http://www.vatican.va/holy_father/benedict_xvi/apost_constitutions/documents/hf_ben-xvi_apc_20091104_anglicanorum-coetibus_en.html>; compare Murray, 'Hands Across the Tiber: Ecumenism in the Wake of *Anglicanorum Coetibus*', *The Tablet* (1 January 2011), 14–15.

[75] See 'it is also of her [the church's] essence, in the degree to which she is human, to have an unchangeable organ of unity' *DC*, 99–100. Here he repeats the traditional claim for the divine institution of the central organs of Catholic unity without asking if and how their performance might be expanded and revised.

[76] See 'Part III. Receptive Ecumenism and Catholic Church Order', *RE&CCL*, 179–252.

[77] See *DC*, 101, 116–31 (particularly 119–20). Again, the concern to maintain consistent focus on the goal of full structural and sacramental unity and not to reduce this to mere co-existence is also central to receptive ecumenism, see *RE&CCL*, 9, 11–12.

[78] *DC*, 131.

[79] See 'As Catholics we believe that our Church is *the* Church' *DC*, 26; also 132–3, 139, 142, 197, 222, 236, 237, 254, 258.

shall see, Congar allows that the catholicity of the church can be enriched and made more manifest through ecumenical reception, it most definitely does not depend upon such reception to be brought into being.[80]

As this suggests and, perhaps, unsurprisingly given the combination of historical ecclesial context in which and personal temperament with which he was working, Congar here espouses a version of the 'ecumenism of return' required by *Mortalium Animos* in 1928. As he writes: 'For us, indeed, the Catholic Church is *the* Church—simply and without qualification—and consequently reunion must be a "return" to this one existing Church.'[81] Along with 'return', the other words Congar uses—always meticulous over use of words—to speak of the goal of structural unity all suggest similar: 'reunion' (most frequently); 'reintegration', and 'reincorporation'.[82] But it is very much a *version* of the ecumenism of return that Congar is advocating here;[83] one significantly shorn of the assumption of a one-way process affecting and requiring something only of the traditions currently separated from Rome but without any substantive implications for the Catholic Church itself.

Congar is quite clear that there are positive things—'elements of truth and inalienable Christian values'—in all the denominational traditions.[84] Indeed, it may well be that these elements have been lived in the other traditions in a manner that far outstrips what has been achieved, thus far, within Catholicism and from which, therefore, Catholicism needs to receive.[85] The growth to Christian unity, to restored communion, is not a one-way street: Catholicism itself has much to learn.[86] Indeed, without such learning, Catholicism is very definitely the poorer: 'what is true in, for instance, the Lutheran or Wesleyan experience is, in its Lutheran or Wesleyan setting, a loss to the Catholic Church of today'.[87] As such, receptive ecumenical learning on Catholicism's behalf and for Catholicism's own good is not simply a desirable but a fundamental necessity.[88] In this Congar can be seen to anticipate by twenty-eight

[80] 'Lastly,...though we must insist that the one Church of Christ is something already existing, we believe that we may give an exact and legitimate meaning to the assertion that the "reunited Church" will be something more rich, more complete, than any existing Christian body...' *DC*, 258; also 253–6; compare 'Catholic Learning—duly discerned...is about becoming more not less Catholic and, hence, more fully, more richly Catholic and, hence, more fully, more richly the church of Christ', *RE&CCL*, 18.

[81] *DC*, 258; also 46, 238, 252.

[82] E.g., for 'reunion', see 135, 221, 238, 247, 249, 250, 252, 253, 254, 257, 258, 259, 262, 266, 268, 271, 272, 273, 274, 275; for 'reintegration', see p. xiv, 45, 46, 188, 252, 253, 255, 256, 266, 267, 271; for 'reincorporation', see 40, 46, 97, 98, 101.

[83] *DC*, 238.

[84] *DC*, 256 and 135; also 40, 41, 242, 250–1, 258.

[85] *DC*, 258.

[86] *DC*, 46; also 47, 136, 255, 271; compare *Fifty Years*, 31.

[87] *DC*, 256; also 254.

[88] Congar speaks here of 'the necessity of each to the other and to the Catholicity of the whole' 260; again compare: 'This is the kind of real ecumenical learning we now so urgently need and

years the related principle, earlier noted, that would come to formal articulation in *LG* § 8 and *UR* § 5–6 and that likewise lies at the heart of receptive ecumenism.

All of this serves to qualify very significantly the sense in which Congar intends to advocate an ecumenism of return in as much as the Catholicism with which he envisages the currently separated traditions being brought into full communion is itself changed in the process.[89] All must grow towards restored communion and intensified catholicity. In this sense, the qualified version of 'return' he retains is not that remarkable. All authentically Catholic ecumenical engagement will, by definition, view restored communion with the Bishop of Rome, even if in necessarily revised form, as one of the abiding gifts that Catholicism has to offer. The language of 'return' breaks down not because there is no appropriate movement towards communion with Rome, appropriately reformed, but because it is a shared journey of growth and renewal that is better figured in terms of moving together to a new place than of 'return', however qualified, to an existing place or earlier state.

Thus far we have been exploring Congar's thinking about the relevance of receptive ecumenical learning to the intrinsic enrichment of catholicity. Equally important, for Congar is the significance it has for any real ecumenical progress. Without it the other traditions will have no confidence that restored communion with Rome can mean anything other than an abandoning of all they hold dear and conformity to the present Catholic state of things.[90] For this reason, whilst the 'business of information, refutation, contact and discussion has its useful and necessary place . . . the true œcumenical work is the one which the Church carries out by her efforts to realize in all its fullness the grace of her Catholicity'.[91]

As such, Catholic ecumenical commitment must, if serious, work hand in glove with commitment to Catholic reform. He asks, '[W]hy should we be scared of that?' and continues, 'The Church is always reforming herself; it is the way she keeps her life.'[92] Once again we hear clear anticipatory resonance with the '*semper purificanda*' of *LG* § 8 and the '*perennem reformationem*' of *UR* § 6. But not just any reforming concern will do. In a line that could be an advertisement for his next great work, *Vraie et fausse réforme dans l'Église*, he writes of the need to discriminate 'between a genuine reform of the Church and a reform based on false principle and inevitably schismatic'.[93] Consequently, recognizing that 'God alone can rebuild Jerusalem and gather together the dispersed of Israel' yet that 'He will not do it apart from His creatures',

which will move us closer to finding ourselves in the other, the other in ourselves, and each in Christ.' *RE&CCL*, 16.

[89] For independent development, compare *RE&CCL*, 6–7, 14–17.
[90] See *DC*, 271; also 40, 46, 250–1, 259.   [91] *DC*, 273.
[92] *DC*, 272.   [93] *DC*, 186.

central to such integral Catholic reform and sound ecumenical engagement must be a peculiar combination of patience and the impulse of a certain graced activism.[94] As he writes:

> While it would be futile to try to picture it to ourselves, planning it beforehand and conducting it as though it were a purely human affair, we can none the less prepare for it ... disposing ourselves to be, with the least possible imperfection, instruments of the peace of God.[95]

A work that ostensibly starts out questioning whether there can be any such thing as Catholic ecumenism, ends having identified ecumenical receptivity and associated Catholic reform as central to the full realization of catholicity and as pertaining to the entirety of Christian vocation.

EXPANDING CATHOLICITY THROUGH ECUMENICITY IN *DIALOGUE BETWEEN CHRISTIANS*

Where *Chrétiens désunis* originated as a series of lectures, Congar's second major work on ecumenism, *Chrétiens en dialogue* (1964), consists of a collection of occasional pieces stretching from 1935 to 1963. It would be foolish to treat such a collection as a uniform whole. Similarly, rather than chart the reprisal of the various themes identified in *Chrétiens désunis*, such continuity will merely be indicated and attention focused in the main on points receiving either significantly more developed or entirely fresh treatment.

Whilst taking a more positive stance in regard to Life and Works ecumenism, he steadfastly reiterates that the goal of ecumenical activity can be nothing less than full structural and sacramental unity. Although the doctrinal agreement this requires need not equate with uniformity of expression, 'vague formulas, wide enough to include all opposing views' serve 'no good purpose'.[96] All such 'confusionism and syncretism' and 'doctrinal indifferentism' is to be rejected.[97]

Again we hear that in Catholic understanding this desired visible unity of the church does not simply await realization in the future but already genuinely exists in the Catholic Church.[98] The more fully realized unity and catholicity that will flow from the overcoming of current divisions 'will lie

---

[94] *DC*, 2; also 135, 249–50.

[95] *DC*, 250; again compare 'In this perspective, the Christian task is not so much to assert and to construct the Kingdom as to lean into its coming; to be shaped and formed in accordance with it so as to become channels for its anticipatory realization and showing in the world.' *RE&CCL*, 11.

[96] *DBC*, 73.   [97] *DBC*, 74 and 120–1; also 72.   [98] See 74, 76, 115, 119–20.

along the line of development of the Catholic Church'[99] but will also very definitely represent an enrichment and expansion thereof:

> In this sense it is true to say that after reunion, and thanks to it, the Church will be something more than she is now. She will be more fully catholic, partly because of the contributions of the dissident sects whose secession has left so sad a void in the body of the Church.[100]

As such, right from the very earliest essays in the volume we find the same distinctly qualified articulation of an ecumenism of return that we found in *Chrétiens désunis*.[101] Once again the distinctive values of the other traditions must not only be respected, 'we must also, through dialogue, be receptive' to them.[102] Moreover, it is more clearly emphasized that in as much as these values and attributes are matters of life and not simply doctrine, then the required ecumenical attention and receptivity must involve other modes of approach, such as the sociological, than the directly theological alone.[103]

Similarly, there is again the correlative emphasis on the need for integral Catholic reform and continuing conversion but itself also given fresh emphasis. Whilst the achievement of reconciled unity is fundamentally God's work rather than ours, in which we share with a spirit of 'active patience',[104] the most appropriate way for us to dispose ourselves for this is by taking responsibility for living the calling of our own tradition well: 'each individual's ecumenical task' is 'in the first place at home among his own people'.[105]

Also corresponding to the recognition that unity and catholicity are both extant in the Catholic Church and yet to be realized more fully and that, as such, 'the Church of eventual reunion . . . lies before both us and our separated brethren',[106] there is an intensified emphasis on the eschatological, forwards-looking dimension to ecumenical aspiration. It proceeds 'not by a return to the past' but 'by a development which will be a step forward towards the kingdom of God'.[107] Frequent reference is made to an orientation towards 'plenitude'.[108] Here heart can be taken from the achievements thus far—'so substantial that one can only see in them a wholly new intervention of God's mercy, the extent of which it is no man's right to limit in advance'.[109]

---

[99] *DBC*, 95, also 97.   [100] *DBC*, 115; also 95–6, 104–5; *Fifty Years*, 56.
[101] See *DBC*, 290–1; also 76, 96, 97, 114–15.   [102] *DBC*, 155 and 111; also 127–8, 311.
[103] *DBC*, 158; also 144–5, 191.
[104] On unity as God's work, see 74–5; on 'The Role of Patience', see 44–5.
[105] *DBC*, 21; also 31, 64; compare '[F]or this process of overcoming stasis to begin, it requires some to take responsibility, to take the initiative, and this regardless of whether others are ready to reciprocate.' *RE&CCL*, 15; also 12.
[106] *DBC*, 95.
[107] *DBC*, 357; also 'Ecumenical Experience', 83; 'Reflections', 407.
[108] *DBC*, e.g., 97, 104.
[109] *DBC*, 357.

Significantly intertwined with this heightened emphasis on the forwards-looking dimension to ecumenical work is the introduction into Congar's thought during this period of the category of 'development'. As he states, 'I have come to a better understanding of the ... riches and the essential nature of the notion of development.'[110] It is this that gives him his needed 'solution of an antinomy ... at the heart of ecumenical work'[111] as to how things can change with integrity intact. In turn, this enables him to begin thinking in terms of the possibility of a genuinely theological receptivity rather than one limited, as in *Chrétiens désunis*, to the levels of cultural expression and spiritual patrimony. This ability to recognize identity across diversity of form is key, as we shall see, to Congar's later attempts to think in terms of doctrinal agreement that does not presuppose uniformity of expression.

Perhaps the single most significant departure in *Chrétiens en dialogue* relates to the attention Congar gives at various points to the actual character of the required dialogical approach and related matters. As he describes: 'it is necessary to foster an initial stage of approach in which all apologetic haste is laid aside and we humbly, simply and laboriously make the effort to put ourselves on the plane of this particular spiritual world and attempt to understand it'.[112] This will require the preparedness both to take the first step, making oneself vulnerable by 'gratuitous acts of candour', and 'to accept the other as 'other', to admit that he may have some contribution to make and to keep one's mind open to it'.[113] With this, one needs to take seriously at least the possibility that the other's position 'may be right, or at least that they may have reasons for thinking differently from us which are valid from certain points of view'.[114]

This last point brings us very close to the issues of truth and plurality that come to focus in discussion of *Diversités et Communion* and the use that is made there of the concept of 'reconciled diversity'. Congar's way of handling these matters in *Chrétiens en dialogue* is essentially to reject a binary logic, wherein positions are either true or false without qualification, and to distinguish between the fact of a belief articulating truth and it articulating such truth in an exhaustively adequate manner. As he puts it: 'Openness to dialogue necessarily entails an adequate realization that I cannot completely identify what I now hold, and in the way in which I hold it, with the absolute truth to which I profess to be dedicated.'[115] In this regard he employs Aquinas' definition of dogma as 'a perception of truth tending towards truth itself'.[116] That is, far from the more qualified understanding of truth-claims that Congar

---

[110] *DBC*, 96 n. 42; also 'the Catholic hierarchy has fostered the possibility of genuine development, adaptation and progress, capable of constituting a true development of tradition and not a purely external change' 78.
[111] *DBC*, 128–9.   [112] *DBC*, 128, 297–8.   [113] *DBC*, 56–7.
[114] *DBC*, 57–8.   [115] *DBC*, 59.   [116] *DBC*, 60, citing *ST*, IIaIIæ 1.a.6.

here advocates being complicit in any form of relativism, it is actually impelled by a very strong understanding of truth as always surpassing our current articulations of it.[117] This is a plenitudinous understanding of truth rather than a relativistic one. It is not that all truth-claims are made relative by each other but that they are made relative by the plenitude of truth which even when they truly express something of such plenitude they can only ever do so in part. 'The acquisition of truth' he tells us 'is a dialectical process': 'Opponents whose conclusions clash' who take 'the time to understand each other better and understand themselves better' may 'come together again at a point at present indeterminate ... beyond their present positions'.[118]

SEEKING CATHOLICITY TRANSFIGURED IN *DIVERSITY AND COMMUNION*

Diversités et Communion has its origins in a seminar course Congar taught in 1980 in the form, as the French subtitle suggests, of a combination of historical documentation and theological analysis (*Dossier historique et conclusion théologique*). The integrating focus is to examine whether one can 'find a foundation for a "pluralist unity" or a "reconciled diversity", which might be the form in which communion is re-established, in the idea of "fundamental articles"?'[119] The context prompting this question was a realization by Congar that further ecumenical progress requires a more constructive approach to the issue of difference and diversity than has frequently prevailed in Christian history.

What he refers to as the 'polemical' approach, of seeking to convince the other, has not succeeded.[120] In turn, ironically, ecumenical engagement has, if anything, 'tended ... to revive and reinforce ... the confessional conscience of the various groups' rather than help overcome such differences.[121] As he later tells us:

> In the study I have made of attempts at union and dialogues carried on down to the present day, I have been struck by the fact that each side jealously preserves its identity, judges the other by comparison with itself and basically is not very open

---

[117] *DBC*, 60–1; compare Murray, *Reason, Truth, and Theology in Pragmatist Perspective*, (Leuven: Peeters, 2004), particularly 73, 98, 113–17.

[118] *DBC*, 66 and 58, citing, in the latter regard, Gilson, 'Reflexions sur la controverse S. Thomas–S. Augustin', in Gilson, *Mélanges Pierre Mandonnet*, I (Paris, 1930), 370–83 (371); also *DBC*, 128.

[119] *D&C*, 1.

[120] *D&C*, 2.

[121] *D&C*, 2.

to that part of the truth with which it is confronted. There is little departure from the 'confessional'.[122]

For its own part, implicated in this also is the Catholic default to 'a uniform and hierarchical conception of unity, of a military kind'.[123]

In the terminology of receptive ecumenism, Congar here identifies the tendency of traditions to focus more on the question as to what they each have to teach their others than on what they themselves have to learn, in such a fashion as leads both to a clearer understanding of respective identities but also a more entrenched confessional stalemate and this regardless of whether or not relationships and pastoral cooperation have become warmer and easier in the process. In this context, he writes in the conviction that we need to recognize differences as real; that we cannot get to unity by either ignoring them and settling for mere 'peaceful coexistence'[124] or treating them as made irrelevant by aiming for a syncretistic loose federation of Christian traditions regardless of continuing significant divergences of belief, structure, and practice.[125] The implication is that the path to unity must be through rather than in spite of difference: by taking differences seriously and asking what they each respectively actually represent; how fundamental they in fact are; whether it is possible to identify inessential differences; and whether and how it is possible to learn across such differences. As he writes:

> What is relatively new is the recognition of the *other* as such. For centuries people have attempted to make others conform to them. ... The new development is marked by an interest in the other precisely where he or she differs.[126]

Noting that the practice of ecumenical dialogue together with his training as an historian have enabled him to realize the 'relativity of more than one position', he states his concern as being to examine the possibility of 'a unity which allows for quite widespread diversity', wherein differences are not necessarily regarded as 'irreconcilable'.[127] It is in this context that he first makes mention of the Lutheran notion of 'reconciled diversity'.[128] Rather than looking for the 'rediscovery' or restoration of a supposedly homogeneous unity that has been 'lost', Congar is in search of 'a unity which allows of [legitimate] diversity...',[129] citing, at one point, Pope John Paul II in official support:

---

[122] *D&C*, 222 n. 3. The resonance with Möhler's language of egocentric preservation of one's own truth rather than concern to bring it into correlation with the whole is again significant.
[123] *D&C*, 41.   [124] *D&C*, 3.
[125] *D&C*, 2, 119; also 3–4.
[126] *D&C*, 35.
[127] *D&C*, 3.
[128] *D&C*, 4, also 149.
[129] *D&C*, 4.

Unity—whether on the universal level or at the local level—does not signify uniformity or the absorption of one group by the other. It is rather at the service of all groups, to help each one to give better expression to the gifts which it has received from the Spirit of God.[130]

With this, he imagines a time in which—as most notably came to pass with the formal endorsement of the *Joint Declaration on the Doctrine of Justification* by the Lutheran World Federation and the Catholic Church in 1999—'the authorities concerned should note publicly at the highest level that in certain terms, on particular points, there is no (or there is no longer any) difference'.[131]

As to how we are to understand all of this in relation to a continued concern for doctrinal truth rather than fudge, Congar appeals again to the Thomistic description of dogma, already drawn upon in *Chrétiens en dialogue*, as 'a perception of divine truth moving towards the truth itself'.[132] Applying this to the ecumenical context he notes that 'each group has only a certain number of experiences and realizes only a part or certain aspects of the truth' and draws the conclusion: 'If ecumenism is a quest for the purity and the fullness of the truth about God and the mysteries of salvation, it must be specifically and supremely a welcoming of differences on the basis of a common point of reference and a common destiny.'[133] But nor is this a process without limit: 'There are demands which we cannot surrender.'[134]

Bringing these lines of thought to focus specifically in relation to Congar's appropriation of the concept of 'reconciled diversity', all that we have seen leads us to assume with some confidence that he will by no means put this to work in such fashion as, in Flynn's terms, 'evades institutional/structural transformation in favour of the harmonious coexistence of separate confessional churches'.[135] Indeed, at the very outset of his most extended treatment of the concept,[136] he identifies as inaccurate the WCC tendency to interpret this phrase in support of the vision of a 'conciliar community' of diverse 'confessional groups', structurally separate yet coexisting alongside each other.[137]

Then, interestingly, he reinforces his rejection of ecumenical federalism—wherein each simply 'agrees to recognize the legitimacy of the others'—by

---

[130] *D&C*, 33, citing Pope John Paul II, 'Address to a Delegation of the Coptic Orthodox Church' (23 June 1979), *AAS* 71 (1979), 1000–1. ET available at: <http://www.vatican.va/holy_father/john_paul_ii/speeches/1979/june/documents/hf_jp-ii_spe_19790622_chiesa-copta-ortodossa_en.html>.

[131] *D&C*, 141, also 1.
[132] *D&C*, 40, see n. 72.
[133] *D&C*, 41.
[134] *D&C*, 43.
[135] Flynn, 'Receptive Ecumenism', 411 n. 22.
[136] *D&C*, 149–52.
[137] *D&C*, 149–50.

lengthy citation from a 1938 essay (one year after the publication of *Chrétiens désunis*) by his Jesuit contemporary, Yves de Montcheuil, from a volume to which Congar also contributed, dedicated to exploring the ecclesiological and ecumenical implications of Möhler's thought.[138] Particularly significant is a balanced pair of principles, each reflecting Möhler's influence, pertaining to the appropriate relation between unity and diversity. First, '[I]t is not enough to recognize the right of the other groups to exist: what is needed is to assimilate the truth possessed by each of the others, excluding their exclusiveness.' And second, 'But also... there is nothing more contrary to true Christian unity than the quest for unification. This always consists in wanting to universalise one particular form, to endorse life in one of its expressions.'[139]

Taking his leave from de Montcheuil, Congar proceeds with his own discussion of Möhler relative to the notion of 'reconciled diversity', particularly in relation to Möhler's distinction in *Einheit* § 46 and elsewhere between *Gegensätze*—contrasts/distinctions—and *Widersprüche*—contradictions.[140] Where *Gegensätze* are partial expressions of a greater, compex, multifaceted, yet unified truth that require to and can be held in tension—'contrasted positions which express different aspects of reality'[141]—*Widersprüche* are articulated in opposition to each other and allow for no higher resolution. Again, where the catholicity of the church is the embodiment of the *Gegensätze*, heresy is the natural manifestation and result of the *Widersprüche*.[142] Of the *Gegensätze* Congar writes: 'When they are held in the living unity of the church which embraces them, each one is corrected by at least a potential openness to the complementary aspect.'[143] From such ideas Congar takes the notion of a restored unity that is not—as he incorrectly takes the Hegelian *aufgehoben* to imply—a flattened, uniform 'reconciliation of contradictions among themselves' but a 'living exchange', a 'unity of diversity which constitutes an organic totality'.[144] Viewed in this way, 'One cannot avoid seeing the church as plenitude.'[145]

In order to corroborate his reading of 'reconciled diversity' as not just a possible Catholic reading but one entirely in accord with recognized Lutheran understanding, Congar includes as an Appendix a series of extracts from a dossier of relevant Lutheran writings sent to him by Harding Meyer.[146] Here

---

[138] See Yves de Montcheuil, 'La Liberté et la diversité dans l'Unité', in Chaillet (ed.), *L'Église est une*, 234–54.

[139] *D&C*, 150.

[140] *D&C*, 151–2; compare Möhler, *Einheit* § 46 (194–8); also § 48 (201–5); § 32 (157–60).

[141] *D&C*, 151.

[142] Somewhat surprisingly, for his own part de Lubac makes no reference whatsoever to Möhler throughout *Catholicism*, even in its later editions, although there are a number of places where the resonance is very striking, see e.g. de Lubac, *Catholicism*, 52–3, 298, 300, 330.

[143] *D&C*, 151.

[144] *D&C*, 151.

[145] *D&C*, 152.

[146] *D&C*, 153–8.

again we find condemned as 'flagrant misunderstanding' the notion that it refers to 'the persistence of the coexistence of separate confessional groups'.[147] The point is that 'reconciliation between the hitherto separated confessions is inconceivable without renewal and change at the heart of the different confessional identities'.[148] Far from leaving the traditions as they were, with continuing significant differences covered over by a mood of peaceable coexistence, 'reconciled diversity', properly understood, presupposes a process 'that could be described as a redefinition of the confessions by dialogue'.[149] And in words that provide fitting closure here: 'It is rather a matter of reconciliation and community through the vigorous affirmation of the other with his otherness *redefined*, in a way which shows its legitimacy.'[150]

CONCLUSION: ABIDING ORIENTATION AND CONTINUING CALL TO THE FULLNESS OF CATHOLICITY

This chapter started out by establishing that an intrinsic dual relationship exists between *ressourcement* and ecumenism: on the one hand, twentieth-century Catholic ecumenism was both dependent in general on the renewal in Catholic theology that *ressourcement* represented and specifically dependent on the work of historical and scriptural *ressourcement* that lay behind many areas of doctrinal progress; on the other hand, ecumenism can itself be seen as a powerful agent of *ressourcement* and Catholic reform in as much as it served to open Catholicism to the challenge and potential of the diverse particular giftedness of the other traditions.

Following this a case was made in favour of there being a fundamental continuity of concern across Congar's ecumenical writings, with identifiable anticipations in the earlier writings of what were later to become developed emphases. The work of Möhler was suggested as a major thread in this line of continuity. As the reading was pursued, it was noted time and again how Congar can be seen to have anticipated and, in many cases, to have significantly developed the key principles that come to articulation in receptive ecumenism: combining steadfast focus on full structural and sacramental unity as the goal of ecumenism, attentiveness to the lived particularity of the various Christian traditions and their respective areas of giftedness and dysfunction, and the need for each to take responsibility for examining seriously

---

[147] *D&C*, 156.   [148] *D&C*, 156.
[149] *D&C*, 157.   [150] *D&C*, 158.

how their respective traditions both can be and need to be renewed, expanded, and enriched, with dynamic integrity in the light of the other traditions.

The final section focused on demonstrating that the concept of 'reconciled diversity' can be given authentic Catholic articulation, providing a challenging vision of an expanded catholicity into which Roman Catholicism still has some considerable way to grow. Taken together with comments made earlier in the chapter, it might even be possible to imagine a scenario wherein—with all necessary doctrinal reconciliation achieved, allowing for appropriate diversity of articulation—diverse, but not fundamentally contradictory, organizational systems could operate as sub-sets of transfigured and expanded Catholic life: either on the model of religious orders, which operate both under their own trans-diocesan organizational systems and under the ordinary jurisdiction of the diocese in which they serve; or on the model of the Eastern Rite Churches in full communion with Rome wherein episcopal jurisdiction can operate either on a traditional geographical-territorial model or, in non-Orthodox countries, on a trans-diocesan basis according to affiliation.

A major gap in this chapter is that whilst focusing on the broad principles of Congar's ecumenical thinking across the course of his writing, there has not been opportunity to engage the detail of any of the many specific areas of Catholic theology and life on which he shone the light of integral renewal: the overcoming of a hierocratic church, the vocation of the laity, the understanding of ministry and that of the ordained, and many more.[151] These and others—most notably the exercise of the office of the Bishop of Rome, the appointment of bishops, the structures of decision making and accountability, the relationship between lay and ordained—still stand today as the unfinished business of Catholic renewal, essential alike both to intrinsic Catholic flourishing and to ecumenical progress. I close by suggesting that the most fitting tribute to Congar both in thought and deed is to commit to engaging these and other such specifics with the same combination of rigour, courage, fidelity, and active patience that he so exemplified and to do so, as first step, by collating and assessing his own relevant contributions—as also those of the other great *ressourcement* theologians and theological fellow travellers—alongside those of the ecumenical dialogues. He continues to help us be responsible both to the inherited past of our tradition and for its future. His is an exemplary performance of what it means to live and work for Catholic plenitude in ecumenical perspective and amidst ecumenical potential.

---

[151] For an authoritative treatment, see Flynn, *Yves Congar's Vision of the Church*.

30

Ressourcement Theology and Protestantism

John Webster

Ressourcement may be thought of as a mode of theology which derives from a substantive account of Christianity, offering both a diagnosis and a remedy in what were judged to be straitened circumstances of Christian reflection. The diagnosis was that salient features of the Christian culture of the first half of the twentieth century—historically myopic neo-scholasticism, autonomous philosophy, Protestant bifurcations of the temporal and the supra-temporal—were symptomatic of the 'separations' introduced from the early fourteenth century, by which natural and supernatural were prised apart. Such formal separations were mirrored in an ecclesiology dominated by juridical categories, cut adrift from the Trinitarian and Christological mysteries of which the church is properly the bodying forth. The proffered remedy was immersion in earlier dogmatic, liturgical, and spiritual tradition offering release from present inhibitions and access to a more spacious and pacific vision of Christianity: 'it is good to disengage oneself where possible from the restrictions of controversy and to consult the ideas of those who worked on these matters in peace ... There one discovers an untroubled situation, a freedom and calm— in short, a climate where many difficulties lose their acute and irritating character.'[1]

Until Vatican II, Protestant theologians were generally inattentive to the work of their *ressourcement* colleagues; since then, much mainstream Protestant theology—especially those strands of English-language, German, and Scandinavian Protestantism with exposure and commitment to the dominant ecumenical theological climate—has come to hold the achievement of *ressourcement* theology in high esteem. In part, this is because of the remarkable widespread ecumenical adoption of some formulations in ecclesiology and the theology of ministry and sacraments which were also typical of *ressourcement*

---

[1] Y. M.-J. Congar, *Tradition and Traditions: An Historical and a Theological Essay*, trans. Michael Naseby and Thomas Rainborough (London: Burns & Oates, 1966), 289.

theology; in part, it is because of an ecumenical approach to overcoming divisive controversy by returning to common early traditions of doctrine and devotion. Further, some recent Protestant theology has invested heavily in the retrieval of earlier tradition; Protestants have been much involved in recovering ancient exegetical practices, for example. This broadly sympathetic response is despite the fact that *ressourcement* thinkers themselves tended to view Protestantism as an instance of the declension of the church which they sought to reverse. *Ressourcement* theologians rarely offered detailed and well-disposed readings of Protestant theology, von Balthasar's remarkable book on Barth being the exception which proves the rule.[2] Their critiques of Protestantism often worked with ideal types, as in Bouyer's *The Spirit and Forms of Protestantism*,[3] or, perhaps more surprisingly, in the lengthy but curiously unperceptive treatments of Protestantism in Congar's *Tradition and Traditions*. Balthasar was not without reasons for his dismay at the lack of deep and wide knowledge of classical and modern Protestantism on the part of his Catholic *confrères*.

The questions to be asked are: what might an alert, self-critical, and expectant Protestant theology learn from the theologians of the *ressourcement*? How might it respond to their critiques of the Reformation tradition? And what opportunities are offered here for mutual enlargement of understandings of the Christian gospel?

RESSOURCEMENT AS A MODE OF THEOLOGY

At the beginning of *Catholicism*, Henri de Lubac felt it necessary to explain to his readers why his text was saturated with quotations from the Fathers: 'I seek only to understand them, and listen to what they have to tell us, since they are our fathers in the faith, and since they received from the church of their time the means to nourish the church of our times as well.'[4] This is an illuminating statement. The characteristic genre of *ressourcement* theology was not the treatise or manual; its practitioners did not place a high premium upon scholarly comprehensiveness, and their work did not fit easily within any of the standard modern theological sub-disciplines, dogmatic, historical, or practical. Instead, they gave themselves eagerly to discursive commentary on the Christian past, the goal being not so much *wissenschaftlich* analysis as

---

[2] H. U. von Balthasar, *The Theology of Karl Barth: Exposition and Interpretation*, trans. Edward T. Oakes, SJ (San Francisco: Ignatius Press, 1992).

[3] L. Bouyer, *The Spirit and Forms of Protestantism*, trans. A. V. Littledale (London: Harvill Press, 1956).

[4] H. de Lubac, *Catholicism: A Study of Dogma in Relation to the Corporate Destiny of Mankind*, trans. Lancelot C. Sheppard (London: Burns, Oates and Washbourne, 1950), p. xiii.

retrieval and commendation of largely forgotten habits of thought and spiritual practice. Their texts were directed to contemplative intelligence, their chief aim being edification by directing the church to the treasures of meaning which lay ready to be discovered in earlier apprehensions of divine revelation. Often this was accomplished simply by loving re-presentation of the sources, 'this immense army of witnesses', as de Lubac called them;[5] hence the catena method of theological portraiture, and the generally a-critical reading of the early Christian centuries and its literature; hence, too, the temptation (not always resisted) to free association, and the potential for overload and distraction by detail (de Lubac's *Corpus Mysticum*[6] is a case in point).

The *ressourcement* desire to practise a different kind of theology was animated by a conviction that revelation is not an external, timeless, and apodictic announcement but a process of transmission, at once temporal and social. Nourishing present theology from past sources is not mere archaism, but the consequence of a judgement that the Christological and pneumatological reality of the church in its historical and social extensions is basic to the order of human being and therefore of human intelligence. The fact that the Fathers are 'such a unique and very precious *locus theologicus*' is for Congar a matter of 'Christian ontology'[7]—a confession that, because they are those whose lives are in Christ, the Fathers are not merely *history* but *tradition*, referring present theology to the mystery of faith because they are 'wholly concentrated on exposition and illustration of the inner direction of revelation and of the saving economy which comes from God through Christ to the church as the sacrament of the new order of salvation'.[8]

What might Protestant theology make of this mode of theological work? One *entrée* into the matter is to reflect on the history of Protestant attitudes to the patristic tradition.

From the early Reformation period, Protestant theologians have commonly (though not unanimously) looked to the patristic era for support in controversy, and for instruction in classic articulations of the Christian faith. They have, however, differentiated—sometimes quite sharply—the gospel from its transmission in and through the church, and given prominence to the supremacy and sufficiency (material and formal) of Holy Scripture, and to a corollary assertion of the fallibility and subordinate status of ecclesial transmission of the gospel, that is, of the instruments and practices of tradition.

Calvin, for example, in the Epistle Dedicatory to his 1536 *Institutes*, argues that opponents of the Reformation 'unjustly set the ancient fathers against us

---

[5] De Lubac, *Catholicism*, p.xiii.

[6] De Lubac, *Corpus Mysticum: The Eucharist and the Church in the Middle Ages*, trans. Gemma Simmonds with Richard Price and Christopher Stephens, eds. Laurence Paul Hemming and Susan Frank Parsons (London: SCM Press, 2006).

[7] Congar, *Tradition and Traditions*, 436.

[8] Congar, *Tradition and Traditions*, 450.

(I mean the ancient writers of a better age of the church)', protesting that 'we do not dispense with the fathers... in fact... I could with no trouble at all prove that the greater part of what we are saying today meets their approval.'[9] Both in commenting on scripture and in his treatises, Calvin draws a good deal on patristic support, and in a polemical context he frequently appeals to the Fathers as 'defenders of our opinion'[10]: one of his chief weapons against Sadolet, for example, is to show that 'the ancient church is clearly on our side'.[11]

Yet Calvin is not without reservations, and feels the need to accentuate the subsidiary status of patristic authority: 'we have always held [the fathers] to belong to the number of those... whose authority we will not so exalt, as in any way to debase the dignity of the Word of our Lord, to which alone is due complete obedience in the church of Jesus Christ', he told the Lausanne assembly.[12] There is a deep principle here, one surely troubling to *ressourcement* theologians, namely the principle that Jesus Christ and the church constitute two distinct orders of reality, such that the exclusivity of Christ's authority must be safeguarded by the subordination of that of the church. God 'must be acknowledged as sole king and legislator'.[13] That Calvin frames the issue as one of legislative authority is telling, indicative, perhaps, of an understanding of the church as a sphere in which Christ rules immediately, and in which revelation is external norm rather than that which takes temporal form in the spiritual and sacramental life of the Christian society. In this ecclesiology, *ad fontes* means back to the *viva vox Dei*, Jesus Christ speaking through the prophets and apostles, and only by derivation back to the Fathers as representative hearers of the gospel. Yet the Fathers remain 'good servants', and

we do them such honour as may according to God be accorded to them, while we attend to them and their ministry, to search the Word of God, in order that, having found it, we should with them listen to and observe it with all humility and reverence, reserving this honour for the Lord alone, who has opened his mouth in the church only to speak with authority.[14]

If Calvin's approach to the patristic writers is more cautious and a good deal less celebratory than that of *ressourcement* theologians, it is so because of a

---

[9] J. Calvin, *Institutes of the Christian Religion* (1536 edition), trans. F. L. Battles (Grand Rapids MI: Eerdmans, 1995), 6.

[10] J. Calvin, 'Two Discourses on the Articles', in J. K. S. Reid (ed.), *Calvin: Theological Treatises* (London: SCM Press, 1954), 40. The setting is the 1536 debate on the so-called Lausanne articles. On Calvin's use of patristic material in polemic, see J. van Ort, 'John Calvin and the Church Fathers', in I. Backus (ed.), *The Reception of the Church Fathers in the West: From the Carolingians to the Maurists* (New York: Brill, 1996), 661–700; A. N. S. Lane, *John Calvin: Student of the Church Fathers* (Edinburgh: T&T Clark, 1999).

[11] J. Calvin, 'Reply to Sadolet', in Reid (ed.), *Calvin: Theological Treatises*, 240.

[12] Calvin, 'Two Discourses on the Articles', 38.

[13] Calvin, 'Two Discourses on the Articles', 39.

[14] Calvin, 'Two Discourses on the Articles', 39.

commitment to the discontinuity of Christ as revealer from the church which his Word alone engenders and sustains.

Amongst the post-Reformation divines, something of the same pattern can be discerned, reinforced by the greater sophistication introduced by the rise of Protestant patrology in the seventeenth century (in figures such as Gerhard, Rivet, or Scultetus).[15] As with Calvin, the Fathers proved allies in controversy, especially in face of Socinian denials of Trinitarian and incarnational orthodoxy. But if the Fathers function as *testes veritatis*, it is only in confirmation of what may be found independent of them by searching scripture. Because of this, post-Reformation Protestants were wary of ideas of the *consensus partrum*, and in those doctrines which separate them from the church of Rome (chiefly teaching about scripture and about the church) the authority of the Fathers is much less in evidence. The later seventeenth-century Swiss Reformed dogmatician Francis Turretin is exemplary.

> The orthodox (although they hold the fathers in great estimation and think them very useful to a knowledge of the history of the ancient church, and our opinion on cardinal doctrines may agree with them) yet deny that their authority, whether as individuals or taken together, can be called authoritative in matters of faith and the interpretation of the scriptures, so that by their judgement we must stand or fall. Their authority is only ecclesiastical and subordinate to the scriptures and of no weight except so far as they agree with them.[16]

The Fathers are, in other words, 'witnesses' rather than 'judges'. Undergirding this is a crucial principle, at once ecclesiological and bibliological: 'The unity of the church may be properly preserved by the unity of faith delivered in the scriptures, not by the consent of the fathers.'[17]

To sum up: the magisterial Reformers and their successors do not consider tradition—especially patristic tradition—as wholly corrupt, and find it an important resource in controversy. But such is their conception of the divine Word and its segregation from human reception that they are uneasy with talk of revelation's transmission or actualization in the church, even the church of a golden age. Revelation is always outside, non-assimilable, non-transferrable,

---

[15] See here P. Fraenkel, *Testimonia Patrum: The Function of Patristic Argument in the Thought of Philip Melanchthon* (Geneva: Droz, 1961); E. P. Meijering, *Melanchthon and Patristic Thought* (Leiden: Brill, 1983); I. Backus, 'The Fathers in Calvinist Orthodoxy: Patristic Scholarship', in I. Backus (ed.), *The Reception of the Church Fathers in the West*, 839–65; E. P. Meijering, 'The Fathers and Calvinist Orthodoxy: Systematic Theology', in I. Backus (ed.), *The Reception of the Church Fathers in the West*, 867–87; R. A. Muller, 'Ad Fontes Argumentorum. The Sources of Reformed Theology in the Seventeenth Century', in *After Calvin: Studies in the Development of A Theological Tradition* (Oxford: Oxford University Press, 2003), 47–62.
[16] F. Turretin, *Institutes of Elenctic Theology*, i, trans. George Musgrave Giger (Phillipsburg NJ: Presbyterian and Reformed, 1992), II.xxi.5 (163).
[17] Turretin, *Institutes*, II.xxi.13 (166).

the exclusive particles *solus Christus* and *sola scriptura* condensing an entire conception of the Christian faith and its enactment in time.

One effect of the rise of the critical history of Christianity in the early nineteenth century was that Protestant theological critiques of the authority of church tradition were detached from the positive use of the Fathers as *testes* and secularized, transformed by modern ideals of critical rationality and of political repudiation of heteronomous institutions into assertions that classical Christian thought is largely alien and unusable. Whether *ressourcement* theologians were right to regard such developments as a natural outgrowth of Protestant separations of revelation and the time of the church remains an open question. What is true is that the idea of the present as qualitatively different from the past has held much modern Protestant theology in its grip. Some of the most dominant strands of Protestant theology in modernity have been acutely responsible to what is taken to be the present cultural situation of the church, and have declined to see de Lubac's 'immense army of witnesses' as either a feature of that present or a guide to its interpretation.

Nevertheless, there have been examples of Protestant theologians for whom loving study of one or other strand of the Christian tradition has proved important in conducting them out of modern habits of mind and enabling them to formulate critical judgements about their present situation. Barth himself—often regarded by *ressourcement* theologians as typifying Protestant separations—operated in certain respects like some of his contemporaries in *nouvelle théologie*. Barth was, of course, far from being an instinctive traditionalist, accomplishing all manner of innovations and usually reluctant to sidestep modern problems simply by appeal to antique tradition. Equally, he had high expectations of what may be learned from the Christian past, especially from dogmatic and exegetical writings, and he was at his most anti-modern in his providential rather than secularized reading of the development of the church and its theology. Barth's break with Liberal Protestantism was only brought to completion when, in the early 1920s, he immersed himself, *ressourcement*-style, in the writings of sixteenth- and seventeenth-century Calvinist divinity. As a result, he came to think of himself as a *church* theologian, not operating in a vacuum but in a given tradition of ecclesial and confessional practice. As he noted in his first cycle of dogmatics lectures: 'The vital interest of the church may be summed up again in the old war cry that the Reformers understood better and more profoundly than the humanists who first raised it: Back to the sources!'[18] At the same time, Barth came to appreciate the primacy for Reformed Christianity of the scripture principle, that is, of the non-continuity between the divine Word and the church. Yet he was clear that the scripture principle offered no licence to private judgement:

---

[18] K. Barth, *The Göttingen Dogmatics: Instruction in the Christian Religion*, trans. Geoffrey W. Bromiley (Grand Rapids MI: Eerdmans, 1991), 40f.

'in the church there can never be any question of overleaping the centuries and immediately (each trusting to the sharpness of his eye and the openness of his heart) linking up with the Bible'.[19] *Sola scriptura* is not a denial that 'it is in the *church* that the Bible is read; it is by the *church* that the Bible is heard. This means that in reading the Bible we should also hear what the church, the church that is distinguished from my person, has up to now read and heard from the Bible.'[20] And so, 'in the church, the same kind of obedience as, I hope, you pay to your father and mother, is demanded of you towards the church's past ... In this obedience to the church's past it is always possible to be a very *free* theologian. But it must be borne in mind that, as a member of the church, as belonging to the *congregatio fidelium*, one must not *speak* without having *heard*.'[21] The massive presence of an immense range of the Christian tradition in the *Church Dogmatics* is part of what makes its title especially apt.

Other Protestant theologians after Barth, especially those sympathetic to a model of ecumenical convergence indebted to *ressourcement* thought, have written out of captivation by catholic tradition. T. F. Torrance's exposition of Nicene orthodoxy in *The Trinitarian Faith* is in some respects a classic of *ressourcement* theology from a Reformed perspective, with its sense of the coherence and authority of ancient Christian thought, its deference to early liturgical and dogmatic tradition, and its working assumption that classical Christian theology unfolds under the impulse of the Spirit in the church.[22] On a grander scale, there have been a number of systematic theologies which share some *ressourcement* attitudes to tradition and modes of theology: the ecumenical dogmatics of the Lutheran Edmund Schlink;[23] the liturgically-oriented treatment of Christian doctrine by the Methodist Geoffrey Wainwright;[24] or Thomas Oden's presentation of the leading themes of Christian doctrine by lengthy report upon classic sources.[25]

At the very least, this historical sketch calls into question Louis Bouyer's rather bitter appraisal of the Reformation tradition as 'individualistic, heretical, and negative'.[26] At its most mature, the Protestant tradition has retained a sense of itself as one mode of universal Christianity, and of its theology as an exercise within the spiritual milieu of the apostolic community of faith. Yet Protestantism emerged out of contest about the character of the truly apostolic church, and especially about the church's relation to the divine Word and

---

[19] Barth, *Credo*, trans. J. Strathearn McNab (New York: Scribner's, 1962), 180.

[20] Barth, *Credo*, 181.

[21] Barth, *Credo*, 181.

[22] T. F. Torrance, *The Trinitarian Faith: The Evangelical Theology of the Ancient Catholic Church* (Edinburgh: T&T Clark, 1988).

[23] E. Schlink, *Ökumenische Dogmatik. Grundzüge* (Göttingen: Vandenhoeck und Ruprecht, 1983).

[24] G. Wainwright, *Doxology: The Praise of God in Worship, Doctrine, and Life: A Systematic Theology* (Oxford: Oxford University Press, 1980).

[25] T. Oden, *Systematic Theology*, 3 vols. (San Francisco: Harper, 1987–92).

[26] Bouyer, *The Spirit and Forms of Protestantism*, 16.

action. For some Protestant theology, divergences over church and revelation are deep, and their resolution difficult to conceive; to these we now turn.

CHURCH AND REVELATION

Ressourcement theology sought to recover an ecclesiology in which the church's temporal visibility is intrinsic to the economy of salvation and its communication to creatures. They did so out of commitment to a doctrine of the *corpus mysticum* in which the church is the enlargement of the hypostatic union: 'There, then, is the church,' wrote de Lubac, 'human and divine at once even in her visibility, "without division and without confusion", just like Christ himself, whose body she mystically is.'[27] This, in turn, prompted critique of what was considered characteristically Protestant over-emphasis upon the purity and incommunica-bility of the work of God, and upon its utter transcendence of the historical Christian community. Protestantism is symptomatic of 'a fatal dissociation of the visible and the invisible',[28] of a failure to see the church as, by virtue of the Spirit, the 'realization of salvation'.[29] *Ressourcement* critics often fastened upon Protestant elevation and isolation of scripture and the consequent rejection of all non-biblical mediation of the divine gift, in which saving revelation is stripped of the forms of ministry and traditions of interpretation by which it makes itself present in the society of believers. An entire trajectory of theology, stretching from late-thirteenth-century nominalism through Wycliffe, the Reformers, and on into modern Protestantism deploys the primacy of scripture in an 'anti-ecclesiastical' way, the result being '*Scripture and the church: two authorities forced into competition.*'[30] What presents initially as a dispute about ecclesial authority is, furthermore, undergirded by a certain Christological constriction (even, perhaps, monophysitism): Protestant theology considers Christ's lordship 'too exclusively in terms of the glorified Christ and not enough as a *de jure* power residing already in Christ made man', and so neglects that he is 'the Lord of time ... not only in himself in heaven but also in his church'.[31]

   The core issue is a cleavage of incarnation and revelation from church, acting 'as if Christ and the church were in a purely extrinsic relation to each other'.[32] The

---

[27] De Lubac, *The Splendour of the Church*, trans. Michael Mason (London: Sheed & Ward, 1956), 69; see, further, Y.M.-J. Congar, *The Mystery of the Temple, or the Manner of God's Presence to his Creatures from Genesis to Apocalypse*, trans. Reginald Frederick Trevett (London: Burns & Oates, 1962).

[28] De Lubac, *Splendour*, 60.

[29] Congar, *Tradition and Traditions*, 130.

[30] Congar, *Tradition and Traditions*, 98.

[31] Congar, *Tradition and Traditions*, 490.

[32] Congar, *Tradition and Traditions*, 491.

revelatory grace embodied in Christ ought not to be isolated from the processes by which it unfolds itself within and is received by the apostolic community. Revelation—the communicative presence of the saving mystery—is not a purely self-contained moment of interruptive grace, permanently external to its 'use'. It is, rather, the presence within time of an inexhaustible pattern or source, that which *makes* rather than arrests history. Hence the principle: 'We are at a point where the concepts of revelation, the church and tradition overlap: what was hidden in God is manifested in time. This manifestation, as knowledge, is revelation and tradition; as a present mystery it is the church, salvation and again tradition, *paradosis* being this content of saving knowledge and practice which the church transmits and by which it lives'.[33] All this culminates in the common *ressourcement* worry that Protestant theology and practice is 'extrinsicist', splitting apart social process and the economy of revelation, 'a complete severance of the natural and the supernatural'.[34] God *first* is distorted into God *alone*.

Such critiques have enjoyed widespread success in recent years amongst ecumenically-minded theologians, reinforced by being prosecuted in somewhat angular form by 'Radical Orthodox' thinkers in whose genealogy of modernity the Reformation is a defection from the unified catholic vision of reality shattered by Scotus and followers.[35] Many Protestant (and especially some notable Lutheran) theologians have felt no need to defend their tradition at this point, conceding the justice of the critique and embracing—for example—a communion ecclesiology privileging the church's historical and social visibility.[36] Others, often somewhat more marginal to the ecumenical consensus, are less sure, and their hesitations are worth exploring, since they give access to some classical Protestant points of theological and spiritual conscience.[37]

---

[33] Congar, *Tradition and Traditions*, 25.

[34] De Lubac, *Catholicism*, 166.

[35] A complex version of the argument—one not entirely allergic to Protestant concerns—can be found in J. Milbank, 'Alternative Protestantism. Radical Orthodoxy and the Reformed Tradition', in J. K. A. Smith and J. H. Olthuis (eds.), *Radical Orthodoxy and the Reformed Tradition: Creation, Covenant and Participation* (Grand Rapids MI: Baker, 2005), 25–41.

[36] See, for example, R. Jenson, *Systematic Theology*, ii (Oxford: Oxford University Press, 1999), 211–27; Jenson, 'The Church as *Communio*', in C. Braaten and R. Jenson (eds.), *The Catholicity of the Reformation* (Grand Rapids MI: Eerdmans, 1996), 1–12. Bonhoeffer gives an interesting anticipation of these developments in *Discipleship*, trans. John D. Godsey (Minneapolis MN: Fortress, 2001), 225–52, on which see the penetrating analysis of D. Yeago, 'The Church as Polity? The Lutheran Context of Robert W. Jenson's Ecclesiology', in C. Gunton (ed.), *Trinity, Time and Church: A Response to the Theology of Robert W. Jenson* (Grand Rapids MI: Eerdmans, 2000), 201–37.

[37] For recent statements, see, for example, H.-P. Grosshans, *Die Kirche-irdischer Raum der Wahrheit des Evangeliums* (Leipzig: Evangelische Verlagsanstalt, 2003); E. Jüngel, 'The Church as Sacrament?', in *Theological Essays I*, trans. John Webster (Edinburgh: T&T Clark, 1989), 189–213; C. Schwöbel, 'The Creature of the Word. Recovering the Ecclesiology of the Reformers', in C. Gunton and D. Hardy (eds.), *On Being the Church: Essays on the Christian Community* (Edinburgh: T&T Clark, 1989), 110–55; Schwöbel, 'Gottes Ökumene. Über das Verhältnis von Kirchengemeinschaft und Gottesverständnis', in *Christlicher Glaube und*

Rather than regarding Protestantism as segregating the supernatural from the natural and as denying any stable or enduring presence of the former in the latter, Protestantism could instead be understood as following through the logic of the distinction between uncreated and created being in thinking about the church and its existence in time. The ecclesiology which to *ressourcement* theologians seems so docetic, so lacking in spacious historical extension, is a function of teaching about God. More closely, classical Protestant doubts about 'intrinsicist' ecclesiologies are rooted in a theology of God's presence to created being. In this theology, the relation of God to creatures—including his relation to the church as the 'creature of the Word'—is always a 'mixed' relation, real on the side of the creature but not on God's side, and therefore a wholly asymmetrical relation in which God's entire perfection remains undiminished apart from the church. The absolute distinction between God and creatures, to which attention is drawn by teaching about *creatio ex nihilo* and *creatio de novo*, prohibits us from thinking of creator and creature as within the same order of being, as may happen in a theology of the *totus Christus*. There is no relaxation of this rule, not even an incarnational or ecclesiological one.

It is this—rather than unrecognized extrinsicist metaphysics derived from the late medieval setting of the Reformation—which lies behind Protestant disquiet about what Balthasar called 'the Catholic passion for couplets'.[38] The 'external' orientation of Protestant ecclesiology, its sense that the discontinuity between the gospel and the church as ecclesiologically basic, is not a denial of the church's historical reality, though it is doubtless susceptible to docetic reduction. Properly formulated, it is a way of registering the fact that the church is an elect and summoned *congregatio fidelium*, wholly constituted by its creator whose life is incommunicable even as he gives himself in loving fellowship as the church's lord and redeemer.

Election, indeed, is a key ecclesiological motif, conveying in a potent way the sheer originality and spontaneity of God's relation to the church as his creature, the community at whose heart lies the divine *fiat!* The church, says Calvin, 'stands by God's election'.[39] This ought not to be pressed in such a way that it eliminates the proper union of Christ and the church. Rather, rooting ecclesiology in election sets the church's union with its head in the context of uncaused divine determination, and gives less weight to the church's historical

---

Pluralismus—Studien zu einer Theologie der Kultur (Tübingen: MohrSiebeck, 2003), 107–32; Schwöbel, 'Kirche als Communio', in *Gott in Beziehung. Studien zur Dogmatik* (Tübingen: MohrSiebeck, 2002), 379–435. See also the document *The Church of Jesus Christ: The Contribution of the Reformation Towards Ecumenical Dialogue on Church Unity* (Frankfurt/M: Lembeck, 1995), with the commentary by M. Beintker, 'The Church of Jesus Christ: An Introduction', *Ecclesiology*, 1 (2005), 45–58.

[38] Balthasar, *The Theology of Karl Barth*, 50.

[39] Calvin, *Institutes of the Christian Religion* (1559 edition), ed. J. T. McNeill (London: SCM Press, 1960), IV.1.iii (1015).

and social materiality as properties of Christ himself. An ecclesiology of union is properly a function of a Christology whose central motifs are the Son's unrepeatable historical work of redemption and his continuing inalienable activity of presenting himself through the Spirit.

Much more follows from the explication of Protestant ecclesiology out of the distinction between uncreated and created being. The church and its acts come to be thought of as witness to the presence of God rather than as internal to that presence or as modes of its extension and embodiment. The gospel is in a very important sense discontinuous from the church, since the gospel is a creative divine word which cannot be identified with any human form, even when it takes human instruments into its service. *Opus dei* and *opera ecclesiae* are to be distinguished, even if not wholly separated (for God elects creaturely means). The church is 'invisible' (or—to use Barth's happier term—'spiritually visible'), that is, constituted as a mode of human community by the action of the Spirit in assembling and giving life to the redeemed. Faithful attention to and attestation of the divine Word is basic to the church's constitution and activity. All this extends into ecclesiology the principle—fundamental to the doctrines of creation, incarnation, and grace alike—that whatever is said of God's relation to creatures is grounded in God's antecedent perfection in himself.

For *ressourcement* theologians, this may simply repeat the bifurcation of the sensible and the transcendent which produced Protestant spiritualism. The objection, it must be conceded, carries some weight: there have been degenerate forms of Protestant practice and theological reflection which have operated with the barest sketch of a doctrine of the church, or sequestered justification into an entirely private realm, or extracted scripture from the history of its reception. But these are no more authentic forms of Protestantism than textbook neo-scholasticism is an authentic reading of Thomas. The ecclesiology of the magisterial Reformers did not deny that life in the society of God takes tangible, social-historical shape. Rather, it sought to establish the external conditions for the church's historical visibility, to suggest that in ecclesiology, creatureliness goes all the way down. The practical-polemical constraints of the early Reformation period, and the Reformers' allergy to speculative divinity, hampered them in articulating the deep background of their ecclesiology. But a calmer setting allows us to see that the animating centre of their doctrine of the church is the doctrine of the triune God: the Father's free act of election, the Son's inparticipable act of redemption, the Spirit's sovereign distribution and realization of the benefits of election and redemption. These missions effect the renewal of time and society, but they are to be understood not only from the vantage point of their enactment in history, but also in terms of their reference back to the immanent divine processions of God's wholly-realized life. If the *ressourcement* question to Protestantism is whether such a doctrine of God's triune purity accords sufficient weight to God's plenitude in the economy, at least one Protestant response (which is not, of course, exclusively Protestant) might be that the economy of God's grace to the church has to be understood as derivative from the antecedent perfection of the creator.

CONCLUSION

The ecclesiology just outlined remains something of a minority report in contemporary Protestant theology. It is certainly a good deal less companionable to *ressourcement* theologies of the church, though not necessarily a less engaging conversation partner, even if the end of the conversation may be more divergence than convergence at the level of doctrinal substance.

These dogmatic differences aside, *ressourcement* theology offers an invitation to Protestant theology to renew its vocation as ecclesial science. *Ressourcement* theologians discovered the emancipating power of history— that poring over the traditions of Christian practice and reflection is not 'an impossible return to the past'[40] but an opportunity to see the present situation of theology for what it is: as a moment in the history of redemption. Modern Protestant theology has often been mesmerized into viewing the history of theology as a string of unrelated moments, each with its unique determining context by which it is shaped and insulated from the others, and so has found it acutely difficult to envisage the history of *theology* as an aspect of the history of the *church*.[41] But if the context of theological work is not simply the present moment as some quasi-absolute constraint but also and more importantly the long past of the Spirit's work, then 'tradition'—the intellectual and spiritual culture of the communion of the saints—is indispensable to the operation of theological reason. Among the many illusions under which some modern Protestant divinity operates are the beliefs that theology can decline to take part in the conversation of tradition and yet somehow remain intact and interesting, and that truly rational activity is always original. One is tempted to say that the future of Protestant divinity rests in some measure on its capacity to absorb and re-articulate the resources of the tradition(s) of Christianity—perhaps more than anything, its exegetical traditions and the modes of theological discourse in which they found expression. To do this, however, means facing a requirement to build a certain kind of theological culture, one whose ties to modern intellectual institutions are looser, one which reaches spiritual judgements about its wider contexts, one which is

---

[40] De Lubac, *Catholicism*, 172.
[41] See S. Holmes, *Listening to the Past : The Place of Tradition in Theology* (Grand Rapids MI: Baker, 2002).

expectant that the Christian past will prove a resource rather than an embarrassment or obstacle in rational work, and one which is open to risk experimenting with genres of theological writing largely lost to Western theology. The establishment of such a culture is, however, not simply a Protestant task, but one for ecumenical ecclesial reason.

31

French *Ressourcement* Theology and Orthodoxy: A Living Mutual Relationship?

Andrew Louth

INTRODUCTION

The purpose of this essay is to trace some of the links between French *ressourcement* theology in (mostly) the second and third quarters of the twentieth century and the Orthodox scholars who came to settle in the West, especially in Paris, in this period. My argument is that the relationship is a mutual one, each side learning from the other, and moreover that in this engagement one can see something of the dynamics of a genuine, mutually receptive, ecumenism.[1] I shall proceed by, first of all, setting the scene in general terms, then looking at some of the principal protagonists, on both sides, and finally look at what each side learnt from the other.

CONTEXT

In very general terms, we are dealing with an engagement between two different movements: on the Western side, with the reaction to the condemnation of Catholic Modernism, and on the Eastern side, with the presence in the West of Russian émigrés, expelled from Russia by Lenin (in 1922, most of them leaving in early 1923), who had themselves been formed by cultural and philosophical movements in nineteenth-century Russia that were inspired by, and also to some extent reacting against, nineteenth-century Western,

---

[1] For the notion of receptive ecumenism, see Paul D. Murray (ed.), *Receptive Ecumenism and the Call to Catholic Learning: Exploring a Way for Contemporary Ecumenism* (Oxford: Oxford University Press, 2008); of closest relevance to the present essay, see Louth, 'Receptive Ecumenism and Catholic Learning: An Orthodox Perspective', 361–72.

especially German, thought. It is immediately evident that, despite the widely different historical circumstances, their differences may not have been that great: neither in their background (Enlightenment, German idealism, etc.), nor in their *esprit*, the sense each had of what they were seeking for. But that is something that may emerge in what is to follow.

Catholic Modernism, as it became referred to, represented a range of belated attempts to catch up with cultural and philosophical developments since the Enlightenment, not least the growth of historical consciousness, and its application to the interpretation of the scriptures.[2] Roman Catholicism had reacted nervously and violently against the movements of thought of the nineteenth-century West. Pius IX, with his encyclical *Quanta Cura* of 1864 and the accompanying *Syllabus Errorum*,[3] set the face of the church, or at any rate the hierarchy, against the spirit of the age. The subsequent naming and condemnation of Modernism in the decree *Lamentabile* and the encyclical *Pascendi* by Pius X in 1907 was aimed at putting an end to all belated Catholic attempts to engage with the intellectual currents of the time.[4]

It is interesting to reflect, in passing, on the fact that one who is maybe the greatest Catholic thinker of the nineteenth century—John Henry Cardinal Newman, now Blessed—was someone who responded positively to the intellectual currents of the time (maybe because he encountered them in a more benign English form) and who certainly developed a sense of historical consciousness, manifest in his theory of development, as well as being fairly serene about the challenges to Victorian faith, in contrast to the panic that inspired the *Syllabus of Errors*. In many ways, he anticipates some of the features of the theological engagement this essay deals with, though he knew nearly nothing about Orthodoxy.

More generally, as a consequence of this repressive anti-Modernist climate, Catholic thinkers, especially if ordained, were well advised to steer clear of areas of thought that might lead them to contravene the anti-Modernist oath of 1910, effectively biblical criticism and dogmatic theology. This led such

---

[2] Within the huge bibliography on Modernism, see, e.g., Michele Ranchetti, *The Catholic Modernists: A Study of the Religious Reform Movement 1864–1907*, trans. Isabel Quigley (London: Oxford University Press, 1970).

[3] Pius IX, *Qanta Cura*. Encyclical Letter condemning Current Errors (8th December 1864), *ASS*, iii (1878), 160–8. ET available at: <http://www.papalencyclicals.net/Pius09/p9quanta. htm>. Also The Syllabus of Errors Condemned by Pius IX (1878), *ASS*, iii (1878), 168–76. ET available at: <http://www.papalencyclicals.net/Pius09/p9syll.htm>.

[4] See Pius X, *Lamentabili Sane*. Syllabus condemning the Errors of the Modernists (3 July 1907), *ASS* xl (1907), 470–8. ET Available at: <http://www.papalencyclicals.net/Pius10/ p10lamen.htm>; *Pascendi Dominici Gregis*. Encyclical Letter on the Doctrines of the Modernists (8 September 1907), *ASS* xl (1907), 593–650. ET available at: <http://www.vatican.va/holy_ father/pius_x/encyclicals/documents/hf_p-x_enc_19070908_pascendi-dominici-gregis_en.html>. For some sense of the crisis as it affected French intellectual life in the early years of the twentieth century, see René Marlé, *Au cœur de la crise moderniste: Le dossier inédit d'une controverse* (Paris: Aubier, 1960).

thinkers in the direction of historical theology, preferably covering less sensitive areas of church history, such as the period between the New Testament and scholasticism. As is treated in greater detail elsewhere in this volume, the dual focus of such intellectual activity came to be the Jesuit house in Lyon-Fourvière, where the presiding genius was Henri de Lubac (later, very much later, to receive the honour of the cardinalate), and the Dominican school of theology, Le Saulchoir, first in Belgium, then in Paris, where the shaping power was Marie-Dominique Chenu.[5]

In turn, the intellectual culture and theological concerns that the Russian émigrés brought with them in 1922/3 were also rooted in the nineteenth century, and again there was a sense of desperately trying to catch up. Russia (and the rest of the Orthodox world, though for different reasons) had missed out on the experience of Renaissance, Reformation, and Enlightenment that had determined the intellectual history of the West. Tsar Peter the Great's opening up of Russia to the West—symbolized by his moving the capital of Russia west to St Petersburg—had a profound effect not only on Russian society but also on its intellectual culture. Although the dominant movement of Slavophilism in the nineteenth century was in reaction against Westernism, at the same time it was deeply indebted to the West, and also conscious of how behind it was in comparison, and how much ground it had to make up. One sometimes gets the impression that Renaissance, Reformation, and Enlightenment had to be compressed into a few decades. But there was, too, especially among the Slavophiles, a sense that Russian thought and culture had been spared something by being shielded from these movements that had so affected western culture. The Russians were different, and indeed had something to offer the West that was already experiencing the strains on society caused by industrialization and capitalism. So, even though Slavophiles—especially Alexei Khomiakov and Ivan Kireevsky—were deeply influenced by German idealism, particularly the form that it took in Schelling (Hegel was a less important influence), there was a strong sense that there was something unique about the Russian experience.

One can point to what this meant in a couple of ways. First, we find a widespread sense that Western society had become characterized by individualism: industrialization and the growth of the city had produced an anonymous society consisting of faceless individuals, identified by their factory number or their address, and no longer gaining a sense of their human meaning from participation in the ordered society of pre-industrial communities. Throughout the nineteenth century, there is a sense that Russia is threatened by Western individualism, and that Russians should hold on to the notion of a person, formed by the society of the village from which they

---

[5] See the chapters by Étienne Fouilloux, Janette Gray, and David Grumett in this volume.

derived their sense of identity and meaning. What is later called 'personalism' was, for the Russians, rooted in the sense of what was in danger of being lost by the influence of Western notions.[6]

But secondly, the Slavophiles were conscious of their Christian, Orthodox heritage; conscious of being the only 'free' Orthodox nation (most of the rest of the Orthodox countries in the nineteenth century were struggling to free themselves from the Ottoman yoke), with, consequently, a responsibility for preserving and articulating the Orthodox tradition. Among other things this meant what in this volume we call *ressourcement*: recourse to the ancient Fathers of the church. Kireevsky spoke of the Fathers as having a kind of originary significance. As he put it, 'The holy Fathers speak of a country they have been to'; in their writings the Fathers bear 'testimony as eyewitnesses'.[7]

Arguably, the origins of this movement of *ressourcement* lie in the previous century with the publication in Venice in 1782 of the *Philokalia of the holy Ascetics* by St Makarios of Corinth and St Nikodimos of the Holy Mountain. This anthology (which is what 'philokalia' means) is a collection of ascetic texts of the Byzantine tradition stretching from the fourth to the fourteenth century. As Sts Makarios and Nikodimos were preparing their edition, from texts traditionally used by the monks of the Holy Mountain of Athos, St Paiisy Velichkovsky was translating a selection of the same texts into Slavonic, which were published as the *Dobrotolyubia* (the word is a calque of 'philokalia', and so suggests to the Slav reader 'love of beauty'). In its Slavonic form it became very popular in Russia, being read by St Seraphim of Sarov and the monks of Optino, a monastery, south of Moscow that became a spiritual centre for the Slavophiles and other intellectuals, such as Tolstoy and Dostoevsky. It fuelled a spiritual revival in Russia, which focused on the use of the Jesus Prayer and the importance of spiritual fatherhood, or *starchestvo* (echoes of which can be heard in Dostoevsky's novel, *The Brothers Karamazov*), but its significance was much greater, for it drew attention to the spiritual and intellectual vision of great Byzantine theologians such as St Maximos the Confessor and St Gregory Palamas. Optina Pustyn became a centre for a patristic revival, publishing translations of Fathers of the 'philokalic' tradition. This translation work was echoed in the Theological Academies, which embarked on a programme of patristic translation, so that, as Olivier Clément put it, 'at the

---

[6] Andrzej Walicki talks of the 'conservative romanticism' of the Slavophiles, something that we can recognize in English Romantics such as Wordsworth and Coleridge. See Walicki, *The Slavophile Controversy* (Oxford: Clarendon Press, 1975); and *A History of Russian Thought from the Enlightenment to Marxism* (Oxford: Clarendon Press, 1980). For 'personalism' *v.* 'individualism', see Tomáš Špidlík, *Die russische Idee: Eine andere Sicht des Menchens* (Würzburg: Der Christliche Osten, 2002), 29–44.

[7] From Kireevsky's 'Fragments'; cited in B. Jakim and R. Bird (trans. and eds.), *On Spiritual Unity: A Slavophile Reader* (Hudson NY: Lindisfarne Books, 1998), 248, 243.

end of the nineteenth century, Russia had at its disposal, in its own language, the best patristic library in Europe'.[8]

PRINCIPAL PROTAGONISTS

The context outlined above complicates the nature of *ressourcement* among the Russian émigrés in Paris in the 1920s and thereafter, for though *ressourcement* was claimed by those, such as Florovsky and Lossky, who saw the future of Orthodox theology as lying in the search for a 'neo-patristic synthesis', in reality *ressourcement* was deeply embedded in the Russian enterprise of theology and characterizes those whom the protagonists of the neo-patristic synthesis saw themselves as opposing. The extent to which this is true can be seen in the methodological statement put forward by Fr Sergii Bulgakov in his treatise on the Eucharist:

> But Orthodoxy has not yet said its word here. For this, it is necessary, first of all, to return to the theology of the fathers (one thousand years into the past), to the patristic doctrine, and to use it as a true guide, creatively to unfold it and apply it to our time. Secondly, it is necessary to make a total change in the *statement* of the question, where one gets away from Catholic cosmism, which reifies the eucharistic problematic, and in the unfolding of this problematic to rely not on Aristotle's *Metaphysics* but on the Gospel. In other words, the question must be returned to the domain of Christology, for it is essentially and wholly a *Christological* question.[9]

Bulgakov's theological method, as expressed here, amounts to a patristic *ressourcement*, not however a simply archaeological disinterment of the patristic texts, but allowing them to challenge our theological approach, enabling us to hear the Gospel, uncluttered by the philosophical language in which theological reflection has come to be expressed. His further suggestion that eucharistic theology must be seen as a *Christological* question is one that has wider application.

Nevertheless, the principal Orthodox figures that feature in drawing out the Orthodox dimension in Catholic *ressourcement* are those associated with the neo-patristic synthesis, in particular, the three Russians, Georges Florovsky, Myrrha Lot-Borodine, and Vladimir Lossky.

---

[8] O. Clément, 'Les Pères de l'Église dans l'Église orthodoxe', *Connaissance des Pères de l'Église*, 52 (December 1993), 25–6; quoted by Boris Bobrinskoy in his 'Le renouveau actuel de la patristique dans l'orthodoxie', in *Les Pères de l'Église au XXe siècle: Histoire-littérature-théologie* (Paris: Cerf, 1997), 437–44 (440).

[9] Bulgakov, *The Holy Grail & the Eucharist*, trans. Boris Jakim (Hudson NY: Lindisfarne Press, 1997), 82.

Before discussing them, however, it might be worth indicating the way in which the Russian émigrés encountered the theologians and philosophers of the West who welcomed them. Central to this encounter was the 'Berdyaev Colloquy', so called because it was convened by Nikolay Berdyaev, a leading figure among the Russian émigrés. Berdyaev himself (1874–1948) was a prolific philosopher who, like many others, moved from Marxism towards Orthodoxy, though his own Orthodoxy was highly idiosyncratic. Already in Moscow, after the revolution, he had founded a Religious-Philosophical Academy, though it was more of a discussion group, and included among its members S. L. Frank, I. A. Il'in, and B. P. Vysheslavtsev. Another enterprise promoted by Berdyaev was the journal, *Put'* ('The Way'), which became a forum for sharing ideas among the Russians in Europe. More important for the subject of this essay, however, was the 'Berdyaev Colloquy', an ecumenical discussion group, started in 1926, membership of which was by invitation only. Its members included, among the Catholics, Jacques Maritain, Gabriel Marcel, Charles du Bos, Lucien Laberthonnière, and occasionally Père Lebreton, Étienne Gilson, and Édouard Leroy. Among the Protestants were Marc Boegner, Wilfred Monod, and August Leeuf, and occasionally Pierre Maury; while the Orthodox members included Berdyaev, Florovsky, Sergii Bulgakov, Vysheslavtsev, and sometimes Lot-Borodine and V. V. Zenkovsky. The group met monthly, usually to hear and discuss a paper given by one of the members. It attracted the disapproval of the Catholic authorities and was abandoned after a couple of years, though later a small Catholic-Orthodox group reconvened. This smaller group lasted until the mid-1930s, when regular meetings ended after a 'terrible clash between Berdyaev and Maritain' (as Florovsky reported).[10]

The importance of the Berdyaev Colloquy is that it seems to have been the crucible in which the Russian émigrés refined their own theological and religious identity and came to understand how the Russian, or more generally, Orthodox tradition differed from the western traditions they found themselves encountering at close quarters in Paris. Although the traditional differences— the *Filioque* and the papal claims—were not neglected, it is not difficult to see that there emerged a sense that the real differences lay deeper. One can begin to understand what this meant in two, at least, of the works of Sergii Bulgakov: his work on the Mother of God, *The Burning Bush*,[11] which has long sections of polemical engagement with Roman Catholic Mariology, and his work on eucharistic theology, *The Eucharistic Dogma*.[12]

[10] All the information in this paragraph (with some corrections) comes from Andrew Blane (ed.), *Georges Florovsky: Russian Intellectual and Orthodox Churchman* (Crestwood NY: St Vladimir's Seminary Press, 1993), 54–5.
[11] See Bulgakov, *The Burning Bush: On the Orthodox Veneration of the Mother of God*, trans. Thomas Allan Smith (Grand Rapids MI/Cambridge: Eerdmans, 2009 (1927)).
[12] Bulgakov, *The Holy Grail & the Eucharist*, trans. Boris Jakim (Hudson NY: Lindisfarne Books, 1997 (original Russian articles published 1930, 1932)), 63–138.

In *The Burning Bush*, Bulgakov focused his criticism of Catholic Mariology on the doctrine of *natura pura*, the idea of a purely natural created state, which has no relation to God, for it is only with the advent of grace that the human person realizes its need for God.[13] It is a criticism that uncannily anticipates Henri de Lubac's criticism of the traditional Catholic understanding of the relationship between nature and grace, expressed in *Surnaturel* (1946), which attracted censure from Rome.[14] This convergence between Bulgakov and one of the promoters of Catholic *ressourcement* is surely not a matter of chance.

In his *The Eucharistic Dogma*, there is an attack on what purports to be St Thomas's doctrine of transubstantiation. Bulgakov does not show much evidence of having studied Aquinas in any depth,[15] but the treatise illustrates his sense that the differences between Orthodox and Catholic theology can be traced back to the rise of scholasticism in the West. The—Catholic—West for Bulgakov meant scholasticism and its greatest representative, Aquinas. Two members of the Berdyaev Colloquy—Jacques Maritain and Étienne Gilson— were leading representatives of the philosophical movement of the first half of the twentieth century known as neo-Thomism. Orthodox in Paris would also have encountered among their Catholic friends, especially clergy, the 'school Thomism' that was taught in the seminaries. These various kinds of Thomism came to represent Western (Catholic) theology, so far as the Orthodox were concerned. The Orthodox themselves found it easy to see their own theological endeavours as an answer or response to such Western latter-day scholasticism.

But there were points of contact, too. Another Catholic member of the Berdyaev Colloquy was Gabriel Marcel (1889–1973), known as a 'Christian existentialist' and compared with Sartre, though his most important works were published before Sartre came on the French scene.[16] Marcel's brand of personalist existentialism has many parallels with the personalism the Russians inherited from the Slavophiles, and it would appear that personalist existentialism provided a framework of ideas that many members of the Berdyaev Colloquy found congenial.

Let us look a little more closely at the three figures mentioned above, associated with the neo-patristic synthesis.[17] It is convenient to begin with

---

[13] See Louth, 'Father Sergii Bulgakov on the Mother of God', *St Vladimir's Theological Quarterly*, 49 (2005), 145–64, esp. 152–3.

[14] Compare John Milbank, *The Suspended Middle: Henri de Lubac and the Debate Concerning the Supernatural* (London: SCM Press, 2005).

[15] See Louth, 'The Eucharist in the Theology of Fr Sergii Bulgakov', *Sobornost*, 27/2 (2005), 36–56, esp. 44.

[16] Marcel's *Journal Métaphysique* is dated 1913–14 and 1915–23, and was published in 1927; his *Être et Avoir* was published in 1935. By contrast Sartre's *L'Être et le néant* was published in 1943.

[17] Extremely useful for biographical information on the émigrés is Antoine Niv'er, *Pravo-slavnye Svyashchennosluzhiteli, Bogoslovy i Tserkovnye Deyateli Russkoy Emigratsii b Zapadnoy Tsentral'noy Evrope 1920–1995: Biograficheskiy Spravochnik* (Moscow/Paris: Russkiy Put'/ YMCA Press, 1970).

Fr Georges Florovsky, as the notion of the neo-patristic synthesis is especially associated with his name, though he was not the oldest of our group. Although not born in Odessa, he moved there when he was one, and always thought of it as his home. It was there he went to university and studied in the historical-philosophical faculty, but also pursued studies in Mathematics, the Philosophy of Mathematics, and Biology and Psychology. Appointed to a chair in 1919, he soon left Russia, and by way of Bulgaria and Prague, found himself in Paris in 1926. He remained there until after the Second World War as professor of Patrology. By this time he was already involved in the ecumenical movement and after the war was one of the leading theologians engaged in the formation of the World Council of Churches, present at the first assembly in Amsterdam in 1948, and serving on the central committee from 1948 to 1961. In 1948 he went to the United States of America, where he remained for the rest of his life. First of all, he held the chair of Dogmatic Theology and Patristics at St Vladimir's Theological Seminary in New York from 1948 to 1955, being Dean from 1950. After a brief time at Holy Cross Greek Orthodox Seminary, he was Professor of the History of Eastern Christianity at Harvard from 1956 to 1964, and finally held a chair at Princeton University from 1964 until he retired in 1972. He died in Princeton in 1979.

The most important period of his life (for our purposes, and perhaps absolutely) was his time in Paris. He was a member of the Berdyaev Colloquy and formed a number of important friendships there, notably with Berdyaev himself and Jacques Maritain, and among the Russians, the Jewish philosopher, Lev Shestov, Myrrha Lot-Borodine, I. I. Fondaminsky, V. V. Rudnev, Lev Zander, and Fr Sergii Chetverikov.[18] The event that determined his theological orientation, however, was his role in the 'controversy over Sophia' (to adopt the title of Lossky's book on the controversy)[19]. Sophiology—speculation over the place of the Wisdom of God, Sophia, in theology—was central to Bulgakov's theological *œuvre*, which began with *The Unfading Light* (1917) and culminated in his great trilogy *On Godmanhood*, the last volume of which, *The Lamb of God*, was published in 1945, one year after his death. For Bulgakov's opponents, his theology was tainted by pantheism, verging on paganism. For Florovsky, Bulgakov demonstrated the bankruptcy of tradition of Russian religious speculation, which was indebted to German idealism.[20] It was against this, as well as against the theological traditions he had encountered in the West, that Florovsky's notion of the 'neo-patristic synthesis' was directed.

[18] See Blane, *Georges Florovsky*, 55–7.
[19] Vladimir Lossky, *Spor o Sofii* (Moscow: Izdatel'stvo Svyato-Vladimirskogo Bratstva, 1996).
[20] For an account of Florovsky's involvement in the Sophiological controversy, see Alexis Klimoff, 'Georges Florovsky and the Sophiological Controversy', *St Vladimir's Theological Quarterly*, 49 (2005), 67–100.

The programme of a 'neo-patristic synthesis' was intended to recall Russian Orthodox theology from what Florovsky called the '"pseudomorphism" of Russia's religious consciousness' or 'a "pseudomorphosis" of Orthodox thought'[21]—borrowing the geological term from Oswald Spengler's analysis of the 'decline of the West'—or more dramatically (echoing this time Martin Luther) 'the "Babylonian captivity" of the Russian Church',[22] which was held to be evident by the eighteenth century, and led, *via* the Slavophiles and wayward genius of Vladimir Solov'ev, to what Florovsky regarded as the near-paganism of sophiology. Florovsky's *Ways of Russian Theology* re-counted the errant wanderings of Russian theology to the point where it needed to be recalled to the 'patristic style and method' which had been 'lost'. This 'patristic theology must be grasped from within', he declared.[23] Florovsky spoke of 'intuition' as well as 'erudition', and argued that to regain this patristic way of thinking, or *phronema*, 'Russian theological thought must still pass through the strictest school of Christian Hellenism'.[24] Florovsky himself had a fine knowledge of the Fathers, but apart from a few articles,[25] his patristic scholarship is mostly found in the books derived from the lectures he gave in Paris in the late 1920s and 1930s,[26] and which found their way to publication through the efforts of Mother Maria Skobstova and the sponsor-ship of Fondaminsky, both of whom died in German concentration camps during the Second World War.

As is evident from the brief biographical account of his life given above, a great deal of Florovsky's post-war energies were caught up in the ecumenical movement. It is probably for this reason that Florovsky never did more than sketch out the lineaments of his neo-patristic synthesis, but it remained a clarion call, and much of the Orthodox theology of the latter half of the twentieth century can be seen as exploring what such a notion might mean. But the very notion of a neo-patristic synthesis demands *ressourcement* and, as we shall see, also came to contribute to it.

The next figure, less often mentioned in the context of the neo-patristic synthesis, is Myrrha Lot-Borodine (1882–1957). Born and educated in St Petersburg, she arrived in Paris in 1906 and became 'docteur de l'université' in 1909. Her principal academic interest, which she shared with her husband, the great medievalist Ferdinand Lot, was the Middle Ages, and especially the

[21] Florovsky, *Ways of Russian Theology*, i. *The Collected Works of Georges Florovsky*, v. (Belmont MA: Nordland Publishing, 1979), 85.

[22] Florovsky, *Ways*, i.121.

[23] Florovsky, *Ways*, ii. *Collected Works*, vi. (Vaduz: Büchervertriebsanstalt, 1987), 294.

[24] Florovsky, *Ways*, ii.297.

[25] Most of which can be found in vols. i–iv of the *Collected Works* (Belmont MA: Nordland Publishing Co., 1972–5).

[26] Published in English translation (not always satisfactory) in *Collected Works*, vols. vii–x (Vaduz: Büchervertriebsanstalt, 1987).

legend of the Holy Grail, her major work on which was published posthumously, with an introduction by Gilson.[27] But she brought to her study of the Latin Middle Ages a distinct Orthodox sensitivity, manifest most clearly perhaps in an article she published in 1951 that criticized Gilson's attempt to identify the grail in *La Quête del Saint Graal* with the scholastic notion of created grace.[28] In this article, she argued that the background of the Grail legend was to be sought in the common monastic heritage of both East and West, rather than in scholasticism, where Gilson sought to locate it. What this common heritage, in danger of being lost in the world of scholasticism, amounted to can be discerned from the articles she wrote expounding the Eastern tradition.

In the 1930s, she wrote a few articles on the doctrine of deification in the Greek Fathers, posthumously published as a book.[29] Another series of articles was published as a book in her lifetime, *Un maître de la spiritualité byzantine au XIVe siècle: Nicolas Cabasilas*.[30] Cabasilas's works include a commentary on the Divine Liturgy and another called *The Life in Christ*, an exposition of the Christian life as flowing from the sacraments of the church. Cabasilas is also generally counted among the supporters of the hesychasts of the fourteenth century. For Lot-Borodine, Orthodox theology was not a theoretical discourse, but concerned with the transformation of humanity made possible by the Incarnation and its continuation in the sacraments of the church. For her, scholasticism represented the danger of an intellectualizing of Christianity, a danger resisted by the monks, led by St Gregory Palamas, in the fourteenth-century hesychast controversy in Byzantium.

Our third figure was much younger, and also died young: Vladimir Lossky (1903–58). Also from St Petersburg, he left Russia together with his parents, as a result of Lenin's decree of 1922. By way of Prague, they arrived in Paris in 1924. Like Lot-Borodine, Lossky became a medievalist with a great love of medieval France. Throughout his life he worked on a dissertation on the Latin works of Meister Eckhart, with the intention of submitting it for a *doctorat d'état*, which was eventually published posthumously, with a preface by Étienne Gilson.[31] In Paris, he supported the Moscow Patriarchate in the confusion of the 1930s, and so did not belong to the Institut St-Serge, but to the rival Institut St-Denys, where he taught, as well as being affiliated to the Centre National de la Recherche Scientifique. He, too, was involved in the

---

[27] Myrrha Lot-Borodine, *De l'amour profane à l'amour sacré* (Paris: Librairie Nizet, 1961).

[28] Lot-Borodine, 'Les Grands Secrets du Saint-Graal dans la Queste du pseudo-Map', in R. Nelli (ed.), *Lumière du Graal* (Paris: Cahiers du Sud, 1951), 151–74, criticizing an article by Gilson, 'La mystique de la grâce dans "la Queste del saint-Graal"', originally published in *Romania*, 51 (1925), 321–47, and reprinted in Gilson, *Les Idées et les lettres* (Paris: Vrin, 1932).

[29] Lot-Borodine, *La déification de l'homme*, preface by Cardinal Jean Daniélou (Paris: Cerf, 1970).

[30] (Paris: Éditions de l'Orante, 1958).

[31] Lossky, *Théologie négative et connaissance de Dieu chez Maître Eckhart* (Paris: Vrin, 1960).

controversy over Sophia, which he opposed even more sharply than did Florovsky, though when Bulgakov died in 1944, he walked across France to be present at his funeral. The only book he published in his lifetime was his *Essai sur la théologie mystique de l'Église d'Orient*,[32] which became a kind of *vade mecum* for the neo-patristic synthesis. This synthesis he identified, far more clearly than did Florovsky, with the hesychast doctrine defended by St Gregory Palamas in the fourteenth century, with its key doctrine of the distinction between the unknowable essence of God and his energies, through which he makes himself known in the world. He also saw hesychasm and the essence-energies distinction as marking out the distinction between Orthodox theology and the West, typified by scholasticism and Aquinas. In another work, published posthumously, *Vision de Dieu*,[33] he sought to demonstrate how scholasticism had abandoned the historical tradition of the church over the vision of God.

The *ressourcement* we find in these three figures is in some respects very different from the French Catholic *ressourcement* with which it was contemporary. It is mostly about interpretation of the patristic tradition, and furthermore an interpretation aimed at providing a sense of identity over and against the West (though both Lot-Borodine and Lossky were fascinated by the—especially French—Middle Ages, and deeply attracted to them).[34] In contrast, French *ressourcement* was more committed to actually providing access to the patristic texts—notably through the series *Sources chrétiennes*, which was originally intended to provide cheap and reliable translations, though soon it became a series of (now very expensive) scholarly editions—and through reflection on these works, especially the works of the Greek Fathers, finding a new and deeper identity, enriching western experience with the witness of the East. Already before the war, however, Fr (later Archbishop) Basile Krivochéine and Fr Dumitru Stăniloae, both of whom did research on Palamas in the 1930s in Paris, were making a start on making available the Greek Fathers in the vernacular. For Stăniloae this blossomed in the Romanian *Philokalia*, a much expanded and more scholarly version of the Greek *Philokalia* published in Venice in 1782. Krivochéine's philological work formed the basis for the critical edition of the works of St Symeon the New Theologian that eventually appeared in *Sources chrétiennes*, the work of editing being completed by the Catholic scholars Darrouzès and Koder. In 1959 a beginning was made in the publication of critical editions of Palamas with John

[32] (Paris: Aubier, 1944). ET, *The Mystical Theology of the Eastern Church*, trans. members of the Fellowship of St Alban and St Sergius (Cambridge/Crestwood NY: James Clarke/St Vladimir's Seminary Press, 1957/1976).
[33] 1962; ET, *The Vision of God*, The Library of Orthodox Theology, 2 (Faith Press, 1964).
[34] See the diary Lossky wrote as the German armies invaded France and he followed the retreating French army, hoping to be able to join up, *Sept jours sur les routes de France: Juin 1940* (Paris: Cerf, 1998).

Meyendorff's edition of the *Triads*. Since then many critical texts of both sides of the hesychast controversy have been published, by both Orthodox and Catholic scholars.

RESSOURCEMENT AND MUTUAL
RECEPTIVE LEARNING

Ressourcement, then, was a collaborative project between Catholics and Orthodox, though, so far as the actual work of editing was concerned, the lion's share of this was done by the Catholics. The publication in fine critical editions, with translation, of the works of the Greek Fathers has been of enormous benefit to Orthodox, who have been able, as a result of this work, to gain a much deeper and more accurate knowledge of their own tradition.

It is obvious from the last few paragraphs that, both in editorial work and in reflection on the patristic tradition, there has been a tendency among Orthodox to focus on the works of Palamas and his supporters. This is part of a broader phenomenon in Orthodoxy that we have already highlighted at the beginning of this essay, when we asserted that the *fons et origo* of *ressourcement* in the Orthodox tradition in the modern period is to be found in the publication of the *Philokalia* in 1782. This collection of texts from the fourth to the fourteenth century culminates in a group of texts from Palamas and his supporters. The texts that lead up to this, while they do not ignore the dogmatic side of the faith (St Maximos is included, with whom no separation between the dogmatic and the spiritual/ascetic is possible), are primarily concerned with the Christian's life of prayer—a life of prayer that demands and effects a transformation of our human nature that the Greek Fathers called deification.

The influence of the *Philokalia* on modern Orthodox reflection has meant that speculative theology has never become detached from a demand to know what difference this is going to make to the way we live and the way we pray (and this is as true of the sophiological reflection of Solov'ev, Florensky, and Bulgakov, as it is of more evidently 'philokalic' writers such as Lossky and Fr Sophrony of Essex). The *Philokalia* has given to most modern Orthodox theology a certain complexion: one might sum this up by saying that the influence of the *Philokalia* has meant that God is approached as one to whom we pray and in encounter with whom we are transfigured and enabled to become vehicles of God's healing and transforming presence in the world—rather than a concept giving us a sense of God as the cause of the world, or the One who underwrites our sense of morality. All the Fathers can be approached in this way, but there is a core engagement with the transfiguring power of

God in Christ into which the 'philokalic' texts provided an initiation. A sense of inwardness to the tradition was something sensed in Lot-Borodine's work by Daniélou, as he remarks in his moving memoir of her that appeared as a preface to her book on deification:

> What made the work of Myrrha Lot-Borodine of exceptional value was not simply her dedication to learned research, but that she had rediscovered the living expression of Byzantine mysticism and she *knew* how to make it felt. Her work was nourished by her reading of the great spiritual authors and theologians of the Greek and Byzantine world. One found there echoes of Gregory and Evagrios, of Maximos the Confessor and Pseudo-Dionysios, of Symeon the New Theologian and Nicolas Cabasilas. She mentioned these authors often, but not by citing them. Her articles had the minimum of scholarly apparatus. That made them difficult to use. The boundaries between the experience of the author and that of her sources were difficult to trace.[35]

This sense of inwardness to a living tradition was, as Daniélou makes clear, an inspiration to him, as it must have been to others. So, though the Orthodox gained immeasurably from the Catholic commitment to *ressourcement*, they also contributed something, at least in terms of inspiration.

Nevertheless, the benefits of *ressourcement*, balanced against the scholarly commitment involved, have been distributed unevenly. Furthermore, in the Catholic world, *ressourcement* has moved on. Recent research on Aquinas, for instance, has detached him from the cold intellectual categories of 'scholasticism', and revealed a priest and friar whose theology was based on and nourished by the Bible, whose intellectual feats—though rigorous and logical—were at the service of an engagement with God, and not an end in themselves.[36] It is not difficult to see how this way of summing up the contrast between Catholic and Orthodox as Aquinas *versus* Palamas came about, but it is a contrast hard to maintain in view of the trends of recent Thomist scholarship.[37] French *ressourcement* was, under God's providence, a movement in which Catholic and Orthodox found themselves gaining mutual benefit from each other. The opportunities for such mutually enriching engagement are still there.

---

[35] Jean Daniélou, 'Introduction', *La déification de l'homme*, 11.

[36] See Nicholas M. Healey, *Thomas Aquinas: Theologian of the Christian Life* (Aldershot/ Burlington VT: Ashgate, 2003).

[37] Such as Healey's *Thomas Aquinas*; Fergus Kerr, OP (ed.), *Contemplating Aquinas*, (London: SCM Press, 2003); Kerr, *After Aquinas* (Oxford: Blackwell Publishing, 2002).

Epilogue

'Ressourcement' in Retrospect

John McDade

Man is separated from the past (even from the past only a few seconds
old) by two forces that go instantly to work and cooperate: the force of
forgetting (which erases) and the force of memory (which transforms)....

(Milan Kundera, *The Curtain*)

INTRODUCTION: REMEMBERING

If Milan Kundera is right, when something is remembered, it is not transcribed
as on to a blank page but is transformed because remembering is an act of
interpretation. At the same time, something else from that same event is erased.
So memory and forgetting are two features of how we engage with the past,
exercising a selectivity in relation to some things and an obliviousness in relation
to others. We do not realize that this is happening, Kundera thinks, because we
always act with a set of assumptions that pre-interpret the world for us and, at the
same time, block our perception of other things. He thinks that the novel, and
literature in general, is how we are taken beyond our pre-interpretative categories
and experience the world differently, more objectively. If we recall that the great
Augustinian scholar, Cornelius Jansenius, thought that 'theology is a discipline of
memory, and not of understanding (*entendement*)', we make an immediate
connection to our theme here because theology as an act of 'remembering',
and remembering better, is central to the project of *ressourcement*.[1] It will also
be concerned with 'forgetting' because it will try to restore features forgotten by

---

[1] J. Orcibal, *Jansénius d'Ypres (1585–1638)* (Paris: *Études augustiniennes*, 1989), 295.

earlier ways of remembering the past. Fortunately for us, readers and heirs of *ressourcement*, the dialectic of memory and forgetting in their hands is not at the expense of 'understanding'.

When we try to locate and assess the project of *ressourcement*, we should not assume that it has run its course. Everyone is agreed that *ressourcement* begins as the offspring of Modernism, unwittingly fathered by an intellectually repressive pontificate at the turn of the twentieth century. That it runs through virtually the whole of the twentieth century is testimony to the energy it unleashed; yet though the Second Vatican Council is its first fruits, the reception of that Council by the church is unfinished and so the dynamic of *ressourcement* is work in progress.

TWENTIETH-CENTURY CATHOLIC AND PROTESTANT *RESSOURCEMENTS*

With what might it be compared? Perhaps only with the massive upheaval of Barth's revision of the Protestant legacy which took place at the same time, his attempt to rescue it from the anthropocentrism and cultural prisons into which it had fallen. There is surely a parallel between what Barth tried to do in establishing a proper autonomy and method for theology based upon God's self-revelation (an Anselmian project) and what *ressourcement* tried to achieve within the Catholic tradition in re-centring the church's grasp of its identity. Where Barth saw a deterioration of Protestantism in the anthropocentrism of Schleiermacher's liberal children, Chenu saw a deterioration in the quality of Thomism among Aquinas' interpreters; both aimed at recovering stronger forms of Christian thought in which the restored actuality of the Reformation on the one hand, and the vigour of Aquinas on the other, would be able to take the church beyond the debilitated traditions previously available.

In the deformed theology against which Barth struggled, 'God was in danger of being reduced to a pious notion: the mythical expression and symbol of human excitation'.[2] (Echoes of the Catholic debates we conveniently call 'Modernism'.) It is no accident that Barth's double targets were Liberal Protestantism and Roman Catholicism, analogous betrayals of God on the basis of a deluded estimate of human nature and its religious impulses, and a violation of God's transcendent sovereignty. Hence Barth's mischievous and serious characterization of Catholicism as *Sancta Maria sopra Minerva*: a Church that over-values human effort, founding its life on 'revelatory sources' which could not convey God.

---

[2] Karl Barth, 'The Humanity of God' (1956) in *Karl Barth: Theologian of Freedom*, ed. C. Green (London: Collins, 1989), 48.

But unlike the Barthians, *ressourcement* theologians did not view their work as a recovery of a fundamental Christian principle that was being destroyed by European cultural processes. Nothing had gone fundamentally wrong with Catholic thought but certainly correction was needed through a better engagement with the Bible, the Fathers, and liturgy: reliable access to the sources of faith was a priority. Certainly they judged that what was promoted as Catholic theology was unhelpful and arid but this could be remedied by a better, more accurate and richer reading of the tradition.

But in Webster's view, the ecclesiology implied and subsequently strengthened by *ressourcement* is characteristically Catholic in the way the church is considered in relation to Incarnation and revelation. It expresses what he calls an 'ecclesiology of union' of Christ and church, in which the church is viewed as 'the enlargement of the hypostatic union'. Möhler's view of the church as an extension or continuation of the Incarnation is surely the inspiration here.[3] By contrast, Reformed ecclesiology is an 'ecclesiology of election' in which a stronger sense of the continued distinction between the divine and the human is preserved. In this Reformed ecclesiology which flows into Barth, 'the church and its acts come to be thought of as witness to the presence of God rather than as internal to that presence or as modes of its extension and embodiment'. Hence the widespread accusation by Congar and others that the Protestant tradition was 'extrinsicist', 'splitting apart social process and the economy of revelation', effecting in de Lubac's words, 'a complete severance of the natural and the supernatural'.[4] There is a fundamental difference in the ecclesial paradigms favoured in both the Barthian and *ressourcement* renewals. This is certainly one factor in explaining why the *ressourcement* theologians were so opposed to such extrinsicism, but it is not the whole story.

A related answer is found in a bulletin to Catholic youth chaplains written by de Lubac in occupied France in 1942, about the weakening of the sense of the sacred, and in some measure it takes us into the heart of the *ressourcement* project.[5] He highlights three features of the theological landscape around him.

---

[3] 'The visible Church ... is the Son of God himself, everlastingly manifesting himself among men in a human form, perpetually renovated, and eternally young—the permanent incarnation of the same.' (Johann Adam Möhler, *Symbolism* (1832), 259). No Barthian could say this. Cf. M. J. Himes, 'Divinising the Church: Strauss and Barth on Möhler's Ecclesiology', in D. J. Dietrich and M. J. Himes (eds.), *The Legacy of the Tübingen School* (New York: Crossroad, 1997), 95–110.

[4] See Y. Congar's *The Mystery of the Temple* (London: Burns & Oates, 1962), 293ff: in Protestant perception, 'God still works [now, in the Church] under the same conditions as formerly in Israel', in the mode of anticipation and promise. By contrast, in Catholic perception, 'the last things are already given to us in the Church' and through the Incarnation there is in the world a 'sacred reality—the body of Christ' existing under three forms: that raised in the resurrection, the Eucharistic species and the church. Cf William of Saint-Thierry, *On the Sacrament of the Altar*, c. 12; quoted in H. de Lubac, *Catholicism*, trans. Lancelot C. Sheppard (London: Burns & Oates, 1962), 245.

[5] De Lubac, *Theology in History*, trans. Anne Englund Nash (San Francisco: Ignatius, 1996), 223–40.

Firstly, 'the proportions of the theological edifice are poorly balanced: certain parts are hypertrophied [over-nourished and abnormally enlarged]; others, on the other hand, are greatly reduced ... because the dominant concern is less to seek an understanding of faith, to be nourished on mystery, than to respond to and oppose heresies'.[6] In other words, the teaching developed in order to combat earlier heresies is not a suitable means of restoring the sense of the sacred in secularized France.

Secondly, he says, 'current theology is not so much modelled on its sources, it is rather these sources that are chosen, interpreted, commented upon according to the need and the partialities of current theology'.[7] An acerbic judgement about how Catholic theologians understand their task: they are accused of visiting the past, raiding it, not in order that their work might be guided and inspired by teachings and procedures canonized in the tradition, but so that modern fashions in theology might be confirmed. Where Barth in similar critical vein accused liberals of doing this, de Lubac's target is a neo-scholasticism with plenty of answers to which no one knows the questions. A Denzinger-like taxonomy of past teachings is informative, not transformative: it does not allow the tradition to re-shape and renew the present, and yet the logic of the Church's identity in which past and present are mutually reinforcing streams of life demands a different strategy. How to get beyond the impasse of excessive taxonomies to which theology has been reduced? An ecclesiology needs to extend beyond limits currently in place, and, without invoking his name, de Lubac points his chaplains towards Newman: '[But] the doctrine of the Church extends far beyond what has been defined, put into formulas, promulgated by the competent authority during the course of the centuries according to the occasion ... How false the perspectives are at times.'[8] De Lubac points away from formal, juridical theology, guilty he implies of creating 'false perspectives', to what Newman calls the 'prophetical tradition', a co-foundational principle within the church, found in

> ... a certain body of Truth, pervading the Church like an atmosphere ... partly written, partly unwritten, partly preserved in intellectual expressions, partly latent in the spirit and temper of Christians; poured to and fro in closets and upon the housetops, in liturgies, in controversial works, in obscure fragments, in sermons, in popular prejudices, in local custom ... her accustomed and unconscious mode of viewing things, and the body of her received notions [rather] than any definite and systematic collection of dogmas elaborated by the intellect.[9]

---

[6] De Lubac, *Theology in History*, 277.
[7] De Lubac, *Theology in History*, 229.
[8] De Lubac, *Theology in History*, 229.
[9] John Henry Newman, *The 'Via Media' of the Anglican Church*, ed. H. D. Weidner (Oxford: Clarendon Press, 1990), 268–9. Congar, too, is surely influenced by Newman when the third of the 'monuments of tradition', following liturgy and the Fathers, is identified as 'ordinary

For Newman, the 'body of received notions', expressed in a range of aspects of ordinary Christian life, is how the episcopal tradition is balanced and complemented by the 'equally Apostolical' principle, that of the prophetical tradition. A differentiated ecclesiology, properly Catholic, biblical, and patristic, is already in view in de Lubac's remarks and the work of *ressourcement* is given one of its central features, a renewed ecclesiology. Congar's *Tradition and the Traditions, Lay People in the Church*, and de Lubac's *Catholicism* and *The Splendour of the Church* are magisterial expressions inspired by the church's prophetical tradition. Already, *Lumen Gentium* is on the horizon.

Thirdly, de Lubac says—and here we see the real reason for his detailed work on grace and nature—the church has fostered an excessively sharp separation of the sacred and the secular, with the consequence that people cannot see any necessity for a religious language because the secular has an autonomy and self-sufficiency, which leaves no role for the supernatural except as something to please 'women and children':

> Is a theory that tends to separate the supernatural from nature a suitable instrument for penetrating the whole reality and life of the authentically sacred? Is it not in danger, on the contrary, of favoring or promoting confusions that place the whole of Christianity in question? Finally, in a shriveled, rationalized world, how will we make the sense of this Sacred spring up anew if we have let ourselves be contaminated by this world to the point of participating, even if only in small amounts, in its shriveling rationalism?[10]

The source of this rationalism, he says, lies in a Christian apologetic in which Christian thinkers insisted so strongly on a rational demonstration of God's existence that we have presented the world with 'a secular God' who can be proved rather than a God whose actuality is perceived in the deepest dimensions of our God-directed nature.[11] God is thought of only in the context of a logical demonstration that God *must* exist if the world exhibits features of order and design. Signs of the supernatural within the dynamic of the natural and living signs of the actuality of God in prayer, experience, and the movements of the heart are ignored in favour of a rational proof about a possible God. With what consequence? By removing the sacred from the secular, we have created the secular and established it as a God-free zone.

'Men, taking us at our word... relegated this supernatural to some distant corner where it could only remain sterile. They exiled it to a separate province, which they willingly abandoned to us, leaving it to die little by little under our care.'[12] Taking Christians seriously when they said that there is a gulf between the

expressions of the Christian life', Congar, *Tradition and Traditions: An historical and a theological essay*, trans. Michael Naseby and Thomas Rainborough (London: Burns & Oates, 1966), 450.
[10]   De Lubac, *Theology in History*, 236.
[11]   De Lubac, *Theology in History*, 235.
[12]   De Lubac, *Theology in History*, 232.

supernatural and the natural, human beings decided that the supernatural has nothing to do with a proper consideration of the way the world is; the Church then finds that it is in a condition of exile as a consequence of an imbalance within theology concerning the supernatural. A certain way of doing theology gives rise to atheism which, in Fergus Kerr's phrase, is 'an inside job' orchestrated unwittingly by Christian apologists.[13] The pastoral problems of the twentieth century, de Lubac implies, are a consequence of a certain way of doing theology, and if they are to be addressed, they cannot be solved by repeating the same theology (heresy-obsessed, formulaic and rationalistic to the point of occluding the mystery of the divine) that gave rise to them in the first place.[14]

The chaplains who read de Lubac's tripartite analysis of the 'internal causes' within the church which brought about a weakened religious sense read him in full flight. No wonder de Lubac presented himself to them in the role of the 'biblical Satan', the accuser, 'the malicious analyst of the faults of the just'[15] who pointed out the things which impeded their mission to the people of France. A theology over-concerned with past heresies, unable to bring the past into a corrective and positive relation to the present and suffering from a rationalistic bias leading to deism and atheism: these are what de Lubac, 'the devil's advocate', asks them to abjure as a prelude to a resourced mission. Significantly, these points are made not to theologians but to youth chaplains because these are primarily pastoral issues rather than issues solely within the technical competence of theologians. They are issues for the whole church to address; de Lubac as a theologian of the *ressource-ment* will play his part in trying to find a way past the impasse.[16]

THE HEART OF *RESSOURCEMENT*

De Lubac's address takes us into the heart of the project of *ressourcement*, articulating a strategy about how the past can be made to speak again to the

---

[13] 'The "death of God", as one might have expected, was an inside job, the result of two or three centuries of "natural theology". By shifting to supposedly neutral religion-free ground to mount proofs of the existence of God, these theologians inaugurated a whole tradition of philosophical theology which dialectically generated its own negation. Historically, atheism would thus be the product of a certain kind of theism.' (Fergus Kerr, OP, 'Aquinas After Marion', *New Blackfriars*, 76 (1995), 354–64).

[14] De Lubac's view that atheism is a consequence of how Christians taught others to think about God is developed by Michael Buckley in *At The Roots of Modern Atheism* (New Haven CT: Yale University Press, 1987).

[15] De Lubac, *Theology in History*, 233.

[16] What would he have made of Iris Murdoch's remark? 'Nor ... does it seem to me that the Christian religion has been able to present us in recent times with any satisfying or powerful picture of ourselves and each other.' *Existentialists and Mystics* (London: Chatto & Windus, 1997), 270.

present and how the church might find what it needs for its mission of awakening faith. It is an example of the correction, revision, and nourishment which the church has the right to expect from its theologians if it is to have an effective mission. Are *correction, revision, and nourishment* all that different? De Lubac would seem to make them necessary aspects of what a theologian ought to do for the church. Can the church be nourished without experiencing correction and revision of its central teachings? Yes, of course, and this is what preaching is meant to do in the ordinary circumstances of the church's life. But on occasion, at times of major upheavals in culture and belief when the church's mission no longer works, correction and revision are needed to enable the church to re-appropriate its identity and fitness for mission.

What makes this both possible and necessary is the connection between *identity* and *history* in the church's sense of itself. The way the church *is* (its identity) and what the church *has been* (its past) form the 'double helix' of its genetic identity: a renewed grasp of its history brings about a changed grasp of identity and a renewed sense of identity recasts the history which informs it. This is the thought world of *ressourcement*: to move between the past and the present in mutually illuminating, corrective, and nourishing ways.

But how is the relationship of past and present to be viewed? Congar suggests that it is not a question of 'the relation of the present to the past': this, he says, is 'too precise an expression', presumably because it suggests two discrete things, one 'then' and the other 'now', which a neutral interpreter has to bring into relationship. He suggests that we think rather of '*the continuing presence of the past in the present*':[17] with this formula, the past is not to be viewed as a foreign country to which we send envoys (*ressourcement* pioneers) commissioned to report back on the features of ancient landscapes. Instead, in the life of the church, past and present are never separated because the present is constituted by the past in an organic, continuing way: think of the Eucharist and the Bible, both of which constitute the actuality of church. The church relates to them not as to historic realities to which it must pay attention, but as two essential principles which make the church what it is. ('Eucharistic ecclesiology', for example, is tautologous, as is 'Christian theology' for the Barthian.)

The distinction Congar makes between *tradition* and *the monuments of tradition* challenges the view that *ressourcement* is primarily a work of historical correction and retrieval. The church is a living interpreter of its own reality (this constitutes tradition); the 'monuments of tradition' (liturgy, Fathers, and ordinary Christian life) are the 'objective historical realities' which this self-interpretation produces in time.[18] (Congar's *Tradition and Traditions* is an extended hermeneutic of the project of *ressourcement*.) The working of 'tradition' cannot be reduced to repeating the elements contained in the 'monuments

---

[17] Congar, *Tradition and Traditions*, 264 (emphasis added).
[18] Congar, *Tradition and Traditions*, 452.

of tradition', but it cannot be done without engaging those monuments as intelligently as possible, and that means an acceptance of the contingent history of those monuments. Historical inquiry and hermeneutics, instead of being perceived threats to timeless, propositional truths, become key instruments by which tradition performs its task of interpreting the Word of God entrusted to it.

The simple statement of *Dei Verbum* § 12 that in scripture 'God has spoken through human agents to humans' validates the task of establishing 'what meaning the Biblical writers had in mind' and thus exegesis, and the history of interpretations of sacred texts, becomes integral to the work of tradition-bearing. Daley speaks of the retrieval by de Lubac 'of a more lively, historically aware understanding of the long tradition in which the church lives', identifying him as 'the first modern scholar to take patristic biblical exegesis seriously' as a factor in how scripture is to be understood. Thus, in the perspective of *ressourcement*, scripture and its reception history belong together, and so de Lubac's procedures, *avant la lettre*, exemplify the way in which *Dei Verbum* says that scripture and tradition are to be related. Going further, Daley describes the Bible as 'a single, continuous book, formed from many layers and parts...a continuing inheritance of earlier interpretive traditions' which generate the church's identity. Consequently, the church 'was formed into a living community of faith around text and interpretive traditions'. *Ab initio*, therefore, the church is an interpretative and self-interpretative community in which exegetical traditions and what flows from them constitute the corpus of its faith: 'Scripture, tradition, and teaching church form and define one another', in Daley's words.

What the *ressourcement* theologians were doing then was not a work of retrieval, but an act of ecclesial self-interpretation conducted by them on behalf of the church. There are good reasons why the defenders of the tradition looked critically at theologians who understood their task to be that of thinking *for the church* in ways that the church needed but did not (yet) acknowledge. Were they misunderstood or understood correctly by their critics? Did Garrigou-Lagrange, now the focus of much theological scorn, get them wrong when he saw them as a continuation of 'Modernism'? Even if one grants that 'Modernism' does not always have consistently identifiable features, the consensus is surely that he was wrong. But he was probably right in seeing that a consequence of their approach was that the church was being pressed to undertake a major paradigm shift in how it saw revelation and history, seeing revelation, in John Webster's words as 'not an external, timeless, and apodictic announcement but a process of transmission, at once temporal and social'.

What the propositionalist apologetics against which *ressourcement* reacted could not see was that the history of its interpretations is built into the character of revelation and that a creative engagement with revelation cannot ignore an engagement with the history of how it is interpreted. In this respect, *ressourcement* is an instance of theology's self-corrective appropriation of its identity, an engagement with the complexity and the historical character of the church's interpretative tradition. But on what basis does this appropriation take place? How does an interpretative, rational tradition such as theology relate to its past? Intelligently and responsibly, and with practical skills such as that identified by Alasdair MacIntyre:

> One has to acquire a certain kind of *knowing how* which enables one to move from the achievements of the past...to the possibility of new achievements, which will depend upon making them in what may be some very different way. It is the possession and transmission of this kind of ability to recognize in the past *what is and what is not a guide to the future* which is at the core of any adequately embodied tradition.[19]

This is exactly what an intellectual tradition such as theology ought to do. Catholic *ressourcement* is aimed not at a nostalgic restoration of earlier forms of thought and life but at 'new achievements' in different, as yet unforeseen contexts. Theology has a history which needs to be constantly revisited for insight or correction. Using MacIntyre again, theology conducted within the Catholic Church is 'a tradition-constituted and tradition-constitutive enquiry'. It begins in 'the beliefs, institutions, and practices of some particular community which constitute a given'; within that community, 'authority has been conferred upon certain texts and certain voices'; no less certainly, texts and utterances become susceptible to incompatible interpretations and divergent views, in which 'confrontations by new situations, engendering new questions, may reveal within established practices and beliefs a lack of resources for offering or for justifying answers to these new questions'. This is de Lubac's situation, the life-setting of the *ressourcement* theologian, in which the attempt to recast identity through a renewed grasp of history results in 'a set of reformulations, re-evaluations, and new formulations and evaluations designed to remedy inadequacies and overcome limitations'.[20]

RESSOURCEMENT: RE-INTERPRETING THE PAST

MacIntyre says that historians of philosophy have two ways of interpreting the philosophies of the past. Either they read them in ways that make them relevant to our modern problems and enterprises, transforming them into

---

[19] Alasdair MacIntyre, *Three Rival Versions of Moral Enquiry* (Notre Dame IN: University of Notre Dame Press, 1990), 127–8 (emphasis added).
[20] MacIntyre, *Whose Justice? Which Rationality?* (London: Duckworth, 1988), 354–5.

what they would be if they were part of our intellectual world. Or they read earlier writers in their own terms, respecting their very different character and presuppositions, 'so that they cannot emerge into the present except as a set of museum pieces'.[21] The choice is between reading earlier writers as a way of addressing present issues or reading them so that they come through to us as distinctly unmodern, alien voices who cannot be absorbed into contemporary debates.

To which of these strategies does *ressourcement* correspond? At first glance, it seems to be a reading of the past, a selective retrieval with an eye on modern concerns, in order to give the church a better grasp of its faith. But if this is the strategy, then do *ressourcement* theologians treat the present as the context where the right *questions* are asked and the past as where the *answers* to those questions are found? How then does it differ from what de Lubac criticized in the arid theological world of 1942 in which elements of the past are 'chosen, interpreted, commented upon according to the need and the partialities of current theology'? But to raise the matter in this way is too crude. A good part of what *ressourcement* theologians did was to learn from earlier writers how the questions ought to be framed in the first place. The outstanding intellectual achievement of the *ressourcement* project is de Lubac's work on grace, and here de Lubac's primary task was to learn and clarify which questions should *not* be asked and why, before the right questions, guided by a rigorous examination of the past, could be posed.[22] The work which Chenu initiates in the study of St Thomas is both an attempt to place him in his thirteenth-century context—thereby making him very different from the flattening portrayal to which centuries of Thomism had subjected him—and simultaneously to propose an analogous, historical engagement on the part of the modern theologian. These ventures, inadequately summarized here, are subtle acts of reading and interpretation.

In the hands of its masters, *ressourcement* is a work of reinterpretation, analogous to Harold Bloom's description of revisionism in literary criticism as 'a re-aiming, or a looking-over-again, leading to a re-esteeming or a re-estimating'. Bloom's description of what a revisionist aims at is not far from what a re-sourcing theologian tries to do: 'to *see* again, so as to *esteem* and *estimate* differently, so as then to *aim* "correctively"'.[23] The aim of the revisionist critic, as of the *ressourcement* theologian, is to effect a changed understanding through a changed reading of authoritative texts, 'monuments', and teaching.

---

[21] MacIntyre, 'The Relation of Philosophy to its Past', in R. Rorty, J. B. Schneewind, and Q. Skinner (eds.), *Philosophy in History* (Cambridge: Cambridge University Press, 1984), 31–48 (31).
[22] John Milbank, *The Suspended Middle: Henri de Lubac and the Debate Concerning the Supernatural* (Grand Rapids MI: Eerdmans, 2005).
[23] Harold Bloom, *A Map of Misreading* (New York: Oxford University Press, 2003), 4.

What is one to make of the cavalier way in which Congar and Chenu take upon themselves the project of 'liquidating Baroque theology', as though a whole swathe of post-Tridentine religion should be wiped from public consciousness in order to allow 'true' tradition to shine through with lambent gleam? This is not the only example: some of the most distinguished exponents of authentically Catholic *ressourcement* in the wake of the Council could be bitter street-fighters. Think of the marginalization of Karl Rahner in the modern church because he does not share the ecclesiology currently in favour.[24] *Ressourcement* has a hard edge to it; there is something of the partisan about some of its theologians who, unprovoked, enjoyed 'biffing' others. In its hostility to 'Baroque theology', or more accurately, post-Tridentine scholastic religious thought, was it being unbalanced? Probably, but that is how things were in those days; *ressourcement* theologians were not unique in having blind spots and prejudices. (Kundera's remark earlier about the co-presence of remembering and erasure is relevant.) In saying this, we are doing no more than recalling that *ressourcement* is as historical, contingent, and limited as any other theological movement, subject no less than they to imbalances and biases.

Ruddy is surely correct in saying that 'it would be a strange *ressourcement*, after all, that simply regarded centuries of thought as a new Dark Ages or that reduced complex eras and theologies to brief, often dismissive summaries in textbooks.' From within the logic of the project of *ressourcement*, this is surely correct and Ruddy is right to propose that post-Tridentine theology has an enduring relevance 'for both the reception of Vatican II and *ressourcement* itself'. It is hardly surprising that the movement so comprehensively rejected by some *ressourcement* theologians should now be proposed for an analogous retrieval; certainly, the logic is beyond challenge, but the timing is uncertain.

While Barth's re-ordering of theology was founded upon restoring God's self-interpretation in Christ to the foundational starting point from which everything would unfold, the project of *ressourcement* has no identifiable starting point with which it might stand comparison with Barth. This, except to those in the grip of theory, is not a weakness. At the end of his first lecture in a German university, Rowan Williams was asked 'What is your methodological starting point?' An intimidating question at the best of times, and even more so in the home of *theologische Wissenschaft*. Williams says that it was at odds with his sense that 'the theologian is always beginning in the middle of things', always and already immersed in a shared way of interpreting human

---

[24] How strange that the essay on Rahner in this volume should carry, in its title, a suggestion that he is 'an alternative' to *ressourcement*. Lennan's excellent essay presents Rahner as deeply engaged in a philosophical *ressourcement* of the highest quality. Rahner distrusts metaphors and theologies that depend on them because they are slippery. While it can be difficult to distinguish between aesthetic and theological criteria in the modern church, it would be a pity if this disqualified him from belonging to the *ressourcement* movement.

life as lived in relation to God.[25] The point is that there is no starting point outside that experience of being in the middle, no panoptic *point de répère* from which one can take detached, neutral bearings and calculate how we stand in relation to God, or more usually, how God stands in relation to us, anxious, preening creatures that we are. Doing theology means standing in that 'middle', attentively, with an eye both on the present state of the church's life and reflection and on how it relates to its complex, often conflicted, past.

Where should we locate the moment of *ressourcement* within theology? Again, Williams will help: he proposes that theology be characterized as an enfolding of three styles: the *celebratory*, the *communicative*, and the *critical*. The *celebratory* style seeks to use the resources of thought and language to construct a theological fullness of vision that reflects the divine glory 'as kingfishers catch fire, dragonflies draw flame', as Hopkins's poem expresses it. Here, theology is the verbal equivalent of an icon, a piece of music, or a religious ritual, conveying through sign and symbol the generative trinitarian mystery of God. In this style, theology aims to communicate the felt presence of God, not as a theme of consciousness but as a direction and a response of the prayerful self/community. It is a theology created, in Balthasar's words, as 'an act of homage to the Lord of the Church' known and worshipped in prayer. (For many people, Balthasar himself is the most effective exponent and interpreter of this style within the trajectory of *ressourcement*.)

This articulation of the experience of God then flows into the *communicative* style, in which theology experiments 'with the rhetoric of its uncommitted environment' and witnesses to the Gospel's 'capacity for being at home in more than one cultural environment'. It signals a move outwards into the public space, through an articulation of Christian faith which 'those imperfectly covenanted' (i.e., Gentiles) might recognize as the completion of what they already know and sense. It is a Pauline mission which assumes a public to whom the church's vocabulary is strange. If this is to happen, there must be a confidence that Christian faith is robust enough to be drastically immersed in other ways of interpreting the world. And of course, this is not always the case: think of the attempted closing down of the Catholic mind in the attack on 'Modernism' during Pius X's pontificate.

In response to the question that must always arise, 'Is what is emerging through the communicative style identical or continuous with what has been believed in the past?', the third style of theology comes into its own, what Williams calls the *critical* (surely more accurately the *self-critical*) style. In its attempt to develop an understanding that is, on the one hand, continuous with its sources and roots, and, on the other, fit for an effective *missio ad gentes*, the

---

[25] Rowan Williams, *On Christian Theology* (Oxford: Blackwell, 2000), pp. xii–xv.

church needs to ensure that the process of translation, adaptation, and transmission (*trahere*) is not at the same time an act of betrayal (*tradere*). At the same time, in this third mode, theology learns to attend to the tensions between its past and its possible future, become attentive to its own irresolutions and uncertainties, and to the difficulty of speaking of God at all. This style is characterized by a 'nagging at fundamental meanings', a worrying sense that because we have no sure grip on divine things, what we say about God can only be an unwarranted act of colonization.

Theology, Williams suggests, does not end with this self-critical moment, but points its newly acquired attentiveness and tentativeness back into its originating task, that of expressing the experience of God: '[theology] may move towards a rediscovery of the celebratory by hinting at the gratuitous mysteriousness of what theology deals with, the sense of a language trying unsuccessfully to keep up with a datum that is in excess of any foresight, any imagined comprehensive structure. And the cycle begins again.'[26]

If we take Williams's scheme of a tripartite theological cycle (a tricycle?) to designate the sources, purpose, and reflexivity of theology, then two points should be made. Firstly, *ressourcement* should be set in the transition between the second and third styles when questions of continuity and self-examination arise as a consequence of an unsuccessful *missio ad gentes*. Secondly, its aim is not the antiquarian repristination of Patristic religion or Tridentine liturgy, but purification and correction. It is not a process by which Christians clothe themselves in older styles, assuming an (imagined) identity appropriate to an earlier age which permits us to bypass modernity. The best Catholic reflection of the twentieth century was impelled by the sense that the church's grasp of its faith was not adequate for what it had to do. As we saw with de Lubac, the project of *ressourcement* is missionary and evangelical in intent, not antiquarian, aiming to place at the church's disposal a Gospel able to speak to modern sensibilities about the sense of the sacred.

REMEMBERING OUR JEWISH ROOTS

We began with an enigmatic remark by Milan Kundera about remembering and forgetting, two sides of how the past comes into the present: when one thing is remembered, another related thing is forgotten. The project of *ressourcement* has set in train the recovery of a forgotten relationship, an erased aspect of identity central to Christian self-definition, namely the relation of the church to the Jewish people. The simple statement in *Nostra Aetate* that the Council

---

[26] Williams, *On Christian Theology*, p. xv.

'remembers the spiritual bonds' between the church and the Jewish people set in motion a remarkable recovery within the church of an insight embedded in the earliest Christian community, namely that the church has an intrinsic and living connectedness to Israel because Christ, said John Paul II, 'carried to its extreme consequences the love demanded by Torah'. In one of the layers in the archaeological *tel* that is the New Testament, Christ instructs the people, 'The scribes and the Pharisees sit on Moses' seat, so practise and observe whatever they tell you—but not what they do' (Mt 23.2). The memory of the Jewish-Christian core of early Christianity, what Jacob Jervell famously called 'the mighty minority', knew that what comes to expression in Christ cannot be detached from what comes to expression in Israel, and therefore Christ-centred life cannot be understood or practised without reference to Israel's relation to God. At this early stage, the church was formed, in the phrases Daley uses to describe de Lubac and *Dei Verbum*, 'into a living community of faith around text and interpretative traditions'. It negotiated then its inheritance of earlier interpretative traditions, such as this text set within the Gospel of Matthew, and an analogous process is happening again, and at the highest levels of the church, with considerable consequences for Christian self-definition.

In the Mainz Synagogue in 1980, Pope John Paul spoke of 'the people of God of the Old Covenant which has never been revoked', and in 1982 he spoke of the unique relations between Christianity and Judaism which are 'linked together at the very level of their identity', relations which are 'founded on the design of the God of the covenant'. In 1998 Joseph Ratzinger wrote that Christians 'ought to acknowledge the decree of God, who has obviously entrusted Israel with *a distinctive mission* in "the time of the Gentiles"'.[27] The Vatican's 'Notes on the Correct Way to present the Jews and Judaism in Preaching and Catechesis' view the persistence of Jewish identity and religion since Christ as divinely willed: 'The permanence of Israel (while so many ancient peoples have disappeared without trace) is a historic fact and a sign to be interpreted within God's design...We must remind ourselves how the permanence of Israel is accompanied by a continuous spiritual fecundity.'[28] These are remarkable teachings, radical reversals of earlier 'teachings of contempt' and supersessionism, fresh yet ancient retrievals within the dynamic of the church's self-understanding.[29]

---

[27] Joseph Ratzinger, 'Interreligious Dialogue and Jewish-Christian Relations', *Communio*, 25 (1998), 29–41 (37). With this little phrase, 'a distinctive mission', Ratzinger summarizes an astonishing and rapid revolution in how the Catholic Church thinks of Jews.

[28] Pontifical Council for Promoting Christian Unity, Commission for Religious Relations with the Jews, 'Notes on the Correct Way to present the Jews and Judaism in Preaching and Catechesis in the Roman Catholic Church', Part VI, § 1. ET available at: <http://www.vatican.va/roman_curia/pontifical_councils/chrstuni/relations-jews-docs/rc_pc_chrstuni_doc_19820306_jews-judaism_en.html>.

[29] Supersessionism is the view that because the particularity of Israel's election by God has now given way to the universality of the church's mission from Christ, the observance of Jewish life *post et extra Christum* can have no role in the working out of God's purposes.

Precisely because they are the recovery of insights embedded in the earliest Christian community centred on Jerusalem, these teachings inaugurate a new, resourced tradition in which a mature church, long since separated from its earliest Jewish matrix, sets itself the task of relating positively to the Jewish people. It recognizes that the church belongs within the dynamic of Israel's election by God and therefore, in spite of its predominantly Gentile character and its creativity in engaging with a broader context of human experience, it has an organic, living connection with covenantal Israel from Abraham which is never left behind. The point is that if Christianity springs from Israel for the sake of the nations as the fulfilment of the Abrahamic covenant, what is brought about in the church belongs within the dynamic of God's dealings with Israel, and therefore church and Israel are as linked as Jesus Christ and Israel were (are) linked. If *ressourcement* is how the church articulates its identity/history, then the specific features of the caesura, the break with Judaism through the emergence of a Pauline Torah-free Gospel must be examined and appropriated in the spirit of *ressourcement*, as Rahner recognized:

> Today, as a matter of fact, perhaps in contrast to patristic and medieval theology, we do not have a clear, reflective theology of this break, this new beginning of Christianity with Paul as its inaugurator; perhaps that will only gradually be worked out in a dialogue with the Synagogue of today.[30]

We can do no more than point to this issue as entirely within the trajectory of *ressourcement*. At first, the work of *ressourcement* involved a re-centring, a deepening, a re-vision, a spiralling inwards in order to renew the specifically Christian core of identity and tradition. This emerging second dimension of *ressourcement* takes relationality *ad extra* as the keynote, specifically the church's relation to Israel. Cardinal Walter Kasper's view that 'Judaism is a sacrament of every otherness that as such the Church must learn to discern, recognise and celebrate' indicates the wider significance of what such a recovery might bring.[31] If carried through, then a correction, revision, and nourishment of the church's faith in relation to Israel may be eventually the most significant achievement of *ressourcement*, especially if it is conducted jointly by both Christians and Jews.

---

[30] Karl Rahner, 'Towards a Fundamental Theological Interpretation of Vatican II', *TS*, 40 (1979), 716–27 (723).

[31] W. Kasper 'Address on the 37th Anniversary of *Nostra Aetate*', quoted in H. Schoot and P. Valkenberg, 'Thomas Aquinas and Judaism', *Modern Theology* 20 (2004), 51–70 (67).

Bibliography

Church Documents

Pope Benedict XIV, *Certiores Effecti*, Bull. Rom. Bened. XIV, XIV, 1.213–213.

Pope Pius VI, *Auctorem Fidei*, Bull. Rom. Cont., 9.395–418.

Pope Pius IX, *Quanta Cura*. Encyclical Letter condemning Current Errors (8 December 1864), *ASS* 3 (1878) 160–8.

——— Syllabus of Errors Condemned by Pius IX, *ASS* 3 (1878), 168–76.

Pope Leo XIII, *Aeterni Patris*. Encyclical Letter on the Restoration of Christian Philosophy (4 August 1879), *Acta Leonis XIII*, 1 (1881), 255–84.

Pope Pius X, *Motu proprio, Tra le sollecetudini* (22 November 1903), *ASS*, 36 (1903–4), 331.

——— *Sacra Tridentina Synodus* S. Congregatio Concilii, *Sacra Tridentia Synodus, ASS*, xxxviii (1905), 400–6.

——— *Pascendi Dominici Gregis*. Encyclical Letter on the Doctrines of the Modernists (8 September 1907), *AAS* 40 (1907), 593–650.

——— *Encyclical Letter (Pascendi): on the Doctrines of the Modernists toe decree (Lamentabili) of July 4, 1907, on Modernist Errors* (London: Catholic Truth Society, 1937).

——— Syllabus Concerning the Errors of the Modernists, *Lamentabili Sane* (3 July 1907), *ASS* 40 (1907), 470–8.

Pope Pius XI, *Mortalium Animos*. Encyclical Letter on Religious Unity (6 January 1928), *AAS* 20 (1928), 5–16.

——— *Mit brennender Sorge*. Encyclical Letter of Pope Pius XI on the Church and the German Reich (14 March 1937), *AAS* 29 (1937), 145–67.

——— *The Papal Encyclicals 1903–1939*, iii (ed.), Claudia Carlen, 5 vols (Raleigh: Pierian, 1990), 525–35.

Pope Pius XII, *Mystici Corporis Christi*. Encyclical Letter on the Mystical Body of Christ (29 June 1943), *AAS* 35 (1943), 195–248.

——— *Divino Afflante Spiritu*. Encyclical Letter on Promoting Biblical Studies (30 September 1943), *AAS* 35 (1943), 297–325.

——— address to the Jesuits, *L'Osservatore Romano* (18 September 1946) and Dominicans, *L'Osservatore Romano*, (22–23 September, 1946).

——— *Humani Generis*. Encyclical Letter concerning some False Opinions Threatening to Undermine the Foundations of Catholic Doctrine (12 August 1950), *AAS* 42 (1950), 561–78.

——— *False Trends In Modern Teaching: Encyclical Letter (Humani Generis)*, trans. Ronald A. Knox, rev. edn. (London: Catholic Truth Society, 1959).

——— 'Applied Psychology. Address to the Rome Congress of the International Association of Applied Psychology' (10 April 1958), *AAS* 50 (1958), 268–82.

Pope John Paul II, 'Address to a Delegation of the Coptic Orthodox Church' (23 June 1979), *AAS* 71 (1979), 1000–1.

Pope John Paul II, *Dives in Misericordia*. Encyclical Letter on the Revelation of Mercy (30 November 1980), *AAS* 72 (1980), 1177–232.

—— *Dominum et Vivificantem*. Encyclical Letter on the Holy Spirit in the Life of the Church and the World (18 May 1986), *AAS* 78 (1986), 809–900.

—— *Ut Unum Sint*. Encyclical Letter on Commitment to Christian Unity (25 May 1995), *AAS* 87 (1995), 921–82.

—— 'Message to the Participants in the Course on the Internal Forum Organized by the Apostolic Penitentiary' (20 March 1998), *AAS* 90 (1998), 608–13.

—— *Ecclesia de Eucharistia*. Encyclical Letter on the Eucharist in its Relationship to the Church (17 April 2003), *AAS* 95 (2003), 433–75.

Pope Benedict XVI, 'Christmas Greetings to the Members of the Roman Curia and Prelature' (22 December 2005), *AAS* 98 (2006), 40–53.

—— 'First Message of His Holiness Benedict XVI at the end of the Eucharistic Concelebration with the Members of the College of Cardinals in the Sistine Chapel', (20 April 2005), *AAS* 97 (2005), 694–9.

—— *Deus Caritas Est*. Encyclical Letter on Christian Love (25 December 2005), *AAS* 98 (2006), 217–52.

—— 'Letter of His Holiness Benedict XVI to the Bishops on the Occasion of the Publication of the Apostolic Letter "Motu Proprio Data" *Summorum Pontificum* on the use of the Roman Liturgy Prior to the Reform of 1970' (7 July 2007), *AAS* 99 (2007), 777–81.

—— Homily for the closing of the 49th International Eucharistic Conference (22 June 2008), *AAS* 100 (2008), 485–8.

—— *Anglicanorum Coetibus*. 'Apostolic Constitution Providing for Personal Ordinariates for Anglicans Entering into Full Communion with the Catholic Church' (4 November 2009), *AAS* 101 (2009), 985–96.

—— 'Pastoral Letter of the Holy Father Pope Benedict XVI to the Catholics of Ireland', 19 March 2010.

'Proposal of the Holy Office' (1960) in *Acta et Documenta Concilio Oecumenico Vaticano II Apparando* i.iii (Vatican: Typis Polyglottis Vaticanis, 1960) 4, 9.

Catechism of the Catholic Church (1992; revised, 1997).

Books and Articles

'La Théologie et ses sources: réponse aux Études critiques de la Revue thomiste (mai-août) 1946', *RSR*, 33 (1946), 385–401.

Henri-Marie Féret: Dominicain: 1904–1992, unpublished pamphlet of the '*Groupe évangélique*' (Paris, 1992).

Le Lyonnais—Le Beaujolais, Dictionnaire du monde religieux dans la France contemporaine, ed. Xavier de Montclos (Paris: Beauchesne, 1994).

Proceedings of the Conference 'Surnaturel: une controverse au Cœur du thomisme au XXe siècle', *RevTh*, 109 (2001), 5–351.

'Henri de Lubac's *Catholicism* at 70 Years', *Communio*, 35 (2008).

RSR, 97/2 (2009).

Acerbi, Antonio, *Due ecclesiologie. Ecclesiologia giuridica ed ecclesiologia di comunione nella 'Lumen Gentium'* (Bologna: Edizioni Dehoniane, 1975).

Afanasíev, Nicholas, 'The Church Which Presides in Love', in John Meyendorff *et al.* (eds.), *The Primacy of Peter in the Orthodox Church*, trans. Katherine Farrer (London: Faith Press, 1963), 57–110.

———— *The Primacy of Peter: Essays in Ecclesiology and the Early Church*, ed. John Meyendorff (repr.) (Crestwood NY: St Vladimir's Seminary Press, 1992).

———— 'Una Sancta', in Michael Plekon (ed.), *Tradition Alive. On the Church and the Christian Life in Our Time* (Lanham MD: Rowman & Littlefield, 2003), 3–30.

Aguettant, Louis, *La vie comme une œuvre d'art: Biographie*, ed. Jacques Longchampt (Paris: L'Harmattan, 2006).

Alberigo, Giuseppe, 'From the Council of Trent to "Tridentinism"', in Raymond F. Bulman and Frederick J. Parrella (eds.), *From Trent to Vatican II: Historical and Theological Investigations* (New York: Oxford University Press, 2006), 19–37.

Alberigo, Giuseppe, and Joseph Komonchak (eds.), *History of Vatican II*, 5 vols (Leuven/Maryknoll: Peeters/Orbis, 1996–2006).

Albertson, James S., 'Instrumental Causality in St. Thomas', *New Scholasticism*, 28 (1954), 409–35.

D'Ambrosio, Marcellino, '*Ressourcement* theology, *aggiornamento*, and the hermeneutics of tradition', *Communio*, 18 (1991).

Ardagh, John, *The New French Revolution: A Social and Economic Survey of France, 1945–1967* (London: Secker & Warburg, 1968).

Arendt, Hannah, *The Origins of Totalitarianism*, 9th edn. (New York: Schocken Books, 2004).

Arnauld, Antoine, *La tradition de l'Église sur le sujet de la pénitence et de la communion* (Paris: Antoine Vitré, 1644).

———— *Œuvres*, 42 vols (Paris: Sigismond d'Arnay, 1775–82).

Aron, Raymond, *L'opium des intellectuals* (Paris: Calman Levy, 1955).

———— *The Opium of the Intellectuals* (Garden City NY: Doubleday, 1957).

Aubert, Roger, *Le problème de l'acte de foi. Données traditionnelles et résultats des controverses récentes* (Louvain: Universitas Catholica Lovaniensis, 1945).

———— 'Discussions récentes autour de la Théologie de l'Histoire', *Collectanea Mechliniensia*, 33 (1948), 129–49.

———— *La Théologie Catholique au milieu du XXe siècle* (Tournai: Casterman, 1954).

———— 'The Modernist Crisis and the Integrist Reaction', in R. Aubert, J. Bruhls, and J. Hajjar (eds.), *The Church in a Secularised Society*, trans. Janet Sondheimer (New York/London: Paulist/Darton, Longman & Todd, 1978), 198–203.

———— '*Humani generis*', in *Dictionnaire d'histoire et de géographie ecclésiastique*, s.v., 334–9.

Auricchio, John, *The Future of Theology* (Staten Island NY: Alba, 1970).

Auvray, Paul, *Richard Simon (1638–1712)* (Paris: Presses Universitaires de France, 1974).

Ayres, Lewis, *Nicaea and its Legacy: An Approach to Fourth-Century Trinitarian Theology* (New York: Oxford University Press, 2006).

———— 'The Soul and the Reading of Scripture: A Note on Henri de Lubac', *Scottish Journal of Theology*, 61 (2008), 173–90.

Backus, I., 'The Fathers in Calvinist Orthodoxy: Patristic Scholarship', in I. Backus (ed.), *The Reception of the Church Fathers in the West*, 839–65.

Backus, I., (ed.), *The Reception of the Church Fathers in the West* (Leiden: Brill, 1997).

Baldovin, John F., 'Hippolytus and the *Apostolic Tradition*: Recent Research and Commentary', *TS*, 64 (2003), 520–42.

von Balthasar, Hans Urs, 'Patristik, Scholastik, und Wir', *Theologie der Zeit*, 3 (1939), 65–104.

———— *Présence et pensée: Essai sur la philosophie religieuse de Grégoire de Nysse* (Paris: Beauchesne, 1942).

———— *Wahrheit der Welt* (Einsiedeln: Benziger, 1947).

———— 'Peace in Theology', *Communio*, 12 (1985), 398–407.

———— *Theo-Drama*, i. *Prolegomena*, trans. Graham Harrison (San Francisco: Ignatius Press, 1988).

———— *Test Everything, Hold Fast to What Is Good: an Interview with Hans Urs von Balthasar by Angelo Scola*, trans. Maria Shrady (San Francisco: Ignatius Press, 1989).

———— *The Theology of Henri de Lubac: An Overview*, trans. Joseph Fessio, SJ and Michael M. Waldstein (San Francisco: Ignatius Press, 1991).

———— 'Who is the Church?', in *Explorations in Theology*, ii, *Spouse of the Word*, trans. A. V. Littledale, Alexander Dru *et al.* (San Francisco: Ignatius Press, 1991), 143–91.

———— *Theology of Karl Barth: Exposition and Interpretation*, trans. Edward T. Oakes (San Francisco: Ignatius Press, 1992).

———— *Theo-drama: Theological Dramatic Theory, vol. 3, The Dramatis Personae: The Person in Christ*, trans. Graham Harrison (San Francisco: Ignatius Press, 1992).

———— *The Theology of Karl Barth: Exposition and Interpretation*, trans. Edward T. Oakes, SJ (San Francisco: Ignatius Press, 1992).

———— 'Bertolt Brecht: the Question about the "Good"', *Explorations in Theology* iii. *Creator Spirit*, trans. Brian McNeil, CRV (San Francisco: Ignatius Press, 1993).

———— *My Work in Retrospect*, trans. Brian McNeil (San Francisco: Ignatius Press, 1993).

———— *Theo-Logic: Theological Logical Theory*, i. *Truth of the World*, trans. Adrian J. Walker (San Francisco: Ignatius Press, 2000).

Barlow, Bernard, *A Brother Knocking at the Door: The Malines Conversations, 1921–1925* (Norwich: Canterbury, 1996).

Bars, Henry, 'Gilson et Maritain', *RTh*, 7 (1979), 237–71.

Barth, Karl, *Fides Quaerens intellectum: Anselms Beweis der Existenz Gottes im Zusammenhang seines theologischen Programms* (Munich: Chr. Kaiser Verlag: 1931).

———— *Natural Theology—Comprising Nature and Grace by Professor Dr Emil Brunner and the reply No1 By Dr Karl Barth* (London: The Centenary Press, 1946).

———— *Dogmatics in Outline*, trans. G. T. Thomson (New York: Harper & Row, 1959).

———— *Credo*, trans. J. Strathearn McNab (New York: Scribner's, 1962).

———— *The Göttingen Dogmatics: Instruction in the Christian Religion*, trans. Geoffrey W. Bromiley (Grand Rapids MI: Eerdmans, 1991).

———— *Church Dogmatics II.1. The Patience and Wisdom of God*. Revised Study Edition (London: T&T Clark, 2009).

Barthes, Roland, *Sade, Fourier, Loyola*, trans. Richard Miller (New York: Hill and Wang, 1976).

Bartlett, Robert, *The Natural and the Supernatural in the Middle Ages* (Cambridge: Cambridge University Press, 2008).

Baum, Gregory (ed.), *The Twentieth Century: A Theological Overview* (Maryknoll NY: Orbis, 1999).

Beauduin, Lambert OSB, *Liturgy the Life of the Church* 3rd edn. (Farnborough: St Michael's Abbey Press, 2002).

Bedouelle, Guy, OP (ed.), *Marie-Dominique Chenu: Moyen-Âge et Modernité* (Paris: Le Centre d'Études du Saulchoir, 1995).

de la Bedoyere, Michael, *The Life of Baron von Hügel* (London: Dent, 1951).

Beintker, M., 'The Church of Jesus Christ: An Introduction', *Ecclesiology*, 1 (2005), 45–58.

Bellarmine, Robert, *Disputationes de controversiis*, 4 (*De Conciliis*).

—— *De controversiis christianae fidei adversus huius temporis haereticos*, Book III, Chapter 2, *Opera Omnia* II (Naples, 1856).

Benoit, Pierre, *Aspects of Biblical Inspiration* (Dubuque IL: Priory Press, 1965).

—— *Inspiration and the Bible* (London: Sheed and Ward, 1965).

—— *Jesus and the Gospel*, i (New York: Herder and Herder, 1973).

Berdiaeff, Nicholas, *Une nouveau Moyen Âge* (Paris: Plon, 1927).

Bergé, Christine, *L'au-delà des Lyonnais: Mages, Médiums et Francs-Maçons du XVIIIe au XXe siècle* (Lyon: Lugd, 1995).

Bertrand, Dominique, 'Patristique et apologétique, *Catholicisme*', in *Bulletin de l'Institut Catholique de Lyon*, 116 (January–March 1997), 17–29.

Bishop, Edmund, 'The Genius of the Roman Rite', in *Liturgica Historica: Papers on the Liturgy and Religious Life of the Western Church* (Oxford: Clarendon Press, 1962 [1918]), 1–19.

Blane, Andrew, (ed.), *Georges Florovsky: Russian Intellectual and Orthodox Churchman* (Crestwood NY: St Vladimir's Seminary Press, 1993).

Blet, Pierre, 'La querelle de la moralité du théâtre avant Nicole et Bossuet', *Revue d'histoire littéraire de la France*, 5–6 (1970), 553–76.

—— 'L'idée de l'épiscopat chez les évêques français du XVIIe siècle', in B. Vogler (ed.), *Miscellanea historiae ecclesiasticae: Colloque de Strasbourg, septembre 1983, sur 'L'institution et les pouvoirs dans les églises de l'antiquité à nos jours'* (Brussels: Nauwelaerts, 1987), 315–19.

Block, Ed, 'Balthasar's literary criticism', in Edward T. Oakes, SJ and David Moss (eds.), *The Cambridge Companion to Hans Urs von Balthasar* (Cambridge: Cambridge University Press, 2004), 207–23.

Blondel, Maurice, *L'Action: Essai d'une critique de la vie et d'une science de la pratique* (Paris: Alcan, 1893).

—— 'Histoire et dogme', *La Quinzaine*, 56 (1904), 145–67, 349–73, 433–58.

—— *Histoire et dogme* (La Chapelle-Montligeon: Libraire de Montligeon, 1904).

—— 'Le Point de départ de la recherche philosophique', *Annales de philosophie chrétienne*, 151 (1906), 337–60; 152 (1906), 225–49.

—— 'The Latent Sources in St. Augustine's Thought', in M. C. D'Arcy, SJ (ed.), *A Monument to St. Augustine* (London: Sheed & Ward, 1930), 317–53.

—— *et al.*, 'La notion de philosophie chrétienne', *Bulletin de la société française de la philosophie*, 31 (1931), 37–93.

—— *Le problème de la philosophie catholique* (Paris: Bloud & Gay, 1932).

Blondel, Maurice, *Lutte pour la civilisation et philosophie de la paix* (Paris: Flammarion, 1939).

────── *Correspondance*, ii (Paris: Aubier, 1957).

────── *Lettres philosophiques* (Paris: Aubier, 1961).

────── *Dialogues avec les philosophes: Descartes; Spinoza; Malebranche; Pascal; Saint Augustin*, Preface, Henri Gouhier (Paris: Aubier, 1966).

────── *Action (1893): Essay on a Critique of Life and a Science of Practice*, trans. Olivia Blanchette (Notre Dame IN: University of Notre Dame Press, 1984).

────── *The Letter on Apologetics and History and Dogma*, trans. and ed., Alexander Dru and Illtyd Trethowan (Grand Rapids MI: Eerdmans, 1994).

────── *Œuvres complètes*, vol. i, ed. Claude Troisfontaines (Paris: PUF, 1995).

────── *Œuvres complètes*, vol. ii, *1888–1913: La philosophie de l'action et la crise moderniste*, ed. Claude Troisfontaines (Paris: PUF, 1997).

────── *Une alliance contre nature: catholicisme et intégrisme, La Semaine sociale de Bourdeaux 1910*, repr. (Brussels: Editions Lessius, 2000).

Bobrinskoy, Boris, 'Le renouveau actuel de la patristique dans l'orthodoxie', in *Les Pères de l'Église au XXe siècle. Histoire-littérature-théologie* (Paris: Cerf, 1997), 437–44.

────── 'Le P. Yves Congar et l'orthodoxie', *Istina*, 48 (2003), 20–3.

Bockmuehl, Markus, *Seeing the Word: Refocusing New Testament Study* (Grand Rapids MI: Baker Academic, 2006).

Boersma, Hans, *Nouvelle Théologie and Sacramental Ontology: A Return to Mystery* (Oxford: Oxford University Press, 2009).

Boissard, Guy *Charles Journet, 1891–1975* (Paris: Salvator, 2008).

Bonhoeffer, D., *Discipleship*, trans. John D. Godsey (Minneapolis MN: Fortress, 2001).

Bonino, Serge-Thomas, OP, 'Historiographie de l'école thomiste: le cas Gilson', in Bonino (ed.), *Saint Thomas au XXe siècle*, 299–313.

────── (ed.), *Saint Thomas au XXe siècle*, Actes du colloque du Centenaire de la *Revue Thomiste* (Paris: Centre National de Livre-Saint Paul, 1994).

Bonnefoy, J.-F., 'La théologie comme science et l'explication de la foi selon S. Thomas d'Aquin', *EphTh*, 14 (1937), 421–46; 15 (1938), 491–516.

────── *La nature de la théologie selon S. Thomas d'Aquin* (Paris/Bruges: Vrin/Beyaerts, 1939).

Borne, Étienne 'Pour refaire une chrétienté', *VI*, 9 (1936).

Botte, Dom B., 'Holy Orders in the Ordination Prayers', in *The Sacrament of Holy Orders* (Collegeville MN: Liturgical Press, 1962), 5–23.

────── 'Collegiate Character of the Presbyterate and Episcopate', in *The Sacrament of Holy Orders* (Collegeville MN: Liturgical Press, 1962), 75–97.

────── 'The Collegial Character of the Priesthood and the Episcopate', *Concilium*, 4/1 (1965), 88–90.

Bouyer, Louis, *L'Incarnation et l'Église: Corps du Christ dans la théologie de saint Athanase* (Paris: Cerf, 1943).

────── *Le Mystère Pascal: (Paschale Sacramentum). Méditation sur la liturgie des trois derniers jours de la Semaine Sainte* (Paris: Cerf, 1945).

────── 'Le Renouveau des études patristiques', *VI*, 15 (1947), 6–25.

────── *The Paschal Mystery: Meditations on the Last Three Days of Holy Week*, trans. Sister Mary Benoit (London: Allen and Unwin, 1951).

—— *The Meaning of the Monastic Life*, trans. Kathleen Pond (London: Burns & Oates, 1955).

—— *Liturgical Piety* (Notre Dame IN: University of Notre Dame Press, 1955).

—— *The Spirit and Forms of Protestantism*, trans. A.V. Littledale (London: Harvill Press, 1956).

—— *The Meaning of Sacred Scripture*, trans. Mary Perkins Ryan (Notre Dame IN: University of Notre Dame Press, 1958).

—— *Introduction to Spirituality*, trans. Mary Perkins Ryan (New York: Desclée, 1961).

—— *The Word, Church and Sacraments in Protestantism and Catholicism*, trans. A. V. Littledale (New York: Desclée, 1961).

—— *Dictionary of Theology*, trans. Charles Underhill Quinn (New York: Desclée, 1965).

—— *Life and Liturgy*, 3rd edn. (London: Sheed & Ward, 1965).

—— 'Liturgie juive et chrétienne,' in Lancelot Sheppard (ed.), *Le Culte en Esprit et en Vérité* (Paris: Desclée et Cie, 1966), 45–62.

—— *The Eternal Son: A Theology of the Word of God and Christology* (Huntington IN: Our Sunday Visitor, 1978).

—— *Le métier de théologien: entretiens avec Georges Daix* (Paris: Editions France-Empire, 1979).

—— *The Church of God, Body of Christ and Temple of the Spirit*, trans. Charles Underhill Quinn (Chicago: Franciscan Herald Press, 1982).

—— *Mystérion: Du Mystère à la mystique* (1986).

—— *The Christian Mystery*, trans. Illtyd Trethowan (Edinburgh: T&T Clark, 1990).

—— *Women Mystics*, trans. Anne Englund Nash (San Francisco: Ignatius Press, 1993).

—— *The Invisible Father: Approaches to the Mystery of the Divinity*, trans. Hugh Gilbert (Petersham MA/Edinburgh: St Bede's/T&T Clark, 1999).

—— *Le métier de théologien* (Geneva: Ad Solem, 2005).

Bouillard, Henri, *Conversion et grâce chez S. Thomas d'Aquin: Étude historique*, Théologie 1 (Paris: Aubier, 1944).

—— 'L'idée chrétienne du miracle', *Cahiers Laënnec*, 8 (1948), 25–37.

—— 'Notions conciliaires et analogie de la vérité', *RSR*, 35 (1948), 251–71.

—— 'L'intention fondamentale de Maurice Blondel et la théologie', *RSR*, 36 (1949), 321f.

—— *Genèse et evolution de la Théologie dialectique*, Théologie 38 (Paris: Aubier, 1957).

—— *Parole de Dieu et existence humaine, 1 & 2* Théologie 39 (Paris: Aubier, 1957).

—— *Blondel et le christianisme* (Paris: Seuil 1961).

—— 'Le Sens de l'apologétique', *Bulletin du comité des études de la Compagnie de Saint-Suplice*, 35 (1961), 311–26.

—— 'Plan d'un cours d'apologétique', *Bulletin du comité des études de la Compagnie de Saint-Suplice*, 35 (1961), 449–52.

—— *Connaissance de Dieu* (Paris: Aubier 1967).

—— *The Logic of Faith* (London: Sheed & Ward, 1967).

Bouillard, Henri, *Blondel and Christianity* trans. James M. Somerville (Washington: Corpus Books, 1969).

——— *Knowledge of God*, trans. Samuel D. Fermiano (New York: Herder and Herder, 1969).

——— *Comprendre ce que l'on croit* (Paris: Aubier, 1971).

——— *Vérité du christianisme*, Théologie (Paris: Desclée De Brouwer, 1989).

Boyer, Charles, 'Nature pure et surnaturel dans le *Surnaturel* du Père de Lubac', *Gr*, 28 (1947), 279–95 (291).

Brambilla, Franco Giulio, '*Theologia del Magistero* e fermenti di rinnovamento nella teologia cattolica', in G. Angelini and S. Macchi (eds.), *La teologia del Novecento: Momenti maggiori e questioni aperte*, Lectio, 7 (Milan: Glossa, 2008), 189–236.

Braun, F.-M., *The Work of Père Lagrange* (Milwaukee WI: Bruce, 1963).

Brechter, H. S., 'Decree on the Church's Missionary Activity', trans. W. J. O'Hara, in H. Vorgrimler (ed.), *Commentary on the Documents of Vatican II*, iv.87–181.

Bredin, J.-D., *The Affair* (New York: Braziller, 1986).

Brosse, Olivier de la, *Le Père Chenu: la liberté dans la foi* (Paris: Cerf, 1969).

Buche, Joseph, *L'École mystique de Lyon (1776–1847): Le grand Ampère, Ballanche, Cl.-Julien Bredin, Victor de Laprade, Blanc Saint-Bonnet, Paul Chenavard, etc.* (Lyon: A. Rey, 1935).

Buclet, Françoise, '"Le Van", Revue lyonnaise de bibliographie, 1921–1939', unpublished Master's dissertation (Université Lumière-Lyon II, 1995).

Buckley, Michael J., SJ, *At the Origins of Modern Atheism* (New Haven: Yale University Press, 1987).

Bugnini, Annibale, CM, *The Reform of the Liturgy 1948–1975*, trans. Matthew J. O'Connell (Collegeville MN: Liturgical Press, 1982).

Bulgakov, Sergei, *The Holy Grail & the Eucharist*, trans. Boris Jakim (Hudson NY: Lindisfarne Press, 1997).

——— *The Burning Bush. On the Orthodox Veneration of the Mother of God*, trans. Thomas Allan Smith (Grand Rapids MI/Cambridge: Eerdmans, 2009).

Buonaiuti, Ernesto, 'The Future of Catholicism', in Claud Nelson and Norman Pittenger (eds.), *Pilgrim of Rome: An Introduction to the Life and Work of Ernesto Buonaiuti*, 1st edn. (Welwyn, Herts: Nisbet, 1969), 102–4.

Burke, Peter, *The French Historical Revolution: the Annales School 1929–89* (Cambridge: Polity Press, 1990).

Burrell, David, *Aquinas: God and Action* (Scranton PA/London: University of Scranton Press, 2008).

Cabié, Robert, *The Church at Prayer II: The Eucharist* (Collegeville MN: The Liturgical Press, 1992).

Cagin, Michel, 'Le mystère de l'Église: En relisant le livre du Père Clérissac', *Nova et vetera* (1991), 28–48.

Calvin, J., 'Two Discourses on the Articles', in J. K. S. Reid (ed.), *Calvin: Theological Treatises* (London: SCM Press, 1954).

——— 'Reply to Sadolet', in J. K. S. Reid (ed.), *Calvin: Theological Treatises* (London: SCM Press, 1960), 240.

——— *Institutes of the Christian Religion* (1559 edition), ed. J. T. McNeill (London: SCM Press, 1960).

—— *Institutes of the Christian Religion* (1536 edition), trans. F. L. Battles (Grand Rapids MI: Eerdmans, 1995).

Castro, Michel, 'Henri Bouillard (1908–1981): éléments de biographie intellectuelle', *Mélanges de science religieuse*, 60 (2003), 43–58.

Cattaneo, Enrico, *Il Culto Cristiano in Occidente* (Rome: CLV, 1992), 458–9.

Cerfaux, Lucien, *La théologie de l'Église suivant saint Paul*, Unam Sanctam, 10 (Paris: Cerf, 1942).

—— *The Christian in the theology of St. Paul* (New York: Herder and Herder, 1967).

Cernera, Anthony J. (ed.), *Continuity and Plurality in Catholic Theology: Essays in Honor of Gerald A. McCool, S.J.* (Fairfield CT: Sacred Heart University Press, 1998).

Certeau, Michel de, 'Lacan: An Ethics of Speech', *Representations*, 3 (1983), 21–39.

Ceyssens, Lucien, 'Le Cardinal Jean Bona et le Jansénisme', *Benedictina*, 10 (1956), 79–119, 267–327.

Chadwick, Henry, *East and West: The Making of a Rift in the Church* (Oxford: Oxford University Press, 2003).

—— *A History of the Popes 1830–1914* (Oxford: Clarendon Press, 1998).

Chadwick, Owen, *The Popes and European Revolution* (Oxford: Oxford University Press, 1981).

Chaim, Jan, *La Dottrina Sacramentale di Louis Bouyer* (Ph.D. thesis, Pontifical Gregorian University, 1984; published excerpts, Rome: Pontifical Gregorian University, 1984).

Chaine, J., *Le livre de la Genèse*, Lectio divina, 3 (Paris: Cerf, 1951).

Chantraine, Georges, SJ, *Henri de Lubac: De la naissance à la démobilisation (1896–1919)*, vol. i, Études lubaciennes, vi (Paris: Cerf, 2007).

—— '*Catholicism*: On "Certain Ideas"', *Communio*, 35 (2008), 520–34.

—— *Henri de Lubac: Les années de formation (1919–1929)*, vol. ii, Études lubaciennes, vii (Paris: Cerf, 2009).

Charlier, Louis, *Essai sur le problème théologique*, Bibliothèque Orientations: Section scientifique, 1 (Thuillies: Ramgal, 1938).

Chédozeau, Bernard, 'La publication de l'Écriture par Port-Royal. Première partie: 1653–1669', *Chroniques de Port-Royal*, 33 (1984), 35–42.

—— 'La publication de l'Écriture par Port-Royal. Deuxième partie: 1672–1693', *Chroniques de Port-Royal*, 35 (1986), 195–203.

—— 'Les grandes étapes de la publication de la Bible catholique française', in Jean-Robert Armogathe (ed.), *Le grand siècle et la Bible*, vi (Paris: Beauchesne, 1989), 341–60.

—— *La Bible et la liturgie en français: l'église tridentine et les traductions bibliques et liturgiques (1600–1789)* (Paris: Cerf, 1990).

—— 'Port-Royal et le jansénisme: la revendication d'une autre forme du tridentinisme?' *XVIIe Siècle*, 43 (1991), 119–25.

—— 'Préfaces de la *Bible de Port-Royal*', *Chroniques de Port-Royal*, 53 (2004), 47–66.

Chenu, Marie-Dominique, OP, 'La théologie comme science au XIIIe siècle. Genèse de la doctrine de Saint Thomas', *Archives d'histoire doctrinale et littéraire du Moyen Age*, 2 (1927), 31–71.

—— 'Le sens et les leçons d'une crise religieuse', *VI*, 13 (1931), 356–80.

Chenu, Marie-Dominique, OP, 'Préface pour la deuxième édition', in Ambroise Gardeil, *Le donné révélé et la théologie*, 2nd edn., 1932, pp. vii–xiv.

——— 'Position de la théologie', *RSPT*, 25 (1935), 232–57.

——— *Une école de théologie: Le Saulchoir* (Kain-lez-Tournai/Étiolles: Le Saulchoir/ Casterman, 1937).

——— 'Aux origines de la "science moderne"', *RSPT*, 29 (1940), 206–17.

——— 'Ratio superior et inferior. Un cas de philosophie chrétienne', *RSPT*, 29 (1940), 84–9.

——— *La théologie comme science au XIIIe siècle*, Pro manuscripto, 2nd edn. (Paris: Vrin, 1943).

——— *Introduction à l'étude de Saint Thomas d'Aquin* (Montreal/Paris: Institut d'études médiévales/Vrin, 1950).

——— 'L'homme et la nature. Perspectives sur la renaissance du XIIe siècle', *Archives d'histoire doctrinale et littéraire du Moyen Age*, 19 (1952), 19–51.

——— *La théologie au douzième siècle* (Paris: Vrin, 1957).

——— *La théologie est-elle une science?*, Je sais—Je crois 2 (Paris: Fayard, 1957).

——— *La théologie comme science au XIIIe siècle* (Paris: Librairie Philosophique J. Vrin, 1957).

——— *St Thomas d'Aquin et la théologie* (Paris: Seuil, 1959).

——— *Toward Understanding Saint Thomas* (Chicago: Henry Regnery, 1964).

——— *La Parole de Dieu I. La Foi dans l'intelligence* (Paris: Cerf, 1964).

——— 'Les Signes des temps', in Y. Congar and M. Peuchmaurd (eds.), *L'Église dans le monde de ce temps: Constitution pastoral 'Gaudium et Spes'* (Paris: Cerf, 1967), 205–25.

——— 'The History of Salvation and the Historicity of Man in the Renewal of Theology', in L. K. Shook (ed.), *Renewal of Religious Thought*, 1 (New York: Herder and Herder, 1968), 153–66.

——— 'What is Theology', in *Faith and Theology*, trans. Denis Hickey (New York: Macmillan, 1968), 15–35.

——— 'Préface', in Claude Geffré, OP (ed.), *Un nouvel âge de la théologie* (Paris: Cerf, 1972), 9.

——— *Jacques Duquesne interroge le Père Chenu: 'un théologien en liberté'* (Paris: Centurion, 1975).

——— 'La théologie en procès', in *Savoir, faire, espérer: les limites de la raison* (Brussels: Facultés Universitaires St Louis, 1976), 691–96.

——— *Une école de théologie: le Saulchoir*, eds. Giuseppe Alberigo, Étienne Fouilloux, Jean Ladrière et Jean-Pierre Jossua (Paris: Cerf, 1985).

——— 'Regard sur cinquante ans de vie religieuse', in C. Geffré (ed.), *L'hommage différé au Père Chenu* (Paris: Cerf, 1990).

——— 'Nature and Man: The Renaissance of the Twelfth Century', in *Nature, Man, and Society in the Twelfth Century* (Toronto: University of Toronto Press, 1997), 1–48.

——— *Aquinas and His Role in Theology*, trans. Paul Philibert, OP (Collegeville MN: Liturgical Press, 2002).

——— 'L'interprète de Saint Thomas d'Aquin', in M. Couratier (ed.), *Étienne Gilson et nous* (Paris: Vrin, 1980), 43–8.

Cherniss, Harold Frederik, *The Platonism of Gregory of Nyssa*, University of California Publications in Classical Philology II, i (Berkeley CA: University of California Press, 1930).

Childs, B. S., *The Book of Exodus: A Critical Theological Commentary* (Philadelphia PA: Westminster, 1974).

Chupungco, Anscar, J., '*Sacrosanctum concilium*: Its Vision and Achievements', *Ecclesia Orans* XIII/3, (1996), 495–514 (498).

Clément, Olivier, 'Les Pères de l'Église dans l'Église orthodoxe', *Connaissance des Pères de l'Église*, 52 (December 1993), 25–6.

Clifford, Catherine E., *The Groupe des Dombes: A Dialogue of Conversion* (New York: Peter Lang, 2005).

Coconnier, Thomas, 'Spéculative ou positive?', *RevTh*, 10 (1902), 629–53.

Colin, Pierre, *L'audace et le soupçon: La crise du modernisme dans le catholicisme français (1893–1914)* (Paris: Desclée de Brouwer, 1997).

Comte, Bernard, 'Un rassemblement de catholiques libéraux: la naissance à Lyon de la revue *Demain* (1905)', in *Les catholiques libéraux au XIXe siècle* (Grenoble: Presses universitaires de Grenoble, 1974), 239–80.

———— '"*Morale et politique*" (1927–1934): collaboration and exchanges between Vialatoux, J. Maritain and H. de Lubac', *Théophilyon*, X/1 (2005), 45–65.

———— 'Jean Lacroix dans les années 30: militant et pédagogue', in *Cahiers Emmanuel Mounier*, 96 (December 2006), 19–44.

———— 'Les jésuites', in *L'intelligence d'une ville: Vie intellectuelle et culturelle à Lyon entre 1945 et 1975* (Lyon: Bibliothèque municipale, 2006), 55–66.

———— 'Le Père de Lubac, un théologien dans l'Église de Lyon', in Jean-Dominique Durand (ed.), *Henri de Lubac: La rencontre au cœur de l'Église* (Paris: Cerf, 2006).

Congar, Yves M.-J., OP, 'La pensée de Möhler et l'ecclésiologie orthodoxe', *Irénikon*, 12 (1935), 321–9.

———— 'Déficit de la théologie', *Sept*, 18 January 1935.

———— *Chrétiens désunis: Principes d'un 'oecuménisme' catholique* (Paris: Cerf, 1937).

———— 'Pour une théologie de l'Église', *VI*, 52 (1937), 97–9.

———— 'L'Esprit des Pères d'après Moehler', *Supplément à la 'Vie Spirituelle'*, 55 (1938), 1–25.

———— 'La signification œcuménique de l'oeuvre de Möhler', *Irénikon*, 15 (1938), 113–30.

———— 'Sur l'évolution et l'interprétation de la pensée de Möhler, *RSPT*, 27 (1938), 205–12.

———— 'Autour du renouveau de l'ecclésiologie: la collection "Unam Sanctam"', *VI*, 51 (1939), 9–32.

———— *Divided Christendom: a Catholic Study of the Problem of Reunion*, trans. M. A. Bousfield (London: Bles, 1939).

———— 'L'hérésie, déchirement de l'unité', in Pierre Chaillet (ed.) *L'Église est une: hommage à Moehler* (Paris: Bloud & Gay, 1939), 255–69.

———— 'Théologie', in A. Vacant, E. Mangenot, and É. Amann (eds.), *Dictionnaire de théologie catholique*, xv. part i, cols. 341–502 (col. 440) (Paris: Letouzey and Ané, 1946).

———— 'Tendances actuelles de la pensée religieuse', *Cahiers du monde nouveau*, 4 (1948), 33–50.

Congar, Yves M.-J., OP, 'Le prophète Péguy', *Témoignage Chrétien*, 26 August 1949, 1.

—— 'Il faut construire l'Église en nous', *Témoignage Chrétien*, 7 July 1950.

—— *Vraie et fausse réforme dans l'Église*, Unam Sanctam, 20 (Paris: Cerf, 1950).

—— 'Bulletin de théologie dogmatique', *RSPT*, 35 (1951), 591–603.

—— *Esquisses du mystère de l'Église*, new edn., Unam Sanctam, 8 (Paris: Cerf, 1953).

—— *Jalons pour une théologie du laïcat* (Paris: Cerf: 1953).

—— *La Tradition et les traditions: essai historique* (Paris: Fayard, 1960).

—— 'Vœux pour le concile: enquête parmi les chrétiens', *Esprit*, 29 (1961), 691–700.

—— *Aspects de l'œcuménisme* (Bruxelles/Paris: La Pensée Catholique/Office Général du Livre, 1962).

—— 'The Council in the Age of Dialogue', trans. Barry N. Rigney, *Cross Currents*, 12 (1962), 144–51.

—— *La Foi et la Théologie*, Théologie dogmatique, 1 (Tournai: Desclée, 1962).

—— 'The Historical Development of Authority in the Church. Points for Christian Reflection', in John M. Todd (ed.), *Problems of Authority* (London: Darton, Longman & Todd, 1962), 119–55.

—— *The Mystery of the Temple, or the Manner of God's Presence to his Creatures from Genesis to Apocalypse*, trans. Reginald Frederick Trevett (London: Burns & Oates, 1962).

—— 'Ecumenical Experience and Conversion: A Personal Testimony', trans. Beatrice Morton, in Robert C. Mackie and Charles C. West (eds.), *The Sufficiency of God: Essays on the Ecumenical Hope in Honour of W. A. Visser 't Hooft* (London: SCM Press, 1963), 71–87.

—— *La Tradition et les traditions: essai théologique* (Paris: Fayard, 1963).

—— *Sainte Église: Études et approaches ecclésiologiques* (Paris: Cerf, 1963).

—— *Chrétiens en dialogue: contributions catholiques à l'oecuménisme*, Unam Sanctam, 50 (Paris: Cerf, 1964).

—— 'De la communion des Églises a une ecclésiologie de l'Église universelle', in Y. Congar and B. D. Dupuy (eds.), *L'Épiscopat et l'Église universelle* (Paris: Cerf, 1964), 227–60.

—— *Tradition and the Life of the Church*, trans. A. N. Woodrow, Faith and Fact Books, 3 (London: Burns & Oates, 1964).

—— *The Mystery of the Church: Studies by Yves Congar*, trans. A. V. Littledale, 2nd rev. edn. (London: Geoffrey Chapman, 1965).

—— *Lay People in the Church*, trans. D. Attwater (London: Geoffrey Chapman, 1965).

—— *Dialogue between Christians: Catholic Contributions to Ecumenism*, trans. Philip Loretz (London: Geoffrey Chapman, 1966).

—— *Tradition and Traditions: An historical and a theological essay*, trans. Michael Naseby and Thomas Rainborough (London: Burns & Oates, 1966).

—— 'L'inspiration: Un catholicisme rajeuni et ouvert bilan et perspectives', *Informations catholiques internationales*, 255 (1966), 5–15.

—— 'L' "Ecclesia" ou communauté chrétienne, sujet intégral de l'action liturgique', in J.-P. Jossua and Y. Congar (eds.), *La Liturgie après Vatican II* (Paris: Cerf, 1967), 241–80.

—— *Situation et tâches présentes de la théologie*, Cogitatio fidei, 27 (Paris: Cerf, 1967).

—— *Cette Église que j'aime*, Foi Vivante, 70 (Paris: Cerf, 1968).

—— *Vraie et fausse réforme dans l'église*, 2nd edn. (Paris: Cerf, 1968).

—— *This Church That I Love*, trans. Lucien Delafuente (Denville, NJ: Dimension Books, 1969).

—— 'Johann Adam Möhler: 1796–1838', *Theologische Quartalschrift*, 150 (1970), 47–51.

—— *L'Église: de saint Augustin à l'époque moderne* (Paris: Cerf, 1970).

—— 'La personne "Église"', *RevTh*, 71 (1971), 613–40.

—— 'Non-Christian Religions and Christianity', in Mariasusai Dhavamony, (ed.), *Evangelisation, Dialogue and Development: Selected Papers of the International Theological Conference, Nagpur (India) 1971*, Documenta Missionalia, 5 (Rome: Gregorian University Press, 1972), 133–45.

—— 'Pneumatology Today', *The American Ecclesiastical Review*, 167 (1973), 435–49.

—— 'St Thomas Aquinas and the Spirit of Ecumenism', *New Blackfriars*, 55 (1974), 196–209.

—— 'Saint Thomas d'Aquin et l'esprit oecuménique', *Freiburger Zeitschrift für Philosophie und Theologie*, 21 (1974), 331–46.

—— '"Review of Bouyer's *Le Consolateur*" in "Chronique de Pneumatologie"', *RSPT*, 64/3 (1980), 445–9 (446).

—— 'Reflections on being a Theologian', trans. Marcus Lefébure, *New Blackfriars*, 62 (1981), 405–9.

—— *Diversités et Communion: dossier historique et conclusion théologique* (Paris: Cerf, 1982).

—— *I Believe in the Holy Spirit*, trans. David Smith, ii (New York/London: Seabury/ Geoffrey Chapman, 1983).

—— *Martin Luther sa foi, sa réforme: études de théologie historique*, Cogitatio Fidei, 119 (Paris: Cerf, 1983).

—— *Diversity and Communion*, trans. John Bowden (London: SCM Press, 1984).

—— *Essais œcuméniques: Le mouvement, les hommes, les problèmes* (Paris: Le centurion, 1984).

—— *La tradition et la vie de l'Église*, 2nd edn, Traditions chrétiennes, 18 (Paris: Cerf, 1984).

—— 'Letter from Father Yves Congar, O.P., trans. Ronald John Zawilla, *Theology Digest*, 32 (1985), 213–216.

—— 'The Brother I have known', trans. Boniface Ramsey, OP, *The Thomist*, 49 (1985), 495–503.

—— 'Moving Towards a Pilgrim Church', in Alberic Stacpoole, OSB (ed.), *Vatican II by Those Who Were There* (London: Geoffrey Chapman, 1986), 129–52.

—— *Fifty Years of Catholic Theology*, ed. Bernard Lauret (Philadelphia: Fortress Press, 1988).

—— 'Dominicains et prêtres ouvriers', *La Vie spirituelle*, 143 (1989), 817–20.

—— 'Le frère que j'ai connu', in Claude Geffré *et al.* (eds.), *L'hommage différé au père Chenu* (Paris: Cerf, 1990), 239–45.

—— 'Hommage au Père M.-D. Chenu', *RSPT*, 75 (1991), 361–504.

Bibliography

Congar, Yves M.-J., OP, *Je crois en l'Esprit Saint*, new edn., ii (Paris: Cerf, 1995).

———— *Journal d'un théologien*, ed. with an introduction by Étienne Fouilloux (Paris: Cerf, 2000).

———— 'Loving Openness Toward Every Truth: A Letter from Thomas Aquinas to Karl Rahner', *Philosophy and Theology*, 12 (2000), 213–19.

———— *Journal d'un théologien (1946–1956)*, ed. with notes Étienne Fouilloux *et al.*, 2nd edn. (Paris: Cerf, 2001).

———— *Mon Journal du Concile*, ed. with notes Éric Mahieu, 2 vols (Paris: Cerf, 2002).

———— *True and False Reform in the Church*, trans. Paul Philibert (Collegeville MN: Liturgical Press, 2011).

Bürki, Bruno, and Klöckener, Martin, Liturgie In Bewegung—Ein Movement (Freiburg/Geneva: Universitätsverlag/Labor et Fides, 2000).

Connolly, James M., *The Voices of France: A Survey of Contemporary Theology in France* (New York: Macmillan, 1961).

Conticello, C. G., '*De Contemplatione* (Angelicum 1920). La thèse inédite de doctorat du P. M.-D. Chenu', *RSPT*, 75 (1991), 363–422.

Conway, Michael A., 'A Positive Phenomenology. The structure of Maurice Blondel's early philosophy', *Heythrop Journal*, 47 (2006), 579–600.

———— 'From Neo-Thomism to St. Thomas: Maurice Blondel's Early Encounter with Scholastic Thought', *EphThL*, 83 (2007).

———— 'A Thomistic Turn? Maurice Blondel's Reading of St Thomas', *EphThL*, 84 (2008), 87–122.

Coppens, J., *La connaissance du bien et du mal et le péché du paradis: contribution à l'interprétation de Gen., II–III* (Louvain: E Nauwelaerts, 1948).

Cordovani, Mariano, 'Per la vitalità della teologia cattolica', *Ang*, 17 (1940), 133–46.

———— 'Truth and Novelty in Theology,' *American Ecclesiastical Review*, 119 (October 1948) 241–3.

Cottier, Georges M.-M., OP, 'L'œuvre de Charles Journet (1891–1975)', *Nova et vetera* (1975), 242–58.

Courcier, Jacques, 'Dominique Dubarle et la Géométrie Projective', *RSPT*, 92 (2008), 623–36.

Couturier, Guy (ed.), *Les Patriarches et l'histoire: autour d'un article inédit du père M.-J. Lagrange*, Lectio divina, hors-série (Paris: Cerf, 1998).

Croce, Benedetto, 'Controriforma', *La Critica*, 22 (1924), 325–33.

———— *Storia dell'età barocca in Italia: Pensiero, poesia e letteratura, vita morale* (Bari: G. Laterza, 1929).

Cross, F. M. Jr., *The Ancient Library of Qumran* (Garden City NY: Anchor, 1961).

Crouzel, Henri, 'Grégoire de Nysse est-il le fondateur de la théologie mystique? Une controverse récente', *Revue d'ascétique et de mystique*, 33 (1957), 189–202.

———— *Les origines du christianisme latin* (Paris: Desclée/Cerf, 1978).

Daley, Brian, 'Is Patristic Exegesis Still Usable? Reflections on Early Christian Interpretation of the Psalms', *Communio*, 29/1 (2002), 181–216.

———— '*La nouvelle théologie* and the Patristic Revival: Sources, Symbols, and the Science of Theology', *IJST*, 7/4 (2005), 362–82.

Daly, Gabriel, *Transcendence and Immanence: A Study in Catholic Modernism and Integralism* (Oxford: Clarendon Press, 1980).

Daniélou, Jean, SJ, 'Les orientations présentes de la pensée religieuse', *Études*, 79 (1946), 5–21.

———— 'Étienne Gilson à l'Académie', *Études*, 251 (1946), 263–4.

———— *Origène*, Le génie du christianisme (Paris: La table ronde, 1948).

———— *Sacramentum futuri: études sur les origines de la typologie biblique* (Paris: Beauchesne, 1950).

———— *Bible et Liturgie: la théologie biblique des sacrements et des fêtes d'après les Pères de l'Église*, Lex Orandi, 11 (Paris: Cerf, 1951).

———— *Platonisme et théologie mystique: Essai sur la doctrine spirituelle de saint Grégoire de Nysse*, Théologie, 2 (Paris: Aubier, 1944, 1954).

———— 'Eunome l'Arien et l'exégèse néo-platonicienne du Cratyle', *Revue des études grecques*, 69 (1956), 412–32.

———— *The Bible and the liturgy*, trans. Michael A. Mathis (Notre Dame IN: University of Notre Dame Press, 1956).

———— 'Le bon Samaritain', in *Mélanges bibliques rédigés en l'honneur d'André Robert* (Paris: Bloud & Gay, 1957), 457–65.

———— *Philon d'Alexandrie*, Les temps et les destins (Paris: Arthème Fayard, 1958).

———— *From shadows to reality: studies in Biblical typology of the Fathers* trans. Wulstan Hibberd (Westminster MD: Newman, 1960).

———— 'Grégoire de Nysse et le néo-platonisme de l'école d'Athènes', *Revue des études grecques*, 80 (1967), 395–401.

———— *L'être et le temps chez Grégoire de Nysse* (Leiden: Brill, 1970).

———— 'Metempsychosis in Gregory of Nyssa', in *Orientalia christiana analecta. The Heritage of the Early Church: Essays in Honor of the very Reverend G.V. Florovsky* (Rome: Pontificia Institutum Studiorum Orientalium, 1973), 227–43.

———— *Et qui est mon prochain?*, *Mémoires* (Paris: Stock, 1974).

———— *Théologie du judéo-christianisme*, 2nd edn., with a preface by M. J. Rondeau (Paris: Desclée/Cerf, 1991).

———— *Message évangélique et culture hellénistique* (Tournai: Desclée et Cie, 1961, 2nd edn. 1991).

———— *A History of Early Christian Doctrine*, ii, *Gospel Message and Hellenistic Culture*, trans. J. A. Baker (London: Darton, Longman & Todd, 1973).

———— *Carnets spirituels*, ed. Marie-Joseph Rondeau (Paris: Cerf, 2007).

Dansette, Adrien, *Religious History of Modern France* (New York: Herder and Herder, 1961).

D'Arcy, M. C., SJ (ed.), *A Monument to St. Augustine* (London: Sheed & Ward, 1930).

Dawkins, Richard, *The God Delusion* (London: Bantam Press, 2006).

De Gandillac, Maurice, 'À propos de Grégoire de Nysse', *Dieu vivant*, 3 (1945), 123–34.

De Jean, Joan, *Ancients against Moderns: Culture Wars and the Making of a Fin de Siècle* (Chicago: University of Chicago Press, 1997).

De Petter, Dominicus-Maria, 'Impliciete intuïtie', *Tijdschrift voor Philosophie*, 1 (1939), 84–105.

DeHart, Paul, 'On Being Heard but Not Seen: Milbank and Lash on Aquinas, Analogy and Agnosticism', *Modern Theology*, 26/2 (2010), 243–77.

Deman, Thomas, 'Französische Bemühungen um eine Erneuerung der Theologie', *TR*, 46 (1950), 64–82.

Deman, Thomas, 'Tentatives françaises pour un renouvellement de la théologie', *Revue de l'Université d'Ottawa*, 20 (1950), 129–67.

Denzinger, Heinrich, *The Sources of Catholic Dogma*, 1954, trans. Roy Defferari, 30th edn. (St Louis MO: Herder, 1957).

Derrida, Jacques, *Of Grammatology*, trans. Gayatri Chakravorty Spivak (Baltimore MD: Johns Hopkins University Press, 1976).

Desmazières, Agnès, 'La "nouvelle théologie", prémisse d'une théologie herméneutique? La controverse sur l'analogie de la vérité (1946–1949)', *RevTh*, 104 (2004), 241–72.

Dohmen, C., *Exodus 19–40*, Herders theologischer Kommentar zum Alten Testament (Freiburg im Breisgau: Herder, 2004).

Donneaud, Henri, 'Les cinquante premières années de la *Revue thomiste*', *RevTh*, 93 (1993), 5–25.

––––––– 'Les origines fribourgeoises de la *Revue thomiste*', *Mémoire dominicaine* V, (Autumn 1994), 43–60.

––––––– (ed.), 'Correspondance Étienne Gilson—Michel Labourdette', *RTh*, 94 (1994), 479–529.

––––––– 'Le Saulchoir: une école, des théologies?' *Gr*, 83 (2002), 433–49.

Donnelly, John Patrick, 'Introduction', in John Patrick Donnelly and Roland J. Teske (trans. and ed.), *Robert Bellarmine: Spiritual Writings* (New York/Mahwah NJ: Paulist, 1989).

Donnelly, Philip J., 'The Gratuity of the Beatific Vision and the Possibility of a Natural Destiny', *TS*, 11 (1950), 374–404.

Doyle, Dennis M., *Communion Ecclesiology* (Maryknoll NY: Orbis, 2000).

Dubarle, Dominique, *L'Ontologie de Thomas Aquinas*, Philosophie & Théologie (Paris: Cerf, 1996).

Duffé, Bruno-Marie, 'Gabriel Matagrin et l'École lyonnaise: Dialogue social et transcendance', in Denis Maugenest (ed.), *Le mouvement social catholique en France au XXe siècle* (Paris: Cerf, 1990), 89–115.

Duffy, Eamon, *Saints & Sinners: A History of the Popes* (New Haven CT: Yale University Press in association with S4C, 1997).

––––––– 'Confessions of a Cradle Catholic', in *Faith of Our Fathers: Reflections on Catholic Tradition* (London: Continuum, 2004), 11–19.

––––––– *Saints & Sinners: A History of the Popes*, 3rd edn. (New Haven/London: Yale University Press, 2006).

Duffy, Stephen J., 'The Problem of Nature and Grace: The Issues and Terms of the Debate', in *The Graced Horizon: Nature and Grace in Modern Catholic Thought* (Collegeville MN: Liturgical Press, 1992), 12–49.

Dulles, Avery, *A History of Apologetics* (New York: Corpus, 1971).

––––––– *The Catholicity of the Church* (Oxford: Oxford University Press, 1987).

––––––– 'A Half Century of Ecclesiology', *TS*, 50 (1989), 419–42 (422).

––––––– 'The Church as Communion', in Bradley Nassif (ed.), *New Perspectives on Historical Theology: Essays in Memory of John Meyendorff* (Grand Rapids MI: Eerdmans, 1996), 125–39.

––––––– *Models of the Church* (New York: Image Books, 2002).

Dunne, Victor, *Prophecy in the Church: The Vision of Yves Congar*, European University Studies, 23 (Frankfurt: Lang, 2000).

Dupré, Louis, 'Hans Urs von Balthasar's Theology of Aesthetic Form', *TS*, 49 (1988), 219–318.

——— 'Ignatian Humanism and Its Mystical Dimension', *Communio*, 18 (1991), 164–82.

——— *Passage to Modernity: An Essay in the Hermeneutics of Nature and Culture* (New Haven CT: Yale University Press, 1993).

Duquesne, Jacques (ed.), *Jacques Duquesne interroge le Père Chenu: 'un théologien en liberté'*, Les Interviews (Paris: Centurion, 1975).

Durand, Jean-Dominique, 'Catholicisme social: l'École lyonnaise', *Théophilyon*, X/1 (2005), 7–143.

——— (ed.), *Les Semaines sociales de France, 1904–2004* (Paris: Parole et Silence, 2006).

Durand, Jean-Dominique, and Bernard Comte (eds.), *Cent ans de catholicisme social à Lyon et en Rhône-Alpes* (Paris: Éditions Ouvrières, 1992).

Duval, André, OP, 'Aux origines de l'"Institut historique d'études thomistes" du Saulchoir (1920 et ss.). Notes et Documents', *RSPT*, 75 (1991), 423–48.

Dych, William, *Karl Rahner* (London: Geoffrey Chapman, 1992).

Eicher, Peter, 'Von den Schwierigkeiten bürgerlicher Theologie mit den katholischen Kirchenstrukturen', in Karl Rahner and Heinrich Fries (eds.), *Theologie in Freiheit und Verantwortung* (Munich: Kösel, 1981), 96–137 (101).

Famerée, Joseph, '"Chrétiens désunis" du P. Congar 50 ans après,' *NRT*, 110 (1988), 666–86.

——— *L'Ecclésiologie d'Yves Congar avant Vatican II: Histoire et Église*, BETL, 107 (Louvain: Leuven University Press, 1992).

——— 'The Contribution of the *Groupe des Dombes* to Ecumenism: Past Achievements and Future Challenges', *LS*, 33 (2008), 99–116.

Famerée, Joseph, and Gilles Routhier, *Yves Congar* (Paris: Cerf, 2008).

Favraux, Paul, *Une philosophie du médiateur: Maurice Blondel* (Paris: Lethielleux, 1986).

Fédou, Michel, 'Karl Rahner et Hans Urs von Balthasar: lecteurs et interprètes des Pères', in Henri-Jérôme Gagey and Vincent Holzer (eds.), *Balthasar, Rahner: deux pensées en contraste* (Paris: Bayard, 2005), 141–59.

——— 'Le judéo-christianisme selon Daniélou', in J. Fontaine (ed.), *Actualité*, 43–56.

Féret, Henri-Marie, *L'Apocalypse de saint Jean: Vision chrétienne de l'histoire*, Témoignages chrétiens (Paris: Corrêa, 1943).

——— 'La théologie concrète et historique et son importance pastorale présente', in Gérard Philips *et al.*, *Le service théologique dans l'Église: Mélanges offerts au Père Yves Congar pour ses soixante-dix ans*, Cogitatio Fidei, 76 (Paris: Cerf, 1974), 193–247.

Fierens, Marc, 'L'Esprit Saint et la Liturgie dans la pneumatologie de Congar', *Questions Liturgiques*, 66 (1985), 221–7.

Flamard, Jacques, *L'idée de médiation chez Maurice Blondel* (Paris: Béatrice-Nauwelaerts, 1969).

Flanner, Janet, *Paris Journal 1944–1965*, ed. William Shawn (New York: Atheneum, 1965).

Fleming, David L., *A Contempory Reading of the Spiritual Exercises: A Companion to St Ignatius' Text* (St Louis MO: Institute of Jesuit Sources, 1980).

Florovsky, Georges, *The Collected Works of Georges Florovsky*, i–iv (Belmont MA: Nordland, 1972–5).

———— *Ways of Russian Theology*, i. *The Collected Works of Georges Florovsky*, v. (Belmont MA: Nordland, 1979).

———— *The Collected Works of Georges Florovsky*, vi–x (Vaduz: Büchervertriebsanstalt, 1987).

———— 'The Eucharist and Catholicity', in Richard S. Haugh (ed.), *Collected Works of Georges Florovsky xiii. Ecumenism i: A Doctrinal Approach* (Vaduz: Büchervertriebsanstalt, 1989), 46–57.

Flynn, Gabriel, 'Book Essay: *Mon journal du Concile* Yves Congar and the Battle for a Renewed Ecclesiology at the Second Vatican Council', *LS*, 28 (2003), 48–70.

———— 'Cardinal Congar's Ecumenism: An "Ecumenical Ethics" for Reconciliation?', *LS*, 28 (2003), 311–25.

———— *Yves Congar's Vision of the Church in a World of Unbelief* (Aldershot/ Burlington VT: Ashgate, 2004).

———— 'Yves Congar and Catholic Church Reform: A Renewal of the Spirit', in Flynn (ed.), *Yves Congar: Theologian of the Church*, 99–133.

———— (Guest ed.), *Louvain Studies*, 29 (Fall–Winter, 2004): 'This Church that I Love: Essays Celebrating the Centenary of the Birth of Yves Cardinal Congar'.

———— (ed.), *Yves Congar: Theologian of the Church*, Louvain Theological and Pastoral Monographs Series 32 (Louvain: Peeters, 2005/Dudley MA: Eerdmans, 2006).

———— (ed.), *Yves Congar: théologien de l'Église* (Paris: Cerf, 2007).

———— 'Receptive Ecumenism and Catholic Learning – Reflections in Dialogue with Yves Congar and B. C. Butler', in Murray (ed.), *Receptive Ecumenism and the Call to Catholic Learning*, 399–412.

Fodor, James, *Christian Hermeneutics: Paul Ricoeur and the Refiguring of Theology* (New York: Oxford University Press, 1995).

Folliet, Joseph, 'L'École mystique de Lyon et la Chronique sociale', in M. Pacaut, J. Gadille, J.-M. Mayeur, and H Beuve-Méry (eds.), *Religion et politique; les deux guerres mondiales; histoire de Lyon et du Sud-Est: mélanges offerts à M. le doyen André Latreille* (Lyon: Marius Audin, 1972), 581–602.

Fontaine, Gaston, 'Présentation des Missels diocésains français du 17ᵉ au 19ᵉ siècle', *La Maison-Dieu*, 141 (1980), 97–166.

Fontaine, Jacques (ed.), *Actualité de Jean Daniélou* (Paris: Cerf, 2006).

Fontaine, Jacques, and Charles Kannengiesser (eds.), *Epektasis: Mélanges patristiques offerts au Cardinal Jean Daniélou* (Paris: Beauchesne, 1972).

Ford, David F. (ed.), *The Modern Theologians: An Introduction to Christian Theology in the Twentieth Century*, ii (Oxford: Blackwell, 1995).

Forte, Bruno, 'Le prospettive della ricera teologica', in Rino Fisichella (ed.), *Il Concilio Vaticano II: Recezione e attualità alla luce del Giubileo* (Milan: San Paolo, 2000), 419–29.

Fouilloux, Étienne, 'Le Saulchoir en procès (1937–42)', in Chenu, *Une école de théologie: le Saulchoir*, eds. Alberigo *et al.*, 37–59.

—— 'Dialogue théologique? (1946–1948)', in Serge-Thomas Bonino (ed.), *Saint Thomas au XXe siècle: actes du colloque centenaire de la 'Revue Thomiste.' Toulouse, 25–28 mars 1993* (Paris: Saint-Paul, 1994).

—— 'Les théologiens romains à la veille de Vatican II', in *Histoire et théologie: Actes de la Journée d'études de l'Assocation Française d'histoire religieuse contemporaine sous la direction de Jean-Dominique Durand* (Paris: Beauchesne, 1994), 137–60.

—— 'Frère Yves, Cardinal Congar, Dominicain: itinéraire d'un théologien', *RSPT*, 79 (1995), 379–404.

—— *La Collection 'Sources chrétiennes': éditer les Pères de l'Église au XXe siècle* (Paris: Cerf, 1995).

——'Du rôle des théologiens au début de Vatican II: un point de vue romain', in A. Melloni, D. Menozzi, G. Ruggieri, and M. Toschi (eds.), *Cristianesimo nella storia, Saggi in onore di Giuseppe Alberigo* (Bologna: Il Mulino, 1996), 279–311.

—— 'Autour d'une mise à l'Index' in *Marie-Dominique Chenu: Moyen Âge et modernité*, Les Cahiers du Centre d'études du Saulchoir, 5 (Paris: Centre d'Etudes du Saulchoir, 1997), 25–56.

—— *Une Église en quête de liberté: La pensée catholique française entre modernisme et Vatican II (1914–1962)*, Anthropologiques (Paris: Desclée de Brouwer, 1998).

—— 'Autour d'un livre (1946–1953)', in Durand (ed.), *Henri de Lubac*, 91–107.

—— 'Une "école de Fourvière"?' *Gr*, 83 (2002), 451–9.

—— 'La vocation tardive de l'abbé Couturier' in *L'œcuménisme spirituel de Paul Couturier aux défis actuels* (Lyon: Profac, 2003), 15–43.

—— 'Le Groupe de travail en commun de Jacques Chevalier (1920–1940)', in *Bulletin de la Société Historique, Archéologique et Littéraire de Lyon* 2002, xxxii (Lyon, 2004), 361–77.

—— 'La "nouvelle théologie" française vue d'Espagne (1948–1951)', *Revue d'histoire de l'Église de France*, 90 (2004), 279–93.

—— '"Nouvelle théologie" et théologie nouvelle (1930–1960)', in Benoît Pellistrandi (ed.), *L'histoire religieuse en France et Espagne*, Collection de la Casa Velázquez, 87 (Madrid: Casa de Velázquez, 2004), 411–25.

—— *Une Église en quête de liberté: la pensée catholique française entre modernisme et Vatican II (1914–1962)*, 2nd edn. (Paris, Desclée de Brouwer, 2006).

Fraenkel, P., *Testimonia Patrum: The Function of Patristic Argument in the Thought of Philip Melanchthon* (Geneva: Droz, 1961).

Franzelin, J. B., *Theses de Ecclesia Christi* (Rome: Typographia Polyglotta, 1887).

Frei, Fritz, SJ, *Médiation unique et transfiguration universelle: Thèmes christologiques et leurs perspectives missionnaires dans la pensée de Jean Daniélou* Europaïsche Hochschulschriften, Reihe 23, Thologie, 173 (Berne-Frankfurt: P. Lang, 1981).

Frey, Christoph, *Mysterium der Kirche, Öffnung zur Welt: Zwei Aspekte der Erneuerung französischer katholischer Theologie*, Kirche und Konfession, 14 (Göttingen: Vandenhoeck & Ruprecht, 1969).

Frost, Robert, 'Revelation', from *A Boy's Will* (1913), in Frost, *Collected Poems, Prose and Plays* (New York: Library of America, 1995), 27–8.

Gabaude, Jean-Marc, *Un demi-siècle de philosophie en langue française (1937–1990): Historique de l'Association des Sociétés de philosophie de langue française* (Montréal: Montmorency, 1990).

Gabellieri, Emmanuel, 'Catholicisme social et "métaphysique en action": La pensée de Joseph Vialatoux', *Théophilyon*, X/1 (2005), 9–43.

——— 'L'esprit de *L'Action*: Lyon et le *Vinculum* blondélien', in *Maurice Blondel et la philosophie française*, 277–90.

Gabellieri, Emmanuel, and Pierre de Cointet (eds.), *Maurice Blondel et la philosophie française*, Colloque tenu à Lyon (Paris: Parole and Silence, 2007).

Gadamer, Hans-Georg, *Truth and Method* (New York: Crossroad, 1975).

Gagey, Henri-Jérôme, and Vincent Holzer (eds.), *Balthasar, Rahner: deux pensées en contraste* (Paris: Bayard, 2005).

Gagnebet, Marie-Rosaire, 'La nature de la théologie spéculative', doctoral thesis (Rome, Angelicum, 1937).

——— *La nature de la théologie spéculative* (Paris: Desclée De Brouwer, 1938).

——— 'La nature de la théologie spéculative', *RevTh*, 44 (1938), 1–39, 213–55 and 645–74.

——— 'Un essai sur le problème théologique', *RevTh*, 45 (1939), 108–45.

——— 'Le problème actuel de la théologie et la science aristotélicienne d'après un ouvrage récent', *Divus Thomas*, 46 (1943), 237–70.

——— *De natura theologiae ejusque methodo secundum sanctum Thomam* (Rome: Angelicum, 1952).

Gaillardetz, Richard, 'The Reception of Doctrine: New Perspectives', in Bernard Hoose (ed.), *Authority in the Roman Catholic Church: Theory and Practice* (Aldershot/Burlington VT: Ashgate, 2002), 95–114.

Gallagher, Tag, *The Adventures of Roberto Rossellini: his Life and Films* (New York: Da Capo Press, 1998).

Gardeil, Ambroise, *Le donné révélé et la théologie*, Bibliothèque théologique, 4 (Paris: Cerf, 1909).

Gardet, Louis, 'Saint Grégoire de Nysse', *RevTh*, 47 (1947), 342–52.

Garrigou-Lagrange, Réginald, *De Deo uno, Commentarium in primam partem S. Thomae*, Bibliothèque de la *Revue thomiste* (Paris: Desclée De Brouwer, 1938), 43–4.

——— 'La nouvelle théologie, où va-t-elle?' *Ang*, 23 (1946), 126–45.

——— 'Les notions consacrées par les Conciles', *Ang*, 24 (1947), 217–30.

——— 'Vérité et immutabilité du Dogme', *Ang*, 24 (1947), 124–39.

——— *De gratia: Commentarius in Summam Theologicam S. Thomæ I^{ae} II^{ae} q. 109–114* (Turin: Berruti, 1947).

——— 'Nécessité de revenir à la définition traditionnelle de la vérité', *Ang*, 25 (1948), 185–98.

——— 'L'immutabilité du dogme selon le concile du Vatican et le relativisme', *RevTh*, 49 (1949), 309–32.

——— 'Le relativisme et l'immutabilité du dogme', *RevTh*, 50 (1950), 219–46.

——— *Reality: A Synthesis of Thomistic Thought*, trans. Patrick Cummins (St Louis MO: Herder, 1950).

——— *Grace: Commentary on the Summa Theologica of St. Thomas, Ia IIae, q.109–14*, trans. by the Dominican Nuns of Corpus Christi Monastery of Menlo Park, California (St Louis MO: Herder, 1952).

Gaver, Falk van, 'Un théologien de métier', *La Nef*, 199 (December 2008), 105.

Gelin, A., *Les Pauvres de Yahvé* (Paris: Cerf, 1953).

—— *The Poor of Yahweh* trans. Kathryn Sullivan (Collegeville MN: Liturgical Press, 1964).

Geffré, Claude, *Un nouvel âge de la théologie* (Paris: Cerf, 1972).

—— 'Le réalisme de l'Incarnation dans la théologie du Père M.-D. Chenu', *RSPT*, 69/3 (1985), 389–99.

Geffré, Claude, and Jean-Pierre Torrell, 'New Problems in Fundamental Theology in the Postconciliar Period', in René Latourelle and Gerald O'Collins (eds.), *Problems and Perspectives in Fundamental Theology* (New York: Paulist Press 1982), 11–22.

Geffré, Claude, *et al.*, *L'hommage différé au Père Chenu* (Paris: Cerf, 1990).

Geneste, Sylvie, 'Édouard Aynard, banquier, député, mécène et homme d'œuvres (1837–1913)', unpublished Ph.D. thesis (Université Jean-Moulin—Lyon III, 1998).

Gibellini, Rosino, *Panorama de la théologie au XXe siècle*, trans. Jacques Mignon, new edn. (Paris: Cerf, 2004).

Gilson, Étienne, *Introduction au système de S. Thomas d'Aquin* (Strasbourg: Vix, 1919).

—— 'L'avenir de la métaphysique augustinienne', *Revue de Philosophie*, 1 (1930), 690–714.

—— 'Reflexions sur la controverse S. Thomas-S. Augustin', in Gilson, *Mélanges Pierre Mandonnet*, i (Paris, 1930), 370–83.

—— *The Spirit of Mediaeval Philosophy*, The Gifford Lectures 1931–1932, trans. A. H. C. Downes (London: Sheed & Ward, 1936).

—— 'Historical Research and the Future of Scholasticism', *Modern Schoolman*, 29 (1951), 1–10.

—— *Being and Some Philosophers* (Toronto: Pontifical Institute of Mediaeval Studies, 1952).

—— 'Les principes et les causes', *RTh*, 52 (1952), 39–63.

—— 'Note sur le *revelabile* selon Cajetan', *Medieval Studies*, 15 (1953), 199–206.

—— 'Introduction', in John Henry Newman, *An Essay in Aid of a Grammar of Assent* (New York: Image Books/Doubleday, 1955), 9–21.

—— 'The Future of Augustinian Metaphysics', trans. Edward Bullough, in *A Monument to St. Augustine* (New York: Meridian Books, 1957), 289–315.

—— *Le philosophe et la théologie* (Paris: Arthème Fayard, 1960).

—— *The Christian Philosophy of Saint Augustine*, trans. L. E. M. Lynch (London: Victor Golancz, 1961).

—— *Les tribulations de Sophie* (Paris: J. Vrin, 1967).

—— *Letters of Étienne Gilson to Henri de Lubac*, trans. Mary Emily Hamilton (San Francisco: Ignatius Press, 1988).

—— *God and Philosophy*, 2nd edn. (New Haven CT/London: Yale University Press, 2002).

Glejzer, Richard, 'Lacan with Scholasticism: Agencies of the Letter', in *American Imago*, 54/2 (1997), 105–22.

Godin, Henri, and Yvan Daniel, *La France: pays de mission?*, 7th edn. (Paris: Cerf, 1950).

Gouhier, Henri, *Études sur l'histoire des idées en France depuis le XVIIe siècle* (Paris: J. Vrin, 1980).

Grabmann, M., 'Il concetto di scienza secondo S. Tommaso d'Aquino e le relazioni della fede e della teologia con la filosofia e le scienze profane', *Rivista di filosofia neoscolastica*, 26 (1934), 127–55.

de Grandmaison, Léonce, *Dogme chrétien: sa nature, ses formules, son développement* (Paris: Beauchesne, 1928).

—— *Jésus Christ: sa personne, son message, ses preuves* (Paris: Beauchesne, 1928).

Granfield, Patrick, *Theologians at Work* (New York/London: Macmillan/Collier-Macmillan, 1967).

Grant, Edward, *God and Reason in the Middle Ages* (Cambridge: Cambridge University Press, 2001).

Greenstock, David L., 'Thomism and the New Theology', *The Thomist*, 13 (1950), 567–96.

Gregory of Nyssa, *Vie de Moïse, Sources chrétiennes*, 1 (Paris: Cerf, 1944, repr. 1955, 1968, 1987).

Grès-Gayer, Jacques-M., 'Le gallicanisme d'Antoine Arnauld: éléments d'une enquête', *Chroniques de Port-Royal*, 44 (1995), 31–51.

Grootaers, J., 'The Drama Continues between the Acts: The "Second Preparation" and its Opponents', in Alberigo and Komonchak (eds.), *The History of Vatican II*, ii.359–514.

Groppe, Elizabeth Teresa, *Yves Congar's Theology of the Holy Spirit* (Oxford: Oxford University Press, 2004).

Grosshans, H.-P., *Die Kirche-irdischer Raum der Wahrheit des Evangeliums* (Leipzig: Evangelische Verlagsanstalt, 2003).

Grumett, David, *De Lubac: A Guide for the Perplexed* with foreword by Avery Cardinal Dulles, SJ (London: Continuum, 2007).

—— 'Eucharist, Matter and the Supernatural: Why de Lubac needs Teilhard', *IJST*, 10 (2008), 165–78.

Guardini, Romano, *The Church and the Catholic and The Spirit of the Liturgy*, trans. Ada Lane (New York: Sheed & Ward, 1935).

Guarino, Thomas G., 'Fundamental Theology and the Natural Knowledge of God in the Writings of Henri Bouillard', Ph.D. thesis (Catholic University of America, 1984).

—— *Foundations of Systematic Theology* (New York: T&T Clark, 2005).

Guelluy, Robert, 'Les Antécédents de l'encyclique "Humani Generis" dans les sanctions Romaines de 1942: Chenu, Charlier, Draguet', *Revue d'histoire ecclésiastique*, 81 (1986), 421–97.

Gutting, Gary, *French Philosophy in the Twentieth Century* (Cambridge: Cambridge University Press, 2001).

Hahn, Scott W., *Covenant and Communion: The Biblical Theology of Pope Benedict XVI* (Grand Rapids MI: Brazos, 2009).

Haight, Roger D., 'The Unfolding of Modernism in France: Blondel, Laberthonnière, Le Roy', *TS*, 35 (1974), 632–66.

—— *The Experience and Language of Grace* (Dublin: Gill and Macmillan, 1979).

Hamer, J., and Y. Congar (eds.), *La Liberté religieuse: declaration Dignitatis humanae personae: texte latin et traduction française*, Unam Sanctam, 60 (Paris: Cerf, 1967).

Hammans, Herbert, *Die neueren katholischen Erklärungen der Dogmenentwicklung* (Essen: Ludgerus-Verlag Hubert Wingen KG, 1965).

Hanvey, James, 'In the Presence of Love: The Pneumatological Realization of the Economy: Yves Congar's *Le Mystère du Temple*', *IJST*, 7 (2005), 383–98.

Harland, R., *Superstructuralism: The Philosophy of Structuralism and Post-Structuralism* (London/New York: Methuen, 1987).

Harris, Sam, *The End of Faith: Religion, Terror, and the Future of Reason* (New York/London: Norton, 2004).

Hauret, C., *Origines de l'univers et de l'homme d'après la Bible (Genèse I–III)* (Paris: Gabalda, 1950, rev. ed. 1952).

——— *Beginnings: Genesis and Modern Science*, trans. John F. McDonnell (Dubuque IA: Priory Press, 1955; rev. ed. 1964).

Hazard, Paul, *European Thought in the Eighteenth Century* (London: World, 1953).

Healey, Nicholas M., *Church, World, and the Christian Life: Practical-Prophetic Ecclesiology* (Cambridge: Cambridge University Press, 2000).

——— *Thomas Aquinas: Theologian of the Christian Life* (Aldershot/Burlington VT: Ashgate, 2003).

Heaney, John J., *The Modernist Crisis: Von Hügel* (London: Geoffrey Chapman, 1968).

Heller, Karin, *Ton Créateur est ton époux, ton rédempteur: contribution à la théologie de l'Alliance à partir des écrits du R. P. Louis Bouyer, de l'Oratoire* (Paris: Téqui, 1996).

Hello, Ernest, *L'Homme* (Paris: Librairie Academique, 1897 [1872]).

Hemming, Laurence, 'Henri de Lubac: On Reading *Corpus Mysticum*', *New Blackfriars*, 90 (2009), 519–34.

Henn, William, *The Hierarchy of Truths According to Yves Congar, OP* (Rome: Gregorian University Press, 1987).

——— Yves Congar and *Lumen gentium*', *Greg*, 86 (2005), 563–92.

Henrici, Peter, 'Blondel und Loisy in der modernistischen Krise', *Internationale katholishe Zeitschrift 'Communio'*, 16 (1987), 513–30.

——— 'De *l'Action* à la critique du *Monophorisme*', *Bulletin des Amis de Maurice Blondel*, nouvelle série 3 (1991), 9–28.

——— 'Simples remarques sur la philosophie sociale de Blondel', in Marc Leclerc (ed.), *Blondel entre L'Action et la Trilogie, Actes du Colloque international sur les 'écrits intermédiaires' de Maurice Blondel, tenu à l'université Grégorienne à Rome du 16 au 18 novembre 2000* (Bruxelles: Lessius, 2003), 361–4.

Hilary of Poitiers, *Traité des mystères*, 1.1, ed. J.-:P. Brisson, *Sources Chrétiennes*, 19bis (Paris: Cerf, 2005).

Himes, Michael J., *Ongoing Incarnation: Johann Adam Möhler and the Beginnings of Modern Ecclesiology* (New York: Crossroad, 1997).

Hitchens, Christopher, *God Is Not Great: How Religion Poisons Everything* (London: Atlantic Books, 2007).

d'Holbach, Baron Paul, *Le bon sens: ou idées naturelles opposées aux idées surnaturelles* (Amsterdam: n.p., 1772).

——— *Common Sense: or Natural Ideas Opposed to Supernatural* (New York: n.p., 1795).

Hollon, Bryan, *Everything is Sacred: Spiritual Exegesis in the Political Theology of Henri de Lubac* (Eugene OR: Cascade, 2009).

Holmes, S., *Listening to the Past: The Place of Tradition in Theology* (Grand Rapids MI: Baker, 2002).

Holsinger, Bruce, *The Premodern Condition: Medievalism and the Making of Theory* (Chicago/London: University of Chicago Press, 2005).

Hours, Henri, 'L'E.P.I.', *Église à Lyon*, 3 February, 1997, 63–4.

Hulshof, Jan, 'The Modernist Crisis: Alfred Loisy and George Tyrrell', trans. Theo Westow, *Concilium*, 113 (1978), 28–39.

Imbelli, Robert, 'The Reaffirmation of the Christic Center', in Stephen J. Pope and Charles Hefling (eds.) *Sic et Non: Encountering Dominus Iesus* (Maryknoll NY: Orbis, 2002), 96–106.

Irenaeus, *Against the Heresies*, in *Ante-Nicene Fathers*, i, trans. and ed. Alexander Roberts and W. H. Rambaut (Peabody MA: Hendrickson, 1996), 315–567.

von Ivánka, Endre, 'Von Platonismus zur Theorie der Mystik (Zur Erkenntnislehre Gregors von Nyssa)', *Scholastik*, 11 (1936), 163–95.

———— *ZkT*, 71 (1949), 231–3.

Jakim, B., and R. Bird (trans. and eds.), *On Spiritual Unity. A Slavophile Reader* (Hudson NY: Lindisfarne Books, 1998).

James, William, 'Pragmatism. A New Name for Some Old Ways of Thinking' (1907), in *The Works of William James*, I., ed. Frederick H. Burkhardt (Cambridge MA: Harvard University Press, 1975).

Jedin, Hubert, *Crisis and Closure of the Council of Trent: A Retrospective View from the Second Vatican Council*, trans. N. D. Smith (London: Sheed & Ward, 1967).

Jeffreys, Derek S., 'A Deep Amazement at Man's Worth and Dignity', in T. Perry (ed.), *The Legacy of John Paul II: An Evangelical Assessment* (Downers Grove IL: Intervarsity Press Academic, 2007), 37–56.

Jenson, R., *Systematic Theology*, ii (Oxford: Oxford University Press, 1999).

———— 'The Church as *Communio*', in C. Braaten and R. Jenson (eds.), *The Catholicity of the Reformation* (Grand Rapids MI: Eerdmans, 1996), 1–12.

Jodock, Darrell (ed.), *Catholicism Contending with Modernity: Roman Catholic Modernism and Anti-Modernism in Historical Context* (Cambridge: Cambridge University Press, 2000).

Johnson, Cuthbert, OSB, *Prosper Guéranger (1805–1875): A Liturgical Theologian: An Introduction to his liturgical writings and work*, Studia Anselmiana, 89 (Rome: Pontificio Ateneo S. Anselmo, 1984).

Johnson, Elizabeth, *Consider Jesus: Waves of Renewal in Christology* (New York: Crossroad, 1992).

Jossua, Jean-Pierre, *Le Père Congar: la théologie au service du peuple de Dieu*, Chrétiens De Tous Les Temps, 20 (Paris: Cerf, 1967).

———— 'L'œuvre œcuménique du Père Congar,' *Études*, 357 (1982), 543–55.

———— 'Le Saulchoir: une formation théologique replacée dans son histoire', *Cristianesimo nella storia*, 14 (1993), 99–124.

———— 'In Hope of Unity', trans. Barbara Estelle Beaumont, OP, in Flynn (ed.), *Yves Congar: Theologian of the Church*, 167–81.

Jounel, Pierre, 'Les Missels diocésains français du 18e siècle', *La Maison-Dieu*, 141 (1980), 91–6.

Journet, Charles, 'Chronique de philosophie', *Nova et vetera* (1927), 406–21.

——— 'Sources chrétiennes', *Nova et vetera* (1944), 25–37.

——— *Vérité de Pascal: Essai sur la valeur apologétique des 'Pensées'* (Saint-Maurice: Éditions Saint-Augustin, 1951).

——— *Primauté de Pierre dans la perspective protestante et dans la perspective catholique* (Paris: Alsatia, 1953).

——— *The Church of the Word Incarnate*, trans. A. H. C. Downes (London: Sheed & Ward, 1955).

——— *Théologie de l'Église* (Paris: Desclée de Brouwer, 1958).

——— 'Regard rétrospectif. À propos du dernier livre du R. P. Congar sur l'Église', *Nova et vetera* (1963), 294–312.

——— 'Cordula ou l'épreuve décisive' *Nova et vetera* (1968), 147–54.

——— 'De la personnalité de l'Église', *RevTh*, 69 (1969), 192–200.

——— 'Églises particulières et Églises locales' *Nova et vetera* (1971), 58–60.

——— *Journet—Maritain Correspondance*, iv, 1950–1957 (Paris: Éditions Saint-Augustin, 2005).

——— *L'Église du Verbe incarné: Essai de théologie speculative*, ii, *Sa structure interne et son unité catholique* (Paris: Éditions Saint-Augustin, 2000).

Judt, Tony, *Past Imperfect: French Intellectuals*, 1944–1956 (Berkeley CA: University of California Press, 1992).

Jüngel, E., 'The Church as Sacrament?' in *Theological Essays I*, trans. John Webster (Edinburgh: T&T Clark, 1989), 189–213.

Kaplan, Grant, *Answering the Enlightenment: The Catholic Recovery of Historical Revelation* (New York: Herder and Herder, 2006).

Kasper, Cardinal Walter, 'Church as *communio*', *Communio*, 13 (1986), 100–117.

——— 'Eucharist—Sacrament of Unity. The Essential Connection between Eucharist and Church', in *Sacrament of Unity: The Eucharist and the Church* (New York: Crossroad, 2004), 117–50.

——— *That They May All Be One: The Call to Unity Today* (London: Burns & Oates, 2004).

——— (ed.), *Logik der Liebe und Herrlichkeit Gottes: Hans Urs von Balthasar im Gespräch*, Festgabe für Karl Kardinal Lehmann zum 70. Geburtstag (Ostfildern: Matthias-Grünewald-Verlag, 2006).

Kehl, Medard, 'Hans Urs von Balthasar: A Portrait', in Medard Kehl and Werner Löser (eds.), *The Von Balthasar Reader*, trans. Robert J. Daly and Fred Lawrence (New York: Crossroad: 1982), 1–54.

Kennedy, Philip, *Schillebeeckx* (London, Chapman, 1983).

Kerr, Fergus, OP, 'Chenu's Little Book', *New Blackfriars*, 66 (1985), 108–12.

——— *After Aquinas* (Oxford: Blackwell, 2002).

——— (ed.), *Contemplating Aquinas* (London: SCM Press, 2003).

——— *Twentieth Century Catholic Theologians. From Neoscholasticism to Nuptial Mysticism* (Oxford: Blackwell, 2007).

Kizhakkeparampil, Isaac, *The Invocation of the Holy Spirit as Constitutive of the Sacraments according to Cardinal Yves Congar* (Rome: Gregorian University Press, 1995).

Klimoff, Alexis, 'Georges Florovsky and the Sophiological Controversy', *St Vladimir's Theological Quarterly*, 49 (2005), 67–100.

Klinger E., and K. Wittstadt (eds.), *Glaube im Prozess: Christsein nach dem II. Vatikanum* (Freiburg: Herder, 1984).

Knasas, John F. X., *Being and Some Twentieth-Century Thomists* (New York: Fordham University Press, 2003).

Koenker, Ernest, *The Liturgical Renaissance in the Roman Catholic Church* (Chicago: University of Chicago Press, 1954).

Komonchak, Joseph, 'Theology and Culture at Mid-Century: The Example of Henri de Lubac', *TS*, 51 (1990), 579–602.

—— 'Concepts of Communion. Past and Present', *Cristianesimo nella Storia*, 16 (1995), 321–40.

—— 'The Struggle for the Council during the Preparation of Vatican II', in Alberigo and Komonchak (eds.), *History of Vatican II*, 167–356.

—— 'Modernity and the Construction of Roman Catholicism', *Cristianesimo nella Storia*, 18 (1997), 353–85.

—— 'Thomism and the Second Vatican Council', in Anthony J. Cernera (ed.), *Continuity and Plurality in Catholic Theology: Essays in Honor of Gerald A. McCool, S.J.* (Fairfield CT: Sacred Heart University Press, 1998) 53–73.

—— 'Returning from Exile: Catholic Theology in the 1930s', in Gregory Baum (ed.), *The Twentieth Century: A Theological Overview* (Maryknoll NY: Orbis, 1999), 35–48.

—— 'The Council of Trent at the Second Vatican Council', in Bulman and Parrella (eds.), *From Trent to Vatican II*, 61–80.

Koskela, Douglas M., *Ecclesiality and Ecumenism: Yves Congar and the Road to Unity*, Marquette Studies in Theology, 61 (Milwaukee WI: Marquette University Press, 2008).

Kosky, J., 'Georges Bataille's Religion without Religion: A Review of the Possibilities Opened by the Publication of "The Unfinished System of Nonknowledge"', *The Journal of Religion*, 84/1 (2004), 78–87.

Koster, Mannes Dominikus, *Ekklesiologie im Werden* (Paderborn: Bonifacius-Druckerei, 1940).

—— *Volk Gottes im Werden* repr. (Mainz: Grünewald, 1971).

Koyré, Alexandre, *Newtonian Studies* (London: Chapman Hall, 1968), 6.

—— *From a Closed to an Infinite World* (Radford: Wilder Publications, 2008).

Krieg, Robert A., *Romano Guardini: A Precursor of Vatican II* (Notre Dame IN: University of Notre Dame Press, 1997).

—— *Catholic Theologians in Nazi Germany* (New York: Continuum, 2004).

Krumenacker, Yves, 'La science historique à l'époque d'"Histoire et Dogme"', *Théophilyon*, 9 (2004), 99–110.

Küng, Hans, *Disputed Truth: Memoirs*, trans. John Bowden (New York: Continuum, 2008).

Labbie, Erin, *Lacan's Medievalism* (Minneapolis MN/London: University of Minnesota Press, 2006).

Labourdette, Marie-Michel, OP, 'La théologie, intelligence de la foi', *RevTh*, 46 (1946), 5–44.

—— 'La théologie et ses sources', *RevTh*, 46 (1946), 353–71.

——— 'Correspondance Étienne Gilson—Michel Labourdette', *RevTh*, 94 (1994), 479–529.

Labourdette, M.-M., OP, *et al.*, *Dialogue théologique: Pièces du débat* (Var: Les Arcades, 1947).

Labourdette, Marie-Michel, and Marie-Joseph Nicolas, 'L'Analogie de la vérité et l'unité de la science théologique', *RevTh*, 47 (1947), 417–66.

Lacan, Jacques, *The Seminar of Jacques Lacan, Bk xii, 1964–1965: Crucial problems for Psychoanalysis*, trans. C. Gallagher. Unpublished. 7.4.65.

——— *The Seminar of Jacques Lacan, Bk xiii: The Object of psychoanalysis, 1965–1966*, trans. Cormac Gallagher. Unpublished, 19.1.66.

——— *The Seminar of Jacques Lacan, Bk xiv: The Logic of Phantasy*, trans. Cormac Gallagher. Unpublished. 7.12.66.

——— *The Seminar of Jacques Lacan, Bk xvi: From the Other to the other, 1968–1969*, trans. C. Gallagher. Unpublished. 4.6.69.

——— 'Geneva Lecture on the Symptom', *Analysis*, 1 (1989), 15.

——— *Television: A Challenge to the Psychoanalytic Establishment*, ed. Joan Copjec, trans. Jeffrey Mehlman (New York/London: Norton, 1990).

——— *The Seminar of Jacques Lacan, Bk i: Freud's Papers on Technique, 1953–1954*, ed. Jacques-Alain Miller, trans. John Forrester (London/New York: W. W. Norton & Company, 1991).

——— *The Seminar of Jacques Lacan, Bk vii: The Ethics of Psychoanalysis, 1959–1960*, ed. Jacques-Alain Miller, trans. Dennis Porter (London: Routledge, 1999).

——— *The Seminar of Jacques Lacan, Bk xx: Encore, 1972–1973*, ed. Jacques-Alain Miller, trans. Bruce Fink (New York/London: Norton, 1999).

——— *Écrits*, trans. Bruce Fink (New York/London: Norton, 2006).

Lacoste, Jean-Yves, *et al.*, *Histoire de la théologie* (Paris: Seuil, 2009).

Ladous, Régis (ed.), *Médecine humaine, médecine sociale: Le Docteur René Biot (1889–1966) et ses amis* (Paris: Cerf, 1986).

Lagrange, M.-J., *Père Lagrange: Personal Reflections and Memoirs* (New York: Paulist Press, 1985).

Lamberigts, M., L. Boeve, and T. Merrigan (eds.) *Theology and the Quest for Truth: Historical and Systematic Theological Studies*, BETL 202 (Louvain/Leuven: Presses Universitaires de Louvain/Peeters, 2007).

Lamioni, C., ed., *Il Sinodo di Pistoia del 1786* (Rome: Herder, 1991).

Lamont, John R. T., 'Conscience, Freedom, Rights: Idols of the Enlightenment Religion', *The Thomist*, 73 (2009), 169–239.

Lancelot, Claude, *Memoires touchant la vie de M. de Saint-Cyran* (1738), ed. Denis Donetzkoff (Paris: Nolin, 2003).

Lane, A. N. S., *John Calvin: Student of the Church Fathers* (Edinburgh: T&T Clark, 1999).

Lane, Dermot A., 'Pneumatology in the Service of Ecumenism and Inter-religious Dialogue: A Case of Neglect?', *LS*, 33 (2008), 136–58.

Laplanche, François, *La crise de l'origine: La science catholique des Évangiles et l'histoire au XXᵉ siècle* (Paris: Albin Michel, 2006).

Larrey, Martin F., 'Towards a re-evaluation of the Counter-Reformation', *Communio*, 7 (1980), 209–24.

Bibliography

Lash, Nicholas, *Voices of Authority* (London: Sheed & Ward, 1976).

—— *Theology for Pilgrims* (London: Darton, Longman & Todd, 2008).

Latourelle, René, *Theology of Revelation* (New York: Alba House, 1966).

Latourelle, René, (ed.), *Vatican II: Assessment and Perspectives Twenty-Five Years After (1962–1987)*, i (New York: Paulist Press, 1988).

Laudouze, André, OP, *Dominicains français et Action Française: 1899–1940. Maurras au Couvent* (Paris: Les Éditions Ouvrières, 1989).

Laulagnier, Rachel, 'Le Groupe lyonnais d'études médicales, philosophiques et biologiques, 1924–1969', unpublished Master's dissertation (Université Lumière-Lyon II, 1997).

Lawrence, Hugh, 'Spiritual Authority and Governance: A Historical Perspective', in Hoose (ed.), *Authority in the Roman Catholic Church*, 37–57.

Le Blond, Jean-Marie, 'L'Analogie de la vérité: Réflexion d'un philosophe sur une controverse théologique', *RSR*, 34 (1947), 129–41.

Lebreton, Jules, '"In Memoriam" Le Père Yves de Montcheuil', *RSR*, 33 (1946), 5–9.

Leclercq, Henri, 'Liturgies Néo-Gallicanes', in F. Cabrol (ed.), *Dictionnaire d'archéologie chrétienne et de liturgie* (Paris: Letouzey et Ané, 1907), ix, 2, cols. 1636–729.

Le Goff, Jacques, *Medieval Civilisation* (Oxford: Blackwell, 1996).

—— 'Le Père Chenu et la société médiévale', *RSPT*, 81 (1997), 371–80.

Legrand, Hervé, 'L'ecclésiologie eucharistique dans le dialogue actuel entre l'Église catholique et l'Église orthodoxe', *Istina*, 51 (2006), 354–74.

Legrand, Hervé-Marie, 'The Presidency of the Eucharist According To the Ancient Tradition', in R. Kevin Seasoltz (ed.), *Living Bread, Saving Cup: Readings on the Eucharist* (Collegeville MN: Liturgical Press, 1987), 196–221.

Leibholz, G., 'Memoir', in Dietrich Bonhoeffer, *The Cost of Discipleship*, trans. R.H. Fuller, with some revision by Irmgard Booth, complete edn. (London: SCM Press, 1959), 9–27.

Lennan, Richard, *The Ecclesiology of Karl Rahner* (Oxford: Clarendon Press, 1995).

—— 'Faith in Context: Rahner on the Possibility of Belief', *Philosophy and Theology*, 17 (2005), 241–8.

Leprieur, François, *Quand Rome condamne: Dominicains et prêtres-ouvriers* (Paris: Cerf, 1989).

Lera, J. M., 'Sacrae paginae studium sit veluti anima Sacrae Theologiae (Notas sobre el origen y procedencia de esta frase)', in A. Vargas Machuca and G. Ruiz (eds.), *Palabra y Vida. Homenaje a José Alonso Díaz en su 70 cumpleaños* (Madrid: Universidad Comillas, 1984), 409–22.

Lesaulnier, Jean, 'Les hébraïsants de Port-Royal', *Chroniques de Port-Royal*, 53 (2004), 29–45.

Le Tourneux, Nicolas, *L'Office de l'Eglise en latin et en françois contenant l'office des dimanches et des fêtes* (Paris: Le Petit, 1650).

Levenson, J. D., *The Hebrew Bible, the Old Testament, and historical criticism: Jews and Christians in biblical studies* (Louisville KY: Westminster/John Knox Press, 1993).

Lewy, Guenter, *The Catholic Church and Nazi Germany* (London: Weidenfeld & Nicolson, 1964).

Lienhard, Marc, *Identité confessionnelle et quête de l'unité: Catholiques et protestants face à l'éxigence œcuménique* (Lyon: Olivétan, 2007).

Lies, Lothar, '*Fundamentaltheologie—Kritik und Theologie. Christliche Glaubens- und Schrifthermeneutik nach Richard Simon (1638–1712)*', TR, 103/4 (2007), 302.

Lindbeck, George, 'Ecumenical Theology', in Ford (ed.), *The Modern Theologians*, ii.255–73.

Lobkowicz, Nicholas, 'What Happened to Thomism? From *Aeterni Patris* to *Vaticanum Secundum*', *American Catholic Philosophical Quarterly*, 69 (1995), 397–425.

Lohfink, Gerhard, *Jesus and Community*, trans. John P. Galvin (New York: Paulist Press, 1984).

Lohfink, Norbert, *Katholische Bibelwissenschaft und historisch-kritische Methode* (Kevelaer: Butzon und Bercker, 1966).

Alfred Loisy, *L'Évangile et l'Église* (Paris: Picard, 1902).

——— *Études bibliques*, 3rd edn. (Paris: Picard, 1903). The first edition of *Études bibliques* had been published in 1894, the second in 1901.

——— *Autour d'un petit livre* (Paris: Picard, 1903), 197.

——— *My Duel with the Vatican: The Autobiography of a Catholic Modernist*, trans. Richard Wilson Boynton (New York: Greenwood Press, 1968).

Lonergan, Bernard, *Insight: A Study in Human Understanding* (London: Darton, Longman & Todd, 1958).

——— *Method in Theology* (London: Darton, Longman & Todd, 1972).

——— *Grace and Freedom: Operative Grace in the Thought of Thomas Aquinas, The Collected Works of Bernard Lonergan*, Frederick E. Crowe and Robert M. Doran (eds.) (Toronto: University of Toronto Press, 2005).

Long, Steven A., 'Nicholas Lobkowicz and the Historicist Inversion of Thomistic Philosophy', *The Thomist*, 62 (1988), 41–75.

——— *Natura Pura: On the Recovery of Nature in the Doctrine of Grace* (New York: Fordham University Press, 2010).

Loonbeek, Raymond, and Mortiau, Jacques, *Un Pionnier Dom Lambert Beauduin (1873–1960): Liturgie et Unité chrétiens* 2 vols. (Louvain-La-Neuve: Collège Érasme, 2001).

Lossky, V., *Essai sur la théologie mystique de l'Église d'Orient* (Paris: Aubier, 1944).

——— *The Mystical Theology of the Eastern Church*, trans. members of the Fellowship of St Alban and St Sergius (Cambridge/Crestwood NY: James Clarke & Co./St Vladimir's Seminary Press, 1957/1976).

——— *The Vision of God*, The library of Orthodox Theology, 2 (Bedfordshire, UK: Faith Press, 1964).

——— *Théologie négative et connaissance de Dieu chez Maître Eckhart* (Paris: Vrin, 1960).

——— *Spor o Sofii* (Moscow: Izdatel'stvo Svyato-Vladimirskogo Bratstva, 1996).

——— *Sept jours sur les routes de France. Juin 1940* (Paris: Cerf, 1998).

Lot-Borodine, Myrrha, 'Les Grands Secrets du Saint-Graal dans la Queste du pseudo-Map', in R. Nelli (ed.), *Lumière du Graal* (Paris: Cahiers du Sud, 1951), 151–74.

Lot-Borodine, Myrrha, *Un maître de la spiritualité byzantine au XIVe siècle: Nicolas Cabasilas* (Paris: Éditions de l'Orante, 1958).

——— *De l'amour profane à l'amour sacré* (Paris: Librairie Nizet, 1961).

——— *La deification de l'homme*, preface by Cardinal Jean Daniélou (Paris: Cerf, 1970).

Loughlin, Gerard, 'Catholic Modernism', in David Fergusson (ed.), *The Blackwell Companion to Nineteenth-Century Theology* (Oxford: Wiley-Blackwell, 2010), 486–508.

Louth, Andrew, *The Origins of the Christian Mystical Tradition from Plato to Denys* (Oxford: Oxford University Press, 1981).

——— 'Father Sergii Bulgakov on the Mother of God', *St Vladimir's Theological Quarterly*, 49 (2005), 145–64.

——— 'The Eucharist in the Theology of Fr Sergii Bulgakov', *Sobornost*, 27/2 (2005), 36–56.

——— 'Receptive Ecumenism and Catholic Learning: An Orthodox Perspective', in Paul D. Murray (ed.), *Receptive Ecumenism*, 361–72.

Lubac, Henri de, SJ, *Catholicisme. Les aspects sociaux du dogme* (Paris: Cerf, 1937).

——— *Catholicisme*, Unam Sanctam 3 (Paris: Cerf, 1938).

——— 'Sur la philosophie chrétienne: Réflexions à la suite d'un débat', *NRT*, 42 (1936), 225–53.

——— *Surnaturel: Études historiques*, Théologie, 8 (Paris: Cerf, 1946).

——— *Corpus Mysticum: l'Eucharistie et l'Église au Moyen Âge. Étude historique* (Paris: Aubier, 1949).

——— *Catholicism*, trans. Lancelot C. Sheppard (London: Burns & Oates, 1950).

——— *Histoire et esprit: l'intelligence de l'Écriture d'après Origène*, Théologie 16 (Paris: Aubier, 1950).

——— 'L'Église notre Mère', *Études*, (1953) 3–19.

——— *Méditation sur l'Eglise* (Paris: Aubier, 1953).

——— *The Splendour of the Church*, trans. Michael Mason (London: Sheed & Ward, 1956).

——— 'Zum katholischen Dialog mit Karl Barth', *Dokumente*, 14 (1958), 448–54.

——— *Exégèse médiévale* i–iv (Paris: Aubier, 1959–1964).

——— *Paradoxes, suivis de Nouveaux Paradoxes* (Paris: Seuil, 1959).

——— *The Mystery of the Supernatural*, trans. Rosemary Sheed (New York: Herder and Herder, 1967).

——— *Athéisme et sens de l'homme: Une double requête de Gaudium et spes* (Paris: Cerf, 1968).

——— *The Sources of Revelation*, trans. Luke O'Neill (New York: Herder and Herder, 1968).

——— *L'Église dans la crise actuelle* (Paris: Cerf, 1969).

——— 'The Church in Crisis', *Theology Digest*, 17 (1969), 312–25.

——— *Pic de la Mirandole: études et discussions* (Paris: Aubier-Montaigne, 1974).

——— *Trois jésuits nous parlent: Yves de Montcheuil 1899–1944, Charles Nicolet 1897–1961, Jean Zupan 1899–1968* (Paris: Lethielleux, 1980).

——— *The Motherhood of the Church: Particular Churches in the Universal Church*, trans. Sergia Englund (San Francisco: Ignatius Press, 1982).

—— *La revelation divine* (Paris: Cerf, 1983).

—— *A Brief Catechegis on Nature and Grace*, trans. Brother Richard Arnauder, FSC (San Francisco CA: Ignatius, 1984).

—— *The Splendour of the Church*, trans. Michael Mason (San Francisco: Ignatius Press, 1986).

—— *Catholicism. Christ and the Common Destiny of Man* trans. Lancelot C. Sheppard and Elizabeth Englund (San Francisco: Ignatius Press, 1988).

—— (ed.), *Letters of Étienne Gilson to Henri de Lubac*, trans. Mary Emily Hamilton (San Francisco: Ignatius Press, 1988).

—— 'Témoignage de P de Lubac', in Karl-Heinz Neufeld (ed.), *Vérité du Christianisme*, 413–414.

—— *Theological Fragments*, trans. Rebecca Howell Balinski (San Francisco: Ignatius Press, 1989).

—— *Christian Resistance to Anti-Semitism: Memories from 1940–1944*, trans. Sister Elizabeth Englund, OCD (San Francisco: Ignatius Press, 1990).

—— *Théologie dans l'histoire. II Questiones disputées et résistance au nazisme*, Théologie (Paris: Desclée de Brouwer, 1990).

—— *Mémoire sur l'occasion de mes écrits*, 2nd edn. (Namur: Culture et Vérité, 1992).

—— *At the Service of the Church: Henri de Lubac Reflects on the Circumstances that occasioned His Writings*, trans. Anne Englund Nash (San Francisco: Ignatius Press, 1993).

—— *The Discovery of God*, trans. Alexander Dru with Marc Sebanc and Cassian Fulsom (Edinburgh: T&T Clark, 1996).

—— *Theology in History*, trans. Anne Englund Nash (San Francisco: Ignatius Press, 1996).

—— *Medieval Exegesis* trans. Mark Sebanc (i), Edward M. Macierowski (ii, iii), 4 vols. (Grand Rapids MI: Eerdmans, 1998–).

—— *The Mystery of the Supernatural*, trans Rosemary Sheed (New York: Crossroad, 1998).

—— *Augustinianism and Modern Theology*, trans. Lancelot Sheppard (New York: Crossroad, 2000).

—— *More Paradoxes*, trans. Anne Englund Nash (San Francisco: Ignatius Press, 2002).

—— *Histoire et esprit: l'intelligence de l'Écriture chez Origène*, 2nd edn. (Paris: Cerf, 2002).

—— *Corpus Mysticum: The Eucharist and the Church in the Middle Ages: Historical Survey*, trans. Gemma Simmonds with Richard Price and Christopher Stephens, eds. Laurence Paul Hemming and Susan Frank Parsons (London: SCM Press, 2006).

—— *Carnets du Concile*, ed. L. Figoureux, i (Paris: Cerf, 2007).

—— *Entretiens autour de Vatican II: Souvenirs et Réflexions*, Théologies, 2nd edn. (Paris: France Catholique/Cerf, 2007).

—— *History and Spirit: The Understanding of Scripture According to Origen*, trans. Anne Englund Nash with Juvenal Merriell (San Francisco: Ignatius Press, 2007).

—— 'The Total Meaning of Man and the World', trans. of the first four sections (of six total) of *Athéisme et sens de l'homme* by D. C. Schindler, *Communio*, 35 (2008), 613–41.

Lustiger, Jean-Marie, 'Homélie à l'occasion des funérailles du Père Louis Bouyer', *Communio* (French ed.) 30/1 (2005).

McBrien, Richard P., '*I Believe in the Holy Spirit*: The Role of Pneumatology in Yves Congar's Theology', in Flynn (ed.), *Yves Congar: Theologian of the Church*, 303–27.

McCabe, Herbert, OP, 'Appendix 4: Analogy' in Thomas Aquinas, *Summa Theologiae* (London: Eyre & Spottiswoode, 1964), vol. 3, Knowing and Naming God, *Ia. 12–13*, 106–107.

McCool, Gerald, 'Twentieth-Century Scholasticism', in David Tracy (ed.), *Celebrating the Medieval Heritage: A Colloquy on the Thought of Aquinas and Bonaventure. Supplement, The Journal of Religion*, 58 (1978), 198–224.

—— *From Unity to Pluralism: The Internal evolution of Thomism* (New York: Fordham University Press, 1989).

MacCulloch, Diarmaid, *Reformation: Europe's House Divided 1490–1700* (London: Penguin, 2004).

McGuinness, Frank, 'Rimbaud', *The Irish Times*, 14 October 2000.

McKanan, Dan, *The Catholic Worker after Dorothy: Practicing the Works of Mercy in a New Generation* (Collegeville MN: Liturgical Press, 2008).

McKenzie, J. L., *The Two-Edged Sword* (Milwaukee WI: Bruce, 1956).

—— *Myths and Realities: studies in Biblical theology* (Milwaukee WI: Bruce, 1963).

McPartlan, Paul, 'Eucharistic Ecclesiology', *One in Christ*, 22 (1986), 314–31.

—— *Sacrament of Salvation. An Introduction to Eucharistic Ecclesiology* (Edinburgh: T&T Clark, 1995).

—— 'The Eucharist, the Church and Evangelization: The Influence of Henri de Lubac', *Communio*, 23 (1996), 776–85.

—— 'The Eucharist as the Basis for Ecclesiology', *Antiphon*, 6 (2001), 12–19.

—— 'Liturgy, Church, and Society', *Studia Liturgica*, 34 (2004), 147–64.

—— *The Eucharist Makes the Church. Henri de Lubac and John Zizioulas in Dialogue* 2nd edn. (Fairfax VA: Eastern Christian Publications, 2006).

—— 'John Paul II and Vatican II', in G. Mannion (ed.), *The Vision of John Paul II: Assessing his Thought and Influence* (Collegeville MN: Liturgical Press, 2008), 45–61.

—— 'Catholic Learning and Orthodoxy—The Promise and Challenge of Eucharistic Ecclesiology', in Murray (ed.), *Receptive Ecumenism*, 160–75.

Macken, John, *The autonomy theme in the Church Dogmatics: Karl Barth and his critics* (Cambridge: Cambridge University Press, 1990).

Macksey, R., and E. Donato, *The Structuralist Controversy: The Languages of Criticism and the Sciences of Man* (Baltimore MD: Johns Hopkins University Press, 1972).

Maggiolini, Alessandro, 'Magisterial Teaching on Experience in the Twentieth Century: From the Modernist Crisis to the Second Vatican Council', trans. Andrew Matt and Adrian Walker, *Communio*, 23 (1996), 225–43.

Malabre, Natalie, 'Le religieux dans la ville du premier vingtième siècle: La paroisse Notre-Dame Saint-Alban d'une guerre à l'autre', unpublished Ph.D. thesis (Université Lumière-Lyon II, 2006).

Maréchal, Joseph, *Le Point de départ de la métaphysique: Leçons sur le développement historique et théorique du problème de la connaissance*, v. *Le Thomisme devant la philosophie critique* (Louvain/Paris: Museum Lessianum/Alcan, 1926).

—— *A Maréchal Reader*, trans. and ed., Joseph Donceel (New York: Herder and Herder, 1970).

Maritain, J., *Le Songe de Descartes* (Paris: Buchet et Chastel, 1932).

———— *Du Régime Temporel et De La Liberté* (Paris: Desclée de Brouwer et Cie, 1934).

———— *De Bergson à Thomas d'Aquin: essais de métaphysique et de morale* (Paris: Hartmann, 1947).

———— *Le Paysan de la Garonne* (Paris: Desclée De Brouwer, 1966).

———— *The Peasant of the Garonne*, trans. Michael Cuddihy and Elizabeth Hughes (London: Geoffrey Chapman, 1968).

Maritain, Jacques, and Jean Cocteau, *Art and Faith: Letters between Jacques Maritain and Jean Cocteau* (New York: Philosophical Library, 1948).

Marlé, René, *Au cœur de la crise moderniste. Le dossier inédit d'une controverse* (Paris: Aubier, 1960).

Martina, Giacomo, 'The Historical Context in Which the Idea of a New Ecumenical Council Was Born', in René Latourelle (ed.), *Vatican II: Assessment and Perspectives Twenty-Five Years After (1962–1987)*, i (New York: Paulist Press, 1988), 3–73.

Meijering, E. P., *Melanchthon and Patristic Thought* (Leiden: Brill, 1983).

———— 'The Fathers and Calvinist Orthodoxy: Systematic Theology', in I. Backus (ed.), *The Reception of the Church Fathers in the West*, 867–87.

Melloni, Alberto, 'The System and the Truth in the Diaries of Yves Congar', in Flynn (ed.), *Yves Congar: Theologian of the Church*, 277–302.

Mercier, Alexis, 'La Revue fédéraliste: Une tentative décentralisatrice lyonnaise, 1918–1928', unpublished Master's dissertation (Université Lumière-Lyon II, 1997).

Merrigan, Terrence, 'The Appeal to Yves Congar in Recent Catholic Theology of Religions: The Case of Jacques Dupuis', in Flynn (ed.), *Yves Congar: Theologian of the Church*, 427–57.

Mersch, Émile, *Le corps mystique du Christ: Études de théologie historique* i and ii (Leuven: Museum Lessianum, 1933).

———— *The Whole Christ: The Historical Development of the Doctrine of the Mystical Body in Scripture and Tradition*, trans. John R. Kelly (Milwaukee WI/London: Bruce/Dennis Dobson, 1938).

———— *Théologie du corps mystique* (Brussels: Éditions Universelles, 1949).

———— *The Theology of the Mystical Body*, trans. Cyril Vollert (St Louis MO: B. Herder, 1951).

Mettepenningen, Jürgen, 'Christus denken naar de mensen toe: De *nouvelle théologie* christologisch doorgedacht door Piet Schoonenberg', *Tijdschrift voor Theologie*, 46 (2006), 143–60.

———— 'Truth as Issue in a Second Modernist Crisis? The Clash between Recontextualization and Retrocontextualization in the French-Speaking Polemic of 1946–47', in M. Lamberigts, L. Boeve, and T. Merrigan (eds.) *Theology and the Quest for Truth*, 119–42.

———— 'Edward Schillebeeckx: Herodero y promotor de la *nouvelle théologie*', *Mayéutica*, 78 (2008), 285–302.

———— 'L'*Essai* de Louis Charlier (1938): Une contribution à la *nouvelle théologie*', *RThL*, 39 (2008), 211–32.

———— *Nouvelle Théologie—New Theology: Inheritor of Modernism, Precursor of Vatican II* (London: Continuum, 2010).

Meuleman, Gezinus Evert, *De ontwikkeling van het dogma in de Rooms Katholieke theologie* (Kampen: Kok, 1951).

Meyer, Hans Bernhard (ed.), *Eucharistie: Geschichte, Theologie, Pastoral*, Gottesdienst der Kirche, 4 vols (Regensburg: Pustet, 1989).

Meyers, Jeffrey, *Edmund Wilson: a biography* (Boston: Houghton Mifflin, 1995).

Milbank, John, *The Suspended Middle: Henri de Lubac and the Debate concerning the Supernatural* (London: SCM Press, 2005).

—— 'Alternative Protestantism. Radical Orthodoxy and the Reformed Tradition', in J. K. A. Smith and J. H. Olthuis (eds.), *Radical Orthodoxy and the Reformed Tradition: Creation, Covenant and Participation* (Grand Rapids MI: Baker, 2005), 25–41.

—— 'Radical Orthodoxy and twentieth-century theology' in John Milbank and Simon Oliver (eds.), *The Radical Orthodoxy Reader* (London: Routledge, 2009), 368–79.

Milik, J. T., *Ten Years of Discovery in the Wilderness of Judea*, Studies in Biblical Theology, 26 (London: SCM Press, 1959).

Minnich, Nelson H., 'The Priesthood of All Believers at the Council of Trent', *The Jurist*, 67 (2007), 341–63.

Moeller, Charles, 'History of *Lumen Gentium*'s Structure and Ideas', in John H. Miller (ed.), *Vatican II: An Interfaith Appraisal* (Notre Dame IN: University of Notre Dame Press, 1966), 123–52.

Möhler, Johann Adam, *Die Einheit in der Kirche oder das Prinzip des Katholizismus* (Mainz: Grünewald, 1825).

—— *Symbolik oder Darstellung der dogmatischen Gegensätze der Katholiken und Protestanten nach ihren öffentlichen Bekenntnisschriften*, i (Cologne: Hegner, 1960).

—— *Unity in the Church or the Principle of Catholicism: Presented in the Spirit of the Church Fathers of the First Three Centuries*, ed. and trans. Peter C. Erb (Washington DC: Catholic University of America Press, 1996).

Moingt, Joseph, 'Avant-Propos', *RSR*, 60/1 (1972), 7.

Mondésert, Claude, *Pour lire les Pères de l'Église dans la Collection 'Sources Chrétiennes'*, Foi Vivante, 230, 2nd edn. (Paris: Cerf, 1988).

Mongrain, Kevin, *The Systematic Thought of Hans Urs Von Balthasar: An Irenaean Retrieval* (New York: Crossroad, 2002).

Montcheuil, Yves de, 'La Liberté et la diversité dans l'Unité', in Pierre Chaillet (ed.) *L'Église est une: hommage à Moehler* (Paris: Bloud & Gay, 1939), 234–54.

—— 'Exigences de la libération', *Cahiers du Témoignage chrétien*, xxvi–xxvii, mai 1944 (309–12).

Montagnes, Bernard, *M.-J. Lagrange: une biographie critique* (Paris: Cerf, 2004).

—— *The Story of M.-J. Lagrange: founder of modern Catholic Bible Study* (New York: Paulist Press, 2006).

Mourroux, Jean, *La Liberté chrétienne* (Paris: Aubier, 1966).

Müller, Wolfgang W., 'Was kann an der Theologie neu sein? Der Beitrag der Dominikaner zur *nouvelle théologie*', *Zeitschrift für Kirchengeschichte*, 110 (1999), 86–104.

Müller, Sascha, and Rudolf Voderholzer, *Richard Simon (1638–1712), Exeget, Theologe, Philosoph und Historiker: eine Biographie* (Würzburg: Echter, 2005).

Muller, R. A., 'Ad Fontes Argumentorum. The Sources of Reformed Theology in the Seventeenth Century', in *After Calvin: Studies in the Development of A Theological Tradition* (Oxford: Oxford University Press, 2003), 47–62.

Mullins, Patrick, 'The Spirit Speaks to the Churches: Continuity and Development in Congar's Pneumatology', *LS*, 29 (2004), 288–319.

Murray, John Courtney, '*Sources Chrétiennes*', *TS*, 9 (1948), 250–55.

Murray, Paul D., *Reason, Truth, and Theology in Pragmatist Perspective* (Leuven: Peeters, 2004).

———— 'Receptive Ecumenism and Catholic Learning—Establishing the Agenda', in Murray (ed.), *Receptive Ecumenism*, 5–25.

Murray, Paul D., 'Receptive Ecumenism and Ecclesial Learning: Receiving Gifts for Our Needs', *LS*, 33 (2008), 30–45.

———— (ed.), *Receptive Ecumenism and the Call to Catholic Learning: Exploring a Way for Contemporary Ecumenism* (Oxford: Oxford University Press, 2008).

———— 'Hands Across the Tiber: Ecumenism in the Wake of *Anglicanorum Coetibus*', *The Tablet* (1 January 2011), 14–15.

Murray, Paul D. and M. J. Guest, 'On Discerning the Living Truth of the Church: Theological and Sociological Reflections on *Receptive Ecumenism and the Local Church*' in Chris Scharen (ed.), *Ecclesiology and Ethnography* (Grand Rapids, MI: Eerdmans, forthcoming).

Napiwodski, Piotr, *Eine Ekklesiologie im Werden* (published on the server of Freiburg University, 2005).

Nelson, Claud, and Norman Pittenger (eds.), *Pilgrim of Rome: An Introduction to the Life and Work of Ernesto Buonaiuti*, 1st edn. (Welwyn, Herts: Nisbet, 1969).

Neufeld, Karl-Heinz, 'Fundamentaltheologie in gewandelter Welt: H. Bouillards theologischer Beitrag', *ZkT*, 100 (1978), 417–40.

———— 'In the Service of the Council: Bishops and Theologians at the Second Vatican Council (for Cardinal Henri de Lubac on His Ninetieth Birthday)', in R. Latourelle (ed.), *Vatican II*, i.74–105.

Karl H. Neufeld, SJ (ed.), *Vérité du Christianisme, Henri Bouillard* (Paris: Desclée de Brouwer, 1989).

———— 'Comment parler de Dieu: Henri Bouillard, 1908–1981' in *Vérité du Christianisme*, 25–7.

———— 'Karl Barth et le catholicisme', in *Vérité du Christianisme*, 101–16.

———— 'Philosophie et Religion Dans L'Œuvre Éric Weil', *Vérité du Christianisme*, 233–316.

———— 'La Théologie fondamentale dans un monde transformé', in *Vérité du Christianisme*, 359–90.

Neuhaus, R. (ed.), *Biblical Interpretation in Crisis: The Ratzinger Conference on Bible and Church* (Grand Rapids MI: Eerdmans, 1989).

J. Neuner and J. Dupuis (eds.), *The Christian Faith in the Doctrinal Documents of the Catholic Church* (New York: Alba House, 1982), 34. ET available at <http://www.vatican.va/holy_father/pius_x/motu_proprio/documents/hf_p-x_motu-proprio_19031122_sollecitudini_it.html>.

Neveu, Bruno, 'Augustinisme janséniste et magistère romain', *XVIIe siècle*, 135 (1982), 191–209.

Newman, John Henry, *Essay on the Development of Christian Doctrine* (London: James Toovey, 1846).

—— 'Faith and Doubt', *Discourses Addressed to Mixed Congregations* (London: Longmans, Green and Co., 1916), 216–17.

—— *Apologia pro Vita Sua* (New York: Doubleday, 1956).

Nichols, Aidan, OP, *From Newman to Congar: The Idea of Doctrinal Development from the Victorians to the Second Vatican Council* (Edinburgh: T&T Clark, 1990).

—— 'Thomism and the Nouvelle Théologie', *The Thomist*, 64 (2000), 1–19.

—— 'Review of "Augustinianism and Modern Theology, Henri de Lubac"', *Irish Theological Quarterly*, 66 (2001), 87–8.

—— *The Thought of Benedict XVI* (London: Burns & Oates, 2005).

—— *Reason with Piety: Garrigou-Lagrange in the Service of Catholic Thought* (Naples FL: Sapientia Press of Ave Maria University, 2008).

Niv'er, Antoine, *Pravoslavnye Svyashchennosluzhiteli, Bogoslovy i Tserkovnye Deyateli Russkoy Emigratsii b Zapadnoy Tsentral'noy Evrope 1920–1995. Biograficheskiy Spravochnik* (Moscow/Paris: Russkiy Put'/YMCA Press, 1970).

Oakes, Edward T., *Pattern of Redemption: The Theology of Hans Urs von Balthasar* (New York: Continuum, 1994).

Oakes, Edward T., SJ, and David Moss (eds.), *The Cambridge Companion to Hans Urs Von Balthasar* (Cambridge: Cambridge University Press, 2004).

Oakley, Francis, *The Conciliarist Tradition: Constitutionalism in the Catholic Church 1300–1870* (Oxford: Oxford University Press, 2003).

O'Collins, Gerald, SJ, 'At the Origins of *Dei Verbum*', *Heythrop Journal*, 26 (1985), 5–13.

—— *Retrieving Fundamental Theology* (Mahwah NJ: Paulist Press, 1993).

—— *Rethinking Fundamental Theology: Toward a New Fundamental Theology* (Oxford: Oxford University Press, 2011).

O'Collins, Gerald, SJ, and M. K. Jones, *Jesus Our Priest: A Christian Approach to the Priesthood of Christ* (Oxford: Oxford University Press, 2010).

O'Connell, Marvin Richard, *Critics on Trial: An Introduction to the Catholic Modernist Crisis* (Washington DC: Catholic University of America Press, 1994).

O'Donnell, John, SJ, *Hans Urs Von Balthasar* (London: T&T Clark, 1991).

Oden, T., *Systematic Theology*, 3 vols. (San Francisco: Harper, 1987–92).

O'Keefe, John, and R. R. Reno, *Sanctified Vision. An Introduction to Early Christian Interpretation of the Bible* (Baltimore: Johns Hopkins University Press, 2005).

O'Malley, John W., *Trent and All That: Renaming Catholicism in the Early Modern Era*, 2nd edn. (Cambridge MA: Harvard University Press, 2000).

—— 'Trent and Vatican II: Two Styles of Church', in Bulman and Parrella (eds.), *From Trent to Vatican II*, 301–20.

—— *What Happened at Vatican II* (Cambridge MA/London: The Belknap Press of Harvard University Press, 2008).

O'Meara, Thomas F., 'Between Schelling and Hegel: The Catholic Tübingen School', in *Romantic Idealism and Roman Catholicism: Schelling and the Theologians* (Notre Dame IN: Notre Dame, 1982), 138–60.

—— '"Raid on the Dominicans": The Repression of 1954', *America*, 170 (1994), 1–8.

Ort, J. van, 'John Calvin and the Church Fathers', in I. Backus (ed.), *The Reception of the Church Fathers in the West*, 661–700.

Palmieri, Domenico, *Tractatus de gratia divina actualis* (Gulpen: M. Alberts, 1885).

Pannenberg, Wolfhart, and Neuhaus, Richard, J., 'The Christian West?' *First Things*, 7 (1990), 24–31 (25–6).

Paramelle, Joseph, 'À la découverte des Pères de l'Église avec Daniélou', in J. Fontaine (ed.), *Actualité*, 105–111.

Parente, Pietro, 'Nuove tendenze teologiche', *L'Osservatore Romano*, 9–10 February 1942, 1.

Pascal, Blaise, *Pensées*, ed. Louis Lafuma (Paris: Seuil, 1962).

——— *Les Provinciales: Pensées et opuscules divers*, eds. Gérard Ferreyroles and Philippe Sellier (Paris: Librairie Générale Française, 2004).

Passelecq, Georges and Bernard Suchecky, *The Hidden Encyclical of Pius XI*, trans. Steven Rendall (New York: Harcourt Brace, 1997).

Paul VI, 'Lettre de Sa Sainteté Paul VI au Cardinal Journet pour son quatre-vingtième anniversaire', *RevTh*, 71 (1971), 197.

Pearcey, N. R., 'Evangelium Vitae', in Perry (ed.), *The Legacy of John Paul II*, 181–204.

Pecklers, Keith F., SJ, *The Unread Vision: The Liturgical Movement in the United States of America 1926–1955* (Collegeville MN: The Liturgical Press, 1998).

——— *Dynamic Equivalence* (Collegeville MN: Liturgical Press, 2003).

——— *Worship*, New Century Theology (London: Continuum, 2003).

——— 'The Jansenist critique and the Liturgical Reforms of the Seventeenth and Eighteenth Centuries', *Ecclesia Orans*, 20 (2003), 325–39.

Peddicord, Richard, *The Sacred Monster of Thomism: An Introduction to the Life and Legacy of Reginald Garrigou-Lagrange* (South Bend IN: St Augustine's, 2005).

Pegis, Anton C., 'Nature and Spirit: Some Reflections on the Problem of the End of Man', *Proceedings of the American Catholic Philosophical Association* 23 (1949), 7–9.

Péguy, C., 'Avertissement', *Cahiers de la quinzaine*, V, 11 (1 March 1904), in R. Burac (ed.), *Œuvres en prose complètes*, La Pléiade, 3 vols (Paris: Gallimard, 1987–92).

Peli, Pinchas, *Torah today: a renewed encounter with scripture* (Washington DC: B'nai B'rith Books, 1987).

——— *Shabbat shalom: a renewed encounter with the Sabbath* (Washington DC: B'nai B'rith Books, 1988).

Périco, Yvette, *Maurice Blondel: Genèse du sens* (Paris: Editions Universitaires, 1991).

Peroli, Enrico, 'Gregory of Nyssa and the Neoplatonic Doctrine of the Soul', *Vigiliae Christianae*, 51 (1997), 117–39.

Perry, Tim (ed.), *The Legacy of John Paul II: An Evangelical Assessment* (Downers Grove IL: Intervarsity Press Academic, 2007).

Petit, Jean-Claude, 'La compréhension de la théologie dans la théologie française au XXe siècle: Vers une nouvelle conscience historique: G. Rabeau, M.-D. Chenu, L. Charlier', *Laval théologique et philosophique*, 47 (1991), 215–29.

——— 'La compréhension de la théologie dans la théologie française au XXe siècle: Pour une théologic qui réponde à nos nécessités: la nouvelle théologie', *Laval théologique et philosophique*, 48 (1992), 415–31.

Petráček, Tomáš, *Le père Vincent Zapletal O.P. (1867–1938): portrait d'un exégète catholique*. Studia friburgensia. Series historica, 6 (Fribourg: Academic Press, 2007).

Petre, Maude D. (ed.), *George Tyrrell's Letters* (London: Fisher and Unwin, 1920).

Philibert, Paul J., OP, 'Retrieving a Masterpiece: Yves Congar's Vision of True Reform', *Doctrine and Life*, 61 (2011), 10–20.

Philips, Gérard, *Achieving Christian Maturity* trans. E. Kane (Dublin: Gill, 1966).

———— *L'Église et son mystère au IIe Concile du Vatican: histoire, texte et commentaire de la Constitution 'Lumen Gentium'*, 2 vols (Paris: Desclée, 1967).

———— 'History of the Constitution', in Herbert Vorgrimler (ed.), *Commentary on the Documents of Vatican II*, i (London: Burns & Oates, 1967), 105–37.

Pillorget, René and Suzanne, *France baroque, France classique 1589–1715 Dictionnaire* (Paris: Laffont, 1995).

Piqué, Nicolas, 'Arnauld, Rome et la tradition', *Chroniques de Port-Royal*, 46 (1997), 169–84.

Plaut, W. G. (ed.), *The Torah: A Modern Commentary* (New York: Union of American Hebrew Congregation, 1981).

Plotinus, *Ennéades*, trans. Émile Bréhier, Collection des Universités de France (Paris: Les belles lettres, 1924–1931).

Potter, Vincent G., 'Karl Barth and the Ontological Argument', *The Journal of Religion*, 45/4 (1965), 309–25.

Pottier, B. 'Le Grégoire de Nysse de Jean Daniélou. Réflexions autour de "Platonisme et théologie mystique"' in J. Fontaine (ed.), *Actualité*, 87–9.

———— 'Le Grégoire de Nysse de Jean Daniélou. *Platonisme et théologie mystique* (1944): *eros* and agapè', *NRT*, 128/2 (2006), 258–73.

Pottmeyer, Hermann J., *Towards a Papacy in Communion: Perspectives from Vatican Councils I & II* (New York: Herder and Herder, 1998).

Propp, W. H. C., *Exodus 1–18* Anchor Bible 2a (New York: Doubleday, 2000).

———— *Exodus 19–40* Anchor Bible 2b (New York: Doubleday, 2006).

Prouvost, Géry, 'Lettres d'Étienne Gilson à Henri Gouhier', *RevTh*, 94 (1994), 460–78.

Pseudo-Dionysius the Areopagite, *Œuvres complètes*, trans. Maurice de Gandillac, Bibliothèque philosophique (Paris: Aubier, 1943).

Puech, Henri-Charles, 'La ténèbre mystique chez le Pseudo-Denys l'Aréopagite et dans la tradition mystique', *Études carmélitaines*, 23 (1938), 33–53.

Puyo, Jean, (ed.), *Jean Puyo interroge le Père Congar: 'Une vie pour la vérité'*, Les Interviews (Paris: Centurion, 1975).

Quantin, Jean-Louis, *Le catholicisme classique et les Pères de l'église—un retour aux sources (1669–1713)* (Paris: Institut d'Études Augustiniennes, 1999).

Quisinsky, Michael, *Geschichtlicher Glaube in einer geschichtlichen Welt: Der Beitrag von M.-D. Chenu, Y. Congar und H.-M. Féret zum II. Vaticanum*, Dogma und Geschichte, 6 (Berlin: LIT, 2007).

Quitslund, Sonya A., *Beauduin: A Prophet Vindicated* (New York: Newman Press, 1973).

Rabeau, G., *Introduction à l'étude de la théologie* (Paris: Bloud & Gay, 1926).

Raffelt, Albert, 'Maurice Blondel und die katholische Theologie in Deutschland', in Albert Raffelt, Peter Reifenberg, and Gotthard Fuchs (eds.), *Das Tun, der Glaube, die Vernunft: Studien zur Philosophie Maurice Blondels 'L'Action' 1893–1993* (Würzburg: Echter, 1995), 180–205.

Rafferty, Oliver P., SJ, (ed.), *George Tyrrell and Catholic Modernism* (Dublin: Four Courts Press, 2010).

Rahner, Karl, SJ, *Free Speech in the Church*, trans. G. Lamb (New York: Sheed and Ward, 1959).

—— *Theological Investigations*, i. God, Christ, Mary and Grace, trans. Cornelius Ernst, OP (London: Darton, Longman & Todd, 1961).

—— *Mission and Grace*, i, trans. Cecily Hastings (London: Sheed and Ward, 1963).

—— *Nature and Grace*, trans. Diana Wharton (London: Sheed and Ward, 1963).

—— *The Dynamic Element in the Church*, trans. W. O'Hara (London: Herder and Herder, 1964).

—— *Inspiration in the Bible*, trans. C. H. Henkey, 2nd rev. edn. (rev. trans. M. Palmer) (New York: Herder and Herder, 1964).

—— 'La situation actuelle de la théologie en Allemagne, conférence donnée à Paris le 28 février 1965', in *Recherches et Débats*, 1965 (cahier 51), 224.

—— *Theological Investigations*, iv, trans. Kevin Smyth (Baltimore/London: Helicon Press/Darton, Longman & Todd, 1966).

—— 'Observations on the Concept of Revelation', in Karl Rahner and Joseph Ratzinger, *Revelation and Tradition*, trans. W. J. O'Hara (London: Burns & Oates, 1966), 9–25.

—— 'The Hierarchical Structure of the Church, with Special Reference to the Episcopate', in Herbert Vorgimler (ed.), *Commentary on the Documents of Vatican II* (London: Burns & Oates, 1967), i.187.

—— 'Salvation', *Sacramentum Mundi*, trans. Cornelius Ernst and Kevin Smyth (London: Burns and Oates, 1970) v.430b.

—— *Theological Investigations*, ii, trans. Karl-Heinz Kruger (New York: Crossroad, 1975).

—— *Theological Investigations*, vii, trans. David Bourke (New York: Crossroad, 1977).

—— *Foundations of Christian Faith*, trans. W. V. Dych (New York: Seabury Press, 1978).

—— *Theological Investigations*, iii, trans. Karl-Heinz and Boniface Kruger (New York: Crossroad, 1982).

—— *Theological Investigations*, iv, trans. Kevin. Smyth (New York: Crossroad, 1982).

—— *Theological Investigations*, vi, trans. Karl-Heinz and Boniface Kruger (New York: Crossroad, 1982).

—— *Theological Investigations*, v, trans. Karl-Heinz Kruger (New York: Crossroad, 1983).

—— *Theological Investigations*, xxi, trans. Hugh Riley (New York: Crossroad, 1988).

—— *Theological Investigations*, xv, trans. Lionel Swain (New York: Crossroad, 1990).

—— *Hearer of the Word: Laying the Foundations for a Philosophy of Religion*, trans. Joseph Donceel (New York: Continuum, 1994).

—— 'Experiences of a Catholic Theologian' in Declan Marmion and Mary Hines (eds.), *The Cambridge Companion to Karl Rahner* (Cambridge: Cambridge University Press, 2005), 306–7.

Ranchetti, Michele, *The Catholic Modernists. A Study of the Religious Reform Movement 1864–1907*, trans. Isabel Quigley (London: Oxford University Press, 1970).

Ratté, John, *Three Modernists* (New York: Sheed & Ward, 1967).

Ratzinger, Joseph, *Volk und Haus Gottes in Augustins Lehre von der Kirche* (München: K. Zink, 1954).

—— 'The Pastoral Implications of Episcopal Collegiality', *Concilium*, 1/1 (1965), 20–34.

—— 'Dogmatic Constitution on Divine Revelation', trans. William Glen-Doepel, in Herbert Vorgrimler (ed.), *Commentary on the Documents of Vatican II* (London: Burns & Oates, 1968), iii.

—— *Das neue Volk Gottes. Entwürfe zur Ekklesiologie* (Düsseldorf: Patmos-Verlag, 1969).

—— 'The Pastoral Constitution on the Church in the Modern World. Chapter I, Part I', in H. Vorgrimler (ed.), *Commentary on the Documents of Vatican II*, v.121.

—— *Theology of History in St. Bonaventure*, trans. Z. Hayes (Chicago: Franciscan Herald Press, 1971).

—— *Principles of Catholic Theology*, trans. Sr Mary Frances McCarthy, SND (San Francisco: Ignatius Press, 1982).

—— with Vittorio Messori, *The Ratzinger Report*, trans. Salvator Attanasio and Graham Harrison (Leominster: Fowler Wright Books Limited, 1985).

—— *Behold The Pierced One. An Approach to a Spiritual Christology*, trans. G. Harrison (San Francisco: Ignatius Press, 1986).

—— '"Consecrate them in the truth", a homily for St. Thomas' day', *New Blackfriars*, 68 (1987), 112–15.

—— *Journey Towards Easter: Retreat Given in the Vatican in the Presence of Pope John Paul II*, trans. M. Groves (Middlegreen: St Paul Publications, 1987).

—— *Church, Ecumenism and Politics* (Slough: St Paul's, 1988).

—— 'The Spiritual Basis and Ecclesial Identity of Theology', *The Nature and Mission of Theology*, trans. Adrian Walker (San Francisco: Ignatius Press, 1995), 45–72.

—— *Salt of the Earth. Christianity and the Catholic Church at the End of the Millennium. An Interview with Peter Seewald*, trans. A. Walker (San Francisco: Ignatius Press, 1997).

—— *Milestones: Memoirs 1927–1977*, trans. E. Leiva-Merikakis (San Francisco: Ignatius Press, 1998).

—— *The Spirit of The Liturgy*, trans. John Saward (San Francisco: Ignatius Press, 2000).

—— 'The Question of the Concept of Tradition: A Provisional Response', in *God's Word* (San Francisco: Ignatius Press, 2005).

—— *Jesus of Nazareth*, trans. A. Walker (London/New York: Bloomsbury/Doubleday, 2007).

—— 'Revelation and Tradition', in Rahner and Ratzinger, *Revelation and Tradition*, 26–49.

Reardon, Bernard M. G. (ed.), *Roman Catholic Modernism* (London/Stanford CA: Black/Stanford University Press, 1970).

Reardon, Michael F., 'Science and Religious Modernism: The New Apologetic in France, 1890–1913', *The Journal of Religion*, 57/1 (1977), 48–63.

Regnault, François, *Dieu Est Inconscient* (Paris: Navarin Éditeur, 1985).

Reno, R. R., 'Theology After the Revolution', *First Things*, 173 (May 2007), 15–21.

Richardson, William, 'Psychoanalysis and the Being-question', in *Psychiatry and the Humanities: Interpreting Lacan*, vi, eds. J. Smith and W. Kerrigan (London: Yale University Press, 1983).

Rigault, Hyppolyte, *Histoire de la querelle des anciens et des modernes* (Paris: Adamant, 2001).

Rivière, J., 'Modernisme', in A. Vacant, E. Mangenot, and É. Amann (eds.), *Dictionnaire de théologie catholique*, x. part ii, cols. 2009–47 (Paris: Letouzey and Ané, 1929).

Rondeau, Marie-Josèphe (ed.), *Jean Daniélou (1905–1974)* (Paris: Cerf, 1975).

——— 'Jean Daniélou théologien', in J. Fontaine (ed.), *Actualité*, 127–54.

Rondet, G.-L.H., 'Nouvelle Théologie', in Karl Rahner (ed.), *Sacramentum Mundi* (New York: Herder, 1964).

Rouet de Journel, M. J. (ed.), *Enchiridion Patristicum*, 23rd edn. (Barcelona: Herder, 1965).

Rousseau, Olivier, OSB, *The Progess of the Liturgy* (Westminster MD: The Newman Press, 1951), 24.

Rousselot, Pierre, SJ, *L'Intellectualisme de saint Thomas* (Paris: Alcan, 1908).

——— 'Les Yeux de la foi', *RSR*, 1 (1910), 241–59, 444–75.

——— *L'Intellectualisme de saint Thomas* (Paris: Beauchesne, 1936).

——— *The Eyes of Faith*, trans. Joseph Donceel, SJ (New York: Fordham University Press, 1990 [1910]).

——— *Intelligence: Sense of Being, Faculty of God*, trans. and ed., Andrew Tallon, Marquette Studies in Philosophy 16 (Milwaukee WI: Marquette University Press, 1998).

Rowland, Tracey, *Ratzinger's Faith. The Theology of Pope Benedict XVI* (Oxford: Oxford University Press, 2008).

Ruddy, Christopher, *The Local Church: Tillard and the Future of Catholic Ecclesiology* (New York: Herder and Herder, 2006).

Ruggieri, G., 'The First Doctrinal Clash', in G. Alberigo and J. A. Komonchak (eds.), *The History of Vatican II*, ii.233–66.

——— 'Beyond an Ecclesiology of Polemics: The Debate on the Church', in Alberigo and Komonchak (eds.), *The History of Vatican II*, ii.281–357.

Russo, Antonio, *Henri de Lubac: teologia e dogma nella storia. L'influsso di Blondel* (Rome: Studium, 1990).

Le Maistre de Sacy, Isaac-Louis, *Les enluminures du fameux Almanach des PP. Iesuites, intitulé la déroute et la confusion des iansenistes, Ou triomphe de Molina Iesuite sur S. Augustin* (n.p: n.pub., 1654).

Sagovsky, Nicholas, *'On God's Side': A Life of George Tyrrell* (Oxford: Clarendon Press).

Sales, M., SJ, F. Jacquin, and M.-J. Rondeau (eds.), 'Les étapes d'une vie et d'une œuvre', in J. Fontaine (ed.), *Actualité de Jean Daniélou*, 219–27.

Sardella, Louis-Pierre, 'Autour de l'École de Lyon et de la revue *Demain*: L'émergence d'une nouvelle forme d'anticléricalisme croyant?', in *L'anticléricalisme croyant (1860–1914): Jalons pour une histoire* (Annecy-le-Vieux: Université de Savoie, 2004), 161–81.

Sauer, Hanjo, *Erfahrung und Glaube: Die Begründung des pastoralen Prinzips durch die Offenbarungskonstitution des II. Vatikanischen Konzils* (Frankfurt: Peter Lang, 1993).

—— 'The Doctrinal and the Pastoral: the Text on Divine Revelation', in Giuseppe Alberigo and Joseph Komonchak (eds.), *History of Vatican II* iv.195–231.

Scarisbrick, J. J., 'An Historian's Reflections on Yves Congar's *Mon Journal du Concile*', in Gabriel Flynn (ed.), *Yves Congar Theologian of the Church*, 249–75.

Scheper-Hughes, Nancy, *Saints, Scholars and Schizophrenics: Mental Illness in Rural Ireland* (Berkeley: University of California Press, 1979).

Scherer, R., 'Besuch bei Heidegger', *Wort und Wahrheit*, 2 (1947), 780–2.

Schillebeeckx, Edward, OP, *Marriage: Secular Reality and Saving Mystery*, trans. N. D. Smith, 2 vols (London: Sheed & Ward, 1965).

—— *Faith and Revelation*, trans. N. D. Smith, 2 vols. (New York: Sheed & Ward, 1967–8).

—— *Revelation and Theology*, ii. *The Concept of Truth and Theological Renewal*, trans. N. D. Smith (London: Sheed & Ward, 1968).

Schindler, David C., 'Towards a Non-Possessive Concept of Knowledge: On the Relation between Reason and Love in Aquinas and Balthasar', *Modern Theology*, 22 (2006), 577–607.

Schleiermacher, F. D. E., *The Christian Faith*, trans. H. R. Mackintosh and J. S. Stewart (Edinburgh: T&T Clark, 1928).

—— *Hermeneutics and Criticism and other Writings*, trans. and ed. Andrew Bowie (Cambridge: Cambridge University Press, 1998).

Schlink, E., *Ökumenische Dogmatik. Grundzüge* (Göttingen: Vandenhoeck und Ruprecht, 1983).

Schmitt, Jean-Claude, 'L'Œuvre médiéviste du Père Chenu', *RSPT*, 81 (1997), 395–406.

Schmitz, Kenneth L., *What has Clio to do with Athena? Étienne Gilson: Historian and philosopher* (Toronto: Pontifical Institute of Mediaeval Studies, 1987).

—— *At the Center of the Human Drama: The Philosophical Anthropology of Karol Wojtyla/Pope John Paul II* (Washington, DC: Catholic University of America Press, 1993).

Schloesser, Stephen, *Jazz Age Catholicism: Mystic Modernism in Postwar Paris, 1919–1933* (Toronto: University of Toronto Press, 2005).

Schoof, Mark, OP, *Breakthrough: Beginnings of the New Catholic Theology*, introduced by E. Schillebeeckx OP, trans. N. D. Smith (Dublin: Gill and Macmillan, 1970 [1968]), 45.

Schoonenberg, Piet, *Theologie als geloofsvertolking: Het proefschrift van 1948*, eds. Leo Kenis and Jürgen Mettepenningen, Documenta Libraria, 36 (Louvain: Faculteit Godgeleerdheid/Maurits Sabbebibliotheek/Peeters, 2008).

Schultenover, David G., SJ, *A View from Rome: On the Eve of the Modernist Crisis* (The Bronx NY: Fordham University Press, 1993).

—— *The Reception of Pragmatism in France & the Rise of Roman Catholic Modernism: 1880–1914* (Washington DC: Catholic University of America Press, 2009).

Schüssler-Fiorenza, Francis, 'From Theologian to Pope', *Harvard Divinity School Bulletin*, 33/2 (2005), 56–62.

Schwöbel, C., 'The Creature of the Word. Recovering the Ecclesiology of the Reformers', in C. Gunton and D. Hardy (eds.), *On Being the Church: Essays on the Christian Community* (Edinburgh: T&T Clark, 1989), 110–55.

―――― *The Church of Jesus Christ: The Contribution of the Reformation Towards Ecumenical Dialogue on Church Unity* (Frankfurt/M: Lembeck, 1995).

―――― 'Kirche als Communio', in *Gott in Beziehung. Studien zur Dogmatik* (Tübingen: Mohr-Siebeck, 2002), 379–435.

―――― 'Gottes Ökumene. Über das Verhältnis von Kirchengemeinschaft und Gottesverständnis', in *Christlicher Glaube und Pluralismus—Studien zu einer Theologie der Kultur* (Tübingen: Mohr-Siebeck, 2003), 107–32.

Scully, Eileen, *Grace and Human Freedom in the Theology of Henri Bouillard* (Bethesda MD: Academia Press, 2007).

Seckler, Max, *Instinkt und Glaubenswille nach Thomas von Aquin* (Mainz: Matthias-Grünewald-Verlag, 1961).

Sedgwick, Alexander, *Jansenism in Seventeenth-Century France: Voices from the Wilderness* (Charlottesville: University Press of Virginia, 1977).

Sellier, Philippe, *Pascal et la liturgie* (Paris: Presses Universitaires de France, 1966).

Sesboüé, Bernard, *Karl Rahner*, Initiations aux théologiens (Paris: Cerf, 2001).

―――― *Yves de Montcheuil (1900–1944): Précurseur en théologie*, Cogitatio Fidei, 255 (Paris: Cerf, 2006).

―――― *La théologie au XXe siècle et l'avenir de la foi: Entretiens avec Marc Leboucher* (Paris: Desclée de Brouwer, 2007).

Sheehy, Michael, *Is Ireland Dying? Culture and the Church in Modern Ireland* (London: Hollis and Carter, 1968).

Shook, Laurence K., *Étienne Gilson* (Toronto: Pontifical Institute of Mediaeval Studies, Toronto, 1984).

Siefer, Gregor, *The Church and Industrial Society: A survey of the Worker-Priest Movement and its implications for the Christian Mission*, trans. Isabel and Florence McHugh (London: Darton, Longman & Todd, 1964).

Smith, Christian, with Melissa Lundquist Denton, *Soul Searching: The Religious and Spiritual Lives of American Teenagers* (New York: Oxford University Press, 2005).

Smith, James K. A., *Introducing Radical Orthodoxy: Mapping a Post-Secular Theology* (Grand Rapids MI: Baker Academic, 2005).

Solages, Bruno de, 'La crise moderniste et les études ecclésiastiques', *Revue apologétique*, 51 (1930), 5–30.

Solano, Jesús, *Sacrae Theologiae Summa*, vol. 3 (Madrid: Biblioteca de Autores Cristianos, 1956).

Špidlík, Tomáš, *Die russische Idee. Eine andere Sicht des Menchens* (Würzburg: Der Christliche Osten, 2002).

Stafin, Roman, *Eucharistie als Quelle der Gnade bei Pius Parsch* (Würzburg: Echter, 2004).

Stegmüller, Franz, 'Review of "Une école de théologie"', *TR*, 38 (1939), 48–51.

Steinmann, Jean, *Richard Simon et les origines de l'exégèse biblique* (Paris: Desclée de Brouwer, 1960).

Stolz, Anselme, *Théologie de la mystique* (Chevetogne: Éd. Bénédictines d'Amay, 1939).

Sullivan, Frank A., SJ, 'The Meaning of *Subsistit in* as explained by the Congregation of the Doctrine of the Faith', *TS*, 67 (2006), 116–24.

—— 'A Response to Karl Becker, SJ, on the Meaning of *Subsistit in*', *TS*, 67 (2006), 395–409.

—— 'Further Thoughts on the Meaning of *Subsistit in*', *TS*, 71 (2010), 133–47.

Sullivan, Maureen, *The Road to Vatican II: Key Changes in Theology* (New York: Paulist Press, 2007).

Synave, Paul, *Prophecy and Inspiration: A Commentary on the* Summa Theologica (New York: Desclée, 1961).

Taft, Robert, F., SJ, 'Return to our Roots: Recovering Western Liturgical Traditions' *America*, 198/18 (May 26–June 2, 2008), 10–13.

Tallon, Alain, *La France et le Concile de Trente (1515–1563)* (Rome: École Française de Rome, 1997).

Taylor, Charles, *The Ethics of Authenticity* (Cambridge MA: Harvard University Press, 1991).

Teilhard de Chardin, Pierre, *Le phénomène humain* (Paris: Seuil, 1955).

—— *The Phenomenon of Man*, trans. Bernard Wall (London: Collins, 1959).

—— *L'Avenir de l'homme* (Paris: Seuil, 1959).

—— *Le Milieu Divin: An Essay on the Interior Life*, trans. Siôn Cowell (London: Collins, 1964).

—— *Hymn of the Universe*, trans. Simon Bartholomew (London: Collins, 1965).

—— *La Messe sur le monde* (Paris: Seuil, 1965).

—— *The Prayer of the Universe*, trans. René Hague (London: Collins, 1968).

—— *The Phenomenon of Man*, rev. ed., trans. Bernard Wall (London: Collins, 1970).

—— *Christianity and Evolution* trans. René Hague (London: Collins, 1971).

—— *Lettres intimes de Teilhard de Chardin* (Paris, Aubier Montaigne, 1974).

Tillard, J. M. R., *Flesh of the Church, Flesh of Christ. At the Source of the Ecclesiology of Communion* (Collegeville MN: Liturgical Press, 2001).

—— 'Théologies et "devotions" au pape depuis le Moyen Âge. De Jean XXII à . . . Jean XXIII', *Cristianesimo nella Storia*, 22 (2001), 191–211.

Timmermans, Linda, *L'accès des femmes à la culture (1598–1715): un débat d'idées, de Saint François de Sales à la marquise de Lambert* (Paris: Champion, 1993).

Torrance, T. F., 'The Problem of Natural Theology in the Thought of Karl Barth', *Religious Studies*, 6/2 (1970), 121–35.

—— *The Trinitarian Faith: The Evangelical Theology of the Ancient Catholic Church* (Edinburgh: T&T Clark, 1988).

Torrell, J.-P., *La théologie catholique*, 2nd edn. (Paris: Cerf, 2008).

Tourpe, Emmanuel (ed.), *Penser l'être de l'Action: La métaphysique du 'dernier' Blondel* (Louvain: Peeters, 2000).

Tracy, David, *The Analogical Imagination: Christian Theology and the Culture of Pluralism* (New York: Crossroad, 1981).

Tranvouez, Yvon, *Catholiques d'abord. Approches du mouvement catholique en France (XIXᵉ–XXᵉ siècle)* (Paris: Les Éditions Ouvrières, 1988).

Tresmontant, Claude, *La Crise moderniste* (Paris: Éditions du Seuil, 1979).

Trethowan, Illtyd, 'Review of Louis Bouyer, *L'Église de Dieu. Corps du Christ et Temple de l'Esprit*', *The Downside Review* 89/296 (July 1971), 250–4.

Trever, John, *The Dead Sea Scrolls: A Personal Account* (Grand Rapids MI: Eerdmans, 1978).

Tshibangu, Tarcisse, *Théologie positive et théologie speculative: Position traditionnelle et nouvelle problématique* (Louvain: Publications universitaires, 1965).

———— *La théologie comme science au XXème siècle* (Kinshasa: Presses universitaires, 1980).

Turner, Denys, 'Guest Editorial', *IJST*, 7 (2005), 343–4.

Turretin, F., *Institutes of Elenctic Theology*, vol. 1, trans. George Musgrave Giger (Phillipsburg: Presbyterian and Reformed, 1992).

Tuyaerts, M. M., OP, *L'Évolution du Dogme. Étude théologique* (Louvain: Nova et Vetera, 1919).

Tyrrell, George (alias Hilaire Bourdon), *L'Église et l'avenir* (1903).

———— *Lex Orandi or Prayer and Creed* (London: Longmans, Green, 1903), 58.

———— *Through Scylla and Charybdis; or, The Old Theology and the New* (London: Longmans, Green, 1907).

———— *Christianity at the Cross-Roads* (London: Longmans, Green & Co., 1909), 92.

———— *Medievalism: A Reply to Cardinal Mercier* (Tunbridge Wells: Burns & Oates, 1994).

Valentini, D., *La Teologia della storia nel pensiero di Jean Daniélou*, Corona Lateranensis 20 (Rome: Lateran University Press, 1970).

Vallin, Pierre, '*Catholicisme*: le Père de Lubac au seuil d'une œuvre', *Théophilyon*, X/1, (2005), 67–108.

Vanhoozer, Kevin J., *Biblical Narrative in the Philosophy of Paul Ricoeur: A Study in Hermeneutics and Theology* (Cambridge: Cambridge University Press, 1990).

Van Steenberghen, Fernand, 'Un incident révélateur au congrès thomiste de 1950', *Revue philosophique de Louvain*, 86 (1988), 379–90.

Van Wijngaerden, Johan, 'Voorstudie tot het denken van E. Schillebeeckx: D.M. De Petter o.p. (1905–1971): Een inleiding tot zijn leven en denken. Deel 1: Een conjunctureel-historische situering', MA thesis (Louvain, 1989).

Varillon, François, 'Feuilles de route', *Chronique sociale*, reproduced in *Beauté du monde et souffrance des hommes, entretiens avec Charles Ehlinger* (Paris: Centurion, 1980), 75.

Vaux, R. de, *Revue biblique*, 57 (1950), 140–1.

Vawter, B., *A Path through Genesis* (New York: Bruce, 1956).

———— *On Genesis* (Garden City NY: Doubleday, 1977).

Venard, O. T., OP, 'The Cultural Backgrounds and Challenges of *La Bible de Jérusalem*', in Philip McCosker (ed.), *What is it that Scripture Says? Essays in Biblical Interpretation, Translation and Reception in Honour of Henry Wansborough OSB*, (London: T&T Clark, 2006), 111–34.

Vidler, Alec R., *A Variety of Catholic Modernists* (Cambridge: Cambridge University Press, 1970), 17–18.

Villain, Maurice, *Portrait d'un précurseur: Victor Carlhian, 1875–1959* (Paris: Desclée de Brouwer, 1965).

Villemin, Laurent, *Pouvoir d'ordre et pouvoir de jurisdiction. Histoire théologique de leur distinction* (Paris: Cerf, 2003).

Vincent of Lérins, *Commonitorium*, ed. Reginald Stewart Moxon (Cambridge: Cambridge University Press, 1915).

Virgoulay, René, *L'Action de Maurice Blondel (1893): Relecture pour un centenaire* (Paris: Beauchesne, 1992).

——— *Philosophie et Théologie chez Maurice Blondel* (Paris: Cerf, 2002).

Visser 't Hooft, W. A., *Memoirs* (London/Philadelphia PA: SCM Press/Westminster Press, 1973).

Viviano, Benedict T., 'The Church in the Modern World and the French Dominicans', *Freiburger Zeitschrift für Philosophie und Theologie*, 50 (2003), 512–21.

——— 'Rezensionen – Richard Simon (1638–1712). Exeget, Theologe, Philosoph und Historiker. Eine Biographie', *Freiburger Zeitschrift für Philosophie und Theologie*, 54/1 (2007), 275.

Voderholzer, Rudolf, 'Die Bedeutung der sogenannten *Nouvelle Théologie* (insbesondere Henri de Lubacs) für die Theologie Hans Urs von Balthasars', in Walter Kasper (ed.), *Logik der Liebe und Herrlichkeit Gottes: Hans Urs von Balthasar im Gespräch* (Ostfildern: Matthias-Grünewald-Verlag, 2006), 204–28.

——— *Meet Henri de Lubac* (San Francisco: Ignatius Press, 2008).

Voisin, Joseph, *Messel Romain, selon le règlement du Concile de Trente* (Paris: de la Haye and Piget, 1660).

Völker, Walther, *Das Volkommenheitsideal des Origenes*, BHTh 7 (Tübingen: Mohr, 1931).

——— *Fortschritt und Vollendung bei Philo von Alexandrien* (Leipzig: Hinrich, 1938).

——— 'Rezensionen', *Theologische Zeitschrift*, 5 (1949), 143–8.

——— *Der wahre Gnostiker nach Clemens Alexandrinus*, Texte und Untersuchungen zur Geschichte der altchristlichen Literatur, Band 57 (Berlin/Leipzig: Akademie Verlag, 1952).

——— *Gregor von Nyssa als Mystiker* (Wiesbaden: Steiner, 1955).

——— *Kontemplation und Ekstase bei Pseudo-Dionysius Areopagita* (Wiesbaden: Steiner, 1958).

——— *Maximus Confessor als Meister des geistlichen Lebens* (Wiesbaden: Steiner, 1965).

Vollert, Cyril, 'Humani Generis and the Limits of Theology', *TS*, 12 (1951), 3–23.

Vorgrimler, Herbert, *Understanding Karl Rahner: An Introduction to his Life and Thought*, trans. John Bowden (New York: Crossroad, 1986).

Vorgrimler, Herbert (ed.), *Commentary on the Documents of Vatican II*, i, trans. Lalit Adolphus, Kevin Smyth, and Richard Strachan (New York/London: Herder and Herder/Burns & Oates, 1967).

——— *Commentary on the Documents of Vatican II*, ii, trans. William Glen-Doepel, Hilda Graef, Richard Strachen, Ronald Walls, and R. A. Wilson (New York/London: Herder and Herder/Burns & Oates, 1968).

——— *Commentary on the Documents of Vatican II*, iii, trans. William Glen-Doepel, Hilda Graef, John Michael Jakubiak, and Simon and Erika Young (New York/London: Herder and Herder/Burns & Oates, 1968).

——— *Commentary on the Documents of Vatican II*, iv, trans. Hilda Graef, W. J. O'Hara, and Ronald Walls (New York/London: Herder and Herder/Burns & Oates, 1969).

—— *Commentary on the Documents of Vatican II*, v, trans. W. J. O'Hara (New York/London: Herder and Herder/Burns & Oates, 1969).

Wagner, Jean-Pierre, *La théologie fondamentale selon Henri de Lubac*, Cogitatio Fidei, 199 (Paris: Cerf, 1997).

—— *Henri de Lubac*, Initiations aux théologiens (Paris: Cerf, 2007).

Wainwright, G., *Doxology: The Praise of God in Worship, Doctrine, and Life. A Systematic Theology* (Oxford: Oxford University Press, 1980).

Waldstein, Michael, 'Johannine foundations of the Church', in L. Melina and C. A. Anderson (eds.), *The Way of Love* (San Francisco: Ignatius Press, 2006), 250–65.

Walgrave, Jan Hendrik, *Unfolding Revelation: The Nature of Doctrinal Development* (Philadelphia PA/London: Westminster/ Hutchinson, 1972).

Walicki, Andrzej, *The Slavophile Controversy* (Oxford: Clarendon Press, 1975).

—— *A History of Russian Thought from the Enlightenment to Marxism* (Oxford: Clarendon Press, 1980).

Walling, Richard William, 'Metamorphosis of the Sacred: Christian Liturgy and the Mystery of the Incarnation in the Work of Louis Bouyer' (unpublished Ph.D. thesis, Catholic University of America, 1990).

Walsh, Christopher J., 'De Lubac's Critique of the Post-conciliar Church', *Communio*, 19 (1992), 404–32.

Walsh, James Joseph, *The Thirteenth, Greatest of Centuries* (New York: Catholic Summer School Press, 1912).

Ward, Maisie, *The Wilfrid Wards and the Transition*, 2 vols (London: Sheed & Ward, 1934–7), vol. 2: Insurrection versus Resurrection, 492–3.

Weakland, Rembert, 'Images of the Church: From "Perfect Society" to "God's People on Pilgrimage"', in Austen Ivereigh (ed.), *Unfinished Journey. The Church 40 Years after Vatican II* (London: Continuum, 2003), 78–90.

Weaver, F. Ellen, 'The Neo-Gallican Liturgies Revisited', *Studia Liturgica*, 16 (1986–7), 62–5.

—— 'Erudition, Spirituality and Women: the Jansenist Contribution', in Sherrin Marshall (ed.), *Women in Reformation and Counter-Reformation Europe: Public and Private Worlds* (Bloomington IN: Indiana University Press, 1989), 189–206.

—— 'Liturgy for the Laity: the Jansenist Case for Popular Participation in Worship in the Seventeenth and Eighteenth centuries', *Studia Liturgica*, 19 (1989), 47–59.

Weber, Eugen, *Action Française: Royalism and Reaction in Twentieth-Century France* (Stanford CA: Stanford University Press, 1962).

Weigel, Gustave, 'The Historical Background of the Encyclical *Humani Generis*', TS, 12 (1951), 208–30.

—— 'Gleanings from the Commentaries on *Humani generis*', TS, 12 (1951) 520–49.

White, Victor, OP, *God the Unknown: And Other Essays* (London: Harvill Press, 1956).

Wicks, Jared, 'Theology, Manualist', in R. Latourelle and R. Fisichella (eds.), *Dictionary of Fundamental Theology* (New York: Crossroad, 1996), 1102–5.

—— 'Review Article: New Light on Vatican Council II', *Catholic Historical Review*, 92 (2006), 609–28.

—— 'Review Article: More Light on Vatican Council II', *Catholic Historical Review*, 94 (2008), 75–101.

Wicks, Jared, 'Six texts by Prof. Joseph Ratzinger as *peritus* before and during Vatican Council II', *Gregorianum*, 89/2 (2008), 233–311.

——— 'Review Article: Further Light on Vatican Council II', *Catholic Historical Review*, 95 (2009), 546–69.

——— 'Vatican II on Revelation—Behind the Scenes', *TS*, 71 (2010), 637–50.

Williams, A. N., 'The Future of the Past: The Contemporary Significance of the *Nouvelle Théologie*', *IJST*, 7 (2005), 347–61.

——— *The Divine Sense: The Intellect in Patristic Theology* (Cambridge: Cambridge University Press, 2007).

Williams, George Huntston, *The Mind of John Paul II: Origins of his Thought and Action* (New York: Seabury Press, 1981).

Wilson, Edmund, *The Scrolls from the Dead Sea* (New York: Oxford University Press, 1955).

Wood, Susan K., *Spiritual Exegesis and the Church in the Theology of Henri de Lubac* (Grand Rapids MI: Eerdmans, 1998).

Wulf, F., 'Decree on the Appropriate Renewal of the Religious Life', in Vorgrimler (ed.), *Commentary on the Documents of Vatican II*, ii.301–70.

Yap, Jake C., '"*Word*" and "*Wisdom*" in the Ecclesiology of Louis Bouyer', unpublished D.Phil. thesis (University of Oxford, 2003).

Yeago, D., 'The Church as Polity? The Lutheran Context of Robert W. Jenson's Ecclesiology', in C. Gunton (ed.), *Trinity, Time and Church: A Response to the Theology of Robert W. Jenson* (Grand Rapids MI: Eerdmans, 2000), 201–37.

Zapelena, Timotheus, *De Ecclesia Christi: Pars Apologetica* (Rome: Gregorian University, 1955).

Žižek, Slavoj and Glyn Daly, *Conversations with Žižek* (Cambridge: Polity Press, 2004).

Zizioulas, John, 'La communauté eucharistique et la catholicité de l'Eglise', *Istina*, 14 (1969), 67–88.

——— 'Episkope and Episkopos in the Early Church: A Brief Survey of the Evidence', in *Episkopē and Episcopate in Ecumenical Perspective*, Faith and Order Paper 102 (Geneva: World Council of Churches, 1980), 30–42.

——— *Being as Communion* (London: Darton, Longman & Todd, 1985).

Zordan, Davide, *Connaissance et Mystère: l'itinéraire théologique de Louis Bouyer*, Théologies (Paris: Cerf, 2008).

Web References

Evans, Dylan, 'Science and Truth', in *The Symptom 10*, <http://www.lacan.com/thesymptom/?p=59> (accessed 20 February 2010).

Lettmann, Reinhard Bishop of Münster, 'Introduction', Bishop von Galen, *Three Sermons in Defiance of the Nazis*, 1–28 (5), available at: <http://www.churchinhistory.org/pages/booklets/vongalen(n).htm> (accessed 9 March 2010).

Marini, Archbishop Piero, Interview with John L. Allen, Jr., Archbishop's House, Westminster, London, 15 December 2007, available at: <http://www.natcath.com/mainpage/specialdocuments/marini_interview.pdf>, 6 (accessed 20 April 2010).

Miller, Jacques-Alain, 'Improvisation on *Rerum Novarum*', <http://www.lacanianreview.com.br/n1/artigos2.asp#> (accessed 20 February 2010).

Pope Pius IX, *Quanta Cura*. Encyclical Letter condemning Current Errors (8 December 1864), <http://www.papalencyclicals.net/Pius09/p9quanta.htm>.

——— The Syllabus of Errors Condemned by Pius IX, <http://www.papalencyclicals.net/Pius09/p9syll.htm> (accessed 22 January 2011).

Pope Leo XIII, *Aeterni Patris*. Encyclical Letter on the Restoration of Christian Philosophy (4 August 1879), <http://www.vatican.va/holy_father/leo_xiii/encyclicals/documents/hf_l-xiii_enc_04081879_aeterni-patris_en.html> (accessed 22 January 2011).

Pope Pius X, *Pascendi Dominici Gregis*. Encyclical Letter on the Doctrines of the Modernists (8 September 1907), <http://www.vatican.va/holy_father/pius_x/encyclicals/documents/hf_p-x_enc_19070908_pascendi-dominici-gregis_en.html> (accessed 22 January 2011).

——— *Lamentabili Sane*. Syllabus condemning the Errors of the Modernists (3 July 1907), <http://www.papalencyclicals.net/Pius10/p10lamen.htm> (accessed 22 January 2011).

Pope Pius XII, *Divino Afflante Spiritu* on Promoting Biblical Studies (30 September 1943), <http://www.vatican.va/holy_father/pius_xii/encyclicals/documents/hf_p-xii_enc_30091943_divino-afflante-spiritu_en.html> (accessed 22 January 2011).

——— *Mystici Corporis Christi*. Encyclical Letter on the Mystical Body of Christ (29 June 1943), <http://www.vatican.va/holy_father/pius_xii/encyclicals/documents/hf_p-xii_enc_29061943_mystici-corporis-christi_en.html> (accessed 22 January 2011).

——— *Humani Generis*. Encyclical Letter concerning some False Opinions Threatening to Undermine the Foundations of Catholic Doctrine (12 August 1950), <http://www.vatican.va/holy_father/pius_xii/encyclicals/documents/hf_p-xii_enc_12081950_humani-generis_en.html> (accessed 22 January 2011).

——— 'Applied Psychology: Address to the Rome Congress of the International Association of Applied Psychology' (10 April 1958), <http://www.papalencyclicals.net/Pius12/P12APPSY.HTM> (accessed 22 January 2011).

Pope John Paul II, 'Message to the Participants in the Course on the Internal Forum Organized by the Apostolic Penitentiary' (20 March 1998), <http://www.vatican.va/holy_father/john_paul_ii/speeches/1998/march/documents/hf_jp-ii_spe_19980320_cardeal-baum_en.html> (accessed 22 January 2011).

——— *Ecclesia de Eucharistia*. Encyclical Letter on the Eucharist in its Relationship to the Church (17 April 2003), <http://www.vatican.va/edocs/ENG0821/__P2.HTM> (accessed 22 January 2011).

Pope Benedict XVI, 'Christmas Greetings to the Members of the Roman Curia and Prelature' (22 December 2005), <http://www.vatican.va/holy_father/benedict_xvi/speeches/2005/december/documents/hf_ben_xvi_spe_20051222_roman-curia_en.html> (accessed 22 January 2011).

——— 'First Message of His Holiness Benedict XVI at the end of the Eucharistic Concelebration with the Members of the Collge of Cardinals in the Sistine Chapel' 20 April 2005, <http://www.vatican.va/holy_father/benedict_xvi/messages/pont-messages/2005/documents/hf_ben-xvi_mes_20050420_missa-pro-ecclesia_en.html> (accessed 20 April 2010).

Pope Benedict XVI, *Deus Caritas Est*. Encyclical Letter on Christian Love (25 December 2005), <http://www.vatican.va/holy_father/benedict_xvi/encyclicals/documents/hf_ben-xvi_enc_20051225_deus-caritas-est_en.html> (accessed 22 January 2011).

———— 'Letter of His Holiness Benedict XVI to the Bishops on the Occasion of the Publication of the Apostolic Letter "Motu Proprio Data" *Summorum Pontificum* on the use of the Roman Liturgy Prior to the Reform of 1970' (7 July 2007), <http://www.vatican.va/holy_father/benedict_xvi/letters/2007/documents/hf_ben-xvi_let_20070707_lettera-vescovi_en.html> (accessed 22 January 2011).

———— Homily for the closing of the 49th International Eucharistic Conference (22 June 2008), <http://www.vatican.va/holy_father/benedict_xvi/homilies/2008/documents/hf_ben-xvi_hom_20080622_quebec_en.html> (accessed 22 January 2011).

———— 'Pastoral Letter of the Holy Father Pope Benedict XVI to the Catholics of Ireland' (19 March 2010), <http://www.vatican.va/holy_father/benedict_xvi/letters/2010/documents/hf_ben-xvi_let_20100319_church-ireland_en.html> (accessed 20 April 2010).

Name Index

Subject Index

Made in the USA
Middletown, DE
30 October 2020